Lecture Notes in Computer Science 15752

Founding Editors

Gerhard Goos
Juris Hartmanis

Editorial Board Members

Elisa Bertino , *Purdue University, West Lafayette, IN, USA*
Wen Gao, *Peking University, Beijing, China*
Bernhard Steffen , *TU Dortmund University, Dortmund, Germany*
Moti Yung , *Columbia University, New York, NY, USA*

The series Lecture Notes in Computer Science (LNCS), including its subseries Lecture Notes in Artificial Intelligence (LNAI) and Lecture Notes in Bioinformatics (LNBI), has established itself as a medium for the publication of new developments in computer science and information technology research, teaching, and education.

LNCS enjoys close cooperation with the computer science R & D community, the series counts many renowned academics among its volume editors and paper authors, and collaborates with prestigious societies. Its mission is to serve this international community by providing an invaluable service, mainly focused on the publication of conference and workshop proceedings and postproceedings. LNCS commenced publication in 1973.

Christina Garman · Pedro Moreno-Sanchez
Editors

Financial Cryptography and Data Security

29th International Conference, FC 2025
Miyakojima, Japan, April 14–18, 2025
Revised Selected Papers, Part II

Editors
Christina Garman
Purdue University
West Lafayette, IN, USA

Pedro Moreno-Sanchez
IMDEA Software Institute
Pozuelo de Alarcón, Spain

ISSN 0302-9743 ISSN 1611-3349 (electronic)
Lecture Notes in Computer Science
ISBN 978-3-032-07034-0 ISBN 978-3-032-07035-7 (eBook)
https://doi.org/10.1007/978-3-032-07035-7

© International Financial Cryptography Association 2026

This work is subject to copyright. All rights are solely and exclusively licensed by the Publisher, whether the whole or part of the material is concerned, specifically the rights of translation, reprinting, reuse of illustrations, recitation, broadcasting, reproduction on microfilms or in any other physical way, and transmission or information storage and retrieval, electronic adaptation, computer software, or by similar or dissimilar methodology now known or hereafter developed.
The use of general descriptive names, registered names, trademarks, service marks, etc. in this publication does not imply, even in the absence of a specific statement, that such names are exempt from the relevant protective laws and regulations and therefore free for general use.
The publisher, the authors and the editors are safe to assume that the advice and information in this book are believed to be true and accurate at the date of publication. Neither the publisher nor the authors or the editors give a warranty, expressed or implied, with respect to the material contained herein or for any errors or omissions that may have been made. The publisher remains neutral with regard to jurisdictional claims in published maps and institutional affiliations.

This Springer imprint is published by the registered company Springer Nature Switzerland AG
The registered company address is: Gewerbestrasse 11, 6330 Cham, Switzerland

If disposing of this product, please recycle the paper.

Preface

The Twenty-Ninth International Conference on Financial Cryptography and Data Security (FC 2025) was held on 14–18 April 2025 at the Hotel Shigira Mirage in Miyakojima, Japan. The conference is organized annually by the International Financial Cryptography Association (IFCA).

The Program Committee used the HotCRP system to organize the reviewing process, with a special thanks to Christian Cachin for graciously setting up a server for these purposes. We received 300 submissions and accepted 46 papers (42 regular papers, 3 short papers and 1 Systematization of Knowledge (SoK) paper). The acceptance rate was 15%. Papers received 2 reviews in a first round of double-blind peer review, with some papers subjected to an early rejection if both reviews were negative. The papers that proceeded to a second round of reviews received an additional 2 reviews. Some papers received a fifth review in a third round of reviews at the discretion of the program chairs.

We provided an open call for the nomination of program committee members. We curated a committee of 126 experts in cryptography, blockchain technology, security, and privacy, with members spanning academia and industry, as well as senior and junior positions. The members also used external reviewers at their discretion. Most members received 7 or 8 submissions to review, which we appreciate is a considerable amount of work. We thank all reviewers for demonstrating their careful consideration of each assigned paper, for providing useful feedback to the authors, and for lively discussions of the merits of each paper. The success of the conference and the final program is in large part due to the efforts of the program committee.

For the conference itself, we visited for the first time the island of Miyakojima in Japan. The conference ran Monday to Thursday, with Friday reserved for 6 workshops. Papers were split into 12 sessions, which are only slightly adjusted for these proceedings. The paper presentations were augmented with one highly engaging keynote. For the keynote, we invited Ed Felten (Offchain Labs) who presented his thoughts on "Toward a Practical Theory of On-Chain Resource Pricing." The program also included a rump session hosted by Andrew Miller, and a general meeting that included an election for members of the steering committee.

The success of FC 2025 would not have been possible without the contributions of a large number of people and organizations. Our general chairs, Kazue Sako and Rafael Hirschfeld, did countless organizational and logistical tasks to secure a beautiful location, ensure the smooth operation of the conference, and provide attendees with a full schedule of fun social activities. We thank the steering committee (listed below) and previous FC 2024 chairs (Jeremy Clark and Elaine Shi) for helpful guidance. We thank our sponsors whose generous support made this event possible. Our platinum sponsors: a16z crypto research, Covenant Holdings, and Sui. Our gold sponsor: Ethereum Foundation. Our silver sponsors: Common Prefix, Flashbots, Input Output, and Silence Laboratories. Thank you to all the authors, presenters, and attendees of the conference. Financial

Cryptography continues to maintain a high academic standard because of your diverse interests and innovation. You are helping sustain a vibrant community through your participation and perspectives.

June 2025

Christina Garman
Pedro Moreno-Sanchez

Organization

General Chairs

Rafael Hirschfeld   Unipay Technologies, The Netherlands
Kazue Sako   Waseda University, Japan

Program Committee Chairs

Christina Garman   Purdue University, USA
Pedro Moreno-Sanchez   IMDEA Software Institute, Spain

Steering Committee

Joseph Bonneau   NYU & a16z crypto, USA
Sven Dietrich   City University of New York, USA
Rafael Hirschfeld   Unipay Technologies, The Netherlands
Andrew Miller   University of Illinois Urbana-Champaign, USA
Monica Quaintance   Zenia Systems, USA
Burton Rosenberg   University of Miami, USA
Kazue Sako   Waseda University, Japan

Program Committee

Hamza Abusalah   IMDEA Software Institute, Spain
Ghada Almashaqbeh   University of Connecticut, USA
Orestis Alpos   Common Prefix, Switzerland
Jayamine Alupotha   University of Bern, Switzerland
Lukas Aumayr   Common Prefix, Switzerland
Zeta Avarikioti   TU Wien & Common Prefix, Austria
Massimo Bartoletti   University of Cagliari, Italy
Soumya Basu   Nuveaux Trading, USA
Don Beaver   Fierce Logic, USA
Adithya Bhat   Visa Research, USA
Alexander R. Block   University of Illinois Chicago, USA
Joseph Bonneau   NYU & a16z crypto, USA
Rainer Böhme   University of Innsbruck, Austria
Stefanos Chaliasos   Imperial College London, UK

Panagiotis Chatzigiannis	Visa Research, USA
James Hsin-yu Chiang	Aarhus University, Denmark
Hao Chung	Carnegie Mellon University, USA
Michele Ciampi	University of Edinburgh, UK
Jeremy Clark	Concordia University, Canada
Bernardo David	IT University of Copenhagen & Common Prefix, Denmark
Rafael Dowsley	Monash University, Australia
Sisi Duan	Tsinghua University, China
Yue Duan	Singapore Management University, Singapore
Muhammed F. Esgin	Monash University, Australia
Aleksander Essex	Western University, Canada
Ittay Eyal	Technion, Israel
Hanwen Feng	University of Sydney, Australia
Christof Ferreira Torres	INESC-ID Instituto Superior Técnico (IST) & University of Lisbon, Portugal
Arthur Gervais	University College London, UK
Noemi Glaeser	University of Maryland, USA
Tiantian Gong	Purdue University, USA
Yue Guo	JP Morgan AI Research, USA
Suyash Gupta	University of Oregon, USA
Lucjan Hanzlik	CISPA Helmholtz Center for Information Security, Germany
Hannes Hartenstein	Karlsruhe Institute of Technology, Germany
Bernhard Haslhofer	Complexity Science Hub, Austria
Ningyu He	The Hong Kong Polytechnic University, China
Lioba Heimbach	ETH Zurich, Switzerland
Jaap-Henk Hoepman	Radboud University & Karlstad University, The Netherlands
Yan Ji	Chainlink Labs, USA
Xiangkun Jia	Institute of Software, Chinese Academy of Sciences, China
Yanxue Jia	Purdue University, USA
Chenglu Jin	CWI Amsterdam, The Netherlands
Tushar Jois	City College of New York, USA
Ari Juels	Cornell Tech, USA
Ghassan Karame	Ruhr-University Bochum, Germany
Harish Karthikeyan	JP Morgan AI Research, USA
Mahimna Kelkar	Cornell University, USA
Lucianna Kiffer	IMDEA Networks, Spain
Jason Kim	Georgia Institute of Technology, USA
Lefteris Kokoris Kogias	Mysten Labs, Greece

Yashvanth Kondi	Silence Laboratories (Deel), USA
Kari Kostiainen	ETH Zurich, Switzerland
Mario Larangeira	Tokyo Institute of Technology & IOG, Japan
Duc V. Le	Visa Research, USA
Eysa Lee	Brown University, USA
Stefanos Leonardos	King's College London, UK
Jacob Leshno	University of Chicago, USA
Jiasun Li	George Mason University, USA
Orfeas Stefanos Thyfronitis Litos	Imperial College London & Common Prefix, UK
Jing Liu	MPI-SP & UC Irvine, Germany
Xiangyu Liu	Purdue University & Georgia Institute of Technology, USA
Zeyan Liu	University of Louisville, USA
Chen-Da Liu-Zhang	Lucerne University of Applied Sciences and Arts & Web3 Foundation, Switzerland
Donghang Lu	TikTok, USA
Yuan Lu	Institute of Software Chinese Academy of Sciences, China
Varun Madathil	Yale University, USA
Akaki Mamageishvili	Offchain Labs, USA
Easwar Vivek Mangipudi	Supra Research, USA
Elisaweta Masserova	Carnegie Mellon University, USA
Shin'ichiro Matsuo	Virginia Tech & Georgetown University, USA
Roman Matzutt	Fraunhofer FIT, Germany
Patrick McCorry	Arbitrum Foundation, USA
Kelsey Melissaris	Aarhus University, Denmark
Johnnatan Messias	MPI-SWS, Germany
Jason Milionis	Columbia University, USA
Pratyush Mishra	University of Pennsylvania, USA
Ciamac Moallemi	Columbia University, USA
Malte Möser	Chainalysis, USA
Neha Narula	MIT, USA
Georgios Palaiokrassas	Yale University, USA
Georgios Panagiotakos	IOG, Greece
Dimitrios Papadopoulos	HKUST, China
Krzysztof Pietrzak	Institute of Science and Technology Austria (ISTA), Austria
Kaihua Qin	Yale University, USA
Alfredo Rial	Nym Technologies, Belgium
Pierre-Louis Roman	None, Switzerland
Tim Roughgarden	Columbia University & a16z crypto, USA
Reihaneh Safavi-Naini	University of Calgary, Canada

Giulia Scaffino	TU Wien & Common Prefix, Austria
Ignacio Amores Sesar	University of Bern, Switzerland
Nibesh Shrestha	Supra Research, USA
Pratik Soni	University of Utah, USA
Alberto Sonnino	Mysten Labs & University College London, UK
Alexander Spiegelman	Aptos Labs, USA
Srivatsan Sridhar	Stanford University, USA
Chrysoula Stathakopoulou	Chainlink Labs, USA
Erkan Tairi	ENS Paris, France
Wenpin Tang	Columbia University, USA
Sri AravindaKrishnan Thyagarajan	University of Sydney, Australia
Daniel Tschudi	Concordium, Switzerland
Taro Tsuchiya	Carnegie Mellon University, USA
Marie Vasek	UCL, UK
Friedhelm Victor	TRM Labs, USA
Yann Vonlanthen	ETH Zurich, Switzerland
Anh V. Vu	University of Cambridge, UK
Jun Wan	Five Rings LLC, USA
Ding Wang	Nankai University, China
Haoyu Wang	Huazhong University of Science and Technology, China
Kanye Ye Wang	University of Macau, China
Qin Wang	CSIRO Data61, Australia
Shouqiao Wang	Columbia University, USA
Xuechao Wang	HKUST (GZ), China
Zhipeng Wang	Imperial College London, UK
Ke Wu	University of Michigan, USA
Matheus Xavier Ferreira	University of Virginia, USA
Zhuolun Xiang	Aptos Labs, USA
Guowen Xu	University of Electronic Science and Technology of China, China
Jiahua Xu	University College London, UK
Yingjie Xue	The Hong Kong University of Science and Technology (Guangzhou), China
Aviv Yaish	Yale University, USA
Zheng Yang	Southwest University, China
Mengqian Zhang	Yale University, USA
Hong-Sheng Zhou	Virginia Commonwealth University, USA
Liyi Zhou	University of Sydney, Australia
Yajin Zhou	Zhejiang University & BlockSec, China

Additional Reviewers

Sharad Agarwal
Jannik Albrecht
Parwat Singh Anjana
Arasu Arun
Gennaro Avitabile
Akhil Bandarupalli
Kyle Beadle
Nidhish Bhimrajka
Hangcheng Cao
Yiyue Cao
Wonseok Choi
Lei Fan
Matthias Grundmann
Jia Hu
Florian Jacob
Yu Shen
Zhenghao Lu
Rujia Li
Enrico Lipparini
Zeyu Liu
Anna Piscitelli

Judith Senn
Yu Xia
Qianyu Yu
Tsz Hon Yuen
Zhelei Zhou
Jiajun Xin
Pengzhi Xing
Jianting Zhang
Mingfei Zhang
Rui Zhang
Bolin Zhang
Hongxiao Wang
Cong Wu
Sravya Yandamuri
Yuchen Ye
Nikhil Vanjani
Ioannis Tzannetos
Giannis Tzannetos
Andrei Tonkikh
Zhelei Zhou

Contents

MEV

Piercing the Veil of TVL: DeFi Reappraised 3
  Yichen Luo, Yebo Feng, Jiahua Xu, and Paolo Tasca

Transaction Fee Mechanism Design for Leaderless Blockchain Protocols 20
  Pranav Garimidi, Lioba Heimbach, and Tim Roughgarden

Seahorse: Efficiently Mixing Encrypted and Normal Transactions 36
  Ben Riva, Alberto Sonnino, and Lefteris Kokoris-Kogias

The Early Days of the Ethereum Blob Fee Market and Lessons Learnt 53
  Lioba Heimbach and Jason Milionis

Quantifying the Value of Revert Protection 72
  *Brian Z. Zhu, Xin Wan, Ciamac C. Moallemi, Dan Robinson,
  and Brad Bachu*

Consensus

Frosty: Bringing Strong Liveness Guarantees to the Snow Family
of Consensus Protocols 91
  *Aaron Buchwald, Stephen Buttolph, Andrew Lewis-Pye,
  Patrick O'Grady, and Kevin Sekniqi*

Consensus Under Adversary Majority Done Right 108
  *Srivatsan Sridhar, Ertem Nusret Tas, Joachim Neu, Dionysis Zindros,
  and David Tse*

On the (in)security of Proofs-of-Space Based Longest-Chain Blockchains 127
  Mirza Ahad Baig and Krzysztof Pietrzak

Constellation: Peer-to-Peer Overlays for Federated Byzantine Agreement
Systems 143
  *Giuliano Losa, Yifan Mao, Shaileshh Bojja Venkatakrishnan,
  and Yunqi Zhang*

Short Paper: A New Way to Achieve Round-Efficient Asynchronous
Byzantine Agreement 160
  Simon Holmgaard Kamp

Proof-of-X and Rewards

Blink: An Optimal Proof of Proof-of-Work 173
   Lukas Aumayr, Zeta Avarikioti, Matteo Maffei, Giulia Scaffino,
   and Dionysis Zindros

Reward Schemes and Committee Sizes in Proof of Stake Governance 191
   Georgios Birmpas, Philip Lazos, Evangelos Markakis, and Paolo Penna

Mining Power Destruction Attacks in the Presence of Petty-Compliant
Mining Pools 208
   Roozbeh Sarenche, Svetla Nikova, and Bart Preneel

A Theoretical Basis for MEV 225
   Massimo Bartoletti and Roberto Zunino

Short Paper: Rewardable Naysayer Proofs 243
   Gennaro Avitabile, Luisa Siniscalchi, and Ivan Visconti

Signatures and Threshold Cryptography

Verification-Efficient Homomorphic Signatures for Verifiable Computation
over Data Streams 255
   Gaspard Anthoine, Daniele Cozzo, and Dario Fiore

Rational Secret Sharing with Competition 273
   Tiantian Gong and Zeyu Liu

The Latency Price of Threshold Cryptosystem in Blockchains 291
   Zhuolun Xiang, Sourav Das, Zekun Li, Zhoujun Ma,
   and Alexander Spiegelman

On Non-Interactive Blind Signatures in the Plain Model Using Complexity
Leveraging 309
   Kazuki Yamamura, Tetsuya Okuda, and Eiichiro Fujisaki

Do Compilers Break Constant-Time Guarantees? 327
   Lukas Gerlach, Robert Pietsch, and Michael Schwarz

Machine Learning

PrivGNN: High-Performance Secure Inference for Cryptographic Graph
Neural Networks 347
   Fuyi Wang, Zekai Chen, Mingyuan Fan, Jianying Zhou, Lei Pan,
   and Leo Yu Zhang

Linking Cryptoasset Attribution Tags to Knowledge Graph Entities:
An LLM-Based Approach 366
   Régnier Avice, Bernhard Haslhofer, Zhidong Li, and Jianlong Zhou

CCBNet : Confidential Collaborative Bayesian Networks Inference 383
   Abele Mălan, Thiago Guzella, Jérémie Decouchant, and Lydia Chen

Author Index 401

MEV

Piercing the Veil of TVL: DeFi Reappraised

Yichen Luo[1], Yebo Feng[2,3](✉), Jiahua Xu[1,3], and Paolo Tasca[3]

[1] Centre for Blockchain Technologies, University College London, London, UK
[2] Nanyang Technological University, Singapore, Singapore
yebo.feng@ntu.edu.sg
[3] DLT Science Foundation, London, UK

Abstract. Total value locked (TVL) is widely used to measure the size and popularity of decentralized finance (DeFi). However, TVL can be manipulated and inflated through "double counting" activities such as wrapping and leveraging. As existing methodologies addressing double counting are inconsistent and flawed, we propose a new framework, termed "total value redeemable (TVR)", to assess the true underlying value of DeFi. Our formal analysis reveals how DeFi's complex network spreads financial contagion via derivative tokens, increasing TVL's sensitivity to external shocks. To quantify double counting, we construct the DeFi multiplier, which mirrors the money multiplier in traditional finance (TradFi). Our measurements reveal substantial double counting in DeFi, finding that the gap between TVL and TVR reached $139.87 billion during the peak of DeFi activity on December 2, 2021, with a TVL-to-TVR ratio of approximately 2. We conduct sensitivity tests to evaluate the stability of TVL compared to TVR, demonstrating the former's significantly higher level of instability than the latter, especially during market downturns: a 25% decline in the price of Ether (ETH) leads to a $1 billion greater decrease in TVL compared to TVR among leading protocols via asset value depreciation and liquidations triggered by derivative tokens. We also document that the DeFi money multiplier is positively correlated with crypto market indicators and negatively correlated with macroeconomic indicators. Overall, our study suggests that TVR is more reliable and stable than TVL.

1 Introduction

Total value locked (TVL) is one of the most widely adopted metrics for assessing both the size and popularity of DeFi. Analogous to the concept of assets under management (AUM) in TradFi, TVL is a similar measure of assets pooled for yield generation (see Definition 1) [4,21]. According to DeFiLlama, the entire DeFi TVL stands at over $200 billion as of November 22, 2025. While

---

We thank Ripple UBRI [5]'s support and Antoine Mouran's insights in double counting and related literature.

Table 1. Survey of DeFi tracing websites with a focus on protocols coverage and TVL-related information disclosure as of February 15, 2025.

DeFi Tracing Website	Protocol Coverage Number	TVL-related Information						
		TVL Presented Methodology	Overall Methodology	Protocol-specific Methodology	Token Price Sources	Constituent Protocols	Code	Double Counting Solution
DeFiLlama	4,477	●	●	●	●	●	●	●
L2BEAT	N/A	●	●	○	○	●	●	○
DappRadar*	4,588	◐	○	○	○	●	○	○
Stelareum	309	●	○	○	○	●	○	○
DeFiPulse	N/A	○	●	○	○	○	○	●

*: Although DappRadar tracks over 4,000 protocols, it discloses the TVL for only around 500 ones.
●: Disclosure. ◐: Partial Disclosure. ○: No disclosure.

blockchain systems were designed to enable automatic reconciliation and a coherent accounting whole without discrepancies [8,9], DeFi protocols and liquidity pools have fragmented shared ledgers into accounting "islands" where double counting thrives. Particularly, highly incentivized practices such as token wrapping and redepositing of borrowed tokens [4,21] can trigger double counting, artificially inflating TVL in the absence of any new capital inflows. Consequently, TVL can be a deceptive metric, misleading investors to make financial decisions based on distorted valuations.[1] Moreover, the culprit for double counting, the "derivative tokens" (see Definition 3), also serves as channels for financial contagion, making TVL highly sensitive during market downturns. Unfortunately, the methods for different DeFi tracing platforms to calculate TVL are yet unstandardized, non-transparent, and often biased (see Table 1), obscuring DeFi's true economic value.

The double counting problem in DeFi is a crucial yet understudied topic in the literature. Many studies use TVL for protocols valuation and risk monitoring [11,12,18,19] but overlook the issue of double counting within TVL. While some existing studies document the complexity and interconnections within DeFi at the token level [16], protocol level [20] and sector level [3], most of them focus on analyzing the topological features and associated risks of DeFi networks rather than their impacts on TVL. Although a theoretical production-network model has been applied to assess the value added and service outputs across various DeFi sectors on Ethereum [3], it fails to address double counting within individual sectors.

In this paper, we propose a novel yet effective measurement framework, termed total value redeemable (TVR), to address the double counting problem at the finest granularity—the token level. TVR excludes the value of complex DeFi derivatives and borrowed tokens, focusing only on the asset component that contributes directly to the underlying value of DeFi that can ultimately be redeemed. By eliminating derivatives, TVR also avoids the inclusion of financial contagion risk, making it a more stable metric than TVL.

We reappraise the DeFi system's value using the TVR framework with data from 3,570 protocols over five years from DeFiLlama and token categories from

---
[1] Value inflation in the blockchain space has also been observed in other metrics, such as throughput [14].

CoinMarketCap. We employ the token category data fetched from CoinMarketCap to identify "plain tokens", i.e. tokens that do not entail any underlying token. The values of these tokens are then aggregated to calculate the TVR for the entire DeFi system. Inspired by TradFi money multiplier, we introduce the DeFi money multiplier, which is defined as the ratio of TVL to TVR. This metric quantifies the extent of double counting in DeFi. Through formalization and sensitivity tests, we compare the stability of TVL with that of TVR. The formalization reveals that TVL is highly sensitive to price shocks such as ETH price decline. This sensitivity arises from the endogeneity of the derivative token price and the quantity of derivative tokens staked in protocols for loanable funds (PLF). We then conduct simulations to assess the stability of TVL compared to TVR. The simulation results align with our formalization.

We summarize our main contributions as follows:

1. By modeling and formalizing TVL, we reveal the double counting mechanism and financial contagion risk under the TVL framework. We find existing methodologies addressing double counting either inconsistent or flawed.
2. To the best of our knowledge, we are the first to introduce an enhanced measurement framework to evaluate value locked within a DeFi system without double counting. Our analysis of 3,570 protocols over five years finds a substantial double counting within the DeFi system, up to $139.87 billion with a TVL-TVR ratio of around 2. This contribution provides DeFi users with more accurate and complete information about the value locked in DeFi, which supports better decision-making within the community.
3. Our sensitivity tests reveal that TVL is highly sensitive to market downturns compared to TVR. A 25% drop in ETH price leads to a significant divergence, resulting in approximately a $1 billion greater decrease in TVL compared to TVR in a system of six representative DeFi protocols in Ethereum.
4. We are also the first to build the DeFi money multiplier based on TVR and TVL in parallel to the TradFi macroeconomic money multiplier to quantify the double counting. We document that the DeFi money multiplier is positively correlated with crypto market indicators and negatively correlated with macroeconomic indicators.

2 Key DeFi Concepts

In this section, we explain key concepts in DeFi. DeFi is an ecosystem of protocols operating autonomously through smart contracts, popularized by Ethereum [7]. These protocols are decentralized applications inspired by traditional centralized finance systems [23].

2.1 TVL

Based on definitions and descriptions from existing literature [6,25], we define TVL as follows:

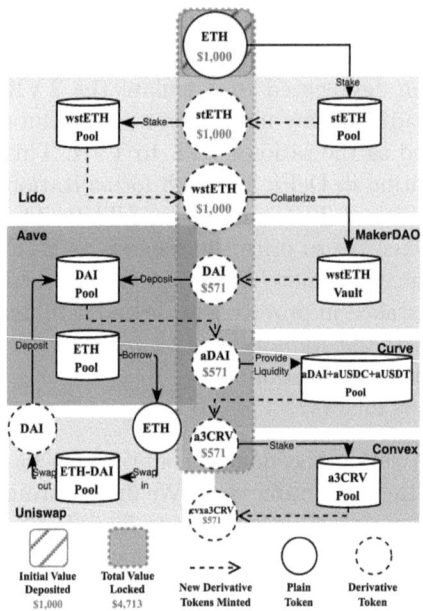
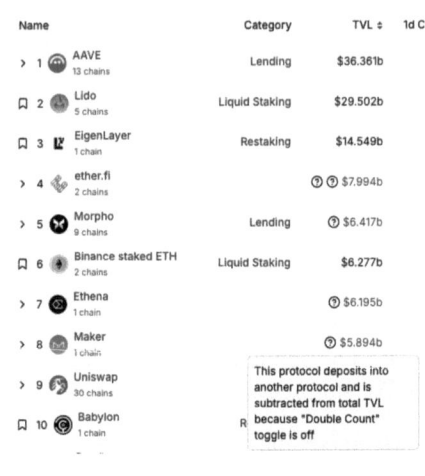

Fig. 1. An example of actions a DeFi user can take to maximize yield, enabled by the DeFi composability.

Fig. 2. DeFiLlama's TVL dashboard after deactivating the "Include in TVL: Double Count" toggle. When a user deactivates this toggle, protocols that deposit into another protocol will be excluded from the total TVL calculation, and their TVL numbers will be grayed out.

Definition 1 (Total Value Locked). *The total value of assets staked in or held by a DeFi protocol, a blockchain, or the entire DeFi ecosystem at a specific moment, usually for yield generation purposes.*

TVL of the DeFi system can be expressed as

$$TVL = \mathbf{p}^T \mathbf{Q} \mathbf{1}, \tag{1}$$

where **1** is a column vector of ones; $\mathbf{Q} = [q_{i,j}]_{m \times n}$ denotes the matrix of staked tokens quantity across all DeFi protocols, with m being the number of token types and n the number of DeFi protocols; $\mathbf{p} = [p_i]_{m \times 1}$ denotes the column vector of token prices for the m token types. We select Lido, MakerDAO, Aave V2, Uniswap V2, Curve, and Convex as an example system (see Fig. 1) to illustrate the complexity of the TVL ecosystem. At the time of writing this paper, these protocols have the highest TVL and are the most representative within their respective category, collectively accounting for approximately 68% of the total TVL. In the illustrative example in Fig. 1, the TVL of these protocols totals $4,713—equivalent to 4.713 times the initial ETH value deposited of $1,000.

DeFi tracing websites disclose key metrics of DeFi protocols including TVL, as shown in Table 1. DeFiLlama, a leading DeFi tracing website, attempts to eliminate double counting by excluding protocols categorized under those feeding tokens into other protocols. The "Include in TVL: Double Count" toggle

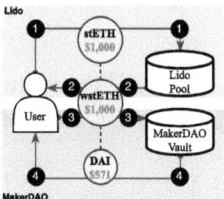 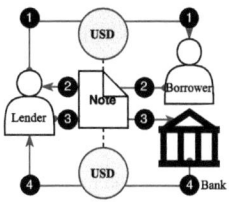

(a) Wrapping in DeFi.   (b) Rehypothecation in TradFi.

Fig. 3. Wrapping and its corresponding TradFi analogy. The process of wrapping in DeFi, as illustrated in Fig. 3a, mirrors the rehypothecation process in TradFi, as shown in Fig. 3b. The black circle (●) with a white number indicates the step.

allows users to filter out the TVL of protocols that deposit into another protocol, as shown in Fig. 2. When such protocols are excluded, the dashboard displays the chain-level DeFiLlama-adjusted TVL (TVL^{Adj}), instead of the standard DeFiLlama TVL that includes double counting (TVL). While DeFiLlama makes efforts to address the issue, it may not fully eliminate double counting. Since different protocols have different degrees of double counting, simply excluding a particular category of protocols does not suffice to address the problem of double counting comprehensively.

2.2 Wrapping

Wrapping and leveraging are two DeFi mechanisms that can result in TVL double counting. As leveraging is less prevalent and has been well documented in [13], we provide its explanation in Appendix §A. Wrapping means DeFi users depositing existing tokens, including tokens that have been wrapped, into smart contracts to generate new tokens. Enabled by DeFi composability, users can repeatedly perform this operation to sustain their liquidity and maximize their interest [4,21,24]. DeFi composability refers to the ability of one DeFi protocol to accept tokens generated from another protocol seamlessly, allowing DeFi tokens to be chained and integrated to create new tokens and financial services. Figure 3a depicts a scenario where an investor initially supplies $1,000 worth of stETH to Lido (step ❶), which is then converted into $1,000 worth of wstETH (step ❷). Subsequently, the investor deposits this wstETH into MakerDAO (step ❸) and issues up to $571 worth of DAI (step ❹)[2]. The wrapping in DeFi is similar to the rehypothecation process in TradFi, illustrated in Fig. 3b. This works as follows. In rehypothecation, lenders who provide loans to borrowers (step ❶) against a promissory note (step ❷), pledge the promissory note (step ❸) and borrow money from the bank (step ❹) [1].

To illustrate the TVL double counting during wrapping, we use a balance-sheet approach to consolidate double-entry bookkeeping (see e.g. [15]) and

---

[2] The calculation of DAI amount is based on the loan-to-value ratio (LTV) of the wstETH low fee vault at the time of this paper and the collateral value.

Table 2. Protocol-perspective balance sheets of the wrapping scenario. We **boldface** the components included in the TVL calculation.

(a) Lido.			(b) MakerDAO.			(c) Consolidated.		
Immediately After	②	④	Immediately After	②	④	Immediately After	②	④
Assets	$	$	*Assets*	$	$	*Assets*	$	$
Value Locked - stETH	**1,000**	**1,000**	**Value Locked - wstETH**	**-**	**1,000**	**Value Locked**	**1,000**	**1,000**
			Receivables - DAI	-	571	Receivables	-	571
Total Assets	**1,000**	**1,000**	**Total Assets**	**-**	**1,571**	**Total Assets**	**1,000**	**1,571**
Liabilities	$	$	*Liabilities*	$	$	*Liabilities*	$	$
Payables - wstETH	1,000	1,000	Payables - wstETH	-	1,000	Payables	1,000	1,571
			New Money - DAI	-	571			
Total Liabilities	**1,000**	**1,000**	**Total Liabilities**	**-**	**1,571**	**Total Liabilities**	**1,000**	**1,571**

describe its financial condition for each protocol. Appendix §B provides a detailed list of bookkeeping entries for common transactions in DeFi protocols. The aggregate value locked can be regarded as a significant element on the asset side of a DeFi protocol's balance sheet [22]. In the context of a DeFi system, we apply the principles of consolidated balance sheets to depict its financial status on an aggregated basis. This type of balance sheet represents the combined financial position of a group, presenting the assets, liabilities, and net position of both the parent company and its subsidiaries as those of a unified economic entity. By employing the principle of non-duplication used in consolidated balance sheet accounting (whereby, accounting entries that are recorded as assets in one company and as liabilities in another are eliminated, before aggregating all remaining items) [17], we can effectively eliminate instances of double counting within a DeFi system. Table 2 shows the balance sheets of Lido and MakerDAO, and the consolidated balance sheet of the DeFi system consists of Lido and MakerDAO. Immediately after step ②, the value of the DeFi system is $1,000. However, if we deposit the receipt token wstETH from Lido into MakerDAO to issue another receipt token DAI, the TVL will be $2,000 under the traditional TVL measurement. The balance sheets are expanded and the TVL is double-counted due to the existence of wstETH. In the consolidated balance sheet, the TVL is adjusted to $1,000 after eliminating the value associated with the wstETH.

3 Enhanced Measurement Framework

In this section, we formalize the double counting problem, identify the instability of TVL, and introduce our enhanced measurement framework TVR.

3.1 Double Counting Problem

We initially classify DeFi tokens into plain tokens and derivative tokens. We provide the following definitions for the plain and underlying tokens:

Definition 2 (Plain Token). *A DeFi token without any underlying token.*

Definition 3 (Derivative Token). *A DeFi receipt token, also known as an I-owe-you (IOU) token or a depositary receipt token, that is generated in a specified ratio by depositing some underlying tokens into the smart contract of a protocol.*

In the example used in Fig. 1, ETH is considered as a plain token because it is initially deposited into the system without having an underlying token. In contrast, other tokens (stETH, wstETH, DAI, aDAI, a3CRV, and cvxa3CRV) are considered derivative tokens since they have underlying tokens. Let $\boldsymbol{\tau} = [\tau_i]_{m\times 1}$, where m is the number of unique tokens and $\tau_i = 1$ if token i is a plain token and 0 otherwise. By decomposing the TVL value, as defined in Eq. 1, into the plain token value and the derivative token value, we can further express the TVL as $TVL = (\mathbf{p} \odot \boldsymbol{\tau})^T \mathbf{Q} \mathbf{1} + [\mathbf{p} \odot (\mathbf{1} - \boldsymbol{\tau})]^T \mathbf{Q} \mathbf{1}$, where $\odot$ denotes the element-wise product. Since the value of derivative tokens can be easily created and inflated through wrapping without injecting any capital into the DeFi system according to Sect. 2.2, there is an urgent need to design a new framework that excludes this inflated value. The new framework should ensure that the underlying value, which cannot be easily manipulated, is accurately reflected.

3.2 Instability of TVL

In addition to the inflation issue, derivative tokens can act as channels for the spread of financial contagion, making the TVL highly sensitive to market downturns. The prices of derivative tokens are endogenously determined by the prices and quantities of their underlying tokens. The pricing mechanism can be described as follows: (i) If the derivative token is a stablecoin generated from a collateralized debt position (CDP) and the aggregate value of its underlying tokens meets or exceeds the value of the stablecoin, the token's price is pegged to its predetermined fiat currency. This peg is maintained through an overcollateralization mechanism, as discussed in Appendix §C. (ii) Otherwise, the token price is determined by the ratio of the underlying tokens' total value to the derivative token's circulating supply. In both cases, a short-term fluctuation term ϵ_d, should be included to account for temporary price variations.

We write the derivative token price as

$$p_d(\mathbf{P}_u, \mathbf{q}_u) = \begin{cases} c_d & \text{if } d \text{ is a CDP stablecoin and } \Gamma \geq c_d \\ \Gamma & \text{otherwise} \end{cases} + \epsilon_d, \quad (2)$$

where $\Gamma = \frac{\mathbf{p}_u^T \mathbf{q}_u}{q_d}$. p_d and q_d are the price and circulating supply of derivative token d. $\mathbf{p}_u = [p_i]_{m \times 1}$ and $\mathbf{q}_u = [q_i]_{m \times 1}$ are the vector of d's underlying token prices and quantities, respectively. c_d is the theoretical pegging price of a CDP stablecoin in USD. The short-term fluctuation ϵ_d is exogenous, associated with the token's supply and demand dynamics as well as the liquidity. For example, the price of stETH deviated from its reference point temporarily in 2022 due to selling pressure from Celsius and market illiquidity. Appendix §D explains in detail the derivative token pegging mechanism that supports Eq. 2. For CDP stablecoins, the deviation of their price, i.e. "depegging", from the predetermined reference point due to the undercollateralization, is denoted as $\Gamma < c_d$.

DeFi composability allows the underlying token of a derivative token to serve as the derivative token of another token, as illustrated in Fig. 1 and Fig. 3a (e.g. wstETH is a derivative token of stETH, which itself is a derivative token of ETH). We can derive the derivative token price function in terms of its ultimate underlying plain token prices and quantities: $p_d(\mathbf{p}_u, \mathbf{q}_u) = \left[p_{d_1} \circ p_{d_2} \ldots \circ p_{d_j}\right](\mathbf{p}_u, \mathbf{q}_u)$, where $\mathbf{p}_u = [p_i]_{v \times 1}$ is the vector of d's ultimate underlying token prices via the recursion of Eq. 2. $\circ$ is the function composition operator. $\left[p_{d_1} \circ p_{d_2} \ldots \circ p_{d_j}\right]$ means we recurse Eq. 2 multiple times until we find the ultimate underlying plain tokens (e.g. ETH as the ultimate plain token of wstETH).

Tokens staked in a PLF, including CDPs such as MakerDAO or lending protocols such as Aave, have a token quantity affected by its token price due to the liquidation mechanism [2,22,24]. Detailed definitions of PLF and its liquidation mechanism are provided in Appendix §C. According to Appendix §C, a change in collateral j's price $p_{j,t} \rightarrow p_{j,t+1}$ will lead to the change of the account i's health factor $h_{i,t+1}(p_{j,t+1})$, a ratio between liquidation threshold-adjusted collateral value to debt value, and the liquidation profit $\Pi_{i,t+1}(p_{j,t+1})$, leading to different scenarios. In liquidation, we should consider the quantity of both collateral tokens and repaid tokens since the liquidator not only withdraws collaterals but also injects liquidity into the protocol via the repayment.

When $h_{i,t+1}(p_{j,t+1}) \geq 1$, the account is deemed safe and the quantity of collateral j in the account remains unchanged, represented by $q_{i,j,t+1}$. When $h_{i,t+1}(p_{j,t+1}) < 1$ and the liquidation profit $\Pi_{i,t+1}(p_{j,t+1}) \leq 0$, the liquidation is considered unprofitable for liquidators, rendering the liquidation unviable and the quantity of collateral in the account also unchanged, represented by $q_{i,j,t+1}$.

When $h_{i,t+1}(p_{j,t+1}) < 1$, the user may face liquidation, where the smart contract transfers and sells varying proportions of collateral to maintain the solvency of PLF. Additionally, when the liquidation profit $\Pi_{i,t+1}(p_{j,t+1}) > 0$, the total collateral value is sufficient to cover the total debt value. In this scenario, the liquidation is deemed profitable for liquidators, leading to a successful liquidation. In a liquidation, the token quantity obeys the following law of motion when $t \rightarrow t+1$:

$$q_{i,j,t+1}(p_{i,j,t+1}) = \begin{cases} q_{i,j,t} + \Delta_{i,j,t+1} & \text{if } h_{i,t+1} < 1 \text{ and } \Pi_{i,t+1} > 0 \\ q_{i,j,t} & \text{otherwise} \end{cases}. \quad (3)$$

Δ and Π depend on the type of PLF and tokens as shown in Table 3a, as explained in Appendix §E.

Given the endogeneity mentioned above, we can then further split the TVL into the following four categories: the value of plain tokens staked in non-PLFs, plain tokens staked in PLFs, derivative tokens staked in non-PLFs, and derivative tokens staked in PLFs:

$$TVL = \underbrace{(\mathbf{p} \odot \boldsymbol{\tau})^T \mathbf{Q}(\mathbf{1}-\boldsymbol{\omega})}_{\substack{\text{plain tokens} \\ \text{staked in non-PLFs}}} + \underbrace{(\mathbf{p} \odot \boldsymbol{\tau})^T \mathbf{Q}\boldsymbol{\omega}}_{\substack{\text{plain tokens} \\ \text{staked in PLFs}}} + \underbrace{[\mathbf{p} \odot (\mathbf{1}-\boldsymbol{\tau})]^T \mathbf{Q}(\mathbf{1}-\boldsymbol{\omega})}_{\substack{\text{derivative tokens} \\ \text{staked in non-PLFs}}} + \underbrace{[\mathbf{p} \odot (\mathbf{1}-\boldsymbol{\tau})]^T \mathbf{Q}\boldsymbol{\omega}}_{\substack{\text{derivative tokens} \\ \text{staked in PLFs}}}, \quad (4)$$

Table 3. Δ and Π in different scenarios, where $V_{\text{liq}} = \min\{\frac{V_c}{1+b}, \delta \cdot V_d\}$ represents the maximum amount of debt that a liquidator can repay at a single liquidation in a lending protocol. b represents the liquidation bonus. δ denotes the close factor. $V_c = \mathbf{c}^T \mathbf{p}_c$ and $V_d = \mathbf{d}^T \mathbf{p}_d$, where $\mathbf{c}$ and $\mathbf{d}$ are vectors of collateral and debt token quantities, represent the total collateral value and total debt value of the position, respectively, as mentioned in Appendix §C. $gasFees$ denotes the gas costs of liquidation.

(a) Quantity increase Δ_{t+1} for token in a CDP or a lending protocol.

	Δ of Repaid Token	Δ of Collateral Token
CDP	0	$-q$
Lending Protocol	$\frac{V_{\text{liq}} \cdot q}{V_d}$	$-\frac{(1+b)V_{\text{liq}} \cdot q}{V_c}$

(b) Liquidation profit Π_{t+1} in a CDP or a lending protocol.

	Π
CDP	$V_c - V_d - gasFees$
Lending Protocol	$V_{\text{liq}} \cdot b - gasFees$

where $\boldsymbol{\omega} = [\omega_i]_{n \times 1}$, $\omega_i = 1$ if protocol i is a PLF and 0 otherwise. The derivative token price depends on its underlying token's price $\mathbf{p}_u$ and quantity (see Eq. 2). In addition, the tokens quantity staked within a PLF is affected by their own price (see Eq. 3). Therefore, the TVL ultimately depends on the prices and quantities of the underlying tokens. Price and quantity shocks to the underlying tokens can lead to a decline in token value, trigger liquidations, and cause depegging for derivative tokens due to the endogenous relationship between derivative and underlying tokens. Derivative tokens amplify the impact of such shocks on the TVL, making the TVL highly sensitive to changes in the prices of plain tokens. Consequently, the existence of derivative tokens not only inflates the TVL but also serves as the channel for the spread of decentralized financial contagion, making the TVL unstable.

3.3 Total Value Redeemable (TVR)

To address the double counting problem, we introduce the metric TVR.

Definition 4 (Total Value Redeemable). *Token value that can be ultimately redeemed from a DeFi protocol or a DeFi ecosystem.*

We can express the TVR of the entire DeFi ecosystem as the sum of the total value of plain tokens including governance tokens, native tokens, and non-crypto-backed (NCB) stablecoins held by smart contracts in the DeFi ecosystem:

$$TVR = (\mathbf{p} \odot \boldsymbol{\tau})^T \mathbf{Q} \mathbf{1} = \underbrace{(\mathbf{p} \odot \boldsymbol{\tau})^T \mathbf{Q}(1 - \boldsymbol{\omega})}_{\text{plain tokens held by smart contracts in non-PLFs}} + \underbrace{(\mathbf{p} \odot \boldsymbol{\tau})^T \mathbf{Q} \boldsymbol{\omega}}_{\text{plain tokens held by smart contracts in PLFs}}, \quad (5)$$

Compared to TVL, TVR excludes the value of derivative and borrowed tokens, considering only the value of plain tokens held by smart contracts to address the double counting problem. The exclusion of inflated values also decreases the complexity of the interplay within the DeFi system, mitigating the high sensitivity of the metric concerning the ultimate underlying plain tokens. We also introduce the protocol-level TVR to address the intra-protocol double counting, as discussed in Appendix §F.

DeFiLlama provides TVL adjusted for double counting of blockchains. Additionally, it aggregates chain-level TVL to compute the adjusted TVL for the entire DeFi ecosystem. However, it does not offer adjusted TVL for specific protocols. Compared to DeFiLlama's adjusted TVL, TVR eliminates double counting with finer granularity by selectively including or excluding tokens during the calculation, resulting in significantly higher accuracy. We provide a detailed comparison in calculation methods between DeFi space ecosystem-wide TVR and DeFiLlama-adjusted TVL in Appendix §G.

To examine the stability of TVL and TVR, we perform comparative sensitivity analyses on the changes in TVL ($\Delta TVL_{t+1} = TVL_{t+1} - TVL_t$) and TVR ($\Delta TVR_{t+1} = TVR_{t+1} - TVR_t$) in response to shocks in the price of plain tokens. These tests are conducted using six representative protocols, as selected in Sect. 2.1. For the plain token price shock, we use the decline in ETH price as the independent variable because ETH is the native token of Ethereum and is widely used across the DeFi platform. Subsequently, we update the token price vector $\mathbf{p}$ from Eq. 2, quantity matrix $\mathbf{Q}$ from Eq. 3 and Eq. 5. Finally, we calculate ΔTVL_{t+1} and ΔTVR_{t+1}.

4 Empirical Analyses

This section details the data used for measurements and presents empirical results under both the traditional TVL framework and our proposed TVR framework. We also introduce the DeFi money multiplier to quantify double counting in DeFi and provide measurement results for individual altchains.

4.1 Data

We fetch the TVL data about DeFi protocols broken down by token and adjusted TVL (TVL^{Adj}) from January 1, 2021 to March 1, 2024 using DeFiLlama API. DeFiLlama offers the most comprehensive universe of DeFi protocols of all blockchains compared to all other DeFi-tracing websites, as discussed in Table 1. TVL^{Adj} is DeFiLlama's improved metric aimed at mitigating the double counting problem and is flawed as discussed in Sect. 2.1. We then break down the TVL of each protocol to obtain the unadjusted TVL per protocol per day (TVL_i). Additionally, we retrieve token categorization lists for native tokens (layer-one and layer-two) and governance tokens from CoinMarketCap, and obtain stablecoin classifications from DeFiLlama. These lists are then used as filters to extract plain tokens from the TVL breakdown data provided by DeFiLlama to calculate the TVR (TVR). We also retrieve the blockchain states from an Ethereum archive node for three key dates: December 2, 2021, marking the peak of DeFiLlama-unadjusted TVL; May 9, 2022, denoting the end of the Luna collapse; and November 8, 2022, representing the end of the FTX collapse.

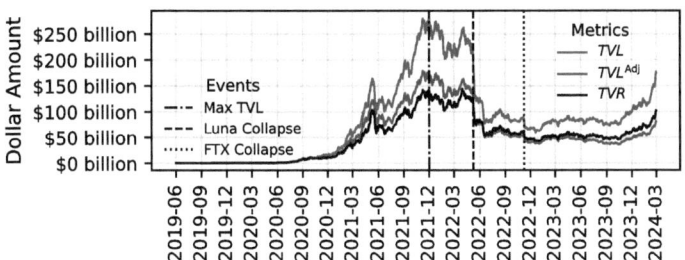

Fig. 4. TVL and TVR over time, where the red, blue, and black lines represent the TVL, TVL^{Adj}, and TVR. (Color figure online)

In Appendix §H, we explore methods to automate this process and eliminate reliance on third-party data.

For the risk analysis, we retrieve the data by crawling blockchain states (e.g. MakerDAO vaults data) and blockchain events (e.g. Aave deposit events) from an Ethereum archive node. Our sample of risk analysis constitutes six leading DeFi protocols with the highest TVL within each respective DeFi protocol category, as shown in Fig. 1. Appendix §I reports the statistics of accounts in sensitivity tests in MakerDAO and Aave on three representative dates.

4.2 TVL, Adjusted TVL, and TVR

Based on the enhanced measurement framework, we build TVR from DeFiLlama TVL breakdown data. Our framework calculates DeFi space ecosystem-wide TVR by summing the value of all **eligible tokens** as described in Sect. 3.3, specifically plain tokens. In contrast, DeFiLlama-adjusted TVL is calculated by first aggregating the TVL of all **eligible protocols** and then summing the TVL across all blockchains, where protocol eligibility is arbitrarily determined by DeFiLlama whose validity we challenge. For instance, although MakerDAO holds both plain tokens (e.g. ETH) that directly contribute to DeFi's underlying value and derivative tokens (e.g. wstETH) that should be excluded, its entire TVL is excluded from the DeFiLlama-adjusted TVL, as illustrated in Fig. 2. Appendix §G conducts a detailed comparison in calculation methods between system-wide TVR and DeFiLlama-adjusted TVL. Figure 4 shows the DeFiLlama unadjusted TVL (TVL), DeFiLlama-adjusted TVL (TVL^{Adj}), and TVR (TVR) for the entire blockchain ecosystem over time. Our empirical measurement reveals the level of double counting within the DeFi ecosystem, with TVL-TVR discrepancies reaching up to \$139.87 billion, and a TVL-TVR ratio of around 2 when the unadjusted TVL reached its maximum value. Moreover, there is a divergence between DeFiLlama-adjusted TVL and the TVR due to differences in methodology. In June 2022, the TVR exceeds DeFiLlama-adjusted TVL because the token value deposited of removed protocols under DeFiLlama's methodology is lower than the actual value that needs to be removed within the TVR framework. Conversely, after June 2022, the TVR falls below DeFiLlama's adjusted

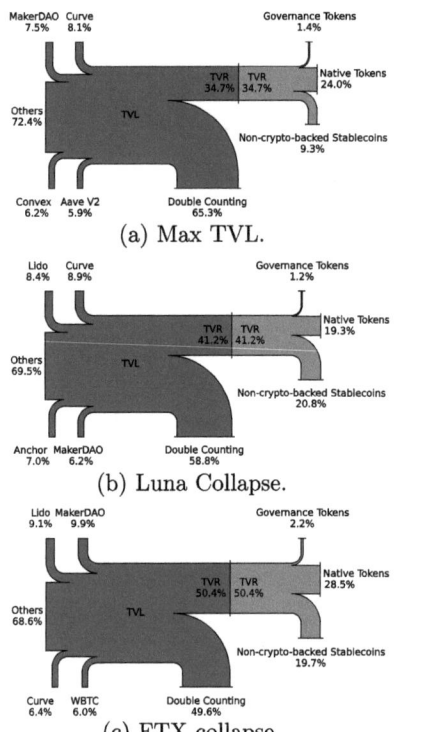
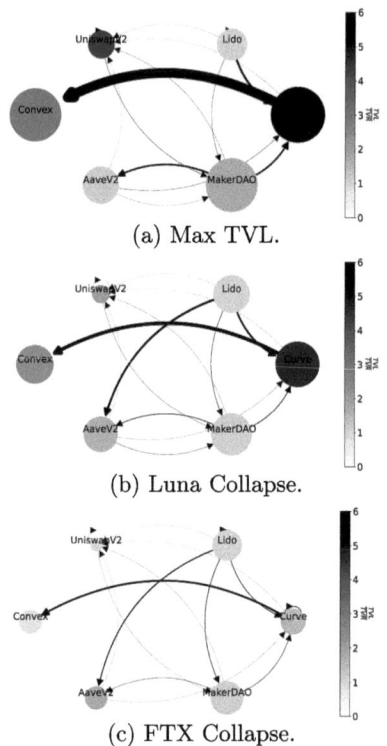

Fig. 5. Decomposition of TVL of the entire DeFi system. We identify four protocols with the highest TVL and group the remaining protocols under the category of "Others". The band width represents the dollar value of tokens. The blue band represents the TVL value, while the orange band represents the TVR value.

Fig. 6. Token wrapping network of six representative protocols. Node size corresponds to the TVL, edge width represents the dollar amount of tokens generated from the source protocol and staked in the target protocol, and node color reflects the ratio between TVL and TVR. A darker color indicates a higher level of double counting.

TVL because the token value deposited of protocols removed by DeFiLlama is higher than the actual value that needs to be removed within the TVR framework. This discrepancy highlights the inaccuracies in DeFiLlama's methodology, which we document in Sect. 3.3.

However, all three metrics show a similar trend, with a surge during the DeFi summer due to increased investor activity and sharp declines following the Luna collapse and the FTX collapse. Figure 5 illustrates the decomposition of TVL in the DeFi system on three key dates. The dominance of the top four protocols increases following the collapse of the Luna and FTX, while the double-counting proportion decreases after these events. The proportion of governance tokens in TVR remains small. The proportion of native tokens decreases after the Luna

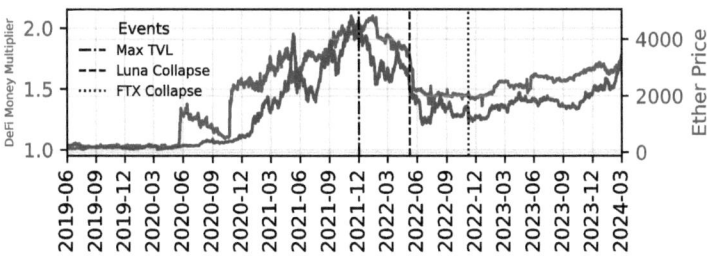

Fig. 7. DeFi money multiplier (red line) and ETH price (blue line). (Color figure online)

collapse but increases following the FTX collapse. Conversely, the proportion of NCB stablecoins rises after the Luna collapse but declines after the FTX collapse. To gain a broader understanding of the double-counting issue, we also analyze two niche alternative chains (Altchains) in Appendix §J.

4.3 DeFi Money Multiplier

The M2 to M0 ratio, known as the traditional money multiplier, indicates the extent to which banks can utilize investor deposits. M0 denotes the money base, which includes cash and bank reserves. M2 denotes the supply of private money, which includes cash, checking deposits, and other short-term deposits. Drawing a parallel, we can divide TVL by TVR to compute the DeFi money multiplier. This ratio reflects the degree of double counting and wrapping effects within the DeFi ecosystem, analogous to the money multiplier in TradFi. Figure 7 plots the DeFi money multiplier.

Table 4 lists the Spearman's rank correlation coefficients between the DeFi money multiplier (M^{DeFi}), key macroeconomic indicators in the US, and representative crypto market indicators. Notably, there is a significant positive correlation between the DeFi money multiplier and cryptocurrency market indicators, such as the S&P Cryptocurrency Broad Digital Market Index ($S\&P$) and Ethereum price (ETH). This suggests that during bullish periods in the cryptocurrency market, investors tend to increase their investments in DeFi and actively engage in leveraged positions. Conversely, the DeFi money multiplier is significantly negatively correlated with the TradFi money multiplier (M^{TradFi}). However, the DeFi money multiplier does not exhibit a significant correlation with the Consumer Price Index (CPI) or the CBOE Volatility Index (VIX). As a robustness test, we also calculate Spearman's rank correlation coefficients between the natural logarithmic return of these indicators to make variables stationary, which is shown in Appendix §K.

5 Risk Analyses

In this section, we present the outcomes of the comparative sensitivity tests. Using the data for the six leading DeFi protocols in Fig. 1, these tests are con-

Table 4. Spearman's rank correlation coefficients between macroeconomic indicators, cryptocurrency market indicators, and DeFi money multiplier computed from TVL and TVR.

	Macroeconomic / TradFi indicators			Cryptocurrency / DeFi indicators		
	CPI_t	VIX_t	M_t^{TradFi}	ETH_t	$S\&P_t$	M_t^{DeFi}
CPI_t	1.00***	-0.19	0.06	0.28*	0.07	0.25
VIX_t	-0.19	1.00***	-0.15	-0.21	-0.19	-0.18
M_t^{TradFi}	0.06	-0.15	1.00***	-0.66***	-0.70***	-0.76***
ETH_t	0.28*	-0.21	-0.66***	1.00***	0.95***	0.91***
$S\&P_t$	0.07	-0.19	-0.70***	0.95***	1.00***	0.91***
M_t^{DeFi}	0.25	-0.18	-0.76***	0.91***	0.91***	1.00***

***, **, and * denote the 1%, 5%, and 10% significance levels, respectively.

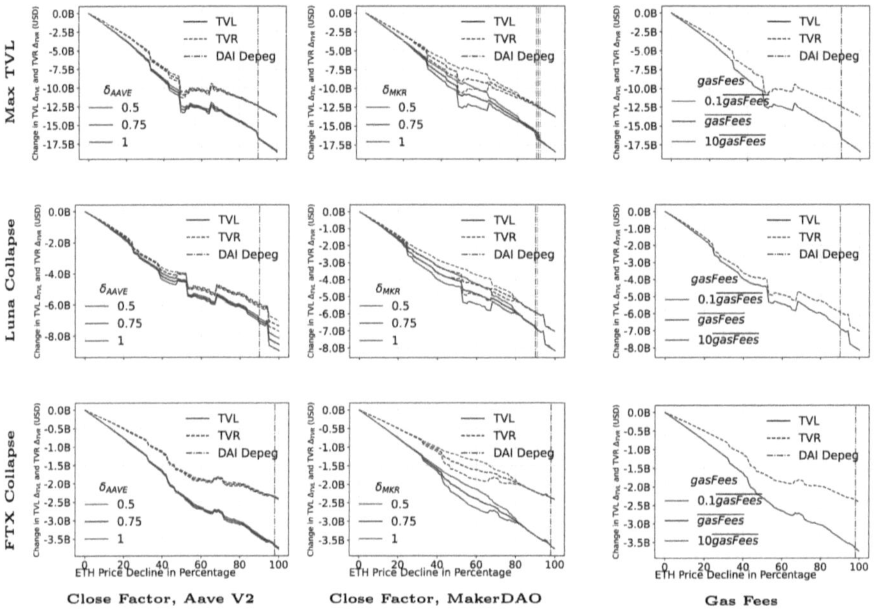

Fig. 8. Change in TVL Δ_{TVL} and TVR Δ_{TVR} as a function of ETH price decline in percentage d_{ETH} on three representative point with different parameter values. Subfigures within a row represent sensitivity tests conducted under the same snapshot, whereas subfigures within a column display sensitivity tests implemented under three different sets of values for a given parameter. Vertical dashed lines indicate the timing of the DAI depeg under different parameter settings.

ducted on three representative date snapshots, each with a different set of parameters. We discuss the default value of certain parameters in Appendix §I. To provide an overview of the simulation environment, we visualize the wrapping network of these protocols in Fig. 6. From this visualization, we observe that both TVL and TVL-to-TVR ratio $\frac{TVL}{TVR}$ of protocols excluding Lido decreases from the point when TVL reaches the maximum value to the subsequent collapse of LUNA and FTX. This trend suggests a reduction in both the overall size of the system and the extent of double-counting within it, which are aligned with the broader dynamics of the overall DeFi system, as depicted in Fig. 4 and Fig. 5.

Figure 8 shows how ΔTVL and ΔTVR vary with ETH price decline d_{ETH}. The ΔTVL and ΔTVR curves with the default parameter setting in Appendix §I are compared with those with hypothetical parameters. Irrespective of parameter values, the ΔTVL curve is more sensitive to d_{ETH} than the ΔTVR curve due to the financial contagion effect of the derivative tokens, which aligns with the reasoning in Sect. 3.

We then discuss how other parameters in Eq. 3 affects ΔTVL and ΔTVR:

1. Close factor (δ): The close factor δ in a lending protocol represents the portion of a loan that a liquidator is allowed to repay when a borrower's health factor falls below one. For instance, consider a liquidable loan position where the loan amount is $100 and the close factor is 0.8; the maximum amount that can be liquidated is then $80 worth of tokens. As shown in Fig. 8, higher δ leads to a greater drop in ΔTVL and ΔTVR, ceteris paribus. This effect is observed for both δ_{AAVE} and δ_{MKR}. The drop in ΔTVL is more sensitive to δ_{MKR} than δ_{AAVE} since MakerDAO has greater exposure to a decline of ETH price compared to Aave V2.
2. Gas fees ($\overline{gasFees}$). We first calculate the average gas fee across daily transactions using $\overline{gasFees} = \overline{gasLimit \times gasPrice}$, and then adjust it by scaling with factors of 0.1, 1, and 10. As shown in Fig. 8, the variations in $\overline{gasFees}$ have a minimal impact on ΔTVL and ΔTVR. This indicates that transaction fees are generally negligible compared to the change of collateral value for most positions.

6 Related Work

Several studies explore the role of TVL in DeFi valuation and risk monitoring. Metelski et al. [11] and Xu et al. [26] investigate the causal relationship between key DeFi performance metrics, such as TVL, protocol revenues, and the DeFi protocol valuations. Stepanova et al. [19] conduct preliminary descriptive and comparison work on TVL of 12 most popular DeFi protocols. Maouchi et al. [12] show that TVL can work as a valuable tool for monitoring market dynamics and assessing the risk of bubbles in the digital financial landscape. Şoiman et al. [18] use TVL divided by market capitalization for DeFi valuation and examine whether this metric drives the DeFi returns.

Some studies examine the DeFi composability and TVL double counting problem in a limited scope. Kitzler et al. [10] measure the composition of DeFi protocols. Saengchote [16] examines the flow of DAI, a DeFi stablecoin, between protocols using high-frequency transaction-level data. The study also explains how TVL accounts for repeat value through the wrapping of DAI. Chiu et al. [3] use a standard theoretical production-network model to assess the value added and service outputs across various DeFi sectors on Ethereum.

7 Conclusion

This paper presents a novel yet effective measurement framework, TVR, to thoroughly address the double counting problem in DeFi. We find a substantial amount of double counting within the DeFi system. Our sensitivity tests show that TVL is highly sensitive during market downturns. We also document that the DeFi money multiplier is positively correlated with crypto market indicators and negatively correlated with macroeconomic indicators. Overall, our findings suggest that TVR is more reliable and stable than TVL.

References

1. Andolfatto, D., Martin, F.M., Zhang, S.: Rehypothecation and liquidity. Eur. Econ. Rev. **100**, 488–505 (2017). https://doi.org/10.1016/J.EUROECOREV.2017.09.010
2. Arora, S., Li, Y., Feng, Y., Xu, J.: SecPLF: secure protocols for loanable funds against oracle manipulation attacks. In: The 19th ACM Asia Conference on Computer and Communications Security, vol. 12, pp. 1394–1405. ACM, New York (2024). https://doi.org/10.1145/3634737.3637681
3. Chiu, J., Koeppl, T.V., Yu, H., Zhang, S.: Understanding Defi through the lens of a production-network model. SSRN Electron. J. (2023). https://doi.org/10.2139/SSRN.4487615
4. Cousaert, S., Xu, J., Matsui, T.: SoK: yield aggregators in DeFi. In: ICBC, pp. 1–14. IEEE (2022). https://doi.org/10.1109/ICBC54727.2022.9805523
5. Feng, Y., Xu, J., Weymouth, L.: University Blockchain Research Initiative (UBRI): boosting blockchain education and research. IEEE Potentials **41**(6), 19–25 (2022). https://doi.org/10.1109/MPOT.2022.3198929
6. Gogol, K., Killer, C., Schlosser, M., Bocek, T., Stiller, B., Tessone, C.: SoK: Decentralized Finance (DeFi) – Fundamentals, Taxonomy and Risks, pp. 1–20 (2024). https://doi.org/10.48550/arXiv.2404.11281
7. Hernandez, W., et al.: Evolution of ESG-focused DLT Research: An NLP Analysis of the Literature (2025). Quant. Sci. Stud. **6**, 810–833 (2025). https://doi.org/10.1162/qss.a.7
8. Ibañez, J.I., Bayer, C.N., Tasca, P., Xu, J.: REA, triple-entry accounting and blockchain: converging paths to shared ledger systems. J. Risk Financ. Manage. **16**(9), 382 (2023). https://doi.org/10.3390/jrfm16090382
9. Ibañez, J.I., Bayer, C.N., Tasca, P., Xu, J.: Triple-entry accounting, blockchain, and next of kin. In: Aggarwal, R., Tasca, P. (eds.) Digital Assets, chap. 9, pp. 198–226. Cambridge University Press (2025). https://doi.org/10.1017/9781009362290.012
10. Kitzler, S., Victor, F., Saggese, P., Haslhofer, B.: Disentangling decentralized finance (DeFi) compositions. ACM Trans. Web **17**(2), 10 (2023). https://doi.org/10.1145/3532857
11. Kumar, A., Le, T., Elnahass, M., Metelski, D., Sobieraj, J.: Decentralized finance (DeFi) projects: a study of key performance indicators in terms of DeFi protocols' valuations. Int. J. Financ. Stud. **10**(4), 108 (2022). https://doi.org/10.3390/IJFS10040108
12. Maouchi, Y., Charfeddine, L., El Montasser, G.: Understanding digital bubbles amidst the COVID-19 pandemic: Evidence from DeFi and NFTs. Finance Res. Lett. **47**, 102584 (2022). https://doi.org/10.1016/J.FRL.2021.102584

13. Perez, D., Werner, S.M., Xu, J., Livshits, B.: Liquidations: DeFi on a knife-edge. In: Borisov, N., Diaz, C. (eds.) FC 2021. LNCS, vol. 12675, pp. 457–476. Springer, Heidelberg (2021). https://doi.org/10.1007/978-3-662-64331-0_24
14. Perez, D., Xu, J., Livshits, B.: Revisiting transactional statistics of high-scalability blockchains. In: IMC, vol. 16, pp. 535–550. ACM, New York (2020). https://doi.org/10.1145/3419394.3423628
15. Richardson, A., Xu, J.: Carbon trading with blockchain. In: Pardalos, P., Kotsireas, I., Guo, Y., Knottenbelt, W. (eds.) MARBLE, chap. 7, pp. 105–124 (2020). https://doi.org/10.1007/978-3-030-53356-4_7
16. Saengchote, K.: Where do DeFi stablecoins go? A closer look at what DeFi composability really means. SSRN Electron. J. (2021). https://doi.org/10.2139/SSRN.3893487
17. Simmonds, A.: Consolidated balance sheet—direct subsidiary. In: Mastering Financial Accounting, pp. 295–318. Palgrave, London (1986). https://doi.org/10.1007/978-1-349-18430-9_17
18. Șoiman, F., Dumas, J.G., Jimenez-Garces, S.: What drives DeFi market returns? J. Int. Financ. Markets Institutions Money **85**, 101786 (2023). https://doi.org/10.1016/J.INTFIN.2023.101786
19. Stepanova, V., Eriņš, I.: Review of decentralized finance applications and their total value locked. TEM J. **10**(1), 327–333 (2021). https://doi.org/10.18421/TEM101-41
20. Tovanich, N., Kassoul, M., Weidenholzer, S., Prat, J.: Contagion in decentralized lending protocols: a case study of compound. In: Workshop on Decentralized Finance and Security, pp. 55–63. ACM, New York (2023). https://doi.org/10.1145/3605768.3623544
21. Xu, J., Feng, Y.: Reap the harvest on blockchain: a survey of yield farming protocols. IEEE Trans. Netw. Serv. Manage. **20**(1), 858–869 (2023). https://doi.org/10.1109/TNSM.2022.3222815
22. Xu, J., Feng, Y., Perez, D., Livshits, B.: Auto.gov: learning-based governance for decentralized finance (DeFi). IEEE Trans. Serv. Comput. **18**(3), 1278–1292 (2025). https://doi.org/10.1109/TSC.2025.3553700
23. Xu, J., Paruch, K., Cousaert, S., Feng, Y.: SoK: decentralized exchanges (DEX) with automated market maker (AMM) protocols. ACM Comput. Surv. **55**(11) (2023). https://doi.org/10.1145/3570639
24. Xu, J., Vadgama, N.: From banks to DeFi: the evolution of the lending market. In: Vadgama, N., Xu, J., Tasca, P. (eds.) Enabling the Internet of Value, chap. 6, pp. 53–66. Springer, Cham (2022). https://doi.org/10.1007/978-3-030-78184-2_6
25. Xu, T.A., Xu, J.: A short survey on business models of decentralized finance (DeFi) protocols. In: FC, pp. 197–206. Springer, Cham (2023). https://doi.org/10.1007/978-3-031-32415-4_13
26. Xu, T.A., Xu, J., Lommers, K.: DeFi versus TradFi valuation using multiples and discounted cash flows. In: Aggarwal, R., Tasca, P. (eds.) Digital Assets, pp. 44–68. Cambridge University Press (2025). https://doi.org/10.1017/9781009362290.004

Transaction Fee Mechanism Design for Leaderless Blockchain Protocols

Pranav Garimidi[1(✉)], Lioba Heimbach[2], and Tim Roughgarden[1,3]

[1] a16z crypto, New York, USA
`pgarimidi@a16z.com`
[2] ETH Zurich, Züurich, Switzerland
`hlioba@ethz.ch`
[3] Columbia University, New York, USA

Abstract. We initiate the study of transaction fee mechanism design for blockchain protocols in which multiple block producers contribute to the production of each block. Our contributions include:
- We propose an extensive-form (multi-stage) game model to reason about the game theory of multi-proposer transaction fee mechanisms.
- We define the *strongly BPIC* property to capture the idea that all block producers should be motivated to behave as intended: for every user bid profile, following the intended allocation rule is a Nash equilibrium for block producers that Pareto dominates all other Nash equilibria.
- We propose the *first-price auction with equal sharing (FPA-EQ)* mechanism as an attractive solution to the multi-proposer transaction fee mechanism design problem. We prove that the mechanism is strongly BPIC and guarantees at least a 63.2% fraction of the maximum-possible expected welfare at equilibrium.
- We prove that the compromises made by the FPA-EQ mechanism are qualitatively necessary: no strongly BPIC mechanism with nontrivial welfare guarantees can be DSIC, and no strongly BPIC mechanism can guarantee optimal welfare at equilibrium.

1 Introduction

1.1 Transaction Fee Mechanisms

A *transaction fee mechanism* is the component of a blockchain protocol responsible for deciding which pending transactions should be included for processing, and what the creators of those transactions should pay for the privilege of execution in the blockchain's virtual machine. For example, the Bitcoin protocol [25] launched with a first-price auction as its transaction fee mechanism

---

L. Heimbach—Work performed in part during an internship at a16z crypto.
T. Roughgarden—Author's research at Columbia University supported in part by NSF awards CCF-2006737 and CNS-2212745.

(which remains in use to this day): users submit bids along with their transactions; should a transaction be included in a block, its bid is transferred from the user to the producer of that block. Block producers are then expected to assemble blocks that maximize their revenue (i.e., the sum of the bids of the included transactions) subject to a block size constraint. The Ethereum protocol also launched with a first-price auction as its transaction fee mechanism [38] but, in order to achieve stronger incentive-compatibility guarantees, the protocol's first-price auction was swapped out in August 2021 in favor of a more sophisticated transaction fee mechanism known as EIP-1559 [6]. Since the initial economic analysis of EIP-1559 [27], a large body of research has been developed to explore the design space of transaction fee mechanisms and to assess different designs through the lenses of incentive-compatibility (both for users and for block producers), collusion-resistance, welfare, revenue, and more; see Sect. 1.4 for an overview.

The entire literature on transaction fee mechanisms considers only *leader-based* blockchain protocols in which each block is assembled unilaterally by a single block producer (like a Bitcoin miner or an Ethereum validator) with monopoly power over the contents of its block. This focus reflects the fact that the vast majority of the major blockchain protocols deployed to-date are leader-based in this sense. For example, all longest-chain protocols in the spirit of Bitcoin and PBFT-type protocols in the vein of Tendermint [5] are leader-based. But the state-of-the-art in consensus protocol design is evolving, and the design of transaction fee mechanisms must evolve with them.

1.2 Leaderless Blockchain Protocols

A new generation of consensus protocols, known as *DAG-based consensus*, is exploring *leaderless* protocol designs (where "DAG" stands for "directed acyclic graph"). In DAG-based consensus protocols, multiple validators build and propose blocks concurrently. Together, the validators build a DAG: whenever a block is proposed by a validator, the block references blocks from previous rounds, effectively voting on these referenced blocks. In each round, some of the blocks (sometimes referred to as anchor blocks) are used as checkpoints in the DAG structure for consensus. When an anchor block is finalized, transactions from all blocks in its causal history that have not been executed previously are deterministically ordered and staged for execution.

Recently, DAG-based consensus protocols have experienced a rise in the blockchain ecosystem, with Sui running Mysticeti in production [35] and other projects such as Aptos planning to transition to DAG-based consensus. The main reason for the rise in popularity of DAG-based consensus protocols is the significant throughput improvements they achieve in comparison to single-leader BFT consensus protocols [4,9,18,33,34]. These throughput improvements stem primarily from two design choices: (1) the separation of the communication and consensus layers, and (2) the use of simultaneous block proposals by all validators to overcome the bottlenecks that arise with the single-leader approach (in effect, spreading what had been a concentrated workload for the leader across all validators). Further, while DAG-based protocols initially suffered from increased latency, current protocols achieve almost optimal latency (up to one extra communication round) [1,2]. Finally, DAG-based protocols have the advantage that they generally recover quickly from crash failures of leaders given that they have backup leaders in place [2].

1.3 Our Contributions

This paper initiates the study of transaction fee mechanism design for blockchain protocols in which multiple block producers contribute to the production of each block. To reason about such mechanisms, several new modeling and design challenges must be addressed:

- Transaction fee mechanism design with a single block producer can focus on equilibria purely from the perspective of users, with the block producer best responding to the resulting bids; with multiple block producers, the "game within the game," meaning the interaction between the incentives of different block producers, must be explicitly modeled and analyzed.
- The design of a transaction fee mechanism must now specify how proposals from multiple block proposers are aggregated into a single block of confirmed transactions.
- The design of a transaction fee mechanism must now specify how any unburned fee revenue from users is distributed between the different block proposers.

This paper offers the following contributions:

- We formally model the game theory of multi-proposer transaction fee mechanisms via extensive-form (multi-stage) games. Further, we define incentive-compatibility for block producers in a multi-proposer transaction fee mechanism, focusing on a condition we call *strongly BPIC*. Intuitively, a transaction fee mechanism is strongly BPIC if, no matter what the user bids, following the intended allocation rule is a Nash equilibrium for block producers that Pareto dominates all other Nash equilibria. While we use our model specifically to study the welfare guarantees achievable by multi-proposer transaction fee mechanisms, it should serve as the appropriate starting point to study a number of other potential benefits of such mechanisms (see Sect. 1.4 below for examples).
- We propose the *first-price auction with equal sharing (FPA-EQ)* mechanism as an attractive solution to the multi-proposer transaction fee mechanism design problem.[1] We prove that the mechanism is strongly BPIC and guarantees near-optimal welfare. Precisely, for every joint distribution over (possibly correlated) user valuations, for every subgame perfect equilibrium of

---

[1] In Sui's current transaction fee mechanism, users pay their bids, and fee revenue is shared with validators pro rata, proportional to validator stake weights (Alberto Sonnino, personal communication, October 2024). The FPA-EQ mechanism can be viewed as the refinement of this mechanism in which transaction fees are shared with validators in proportion to the number of blocks they have contributed to.

the mechanism in which block producers play only Pareto-dominant Nash equilibria, the expected equilibrium welfare is at least $1 - \frac{1}{e} \approx 63.2\%$ of the maximum possible. Our analysis here brings, for the first time, the powerful toolbox on "price of anarchy" bounds to bear on the analysis of transaction fee mechanisms. A simple example shows that the bound of 63.2% is tight in the worst case.
- We prove that the compromises made by the FPA-EQ mechanism are qualitatively necessary: no strongly BPIC mechanism with non-trivial welfare guarantees can be DSIC (i.e., with truthful bidding a dominant strategy for users), and no strongly BPIC mechanism can guarantee optimal welfare at equilibrium.

1.4 Related Work

General TFM Literature. There is a long line of work studying transaction fee mechanisms for single-leader protocols, particularly focusing on Ethereum and Bitcoin. Our model of transaction fee mechanism design closely follows the line of work initiated by Roughgarden [28] to analyze the EIP-1559 mechanism [6]. Before this, research on Bitcoin's fee market focused on monopolistic pricing mechanisms [21,41]. More recent work in this area includes [26] and [13]. Building off Roughgarden's model, Chung and Shi [8] show that achieving an ideal TFM is impossible. They attempt to address these impossibilities using cryptography [30,39], but even with cryptographic methods, perfect TFMs remain unachievable. Furthermore, Chung et al. [7] and Gafni and Yaish [14] show that no mechanism can be incentive compatible for the users and the block producers while also being collusion-resistant. All of these impossibility results carry over to our context, as a single-leader protocol is a special case of a multiple-leader protocol. Although the majority of this work is prior-free, Zhao et al. [43] consider a Bayesian setup, demonstrating ways to circumvent these impossibility results in cases where bidders have i.i.d. valuations. Other works explore TFM dynamics over multiple blocks [10,22] and incorporate maximal extractable value (MEV) into traditional TFM models [3].

DAG-Based Consensus. Hashgraph [4] was the first protocol to introduce a DAG-based consensus protocol. It separated the communication layer and the consensus logic, with the communication layer constructing a DAG of messages which is then used by the consensus protocol. Later protocols adopted a round-based structure within the DAG to design more efficient asynchronous BFT protocols [9,16,18,33]. Among these, Bullshark's partially synchronous variant became the first widely deployed DAG-based consensus protocol, notably used in the Sui blockchain [34]. Since Bullshark's deployment, a number of papers have focused on reducing the latency of DAG-based consensus protocols [1,2,19,23,31,32]. The designs in these papers generally either move towards uncertified DAGs (which do not require explicit certification) or interleave multiple instances of the Bullshark protocol on a shared DAG. Mysticeti [2] has replaced Bullshark as the consensus protocol used by the Sui blockchain [35].

Economics of Multiple Leaders. There is a modest amount of work concerning the incentives faced by validators in multi-leader protocols. Zhang and Kate [42] show how DAG-based consensus protocols can be manipulated for MEV, while Malkhi et al. [24] propose MEV protection for such protocols. Fox et al. [11] look at the cost of censorship in single-leader protocols and show how TFMs specific to multi-leader protocols could potentially be used to significantly increase the cost of censorship. The Solana community has been considering whether to introduce multiple leaders to promote competition between block producers for the benefit of users [40], and Ethereum is planning on incorporating some of the ideas from multi-proposer architectures through FOCIL [37] to increase Ethereum's censorship resistance. The present work does not directly address questions around MEV, censorship, or explicit competition between block producers, but we believe that the model that we introduce in the next section can serve as the starting point for a formal study of these questions.

2 The Model

This section defines our game-theoretic model, the design space of transaction fee mechanisms, several notions of incentive-compatibility, and approximate welfare guarantees.

2.1 The Players

Games have three ingredients: players, strategy spaces, and payoffs. For transaction fee mechanisms (TFMs), there are two types of self-interested players, users and block producers (BPs). We discuss each in turn.

We assume that the set $I = \{1, 2, \ldots, n\}$ of users is known, and that each is identified with a single transaction; we refer to users and transactions interchangeably. We assume that user i has a private valuation v_i for the inclusion of its transaction in the next block, and that transaction validity does not depend on transaction ordering. When discussing Bayes-Nash equilibria (as is necessary when discussing TFMs without dominant strategies, such as variants of first-price auctions), we assume that user valuations $\mathbf{v}$ are drawn from a prior distribution $\mathbf{D}$ that is common knowledge among the users.[2] User valuations may be correlated; that is, $\mathbf{D}$ need not be a product distribution.

We consider TFMs in which each user attaches a nonnegative bid b_i to its transaction (thus, the strategy space of user i is the possible choices of b_i). We assume that each user has a quasi-linear utility function, meaning that its payoff is the value it receives (v_i if its transaction is included in the next block and 0 otherwise) minus the payment it makes. (Utilities functions will be stated more formally following the definition of TFMs; see Sect. 2.4.)

---

[2] We allow valuation distributions to have atoms at zero (or at other values), in which case the number of (non-null) players can be thought of as stochastic rather than known.

We also consider a set $J = \{1, 2, \ldots, m\}$ of BPs. BP strategies correspond to blocks, where for a known block size k, a *block* is a set of at most k transactions (together with the bids of those transactions). We assume that each BP $j \in J$ has an associated subset S_j of transactions that it can include in its block; we refer to the special case in which $S_j = I$ for all $j \in J$ as the *BP-symmetric setting* and the case of general S_j's as the *BP-asymmetric setting*. A block is *feasible* for BP j if it includes only transactions of S_j and, possibly, additional transactions created by j itself (e.g., in order to manipulate a TFM's payment rule). We assume that the S_j's are common knowledge. The payoff of a BP is defined as the revenue it earns from transactions other than its own minus.

2.2 The Game

TFM outcomes are, intuitively, determined by a two-stage process: users decide which bids to attach to their transactions, and BPs then decide which transactions to include. Previous work on TFMs, with a single BP, could essentially model the process with one stage (with the understanding that the BP will respond to users' bids with its favorite block). With multiple BPs best responding to each other (in addition to users' bids), it is important to explicitly model the block formation process as a two-stage game. We do this next, using the standard formalism for extensive-form games (e.g. [12]).

Game Trees. To review, an extensive form game is defined by a rooted tree (the *game tree*). Each node represents a single action to be taken by a single player, with the node labeled with that player and edges leading to the node's children labeled with the possible actions. Each leaf of the tree corresponds to an outcome of the game, and is labeled with players' payoffs in that outcome. Thus, root-leaf paths of the game tree correspond to action sequences that terminate in an outcome of the game. It is a convenient tradition to allow nodes that are labeled with a non-strategic "Nature" player, indicating that the action at that node is chosen at random from a distribution that is common knowledge. Finally, for each player, the nodes labeled with that player are partitioned into information sets. An information set represents a set of nodes that are indistinguishable to the player at the time it must take an action (and thus, the same action must be taken by a player at all nodes in the same information set).

To model behavior in TFMs with multiple BPs, we consider a game tree with $n + m + 1$ levels. (The outcomes and payoffs at the leaves of this tree will depend on the choice of the TFM, but the tree structure is independent of the particular TFM.) At level 0, Nature moves and chooses valuations $\mathbf{v}$ for all users from the assumed prior $\mathbf{D}$. At each level $l = 1, 2, \ldots, n$, user l selects its bid b_l. Information sets are defined for user l so that its choice of bid depends only on its own valuation v_l (and not on the other valuations $\mathbf{v}_{-l}$ determined at level 0 or the bids chosen by users $i \in \{1, 2, \ldots, l-1\}$ at earlier levels). At each level $l = n+1, n+2, \ldots, n+m$, BP $j = l - n$ selects its block B_j. Information sets are defined for a BP so that its choice of block can depend on the bids **b** chosen by users but not on the blocks chosen by the other BPs. [3]

Subgame Perfect Equilibria. Our analysis uses what is arguably the most canonical equilibrium concept in extensive-form games, namely subgame perfect equilibria. In such a game, a strategy for a player is defined by a mapping from each of its information sets to one of the actions available at that information set. In our model of TFMs, a user has one information set for each realization of its valuation, and a BP has one information set for each user bid vector. Thus, a user strategy is simply a bidding strategy, meaning a mapping $v_i \mapsto b_i$ from valuations to bids. A BP strategy is a mapping $\mathbf{b} \mapsto B_j$ from user bid vectors to feasible blocks. Thus, leaves of the game tree are effectively labeled by **v** (Nature's action at level 0), **b** (users' actions at levels 1 through n), and **B** (BPs' actions at levels $n+1$ through $n+m$); these, in conjunction with the choice of a TFM, will define the player payoffs at this outcome.

A strategy profile in an extensive-form game is called a Nash equilibrium if the usual best-response condition holds: no player can strictly improve its expected payoff through a unilateral deviation to a different mapping of its information sets to actions. That is, each player is best responding to the strategies chosen by the other players.

Every node of a game tree induces a rooted subtree that can be regarded as an extensive-form game in its own right. Similarly, every strategy of an extensive-form game induces a strategy in each of its subgames. A strategy profile of an extensive-form game is called a *subgame perfect equilibrium (SPE)* if, for each if its subgames, the induced strategy profile is a Nash equilibrium. Intuitively, even after "fast forwarding" to an arbitrary node of the game tree, play from then on constitutes a Nash equilibrium.[4]

Intuitively, in our model of TFMs with multiple BPs, the SPE condition translates to (i) users play a Bayes-Nash equilibrium relative to the BP equilibrium strategies; (ii) BPs play a Nash equilibrium relative to the user bids.[5]

---

[3] Thus, BPs engage in a complete-information game, with the full bid vector **b** and the S_j's known to all BPs. A good (though possibly difficult) direction for future work is to consider an incomplete-information generalization of our model. With our assumptions, users can effectively treat BPs as carrying out the welfare-maximizing allocation rule. In an incomplete-information setup, users would effectively be submitting bids to a randomized allocation rule induced by some (perhaps impossible-to-characterize) Bayes-Nash equilibrium played by the BPs.

[4] Without the subgame perfect refinement, Nash equilibria of extensive-form games allow players to play arbitrary strategies in subgames that are reached with probability 0.

[5] We do not model how BPs coordinate on a given equilibrium. Microfounding the assumption that BPs reach an equilibrium (e.g., through experience from repeated play, explicit coordination based on transaction hashes, or other means) is an interesting direction for future research.

2.3 Transaction Fee Mechanisms

A TFM is specified by four ingredients: an inclusion rule (the blocks of transactions that the BPs are expected to contribute), a confirmation rule (given the proposed blocks, which transactions are confirmed for execution), a payment rule (given the proposed blocks, what the creators of confirmed transactions pay), and a distribution rule (given the proposed blocks, the revenue received by BPs). Because BPs have unilateral control over the transactions they include, the inclusion rule can only be viewed as a recommendation to BPs; the other three rules are hard-coded into the code of a blockchain protocol and cannot be manipulated by BPs.

We next define these four ingredients formally, along with a number of examples that illustrate the definitions and demonstrate the richness of the TFM design space with multiple BPs. (Many of the examples are deferred to Appendix A.1 of the full version of this paper [15].) These rules are all defined with respect to a commonly known *game structure*, meaning a player set I, a BP set J, BP transaction sets $S_1, \ldots, S_m$, and a block size k.[6] Recall that a block B_j is *feasible for* j if it includes only transactions of S_j and, possibly, transactions that j itself created (along with the bids attached to the included transactions). When we are concerned only with the transactions included in a block and not the attached bids, we sometimes abuse notation and treat a block as a subset of I. We call a profile $\mathbf{B} = (B_1, \ldots, B_m)$ of block choices an *allocation*, and call an allocation *feasible* if each of its blocks B_j is feasible for the corresponding BP j. We call an allocation *shill-free* if, for each of its blocks, only user-submitted transactions are included (i.e., $B_j \subseteq S_j$ for every BP j). Note that the same transaction may be included in more than one block of an allocation. We denote by $T(\mathbf{B}) = \cup_{j \in J} B_j$ the transactions that are included (at least once) in an allocation $\mathbf{B}$.

Inclusion Rules. An inclusion rule can be thought of as a recommendation of the strategies that BPs should play in each information set of the extensive-form game described in Sect. 2.2. Formally, with respect to a game structure, an *inclusion rule* is a function $\mathbf{y} : \mathbf{b} \mapsto \mathbf{B}$ mapping user bids vectors to feasible allocations.

For example, the *welfare-maximizing (WM)* inclusion rule maps each bid vector to a feasible shill-free allocation that maximizes the sum of the bids of the included transactions (breaking ties using some consistent rule). For TFMs with first-price payment rules (see below), this inclusion rule can be interpreted as maximizing the total fees paid by users.[7]

Confirmation Rules. A confirmation rule specifies which of the included transactions are confirmed for execution. Formally, with respect to a game structure, a *confirmation rule* is a function $\mathcal{C} : \mathbf{B} \mapsto \mathcal{B}$ that maps each feasible allocation $\mathbf{B}$

---

[6] The valuation distribution $\mathbf{D}$ is not part of the game structure; in this sense, a TFM is by definition prior-free.

[7] For another example, the *serial dictatorship* inclusion rule is described in Appendix A.1 of the full version of this paper [15].

to a set $\mathcal{B} \subseteq T(\mathbf{B})$ of confirmed transactions. Note that while a transaction may be included in multiple blocks, it can only be confirmed once.

For example, the *first-price auction (FPA) confirmation rule* confirms every transaction that is included at least once: $\mathcal{C}(\mathbf{B}) = T(\mathbf{B})$.[8]

Payment Rules. A payment rule specifies the transaction fee paid by the creator of an included transaction. Formally, with respect to a game structure, a *payment rule* is a function $\mathbf{p}$ that maps each feasible allocation $\mathbf{B}$ to a set of n nonnegative numbers (one per user).

For example, the *first-price auction (FPA) payment rule* charges the creator of an included transaction its bid: $p_i(\mathbf{B}) = b_i$ if $i \in T(\mathbf{B})$ and $p_i(\mathbf{B}) = 0$ otherwise.[9]

Distribution Rules. A distribution rule specifies the revenue earned by each BP from the set of included transactions. Formally, with respect to a game structure, a *distribution rule* is a function π that maps each feasible allocation $\mathbf{B}$ to a set of m nonnegative numbers (one per BP).

For example, the *equal-share* distribution rule (FPA version) splits the bid of each included transaction equally between the BPs: for all j,

$$\pi_j(\mathbf{B}) = \frac{1}{m} \sum_{i \in T(\mathbf{B})} b_i. \tag{1}$$

Many other examples are possible (e.g., splitting the bid of a transaction between only the BPs that include it in their blocks); see Appendix A.1 of the full version of this paper [15] for details.

TFMs. A *transaction fee mechanism (TFM)* is then a tuple $(\mathbf{y}, \mathcal{C}, \mathbf{p}, \pi)$. We restrict attention to TFMs that satisfy the following properties (which are also shared by all TFMs that have been deployed in practice to-date): (i) *deterministic*, meaning that $\mathbf{y}, \mathcal{C}, \mathbf{p}$, and π are all deterministic functions of their inputs; and (ii) *ex post individually rational*, meaning that $p_i(\mathbf{B}) = 0$ if user i's transaction is not confirmed by the TFM (i.e., $i \notin \mathcal{C}(\mathbf{B})$) and $p_i(\mathbf{B}) \leq b_i$ otherwise; (iii) *weakly budget-balanced*, meaning that users' payments always cover BP revenue: $\sum_{j \in J} \pi_j(\mathbf{B}) \leq \sum_{i \in I} p_i(\mathbf{B})$ for every feasible allocation $\mathbf{B}$.[10] We do allow the user payments to exceed the BP revenue, in which we case the remaining

---

[8] One reason to include unconfirmed transactions is to use their bids to set prices for the confirmed transactions, in the spirit of a second-price auction. For more details, see the *second-price auction (SPA) confirmation rule* described in Appendix A.1 of the full version of this paper [15].

[9] For another example, the *second-price auction (SPA) payment rule* is described in Appendix A.1 of the full version of this paper [15].

[10] As an extension to (iii), money-printing in the form of inflationary rewards (like a block reward) can be added to a TFM without affecting its incentive or welfare properties, provided the rewards are the same no matter which feasible allocation $\mathbf{B}$ is chosen by the BPs.

user payments are burned (or otherwise redirected away from BPs, for example to a foundation).

TFMs can be assembled from different inclusion, confirmation, payment, and distribution rules in many natural ways; see Appendix A.1 of the full version of this paper [15] for an incomplete list.

2.4 Incentive Compatibility

Intuitively, a mechanism is incentive-compatible if its participants are motivated to behave in a prescribed way, such as by bidding truthfully (in the case of users) or by choosing blocks as instructed by a TFM's inclusion rule (in the case of BPs). We next formalize these two incentive-compatibility properties (one for users, one for BPs).

Dominant-Strategy Incentive-Compatibility (DSIC). We first observe that the composition of an (intended) inclusion rule $\mathbf{y}$ and confirmation rule $\mathcal{C}$ of a TFM induce an (intended) *allocation rule* $\mathbf{x}$, with $x_i(\mathbf{b}) = 1$ if $i \in \mathcal{C}(\mathbf{y}(\mathbf{b}))$ and $x_i(\mathbf{b}) = 0$ otherwise. That is, $\mathbf{x}(\mathbf{b})$ is the characteristic vector of the confirmed transactions with user bids $\mathbf{b}$, assuming that the BPs carry out the intended inclusion rule. Under the same assumption, the payoff of user i under bid vector $\mathbf{b}$ in the TFM $(\mathbf{y}, \mathcal{C}, \mathbf{p}, \pi)$ is

$$u_i(\mathbf{b}) = v_i \cdot x_i(\mathbf{b}) - p_i(\mathbf{y}(\mathbf{b})). \tag{2}$$

A TFM is then *dominant-strategy incentive-compatible (DSIC)* if, for every user i, valuation v_i, and bid vector $\mathbf{b}$, $u_i(v_i, \mathbf{b}_{-i}) \geq u_i(\mathbf{b})$. That is, after fixing the BP strategies to be those recommended by the TFM's inclusion rule, truthful bidding is a dominant strategy for every user. For example, in the BP-symmetric setting (with $S_j = I$ for all $j \in J$), the SPA-EQ and SPA-Shapley TFMs (see Appendix A.1 of the full version of this paper [15]) are DSIC. TFMs that use the FPA payment rule are never DSIC, as users are incentivized to shade their bids.

Block Producer Incentive-Compatibility (BPIC). The payoff of BP j is $\pi_j(\mathbf{B})$ in an outcome of a TFM $(\mathbf{y}, \mathcal{C}, \mathbf{p}, \pi)$, specified by the bids $\mathbf{b}$ chosen by users and the feasible allocation $\mathbf{B}$ chosen by BPs. A TFM is then *block producer incentive-compatible (BPIC)* if, for every bid vector $\mathbf{b}$ with corresponding intended allocation $\mathbf{y}(\mathbf{b}) = \mathbf{B} = (B_1, \ldots, B_m)$, every BP j, and every block B_j' feasible for j, $\pi_j(\mathbf{B}) \geq \pi_j(B_j', \mathbf{B}_{-j})$. That is, after fixing the user bids to $\mathbf{b}$, the feasible allocation recommended by the TFM's inclusion rule is a Nash equilibrium among the BPs.

For example, the SPA-EQ and SPA-Shapley TFMs from Appendix A.1 of the full version of this paper [15] are not BPIC, as BPs generally have an incentive to deviate from the WM allocation rule by including their own transactions in order to boost their overall revenue. The FPA-Shapley TFM (see Appendix A.1 of the full version of this paper [15]) fails to satisfy BPIC for a different reason: BPs are generally incentivized to redundantly include a high-bid transaction multiple times rather that following the WM allocation rule (in which each transaction is included at most once).

Strong BPIC. Despite the fact that many natural TFMs fail to satisfy it, the BPIC condition is relatively weak. For example, any TFM that uses the null distribution rule (with all transaction fees burned) is trivially BPIC, with all BPs indifferent across all outcomes. Thus, the BPIC condition does not generally provide much force toward BPs carrying out the intended inclusion rule.

The next condition, a strengthening of BPIC, states that the intended allocation should not merely be a Nash equilibrium, but should also be strictly superior to all non-equivalent Nash equilibria. Formally, a TFM $(\mathbf{y}, \mathcal{C}, \mathbf{p}, \pi)$ is *strongly BPIC* if, for every user bid vector $\mathbf{b}$, the following conditions hold:

1. the recommended feasible allocation $\mathbf{B} = \mathbf{y}(\mathbf{b})$ is a Nash equilibrium among the BPs (holding user bids fixed at $\mathbf{b}$);
2. every Nash equilibrium $\mathbf{B}'$ among the BPs (again, with fixed bids $\mathbf{b}$) is either equivalent to or Pareto dominated by $\mathbf{B}$.

Intuitively, two feasible allocations are "equivalent" if they are the same up to tie-breaking and the inclusion of zero-bid transactions. Formally, for a TFM $(\mathbf{y}, \mathcal{C}, \mathbf{p}, \pi)$, feasible allocations $\mathbf{B}$ and $\mathbf{B}'$ are *equivalent* if the multi-sets of the positive bids of the confirmed transactions $\mathcal{C}(\mathbf{B})$ and $\mathcal{C}(\mathbf{B}')$ are identical. We say that one allocation $\mathbf{B}$ *Pareto dominates* another allocation $\mathbf{B}'$ if: (i) $\pi_j(\mathbf{B}) \geq \pi_j(\mathbf{B}')$ for all $j \in J$; and (ii) $\pi_j(\mathbf{B}) > \pi_j(\mathbf{B}')$ for some $j \in J$. We'll see in Sect. 3.2 an example of a strongly BPIC TFM (the FPA-EQ TFM).

2.5 Approximate Welfare Guarantees

We assess the outcome quality of different TFMs using the welfare objective $W(\cdot)$, defined as the total value of the confirmed transactions. That is, for a TFM $(\mathbf{y}, \mathcal{C}, \mathbf{p}, \pi)$ and feasible allocation $\mathbf{B}$, $W(\mathbf{B}) = \sum_{i \in \mathcal{C}(\mathbf{B})} v_i$. TFMs can suffer from welfare loss for three distinct reasons. First, even if all participants behave as desired, a TFM's inclusion rule may result in a suboptimal feasible allocation. Second, even with the WM allocation rule and truthful bids, BPs may coordinate on a suboptimal Nash equilibrium. Third, even with the WM allocation rule and BPs that coordinate on the intended Nash equilibrium, non-truthful bidding by users can lead to suboptimal allocations. (See Appendix A.2 of the full version of this paper [15] for examples of all three types.) Thus, a equilibrium welfare approximation guarantee is a guarantee that the welfare loss *from all three of these sources combined* is relatively modest.

3 FPA-EQ: A Strongly BPIC and Near-Optimal TFM

3.1 What Can We Hope For?

We have highlighted three desirable properties of TFMs (in addition to our standing requirements that TFMs be deterministic and ex post individually rational): (i) DSIC; (ii) strong BPIC; and (iii) optimal or near-optimal welfare at equilibrium. In this work, we take the strong BPIC condition (ii) as a hard constraint. (If

BPs are not properly motivated to carry out the intended inclusion rule, which in turn determines the confirmed transactions and their payments, it's unclear how to interpret a proposed TFM.) In Theorem 4 in Appendix B.1 of the full version of this paper [15], we prove that no DSIC and strongly BPIC TFM can achieve a non-trivial equilibrium welfare guarantee. This result implies that we have no choice but to consider non-DSIC TFMs. In Theorem 5 in Appendix B.2 of the full version of this paper [15], we prove that no (possibly non-DSIC) strongly BPIC TFM can guarantee optimal welfare at equilibrium. In light of these negative results, the best-case scenario is a strongly BPIC TFM that guarantees near-optimal welfare at equilibrium. We present such a TFM next.

3.2 The FPA-EQ TFM

The rest of this section analyzes the *first-price auction with equal sharing (FPA-EQ)* TFM. The ingredients of this TFM were all introduced in Sect. 2.3:

- the welfare-maximizing (WM) inclusion rule (i.e., with $\mathbf{y}(\mathbf{b}) = \mathbf{B}$ chosen to maximize the sum of the bids $\sum_{i \in T(\mathbf{B})} b_i$ of the included transactions, with ties broken according to some consistent rule);
- the FPA confirmation rule (with all included transaction confirmed: $\mathcal{C}(\mathbf{B}) = T(\mathbf{B})$);
- the FPA payment rule (with each user of a confirmed transaction paying its bid);
- the equal share (FPA version) distribution rule (with the payment for each confirmed transaction split equally between the m block producers, as in (1)).

Because of its FPA payment rule, the FPA-EQ TFM is not DSIC; bidders are incentivized to shade their bids. Unlike many other natural TFMs, however, the FPA-EQ TFM is strongly BPIC. The proof of this fact leans heavily on the choice of the equal-share distribution rule, and also on the matroid structure of feasible allocations.

Proposition 1 (FPA-EQ Is Strongly BPIC) *For every game structure, the FPA-EQ TFM is strongly BPIC.*

Proof. Fix a game structure and a user bid vector $\mathbf{b}$. The payoff of every BP is proportional to the total amount paid by users (due to the equal-share distribution rule), and therefore to the sum of the bids of the confirmed transactions (due to the FPA payment rule), and therefore to the sum of the bids of the included transactions (due to the FPA confirmation rule). Because the WM allocation rule instructs BPs to maximize the sum of the bids of the included transactions over feasible allocations, the intended allocation $\mathbf{B}^*$ is a Nash equilibrium among the BPs (holding user bids fixed at $\mathbf{b}$). By the same reasoning, $\mathbf{B}^*$ Pareto dominates every Nash equilibrium allocation that fails to maximize the sum of the bids of the included transactions. Finally, because the subsets of transactions that can be included in a feasible allocation form a matroid (see Proposition 6 in Appendix B.3 of the full version of this paper [15]) and due to the lexicographic optimality property of matroids (see Proposition 7 in Appendix B.3 of the full version of this paper [15]), every feasible allocation **B** that maximizes the sum of the included bids is equivalent to $\mathbf{B}^*$ (i.e., after ignoring zero-bid transactions, the multi-sets of bids of transactions in $\mathcal{C}(\mathbf{B})$ and $\mathcal{C}(\mathbf{B}^*)$ are identical).

3.3 An Approximate Welfare Guarantee for FPA-EQ

Our main result in this section is that the FPA-EQ TFM, in addition to satisfying the strong BPIC property (Proposition 1), achieves near-optimal welfare at equilibrium. Precisely, in the extensive-form game induced by this TFM $(\mathbf{y}, \mathcal{C}, \mathbf{p}, \pi)$ (see Sect. 2.2), call a strategy profile *inclusion-rule respecting (IRR)* at **b** if, in the subgame corresponding to **b**, the BPs choose a feasible allocation that is equivalent to $\mathbf{y}(\mathbf{b})$. (As in Sect. 2.4, two feasible allocations are equivalent if the resulting sets of confirmed transactions share the same multi-sets of positive bids.) A subgame-perfect equilibrium is then called inclusion-rule respecting if it is IRR at every user bid vector **b**. For a strongly BPIC TFM like FPA-EQ, there is good reason to focus on its IRR SPE—in any other SPE, there are bids vectors for which BPs inexplicably coordinate on a subgame equilibrium that is Pareto dominated by the one suggested by the TFM's inclusion rule.

Theorem 2 (FPA-EQ Is Approximately Welfare-Optimal). *For every game structure and valuation distribution* **D**, *every inclusion-rule-respecting subgame perfect equilibrium of the FPA-EQ TFM has expected welfare at least $1 - \frac{1}{e} \approx 63.2\%$ of the maximum possible.*

The proof of Theorem 2 proceeds in two steps. The first step establishes an equivalence between the IRR SPE of the FPA-EQ TFM and the Bayes-Nash equilibria of a (single-shot) winner-pays-bid matroid auction. Intuitively, with the BP behavior fixed (up to allocation equivalence) in an IRR SPE, we can analyze users as if they are competing in a single-stage game. See Lemma 3 in Appendix B.4 of the full version of this paper [15] for details.

The second step of the proof applies the theory of smooth games (see e.g. [29]) to prove a worst-case bound on the expected welfare of the Bayes-Nash equilibria of winner-pays-bid matroid auctions.[11] The details are fairly technical and deferred to Appendix B.4 of the full version of this paper [15].

We can obtain stronger guarantees if we impose symmetry conditions on the BPs and users. In the BP-symmetric setting (see Sect. 2.1), a simple exchange argument shows that *every* SPE of the FPA-EQ TFM is IRR. Thus:

Corollary 1. *In the BP-symmetric setting, for every game structure and valuation distribution* **D**, *every subgame perfect equilibrium of the FPA-EQ TFM has expected welfare at least $1 - \frac{1}{e} \approx 63.2\%$ of the maximum possible.*

Adapting an example of Syrgkanis [36] for first-price auctions to the present setting gives a lower bound showing that the approximation factor of $1 - \frac{1}{e}$ in

---

[11] Such a bound was proved in [17] for the special case of independent user valuations; the bound here for correlated user valuations appears to be new.

Theorem 2 and Corollary 1 is tight (see Appendix B.4 of the full version of this paper [15] for details).

Proposition 3 (Theorem 2 Is Tight) *There exists a game structure, valuation distribution* $\mathbf{D}$, *and an inclusion-rule-respecting subgame perfect equilibrium of the FPA-EQ TFM with expected welfare* $1 - \frac{1}{e}$ *times the expected maximum welfare.*

If we further assume that users are symmetric, meaning that their valuations are drawn i.i.d. from a common distribution, then every SPE of the FPA-EQ TFM is in fact fully efficient. The following corollary follows from Lemma 3 (in Appendix B.4 of the full version of this paper [15]) and the full efficiency of Bayes-Nash equilibria in multi-unit auctions with symmetric unit-demand bidders (see e.g. [20]):

Corollary 2 (Optimal Welfare in Symmetric Settings). *In the BP-symmetric setting, for every game structure and i.i.d. valuation distribution, every subgame perfect equilibrium of the FPA-EQ TFM achieves the maximum-possible expected welfare.*

As noted in Sect. 2.2, these positive results assume that BPs are capable of coordinating on an equilibrium of the appropriate type. It would be interesting to investigate how our guarantees would change under weaker versions of this assumption.

References

1. Arun, B., Li, Z., Suri-Payer, F., Das, S., Spiegelman, A.: Shoal++: high throughput DAG BFT can be fast! arXiv preprint arXiv:2405.20488 (2024)
2. Babel, K., Chursin, A., Danezis, G., Kokoris-Kogias, L., Sonnino, A.: Mysticeti: low-latency DAG consensus with fast commit path. arXiv preprint arXiv:2310.14821 (2023)
3. Bahrani, M., Garimidi, P., Roughgarden, T.: Transaction fee mechanism design in a post-mev world. In: Böhme, R., Kiffer, L. (eds.) 6th Conference on Advances in Financial Technologies, AFT 2024, Vienna, Austria, 23–25 September 2024. LIPIcs, vol. 316, pp. 29:1–29:24. Schloss Dagstuhl - Leibniz-Zentrum für Informatik (2024). https://doi.org/10.4230/LIPICS.AFT.2024.29
4. Baird, L.: The swirlds hashgraph consensus algorithm: fair, fast, byzantine fault tolerance. Swirlds Tech Reports SWIRLDS-TR-2016-01, Technical report, vol. 34, pp. 9–11 (2016)
5. Buchman, E.: Tendermint: Byzantine fault tolerance in the age of blockchains. Ph.D. thesis, University of Guelph (2016)
6. Buterin, V., Conner, E., Dudley, R., Slipper, M., Norden, I., Bakhta, A.: EIP-1559: fee market change for eth 1.0 chain (2024). https://github.com/ethereum/EIPs/blob/master/EIPS/eip-1559.md. Accessed 10 Oct 2024
7. Chung, H., Roughgarden, T., Shi, E.: Collusion-resilience in transaction fee mechanism design. arXiv preprint arXiv:2402.09321 (2024)

8. Chung, H., Shi, E.: Foundations of transaction fee mechanism design. In: Proceedings of the 2023 Annual ACM-SIAM Symposium on Discrete Algorithms (SODA), pp. 3856–3899. SIAM (2023)
9. Danezis, G., Kokoris-Kogias, L., Sonnino, A., Spiegelman, A.: Narwhal and tusk: a DAG-based mempool and efficient BFT consensus. In: Proceedings of the Seventeenth European Conference on Computer Systems, pp. 34–50 (2022)
10. Ferreira, M.V.X., Moroz, D.J., Parkes, D.C., Stern, M.: Dynamic posted-price mechanisms for the blockchain transaction-fee market. In: Proceedings of the 3rd ACM Conference on Advances in Financial Technologies, pp. 86–99 (2021)
11. Fox, E., Pai, M.M., Resnick, M.: Censorship resistance in on-chain auctions. In: Bonneau, J., Weinberg, S.M. (eds.) 5th Conference on Advances in Financial Technologies, AFT 2023, Princeton, NJ, USA, 23–25 October 2023. LIPIcs, vol. 282, pp. 19:1–19:20. Schloss Dagstuhl - Leibniz-Zentrum für Informatik (2023). https://doi.org/10.4230/LIPICS.AFT.2023.19
12. Fudenberg, D., Tirole, J.: Game Theory. MIT Press (1991)
13. Gafni, Y., Yaish, A.: Greedy transaction fee mechanisms for (non-) myopic miners. arXiv preprint arXiv:2210.07793 (2022)
14. Gafni, Y., Yaish, A.: Barriers to collusion-resistant transaction fee mechanisms. arXiv preprint arXiv:2402.08564 (2024)
15. Garimidi, P., Heimbach, L., Roughgarden, T.: Transaction fee mechanism design for leaderless blockchain protocols (2025). https://arxiv.org/abs/2505.17885
16. Gkagol, A., Leśniak, D., Straszak, D., Świętek, M.: Aleph: efficient atomic broadcast in asynchronous networks with byzantine nodes. In: Proceedings of the 1st ACM Conference on Advances in Financial Technologies, pp. 214–228 (2019)
17. Hartline, J., Hoy, D., Taggart, S.: Price of anarchy for auction revenue. In: Proceedings of the 15th ACM conference on Economics and Computation, pp. 693–710 (2014)
18. Keidar, I., Kokoris-Kogias, E., Naor, O., Spiegelman, A.: All you need is DAG. In: Proceedings of the 2021 ACM Symposium on Principles of Distributed Computing, pp. 165–175 (2021)
19. Keidar, I., Naor, O., Poupko, O., Shapiro, E.: Cordial miners: fast and efficient consensus for every eventuality. arXiv preprint arXiv:2205.09174 (2022)
20. Krishna, V.: Auction Theory. Academic Press (2009)
21. Lavi, R., Sattath, O., Zohar, A.: Redesigning bitcoin's fee market. ACM Trans. Econ. Comput. **10**(1), 1–31 (2022)
22. Leonardos, S., Monnot, B., Reijsbergen, D., Skoulakis, S., Piliouras, G.: Dynamical analysis of the EIP-1559 Ethereum fee market. In: Proceedings of the 3rd ACM Advances in Financial Technologies (2021)
23. Malkhi, D., Stathakopoulou, C., Yin, M.: BBCA-chain: one-message, low latency BFT consensus on a DAG. arXiv preprint arXiv:2310.06335 (2023)
24. Malkhi, D., Szalachowski, P.: Maximal extractable value (MEV) protection on a DAG. In: 4th International Conference on Blockchain Economics, Security and Protocols, p. 1 (2023)
25. Nakamoto, S.: A peer-to-peer electronic cash system (2008)
26. Nisan, N.: Serial monopoly on blockchains (2023)
27. Roughgarden, T.: Transaction fee mechanism design for the Ethereum blockchain: an economic analysis of EIP-1559. arXiv preprint arXiv:2012.00854 (2020)
28. Roughgarden, T.: Transaction fee mechanism design. ACM SIGecom Exchanges **19**(1), 52–55 (2021). Full version at https://arxiv.org/abs/2106.01340
29. Roughgarden, T., Syrgkanis, V., Tardos, E.: The price of anarchy in auctions. J. Artif. Intell. Res. **59**, 59–101 (2017)

30. Shi, E., Chung, H., Wu, K.: What can cryptography do for decentralized mechanism design. arXiv preprint arXiv:2209.14462 (2022)
31. Shrestha, N., Shrothrium, R., Kate, A., Nayak, K.: Sailfish: towards improving latency of DAG-based BFT. Cryptology ePrint Archive (2024)
32. Spiegelman, A., Arun, B., Gelashvili, R., Li, Z.: Shoal: improving DAG-BFT latency and robustness. arXiv preprint arXiv:2306.03058 (2023)
33. Spiegelman, A., Giridharan, N., Sonnino, A., Kokoris-Kogias, L.: Bullshark: DAG BFT protocols made practical. In: Proceedings of the 2022 ACM SIGSAC Conference on Computer and Communications Security, pp. 2705–2718 (2022)
34. Spiegelman, A., Giridharan, N., Sonnino, A., Kokoris-Kogias, L.: Bullshark: the partially synchronous version. arXiv preprint arXiv:2209.05633 (2022)
35. Sui Foundation: Sui Consensus Architecture (2024). https://docs.sui.io/concepts/sui-architecture/consensus. Accessed 09 Oct 2024
36. Syrgkanis, V.: Efficiency of mechanisms in complex markets. Ph.D. thesis, Cornell University (2014)
37. Thomas, Barnabe, Francesco, Julian: Fork-choice enforced inclusion lists (focil): a simple committee-based inclusion list proposal (2024). https://ethresear.ch/t/fork-choice-enforced-inclusion-lists-focil-a-simple-committee-based-inclusion-list-proposal/19870
38. Wood, G.: Ethereum: a secure decentralised generalised transaction ledger (2014). https://ethereum.github.io/yellowpaper/paper.pdf. Accessed 10 Oct 2024
39. Wu, K., Shi, E., Chung, H.: Maximizing miner revenue in transaction fee mechanism design. In: Guruswami, V. (ed.) 15th Innovations in Theoretical Computer Science Conference, ITCS 2024, Berkeley, CA, USA, 30 January–2 February 2024. LIPIcs, vol. 287, pp. 98:1–98:23. Schloss Dagstuhl - Leibniz-Zentrum für Informatik (2024)
40. Yakovenko, A.: Multiple concurrent leaders . https://x.com/aeyakovenko/status/1810222589991583922. Accessed 11 Oct 2024
41. Yao, A.C.C.: An incentive analysis of some Bitcoin fee designs. In: Proceedings of the 47th International Colloquium on Automata, Languages, and Programming (ICALP) (2020)
42. Zhang, J., Kate, A.: No fish is too big for flash boys! frontrunning on DAG-based blockchains. Cryptology ePrint Archive, Paper 2024/1496 (2024). https://eprint.iacr.org/2024/1496
43. Zhao, Z., Chen, X., Zhou, Y.: Bayesian-Nash-incentive-compatible mechanism for blockchain transaction fee allocation. arXiv preprint arXiv:2209.13099 (2022)

Seahorse: Efficiently Mixing Encrypted and Normal Transactions

Ben Riva[1(✉)], Alberto Sonnino[1,2], and Lefteris Kokoris-Kogias[1]

[1] Mysten Labs, Palo Alto, USA
{benriva,alberto,lefteris}@mystenlabs.com
[2] University College of London (UCL), London, UK

Abstract. Blockchains have been proposed as solution against lack of transparency in the traditional finance domain. However, this does not directly prevent arbitrage, but it at least exposes it publicly. In response MEV (Miner Extractable Value) resilience mechanism have been proposed with one significant class of proposals focusing on encrypting sensitive transactions. These solutions, however, face a critical challenge in balancing transaction privacy, efficiency, and execution speed for non-encrypted transactions. Specifically, prior approaches either compromise privacy for non-committed transactions to achieve low latency or significantly increase communication complexity and processing time to maintain strong privacy guarantees against MEV attacks.

This paper presents a novel hybrid approach specifically designed for MEV-resilience of blockchains. Our method employs a dual encryption scheme for each transaction: a per-transaction encryption that keeps contents private until commitment, and a per-event encryption enabling communication efficient batch processing after commitment. This technique maintains transaction confidentiality from submission until just before execution, while minimizing the delay non-encrypted transactions face. Our construction achieves $O(n+B)$ communication complexity for B encrypted transactions and n nodes in optimistic environments, substantially improving upon existing MEV-resistant protocols.

Keywords: Blockchain · MEV · Consensus · Cryptography

1 Introduction

The primary function of a blockchain involves blockchain nodes receiving transactions from users and proposing them to other nodes, ensuring that all blockchain nodes reach a consensus on an ordered list of *committed* transactions [2]. These committed transactions then update the blockchain's state in a consistent manner based on the established order.

One popular class of applications that use such blockchain infrastructure is Decentralized Finance (DeFi), where apps offering users transparency and the absence of intermediaries have been managing billions of USD. One reason why DeFi is preferred to classic centralized finance (CeFi) is that centralized actors are known to abuse their position either to arbitrage [26] or to censor [18] users. Unfortunately in DeFi such attacks have also been seen by nodes (and in cases of public mempools, external observers as well) who use their advantage of seeing all transactions before they are committed, and interject other transactions to unfairly gain profit. Those types of attacks are called Maximal Extractable Value (MEV) attacks [14] and include frontrunning and sandwich attacks. A byproduct of MEV attacks is that it incentivizes nodes to slow down block creation to increase their profit.

In this paper, we explore ways to limit MEV. One of the promising approaches for mitigating MEV attacks is to encrypt transactions:

The blockchain generates a public key pk under which users can encrypt their transactions. The nodes then commit those encrypted transactions and, once committed, collaborate to decrypt them (i.e., threshold decryption), allowing execution to complete. For simplicity, as we focus on the cryptographic and distributed computation protocols, throughout this work, we assume the extreme case in which encrypted transactions fully hide everything about the transaction except for what is needed for paying basic network fees.

As a public infrastructure, blockchains support a wide variety of transaction types, not all of which require MEV protections (e.g., simple payments or object transfers [8]). However, current MEV protection proposals present a challenge when dealing with mixed transaction lists. For example, consider a sequence of transactions tx_1, etx_2, tx_3, where tx_1 and tx_3 are normal transactions and etx_2 is an encrypted one. When this list needs to be finalized for execution, transactions following an encrypted transaction (tx_3) are blocked until the encrypted transaction (etx_2) is decrypted and executed. We define the time between the commitment of tx_3 and its execution as the *delay duration*, which represents the additional latency imposed on normal transactions that follow encrypted ones (assuming execution time is negligible). This delay may be minor for networks with infrequent commits, as the decryption of a block may complete before subsequent commits. However, for blockchains with low latency and high commit rates, tx_3 and consecutive transactions could be significantly delayed by the decryption of etx_2.

There are currently two types of threshold decryption approach used for MEV protection. The first is to use *per-transaction* decryption, where the nodes jointly decrypt each of the encrypted transactions committed separately [6,27,33]. Decrypting a transaction requires $O(1)$ values from each of the nodes. To minimize the delay duration, the nodes can broadcast these values to each other, requiring $O(n)$ communication from each node per transaction, which is a large communication overhead in practice. A cheaper alternative is to send those values to a leader/aggregator, who would then collect messages from all nodes and only broadcast the decrypted transactions. Although this option reduces communication per transaction to $O(1)$ values from each node in the happy case, it might dramatically increase the delay duration in case of a slow or byzantine leader/aggregator. Note that the *minimal delay duration* we can hope for is the time it takes to communicate one message between any set of parties (i.e., 1/2

RTT) or even zero in case the threshold decryption and consensus protocols are coupled [6,31]. Hence, the first option above achieves the minimal delay duration but requires large communication, while the second option has a reasonable communication overhead but potentially larger delay duration.

The second type of threshold decryption being used is what we call a *per-event* decryption [15,28] where encryptions are associated with a blockchain event *in the future*, and once that event occurs, the nodes jointly compute an ephemeral key that allows decrypting *all* encryptions associated with that event. Time-lock encryption (e.g., [17]) is an example of time-based events, and in general Identity Based Encryption (IBE) (e.g., [9]) can be used for any type of events defined by the network (e.g., the event that block i was committed can be represented by the unique identity block:i). Users would now encrypt their transactions to a close-in-the-future event $\mathcal{E}$ and send them to the blockchain. Some of those transactions would be committed before event $\mathcal{E}$ and be considered valid whereas the rest would be considered invalid. Once $\mathcal{E}$ occurs, the nodes jointly compute the ephemeral key for $\mathcal{E}$, and all encrypted transactions to $\mathcal{E}$ can be decrypted and executed, unblocking also the execution of subsequent committed transactions.

Ideally, to minimize the delay duration, nodes may use a different ordering for execution: All committed transactions that are encrypted for event $\mathcal{E}$ are not scheduled for execution until $\mathcal{E}$ occurs, unblocking the execution of subsequent committed normal transactions. Transactions committed after $\mathcal{E}$ might be delayed due to the decryption process. However, jointly computing the ephemeral key for an event requires only $O(1)$ values from each of the nodes, independent of the number of encrypted transactions that are waiting for that key, thus a simple broadcast (with $O(n)$ communication per node) is sufficient and requires only the minimal delay duration.

The main drawback of per-event decryption is that all encrypted transactions ordered after event $\mathcal{E}$ (or even not committed but still known to nodes) will be considered invalid but still decryptable, since the decryption key for $\mathcal{E}$ is public. As a result, they leak private information about the transaction that could be used to extract MEV (e.g., in case the user just retries the same transaction with a different event $\mathcal{E}'$). Privacy aware users are likely to hesitate to encrypt for a close-by event as they risk not making their transactions on time but losing privacy, considerably increase latency of encrypted transactions. In contrast, per-transaction decryption does not leak such information as only committed transactions are decrypted, but the system needs to either "pay" with large communication overhead or a long delay duration in case of node faults.

In this work we explore a middle ground solution between per-transaction and per-event encryptions, where we minimize the delay duration while guaranteeing privacy for non-committed transactions without introducing chokepoints in the process.

1.1 Our Contribution

We propose a new hybrid approach that achieves low delay duration while maintaining the highest level of privacy and requiring only $O(n + B)$ communication for a batch of B encrypted transactions from each node when the network is synchronous and parties are not faulty. In high-level, each transaction is encrypted twice, requiring both encryptions to be decrypted. The first encryption is using per-transaction key, guaranteeing privacy for non-committed transactions while not affecting the delay duration. The second encryption uses a fast per-event decryption together with other encrypted transactions for the same event. Execution order is defined only with respect to the per-event decryption, thus the delay duration is minimal.

We present a construction that is simple and uses two IBE encryptions, one per-transaction and one per-event. We use the fact that the derived keys of IBE encryption schemes are publicly verifiable, thus decryption can be verified as well given access to those decryption keys. The transaction itself is encrypted using symmetric encryption with a fresh key k. We split k into a random string k_1 and a string $k_2 = k \oplus k_1$. The k_1 is encrypted using per-transaction encryption and k_2 using per-event encryption. Once the transaction is committed by the network, nodes start the decryption of k_1 without blocking the execution of normal transactions. This is done efficiently using aggregators needing a small number of communication hops in case of non-faulty parties, and $O(f)$ in the worse case. Once the value of k_1 is committed by the network, the nodes block execution and jointly recover the decryption key associated with the next event, allowing them to decrypt *all* the transactions for that event. Last, the nodes locally decrypt the k_2 component of all relevant transactions, fully decrypt the transactions, and resume execution.

Table 1 compares the main existing approaches with ours.

Table 1. A comparison of the different approaches with minimal duration for n nodes. In all schemes, the additional committed transaction size is $O(1)$. Communication is per node and a batch of B encrypted transactions, ignoring the committed transaction itself. Privacy is of non-committed encrypted transactions. Latency is the additional latency of encrypted transactions on top of the first transaction commit, measured by one-way communication latency (ow) and commit latency (c), assuming that the minimal duration latency is 1 ow. For our construction we compare communication and latency for the happy case and the worst case (in red).

Scheme	Communication	Privacy	Latency
Per-tx [6,27,33]	$O(nB)$	✓	1 ow
Per-event [15,28]	$O(n)$	✗	1 ow
Our construction	$O(n+B)$	✓	2 ow + 1 c
	$O(n+Bf)$		$O(cf)$

More Related Work. Other types of protocols that use encrypted transactions include commit-and-reveal protocols that require the user to also decrypt its transactions, resulting in possibly biasable outputs, encryption using Publicly Verifiable Secret Sharing that require large transactions (e.g., [24]), or, depending on third party entities to decrypt transactions (e.g., trusted enclaves, or small MPC committees).

Recently [12] presented a new cryptographic primitive called Batched Threshold Encryption that allows nodes to decrypt a batch of per-event encryptions without revealing information about non-committed encryptions for the same event, using only $O(1)$ elements from each node. This is a very promising direction for achieving our goals, but more work needs to be done on optimizing its performance in practice (e.g., likely more than a minute for a setup with only 50 parties, and more than 18 s for a per-event precomputation for the same number of parties).

Last, we mention other mitigations for MEV: MEV-aware application designs (e.g., [5,19,25]), time-based fair ordering of transactions (e.g., [11,22,23]), MEV auctions (e.g. [10,16]), secure enclaves (e.g., [7]). See [4,20,32] for more comprehensive systemization of knowledge of the topic.

Scope Limitations. MEV attacks also include scenarios in which nodes can detect public onchain state that can be exploited, and exploit it first as they produce the blocks, e.g., quickly purchase a new collection of NFTs sold on a sale. Those types of attacks do not use user transactions at all, thus the solutions described in this work do not help with them, but they can be combined with other solutions (e.g., randomizing the order after commit [21,27]).

This work assumes deterministic finalization of transactions as privacy relies on the fact that transactions are decrypted only *after* nodes know that all other honest nodes would eventually commit them.

Last, our focus is supporting encrypted transactions in the blockchain protocol layer, as opposed to the application/smart contract layer. The latter may indeed be simpler to design as different applications may process their incoming encrypted requests independently, especially independently of normal transactions. However, it breaks composition since calls to different smart contracts in this case are not atomic.

2 Preliminaries

Bilinear Pairings. Let $\mathbb{G}, \mathbb{G}', \mathbb{G}_T$ be groups of prime order q, let $G \in \mathbb{G}, G' \in \mathbb{G}', G_T \in \mathbb{G}_T$ be generators and $\mathbb{Z}_q$ be its scalar field. We assume the existence of an efficiently computable bilinear pairing map $e : \mathbb{G} \times \mathbb{G}' \to \mathbb{G}_T$, satisfying (Bilinearity) $\forall (P, Q, a, b) \in (\mathbb{G} \times \mathbb{G}' \times \mathbb{Z}_q \times \mathbb{Z}_q): e(aP, bQ) = b \cdot e(aP, Q) = a \cdot e(P, bQ) = ab \cdot e(P, Q)$, and (Non-degeneracy) $e(G, G') \neq 1$. Last, let $\mathsf{H}_{\mathbb{G}}(\cdot)$ be a hash function that maps strings to $\mathbb{G}$.

For the elliptic curves of BLS12-381, a multiplication in $\mathbb{G}$ or an evaluation of $\mathsf{H}_{\mathbb{G}}$ is roughly twice faster than a multiplication in $\mathbb{G}'$, and about six times faster than an evaluation of the pairing map e.

Threshold IBE Encryption. (t,n)-Threshold Identity Based Encryption (TIBE) is initialized with a public key pk and a set of public keys $\mathsf{pk}_1,\ldots,\mathsf{pk}_n$ such that the i-th party knows sk_i that corresponds to pk_i. Anyone can run $c = \mathsf{Enc}(m, u, \mathsf{pk})$ to encrypt message m using pk for identity u. A party can compute $\mathsf{PartialKey}(\mathsf{sk}_i, u)$ as the i-th partial decryption key k_i^u for identity u. Anyone can verify the partial decryption key k_i^u for identity u using $\mathsf{Verify}(k_i^u, u, \mathsf{pk}_i)$. Given a set D of t valid partial decryption keys, anyone can run $\mathsf{Combine}(D)$ for computing the decryption key k^u for identity u. $\mathsf{Verify}(k^u, u, \mathsf{pk})$ can be used for verifying that key as well. Last, an encryption c for identity u can be decrypted with the decryption key k^u using $\mathsf{Dec}(c, k^u)$.

Recall the IBE encryption scheme of [9]. The secret key is $\mathsf{sk} \in \mathbb{Z}_q$ and the public key is $\mathsf{PK} = \mathsf{sk} \cdot G' \in \mathbb{G}'$. In the threshold setting, sk is distributed between nodes using DKG protocol such that sk_i is a linear t-out-of-n share of sk. An encryption of message m for identity u is $\mathsf{Enc}(m, u, \mathsf{PK}) = (u, rG', H(e(r\mathsf{H}_\mathbb{G}(u), \mathsf{PK})) \oplus m)$ where $r \leftarrow_R \mathbb{Z}_q$ and $H(\cdot)$ is a hash function with sufficient length, modeled as a random oracle. $\mathsf{PartialKey}(\mathsf{sk}_i, u) = \mathsf{sk}_i \mathsf{H}_\mathbb{G}(u)$ and $\mathsf{Verify}(k_i^u, u, \mathsf{PK}_i)$ checks if $e(\mathsf{H}_\mathbb{G}(u), \mathsf{PK}_i) = e(\mathsf{PartialKey}(\mathsf{sk}_i, u), G')$. Given the decryption key $k^u = \mathsf{sk} \cdot \mathsf{H}_\mathbb{G}(u) \in \mathbb{G}$, $\mathsf{Dec}((u, c_1, c_2), k^u)$ outputs $c_2 \oplus H(e(k^u, c_1))$.

Blockchain Substrate. We follow the modular view of a blockchain introduced in recent work [1,13], illustrated in Fig. 1. Since we do not focus on the transaction dispersal we bundle the three first layers into a Total Order Broadcast (TOB) black-box that continuously accepts transactions from clients and outputs a total order list of blocks of (ordered) transactions. The TOB guarantees that a transaction sent by an honest client is eventually included in a block, and, that all honest nodes eventually output the same list of blocks.

Our contribution is to introduce an intermediate layer between the (TOB) and the Execution Layer (EL), which we call the MEV Resilient Layer (MEV-R). MEV-R takes as input the total order of blocks and deterministically reorders some of the transactions in a way that mitigates MEV attacks. Our specific focus is on a MEV-R that handles encrypted transactions, but other works have focused on a MEV-R that provides fair timestamping [22]. The final reordered stream of transaction is then provided as input into the EL.

The EL as before simply maintains a state and updates it in a deterministic manner given a continuous, ordered stream of blocks.

We assume that in addition to user transactions, sequenced blocks may include (explicitly or implicitly) unique "synthetic" event messages. An event message indicates an event that is agreed by all honest nodes, e.g., the block height, or an approximated time agreed by the chain. For simplicity we assume that events are committed last in their blocks.

Properties of a MEV-R Layer. We informally define the properties of the MEV-R layer:

- **MEV-Resilience:** We say that a protocol has MEV-Resilience if the adversary does not learn information about transactions of honest users that are

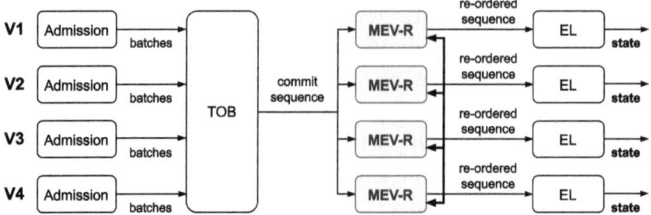

Fig. 1. Overview of a system with 4 nodes (V_1, V_2, V_3, V_4) submitting batches to the Total Order Broadcast (TOB) layer. Each node locally runs a MEV-R layer over the commit sequence and re-order it. Finally the Execution layer (EL) consumes this sequence and outputs the state of the system.

not yet assigned a sequence number as part of their input in the execution layer. MEV-Resilience has different privacy flavors for transactions that are committed and for transactions failed to commit. For committed valid transactions privacy is only guaranteed until the sequence number is assigned. Afterwards the transaction is revealed so that execution can proceed. For the rest of the transactions, including ones that are committed and ignored by the network (e.g., have an invalid nonce), transactions that are never committed, or even never submitted to the TOB, we want perpetual privacy.[1]

– **Safety:** We say that a protocol is safe if for two honest nodes that get the same ordering of transactions as input from the TOB into the MEV-R layer then they get the same output.
– **Liveness:** We say that a protocol is live if for an honest node that gets an ordering of transactions as input from the TOB into the MEV-R layer, then they will eventually get all input transactions as output.

3 Warm Up: Optimizing Execution Order

Most blockchains execute transactions according to a deterministic order that depends on the commit order (e.g., ordered by fee, per block) [3,29,30]. However, when mixing with encrypted transactions, it is better to order the execution of normal transactions first (with the standard ordering logic), and only after that order the encrypted ones. E.g., given a block with transactions $tx_1, tx_2, etx_3, tx_4, etx_5$, the MEV-R layer would order tx_1, tx_2, tx_4 first, and then etx_3, etx_5. This change does not break any fairness or security assumptions, while it reduces the delay duration of transactions that are committed in the same

---

[1] In the security analysis we use ad-hoc games that are similar to CPA security to capture those informal guarantees. We leave to future work the question of whether our protocols can be proven to be secure for stronger notions of security that use ideal functionalities and simulation. Those notions may, for example, capture "adaptive" attacks in which the adversary chooses which transactions to commit depending on the ciphertexts.

block with encrypted ones to zero, as they can be executed independently of the decryption process.

Similarly, when per-event decryption is used, the execution of encrypted transactions should not be ordered after the normal transactions from the same block, but instead at the end of the block that commits the target event. In other words, transactions that are encrypted for event $\mathcal{E}$ and committed before $\mathcal{E}$ is committed, are executed after the normal transactions of block b that includes the target event $\mathcal{E}$. This way, all normal transactions that are committed up to and including block b are not affected by transactions encrypted for $\mathcal{E}$. For example, say we have a block with $\mathsf{etx}_1, \mathsf{tx}_2$, one with $\mathsf{tx}_3, \mathsf{etx}_4, \mathcal{E}$, and another with tx_5. The MEV-R layer will order $\mathsf{tx}_2, \mathsf{tx}_3$ first, $\mathsf{etx}_1, \mathsf{etx}_4$ after, and last tx_5 (which will be blocked on the decryption of the previous two transactions).

Note that even after the above two optimizations, the execution of normal transactions from block b_{i+1} might be blocked on the execution of encrypted transactions from the previous block b_i, impacting the delay duration (as happens with tx_5 in the last example). For blockchains with fast consensus protocols that may commit multiple times per second, this delay can be dramatic. In the next section we show how to reduce this overhead.

4 The Seahorse Design

As the system is designed for blockchains, for simplicity, we assume that all transactions are authenticated. Recall that an encrypted transaction still needs to pay basic network fees even if the encrypted data is invalid. We represent an encrypted transaction etx by $(sender, nonce, blob, sig)$ where $sender$ is the entity that sent the transaction and pays the fees, $nonce$ is a random nonce chosen by the sender per transaction (which may or may not be used by the network for replay attack prevention), $blob$ is the encrypted data, and sig is a signature on $sender, nonce, blob$ using the signature key associated in the network with $sender$ (sig may include other inputs as defined by the network for normal transactions). We denote by $\mathsf{sender}(\cdot)$ the sender of a given transaction and by $\mathsf{nonce}(\cdot)$ the associated nonce.

Let π_i be a deterministic permutation of the node ids, where i is an index, and let $\pi_i[j]$ be the j-th value of π_i. (Those permutations can be constructed, for example, using a pseudorandom function seeded by the hash of the chain at a specific commit, or seeded by i).

For simplicity and generality, we do not specify the details of the DKG protocol and assume that all parties initialize TIBE and agree on the public key pk. Also, we assume that there is a continuous series of "synthetic" events $\mathcal{E}_1, \mathcal{E}_2, \ldots$ committed by the nodes, e.g. an event for every tenth block. The exact frequency should be set considering the trade-off between the cost per event vs latency.

4.1 Our Construction

While for simplicity the construction below uses TIBE also for per-transaction encryption, any threshold encryption can be used for that layer (e.g., TDH2 from

[33]) as long as the encryption can be bounded to the transaction sender and the nonce.

In the following, we explain the protocol in high level. See Figs. 2, 3 and 4 for the algorithms and Fig. 5 for an end-to-end example execution that we describe in more detail below.

Encrypting A Transaction for Event $\mathcal{E}_i$ in the Future. Given a transaction tx, the user follows the next steps: First, it selects a random nonce *nonce* of sufficient length (i.e., 40 bits). Second, it selects random strings k_1, k_2 of the length of a symmetric key and sets the identity $u = \mathsf{sender}(\mathsf{tx}) \mid nonce$. Then, the user computes $c_1 = \mathsf{H}(k_1 \mid k_2) \oplus \mathsf{tx}$ where hash function H has a sufficiently long output (and modeled as a random oracle),[2] $c_2 = \mathsf{TIBE.Enc}(k_1, u, \mathsf{pk})$, and $c_3 = \mathsf{TIBE.Enc}(k_2, \mathcal{E}'_i, \mathsf{pk})$ where $\mathcal{E}'_i$ is an event associated with $\mathcal{E}_i$ that will be emitted below, e.g., $\mathcal{E}_i$ can be the message event:i and $\mathcal{E}'_i$ be the message postevent:i. If the length of the transaction tx should remain private as well, we assume that the transaction is padded to a fixed size before being encrypted. Lastly, it outputs $(\mathcal{E}_i, c_1, c_2, c_3)$ as the blob of the encrypted transaction.

The blob is cryptographically bound to the transaction sender via the identity u. This binding prevents adversaries from copying transactions with the same identity, as u is computed by the network based on the sender of an authenticated transaction. The security implications of this binding are significant. If u were instead a random string, an adversary could potentially intercept a user's transaction, generate an alternative encrypted transaction with an identical identity, commit it to the network, await its decryption, and subsequently use the revealed decryption key to decrypt the original user's transaction, despite it not being committed. This vulnerability underscores the critical nature of the secure binding between the blob and the transaction sender in maintaining the integrity of the encryption scheme and preventing unauthorized access to transaction contents.

```
   // pk is the TIBE's public key.
   // auth is the sender's authentication key.
   // i is the index of a future event.
1: procedure SUBMITTX(auth, pk, tx, i)
2:     nonce ←_R {0,1}^40, k_1, k_2 ←_R {0,1}^128        ▷ Sample random nonce and keys
3:     Let the identity associated with the i-th event be ℰ'_i = postevent:i.
4:     u ← sender(tx) | nonce
5:     c_1 ← H(k_1 | k_2) ⊕ tx
6:     c_2 ← TIBE.Enc(k_1, u, pk)                        ▷ Per-transaction encryption
7:     c_3 ← TIBE.Enc(k_2, ℰ'_i, pk)                     ▷ Per-event encryption
8:     blob ← (ℰ_i, c_1, c_2, c_3)
9:     sig ← SIGN((sender(tx), nonce, blob), auth)       ▷ Signature using auth
10:    etx ← (sender(tx), nonce, blob, sig)
11:    SUBMITTOTOB(etx)
```

Fig. 2. Client protocol.

---

[2] Other option is to use $\mathsf{H}(k_1 \mid k_2)$ as a key to a symmetric encryption that is used to encrypt tx.

High level flows: For each committed block of transactions, a node calls PROCESS-NORMALTX sequentially for all normal transactions, and then calls PROCESSCOMMIT. In parallel it also calls PROCESSETX sequentially for all committed encrypted transactions to initiate the per-transaction decryption. Additionally, the nodes concurrently run AGGREGATEPERTXKEY and AGGREGATEPEREVENTKEY to aggregate signatures. Events $\mathcal{E}_1, \mathcal{E}_2, \ldots$ are emitted implicitly by the TOB or the MEV-R layers, while events $\mathcal{E}'_1, \mathcal{E}'_2, \ldots$ are emitted below by the MEV-R layer.

A node maintains locally the following data structures:
- ongoingEventDec - an set of indexes of the events for which per-event decryption is running, initially empty.
- W - a set of transactions for which the per-tx key is not known, initially empty.
- $\mathsf{CT}(\cdot)$ - a set of encrypted transactions for a given event.
- A - a map between an identity to a set of partial signatures, initially empty.

// Process a normal transaction (step (❸) of Figure 5).
1: **procedure** PROCESSNORMALTX(tx)
2:    Wait until ongoingEventDec is empty
3:    SUBMITTOEL(tx)   ▷ Output to EL layer

// Process an encrypted transaction (step (❹) of Figure 5).
// This function is also used for rotating aggregators.
// - S - the committed sequence.
// - K - the number of commits before rotating aggregators, protocol configured.
4: **procedure** PROCESSETX(S, etx)
5:    Parse etx as $(sender, nonce, (\mathcal{E}_i, c_1, c_2, c_3), sig)$ ▷ sig is verified by the TOB layer
6:    ABORTTRANSACTION(etx) if $\mathcal{E}_i$ appears before etx in S and **return**
7:    $m \leftarrow$ COMMITINDEX(etx)   ▷ Index of the committed block containing etx
8:    $m' \leftarrow$ LASTCOMMITINDEX(S)   ▷ Index of the last committed block
9:    **require** $(m' - m) \mod K == 0$ ▷ Abort call if too early for the next leader
10:   $u \leftarrow$ sender(tx) | nonce
11:   $k_j^u \leftarrow$ TIBE.PartialKey(sk_j, u)
12:   $ag \leftarrow \pi_m\lfloor\frac{m'-m}{K}\rfloor$
13:   SEND($ag, (u, k_j^u)$)   ▷ Send the partial decryption to the current aggregator
14:   $\mathsf{CT}(\mathcal{E}_i) \leftarrow$ etx
15:   $W \leftarrow W \cup \{\text{etx}\}$

// Process committed block.
// - S - the committed sequence.
16: **procedure** PROCESSCOMMIT(S)
17:   Wait until ongoingEventDec is empty
18:   **for** etx $\in W$ **do**
19:     **if** GETPERTXKEY(S, etx) returns a value **then** ▷ Per-tx key in the last block
20:       $W \leftarrow W \setminus \{\text{etx}\}$
21:     **else if** COMMITINDEX(etx) $\neq$ LASTCOMMITINDEX(S) **then**
22:       PROCESSETX(S, etx)   ▷ Try to rotate aggregator
23:   **for** $\mathcal{E}_i \in S$ such that $\mathcal{E}'_i \notin S$ and $\mathsf{CT}(\mathcal{E}_i) \neq \emptyset$ **do**   ▷ In order
24:     Let $C = \mathsf{CT}(\mathcal{E}_i) \cap W$
25:     **if** $C == \emptyset$ **then**   ▷ Step (❺) of Figure 5
26:       EMIT($\mathcal{E}'_i$)   ▷ Emit the blockchain event $\mathcal{E}'_i =$ postevent:i
27:       ongoingEventDec $\leftarrow$ ongoingEventDec $\cup \{i\}$
28:       $k_j^{\mathcal{E}'_i} \leftarrow$ TIBE.PartialKey($sk_j, \mathcal{E}'_i$)
29:       DISSEMINATE($\mathcal{E}_i, k_j^{\mathcal{E}'_i}$)   ▷ Send $k_j^{\mathcal{E}'_i}$ to all nodes

Fig. 3. MEV-R Layer of node j with key sk_j, part one.

In certain scenarios, the entity encrypting the transaction may differ from the one responsible for network fees. Consequently, setting u to sender(etx) becomes problematic, as the fee-paying entity could potentially execute the aforemen-

```
// Called by the designated aggregator (step (❹) of Figure 5).
 1: procedure AggregatePerTxKey((u, k_j^u))
 2:     require TIBE.Verify(k_j^u, u, pk)
 3:     A[u] ← A[u] ∪ {k_j^u}
 4:     return if HasThreshold(A[u]) is false
 5:     k^u ← TIBE.Combine(A[u])
 6:     w ← (u, k^u)
 7:     SubmitToTOB(w)

// Called by all nodes upon receiving ℰ_i, k_j^{ℰ'_i} from node j (step (❻) of Figure 5).
// Incoming messages are collected, but processed only once i ∈ ongoingEventDec.
// - S - the committed sequence.
 8: procedure AggregatePerEventKey(S, ℰ_i, k_j^{ℰ'_i})
 9:     require CT(ℰ_i) ≠ ∅
10:     require TIBE.Verify(k_j^{ℰ'_i}, ℰ'_i, pk_j)
11:     A[ℰ'_i] ← A[ℰ'_i] ∪ {k_j^{ℰ'_i}}
12:     return if HasThreshold(A[ℰ'_i]) is false      ▷ Proceed only if enough partial keys
13:     k^{ℰ'_i} ← TIBE.Combine(A[ℰ'_i])
14:     Wait until i = min(ongoingEventDec)            ▷ Guarantee consistent order
15:     for etx ∈ CT(ℰ_i) do                           ▷ According to a deterministic order
16:         Parse the blob of etx as (ℰ_i, c_1, c_2, c_3)
17:         (u, k^u) ← GetPerTxKey(S, etx)
18:         k_1 ← TIBE.Dec(c_2, k^u)
19:         k_2 ← TIBE.Dec(c_3, k^{ℰ'_i})
20:         tx ← H(k_1 | k_2) ⊕ c_1
21:         SubmitToEL(tx)                             ▷ Output to EL layer
22:     CT(ℰ_i) ← ∅
23:     ongoingEventDec ← ongoingEventDec \ {i}
```

Fig. 4. MEV-R Layer of node j with key sk_j, part two.

tioned attack. To address this issue in such settings, an alternative approach utilizing a signature scheme is proposed. The user encrypting the blob generates a (one-time) signature key pair (sk, pk), employing pk in place of sender(etx) in the identity computation. Subsequently, the user signs the encrypted transaction using sk. This method maintains security by preventing adversaries from creating a signed encrypted blob for the same pk, thereby precluding unauthorized use of the network to compute the decryption key for u unless the legitimate user's transaction is committed.

Committing Encrypted Transactions. Encrypted transactions are committed by the TOB layer as normal ones. Let the blob of an encrypted transaction be $(ℰ_i, c_1, c_2, c_3)$. The MEV-R layer aborts the transaction if $ℰ_i$ was committed already. Otherwise, the MEV-R layer stores internally this encryption and triggers the per-tx decryption below. (Note that MEV-R layer continues processing following transactions).

Per-tx Decryption of etx [Slow Path]. The MEV-R layer of node j sends TIBE.PartialKey(sk_j, u) to node $\pi_m[0]$, where u is calculated as defined above for etx, and m is the index of the commit that included etx. Node $\pi_m[0]$, which we call the *primary* node or aggregator of commit m, checks the partial keys using TIBE.Verify and once it has enough valid partial decryptions for the encrypted transaction etx, it computes k^u using TIBE.Combine and sends it to the TOB along with a reference to etx (e.g., its digest). This process is asynchronous and does not block the execution of other transactions.

A malicious node $\pi_m[0]$ may refuse to follow the protocol. To solve this issue, we use the deterministic order of π_m to all other nodes who would act as *backup nodes*. All nodes keep track of all encrypted transactions that are committed and monitor the work of node $\pi_m[0]$. If nodes fail to observe a key k^u associated with one of the encrypted transactions of commit m after a fixed (protocol specified) number of commits, the nodes replace the primary node $\pi_m[0]$ with the backup node $\pi_m[1]$ and send to it the values TIBE.PartialKey(sk_j, u) as described above. If needed, this process continues with the next backup node, i.e., if $\pi_m[1]$ fails to publish the expected keys on the TOB within the fixed number of commits, the nodes follow to the next backup node $\pi_m[2]$, and so on. Note that once the decryption keys associated with all encrypted transactions of commit m are committed, the nodes proceed to the next step of the protocol, independently of the party that submitted the decryption keys (thus in case, e.g., the primary node was honest but committed the decryption keys one commit after the deadline, the protocol does not need to wait for the backup nodes).

Inserting k^u into the TOB also allows full nodes and auditors following the output of TOB to ensure that no fully corrupted group of nodes censored encrypted transactions by refusing to decrypt them.

Per-Event Decryption and Execution [Fast Path]. Let $\mathsf{CT}(\mathcal{E}_i)$ be the set of committed, encrypted transactions for $\mathcal{E}_i$ that were committed up to event $\mathcal{E}_i$. Once the per-tx decryption keys for all the transactions of $\mathsf{CT}(\mathcal{E}_i)$ are committed, and $\mathcal{E}_i$ is also committed (implying no more encrypted transactions for $\mathcal{E}_i$ will be decrypted), the MEV-R layer implicitly emits $\mathcal{E}'_i$ and pauses executing following transactions. Nodes then jointly generate the per-event decryption key $k^{\mathcal{E}'_i}$. This is achieved by every node disseminates its partial decryption key to all other nodes. When the decryption key is known to the MEV-R layer, it uses it to decrypt pending encrypted transactions for $\mathcal{E}'_i$, outputs their decrypted variants, and resumes to execute subsequent transactions. While the above process is synchronous and blocks the execution of other non-encrypted transactions, it is cheaper than the per-transaction decryption process as it only requires the generation of a single per-event decryption key which can be implemented with a simple broadcast. Note that more than one per-event decryption can be triggered from a single committed block as per-transaction decryption keys from multiple events may be published in any order. The order of events does not impact for the security of the protocol, but for safety all nodes must output the same order of decrypted transactions, and thus nodes keep track of the ongoing per-event decryptions and execute the decrypted transactions according to a deterministic order that depends on the order of committed transactions and their events.

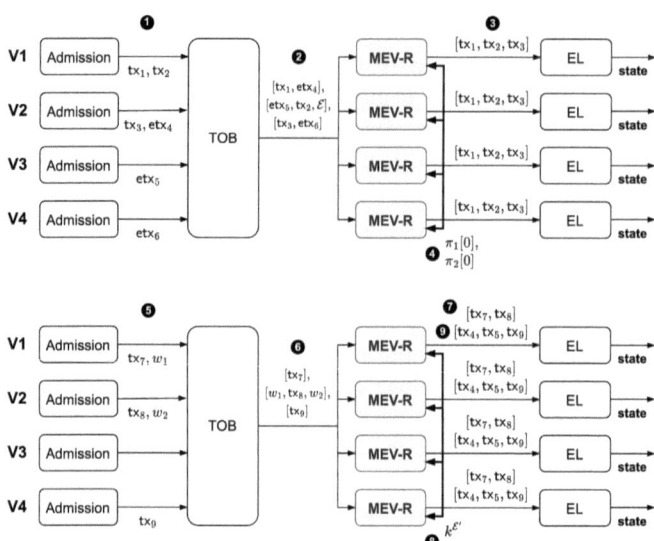

Fig. 5. Example execution performed over the input transactions tx_1, tx_2, tx_3 and the encrypted transactions etx_4, etx_5, etx_6 for event $\mathcal{E}$, followed by transactions tx_7, tx_8, tx_9.

Sharding the Aggregators. The per-tx decryption process leverages a leader to reduce communication complexity. To avoid placing all the communication and computation burden of collecting and processing partial decryptions over a single node at the time, we may logically create l shards (e.g., $l = 5$). Each shard starts with a different primary node and sequence of backup nodes (i.e., using different permutations $\pi_m^1, \ldots, \pi_m^l$). We then deterministically assign each committed etx to a shard (e.g., in a round-robin fashion). This simple sharding strategy allows a parallel resources utilization of honest nodes and a lower latency.

Putting It All Together - An Example. Figure 5 illustrates an end-to-end example execution. Say normal (unencrypted) transactions tx_1, tx_2, tx_3 and encrypted transactions etx_4, etx_5, etx_6 for event $\mathcal{E}$ are sent to the nodes (❶). Nodes call the TOB and receive a list of three blocks, first with tx_1, etx_4, second with $etx_5, tx_2, \mathcal{E}$, and third with tx_3, etx_6 (❷). When a node calls the MEV-R layer on those blocks, the MEV-R layer outputs tx_1, tx_2, tx_3, since those transactions should not be blocked on encrypted transactions for $\mathcal{E}$ (❸). etx_6 is aborted as it was committed after $\mathcal{E}$. Once the MEV-R layer sees etx_4, etx_5 it sends to nodes $\pi_1[0], \pi_2[0]$ the partial decryptions for those transactions (❹). Assuming those nodes are honest and responsive, they receive enough partial decryptions to reconstruct the full decryption keys w_1, w_2 for the c_2 components of etx_4, etx_5 and send them to the TOB (❺).

Let the following blocks returned from the TOB include the block tx_7, block w_1, tx_8, w_2, and block tx_9 ($\mathcal{E}'$ is not explicitly included in the second block as it can be deducted from the output of the TOB) (❻). When a node calls the MEV-R layer on those blocks, it outputs $\mathsf{tx}_7, \mathsf{tx}_8$ as those transactions should not be blocked on encrypted transactions for $\mathcal{E}$ (❼). Once the MEV-R observes that w_1, w_2 are included in a block (and are valid decryption keys), it pauses executing following transactions (i.e., tx_9 is pending), and broadcasts to all nodes the partial decryption key for event $\mathcal{E}'$ (❽). Once the layer receives enough partial decryption keys to construct the full decryption key for $\mathcal{E}'$, it decrypts $\mathsf{etx}_4, \mathsf{etx}_5$ and gets $\mathsf{tx}_4, \mathsf{tx}_5$, and then outputs transactions $\mathsf{tx}_4, \mathsf{tx}_5, \mathsf{tx}_9$ (❾).

4.2 Analysis

Lemma 1. *The decryption key for identity $u = \mathsf{sender}(\mathsf{tx}) \mid \mathsf{nonce}$ is revealed only if user $\mathsf{sender}(\mathsf{tx})$ sent an encrypted transaction for identity u and nonce nonce, and that transaction was committed before its associated event $\mathcal{E}_i$.*

This follows the finality and safety of the TOB (i.e., all honest nodes see the same ordered transactions), the fact that transactions are authenticated (i.e., no other party can send a message with the same $\mathsf{sender}(\mathsf{etx})$), the security of TIBE (i.e., less than t parties cannot recover the key for u), and that u is derived explicitly by nodes and therefore cannot be faked by the adversary.

MEV-Resilience of Committed Transactions. We require that the adversary cannot win the CPA security of IBE with respect to the encryption of k_2 and a chosen identity $\mathcal{E}^*$: Recall that in that game, the challenger chooses a random bit b, generates a key pair sk, PK and sends PK to the adversary. The adversary can once send (id, m_0, m_1) and ask the challenger for a challenge encryption $\mathsf{Enc}(m_b, id, \mathsf{PK})$. In addition it can repeatedly ask the challenger for a decryption key d^u for any identity u as long as $u \neq id$. The adversary sends b' to the challenger and the challenger outputs $b = b'$.

In our variant, an adversary chooses $\mathcal{E}^*$ as the chosen challenge identity, to represent the fact that $\mathcal{E}'$ was not emitted, auxiliary identity u^* and two messages m_0, m_1 such that $|m_0| = |m_1|$. It gets back the encrypted transaction for those inputs, with $\mathsf{tx} = m_b$. The adversary sends b' to the challenger and the challenger outputs $b = b'$.

Say that adversary $\mathcal{A}$ wins the above game with non-negligible advantage ϵ. We can define a simulator $\mathcal{S}$ that breaks the security of the IBE by emulating the honest parties for $\mathcal{A}$. $\mathcal{S}$ passes the public key from the IBE experiment to $\mathcal{A}$ and tunnels requests to decryption keys directly to the IBE experiment challenger (both modified according to the threshold variant of the protocol). When $\mathcal{A}$ requests a challenge encryption (providing $\mathcal{E}^*, u^*, m_0, m_1$), $\mathcal{S}$ chooses random k_1, k_2, computes $c_2 = \mathsf{Enc}(k_1, u^*, \mathsf{PK})$, sends $(\mathcal{E}^*, k_2, 0)$ (where k_2 and 0 are the two messages for the challenge for identity $\mathcal{E}^*$) to the IBE challenger and receives back an encryption c which is used as c_3, and sets c_1 to $\mathsf{H}(k_1 \mid k_2) \oplus m_b$. $\mathcal{S}$

outputs whatever $\mathcal{A}$ outputs. When the IBE experiment challenger's bit is 1, c_1 is statistically hiding m_b and thus the adversary cannot guess b with significant advantage. When the bit is 0, the advantage of guessing b is the same as in the above experiment, thus overall the advantage of winning this experiment is $\epsilon/2$. Following the security of the IBE in use, this advantage is negligible.

MEV-Resilience of Non-committed Transactions. We require that the adversary cannot win an experiment similar to the above one with non-negligible advantage, where the only difference is that here we restrict the requested decryption keys to not include u^* (instead of $\mathcal{E}^*$), to represent the fact that the per-tx decryption key is not revealed if the transaction was not committed before its associated $\mathcal{E}$, following Lemma 1.

We omit the reduction to the security of the IBE encryption as it is similar to the one above.

Safety. Safety directly follows from the safety property of TOB, and the determinism of the MEV-R and EL layers. Let's assume two honest nodes V and V' hold a conflicting state. Honest nodes only execute transactions once they are output by the MEV-R layer, which in turn only processes transactions once they are output from the TOB layer. As a result, there are three cases: (1) V and V' receive different outputs from the TOB layer, which is impossible as it would contradict the safety property of the TOB; (2) The MEV-R layer of V and V' receive the same inputs but produce different outputs. This is impossible following the specification of the protocol, as the MEV-R layer output is deterministic given the inputs from the TOB layer, together with the fact that decryption keys in use are verifiable, thus the decryption process is deterministic; and, (3) The EL layer of V and V' receive the same inputs from the MEV-R but produce a different state, which would be a violation of the determinism property of the EL layer.

Liveness. Our protocol is live provided that there exists at least t correct nodes. Liveness of the MEV-R layer follows the correctness property of the TIBE scheme (Sect. 2) under the threshold t and the livenss of the TOB layer. Notice that the TOB layer might reorder inputs or delay them but it will eventually output all of them.

The liveness of the TOB layer ensures that an encrypted transaction etx' encrypted for event $\mathcal{E}$ and correctly submitted (possibly multiple times) by a correct user into the TOB is eventually committed before $\mathcal{E}$ is triggered. At this point, all t correct nodes observe it and send their partial decryption key to the primary aggregator. We then distinguish two cases: (i) Assuming the correctness of the TIBE scheme, if the primary aggregator is honest, it decrypts the transaction into a plaintext tx' and submits it to the TOB. (ii) If the primary aggregator is dishonest and drops the transaction, the honest nodes, eventually, send their partial decryption key to some future honest scheduled backup node;

we are then back to case (i). Hence eventually all transactions output by TOB will be decrypted.

Since we use broadcast, the per-event decryption eventually progresses given at least t correct nodes.

Communication Complexity. A user transaction of length $|\text{tx}|$ bytes requires additional two IBE encryptions of short keys. In case an aggregator is honest, each node sends $O(1)$ group elements per committed encrypted transaction during the per-tx decryption, or $O(f+1)$ group elements in the worst case that f consecutive aggregators are malicious. Last, each node sends $O(n)$ group elements in total per event.

References

1. Al-Bassam, M.: Lazyledger: a distributed data availability ledger with client-side smart contracts. arXiv preprint arXiv:1905.09274 (2019)
2. Bano, S., et al.: SoK: consensus in the age of blockchains. In: ACM AFT, pp. 183–198 (2019)
3. Baudet, M., et al.: State machine replication in the libra blockchain. The Libra Assn., Technical report **7** (2019)
4. Baum, C., Chiang, J.H., David, B., Frederiksen, T.K., Gentile, L.: SoK: mitigation of front-running in decentralized finance. In: Financial Cryptography and Data Security, pp. 250–271. Springer, Cham (2022)
5. Baum, C., David, B., Frederiksen, T.K.: P2dex: privacy-preserving decentralized cryptocurrency exchange. In: ACNS, pp. 163–194. Springer, Cham (2021)
6. Bebel, J., Ojha, D.: Ferveo: threshold decryption for mempool privacy in BFT networks. Cryptology ePrint Archive, Paper 2022/898 (2022). https://eprint.iacr.org/2022/898
7. Bentov, I., Ji, Y., Zhang, F., Breidenbach, L., Daian, P., Juels, A.: Tesseract: real-time cryptocurrency exchange using trusted hardware. In: ACM SIGSAC Conference on Computer and Communications Security, pp. 1521–1538. ACM (2019)
8. Blackshear, S., et al.: Sui lutris: a blockchain combining broadcast and consensus (2024). https://arxiv.org/abs/2310.18042
9. Boneh, D., Franklin, M.: Identity-based encryption from the Weil pairing. In: Kilian, J. (ed.) CRYPTO 2001. LNCS, vol. 2139, pp. 213–229. Springer, Heidelberg (2001). https://doi.org/10.1007/3-540-44647-8_13
10. Buterin, V.: Proposer/block builder separation-friendly fee market designs (2021). https://ethresear.ch/t/proposer-block-builder-separation-friendly-fee-market-designs/9725/1
11. Cachin, C., Micic, J., Steinhauer, N., Zanolini, L.: Quick order fairness. In: Financial Cryptography and Data Security, pp. 316–333. Springer, Cham (2022)
12. Choudhuri, A.R., Garg, S., Piet, J., Policharla, G.V.: Mempool privacy via batched threshold encryption: attacks and defenses. In: USENIX Security, pp. 3513–3529. USENIX Association (2024)
13. Cohen, S., Goren, G., Kokoris-Kogias, L., Sonnino, A., Spiegelman, A.: Proof of availability and retrieval in a modular blockchain architecture. In: International Conference on Financial Cryptography and Data Security, pp. 36–53. Springer, Cham (2023)

14. Daian, P., et al.: Flash boys 2.0: frontrunning in decentralized exchanges, miner extractable value, and consensus instability. In: IEEE Symposium on Security and Privacy, pp. 910–927. IEEE (2020)
15. Döttling, N., Hanzlik, L., Magri, B., Wohnig, S.: Mcfly: verifiable encryption to the future made practical. In: Financial Cryptography and Data Security, pp. 252–269. Springer, Cham (2024)
16. Flashbots. https://www.flashbots.net/
17. Gailly, N., Melissaris, K., Romailler, Y.: tlock: practical timelock encryption from threshold BLS. Cryptology ePrint Archive, Paper 2023/189 (2023). https://eprint.iacr.org/2023/189
18. Gamestop, AMC trading restricted by robinhood, interactive brokers. https://www.investopedia.com/robinhood-latest-broker-to-restrict-trading-of-gamestop-and-others-5100879
19. Heimbach, L., Wattenhofer, R.: Eliminating sandwich attacks with the help of game theory. In: ASIA CCS (2022)
20. Heimbach, L., Wattenhofer, R.: SoK: preventing transaction reordering manipulations in decentralized finance. In: 4th ACM AFT (2022)
21. Kavousi, A., Le, D.V., Jovanovic, P., Danezis, G.: BlindPerm: efficient MEV mitigation with an encrypted mempool and permutation. Cryptology ePrint Archive, Paper 2023/1061 (2023). https://eprint.iacr.org/2023/1061
22. Kelkar, M., Deb, S., Long, S., Juels, A., Kannan, S.: Themis: fast, strong order-fairness in byzantine consensus. In: ACM SIGSAC Conference on Computer and Communications Security, pp. 475–489. Association for Computing Machinery (2023)
23. Kelkar, M., Zhang, F., Goldfeder, S., Juels, A.: Order-fairness for byzantine consensus. In: Micciancio, D., Ristenpart, T. (eds.) CRYPTO 2020. LNCS, vol. 12172, pp. 451–480. Springer, Cham (2020). https://doi.org/10.1007/978-3-030-56877-1_16
24. Malkhi, D., Szalachowski, P.: Maximal extractable value (MEV) protection on a DAG. In: 4th International Conference on Blockchain Economics, Security and Protocols, Tokenomics 2022, pp. 6:1–6:17. Schloss Dagstuhl (2022)
25. McMenamin, C., Daza, V., Fitzi, M.: Fairtradex: a decentralised exchange preventing value extraction. In: ACM CCS Workshop on Decentralized Finance and Security (2022)
26. Payment for order flow — Wikipedia, the free encyclopedia. https://en.wikipedia.org/wiki/Payment_for_order_flow
27. Piet, J., Nair, V., Subramanian, S.: Mevade: an mev-resistant blockchain design. In: 2023 IEEE International Conference on Blockchain and Cryptocurrency (ICBC), pp. 1–9 (2023)
28. Shutter network: Announcing rolling shutter (2022). https://blog.shutter.network/announcing-rolling-shutter/
29. Sui (2024). https://sui.io
30. Tikhomirov, S.: Ethereum: state of knowledge and research perspectives. In: Foundations and Practice of Security, pp. 206–221. Springer, Cham (2018)
31. Xiang, Z., Das, S., Li, Z., Ma, Z., Spiegelman, A.: The latency price of threshold cryptosystem in blockchains (2024). https://arxiv.org/abs/2407.12172
32. Yang, S., Zhang, F., Huang, K., Chen, X., Yang, Y., Zhu, F.: SoK: MEV countermeasures: theory and practice (2023). https://arxiv.org/abs/2212.05111
33. Zhang, H., Merino, L.H., Qu, Z., Bastankhah, M., Estrada-Galiñanes, V., Ford, B.: F3B: a low-overhead blockchain architecture with per-transaction front-running protection. In: Conference on Advances in Financial Technologies (2022)

The Early Days of the Ethereum Blob Fee Market and Lessons Learnt

Lioba Heimbach[1](✉) and Jason Milionis[2]

[1] ETH Zurich, Zürich, Switzerland
hlioba@ethz.ch
[2] Department of Computer Science, Columbia University, New York, NY 10027, USA
jm@cs.columbia.edu

Abstract. Ethereum has adopted a rollup-centric roadmap to scale by making rollups (layer 2 scaling solutions) the primary method for handling transactions. The first significant step towards this goal was EIP-4844, which introduced blob transactions that are designed to meet the data availability needs of layer 2 protocols. This work constitutes the first rigorous and comprehensive empirical analysis of transaction- and mempool-level data since the institution of blobs on Ethereum on March 13, 2024. We perform a longitudinal study of the early days of the *blob fee market* analyzing the landscape and the behaviors of its participants. We identify and measure the inefficiencies arising out of suboptimal block packing, showing that at times it has resulted in up to 70% relative fee loss. We hone in and give further insight into two (congested) peak demand periods for blobs. Finally, we document a market design issue relating to subset bidding due to the inflexibility of the transaction structure on packing data as blobs and suggest possible ways to fix it. The latter market structure issue also applies more generally for any discrete objects included within transactions.

Keywords: Ethereum · blobs · EIP-4844 · layer 2 · rollup

1 Introduction

1.1 The Blob Fee Market

Ethereum's journey towards enhanced scalability has been a central focus in its development roadmap [6], driven by the need to address increasing network demand while preserving decentralization and security. As part of this effort, *Ethereum Improvement Proposal (EIP)* 4844 introduced a novel transaction type that enables the use of *blobs*—large, temporary data objects that are particularly critical for *layer-2 (L2)* solutions. These blobs, by virtue of their enshrined short

---

L. Heimbach and J. Milionis—Work performed in part during an internship at a16z crypto.
Jason's research was supported in part by NSF awards CNS-2212745, CCF-2212233, DMS-2134059, and CCF-1763970, by an Onassis Foundation Scholarship, and an A.G. Leventis educational grant.

© International Financial Cryptography Association 2026
C. Garman and P. Moreno-Sanchez (Eds.): FC 2025, LNCS 15752, pp. 53–71, 2026.
https://doi.org/10.1007/978-3-032-07035-7_4

lifespans, are designed to offer a significant reduction in the cost of storing L2 data on-chain, thus aligning with Ethereum's broader goal of scaling through L2s.

The introduction of blobs under EIP-4844 also brought about a transformative shift in Ethereum's fee market by establishing a separate yet intertwined *blob fee market*, a critical step in the paradigm of multi-dimensional resource pricing. Previously, there was a unified transaction fee priced after fixing the relative prices of all operations (including storage ones) in multiples of a single unit of account (the so-called gas unit), which was then multiplied by the fee given by the transaction originator per gas unit. Such a technique, however, inhibits a scenario where the relative prices of resources shift regimes through time, and would be particularly inflexible with very distinct resources constantly shifting demand like execution and (temporary) storage. With the advent of blob transactions, Ethereum also introduced a new, parallel, dynamically varying blob gas fee (the inner workings of which we elucidate in Sect. 2.2) that varies separately from the (traditional) EIP-1559 *execution gas fee*.

Our key focus is this *blob fee market* and economic outcomes within this type of temporary storage, especially as they relate to rollups. While this fee market significantly reduced transaction fees for rollups, it also introduced complexities in terms of transaction structuring, optimal block packing, and economic incentives.

1.2 Main Contributions

This work delivers the first rigorous and comprehensive analysis of the Ethereum blob fee market during its initial months, empirically studying it and the behavior of its participants. Our extensive data collection and empirical analysis allows obtaining novel insights on the market internals of this temporary storage and contributes to the ongoing, active debate about the blob space on Ethereum.

Analyzing transaction- and mempool-level data we look into behavioral patterns of the market participants and their effects on-chain. Two major events that spiked demand for blobs may provide a clearer picture of what a congested blob market would look like (especially in a world like the roadmap envisions with more active utilization of blobspace) and we hone in on these periods.

We show that a surprisingly large percentage of blocks are suboptimally packed with blob transactions, leading to up to 70% fee losses for the builders who build these suboptimal blocks compared to the optimally built block. We document that the market has been becoming slightly more efficient over time, but is still stunningly inefficient. We believe the reason for this to be the underinvestment in needed infrastructure due to the low amount of direct economic incentives. Further than that, in Sect. 6.2, we identify a structural market design flaw having to do with the rigid structure of transactions preventing the most efficient use of available blob space, that we term subset bidding. We offer solutions and improvement suggestions for these inefficiencies of the market, as well as point out fruitful future avenues of research. Importantly, we note that the market structure problem and solution we identify does *not only* apply to blobs included in transactions, but *any* potentially discrete "object" allocated in the same all-or-nothing way through the standard Ethereum transaction format.

2 Background

In the following, we introduce the relevant background regarding blobs on Ethereum (see Sect. 2.1), the fees paid by transactions including them (see Sect. 2.2), and Ethereum block building (see Sect. 2.3).

2.1 Blobs

To tackle Ethereum scalability issues, EIP-4844 introduced a new type of transactions—referred to as *type-3 transactions* or *blob transactions*—which allow the sender to submit blobs of data. L2s primarily use these blobs for transaction settlement on the L1. Blobs only persist for a short period (around 18 days) on the network, long enough for them to be retrieved but short enough to prevent excessive long-term usage of storage. This temporary nature allows blobs to be priced lower than calldata,[1] which must be permanently stored on the blockchain and contribute to state growth. Up to six blobs may be included on each block, and a type-3 transaction can have between one and six blobs. There is space for 128kb of data in each blob and a transaction always pays for the entire blob even if it only uses a partial portion of the allowable storage space it provides.

Similarly to all other types of transactions, type-3 transactions that are publicly broadcast are stored in Ethereum's execution layer network *mempool*, i.e., the public waiting area for transactions. Importantly, the blob data itself is not propagated in the execution layer network. Instead, blobs are propagated in the consensus layer network. Thus, type-3 transactions propagated through the execution layer network and included on-chain will only contain a reference to the blob.

2.2 Blob Fees

Type-3 transactions simultaneously pay gas fees in: (1) the "normal" Ethereum gas market, and (2) the blob gas market.

Similar to other types of transactions, type-3 transactions can include calldata, transfer Ether, or interact with a smart contract. The fees paid by a type-3 transaction tx included in block n in the "normal" gas market, which we will refer to as the EIP-1159 gas market throughout, are as follows.

---

[1] Before blobs were introduced, L2s used Ethereum calldata for settlement of L2 data on the L1.

$$\text{FEE}_{1559}(tx, n) = \text{GAS}(tx) \cdot (\text{BASE\_FEE}(n) + \text{PRIORITY\_FEE}(tx)),$$

where $\text{GAS}(tx)$ is the transaction gas usage. Further, $\text{BASE\_FEE}(n)$ is the block's base fee charged per unit of gas: it represents the minimum fee transactions must pay in the block and automatically updates based on past block gas usage [7]. Finally, $\text{PRIORITY\_FEE}(tx)$ is the transaction's priority fee charged per unit of gas. Importantly, the part of the fee paid by transaction tx associated with the base fee (i.e., $\text{GAS}(tx) \cdot \text{BASE\_FEE}(n)$) is burned. Only the remaining fees ($\text{GAS}(tx) \cdot \text{PRIORITY\_FEE}(tx)$) are received by the block's fee recipient.

Additionally, type-3 transactions also pay fees per blob included in the blob gas market, which we will refer to as the EIP-4844 gas market throughout. To be precise, the fees a transaction tx included in block n pays in the EIP-4844 gas market are

$$\text{FEE}_{4844}(tx, n) = \text{NUM\_BLOBS}(tx) \cdot \text{BLOB\_BASE\_FEE}(n),$$

where $\text{NUM\_BLOBS}(tx)$ is the number of blobs included by the transaction and $\text{BLOB\_BASE\_FEE}(n)$ is the blob base fee in block n which is charged per blob gas. The blob base fee for block n is derived as follows

$$\text{BLOB\_BASE\_FEE}(n) = \text{MIN\_FEE} \cdot \exp\left(\frac{\text{TOTAL\_EXCESS\_GAS}(n-1)}{\text{UPDATE\_FRACTION}}\right),$$

where $\text{TOTAL\_EXCESS\_GAS}(n-1)$ is the total blob gas used in excess of the target before the current block. Note that while there is space for six blobs per block, the target is three. Thus, whenever more than three blobs are included in a block the excess increases and decreases when less than three are included. Additionally, MIN_FEE is a constant currently set to 1 wei, and UPDATE_FRACTION is a constant set such that the maximum increase in the blob base fee per block is 12.5% [8]. Importantly, all fees associated with the EIP-4844 gas market are burned, i.e., the block's fee recipient receives no fees for blobs included.

2.3 Block Building

The vast majority of blocks ($\approx$90%) in Ethereum are built through a scheme called *Proposer-Builder Separation (PBS)* [40]. With PBS the validator chosen as the block proposer is only responsible for proposing the block, while specialized *builders* are responsible for building the blocks. The idea is that these specialized builders are better at building high-value blocks, i.e., blocks with significant fee revenue. Additionally, these specialized builders likely have access to value private order flow, i.e., transactions that are not broadcast to the public mempool. Note that in the current implementation of the scheme, validators and builders communicate with each other through a relay: a party trusted by the two [12].

3 Related Work

EIP-1559 Fee Market. The first major shift in the Ethereum transaction fee mechanism was the deployment of EIP-1559 in 2021. Before deployment, Roughgarden [30] presented a game-theoretic analysis of the mechanism, while Ferreira et al. [11], Leonardos et al. [17] conducted studies focusing on the dynamic update rule of the base fee. On the empirical side, multiple studies [18,19,26] demonstrate that the introduction of EIP-1559 made gas fees more predictable despite the short-term oscillation in block size. In addition, for farsighted validators, it can be rational to attack the mechanism leading to greater unpredictability of fees [4,15]. On the other hand, our work focuses on the blob fee market, which was introduced through EIP-4844.

Multidimensional Fee Markets. A recent line of literature explores multidimensional blob markets. Diamandis et al. [10] propose an efficient pricing mechanism for multiple resources, while Angeris et al. [3] show that these multidimensional blockchain fee markets are essentially optimal. In contrast, we empirically explore the blob fee market, which added a second dimension to Ethereum's fee market.

Blob Fee Market. Crapis et al. [9] conducted an economic analysis of the blob market at its launch, examining whether rollups would prefer posting data in blobs or calldata (the original market). Their study concludes that large rollups with high transaction rates would opt for blobs, while those with lower rates would favor the original market. Our empirical findings, however, show that even when the blob market is congested and more expensive than calldata, rollups do not revert to the original market.

Soltani and Ashtiani [31] analyze the delays of blob transactions in a *time-average* fashion to conclude that average delays are lower if all transactions only carry a small number of blobs; this is a consequence of mainly standard limited-resource congestion. Contrary to that, one of our multifaceted contributions deals with examining the delays as a consequence of inefficiencies in block packing, where we study how this has changed *throughout time* and its sensitivity, especially in demand-congested periods.

In the period before the introduction of blobs, Messias et al. [20] performed a comprehensive transaction analysis focusing on inscriptions, which triggered the first significant demand for blob space on Ethereum. Their work, however, does not delve into the internal workings of the blob market, which is the central focus of our study.

A recent research post performs an empirical evaluation of the blob market, focusing on the blob base fees paid and the consequences of increasing the parameter of the minimum base fee [2]. Concurrent work by Lee [16] explores the possibility of rollups sharing blob space among each other (a practice called *blob sharing*) and simulates the impact using the first 180 days of blobs on Ethereum. Their goal is to minimize the costs for rollups. In contrast, our work focuses on the *blob fee market* as a whole and its participants (with an emphasis on *block builders*) while also identifying and documenting market design issues, offering potential solutions to those. Finally, likewise, auction considerations have been previously connected to market mechanisms, including in decentralized finance infrastructure [21–23].

4 Data Collection

To study the Ethereum blob market, we gather three different types of data: Ethereum blockchain, PBS, and Ethereum mempool data. Our data collection spans the range from block 19,426,589 – the block marking the Dencun hardfork that introduced blobs on March 13, 2024 – to block 20,866,918, capturing the final block as of September 30, 2024. Consequently, this dataset encompasses the entire timeline of the blob market's activity up until the end of September 2024.

Ethereum Blockchain. We run a Reth execution layer node [29] and a Lighthouse consensus layer node [25] to gather Ethereum blockchain data. We parse the blockchain for blob transactions, recording relevant details such as the number of blobs submitted and the fees paid. Type-3 transactions pay fees for both regular Ethereum gas in the EIP-1559 market (base and priority fees) and blob gas in the EIP-4844 market (blob base fee). Additionally, transactions may tip block fee recipients via direct transfers.

PBS. We collect data from eight relays that were active during the study period: Aestus, Agnostic, bloXroute (Max Profit), bloXroute (Regulated), Eden, Flashbots, Manifold, and UltraSound. These relays provide public APIs that allow access to the blocks they deliver to proposers. We use the PBS data to obtain information about the block builder. The reason we use this builder-specific information is to investigate whether specific block builders have different strategies on (optimal) transaction choice with blob transactions.

Ethereum Mempool. Finally, we gather Ethereum mempool data from the Mempool Dumpster project [13]. The mempool data allows us to observe the blob mempool, i.e., the blobs waiting for block inclusion in the public P2P network, so that we can then analyze the efficiency of blob inclusion for each builder and the waiting time for blob transactions to be posted on-chain. It is important to note that there is minimal private submission of blob transactions throughout the entire period, and negligible during the congested periods that we focus on.

5 Blob Adoption

We commence our analysis by analyzing the adoption of blobs. Figure 1a visualizes the daily number of blobs included on Ethereum along with the daily target (left y-axis). While we notice a general increase in the daily number of blobs, the number of blobs has not sustainably reached the target. Instead, they have only approached the target on two occasions: (1) the Blobscription heavy interest period ("craze") starting at the end of March 2024 [24] and (2) the LayerZero airdrop on Arbitrum on June 20, 2024 [32]. During these demand increases, we also observe very significant spikes in the blob base fee (see right y-axis in Fig. 1a). Astonishingly during the second incident blob fees increase by nearly 15 orders of magnitude from 1 wei (the minimum blob base fee) to 10^{15} wei. However, while there was little variance (except for the individual incidents) in the first two months of the blob market, the blob base fee variance has risen from June 2024 along with the general increase in blob usage. At the same time, this variance has come down slightly in the past months as demand for blobs has also decreased again. Given that there is no sustained demand for blobs at their target number, the blob base fees have generally been meager, as market economics of demand and supply would dictate.

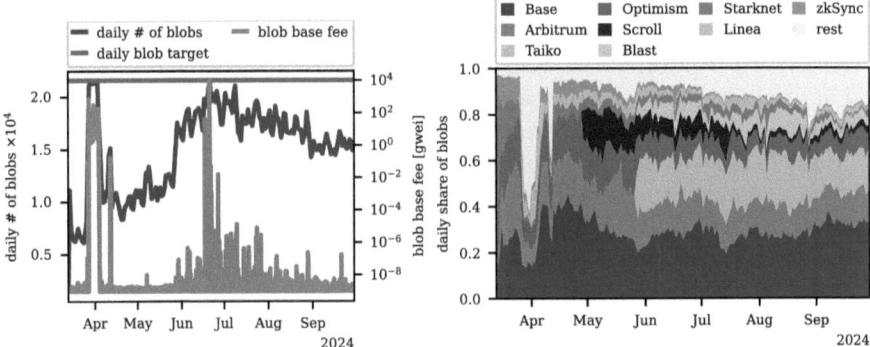

(a) Daily number of blobs (blue line) and **daily** blob target (red line) on the left y-axis. We further plot the blob base fee (green line) on the right y-axis.

(b) Daily share of blobs submitted by L2s. The biggest nine blob submitters are shown separately and the rest are grouped together.

Fig. 1. Blob usage by L2s. Figure 1a shows the overall demand, while Fig. 1b visualizes the individual blob usage of the biggest L2s. (Color figure online)

In Fig. 1b we visualize the proportion of blobs posted by individual senders on a daily basis. The nine largest L2s, in terms of the total number of blobs submitted, are shown separately and ordered by size while the rest are grouped together. We start by noting that, generally, these nine L2s are responsible for more than 80% of blob usage. This figure decreases slowly during our measurement period, indicating that blob demand has extended to a wider group of projects. Additionally, blob demand extended beyond the biggest L2s surrounding the Blobscription craze starting at the end of March 2024. In regards to the biggest L2s, we notice that Base consistently uses more than one-fifth of blobs daily, with Arbitrum being the second biggest blob user. After that, the picture becomes more fragmented with some L2s only starting to post blob a couple of months into our data collection window (e.g., Taiko) or losing market share with time (e.g., zkSync). Overall, the market appears to grow less concentrated over time.

5.1 Fees

Recall, that since the introduction of blobs on Ethereum, the blob base fee has been very low outside of our two outlined major events that spiked demand. In the following, we analyze how the blob base fees paid by type-3 transactions compare to the fees they pay in the EIP-1559 fee market. Figure 2 visualizes the cumulative fees paid by type-3 transactions. The cumulative EIP-4844 base fee paid increased abruptly on two occasions: Blobscriptions and the LayerZero airdrop. Outside of these events, the cumulative EIP-4844 base fee appears almost constant. The two EIP-1559 market fee components (base and priority fee) increase much more steadily. For both, we notice an increase in growth at the beginning of June 2024, which corresponds to a general increase in blob demand (see Fig. 1a). Overall, blob transactions have paid 1,020 ETH in the EIP-4844 base fee, 1,602 ETH in the EIP-1559 base fee, and 372 ETH in the EIP-1559 priority fee. While the 2,993 ETH (approximately US$ 8 M) paid in total fees by type-3 transaction initially appears large, this only amounts to 1% of the fees paid on Ethereum in the same period. Furthermore, only the 372 ETH in priority fees are not burned given that no type-3 transaction has included a coinbase transfer. Thus, these 372 ETH are the sole financial incentive for block builders to include type-3 transactions (i.e., approx US$ 0.7 per block at the current ETH price). In contrast, the average fee revenue from a block is around US$ 200. These small financial incentives builders have to include type-3 transactions that hint at some of the present issues in the blob market (see Sect. 6).

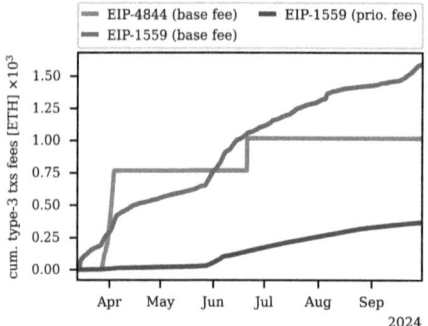 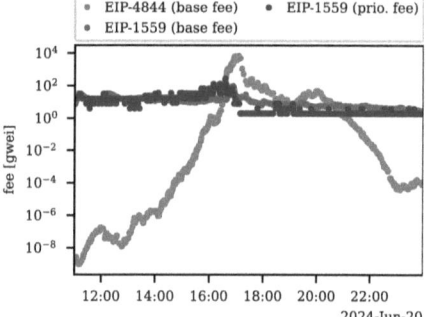

Fig. 2. Cumulative fees paid by blob transactions over time. We separate the EIP-4844 fee market (base fee) from the EIP-1559 fee market (base and priority fee).

Fig. 3. Development of various fee components during the spike in blob demand caused by LayerZero airdrop on 20 June 2024.

We further analyze how the various fee components react to a sudden spike in demand and plot the various fee components from 11:00 to 23:00 on 24 June 2024 in Fig. 3. For each blob transaction, we draw a dot for each of the three components. First note that while the EIP-4844 base fee increases by around 15 orders of magnitude within six hours, there is comparatively little movement in the EIP-1559 fee market. Blob transactions seem to increase their priority fees slightly (by around one order of magnitude), and the EIP-1559 base fee is largely unaffected given that blob transactions are only a small proportion of the overall transaction demand (i.e., blob transactions make up around 0.5%). We further highlight that the EIP-1559 fees recovered a lot quicker, while it took some time for the EIP-4844 to come down again. In addition to taking a long time to recover, the base fee also took several hours to increase. This slow price discovery is a consequence of the blob base fee rule update rule (see Sect. 2.2) taking more than ten blocks to increase or decrease by an order of magnitude.

As a consequence of the slow price discovery, one would expect the rollups to compete in a first price auction [2,5]. However, we only mildly observe this behavior as the priority fee only changes by around one order of magnitude, which does not reflect the 15 orders of magnitude jump of the base fee. Additionally, to the best of our knowledge, our data indicates that none of the rollups moved to the original market and used calldata even though it would have been cheaper to do so—a sign that they were not prepared for such an extreme congestion event.

5.2 Behavior of L2s

In the following, we analyze the behavior of L2s when submitting type-3 transactions, focusing on the number of blobs per transaction and how this changes over time. Figure 4 shows different strategies by L2s: Taiko and Scroll consistently submit one blob, while others, like Blast, Starknet, Linea, and zkSync, vary their blob counts. These four potentially adjust to demand on their own networks or demand for blobs. Finally, large L2s (e.g., Base, Arbitrum, Optimism) tend to use a fixed number of blobs but adjust their strategy over time. Potentially reacting to long-term changes in demand, and on specific occasions (i.e., the LayerZero airdrop indicated by the vertical gray line). One change we observed among most type-3 transaction senders is that starting around June 2024, many of them either diversified how they submit type-3 transactions or adjusted their strategy. This is likely a result of the long-term increase in demand picking up in June 2024. For example, Base and Optimism moved from submitting six blobs per transaction, i.e., taking up the entire blob space in a block, to only submitting five per transaction, i.e., leaving space for one additional blob. Arbitrum similarly adjusted from submitting six blobs per transaction to three. These adjustments could also be related to delays experienced as a result of inefficiencies in the blob market which we will discuss in detail in Sect. 6.

Next, we consider the priority fees and gas usage of type-3 transactions in the EIP-1559 market (see Fig. 5). Recall, that type-3 transactions, in addition to paying for the blobs they include, also pay fees in the EIP-1559 market for any gas they use. In Fig. 5a, we make a violin plot of the gas usage of the biggest L2s for their type-3 transactions. Note that a violin plot combines a boxplot, which displays the lower quartile, median, and upper quartile, with a kernel

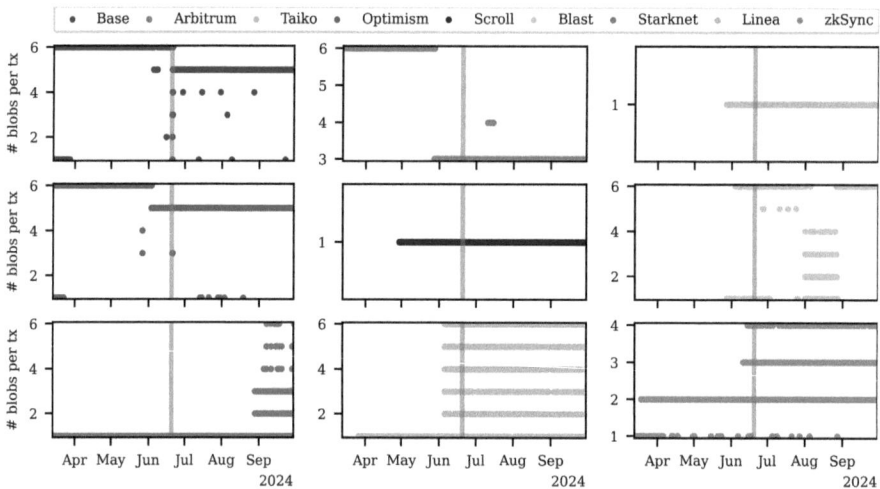

Fig. 4. Number of blobs submitted by the biggest nine L2s per type-3 transaction over time, each dot represents one type-3 transaction submitted by the respective L2. The grey vertical line indicates the spike in demand on 20 June 2024 related to the LayerZero airdrop.

density plot to represent the distribution of values. Base, Optimism, and Blast consistently use the minimum amount of gas possible on Ethereum: 21,000 [41]. Note that these are all optimistic rollups, i.e., they only post data. The two further optimistic rollups (i.e., Arbitrum and Taiko) have significantly higher gas usage but that of Arbitrum is still extremely consistent. For the four zk rollups (i.e., Scroll, Starknet, Linea, zkSync), we generally observe a higher gas usage with higher variance. Note that this is expected as zk rollups execute validity proofs that verify the execution of their transactions.

Regarding priority fees, we also observe different patterns between the biggest type-3 transaction senders (see Fig. 5b). Scroll and Starknet consistently have extremely low priority fees with averages of 0.07 and 0.1 gwei respectively. Note that all type-3 transactions from these two senders are below 1 gwei which is the minimum priority fee accepted by the geth builder [34] – the biggest execution layer client [1]. The remaining senders all have similar priority fees between 1.5 gwei and 3.5 gwei but different distributions. Interestingly, type-3 transactions only have 1.9 gwei average priority fee, and around 20% have a priority fee below 1 gwei. Further, this figure is also lower than the average priority fee of all transactions (i.e., 3.2 gwei during the same period).

We further note that the L2s that posted type-3 transactions with different numbers of blobs consistently for an extended period often do not increase the priority fee depending on the number of blobs they include.

Finally, we visualize the inclusion delay in seconds for each of the biggest nine blob posters in Fig. 5c. Taiko type-3 transactions wait for the shortest time on average with ten seconds, two seconds less than the time between two blocks.

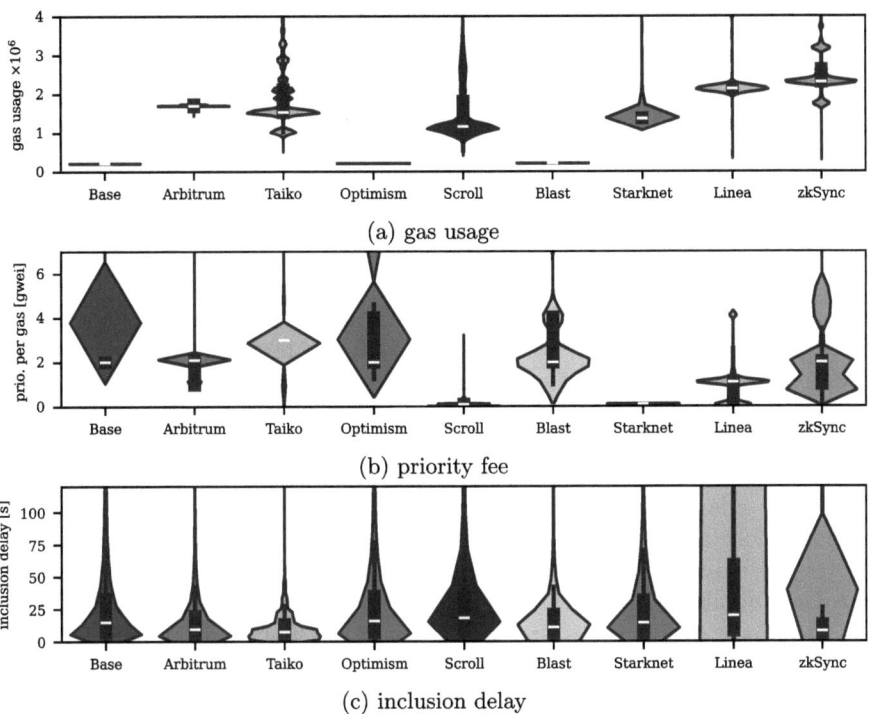

Fig. 5. Distribution of priority fee (see Fig. 5b), gas usage (see Fig. 5a) and inclusion delay (see Fig. 5c) of type-3 transactions submitted by the nine biggest L2s.

On, the other hand, Linea type-3 transactions wait for 100 s on average, i.e., more than eight blocks. Interestingly, Scroll and Starknet which have the lowest priority fees, do not wait for block inclusion significantly longer than many of the other senders that pay much higher priority fees.

6 Inefficiencies in the Blob Market

In the previous sections, we hinted at L2s potentially adjusting the number of blobs they include per transaction to respond to the delay they possibly experience as a result of inefficiencies in the blob market. We look into these issues in this section.

6.1 Block Packing

Recall that there is space for at most six blobs in a block and that each transaction can include between one and six blobs. Solving the packing problem optimally is equivalent to solving knapsack which is NP-hard to optimally solve. On the other hand, a naive, greedy implementation would sort type-3 transactions by priority fee and select transactions as long as there is still space. To see why this is not optimal consider the following example where each transaction is a tuple (GAS_USAGE, NUM_BLOBS, PRIORITY_FEE): there are three type-3 transactions represented by $(1, 5, 2)$, $(1, 3, 1.99)$ and $(1, 3, 1.99)$. The naive algorithm would choose the first transaction but would have no space to include the other two while the optimal algorithm (assuming there is enough gas) would pick the last two transactions and receive nearly double the fees (i.e., 3.98 instead of 2).

Despite the worst-case infeasibility of solving knapsack (an NP-hard problem), since there is only space for six blobs, one can actually *easily* solve the blob packing problem optimally and reasonably quickly. We do these calculations to investigate whether blobs in blocks were optimally packed with respect to the builder's fee income. In case they were not, we quantify the suboptimality, which at times reaches high double-digit percentages (up to 70% suboptimal). For this, we use the mempool data to determine which type-3 transactions were waiting in the mempool. Importantly, we consider only type-3 transactions that were included in a later block and were first observed in the mempool at least four seconds before the block's expected time, but no more than 120 s prior. This ensures the block builder had sufficient time to see the type-3 transaction and that it was unlikely to be cleared from the builder's local mempool. We further note that most transactions are submitted to the public mempool except for type-3 transactions from Taiko being submitted privately starting from September 2024. Finally, we exclude blocks without blobs from this analysis as not including blobs by the block builder might be a choice. In summary, whenever we observe suboptimal blob packing we can be fairly certain that it was suboptimal but the actual suboptimality may have been slightly *higher*.

We start by analyzing what proportion of blocks are packed optimally, suboptimally, whether the naive algorithm achieves the same result as the optimal one (i.e., what we call "unknown"), or whether the block would exceed the maximum allowable gas in an Ethereum block with the optimal blob packing[2] (i.e., what we call "out of gas"). We do the analysis both for block build through PBS (see Fig. 6a) as well as non-PBS blocks (see Fig. 6b). We start by noting that on average there are 1.9 blobs per block for PBS blocks and 2.2 blobs per block for non-PBS blocks. Further, PBS blocks are built by specialized builders, while non-PBS blocks are less likely to be.

Thus, one would expect blobs in PBS blocks to be packed optimally with respect to the block builder's fee income. In Fig. 6a, we notice that this is stunningly not the case. Instead, we can only be sure that 19% of blocks PBS had an optimal blob packing, while 44.6% had a suboptimal packing. Furthermore, only a very minor proportion of blocks would exceed the gas limit with optimal blob packing, running into an execution layer restriction that would prevent them from including the income-optimal number of blobs. In general, we notice that

---

[2] Therefore, in this "out of gas" case, the builder has a clear reason not to include this particular transaction combination yielding the optimal blob packing, as it would lead other potentially profitable bundles to not be able to be included in the built block.

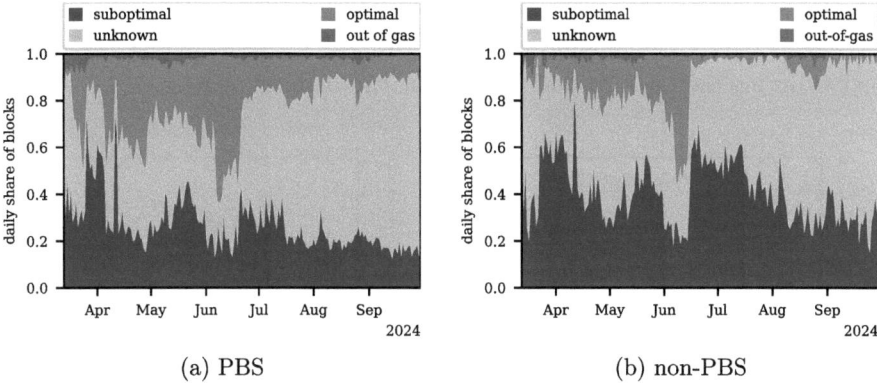

Fig. 6. Daily breakdown of blocks by blob packing: suboptimal, optimal, matching naive and optimal algorithms ("unknown"), or out of gas with optimal packing. Figure 6a shows the breakdown for PBS blocks and Fig. 6b for non-PBS blocks.

over time the proportion of suboptimal blocks has decreased, while the proportion of blocks where it is unknown whether the blob packing algorithm is optimal is increasing. In part, this could be due to type-3 transactions including fewer blobs on average over time (see Fig. 4). Additionally, there may be several reasons why specialized builders pack blobs suboptimally. For one, the investment into an optimal blob building might not be worth it given the low fee revenue (see Fig. 2). Another possibility is related to a race condition (time taking for blocks with more data, i.e., blobs, to propagate across clients) and timing games being played by builders submitting late blocks into the slot to the PBS system. Builders might submit blocks with a varying number of blobs to relays, hence for latency reasons, sometimes blocks with no blobs win the PBS auction and get published instead of their blob-including counterparts.

Figure 6b visualizes the same data for non-PBS blobs. We notice that while there are more suboptimal blocks (i.e., 47% on average) and less optimal blocks (i.e., 9% on average), the difference between PBS and non-PBS blocks is not significant in terms of blob packing. This contrasts with the comparison of the two in terms of overall fee revenue, MEV, etc. [14].

Finally, notice that the number of suboptimal blocks peaked at the end of March 2024 during the Blobscriptions craze – the first peak in blob demand. In the following, we investigate the effects of these suboptimal blob packings in detail (see Fig. 7). We start by analyzing the delay in Fig. 7a and notice that in general, the blobs do not have to wait more than two blocks as a result of suboptimal blob packing. The one big exception is the Blobscriptions craze starting at the end of March 2024, during this period type-3 transactions were delayed by an average of more than eight blocks as a result of suboptimal packings. Regarding loss in fee revenue for the builders of blocks with suboptimal blob packings, we observe a slightly different packing. In general, with time the relative loss decreases. Further, the relative loss is highest during the Blobscriptions craze reaching a relative loss of 70%. There is a further increase in the relative loss during the increase in blob demand starting at the beginning of June which peaked during the LayerZero airdrop at the end of June.

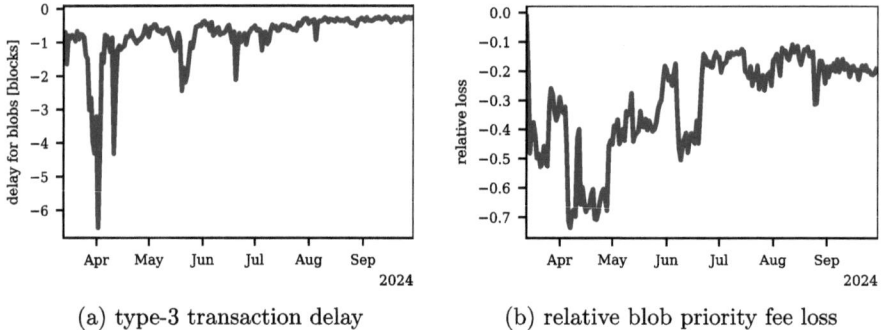

(a) type-3 transaction delay   (b) relative blob priority fee loss

Fig. 7. Delay (see Fig. 7a) and relative blob priority fee loss (see Fig. 7b as a result of suboptimal blob packing.

6.2 Market Design Issue: Subset Bidding

Beyond the above blob packing issues, a different but related—this time fundamental to market design—problem has to do with the transaction format of blob inclusion. In short, recall that a blob (also known as type-3) transaction on Ethereum contains a number of blobs, between 1 and 6 blobs. Only 6 blobs may be included per block, regardless of the number of transactions. The key part is that, if a blob transaction is included, then *all blobs it contains must be included* in the block (self-evidently). Consider, then, what would happen in the case that a transaction with a large number of blobs (e.g., 6) is submitted (showcasing a large demand for blobs from the submitter) and at the same time, a smaller but *sufficiently higher-paying* transaction is already in the mempool (e.g., this transaction has high priority for only including 1 blob). Since the Ethereum block has a six-blob limit, none of the blobs from the larger transaction would be included, and only one blob would make it into the block; this is clearly and grossly inefficient.

A straightforward solution would be for the submitter to instead submit six transactions with only one blob requested in each (or any other subdivision they might deem appropriate). However, this is an incomplete solution in that there is at least two issues with it: first, it would cause mispricing in the execution market: now, additional EIP-1559 gas would *have* to be consumed; this would therefore be suboptimal. Second, suppose for some reason[3] the submitter had

---

[3] There is a natural motivation for providers wanting such adjusted utility functions for blob inclusions in more intricate settings that include, e.g., coordination of multiple rollups.

super-additive value for simultaneous inclusion of multiple of their blobs at the same block; this naive solution would *not allow* the submitter to provide such a super-additive premium for including more than one blob of theirs. The reason for this is that, among a number of blob transactions, a block builder or validator may include their favorite subset of these.[4]

7 Improving the Blob Market

The blob market is still in its early days and we have not consistently observed blob demand at the target. Still, type-3 transaction senders collectively pay a significant fee – especially during congested periods such as the Blobscriptions craze and the LayerZero airdrop. However, most fees paid by type-3 transactions are either the EIP-4844 base fee or the EIP-1559 base fee, and only a small proportion of these fees is collected by the block's fee recipient. As a result, the financial incentives to include blobs are minimal. Even more so, the incentives for infrastructure investments are small and we presume that as a result, we have observed slow infrastructure development regarding blobs. One example would be the inefficiencies in blob packing we observe. Similarly, Geth (i.e., the biggest execution layer client) released a version with a bug in the blob mempool and it took nearly ten days to notice and fix [33, 35–37]. As a result of this bug, clients only had access to a small fraction of blob transactions. A similar bug for non-blob transactions persisting in the biggest execution layer client for more than ten days appears almost unimaginable.

These incidents highlight the need for infrastructure investment in the blob market, for which the financial incentives currently do not appear to suffice.

7.1 Blob (Priority) Fees

Some of the following steps could be taken to ensure that the ecosystem has the incentives to improve the blob market.

Multidimensional (Priority) Fee Market. Since the Decun hard fork, Ethereum has implemented a multidimensional gas market, separating the blob fee market from the general fee market. There are ongoing discussions to further divide non-blob gas usage into categories like computation, storage, and bandwidth [5]. Adding priority fees for each dimension would help scale fees appropriately during congestion. This approach addresses issues like those seen during the LayerZero airdrop, where EIP-1559 priority fees did not adjust adequately.

Increasing the Blob Target Gradually. There are ongoing discussions within the Ethereum community about increasing the blob target soon. This increase is crucial for scaling the Ethereum ecosystem. However, a rapid target increase

---
[4] Such a more "global" optimization on part of the block builder might make it optimal for them, in such a secnario of the naive solution, not to include blob transactions in the intended sequence by the submitting rollup or otherwise blob submitter.

risks a mismatch, where demand takes months to catch up, resulting in extremely lower fees for type-3 transactions. A gradual, steady increase may help balance supply and demand. Nonetheless, creating an appropriate schedule for such a gradual increase presents its own challenges.

Speedup Price Discovery. During the LayerZero airdrop the base fee took more than six hours for price discovery to be achieved. This slow price discovery, in part, is a result of the minimum fee per blob gas being low and the maximum increase per block being 12.5%. Thus, it is no surprise that price discovery took several hours when the base fee had to increase by 15 orders of magnitude. To address this issue, EIP-7762 seeks to increase the minimum blob fee per gas [27,28]. As a result of setting this minimum higher, the base fee would start higher and not have to move as much in times of congestion. Beyond that, this increase should not greatly impact blob transaction senders as they are still expected to pay less in the EIP-4844 gas market than they already do in the EIP-1559 gas market [2].

7.2 Blob and Block Packing

In addition to providing financial incentives to invest in the blob market, we must also outline the specific actions we can take.

Better Packing Algorithms. Our work shows that non-PBS and PBS blocks are often packed inefficiently. While some of this may result from builders avoiding blocks with blobs due to delayed propagation in the trusted-relay PBS system, many observed inefficiencies cannot be explained by this alone. If financial incentives in the blob market increase, better block-packing algorithms should emerge, especially for blob transactions. Importantly, block packing in a multidimensional market is complex, still, our proposed strategy shows potential improvements of up to 70%. Since highly specialized builders currently construct most blocks through PBS, this added complexity is unlikely to pose a barrier.

Subset Bidding. Section 6.2 makes the case for changing the market design for blob transactions. To fully resolve this structural market design issue that we point out, blobs would either need to go through a modified (more flexible) implementation of a mempool, or the transaction standard would need to be adjusted. The fix that we delineate below is relatively straightforward in its description, even though it would require pervasive changes within most Ethereum clients: in its most general form, the standard should allow bidding for any subset of blobs in a transaction, and only a subset of those to be included on-chain (with the rest skipped in the final transaction). Another way of implementing this change is to include transaction signatures for multiple subsets of blobs, in such a way that they are mutually exclusive so that only one can be chosen to be included on-chain at a time.

A special solution to this market design challenge has been introduced by Titan Builder, enabling senders to submit multiple permutations of blob transactions [38,39]. These blobs are then individually sorted to find the optimal combination before being included in a block. This feature would attempt to alleviate the issue in Sect. 6.2 without changing the way type-3 transactions work (only for blobs submitted *privately* through Titan Builder, when they win the block). While this improvement appears promising, we do not find signs of it being utilized to the extent it could and we conjecture that this might be related to the absence of congested periods since the feature's launch.

8 Conclusion

In conclusion, while the innovation of blob transactions through Ethereum's EIP-4844 offers promising advantages, including cost reductions for L2 data settlement, our study reveals several inefficiencies. Such inefficiencies in block packing and economic incentives seem to have emerged as issues expected to be critical in a world where the temporary storage of blobs is dominant for Ethereum. We documented periods of up to 70% fee loss due to suboptimal blob packing, highlighting the need for better utilization of blob space which would result in both higher builder profits and less blob inclusion delay. The lack of significant financial incentives for builders to prioritize blob transactions likely contributes to these inefficiencies, as most fees associated with blob transactions are burnt, leaving builders with minimal rewards.

This work provides valuable insights into the early days of blobs on Ethereum, shedding light on both the potential and challenges of this scaling solution. As Ethereum continues to evolve, we hope for these findings to inform future network upgrades, contributing to more efficient and scalable decentralized systems.

Acknowledgments. We thank Edward Felten, Pranav Garimidi, Scott Duke Kominers, and Tim Roughgarden for helpful discussions on the subject matter of our paper.

References

1. Ether Alpha. Client diversity (2024). https://clientdiversity.org/. Accessed 10 Oct 2024
2. Data Always and Flashbots Research. Understanding minimum blob base fees (2024). https://ethresear.ch/t/understanding-minimum-blob-base-fees/20489. Accessed 10 Oct 2024
3. Angeris, G., Diamandis, T., Moallemi, C.: Multidimensional blockchain fees are (essentially) optimal. arXiv preprint arXiv:2402.08661 (2024)
4. Azouvi, S., Goren, G., Heimbach, L., Hicks, A.: Base fee manipulation in Ethereum's EIP-1559 transaction fee mechanism. In: 37th International Symposium on Distributed Computing (2023)
5. Buterin, V.: Multidimensional gas pricing (2024). https://vitalik.eth.limo/general/2024/05/09/multidim.html. Accessed 10 Oct 2024
6. Buterin, V.: Tweet on ethereum roadmap (2024). https://x.com/VitalikButerin/status/1741190491578810445?s=20. Accessed 10 Oct 2024

7. Buterin, V., Conner, E., Dudley, R., Slipper, M., Norden, I., Bakhta, A.: EIP-1559: fee market change for eth 1.0 chain (2024). https://github.com/ethereum/EIPs/blob/master/EIPS/eip-1559.md. Accessed 10 Oct 2024
8. Buterin, V., Feist, D., Loerakker, D., Kadianakis, G., Garnett, M., Taiwo, M., Dietrichs, A.: EIP-4844: shard blob transactions (2024). https://github.com/ethereum/EIPs/blob/master/EIPS/eip-4844.md. Accessed 10 Oct 2024
9. Crapis, D., Felten, E.W., Mamageishvili, A.: EIP-4844 economics and rollup strategies. arXiv preprint arXiv:2310.01155 (2023)
10. Diamandis, T., Evans, A., Chitra, T., Angeris, G.: Designing multidimensional blockchain fee markets. In: 5th Conference on Advances in Financial Technologies (AFT 2023). Schloss Dagstuhl-Leibniz-Zentrum für Informatik (2023)
11. Ferreira, M.V.X., Moroz, D.J., Parkes, D.C., Stern, M.: Dynamic posted-price mechanisms for the blockchain transaction-fee market. In: Proceedings of the 3rd ACM Conference on Advances in Financial Technologies, pp. 86–99 (2021)
12. Flashbots. MEV-boost relay (2024). https://github.com/flashbots/mev-boost-relay. Accessed 10 Oct 2024
13. Flashbots. Mempool dumpster (2024). https://github.com/flashbots/mempool-dumpster. Accessed 10 Oct 2024
14. Heimbach, L., Kiffer, L., Torres, C.F., Wattenhofer, R.: Ethereum's proposer-builder separation: promises and realities. In: Proceedings of the 2023 ACM on Internet Measurement Conference, pp. 406–420 (2023)
15. Hougaard, J.L., Pourpouneh, M.: Farsighted miners under transaction fee mechanism EIP1559. In: 2023 IEEE International Conference on Blockchain and Cryptocurrency (ICBC), pp. 1–9. IEEE (2023)
16. Lee, S.: 180 days after EIP-4844: will blob sharing solve dilemma for small rollups? arXiv preprint arXiv:2410.04111 (2024)
17. Leonardos, S., Monnot, B., Reijsbergen, D., Skoulakis, E., Piliouras, G.: Dynamical analysis of the EIP-1559 Ethereum fee market. In: Proceedings of the 3rd ACM Conference on Advances in Financial Technologies, pp. 114–126 (2021)
18. Leonardos, S., Reijsbergen, D., Monnot, B., Piliouras, G.: Optimality despite chaos in fee markets. In: International Conference on Financial Cryptography and Data Security, pp. 346–362. Springer, Cham (2023)
19. Liu, Y., Lu, Y., Nayak, K., Zhang, F., Zhang, L., Zhao, Y.: Empirical analysis of EIP-1559: transaction fees, waiting times, and consensus security. In: Proceedings of the 2022 ACM SIGSAC Conference on Computer and Communications Security, pp. 2099–2113 (2022)
20. Messias, J., Gogol, K., Silva, M.I., Livshits, B.: The writing is on the wall: analyzing the boom of inscriptions and its impact on EVM-compatible blockchains. arXiv preprint arXiv:2405.15288 (2024)
21. Milionis, J., Hirsch, D., Arditi, A., Garimidi, P.: A framework for single-item NFT auction mechanism design. In: Proceedings of the 2022 ACM CCS Workshop on Decentralized Finance and Security, DeFi 2022, pp. 31–38. Association for Computing Machinery, New York (2022). https://doi.org/10.1145/3560832.3563436. ISBN 9781450398824
22. Milionis, J., Moallemi, C.C., Roughgarden, T.: Complexity-approximation trade-offs in exchange mechanisms: amms vs. lobs. In: Baldimtsi, F., Cachin, C. (eds.) Financial Cryptography and Data Security, pp. 326–343. Springer, Cham (2024). ISBN 978-3-031-47754-6
23. Milionis, J., Moallemi, C.C., Roughgarden, T.: A myersonian framework for optimal liquidity provision in automated market makers. In: Guruswami, V.

(ed.) 15th Innovations in Theoretical Computer Science Conference (ITCS 2024). Leibniz International Proceedings in Informatics (LIPIcs), vol. 287, pp. 81:1–81:19. Schloss Dagstuhl – Leibniz-Zentrum für Informatik, Dagstuhl, Germany (2024). https://doi.org/10.4230/LIPIcs.ITCS.2024.81. https://drops.dagstuhl.de/entities/document/10.4230/LIPIcs.ITCS.2024.81. ISBN 978-3-95977-309-6
24. Nijkerk, M.: Ethereum hit by blobscriptions in first stress test of blockchain's new data system. CoinDesk (2024). https://www.coindesk.com/tech/2024/03/28/ethereum-hit-by-blobscriptions-in-first-stress-test-of-blockchains-new-data-system/. Accessed 10 Oct 2024
25. Sigma Prime. Lighthouse: A book on Ethereum (2024). https://lighthouse-book.sigmaprime.io/. Accessed 10 Oct 2024
26. Reijsbergen, D., Sridhar, S., Monnot, B., Leonardos, S., Skoulakis, S., Piliouras, G.: Transaction fees on a honeymoon: Ethereum's EIP-1559 one month later. In: 2021 IEEE International Conference on Blockchain (Blockchain), pp. 196–204. IEEE (2021)
27. Resnick, M.: EIP-7762: Increase min_base_fee_per_blob_gas (2024). https://eips.ethereum.org/EIPS/eip-7762. Accessed 10 Oct 2024
28. Resnick, M.: Tweet on blob base fee discovery (2024). https://x.com/MaxResnick1/status/1822400161018167478. Accessed 10 Oct 2024
29. Reth. Reth: A rust Ethereum client (2024). https://reth.rs/. Accessed 10 Oct 2024
30. Roughgarden, T.: Transaction fee mechanism design for the Ethereum blockchain: an economic analysis of EIP-1559. arXiv preprint arXiv:2012.00854 (2020)
31. Soltani, P., Ashtiani, F.: Delay analysis of EIP-4844. arXiv preprint arXiv:2409.11043 (2024)
32. Stevens, R.: Arbitrum cashed in on layerzero airdrop but the boost was short-lived. The Block (2024). https://www.theblock.co/post/302945/arbitrum-cashed-in-on-layerzero-airdrop-but-the-boost-was-short-lived. Accessed 10 Oct 2024
33. Szilagyi, P.: Tweet on geth blob mempool 4 (2024). https://x.com/peter_szilagyi/status/1839626057713864736. Accessed 10 Oct 2024
34. Szilagyi, P.: Tweet on geth blob priority fees (2024). https://x.com/peter_szilagyi/status/1790727197642182737. Accessed 10 Oct 2024
35. Szilágyi, P.: Tweet on geth blob mempool 1 (2024). https://x.com/peter_szilagyi/status/1836062023668387877. Accessed 10 Oct 2024
36. Szilágyi, P.: Tweet on geth blob mempool 2 (2024). https://x.com/peter_szilagyi/status/1836089316067393583. Accessed 10 Oct 2024
37. Szilágyi, P.: Tweet on geth blob mempool 3 (2024). https://x.com/peter_szilagyi/status/1839591535278498001. Accessed 10 Oct 2024
38. Titan Builder. Tweet on eth_sendblobs (2024). https://x.com/titanbuilderxyz/status/1809231370243211601
39. Titan Builder. Eth_sendblobs api documentation (2024). https://docs.titanbuilder.xyz/api/eth_sendblobs. Accessed 10 Oct 2024
40. Wahrstätter, T.: MEV-boost dashboard (2024). https://mevboost.pics/. Accessed 10 Oct 2024
41. Wood, G.: Ethereum: a secure decentralised generalised transaction ledger (2014). https://ethereum.github.io/yellowpaper/paper.pdf. Accessed 10 Oct 2024

Quantifying the Value of Revert Protection

Brian Z. Zhu[1]([✉]), Xin Wan[2], Ciamac C. Moallemi[1,2,3], Dan Robinson[3], and Brad Bachu[2]

[1] Columbia University, New York, USA
bzz2101@columbia.edu, ciamac@gsb.columbia.edu
[2] Uniswap Labs, New York, USA
{xin,brad.bachu}@uniswap.org
[3] Paradigm, Walnut Creek, USA
dan@paradigm.xyz

Abstract. Revert protection is a feature provided by some blockchain platforms that prevents users from incurring fees for failed transactions. We study the economic implications and benefits of revert protection in the context of priority gas auctions and maximal extractable value. We develop a model in which searchers bid for a top-of-block arbitrage opportunity under varying degrees of revert protection. This model applies to a broad range of settings, including bundle auctions on L1s and priority ordering sequencing rules on L2s. We quantify, in closed form, how revert protection improves equilibrium auction revenue, market efficiency, and blockspace efficiency.

Keywords: Blockchain · Priority gas auction · Revert protection · MEV

1 Introduction and Background

Revert protection is a feature for blockchains that block builders and sequencers can provide where they exclude transactions that would otherwise fail, protecting users from paying fees for failed transactions. However, failed transactions would pay fees, which often accrue to the block builder or sequencer. So is it in their interest to offer revert protection?

In this paper, we argue that revert protection is indeed in their interest and quantify the value of revert protection on blockchain platforms, particularly on the auctions that many of those platforms use to capture and allocate maximal extractable value (MEV). We show that in various relevant settings, revert protection is beneficial for auctioneer revenue, as well as for other relevant outcomes like price discovery and blockspace efficiency.

The analysis is complicated by the wide range of rules—across the complex Ethereum block builder market and on a variety of L2s—for how transactions are selected for inclusion and ordered, how fees are collected, and who those fees go to, as well as how applications behave under those rules. We propose a model that can be parameterized to cover a wide variety of these settings, and use that model to solve for the equilibrium behavior of MEV searchers as a function of those parameters.

1.1 Revert Protection

On Ethereum and similar blockchains, users interact with smart contracts using atomic transactions. In the execution of a transaction, a smart contract may trigger a "revert" in the transaction, causing the entire transaction to fail. Normally, if the transaction is included, the user who sent the reverting transaction is still charged some transaction fee, even though the transaction has no other effect on the blockchain state. The fee charged is typically given by the product of *gas price* of and the *gas used* by the transaction before it either completes or reverts. The gas price can be separated into the "base fee"—a flat fee that must be paid by any transaction in the block—and the "priority fee"—an additional fee paid to the builder that often affects inclusion and ordering (particularly when blocks are full).

The gas used in the transaction is a function of how much of the transaction was executed—a transaction that reverts uses only some portion of the gas that it would have used had it succeeded. For example, on an automated market maker, typical reverting transactions may use only around 10-20% of the gas that a successful transaction would use. "Revert protection" is thereby the feature that block builders and sequencers may choose to implement in which failed transactions are excluded entirely from blocks. This feature improves user experience, as users only have to pay fees if their transaction succeeds. However, it also has significant effects on the behavior of the profit-seeking bots known as "searchers," which we now describe.

1.2 Block-Building Auctions

Public blockchains have abundant opportunities for MEV. As an example, one major type of MEV is the arbitraging of prices between decentralized and centralized exchanges, also called "CEX-DEX arbitrage," as discussed in [4] and [13]. On these blockchains, independent actors known as "searchers" seek out MEV opportunities and compete to fill them.

Some block builders use different types of auctions to allocate these opportunities to searchers. For a given MEV opportunity, each transaction attempting to claim it can be thought of as a "bid." Generally, only one transaction trying to claim a given opportunity will succeed in extracting the value from it. Revert protection is therefore very relevant for these auctions, because it protects bidders on a given MEV opportunity from having to pay for failed bids if they do not win the opportunity. Two examples of block building auctions include the "bundle auctions" run by builders such as Flashbots on Ethereum mainnet and the "priority ordering" rule implemented by sequencers on Ethereum L2s.

Bundle Auctions. On Ethereum mainnet, blocks are typically built by profit-maximizing "builders." Many of these builders run "bundle auctions" in which they allow any searcher to submit transactions, and use those searchers' bids as a factor when deciding which transactions to include and how to order them.[1]

Bids can be expressed in two ways for this auction: (i) through the priority fee on the transaction or (ii) through a direct payment as part of the logic of the transaction by calling `coinbase.transfer` [6]. The relevant difference between these methods of payment is that some portion of priority fees are paid *even if the transaction reverts*, whereas if the transfer is made as part of the transaction, then it will be conditional on whether the transaction succeeds.

On Ethereum mainnet, the two components of gas price (base and priority fee) are paid in ETH and accrue to different users: base fees are burned, meaning they ultimately accrue to all ETH holders, rather than the builder; priority fees accrue to the block builder.[2] Many builders, such as Flashbots [8], provide revert protection for transactions submitted to them, even though it is not required by the Ethereum protocol and they might receive more in transaction fees by including it. Our results in this paper help explain this choice by showing that it likely increases their expected revenue in equilibrium.

Priority Ordering. On Layer 2 blockchains today, blocks are typically built by a single sequencer, which often follows a deterministic algorithm for transaction inclusion and ordering. One of the most popular algorithms for this is "priority ordering," in which transactions in a block are ordered in descending order of their gas price.

Priority ordering can be thought of as an auction in which transactions bid with the discretionary part of their gas price (i.e. their priority fee) to be included earlier in the chain. By default, this means that certain kinds of MEV (such as top-of-block CEX-DEX arbitrage) will generally accrue to the sequencer through priority fees. This means that when transactions fail, they still pay some of their priority fee to the sequencer. However, there is a mechanism called MEV taxes [16] that applications can use to capture all but a negligible portion of the value that would otherwise be paid through priority fees. Since MEV taxes are paid as part of the transaction and revert if the transaction fails, these fees will only be paid if the transaction succeeds.

Considering All Cases. Even within these two settings of L1 block builders and L2 priority-ordered sequencers, we now need to consider at least seven cases that differ in who fees go to and how much is paid when the transaction reverts. Table 1 shows the differences between these cases. Our model is general enough

---

[1] Block builders also play the role of bidders themselves in the "MEV-Boost" auction [7], in which they bid to have their block included by the current proposer. As "bids" are complete blocks in PBS auctions, revert protection is not as relevant here, and we will mostly set this case aside for the purposes of this paper.

[2] These bids, whether paid via priority fee or Coinbase transfer, technically go to the *proposer*, not the builder who is assembling the block. However, since they reduce the amount that the builder has to pay to the proposer to win the MEV-Boost auction, we can think of these payments as a value transfer to the builder.

to capture the distribution of transaction fees and revert behavior for all of these cases. We can compute in closed-form the expected base fee and remaining fee (i.e. priority fee, Coinbase transfer, or MEV tax) for all listed settings as well. For the remainder of the paper, we will use the terms "builder" and "sequencer" interchangeably.

Table 1. Transaction Fee Distribution and Revert Behavior for Various Settings.

Setting	Base fee goes to:	Rest of bid goes to:	Is base fee paid when TX fails?	Is rest of bid paid when TX fails?
L1 block builder with bids paid via priority fees	ETH holders	Builder	Partial	Partial
L1 block builder with bids paid via Coinbase transfer	ETH holders	Builder	Partial	No
L2 sequencer with priority ordering	Sequencer	Sequencer	Partial	Partial
L2 sequencer with priority ordering for apps using MEV taxes	Sequencer	Application	Partial	No
L1 block builder with revert protection	ETH holders	Builder	No	No
L2 sequencer with revert protection	Sequencer	Sequencer	No	No
L2 sequencer with revert protection for apps using MEV taxes	Sequencer	Application	No	No

1.3 Implementation Costs of Revert Protection

This paper is primarily concerned with the potential effects of revert protection, not with its implementation. We note that feasible revert protection is a difficult technical challenge: knowing whether a transaction will revert usually requires a builder to execute part of the transaction itself, which consumes computational resources. If the builder does not charge the sender anything for that reverted transaction, denial-of-service (DOS) attacks are possible by spamming the builder with an overwhelming number of reverting transactions.

There are some methods to mitigate this kind of attack. In some settings, the builder can use out-of-band spam prevention techniques (such as IP blocking) to make DOS attacks infeasible. For certain cases—including the auction-like use cases described above—it is also possible for the builder to determine statically whether a transaction will fail or not.

We abstract away from these challenges in our baseline model, assuming that the builder can implement revert protection with negligible cost. In our extensions, we study two schemes to deal with the implementation costs of revert protection where (i) costs are internalized by the sequencer and (ii) searchers pay a fixed amount for revert protection services.

1.4 Our Contributions

The contributions of this paper are as follows:

- We introduce a novel and unified game-theoretic model that can be used to analyze revert protection in a variety of settings such as L1 block builders, L2 priority-ordered sequencers, MEV taxes, etc.
- We characterize equilibria of our model in closed form, in terms of the model parameters: the value of the MEV opportunity, base fee, revert penalty parameters, and number of participating agents.
- Using our model equilibrium, we can quantify the benefits of revert protection versus not offering revert protection:
  - **Revert protection offers higher auction revenue.** The auctioneer extracts the full value of the MEV opportunity when the auction clears. However, in the absence of revert protection, agents randomize when they participate, and there is a non-zero probability that the auction does not clear and value is lost. This results in reduced sequencer revenue.
  - **In the context of automated market makers, revert protection offers better market efficiency.** Here, the auction represents a CEX-DEX arbitrage opportunity. In the absence of revert protection, there is some chance that auctions do not clear, leaving arbitrage opportunities unexploited and hence prices less accurate.
  - **Revert protection offers better blockspace efficiency.** With revert protection, only a single, winning transaction consumes block space. On the other hand, without revert protection, all submitted transactions consume block space.
- Our model allows for different revert penalty rates for the base fee and priority fees. While the penalty rate for priority fees influences bidder behavior, we show that it does not affect aggregate outcomes (e.g. revenue, number of submitted transactions).
- When implementation costs are non-negligible but not too large, we show that charging a fixed fee to searchers for offering revert protection results in more auction revenue than builders internalizing the costs themselves.

1.5 Literature Review

We contribute to the literature on on-chain MEV auctions, first explored in the seminal work of Daian et al. [4]. Studies have focused on aspects in the L1 block building environment, such as censorship resistance [5], advantages for integrated searcher-builders [14], private mempools [3], and proposer-builder separation [2]. Other studies have focused on designing on-chain auctions and analyzing auction equilibria for L2 networks with various sequencing rules, including auctions where bidders are required to pay deposits [17], auctions under shared sequencing [12], taxes on MEV for applications [16], and the TimeBoost mechanism [11] proposed for Arbitrum [10] (a L2 network with a first-come first-serve sequencing rule). Relative to these studies, our paper offers a novel analysis on the effect of revert protection on on-chain auctions. Prior work has mentioned the congestion effects of reverting transactions in [15], and the whitepaper for Unichain, an L2 network that plans to offer revert protection, claims that it benefits swapping on decentralized exchanges [1].

In the context of the economic literature on auctions, our model is a common-value all-pay auction with a reserve price and differential partial refunds for failed bids on the minimum bid and amount above the minimum bid. Common-value auction models are frequently used in the analysis of on-chain auctions [2,3,12,14] and in the traditional economics literature as well. Closest to our work is [9], which also considers a common-value all-pay auction with a reserve price, however does not allow for partial refunds on failed bids, and [18], whose model allows for a wide range of payoff and cost functions but has a more constrained strategy space for the bidders.

2 Model

2.1 Auction Description

We present a stylized model of a priority ordering auction for an MEV opportunity. There are $N \geq 2$ agents, indexed by $i \in [N]$, bidding for a single MEV opportunity in a block with common value $V > 0$, and the base gas fee for the block is $g > 0$.

Agent i may choose to abstain or submit a bid ("priority gas fee") $b_i \geq 0$; we denote the action of abstaining by $b_i = \varnothing$. The winner, denoted by w, extracts value V from the MEV opportunity and pays $g + b_w$. In the event of a tie, the winner is randomly selected among the highest bids. Any losing agent j does not receive any value and incurs a revert cost of $r_1 g + r_2 b_j$, where $r_1, r_2 \in [0, 1]$ are the revert penalty rates on the base gas and priority gas fees, respectively.[3]

This model provides a unified setting that captures a variety of proposed and currently in-use block building protocols among popular blockchains, including those discussed in Sect. 1.2 and listed in Table 1. Table 2 illustrates how the revert penalty parameters may be set in various settings. For example, with an L1 block builder and bids paid via priority fee, we would expect $r_1 = r_2 > 0$, and these parameters might take a value of 10–20% for automated market maker swap transactions.

In the cases involving MEV taxes in Table 2, observe that $r_2 = 0$. This is because with MEV taxes, applications can decide what fraction of the priority fees to capture themselves versus giving to the sequencer. Priority fees that are

---

[3] This model corresponds to a common value, all-pay auction with a minimum bid g and differential refunds $(1 - r_1)g$ and $(1 - r_2)b_j$ for the base bid amount g and additional bid amount b_j, respectively.

Table 2. Revert Penalty Parameters for Settings in Table 1

Setting	Revert penalty on base fee	Revert penalty on rest of bid
L1 block builder with bids paid via priority fees	$r_1 = r_2 \in (0, 1]$	
L1 block builder with bids paid via Coinbase transfer	$r_1 \in (0, 1]$	$r_2 = 0$
L2 sequencer with priority ordering	$r_1 = r_2 \in (0, 1]$	
L2 sequencer with priority ordering for apps using MEV taxes	$r_1 \in (0, 1]$	$r_2 = 0$
L1 block builder with revert protection	$r_1 = r_2 = 0$	
L2 sequencer with revert protection	$r_1 = r_2 = 0$	
L2 sequencer with revert protection for apps using MEV taxes	$r_1 = r_2 = 0$	

captured by the application are fully refunded on revert. As we will see later on (cf. Theorem 4.1), the total priority fee revenue does not depend on the choice of r_2. Hence, applications are incentivized to capture all but a negligible portion of the priority fee, and thus $r_2 = 0$. We make the following assumption to avoid trivialities:[4]

Assumption 2.1. *Assume that the value exceeds the base fee, i.e., $V > g$.*

2.2 Strategy Spaces and Payoffs

Payoffs Under Pure Strategies. Under pure strategies, agent i has strategy space $\mathcal{B} = \emptyset \cup [0, \infty)$ and chooses an action $b_i \in \mathcal{B}$. Given a strategy profile $b = (b_i)_{i \in [N]}$, the payoff of agent i, denoted u_i, is

$$u_i(b_i | b_{-i}) = \begin{cases} (V - g - b_i)\mathbb{P}(w = i | b) \\ \quad - (r_1 g + r_2 b_i)(1 - \mathbb{P}(w = i | b)) & \text{if } b_i \geq 0, \\ 0 & \text{if } b_i = \emptyset, \end{cases}$$

---

[4] This is because, if $V \leq g$, then the utility an agent receives when winning the action cannot be positive, even if the priority fee is zero, since the value does not exceed the base fee. Thus, all agents abstaining is a dominant strategy equilibrium.

where $\mathbb{P}(w = i|b)$ denotes the probability of agent i winning under the strategy profile b, i.e.,

$$\mathbb{P}(w = i|b) = \frac{\mathbb{1}\{b_i = b_M\}}{1 + \sum_{j \neq i} \mathbb{1}\{b_j = b_i\}}.$$

where $b_M \triangleq \max\{b_i \colon b_i \geq 0\}$, i.e., the highest participating bidder wins, with ties broken at random. The first term in the payoff for participating bidders captures the case when agent i has the highest bid; their payoff is the net value gained, $(V - g - b_i)$, scaled by the probability of winning. The second term captures the payment in the case when agent i does not win the auction.

Payoffs Under Mixed Strategies. We now allow agents to probabilistically randomize between the actions of abstaining from the auction and bidding a continuum of possible values. Specifically, agent i now chooses $\beta_i \equiv (p_i, F_i)$ where $p_i \in [0, 1]$ is the probability of abstaining ($b_i = \varnothing$), and F_i is a continuous cdf supported on $b_i \geq 0$ specifying the distribution that agent i bids according to, conditional on agent i choosing to participate in the auction. Given a strategy profile $\beta = (\beta_i)_{i \in [N]}$, the expected payoff $\bar{u}_i$ of agent i conditional on realizing b_i and assuming that agents' actions are chosen independently, is

$$u_i(b_i|\beta_{-i}) = \begin{cases} (V - g - b_i)\mathbb{P}(w = i|b_i, \beta_{-i}) \\ \quad -(r_1 g + r_2 b_i)(1 - \mathbb{P}(w = i|b_i, \beta_{-i})) & \text{if } b_i \geq 0, \\ 0 & \text{if } b_i = \varnothing, \end{cases} \quad (1)$$

where $\mathbb{P}(w = i|b_i, \beta_{-i})$ is the probability that agent i wins conditional on realizing b_i and the other agent's strategies. For the assumptions above, we have

$$\mathbb{P}(w = i|b_i, \beta_{-i}) = \prod_{j \neq i}(p_j + (1 - p_j)F_j(b_i)), \quad (2)$$

noting that ties occur with probability zero under continuous distributions. The expected utility $\bar{u}_i$ for agent i over their random choice of action b_i is then

$$\bar{u}_i(\beta_i, \beta_{-i}) \triangleq \mathbb{E}\left[u_i(b_i|\beta_{-i})\right] = (1 - p_i) \int_0^\infty u_i(b|\beta_{-i})\, dF_i(b). \quad (3)$$

3 Equilibrium

3.1 Pure Strategies

A pure strategy profile b^* as defined in the previous section is a Nash equilibrium in pure strategies if no agent can unilaterally deviate to increase their payoff, i.e. for all $i \in [N]$, we have $u_i(b_i^*|b_{-i}^*) \geq u_i(b_i|b_{-i}^*)$ for any $b_i \in \mathcal{B}$.

Theorem 3.1. *If $r_1 = r_2 = 0$, then a pure strategy profile b where bids are ordered such that $b_1 \leq b_2 \leq \cdots \leq b_N$ (with abstentions represented by bids less than zero) is a Nash equilibrium if and only if $b_{N-1} = b_N = V - g$.*

Intuitively, when there is no cost incurred upon losing the auction, the agents have no disincentive associated with large bids, resulting in an equilibrium when at least two agents bid the breakeven bid, i.e., the highest possible amount yielding a nonnegative utility, which is the value of the arbitrage opportunity less the base gas fee.

Theorem 3.2. *If at least one of r_1 and r_2 is nonzero, then there does not exist a Nash equilibrium in pure strategies.*

Conversely, when agents incur any cost upon losing the auction, whether on the base or priority gas fee, there is no Nash equilibrium in pure strategies. The revert cost penalty results in a situation where at least one agent can benefit from unilaterally deviating given any pure strategy profile. Having characterized the pure-strategy Nash equilibrium and lack thereof, we now look at mixed-strategy equilibria.

3.2 Mixed Strategies

A mixed strategy profile β^* as defined in the previous section is a Nash equilibrium if $\bar{u}_i(\beta_i^*, \beta_{-i}^*) \geq \bar{u}_i(\beta_i, \beta_{-i}^*)$ for all agents i and for any other mixed strategy β_i^*. For tractability, we focus on solving for *symmetric equilibria*, i.e., mixed-strategy Nash equilibria where all agents' strategies β_i are identical.

Theorem 3.3. *If at least one of r_1 and r_2 is nonzero, then the unique symmetric mixed-strategy equilibrium is given by*

$$p_i^* = p^* \triangleq \left(\frac{r_1 g}{V - g + r_1 g} \right)^{\frac{1}{N-1}},$$

$$F_i^* = F^*(b) \triangleq \frac{1}{1 - p^*} \left(\left(\frac{r_1 g + r_2 b}{V - g - b + r_1 g + r_2 b} \right)^{\frac{1}{N-1}} - p^* \right),$$

for bids $b \in [0, V - g]$ and agents $i \in [N]$. The expected payoff of every agent in equilibrium is zero.

We remark that this equilibrium is unique among symmetric mixed-strategy Nash equilibria, but there may exist non-symmetric equilibria. A complete characterization of all possible equilibria of the auction is outside the scope of this paper, and we focus on the symmetric equilibrium for the rest of the paper.

In order for a mixed-strategy Nash equilibrium to arise, arbitrageurs must be indifferent over all possible actions supported by the mixed strategy. Thus, when the equilibrium assigns a positive probability mass to abstaining from the auction, an action which yields zero payoff, it follows that the equilibrium expected payoff of each arbitrageur is zero. It turns out that under the equilibrium in Theorem 3.3, equilibrium expected payoff for arbitrageurs is zero even in cases where they always choose to participate.

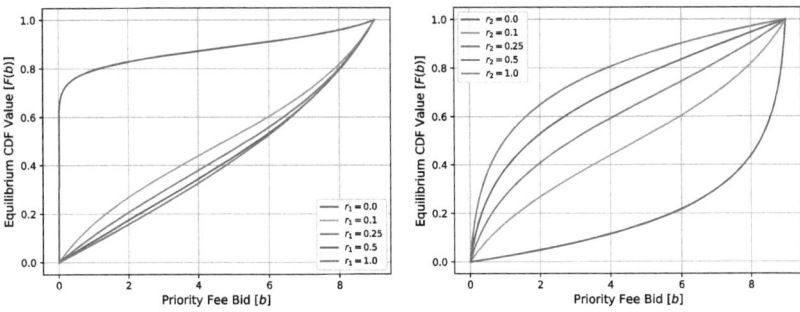

Fig. 1. Equilibrium CDF for Priority Fee Bids. We set $V = 10$, $g = 1$, $N = 20$, $r_2 = 0.1$ for the left plot, and $r_1 = 0.1$ for the right plot.

When $r_1 > 0$, the symmetric equilibrium strategy is characterized by a non-zero probability of abstention and a non-degenerate continuous CDF specifying the distribution from which to draw the priority gas fee bid. In the special case of $r_1 = 0$, all arbitrageurs participate with probability one. Figures 1 and 2 plot the equilibrium CDF and abstention probability for various parameters.[5]

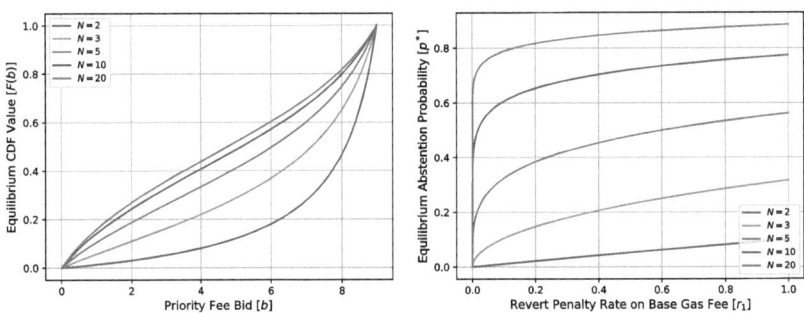

Fig. 2. Equilibrium CDF for Priority Fee Bids (left) and Abstention Probability (right). We set $V = 10$, $g = 1$, and $r_1 = r_2 = 0.1$ for the left plot.

We note that Theorem 3.3 is consistent with Theorem 3.1. When $r_1 = r_2 = 0$, Theorem 3.3 yields $p^* = 0$ and $F^*(b) = 0$ for all $b \in [0, V-g)$. Compare this with the pure strategy equilibrium given in Theorem 3.1, which corresponds to a symmetric mixed-strategy Nash equilibrium given by $p^* = 0$, $F^*(b) = 0$ for all $b \in [0, V-g)$, and $F^*(V-g) = 1$. Indeed, one can show that $F^*(b)$ converges pointwise to the function $\mathbb{1}\{b = V-g\}$ as $(r_1, r_2) \to (0,0)$.

---

[5] In ??, we discuss comparative statics for the the equilibrium CDF and the abstention probability.

4 Implications for Sequencer Design

In this section, we examine the comparative statistics of equilibrium quantities that are relevant to sequencer design.

4.1 Auction Revenue and Market Efficiency

Auction Revenue. Given a realization of the mixed strategy, the auctioneer takes the base fee and priority fee bid of the winner (if one exists), and r_1 times the base fee plus r_2 times the priority fee bids of the remaining participating arbitrageurs. The revenue can be split into two terms: one capturing the revenue from the base fee, and the other capturing revenue from priority fee bids. The expected revenue over all possible realizations along with its decomposition into base and priority components is characterized by the following theorem.

Theorem 4.1. *If at least one of r_1 and r_2 is nonzero, then under the symmetric mixed-strategy Nash equilibrium:*

- *The expected revenue from the auction is*

$$\mathbb{E}[\text{Revenue}] = \left(1 - (p^*)^N\right) V = \left(1 - \left(\frac{r_1 g}{V - g + r_1 g}\right)^{\frac{N}{N-1}}\right) V.$$

- *Expected revenue decreases in r_1, does not depend on N when $r_1 = 0$, decreases in N when $r_1 \neq 0$, and does not depend on r_2.*
- *Expected revenue can be decomposed into components representing revenue from base gas fees and priority gas fees given by*

$$\mathbb{E}[\text{BaseRevenue}] = \left(1 - (p^*)^N\right) g + \left((1 - p^*)N - \left(1 - (p^*)^N\right)\right) r_1 g,$$

$$\mathbb{E}[\text{PriorityRevenue}] = \left(1 - (p^*)^N\right)(V - g) - \left((1 - p^*)N - \left(1 - (p^*)^N\right)\right) r_1 g.$$

- *If $r_1 \neq 0$, then as the number of arbitrageurs N tends to infinity, the expected revenues converges to a finite limit, with*

$$\lim_{N \to \infty} \mathbb{E}[\text{Revenue}] = \frac{V(V - g)}{V - g + r_1 g},$$

$$\lim_{N \to \infty} \mathbb{E}[\text{BaseRevenue}] = \frac{(V - g)(g - r_1 g)}{V - g + r_1 g} - r_1 g \log\left(1 + \frac{V - g}{r_1 g}\right),$$

$$\lim_{N \to \infty} \mathbb{E}[\text{PriorityRevenue}] = (V - g) + r_1 g \log\left(1 + \frac{V - g}{r_1 g}\right).$$

The intuition behind the expression for total revenue is straightforward. Since the arbitrageurs earn a combined expected payoff of zero in equilibrium and the winning arbitrageur extracts a value of V, the total payments made to the sequencer should also equal V, as long as least one arbitrageur participates. We then take a simple expectation over the events "a value extraction of V occurs" and "no value extraction occurs" which have probabilities $1 - (p^*)^N$ and $(p^*)^N$, respectively, for the result. This phenomena is known as "rent dissipation" [9]: any value that is realized entirely goes to the sequencer.

Theorem 4.1 shows that expected revenue decreases in r_1, the revert penalty rate on the base gas fee. This implies that holding all other auction parameters equal, the revenue-maximizing choice of r_1 in expectation is zero, corresponding to a sequencer with full RP the base gas fee. Furthermore, expected revenue is constant in N under full RP while it decreases in N for nonzero r_1, highlighting additional losses when full RP is not implemented.

Interestingly, expected revenue does not depend on r_2, the revert penalty rate for priority gas fees. The intuition behind this is that value extraction only depends on participation, which is independent of r_2. Another interpretation is that r_2 does not matter for the "marginal bidder" who participates but bids a priority fee of zero. Consequently, sequencers and applications can adjust r_2 without affecting the expected total payments collected from participants.

This is relevant to considering MEV taxes imposed by applications, which not only change the distribution of the non-base portion of the fee (causing a share of it to go to the application, rather than the sequencer), but also affect r_2 (since MEV taxes are only paid when the transaction succeeds, while a portion of priority fees are paid even on revert). Since r_2 does not affect total revenue, this helps justify the assumption we made in Sect. 2.1 that an application will parameterize its MEV taxes as high as possible in order to maximize the revenue that it earns.

The expression for expected auction revenue coming from base gas fees is obtained by first conditioning on the number of participating arbitrageurs k. Given k participants, the sequencer will earn $r_1 g$ from $k - 1$ of them and g from the remaining one. Subtracting this from the total revenue thus gives the component coming from priority gas fee bids. Notably, these components also do not depend on r_2.

As previously mentioned, the probability of a value extraction occurring lowers as N increases, stemming from the disincentive to participate brought on by a more competitive environment, but this probability converges to a finite limit as N tends to infinity. This provides a minimum guarantee on expected revenue for any number of arbitrageurs.

Market Efficiency. Revenue is deeply connected with market efficiency in automated market makers. Recall that the probability that value from the arbitrage opportunity is extracted is $1 - (p^*)^N$. When this quantity is high, on-chain arbitrages are frequent, thereby improving market efficiency. On the other hand, when this quantity is low, on-chain arbitrages are less likely to occur, leaving arbitrage opportunities unexploited and generating zero value for the auction. It is straightforward to see that r_1 has the same directional impact on market efficiency (when measured by the probability that a value extraction occurs) as expected auction revenue described in Theorem 4.1, so more revert protection (lower r_1) implies a higher market efficiency.

4.2 Blockspace and Mempool Usage

We proceed to analyze blockspace and memory pool usage. If an arbitrageur decides to participate, they submit a transaction to the mempool. When transactions are not fully revert-protected, they will still appear on-chain, which is prevented by full revert protection. The following theorem characterizes these quantities in equilibrium.

Theorem 4.2. *If at least one of r_1 and r_2 is nonzero, then under the symmetric mixed-strategy Nash equilibrium:*

- *The expected number of submitted transactions is*

$$\mathbb{E}[\mathsf{SubmittedTXs}] = (1 - p^*)N = \left(1 - \left(\frac{r_1 g}{V - g + r_1 g}\right)^{\frac{1}{N-1}}\right) N.$$

- *Expected transactions submitted decreases in r_1 and does not depend on r_2.*
- *If $r_1 \neq 0$, then as the number of arbitrageurs N tends to infinity, expected transactions submitted converge to a finite limit, with*

$$\lim_{N \to \infty} \mathbb{E}[\mathsf{SubmittedTXs}] = \log\left(1 + \frac{V - g}{r_1 g}\right).$$

Theorem 4.2 implies that a higher revert penalty rate r_1 on the base gas fee has a dampening effect on arbitrageur participation, with the expected number of submitted transactions decreasing in r_1. Similarly to expected revenue, expected transactions submitted is constant in r_2 since submission only depends on the participation probability.

Under full revert protection, all arbitrageurs will participate, so as N tends to infinity, so does the number of submitted transactions. When transactions are not fully protected, expected transactions submitted are bounded irrespective of the number of arbitrageurs. In terms of blockspace efficiency, full revert protection is more efficient, particularly as V grows large, since only the winning arbitrageur's transaction will appear on the block as opposed to all participating arbitrageur's transactions when full RP is not in place. However, under full RP, there may be arbitrarily many transactions submitted to the mempool as N grows large, compared to a bounded number of submitted transactions otherwise.

4.3 Discussion: Full Revert Protection

We summarize the impact of full revert protection on arbitrage dynamics within a blockchain by analyzing and contrasting the expected number of participants and auction revenue in equilibrium under two conditions: one where $r_1 \neq 0$,

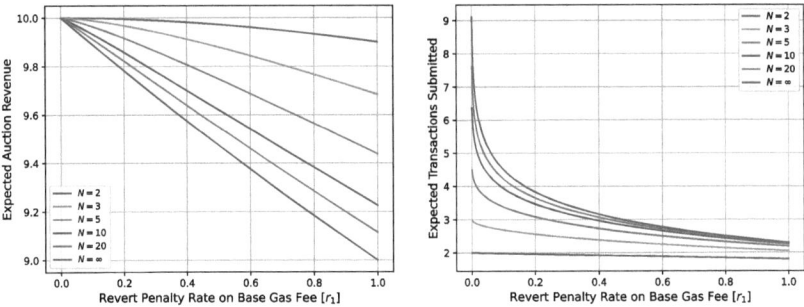

Fig. 3. centering Expected Auction Revenue (left) and Transactions Submitted (right). We set $V = 10$ and $g = 1$.

and the other where $r_1 = 0$, i.e., full revert protection (for the base gas fee component). Figure 3 shows these quantities for various values of r_1 and N.

With full revert protection, the sequencer is always able to capture the full value of an arbitrage opportunity, resulting in an expected auction revenue of V. In this scenario, since there is no deterrent to submitting bids, all arbitrageurs are incentivized to bid up to the breakeven point. As the number of arbitrageurs increases, this can present a spam risk to the sequencer. However, because reverts do not occur on-chain, at most one transaction appears on-chain when an arbitrage opportunity arises, or none otherwise. Thus, the primary challenge for the sequencer under a full revert protection is managing spam effectively.

When revert protection is not in place, the number of participants in an auction asymptotically approaches a finite number as the number of arbitrageurs grows indefinitely. Conversely, auction revenue is reduced by a factor of at most $(1 - (p^*)^N)$ compared to the case of full revert protection. While full revert protection can enhance auction revenue and improve blockspace efficiency, it introduces the risk of increased spamming as the number of arbitrageurs grows. The central trade-off, therefore, lies between these benefits and the elevated risk of spam due to potentially unlimited bids as more arbitrageurs enter the system.

5 Extensions

So far, we assumed that revert protection can be implemented with negligible cost. This may not hold in practice, with block builders bearing non-negligible costs for implementing revert protection. We now take these costs into consideration and analyze two schemes in which costs are (i) internalized by the sequencer and (ii) passed on to searchers/arbitrageurs. In both scenarios, we now suppose that the cost of implementing RP per transaction submitted to the mempool is given by $c > 0$. To avoid trivialities, we make the following assumption:

Assumption 5.1. *Assume that the cost per transaction does not exceed the value less base fee, i.e., $c < V - g$.*

Scheme 1: Sequencer Internalizes Costs. Here, the sequencer incurs costs themselves. While the equilibrium for the searchers does not change, the sequencer's expected revenue under internalization, denoted $\mathbb{E}[\mathsf{Profit}]$, is

$$\mathbb{E}[\mathsf{Profit}] = \mathbb{E}[\mathsf{Revenue}] - c \cdot \mathbb{E}[\mathsf{SubmittedTXs}] = (1 - (p^*)^N)V - c(1 - p^*)N.$$

Since p^* depends on r_1, the revert penalty rate on the base fee, we can optimize over r_1 to find the profit-optimal rate.

Theorem 5.1. *If at least one of r_1 and r_2 is nonzero, then under the symmetric mixed-strategy Nash equilibrium, the profit-optimal r_1 is*

$$r_1^* = \frac{c(V-g)}{(V-c)g} \cdot \mathbb{1}\{c \le g\} + \mathbb{1}\{c > g\}$$

Unlike the baseline model, where full revert protection maximized revenue, a nonzero revert penalty rate now maximizes profits when sequencers internalize the costs of implementing RP. This result highlights a tradeoff between offering full RP to searchers and optimizing profit while covering the costs of full RP.

Scheme 2: Costs Passed Onto Searchers. Here, searchers pay the builders an amount c upfront for the cost of simulating their transactions. The cost c can also represent a "cost of searching" incurred by searching for MEV opportunities. The searcher's payoff is

$$u_i(b_i|\beta_{-i}) = \begin{cases} (V - g - b_i)\mathbb{P}(w = i|b_i, \beta_{-i}) \\ \quad -(r_1 g + r_2 b_i)(1 - \mathbb{P}(w = i|b_i, \beta_{-i})) - c & \text{if } b_i \ge 0, \\ 0 & \text{if } b_i = \varnothing. \end{cases}$$

We resolve for the equilibrium and implications for sequencer design under the modified payoffs.

Theorem 5.2. *Suppose that the searchers pay a fixed cost c for revert protection.*

- *If $r_1 = r_2 = 0$, then a pure strategy profile b where bids are ordered such that $b_1 \le b_2 \le \cdots \le b_N$ (with abstentions represented by bids less than zero) is a Nash equilibrium if and only if $b_{N-1} = b_N = V - g - c$.*
- *If at least one of r_1 and r_2 is nonzero, then a pure-strategy Nash equilibrium does not exist. The unique symmetric mixed-strategy equilibrium is given by*

$$p_i^* = p^* \triangleq \left(\frac{r_1 g + c}{V - g + r_1 g}\right)^{\frac{1}{N-1}},$$

$$F_i^* = F^*(b) \triangleq \frac{1}{1-p^*}\left(\left(\frac{r_1 g + r_2 b + c}{V - g - b + r_1 g + r_2 b}\right)^{\frac{1}{N-1}} - p^*\right),$$

for bids $b \in [0, V - g]$ and agents $i \in [N]$. The expected payoff of every agent in equilibrium is zero.

- *Expected revenue decreases in r_1.*

Comparison of Schemes and Design Implications. Having analyzed the effects of revert protection costs on searchers and the sequencer in both schemes, we now compare the two and draw implications for sequencer design.

Theorem 5.3. *For c sufficiently small, expected revenue in Scheme 2 is greater than the expected profit in Scheme 1 under the profit-optimal choice of r_1.*

This result states that if the computational cost of implementing revert protection is sufficiently small, then having searchers pay the cost results in a greater expected profit to the sequencer than having the sequencer subsidize the costs itself. Besides yielding greater profits under small computational costs, the second scheme is also preferred in the sense that whereas the optimal r_1 needs to be adjusted based on auction parameters in the first scheme and is not necessarily zero, full revert protection is still optimal under the second scheme, with users paying a fixed cost rather than a penalty proportional to their bid, thus encouraging maximum participation in the PGA auction.

A Appendix

All proofs can be found in the online version of our paper.

References

1. Adams, H., et al.: Unichain (2024). https://docs.unichain.org/whitepaper.pdf
2. Capponi, A., Jia, R., Olafsson, S.: Proposer-Builder Separation, Payment for Order Flows, and Centralization in Blockchain. SSRN Working Paper 4723674 (2024)
3. Capponi, A., Jia, R., Wang, K.Y.: Maximal extractable value and allocative inefficiencies in public blockchains. J. Financ. Econ. Revise and Resubmit (2024)
4. Daian, P., et al.: Flash Boys 2.0: frontrunning, transaction reordering, and consensus instability in decentralized exchanges. arXiv Preprint arXiv:1904.05234 (2019)
5. Fox, E., Pai, M., Resnick, M.: Censorship resistance in on-chain auctions. In: 5th Conference on Advances in Financial Technologies (AFT 2023), pp. 19:1–19:20 (2023)
6. Flashbots. Flashbots Builders: coinbase.transfer (2024). https://docs.flashbots.net/flashbots-auction/overview. Accessed 09 Oct 2024
7. Flashbots. Flashbots Builders: Overview (2024). https://docs.flashbots.net/flashbots-auction/overview. Accessed 09 Oct 2024
8. Flashbots. Flashbots Protect: Overview (2024). https://docs.flashbots.net/flashbots-protect/overview. Accessed 09 Oct 2024
9. Hillman, A., Samet, D.: Dissipation of contestable rents by small numbers of contenders. Public Choice **54**(1), 63–82 (1987)
10. Kalodner, H., Goldfeder, S., Chen, X., Matthew Weinberg, S., Felten, E.W.: Arbitrum: scalable, private smart contracts. In: 27th USENIX Security Symposium (2018)

11. Mamageishvili, A., Kelkar, M., Schlegel, J.C., Felten, E.W.: Buying time: latency racing vs. bidding for transaction ordering. In: 5th Conference on Advances in Financial Technologies (AFT 2023), pp. 23:1–23:22 (2023)
12. Mamageishvili, A., Schlegel, J.C.: Shared sequencing and latency competition as a noisy contest. arXiv preprint arXiv:2310.02390 (2024)
13. Milionis, J., Moallemi, C.C., Roughgarden, T., Zhang, A.L.: Automated market making and loss-versus-rebalancing. arXiv preprint arXiv:2208.06046 (2022)
14. Pai, M., Resnick, M.: Structural advantages for integrated builders in MEV-boost. In: Financial Cryptography and Data Security. FC 2024 International Workshops: Voting, DeFI, WTSC, CoDecFin, Willemstad, Curaçao, 4–8 March 2024, Revised Selected Papers, pp. 128–132 (2024)
15. Rasheed, Y.C., Desai, P., Gujar, S.: MEV ecosystem evolution from ethereum 1.0. arXiv Preprint arXiv:2406.13585v1 (2024)
16. Robinson, D., White, D.: Priority is all you need (2024). https://www.paradigm.xyz/2024/06/priority-is-all-you-need. Accessed 08 Oct 2024
17. Schlegel, J.C., Mamageishvili, A.: On-chain auctions with deposits. In: Financial Cryptography and Data Security. FC 2022 International Workshops: CoDecFin, DeFi, Voting, WTSC, Grenada, 6 May 2022, Revised Selected Papers, pp. 207–224 (2022)
18. Siegel, R.: All-pay contests. Econometrica **77**(1), 71–92 (2009)

Consensus

Frosty: Bringing Strong Liveness Guarantees to the Snow Family of Consensus Protocols

Aaron Buchwald[1], Stephen Buttolph[1], Andrew Lewis-Pye[2]([✉]),
Patrick O'Grady[1], and Kevin Sekniqi[1]

[1] Ava Labs, New York, USA
[2] London School of Economics, London, UK
a.lewis7@lse.ac.uk

Abstract. Snowman is the consensus protocol used by blockchains on Avalanche and is part of the Snow family of protocols, first introduced in the Avalanche whitepaper [28]. A major advantage of Snowman is that each consensus decision only requires an expected constant communication overhead per processor in the 'common' case that the protocol is not under substantial Byzantine attack, i.e. it provides a solution to the scalability problem which ensures that the expected communication overhead per processor is independent of the total number of processors n during normal operation. This is the key property that would enable a consensus protocol to scale to 10,000 or more independent validators (i.e. processors). On the other hand, the two following concerns have remained:
1. Providing formal proofs of consistency for Snowman has presented a formidable challenge.
2. Liveness attacks exist in the case that a Byzantine adversary controls more than $O(\sqrt{n})$ processors, slowing termination to more than a logarithmic number of steps.

In this paper, we address the two issues above. We consider a Byzantine adversary that controls at most $f < n/5$ processors. First, we provide a simple proof of consistency for Snowman. Then we supplement Snowman with a 'liveness module' that can be triggered in the case that a substantial adversary launches a liveness attack, and which guarantees liveness in this event by *temporarily* forgoing the communication complexity advantages of Snowman, but without sacrificing these low communication complexity advantages during normal operation.

Keywords: Consensus · Communication complexity · Liveness

1 Introduction

Recent years have seen substantial interest in developing consensus protocols that work efficiently at scale. In concrete terms, this means looking to minimize the latency and communication complexity per consensus decision as a function of the number of processors (participants/validators) n. The Dolev-Reischuk bound [14], which asserts that deterministic protocols require $\Omega(n^2)$ communication complexity per consensus decision, presents a fundamental barrier in this regard: deterministic protocols that can tolerate a Byzantine (i.e. arbitrary) adversary of size $O(n)$ must necessarily suffer a quadratic blow-up in communication cost as the size of the network grows. It is precisely this relationship that makes these protocols susceptible to considerable slowdown when a high number of processors is present.

Probabilistic Sortition. One approach to dealing with this quadratic blow-up in communication cost, as employed by protocols such as Algorand [10], is to utilize probabilistic *sortition* [1,20]. Rather than have *all* processors participate in every consensus decision, the basic idea is to sample a *committee* of sufficient size that the proportion of Byzantine committee members is almost certainly close to the proportion of all processors that are Byzantine. Sampled committees of constant bounded size can then be used to implement consensus, thereby limiting the communication cost. In practical terms, however, avoiding Byzantine control of committees requires each committee to have a number of members sufficient that the *quadratic communication cost for the committee* is already substantial, e.g. Algorand requires committees with k members, where k is of the order of one thousand, meaning that k^2 is already large.

The Snow Family of Consensus Protocols. In [28], a family of consensus protocols was specified, providing an alternative approach to limiting communication costs. These protocols are all based on a common approach that is best described by considering a binary decision game. For the sake of simplicity, let us initially consider the Snowflake protocol[1], which uses three parameters: k, $\alpha > k/2$, and β (for the sake of concreteness, in this paper we will focus on the example that $k = 80$). Suppose that each processor begins with an initial color, either red or blue. Each processor p then proceeds in rounds. In each round, p randomly samples k processors from the total population and asks those processors to report their present color. If at least α of the reported values are the opposite of p's present color, then p adopts that opposite color. If p sees β consecutive rounds in which at least α of the reported values are red, then p decides red (and similarly for blue).

The outcome of this dynamic sampling process can be informally described as follows when the adversary is sufficiently bounded (a formal analysis for a variant of Snowflake that we call Snowflake$^+$ is given in Sect. 4). Once the proportion of the population who are red, say, passes a certain tipping point, it holds with high probability that the remainder of the (non-Byzantine) population will quickly become red (and symmetrically so for blue). If β is set appropriately, then the chance that any correct processor decides on red before this tipping point is reached can be made negligible, meaning that once any correct processor decides on red (or blue), they can be sure that all other correct processors will quickly decide the same way. The chance that correct processors decide differently can

---

[1] In [28], other variants such as the Slush and Snowball protocols are also described.

thus be made negligible through an appropriate choice of parameter values. If correct processors begin heavily weighted in favor of one color, then convergence on a decision value will happen very quickly, while variance in random sampling is required to tip the population in one direction in the case that initial inputs are evenly distributed.

While the discussion above considers a single binary decision game, the 'Snowman' protocol, formally described and analysed for the first time in this paper, shows that similar techniques can be used to efficiently solve State Machine Replication (SMR) [30]. The transition from simple consensus (Byzantine Agreement [21]) to an efficient SMR protocol is non-trivial, and is described in Sect. 5 (and in more detail in the online version of the paper, which can be found at https://arxiv.org/abs/2404.14250). A major benefit of the approach is that it avoids the need for all-to-all communication. In an analysis establishing that there is only a small chance of consistency failure, the value of k can be specified independent of n, and each round requires each processor to collect reported values from only k others.

Our Contribution. The Snowman protocol is presently used by blockchains on Avalanche to implement SMR. However, the two following concerns have remained:

1. Providing formal proofs of consistency for Snowman has presented a formidable challenge.
2. Liveness attacks exist in the case that a Byzantine adversary controls more than $O(\sqrt{n})$ processors [28], meaning that finalization is no longer guaranteed to occur in a logarithmic number of steps.

In this paper, we consider a Byzantine adversary that controls at most $f < n/5$ processors, and address the two issues above. With respect to issue (1):

- We describe a variant of Snowflake, called Snowflake$^+$.
- For appropriate choices of parameter values, we give a simple proof that Snowflake$^+$ satisfies 'validity' and 'agreement' except with small error probability.
- We give a complete specification of a version of Snowman that builds on Snowflake$^+$. This is the first formal description of the Snowman protocol.
- For appropriate choices of parameter values, we give a simple proof that the resulting Snowman protocol satisfies consistency except with small error probability.
- We also describe a variant of Snowflake$^+$ called Error-driven Snowflake, that can be used to give very low latency in the 'common case'.

With regard to issue (2), we note that malicious liveness attacks on Avalanche have not been observed to date. It is certainly desirable, however, to have strong guarantees in the case that a large adversary launches an attack on liveness. The approach we take in this paper is therefore to strike a practical balance. More specifically, we aim to specify a protocol that is optimised to work efficiently in the 'common case' that there is no substantial Byzantine attacker, but which also provides a 'fallback' mechanism in the worst case of a substantial attack on liveness. To this end, we then describe how to supplement Snowman with a 'liveness module'. The basic idea is that one can use Snowman to reach fast consensus under normal operation, and can then trigger an 'epoch change' that temporarily implements some standard quorum-based protocol to achieve liveness in the case that a substantial adversary attacks liveness: this approach is similar to that used by other protocols (e.g. [18]) to flip between different modes of operation. In the (presumably rare) event that a substantial adversary attacks liveness, liveness is thus ensured by *temporarily* forgoing the communication complexity advantages of Snowman during normal operation. The difficulty in implementing such a module is to ensure that interactions between the different modes of operation do not impact consistency. We give a formal proof that the resulting protocol, called Frosty, is consistent and live, except with small error probability.

Paper Structure. Section 2 describes the formal model. Section 3 describes Snowflake$^+$ and gives pseudocode for the protocol. Section 4 gives a proof of agreement and validity for Snowflake$^+$. Section 5 gives an overview of the Snowman protocol: the formal specification and proof of consistency can be found in the online version of the paper at https://arxiv.org/abs/2404.14250. Section 6 gives an overview of the liveness module. The formal specification and analysis of the liveness module appear in the online version, along with a description of Error-driven Snowflake. Section 7 describes related work, and Sect. 8 gives some final comments.

2 The Model

We consider a set $\Pi = \{p_0, \ldots, p_{n-1}\}$ of n processors. Processor p_i is told i as part of its input. We assume a static adversary that controls up to f of the processors, where f is a known bound. Generally, we will assume $f < n/5$. This bound is chosen only so as to give as simple proofs, and providing an analysis for larger f is the subject of future work. A processor that is controlled by the adversary is referred to as *Byzantine*, while processors that are not Byzantine are *correct*. Byzantine processors may display arbitrary behaviour, modulo our cryptographic assumptions (described below).

Cryptographic Assumptions. Our cryptographic assumptions are standard for papers in distributed computing. Processors communicate by point-to-point authenticated channels. We use a cryptographic signature scheme, a public key infrastructure (PKI) to validate signatures, and a collision-resistant hash function H. We assume a computationally bounded adversary. Following a common standard in distributed computing, and for simplicity of presentation (to avoid the analysis of certain negligible error probabilities), we assume these cryptographic schemes are perfect, i.e. we restrict attention to executions in which the adversary is unable to break these cryptographic schemes. In a given execution of the protocol, hash values are thus assumed to be unique.

Communication. As noted above, processors communicate using point-to-point authenticated channels. We consider the standard synchronous model: for some known bound Δ, a message sent at time t must arrive by time $t + \Delta$.

The Binomial Distribution. Consider k independent and identically distributed random variables, each of which has probability x of taking the value 'red'. We let $\mathrm{Bin}(k, x, m)$ denote the probability that m of the k values are red, and we write $\mathrm{Bin}(k, x, \geq m)$ to denote the probability that *at least* m values are red (and similarly for $\mathrm{Bin}(k, x, \leq m)$).

A Comment on the Use of Synchrony. We simplify our analysis by having correct processors execute the protocol executions in cleanly defined *rounds*. Each correct processor thus samples the values of some others in round 1, before adjusting local values based on that sample. All correct processors then proceed to round 2, and so on. As discussed in Sect. 8, a follow-up paper will show how the analysis here can be extended to deal with a *responsive* version of the protocol in which each correct processor can proceed through rounds as fast as local message delays allow, i.e. a processor may proceed to round $s + 1$ as soon as they receive sufficiently many responses for round s (and without waiting for other processors to proceed to round $s + 1$).

3 Snowflake+

We begin by describing a simple probabilistic protocol for binary Byzantine Agreement, called Snowflake+, which will act as a basic building block for the Snowman protocol (described later in Sect. 5 and in more detail in the online version). While a similar analysis could be given for Snowflake (as described in the original whitepaper [28]), an advantage of Snowflake+ is that it allows for a simpler proof to establish that error probabilities are small and, as described in further detail in the online version of the paper, Snowflake+ is also easily adapted to give a protocol called Error-Driven Snowflake which uses flexible termination conditions to give low latency in the good case that most processors are correct. Similar considerations also apply when comparing Snowflake+ and Snowball (also described in the original whitepaper [28]).

The Inputs. Each processor p_i begins with a value $\mathtt{input}_i \in \{0, 1\}$.

The Requirements. A probabilistic protocol for Byzantine agreement is required to satisfy the following properties, except with small error probability:
Agreement: No two correct processors output different values.
Validity: If every correct processor i has the same value $\mathtt{input}_i$, then no correct processor outputs a value different than this common input.
Termination: Every correct processor gives an output.

Snowflake+ is similar to Snowflake (as described in Sect. 1), except that we now use two parameters α_1 and α_2, rather than a single parameter α.

The Protocol Parameters for Snowflake$^+$. The protocol parameters are $k, \alpha_1, \alpha_2, \beta \in \mathbb{N}_{>0}$ and satisfy the constraints that $\alpha_1 > k/2$ and $\alpha_2 \geq \alpha_1$. Each processor p_i also maintains a variable $\mathtt{val}_i$, initially set to $\mathtt{input}_i$. The parameter k determines sample sizes. The parameter α_1 is used to determine when processor p_i changes $\mathtt{val}_i$. Parameters α_2 and β are used to determine the conditions under which p_i will output and terminate.

The Protocol Instructions for Snowflake$^+$. The instructions are divided into rounds, with round s occurring at time $2\Delta s$. In round s, processor p_i:

1. Sets $\langle p_{1,s}, \ldots p_{k,s}\rangle$ to be a sequence of k processors (specific to p_i). For $j \in [1, k]$, $p_{j,s}$ is sampled from the uniform distribution[2] on all processors (so sampling is "with replacement").
2. Requests each $p_{j,s}$ (for $j \in [1, k]$) to report its present value $\mathtt{val}_j$.
3. Waits time Δ and reports its present value $\mathtt{val}_i$ to any processor that has requested it in round s.
4. Waits another Δ and considers the values reported in round s:
   - If at least α_1 of the reported values are $1 - \mathtt{val}_i$, then p_i sets $\mathtt{val}_i := 1 - \mathtt{val}_i$.
   - If p_i has seen β consecutive rounds in which at least α_2 of the reported values are equal to $\mathtt{val}_i$, then p_i outputs this value and terminates.

The pseudocode is described in Algorithm 1.

In Sect. 4, we will show that Snowflake$^+$ satisfies agreement and validity for appropriate choices of the protocol parameters, and so long as $f < n/5$. We do not give a formal analysis of termination for Snowflake$^+$: Once Snowflake$^+$ has been used to define Snowman in Sect. 5, in Sect. 6 we will describe how to augment Snowman with a liveness module (guaranteeing termination), which is formally analysed in the online version of the paper.[3] For an analysis of non-trivial conditions under which termination is satisfied except with small error probability, see [2]: the analysis there is stated in terms of the Slush protocol, but the conclusion that the protocol reaches a stable consensus in $O(\log n)$ rounds, and that this holds even when the adversary can influence up to $O(\sqrt{n})$ processors, carries over directly to Snowflake$^+$.

4 Security Analysis of Snowflake$^+$

We assume $f < n/5$. For the sake of concreteness, we establish satisfaction of agreement and validity for $k = 80$, $\alpha_1 = 41$, $\alpha_2 = 72$, and $\beta = 12$, under the assumption that the population size $n \geq 500$. We make the assumption that $f < n/5$ and $n \geq 500$ only so as to be able to give as simple a proof as possible: a more fine-grained analysis for smaller n is the subject of future work.

---

[2] In proof-of-stake implementations, sampling will be stake-weighted, but, for the sake of simplicity of presentation, we ignore such issues here.

[3] See https://arxiv.org/abs/2404.14250.

Algorithm 1 Snowflake$^+$: The instructions for processor p_i

1: **Inputs**
2: $\text{input}_i \in \{0, 1\}$ ▷ p_i's input
3: $\Delta, k, \alpha_1, \alpha_2, \beta \in \mathbb{N}$ ▷ Protocol parameters
4: **Local variables**
5: val_i, initially set to input_i ▷ p_i's present 'value'
6: count, initially set to 0 ▷ Output once count reaches β
7: $v_i(j, s)$, initially undefined ▷ Stores at most one received value per round
8:
9: **The instructions for round s, beginning at time $2\Delta s$:**
10:     Form sample sequence $\langle p_{1,s}, \ldots p_{k,s} \rangle$; ▷ Sample with replacement
11:     For $j \in [1, k]$, send s to $p_{j,s}$; ▷ Ask $p_{j,s}$ for present value
12:     Wait Δ;
13:     For each j such that p_i has received s from p_j:
14:         Send (s, val_i) to p_j;
15:     Wait Δ;
16:     For each $j \in [1, k]$:
17:         **If** p_i has received a first message (s, v) from $p_{j,s}$:
18:             Set $v_i(j, s) := v$;
19:         **Else** set $v_i(j, s) := \bot$;
20:     **If** $|\{j : 1 \leq j \leq k, v_i(j, s) == 1 - \text{val}_i\}| \geq \alpha_1$, set $\text{val}_i := 1 - \text{val}_i$, $\text{count} := 0$;
21:     **If** $|\{j : 1 \leq j \leq k, v_i(j, s) == \text{val}_i\}| < \alpha_2$, set $\text{count} := 0$;
22:     **If** $|\{j : 1 \leq j \leq k, v_i(j, s) == \text{val}_i\}| \geq \alpha_2$, set $\text{count} := \text{count} + 1$;
23:     **If** $\text{count} \geq \beta$, output val_i and terminate.

Coloring the Processors. Since 0 and 1 are not generally used as adjectives, let us say a correct processor p_i is 'blue' in round s if $\text{val}_i = 0$ at the beginning of round s, and that p_i is 'red' in round s if $\text{val}_i = 1$ at the beginning of round s. Recall (from Algorithm 1) that $v_i(j, s)$ is the color that p_j reports to p_i in round s. We'll say a correct processor p_i 'samples x blue' in round s if $|\{j : 1 \leq j \leq k, v_i(j, s) = 0\}| = x$ (and similarly for red). We'll also extend this terminology in the obvious way, by saying that a processor outputs 'blue' if it outputs 0 and outputs 'red' if it outputs 1. In the below, we'll focus on the case that, in the first round in which a correct processor outputs (should such a round exist), some correct processor outputs red. A symmetric argument can be made for blue.

In the following argument, we will identify certain events as occurring with *small* probability (e.g. with probability $< 10^{-20}$), and may then condition on those events not occurring. To deal with the accumulation of small error probabilities, we suppose that at most 10,000 processors execute the protocol for at most 1000 years, executing at most 5 rounds per second.

Establishing Agreement. The argument consists of four parts:

Part 1. First, let us consider what happens when the proportion of correct processors that are red reaches a certain threshold. In particular, let us consider what happens when at least 75% of the correct processors are red in a given round s. A direct calculation for the binomial distribution shows that the probability a given correct processor is red in round $s+1$ is then at least 0.9555, i.e. $\text{Bin}(80, 0.8 \times 0.75, \geq 41) > 0.9555$. Assuming a population of at least 500, of which at least 80% are correct (meaning that at least 400 are correct), another direct calculation for the binomial distribution shows that the probability that it fails to be the case that more than 5/6 of the correct processors are red in round $s+1$ is upper bounded by 1.59×10^{-20}, i.e. $\text{Bin}(n, 0.9555, \leq 5n/6) < 1.59 \times 10^{-20}$ for $n \geq 400$. Note that this argument requires no knowledge as to the state of each processor in round s, other than the fact that at least 75% of the correct processors are red.

The analysis above applies to any single given round s. Next, we wish to iterate the argument over rounds in order to bound the probability that the following statement holds for *all* rounds:

($\dagger_1$) If at least 75% of the correct processors are red in any round s, then, in all rounds s' with $s' > s$, more than 5/6 of the correct processors are red.

To bound the probability that ($\dagger_1$) fails to hold, we can bound the number of rounds, and then apply the union bound to our analysis of the error probability in each round. Suppose that the protocol is executed for at most 1000 years, with at most 5 rounds executed per second. This means that less than 1.6×10^{11} rounds are executed. The union bound thus gives a cumulative error probability of less than $(1.6 \times 10^{11}) \times (1.59 \times 10^{-20}) < 3 \times 10^{-9}$, meaning that ($\dagger_1$) fails to hold with probability at most 3×10^{-9}.

Part 2. A calculation for the binomial distribution shows that if at least 75% of correct processors are red in a given round s, then the probability that a given correct processor p_i samples at least 72 blue in round s is upper bounded by 1.18×10^{-20}, i.e. $\text{Bin}(80, 0.2 + (0.8 \times 0.25), \geq 72) < 1.18 \times 10^{-20}$. If at most 10,000 processors execute the protocol for at most 1000 years, executing at most 5 rounds per second, we can then apply the union bound to conclude that the following statement fails to hold with probability at most $(1.18 \times 10^{-20}) \times 10000 \times (1.6 \times 10^{11}) < 2 \times 10^{-5}$:

($\dagger_2$) If at least 75% of the correct processors are red in any round s, then no correct processor samples at least 72 blue in round s.

Part 3. Another direct calculation for the binomial distribution shows that, if *at most* 75% of correct processors are red in a given round s, then the probability a given correct processor p samples 72 or more red in round s is upper bounded by 0.0131, i.e. $\text{Bin}(80, (0.75 \times 0.8) + 0.2, \geq 72) < 0.0131$. If, for some $x \geq 1$ it then holds that at most 75% of correct processors are red in round $s + x$, then (independent of previous events), the probability p samples 72 or more red in round $s + x$ is again upper bounded by 0.0131. So, if we consider any 12 given consecutive rounds and any given correct processor p, the probability that at most 75% of correct processors are red in all 12 rounds and p samples at least 72 red in all 12 rounds is upper bounded by $0.0131^{12} < 10^{-22}$. If at most

10,000 processors execute the protocol for at most 1000 years, executing at most 5 rounds per second, we can then apply the union bound to conclude that the following statement fails to hold with probability at most $10^{-22} \times 10000 \times (1.6 \times 10^{11}) < 2 \times 10^{-7}$:

($\dagger_3$) If a correct processor outputs red in any round of the execution, $s + 11$ say, then, for at least one round $s' \in [s, s+11]$, at least 75% of correct processors are red in round s'.

Part 4. Now we put parts 1–3 together. From the union bound and the analysis above, we may conclude that ($\dagger_1$)–($\dagger_3$) all hold, except with probability at most $(3 \times 10^{-9}) + (2 \times 10^{-5}) + (2 \times 10^{-7}) < 3 \times 10^{-5}$. So, suppose that ($\dagger_1$) – ($\dagger_3$) all hold. According to ($\dagger_3$), if a correct processor is the (potentially joint) first to output and outputs red after sampling in round $s + 11$, at least one round $s' \in [s, s+11]$ must satisfy the condition that at least 75% of correct processors are red in round s'. From ($\dagger_1$), it follows that at least 5/6 of the correct processors must be red in all rounds $> s'$. From ($\dagger_2$), it follows that no correct processor ever outputs blue. This suffices to show that Agreement is satisfied, except with small error probability.

Establishing Validity. A similar (but even simpler) argument suffices to establish validity. Suppose that all correct nodes have the same input, red say (i.e. 1). By the same reasoning as above, since round 0 satisfies the condition that at least 75% (in fact 100%) of correct processors are red, the following statement fails to hold with probability at most 3×10^{-9}:

($\dagger_4$) In every round, more than 5/6 of the correct processors are red.

From ($\dagger_2$) and ($\dagger_4$) it follows that no correct processor outputs blue, as required.

Dealing with Alternative Parameter Values. The version of the paper online describes how the argument above is easily adapted to deal with alternative parameter values and also describes how Snowflake$^+$ can be modified to give a protocol called Error-driven Snowflake, which simultaneously uses multiple termination conditions to give low latency in the good case.

5 The Snowman Protocol

Since the Snowman protocol is not specified in the original whitepaper [28], we give an overview in this section. A precise description and analysis are given in the online version of the paper. In Sect. 6 we will describe how to augment Snowman with a module guaranteeing liveness, which is also formally defined and analysed in the online version of the paper.

5.1 Transactions and Blocks

To specify a protocol for State-Machine-Replication (SMR), we suppose processors are sent (signed) transactions during the protocol execution: Formally this can be modeled by having processors be sent transactions by an *environment*, e.g. as in [22]. Processors may use received transactions to form *blocks* of transactions. To make the analysis as general as possible, we decouple the process of block production from the core consensus engine. We therefore suppose that some given process for block generation operates in the background, and that valid blocks are gossiped throughout the network. We do not put constraints on the block generation process, and allow that it may produce equivocating blocks, etc. In practice, block generation could be specified simply by having a rotating sequence of leaders propose blocks, or through a protocol such as Snowman^{++}, as actually used by the present implementation of the Avalanche blockchain.[4]

Blockchain Structure. We consider a fixed *genesis block* b_0. In a departure from the approach described in the original Avalanche whitepaper [28], which built a directed acyclic graph (DAG) of blocks, we consider a standard blockchain architecture in which each block b other than b_0 specifies a unique *parent*. If b' is the parent of b, then b is referred to as a *child* of b'. In this case, the ancestors of b are b and any ancestors of b'. Every block must have b_0 as an ancestor. The descendants of any block b are b and any descendants of its children. The *height* of a block b is its number of ancestors other than b, meaning that the height of b_0 is 0. By a *chain* (ending in b_h), we mean a sequence of blocks $b_0 * b_1 * \cdots * b_h$, such that $b_{h'+1}$ is a child of $b_{h'}$ for $h' < h$.[5]

5.2 Overview of the Snowman Protocol

To implement SMR, our approach is to run multiple instances of Snowflake$^+$. To keep things simple, consider first the task of reaching consensus on a block of height 1. Suppose that multiple children of b_0 are proposed over the course of the execution and that we must choose between them. To turn this decision problem into multiple binary decision problems, we consider the hash value $H(b_1)$ of each proposed block b_1 of height 1, and then run one instance of Snowflake$^+$ to reach consensus on the first bit of the hash. Then we run a second instance to reach consensus on the second bit of the hash, and so on. Working above a block of any height h, the same process is then used to finalize a block of height $h + 1$. In this way, multiple instances of Snowflake$^+$ are used to reach consensus on a chain of hash values $H(b_0) * H(b_1) * \ldots$.

This process would not be efficient if each round required a separate set of correspondences for each instance of Snowflake$^+$, but this is not necessary. Just as in Snowflake$^+$, at the beginning of each round s, processor p_i samples a single sequence $\langle p_{1,s}, \ldots p_{k,s} \rangle$ of k processors. Since we now wish to reach consensus

---

[4] For a description of Snowman^{++}, see https://medium.com/avalancheavax/apricot-phase-four-snowman-and-reduced-c-chain-transaction-fees-1e1f67b42ecf.
[5] Throughout this paper, '$*$' denotes concatenation.

on a sequence of blocks, each processor $p_{j,s}$ in the sample is now requested to report its presently preferred chain, rather than a single bit value. The first bit of the corresponding hash sequence is then used by p_i as the response of $p_{j,s}$ in a first instance of Snowflake$^+$. If this first bit agrees with p_i's resulting value in that instance of Snowflake$^+$, then the second bit is used as the value reported by $p_{j,s}$ in a second instance of Snowflake$^+$, and so on.

As stated earlier, the Snowman protocol is formally specified and analysed in the online version of the paper. In the next section, we will reference some of the variables used in the formal specification of the protocol: at any moment in time, the local variable `pref` is the initial segment of the chain of hash values that p_i presently prefers, while `final` is the initial segment of the chain of hash values that p_i has finalized.

The online version of the paper shows how a slight modification of the proof of Sect. 4 can be used to establish consistency for Snowman.

6 Frosty

Recall that our next aim is to augment Snowman with a liveness module, allowing us to guarantee liveness in the case that $f < n/5$.

6.1 Overview of Frosty

In what follows, we assume that all messages are signed by the processor sending the message. We also suppose that $f < n/5$. Recall that the local variable `pref` is a processor's presently preferred chain and that `final` is its presently finalized chain.

The Use of Epochs. As outlined in Sect. 1, the basic idea is to run the Snowman protocol during standard operation, and to temporarily fall back to a standard 'quorum-based' protocol in the event that a substantial adversary attacks liveness for Snowman. We therefore consider instructions that are divided into *epochs*. In the first epoch (epoch 0), processors implement Snowman. In the event of a liveness attack, processors then enter epoch 1 and implement the quorum-based protocol to finalize the next block. Once this is achieved, they enter epoch 2 and revert to Snowman, and so on. Processors only enter each odd epoch and start implementing the quorum-based protocol if a liveness attack during the previous epoch forces them to do so. The approach taken is reminiscent of protocols such as Jolteon and Ditto [16], in the sense that a view/epoch change mechanism is used to move between an optimistic and fallback path.

Adding a Decision Condition. In even epochs, and when a processor sees sufficiently many consecutive rounds during which its local value `final` remains unchanged, it will send a message to others indicating that it wishes to proceed to the next epoch. Before any correct processor p_i enters the next epoch, however, it requires messages from at least $1/5$ of all processors indicating that they wish to do the same. This is necessary to avoid the adversary being able to trigger a change of epoch at will, but produces a difficulty: some correct processors may wish to enter the next epoch, but the number who wish to do so may not be enough to trigger the epoch change. To avoid such a situation persisting for an extended duration, we introduce an extra decision condition. Processors now report their value final as well as their value pref when sampled. We consider an extra parameter α_3: for our analysis here, we suppose $\alpha_3 = 48$ (since $48 = \frac{3}{5} \cdot 80$). If p_i sees two consecutive samples in which at least α_3 processors report final values that all extend σ, then p_i will regard σ as final. For $k = 80$, $\alpha_3 = 48$ and if $f < n/5$, the probability that at least $3/5$ of p_i's sample sequence in a given round are Byzantine is less than 10^{-14}, so the probability that this happens in two consecutive rounds is small. Except with small probability, the new decision rule therefore only causes p_i to finalize σ in the case that a correct processor has already finalized this value, meaning that it is safe for p_i to do the same. Using this new decision rule, we will be able to argue below that epoch changes are triggered in a timely fashion: either the epoch change is triggered soon after any correct p_i wishes to change epoch, or else sufficiently many correct processors do not wish to trigger the change that p_i is quickly able to finalize new values.

Epoch Certificates. While in even epoch e, and for a parameter γ (chosen to taste),[6] p_i will send the (signed) message (stuck, e, final) to all others when it sees γ consecutive rounds during which its local value final remains unchanged. This message indicates that p_i wishes to enter epoch $e + 1$ and is referred to as an 'epoch $e + 1$ message'. For any fixed σ, a set of messages of size at least $n/5$, each signed by a different processor and of the form (stuck, e, σ), is called an *epoch certificate* (EC) for epoch $e + 1$.[7] When p_i sees an EC for epoch $e + 1$, it will send the EC to all others and enter epoch $e + 1$. This ensures that when any correct processor enters epoch $e + 1$, all others will do so within time Δ.

Ensuring Consistency Between Epochs. We must ensure that the value finalized by the quorum-based protocol during an odd epoch $e + 1$ extends all final values for correct processors. To achieve this, the rough idea is that we have processors send out their local pref values upon entering epoch $e + 1$, and then use these values to extract a chain that it is safe for the quorum based protocol to build on. Upon entering epoch $e + 1$, we therefore have p_i send out the message (start, $e+1$, pref). This message is referred to as a *starting vote* for epoch $e+1$ and, for any string σ, we say that the starting vote (start, $e+1$, pref) extends σ if $\sigma \subseteq$ pref. By a *starting certificate* (SC) for epoch $e + 1$ we mean a set of at least $2n/3$ starting votes for epoch $e + 1$, each signed by a different processor. If S is an SC for epoch $e + 1$, we set Pref*(S) to be the longest σ extended by more than half of the messages in S. The basic idea is that Pref*(S) must extend all final values for correct processors, and that consistency will

---

[6] For the formal analysis in the online version of the paper, we suppose $\gamma \geq 300$.
[7] To ensure ECs are strings of constant bounded length (independent of n), one could use standard 'threshold' cryptography techniques [7,31], but we will not concern ourselves with such issues here.

therefore be maintained if we have the quorum-based protocol finalize a value extending this string.

To argue that this is indeed the case, recall the proof described in Sect. 4 (and recall that $f < n/5$). We argued there that, if any correct processor p_i outputs red in a given round, then (except with small error probability), more than $5/6$ of the correct processors must be red by the end of that round, and that this will also be the case in all subsequent rounds. Similarly, we show for Snowman in the online version of the paper that, if any correct processor p_i finalizes σ in a given round, then (except with small error probability), more than $5/6$ of the correct processors must have local pref values that extend σ by the end of that round, and that this will also be the case in all subsequent rounds. This might seem to ensure that Pref*(S) will extend σ: since $\frac{5}{6} \cdot \frac{4}{5} = \frac{2}{3}$, and since S contains at least $2n/3$ starting votes, it is tempting to infer that more than half the votes in S must extend σ. A complexity here, however, is that this reasoning only applies if all Pref values are reported *in the same round*. We can't (easily) ensure that all correct processors enter $e+1$ epoch in the same round, meaning that some correct processors may send their Pref values in one round, while others send them in the next round. To deal with this, we increase the β parameter from 12 to 14. This ensures (except with small error probability) that, when a correct processor p_i finalizes σ, more than $11/12$ of correct processors have local pref values that extend σ by the end of the previous round, and that this is also true in all subsequent rounds. If s and $s+1$ are two consecutive rounds after p_i finalizes σ, and if we partition the correct processors arbitrarily so that some report their pref value in round s, while the rest do so in round $s+1$, then at least $5/6$ of the correct processors must report values extending σ.

The Choice of Quorum-Based Protocol. While any of the standard quorum-based protocols could be implemented during odd epochs, for the sake of simplicity we give an exposition (in the online version of the paper) that implements a form of Tendermint. We structure the instructions for odd epochs so as to ensure the finalization of one more block before switching back to Snowman for the next even epoch, rather than so as to ensure the finalization of at least one more block produced by a correct leader. One could alternatively achieve the latter result simply by running odd epochs until at least $f+1$ distinct leaders have produced finalized blocks. Another (perhaps more flexible) alternative would be to switch back to Snowman (and the next even epoch) whenever a quorum of validators express their intention to do so (similar to a standard view-change mechanism).

The Frosty protocol is formally specified and analysed in the online version of the paper.

7 Related Work

The Snow family of consensus protocols was introduced in [28]. Subsequent to this, Amores-Sesar, Cachin and Tedeschi [3] gave a complete description of the

Avalanche protocol[8] and formally established security properties for that protocol, given an $O(\sqrt{n})$ adversary and assuming that the Snowball protocol (a variant of Snowflake$^+$) solves probabilistic Byzantine Agreement for such adversaries. The authors also described (and provided a solution for) a liveness attack. As noted in [3], the original implementation of the Avalanche protocol used by the Avalanche blockchain (before replacing Avalanche with a version of Snowman that totally orders transactions) had already introduced modifications avoiding the possibility of such attacks.

In [2], Amores-Sear, Cachin and Schneider consider the Slush protocol and show that coming close to a consensus already requires a minimum of $\Omega\left(\frac{\log n}{\log k}\right)$ rounds, even in the absence of adversarial influence. They show that Slush reaches a stable consensus in $O(\log n)$ rounds, and that this holds even when the adversary can influence up to $O(\sqrt{n})$ processors. They also show that the $\Omega\left(\frac{\log n}{\log k}\right)$ lower bound holds for Snowflake and Snowball.

There is a vast literature that considers a closely related family of models, from the *Ising model* [9] as studied in statistical mechanics, to *voter models* [19] as studied in applied probability and other fields, to the *Schelling model of segregation* [29] as studied by economists (and more recently by computer scientists [4,8] and physicists [23–25]). Within this family of models there are many variants, but a standard approach is to consider a process that proceeds in rounds. In each round, each participant samples a small number of other participants to learn their present state, and then potentially updates their own state according to given rule. A fundamental difference with our analysis here is that, with two exceptions (mentioned below), such models do not incorporate the possibility of Byzantine action. Examples of such research aimed specifically at the task of reaching consensus include [6,11–13,15,17] (see [5] for an overview). Amongst these papers, we are only aware of [6] and [13] considering Byzantine action, and those two papers deal only with an $O(\sqrt{n})$ adversary.

FPC-BI [26,27] is a protocol which is closely related to the Snow family of consensus protocols, but which takes a different approach to the liveness issue (for adversaries which are larger than $O(\sqrt{n})$) than that described here. The basic idea behind their approach is to use a common random coin to dynamically and unpredictably set threshold parameters (akin to α_1 and α_2 here) for each round, making it much more difficult for an adversary to keep the correct population split on their preferred values. Since the use of a common random coin involves practical trade-offs, their approach and ours may be seen as complementary.

8 Final Comments

In this paper, we have considered the case that the adversary controls at most $f < n/5$ processors. We described the protocol Snowflake$^+$ and showed that it

---

[8] The Avalanche protocol is a DAG-based variant of Snowman that does not aim to produce a total ordering on transactions, and was only described at a high level in [28]. It is not used in the present instantiation of the Avalanche blockchain.

satisfies validity and agreement, except with small error probability. We showed how Snowflake$^+$ can be adapted to give an SMR protocol, Snowman, which satisfies consistency, except with small error probability. We then augmented Snowman with a liveness module, to form the protocol Frosty, which we proved satisfies liveness and consistency except with small error probability. We note that Avalanche presently implements Snowflake, rather than Snowflake$^+$, and uses different parameters than those used in the proofs here. Snowflake$^+$ was implemented a few months prior to the writing of this paper, but is not yet activated. Error-driven Snowflake$^+$ is planned for implementation in the coming months. The community may consider adopting the parameters proposed in this paper because they provide a good tradeoff between consistency and latency.

In future work, we aim to expand the analysis here as follows:

(i) The bounds $f < n/5$ and $n \geq 500$ were used only so as to be able to give as simple a proof as possible in Sect. 4. In subsequent papers, we intend to carry out a more fine-grained analysis for smaller n and larger f.
(ii) The analysis here was simplified by the assumption that processors execute instructions in synchronous rounds. In a follow-up work, we will show how the methods described here can be adapted to give formal proofs of consistency and liveness for a *responsive* form of the protocol, allowing each processor to proceed individually through rounds as fast as network delays allow.
(iii) While the liveness module described here achieves (probabilistic) liveness when $f < n/5$, we aim to explore ways in which *slashing* can be implemented for liveness attacks. For $f < n/3$ this may be possible, if one can show that liveness attacks require the adversary either to give provably false information to others, or else execute sampling that is provably biased.

References

1. Abraham, I., et al.: Communication complexity of byzantine agreement, revisited. In: Proceedings of the 2019 ACM Symposium on Principles of Distributed Computing, pp. 317–326 (2019)
2. Amores-Sesar, I., Cachin, C., Schneider, P.: An analysis of avalanche consensus. arXiv preprint arXiv:2401.02811 (2024)
3. Amores-Sesar, I., Cachin, C., Tedeschi, E.: When is spring coming? A security analysis of avalanche consensus. arXiv preprint arXiv:2210.03423 (2022)
4. Barmpalias, G., Elwes, R., Lewis-Pye, A.: Digital morphogenesis via schelling segregation. In: 2014 IEEE 55th Annual Symposium on Foundations of Computer Science, pp. 156–165. IEEE (2014)
5. Becchetti, L., Clementi, A., Natale, E.: Consensus dynamics: an overview. ACM SIGACT News **51**(1), 58–104 (2020)
6. Becchetti, L., Clementi, A., Natale, E., Pasquale, F., Trevisan, L.: Stabilizing consensus with many opinions. In: Proceedings of the Twenty-Seventh Annual ACM-SIAM Symposium on Discrete Algorithms, pp. 620–635. SIAM (2016)
7. Boneh, D., Lynn, B., Shacham, H.: Short signatures from the Weil pairing. In: Boyd, C. (ed.) ASIACRYPT 2001. LNCS, vol. 2248, pp. 514–532. Springer, Heidelberg (2001). https://doi.org/10.1007/3-540-45682-1_30

8. Brandt, C., Immorlica, N., Kamath, G., Kleinberg, R.: An analysis of one-dimensional schelling segregation. In: Proceedings of the Forty-Fourth Annual ACM Symposium on Theory of Computing, pp. 789–804 (2012)
9. Brush, S.G.: History of the lenz-ising model. Rev. Mod. Phys. **39**(4), 883 (1967)
10. Chen, J., Micali, S.: Algorand. arXiv preprint arXiv:1607.01341 (2016)
11. Cooper, C., Elsässer, R., Radzik, T.: The power of two choices in distributed voting. In: Esparza, J., Fraigniaud, P., Husfeldt, T., Koutsoupias, E. (eds.) ICALP 2014. LNCS, vol. 8573, pp. 435–446. Springer, Heidelberg (2014). https://doi.org/10.1007/978-3-662-43951-7_37
12. Cruciani, E., Mimun, H.A., Quattropani, M., Rizzo, S.: Phase transitions of the k-majority dynamics in a biased communication model. In: Proceedings of the 22nd International Conference on Distributed Computing and Networking, pp. 146–155 (2021)
13. Doerr, B., Goldberg, L.A., Minder, L., Sauerwald, T., Scheideler, C.: Stabilizing consensus with the power of two choices. In: Proceedings of the Twenty-Third Annual ACM Symposium on Parallelism in Algorithms and Architectures, pp. 149–158 (2011)
14. Dolev, D., Reischuk, R.: Bounds on information exchange for byzantine agreement. J. ACM (JACM) **32**(1), 191–204 (1985)
15. Elsässer, R., Friedetzky, T., Kaaser, D., Mallmann-Trenn, F., Trinker, H.: Brief announcement: rapid asynchronous plurality consensus. In: Proceedings of the ACM Symposium on Principles of Distributed Computing, pp. 363–365 (2017)
16. Gelashvili, R., Kokoris-Kogias, L., Sonnino, A., Spiegelman, A., Xiang, Z.: Jolteon and Ditto: network-adaptive efficient consensus with asynchronous fallback. In: International Conference on Financial Cryptography and Data Security, pp. 296–315. Springer, Cham (2022)
17. Ghaffari, M., Lengler, J.: Nearly-tight analysis for 2-choice and 3-majority consensus dynamics. In: Proceedings of the 2018 ACM Symposium on Principles of Distributed Computing, pp. 305–313 (2018)
18. Guerraoui, R., Knežević, N., Quéma, V., Vukolić, M.: The next 700 BFT protocols. In: Proceedings of the 5th European conference on Computer Systems, pp. 363–376 (2010)
19. Holley, R.A., Liggett, T.M.: Ergodic theorems for weakly interacting infinite systems and the voter model. Ann. Probab. 643–663 (1975)
20. King, V., Saia, J.: Breaking the o (n 2) bit barrier: scalable byzantine agreement with an adaptive adversary. J. ACM (JACM) **58**(4), 1–24 (2011)
21. Lamport, L., Shostak, R., Pease, M.: The byzantine generals problem. ACM Trans. Program. Lang. Syst. (TOPLAS) **4**(3), 382–401 (1982)
22. Lewis-Pye, A., Roughgarden, T.: Permissionless consensus. arXiv preprint arXiv:2304.14701 (2023)
23. Omidvar, H., Franceschetti, M.: Self-organized segregation on the grid. In: Proceedings of the ACM Symposium on Principles of Distributed Computing, pp. 401–410 (2017)
24. Omidvar, H., Franceschetti, M.: Improved intolerance intervals and size bounds for a schelling-type spin system. J. Stat. Mech: Theory Exp. **2021**(7), 073302 (2021)
25. Ortega, D., Rodríguez-Laguna, J., Korutcheva, E.: A schelling model with a variable threshold in a closed city segregation model. Analysis of the universality classes. Physica A: Stat. Mech. Appl. **574**, 126010 (2021)
26. Popov, S., Buchanan, W.J.: FPC-BI: fast probabilistic consensus within byzantine infrastructures. J. Parallel Distrib. Comput. **147**, 77–86 (2021)

27. Popov, S., Müller, S.: Voting-based probabilistic consensuses and their applications in distributed ledgers. Ann. Telecommun. 1–23 (2022)
28. Rocket, T., Yin, M., Sekniqi, K., van Renesse, R., Sirer, E.G.: Scalable and probabilistic leaderless BFT consensus through metastability. arXiv preprint arXiv:1906.08936 (2019)
29. Schelling, T.C.: Models of segregation. Am. Econ. Rev. **59**(2), 488–493 (1969)
30. Schneider, F.B.: Implementing fault-tolerant services using the state machine approach: a tutorial. ACM Comput. Surv. (CSUR) **22**(4), 299–319 (1990)
31. Shoup, V.: Practical threshold signatures. In: Preneel, B. (ed.) EUROCRYPT 2000. LNCS, vol. 1807, pp. 207–220. Springer, Heidelberg (2000). https://doi.org/10.1007/3-540-45539-6_15

Consensus Under Adversary Majority Done Right

Srivatsan Sridhar[1(✉)], Ertem Nusret Tas[1], Joachim Neu[2], Dionysis Zindros[3], and David Tse[1]

[1] Stanford University, Stanford, CA, USA
{svatsan,nusret,dntse}@stanford.edu
[2] a16z Crypto Research, New York, NY, USA
jneu@a16z.com
[3] Common Prefix, Athens, Greece
dionyziz@commonprefix.com

Abstract. A specter is haunting consensus protocols—the specter of adversary majority. Dolev and Strong in 1983 showed an early possibility for up to 99% adversaries. Yet, other works show impossibility results for adversaries above 50% under synchrony, seemingly the same setting as Dolev and Strong's. What gives? It is high time that we pinpoint a key culprit for this ostensible contradiction: the modeling details of *clients*. Are the clients *sleepy* or *always-on*? Are they *silent* or *communicating*? Can validators be *sleepy* too? We systematize models for consensus across four dimensions (sleepy/always-on clients, silent/communicating clients, sleepy/always-on validators, and synchrony/partial-synchrony), some of which are new, and tightly characterize the achievable safety and liveness resiliences with matching possibilities and impossibilities for each of the sixteen models. To this end, we unify folklore and earlier results, and fill gaps left in the literature with new protocols and impossibility theorems.

1 Introduction

What fraction of parties running a protocol can be controlled by an adversary while guaranteeing security? When it comes to *Byzantine state-machine replication (SMR) consensus* protocols, where security means safety and liveness, the landscape is seemingly contradictory. The oft-cited Dolev–Strong protocol [20], along with recent works [11,25,26] that extend it from broadcast to SMR consensus, tolerates up to 99% adversary parties (we say that it has 99% *resilience*). This stands in contrast to the, perhaps equally-oft-cited, "51% attack" [1] that renders many blockchains based on Nakamoto's longest chain consensus protocol [16,19] insecure as soon as more than 50% of the parties are corrupted.

Due to space constraints, some lemmas, theorems, algorithms, proofs, etc. are not included in this short version, but are found in the appendices of the full version [53]. SS and ENT contributed equally and are listed alphabetically. A part of Sect. 3.2 appeared in an earlier preprint [54] by SS, DZ, and DT.

What is more, prior work (*e.g.*, [48, Thm. 3]) claims that no protocol can achieve 50% or higher resilience. This impossibility holds even if we assume a known set of parties, strong cryptographic functionalities like a public-key infrastructure (PKI), allow for randomized protocols, and consider a network model where the messages arrive within a known delay-bound (*i.e.*, synchrony)[1]; thus, seemingly the same (or stronger) assumptions under which Dolev–Strong claims its 99% resilience. How do we explain the difference and resolve the conundrum?

The Crucial Role of Clients. The impossibility [48, Thm. 3] crucially relies on the requirement that parties who join late, *i.e.*, did not observe the protocol since its start, should still be able to output an up-to-date log of confirmed transactions. In contrast, the 99% resilience of Dolev–Strong [20] and similar protocols [11,25,26] is only guaranteed for parties who are always online, *i.e.*, constantly monitor the protocol from its start to continuously learn the correct confirmed transaction sequence. This key differentiating factor pertains specifically to the parties who attempt to learn the protocol's output, *i.e.*, the *clients*. In blockchains, these clients may be merchants who monitor the chain for payments and ship merchandise in response. They are usually not actively running the protocol to maintain consensus—that is done by the *validators* who are selected for instance through a mechanism such as proof-of-stake.[2] Despite the important role of clients in determining the maximum achievable resilience, the modeling of the clients' capabilities has received little attention in the literature. In this work, we focus on the role of clients. To do so, we level the playing field with respect to other modeling aspects. Specifically, for the remainder of the paper, we adopt a permissioned setting with PKI and allow the use of cryptographic primitives and randomization for all considered protocols— a setting that enables fair comparisons between both Dolev–Strong and permissioned instantiations of longest-chain protocols [16,19],[3] used for instance in the Cardano blockchain system, as well as the other protocols considered in the paper.

Types of Clients. Two specific characteristics of clients are relevant: (1) *Sleepiness:* Clients may only follow the chain intermittently (*e.g.*, a merchant during business hours), or may turn to a chain only long after its inception. We then call this the *sleepy* client model, in analogy to sleepy validators in [49]. In contrast, in the *always-on* client model, we expect clients to follow the chain continuously, such as in the case of block explorers or wallet providers for blockchains. (2) *Interactivity:* In the *silent* client model, clients may be constrained to only *listen* to messages from validators. In contrast, in the *communicating* client model, they may be able to relay messages to validators or other clients, for instance, through a system-wide gossip protocol. Consensus is easier when clients are always-on rather than sleepy, and communicating rather than silent.

---

[1] We repeat the proof of [48, Thm. 3] for this precise setting in Theorem 3.
[2] It may happen, in practice, that a party acts both as a validator and as a client, but conceptually these are two different roles.
[3] The protocols of [16,19], at their core, run a permissioned SMR protocol with a fixed validator set, and then rotate this validator set from epoch to epoch. We focus on this permissioned core protocol. Rotating the validator set is orthogonal.

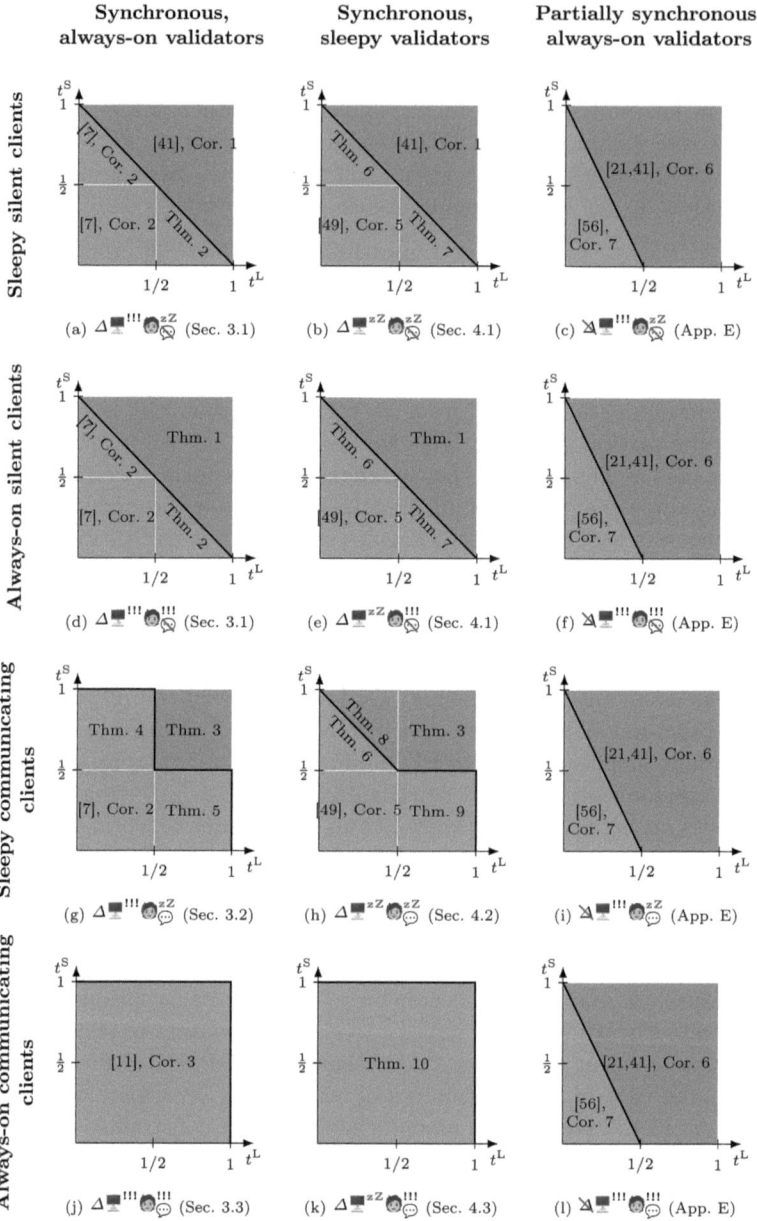

Fig. 1. Tight achievable (■) and impossible (■) safety resilience t^S and liveness resilience t^L bounds for different models (cf. Fig. 2), each with four aspects: *Network delay:* synchrony 🔺 vs. partial synchrony 🔻; *Validator sleepiness:* always-on validators 🖥️!!! vs. sleepy validators 🖥️zZ; *Client sleepiness:* always-on clients 😀!!! vs. sleepy clients 😀zZ; *Client interactivity:* communicating 😀💬 vs. silent 😀🔇. Citations with corollaries, or theorems, indicate previously known, or new results, respectively.

In synchronous networks, longest-chain consensus makes only the weakest client assumptions, *sleepy silent* clients, but achieves only 49% resilience—which is optimal for that model [48,49,51]. In contrast, the Dolev–Strong 99%-resilience holds under the assumption of *always-on communicating* clients, i.e. the strongest client assumptions [11]. (The original Dolev–Strong work was developed in a model with only validators and no clients.) What about the intermediate client assumptions, *sleepy communicating* clients or *always-on silent* clients? What about if the validators themselves can also be sleepy instead of being always-on as in longest-chain consensus [16,19]? And what about if the network is partially synchronous instead of synchronous?

Our Contributions. The main contribution of this paper is a full characterization of the achievable security in all such scenarios. The results are summarized in Fig. 1 in terms of tight achievable *safety* and *liveness resiliences* under each scenario. *Safety resilience* of a protocol is the maximum fraction of adversary validators such that safety is guaranteed, and *liveness resilience* of a protocol is the maximum fraction of adversary validators such that liveness is guaranteed [41,44]. Traditional *resilience* of a protocol, the maximum fraction of adversary validators such that it is *both safe and live*, is the minimum of the protocol's safety and liveness resiliences. Separate safety and liveness resiliences provide a meaningfully more fine-grained measure of a protocol's security since the impact of safety loss and liveness loss to a client is often different.

Figure 2 shows the relationship of all the scenarios we considered in this paper.

Synchronous Network with Always-On Validators: The first column of Fig. 1 shows the results in the synchronous network model. Figure 1j shows that one can achieve 99% resilence when clients are always-on and communicating, i.e., the Dolev–Strong client model. Figure 1a shows that one can achieve 49% resilence when clients are sleepy and silent, i.e., the longest-chain client model. Figure 1d and Fig. 1g are the two intermediate client settings; our impossibility results show that the achievable resilences in both settings do not improve over the longest-chain client model, i.e., 49% resilience. However, the similarity ends when one looks at safety and liveness resiliences separately. In particular, we show a new protocol for sleepy communicating clients that can achieve 99% safety resilience and 49% liveness resilience *simultaneously* (Fig. 1g, Theorem 4), a resilience pair that is impossible for sleepy silent clients (Fig. 1a), and strictly dominates classical protocols like the longest-chain that achieve only 49% safety resilience and 49% liveness resilience. We show another protocol for sleepy communicating clients that achieves 49% safety and 99% liveness resilience (Fig. 1g, Theorem 5). On the other hand, we show that silent clients do not benefit from being always-on rather than sleepy in synchronous networks even when one considers safety and liveness resiliences separately (Figs. 1a and 1d, Theorems 1 and 2).

Synchonous Network with Sleepy Validators: The concept of "sleepy" parties was previously introduced in the sleepy model [49] where it pertains to

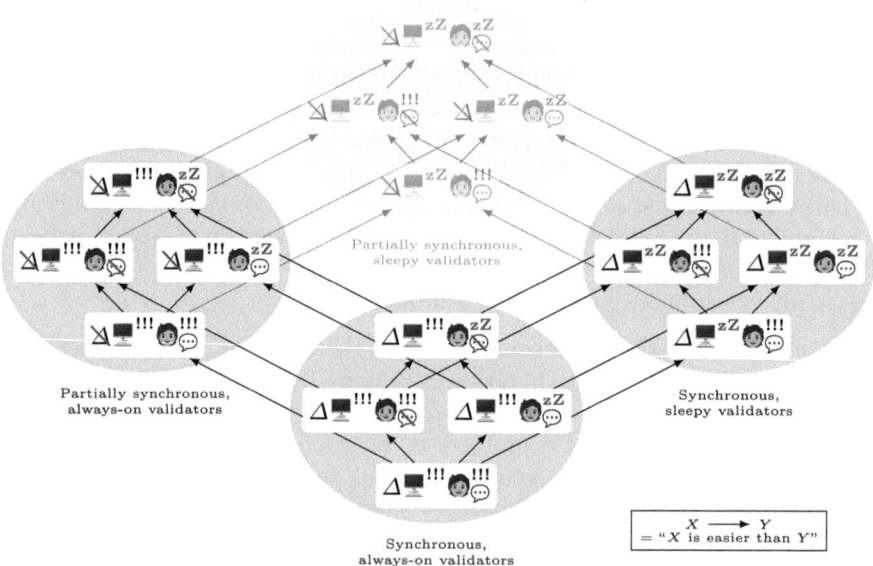

Fig. 2. Hasse diagram illustrating the relative difficulty of consensus in all the different models we study (proof: Lem. 1). Each small white box indicates a different model (see Fig. 1 for icon legend). Models are grouped in a shaded circle when they share validator model and network model but the client model differs. Group (🚫🖥️, 🖥️^{zZ}) is faded out because consensus is impossible [23,32,46].

validators rather than clients. That model features—in addition to adversary Byzantine faults—relatively-benign mobile crash-faults. Each validator is either honest, crashed, or adversary, and liveness must hold even when many validators are crashed [46,47]. We show that under synchrony with silent or with always-on communicating clients, validator sleepiness does not affect achievable safety–liveness pairs (Figs. 1a, 1b, 1d, 1e, 1j and 1k). Validator sleepiness *does* affect, though, what's achievable for sleepy communicating clients (Figs. 1g and 1h). Specifically, while 49% safety and 99% liveness resilience remain simultaneously achievable (Fig. 1h, Theorem 9), that is not the case for 99% safety and 49% liveness resilience (Fig. 1h, Theorems 6 and 8).

Partially Synchronous Network: Finally, the astute reader will note that—whether validators are sleepy or always-on—our discussion above regarding Dolev–Strong and longest-chain consensus assume *synchrony*, where the protocol is parameterized by an upper bound Δ on the delay of message propagation among honest parties. In contrast, PBFT-style protocols [12,13,18,52,56] are designed for *partial synchrony*, where such a delay bound is guaranteed to hold only *eventually*, after an initial period of unknown duration with arbitrary network delay. Network delay constitutes the fourth and last aspect of our models (Fig. 2). Interestingly, the safety–liveness resilience pairs achievable under partial synchrony do not depend on client sleepiness or client interactivity (Figs. 1c,

1f, 1i and 1l—with sleepy validators, safety under partial synchrony is impossible [23,32,46]; cf. Fig. 2). This "robustness" of the partially synchronous model to different client assumptions is perhaps why clients have so far often been an afterthought in the distributed-systems literature.

2 Model

We focus on the most relevant model aspects. Other standard aspects: App. B.

Parties. A fixed set $\mathcal{N}$ of parties called *validators* is known to all parties. Define $n = |\mathcal{N}|$. Each validator has a secret key with which they may sign their messages, and all parties know validators' public keys. We assume a permissioned setting [10,33,49] with a fixed and known set of validators, and defer the proof-of-stake setting to App. A. Unlike validators, the number and identities of the *clients* is not known to all parties, and clients do not have public keys.

Adversary. At the beginning of the execution, before any randomness is drawn, the PPT adversary $\mathcal{A}$ controls f adversary validators (a.k.a. Byzantine faults). $\mathcal{A}$ may also corrupt any number of clients. All our theorems hold for any number of adversary clients. We discuss adaptive corruption in App. A.

Validator Sleepiness (cf. [49]). At every round r, a subset $\mathsf{awake}_r \subseteq \mathcal{N}$ of validators are awake while the rest are *asleep*. When asleep, validators behave like temporarily crashed nodes: they do not run computation or send messages. Whenever a validator is awake, it knows the current round (*i.e.*, it wakes up with a synchronized clock). In the *always-on validators* model, all validators are always awake, ($\forall r\colon \mathsf{awake}_r = \mathcal{N}$). In the *sleepy validators* model, $\mathcal{A}$ selects awake_r, and adversary validators are always awake.

Client Models. We classify clients along two orthogonal criteria. *Interactivity*: *Communicating* clients may send messages to other parties, *silent* clients do not. *Sleepiness*: *Always-on* clients are always awake while *sleepy* clients may be put to sleep by $\mathcal{A}$. When asleep, clients do not perform any computation, send messages, or output new logs. This results in the four client models shown in Fig. 2. For example, the *sleepy communicating* model means that all clients are sleepy and communicating.

Communicating clients are new in this work and more accurately depict blockchain implementations in which communication is facilitated by a non-eclipsed gossip network comprised of both clients and validators. Since clients' messages cannot be authenticated due to their lack of PKI, really the best they can do is relay messages received from validators to other clients. Yet, communicating clients circumvent impossibility results for silent clients (Fig. 1). Relaying transactions, blocks, and votes is already in the client specifications of major blockchains like Ethereum [5] and Tendermint [2]. Furthermore, since clients only relay messages sent by validators, the communication/computation overhead for all parties easily remains bounded by forwarding/processing only valid messages and only once.

Network Delay Models. We consider two standard network models. In the *synchronous* model, there is a known constant Δ such that if an honest party sends a message at round r, then every honest party receives the message by round $r + \Delta$.[4] The partially synchronous model is described in App. B.

In both models, messages are delivered to asleep parties, but they can only process them after awakening. In practice, equivalent behavior can be achieved by having the awakening party query online parties who reply with the 'important' past messages (*e.g.*, 'initial block download' [8]). Thus, although sleepy parties receive all the same messages as always-on parties, they are less powerful since they cannot record the time of message receipt.

SMR. At the start of each round, each awake party may receive some transactions as input. At the end of every round r, each awake honest client k outputs a log (sequence of transactions) $\boldsymbol{L}_k^r$. For a client k asleep at round r, let $\boldsymbol{L}_k^r = \boldsymbol{L}_k^{r-1}$. For all clients k, $\boldsymbol{L}_k^0 = L_{\text{genesis}}$. We use $A \preceq B$ to denote that log A is a (not necessarily strict) prefix of the log B. We use $A \sim B$ ('A is consistent with B') as a shorthand for $A \preceq B \vee B \preceq A$.

Definition 1 (Safety). *An SMR protocol Π is safe iff for all rounds r, s and all honest clients k, k', $\boldsymbol{L}_k^r \sim \boldsymbol{L}_{k'}^s$.*

Definition 2 (Liveness). *An SMR protocol Π is live with latency u iff for all rounds r, if a transaction tx was received by an awake honest validator or communicating client before round $r - u$, then for all honest clients p awake during rounds $[r - u, r]$, tx $\in \boldsymbol{L}_p^r$.*[5]

Definition 3 (Resilience). *For always-on validators, a family of SMR protocols $\Pi(n)$ achieves safety resilience $t^S \in [0, 1]$ and liveness resilience $t^L \in [0, 1]$ if for all n,[6] $\Pi(n)$ is safe with overwhelming probability over executions with $f \leq t^S n$ and live with overwhelming probability over executions with $f \leq t^L n$. For sleepy validators, denote the adversary fraction $\frac{f}{\min_r \text{awake}_r}$ by β. Then, a protocol Π achieves safety resilience $t^S \in [0, 1]$ and liveness resilience $t^L \in [0, 1]$ if Π is safe with overwhelming probability over executions with $\beta \leq t^S$ and live with overwhelming probability over executions with $\beta \leq t^L$.*

3 Synchrony with Always-On Validators

3.1 Sleepy Silent, Always-On Silent Clients (Fig. 1a, Fig. 1d)

We group the protocols and impossibility results for sleepy silent and always-on silent clients in this section because the results are the same for both (Figs. 1a and 1d). Due to Lem. 1, we prove impossibility results for the easier always-on silent client model and show protocols for the harder sleepy silent client model.

---

[4] Gossip networks have been shown to maintain connectivity, and thus synchrony, even under adversary majority [15,35,36].
[5] Clients may not output new logs for a few rounds after awakening. We use a single parameter u for the maximum of such delay and the protocol's latency.
[6] The number of parties is constrained to be polynomial in the security parameter.

Impossibility for Always-On Silent Clients

Theorem 1. *In a synchronous network with always-on validators and always-on silent clients, no protocol can achieve resiliences (t^L, t^S) such that $t^L + t^S \geq 1$.*

Theorem 1 is due to a split-brain attack. Suppose a protocol has resilience (t^L, t^S) such that $t^L + t^S = 1$. Then, the protocol must remain live given $f = t^L n$ adversary validators and safe given $f = (1 - t^L)n$ adversary validators. Then, consider a set of $(1 - t^L)n$ adversary validators that emulate in their heads two apparently honest executions with two different transactions.[7] These validators can ensure that two clients, each hearing only one of the emulated executions, output different logs. Thus, the protocol cannot ensure safety under $(1 - t^L)n = t^S n$ adversary validators, which is a contradiction. Note that the success of the split-brain attack crucially requires the clients to remain isolated, *i.e.*, to be silent. The full proof is in App. C.1.1. For sleepy silent clients, Corollary 1 follows from Theorem 1 and Lem. 1, and a similar proof is also in [41,45].

Corollary 1. *In a synchronous network with always-on validators and sleepy silent clients, no protocol can achieve (t^L, t^S) such that $t^L + t^S \geq 1$.*

Achievability for Sleepy Silent Clients (Safety-Favoring)

Corollary 2. *In a synchronous network with always-on validators and sleepy silent clients, for all (t^L, t^S) with $t^L + t^S < 1$ and $t^L < 1/2$, Sync HotStuff [7] with a quorum size of $q \in (t^S n, (1 - t^L)n]$ achieves (t^L, t^S).*

Corollary 2 follows from [7, Theorems 3 and 4], by replacing the quorum sizes by $q \in (n/2, n]$. A similar construction and its security proof can be found in [41]. Other protocols such as Sync Streamlet [14] can also be adapted with quorums $q \in (n/2, n]$ to achieve the same result. Due to Lem. 1, the protocol achieves the same resiliences in a synchronous network with always-on silent clients.

Achievability for Sleepy Silent Clients (Liveness-Favoring). We next describe a family Π^q_{live} of protocols (Algorithm 1, Fig. 3) parameterized by the integers $q \in [0, n/2]$, one for each resilience pair satisfying $t^L + t^S < 1$ and $t^L \geq t^S$. The protocol Π^q_{live} consists of an *internal protocol* Π_{int} and a *liveness queue*. The internal protocol can be any SMR protocol that achieves all $t^S < 1/2, t^L < 1/2$ under synchrony (*e.g.*, Sync HotStuff [7]).

Each honest validator v participates in the internal protocol. Upon receiving a transaction tx for the first time, v signs tx and sends tx and its signature to all parties (Algorithm 1 l. 5). Each client locally maintains a liveness queue. If a transaction tx gathers q or more signatures, it is added to the queue (Algorithm 1 l. 13). Each client also maintains an *internal log* L_{int} output from the internal protocol (see Fig. 3). To output its log at a round r, a client k appends transactions added to the liveness queue at rounds $r' \leq r - u_{\text{int}}$ (where u_{int} is the internal protocol's latency) to its internal log at round r, discarding duplicates (Algorithm 1 l. 17). The augmented internal log is then output as the log at round r.

---

[7] Since each execution requires a polynomial amount of computation, a polynomial-time adversary can emulate both these executions.

Algorithm 1. Liveness-favoring SMR protocol Π_{live}^q for sleepy silent clients

```
 1  ▷ Code for validator v
 2  on INIT(N, L_genesis)
 3     P_int ← new Π_int(N, L_genesis)              ▷ instantiate a new Π_int validator
 4  on receiving transaction tx or ⟨tx⟩_{v'} for some v' ∈ N
 5     gossip(⟨tx⟩_v)                               ▷ send tx and signature on tx to all parties
 6     P_int.input(tx)                              ▷ input tx to the internal protocol

 7  ▷ Client code
 8  on INIT(N, L_genesis)
 9     P_int ← new Π_int(N, L_genesis)              ▷ instantiate a new Π_int client
10     Q ← ∅                                        ▷ liveness queue: txs seen so far
11     L ← L_genesis                                ▷ output log of the combined protocol Π_live^q
12  on {⟨tx⟩_v}_{v∈V} such that V ⊆ N, |V| ≥ q at round r
13     Q.enqueue((tx, r))                           ▷ add tx to the liveness queue on receiving at least q signatures
14  on every round r
15     L_int ← output by P_int at round r
16     for (tx, r') ∈ Q such that r' ≤ r − u_int and tx ∉ L_int
17        L_int ← L_int ∥ tx
18     L ← L_int                                    ▷ output log
```

Fig. 3. A family of protocols that achieves any resilience $t^L + t^S < 1$ and $t^S < t^L$ for sleepy silent or always-on silent clients (lower right triangle of Figs. 1a and 1d). The internal protocol Π_{int} is any SMR protocol achieving all resilience pairs $t^S < 1/2, t^L < 1/2$ for sleepy silent clients (e.g. Sync HotStuff [7]). On receiving transaction tx, validators sign it and broadcast the signature before processing it as an input to Π_{int}. A client, on receiving transaction tx signed by $q > t^S n$ validators, and after waiting u_{int} rounds (where u_{int} is the maximum latency of Π_{int}), if tx is not included in the log L_{int} output by the client from Π, concatenates tx to L_{int} to output the final confirmed log L.

Theorem 2. *In a synchronous network with always-on validators and sleepy silent clients, for all (t^L, t^S) with $t^L + t^S < 1$ and $t^L \geq 1/2$, the protocol Π_{live}^q with $q \in (t^S n, (1 − t^L)n]$ achieves (t^L, t^S).*

When $f \leq t^L n$ validators are adversary, all transactions input to an honest validator gather q signatures and enter the liveness queues and eventually enter the output log, ensuring liveness with resilience t^L. When $f \leq t^S n$ (which implies $f \leq t^L n$, since $t^L + t^S < 1$ and $t^L \geq 1/2$), the internal protocol is safe *and* live, and adversary validators cannot produce q signatures without an honest validator. Therefore, any transaction tx added to the liveness queue must be known to an honest validator and processed by the internal protocol. By the internal protocol's liveness, tx enters the internal log within u_{int} rounds. Thus, no transaction is ever appended to the internal log. Safety then follows from the internal protocol's safety. The full proof is in App. C.1.2

3.2 Sleepy Communicating Clients (Fig. 1g)

Impossibility for Sleepy Communicating Clients

Theorem 3. *Under synchrony, with always-on validators and sleepy communicating clients, no protocol can achieve resiliences* $(t^L, t^S) \in [1/2, 1] \times [1/2, 1]$.

Suppose a protocol can achieve $t^L = t^S = 1/2$. Let P and Q be two disjoint sets of $n/2$ validators and k_1, k_2 be two clients. Consider two worlds where the (P, k_1) and (Q, k_2) are adversary respectively. In both worlds, the adversary parties initially do not communicate with honest parties. By liveness, in world $i \in \{1, 2\}$, client k_i awake since the start outputs transaction tx_i by round u after hearing from the honest validators. In both worlds, a client k_3 awakes after round u and hears from *all parties* including the adversary ones. By liveness, k_3 also outputs tx_i in world i. However, the two worlds are indistinguishable for k_3 because $P - Q$ and $k_1 - k_2$ exchange their roles in the two worlds, implying its log is the same and must contain both tx_1 and tx_2 in both worlds, leading to a safety violation in at least one world. The full proof is in App. C.2.1.

Achievability for Sleepy Communicating Clients (Safety-Favoring)
This protocol achieves (t^L, t^S) for all $t^L < 1/2$ and $t^S = 1$. In particular, it is *always* safe. It uses a *freezing gadget* applied to an internal SMR protocol Π_{int} that is *certifiable* [31,47] (cf. public verifiability [41]). Quorum-based protocols such as HotStuff [39,56], Streamlet [14], Tendermint [9], Casper [12], and their synchronous variants such as Sync HotStuff [7] and Sync-Streamlet [14, Sec. 4][8] are certifiable. In these protocols, clients output a log on receiving enough quorum certificates which form a *certificate* that other clients can verify *non-interactively*. Certifiable safety means that adversaries controlling $\leq t^S$ validators cannot forge certificates certifying two conflicting logs.

Definition 4 (Certifiable protocol). *An SMR protocol Π is certifiable if there exists a computable functionality $\mathcal{W}$ (the* certificate producer*) and a computable deterministic non-interactive function $\mathcal{C}$ (the* certificate consumer*) such that when a client p invokes $\mathcal{W}()$ at round r, it produces a certificate C such that $\mathcal{C}(C) = \mathbf{L}_p^r$. A certifiable protocol Π is certifiably safe if Π is safe, and moreover, if at any round r, the adversary outputs a certificate C such that $\mathcal{C}(C) = L$, then for all clients q, for all rounds s, $L \sim \mathbf{L}_q^s$. A certifiable protocol Π achieves certifiable safety resilience t^S if Π is certifiably safe with overwhelming probability over executions with $f \leq t^S n$.*

The protocol is described in Algorithm 2 and is illustrated as a block diagram in Fig. 4. Each client runs a client for the internal protocol Π_{int} (see Π_{int} in Fig. 4, Algorithm 2 l. 3), periodically outputs a certificate C for the internal log L_{int}, and gossips it to the network. It similarly processes certificates received from

---
[8] The synchronous variants can be made certifiable by having validators broadcast a signature on their 'committed'/'finalized' logs [41, Sec. 4.2].

Algorithm 2. Freezing protocol for sleepy communicating clients

```
 1  ▷ Code for client
 2  on INIT(N, L_genesis)
 3      P_int ← new Π_int(N, L_genesis)              ▷ instantiate a new Π_int client
 4      S ← ∅                                        ▷ set of valid logs seen so far
 5      L ← L_genesis                                ▷ output log of the combined protocol Π_frz
 6  on certificate C output by P_int.W() once per round or C received from network
 7      L_int ← C(C)                                 ▷ extract log from certificate
 8      S ← S ∪ {L_int}                              ▷ add L_int to set of logs seen so far
 9      gossip(C)                                    ▷ send the transcript to all parties
10      wait(Δ)                                      ▷ meanwhile, continue processing other events
11      if L_int ⊀ L and ∀L' ∈ S: L_int ∼ L'         ▷ log has grown, no conflicting logs
12          L ← L_int
```

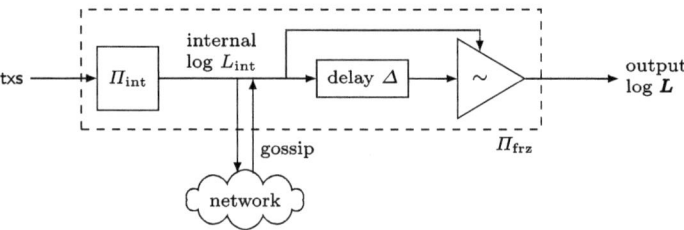

Fig. 4. The freezing protocol Π_{frz} that achieves $t^L < 1/2, t^S = 1$ for sleepy communicating clients. The internal protocol Π_{int} is any certifiable SMR protocol that can achieve all $t^S, t^L < 1/2$. On seeing a log L_{int} from Π_{int} or the network, the client gossips L_{int} (formally, the corresponding certificate), and waits for Δ rounds. The *conflict resolution* component ▷ remembers the set S of all logs it ever received at the input port on its top. On receiving L at the input port on its left, this component outputs L if there were no conflicting logs in S (see Algorithm 2 ll. 11 and 12).

other clients. After waiting Δ rounds (Algorithm 2 l. 10), the client outputs the log L_{int} iff it has seen no conflicting logs (Algorithm 2 ll. 11 and 12).

Applying this gadget to an internal protocol Π_{int} with certifiable safety and liveness resilience $t^L_{\text{int}} < 1/2, t^S_{\text{int}} < 1/2$ (e.g., Sync HotStuff [7]) results in a protocol Π_{frz} (Fig. 4) with resilience $t^L < 1/2, t^S = 1$. Safety of Π_{frz} is ensured by the freezing gadget. See Fig. 5 for a visual safety proof. Liveness of Π_{frz} comes from the internal protocol's liveness and certifiable safety, which guarantee that new transactions are included in the internal log and no conflicting certificates are seen. The full proof is in App. C.2.2.

Similar to our freezing protocol, the Tendermint client implementation 'panics' [4] upon detecting [3] two blocks confirmed at the same height. But the client may have already confirmed one of the blocks before panicking, potentially causing a safety violation. If Tendermint clients instead waited for Δ time before confirming blocks (and remained online after panicking to relay evidence of misbehavior), they would have implemented our freezing protocol. This further shows that the client protocols we study in the paper are practical and reflect real implementations.

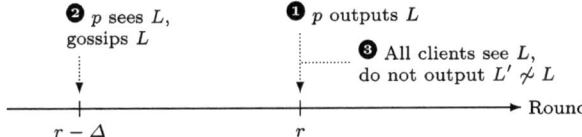

Fig. 5. Illustration for the freezing protocol's safety which is maintained during adversary majority (Theorem 4). ❶ Suppose that at round r, a client p outputs a log L. ❷ The client must have seen L (and its certificate C) either from the internal protocol Π or from the network latest by round $r - \Delta$, at which point it must have sent L (and C) to all other clients. ❸ Thus, by round r, all clients must have seen L and thereafter will never output a log that conflicts with L.

Theorem 4. *In a synchronous network with always-on validators and sleepy communicating clients, for all (t^L, t^S) with $t^L < 1/2$ and $t^S \leq 1$, Π_{frz} with Sync HotStuff as its internal protocol achieves (t^L, t^S).*

Achievability for Sleepy Communicating Clients (Liveness-Favoring). The protocol Π^*_{live} achieves any (t^L, t^S) with $t^L = 1, t^S < 1/2$ under always-on validators. The protocol is very similar to Π^q_{live} the liveness-favoring protocol for sleepy silent clients (Sect. 3.1) but simpler, so we only describe the key difference. Unlike silent clients in Π^q_{live} (Sect. 3.1), *communicating* clients add transactions to their liveness queue as soon as they receive them. This is because while silent clients require signatures from $q > t^S n$ validators to infer that at least one honest validator received the transaction, communicating clients can do so by gossiping the transaction themselves. The full protocol and security proof are in App. C.2.3.

Theorem 5. *In a synchronous network with always-on validators and sleepy communicating clients, for all (t^L, t^S) with $t^L \leq 1, t^S < 1/2$, Π^*_{live} with Sync HotStuff as its internal protocol achieves (t^L, t^S).*

3.3 Always-On Communicating Clients (Fig. 1j)

Achievability for Always-On Communicating Clients. Dolev and Strong [20], and Lamport, Shostak, and Pease [28] presented protocols for the Byzantine Generals problem when all but one validator are adversary. In their problem setting, there are no clients. Instead, a designated leader ('general') broadcasts a value and all honest validators ('lieutenants') must agree on a common value, which matches the leader's value if the leader is honest. However, the Dolev-Strong protocol can be extended to support always-on communicating clients; the client follows the same rules a validator uses to output a value.

An SMR protocol can be created by having each validator propose a block as the leader in an instance of the Dolev-Strong protocol, allowing always-on communicating clients to agree on a unique block (possibly a default empty block) per leader. The client's log is formed by concatenating these blocks in a set order, repeating the process to grow the log. This approach is presented in [11,26], with optimizations in [25]. We recap the protocol from [11] in Alg. 5 and prove its security in App. C.3.1.

Corollary 3. *In a synchronous network with always-on validators and always-on communicating clients, for all (t^L, t^S) with $t^L, t^S < 1$, Alg. 5 achieves (t^L, t^S).*

We note that no protocol can achieve $t^L = t^S = 1$ (cf. App. D.3.2).

4 Synchrony with Sleepy Validators

4.1 Sleepy Silent, Always-On Silent Clients (Figs. 1b and 1e)

Impossibility for Always-On Silent Clients. This follows from Theorem 1 and Lem. 1.

Corollary 4. *In a synchronous network with sleepy validators and always-on silent clients, no protocol can achieve resiliences (t^L, t^S) such that $t^L + t^S \geq 1$.*

Achievability for Sleepy Silent Clients (Equal Resiliences). This follows from Sleepy Consensus [49, Theorem 1] and Goldfish [17, Theorem 2].

Corollary 5. *In a synchronous network with sleepy validators and sleepy silent clients, for all (t^L, t^S) with $t^L < 1/2, t^S < 1/2$, the Sleepy Consensus protocol [49] and Goldfish [17] achieve (t^L, t^S).*

Achievability for Sleepy Silent Clients (Safety-Favoring). To achieve any resilience (t^L, t^S) with $t^L + t^S < 1$ and $t^L < t^S$, we modify the Goldfish protocol [17]. In a nutshell, in Goldfish, voters select a block to vote for by walking down a tree of blocks, and at each fork, selecting the subtree with the largest number of votes from the previous slot. Our key modification is to instead select the subtree with at least ϕ fraction of the total votes from the previous slot, where $\phi \in (t^S, 1 - t^L]$. The details of this protocol are in App. D.1.1.

Theorem 6. *In a synchronous network with sleepy validators and sleepy silent clients, for all (t^L, t^S) with $t^L + t^S < 1$ and $t^L < 1/2$, Goldfish modified with $\phi \in (t^S, 1 - t^L]$ achieves (t^L, t^S).*

Achievability for Sleepy Silent Clients (Liveness-favoring). For any resilience (t^L, t^S) with $t^L + t^S < 1$ and $t^L \geq t^S$, we show a protocol Π_{live}^ϕ achieving (t^L, t^S). The protocol is very similar to Π_{live}^q, the liveness-favoring protocol for sleepy silent clients under always-on validators (Sect. 3.1). The key difference is that to add a transaction to the liveness queue, clients require a fraction ϕ of validators to sign the transaction (unlike a fixed number q in Π_{live}^q). More precisely, at every round $r = \ell\Delta$ for some $\ell \in \mathbb{Z}$, each client calculates the number T_{tx} of validators that signed a transaction tx. It also calculates the number $T_{\ell-1}$ of unique validators that have either sent a 'heartbeat' message for round $(\ell-1)\Delta$ or a signature on some transaction in the past. Then, if $T_{\text{tx}}/T_{\ell-1} \geq \phi$, the client adds tx to its liveness queue. The full protocol and security proof are in App. D.1.2.

Theorem 7. *In a synchronous network with sleepy validators and sleepy silent clients, for all (t^L, t^S) with $t^L + t^S < 1$ and $t^L \geq 1/2$, the protocol Π_{live}^{ϕ} with $\phi \in (t^S, 1 - t^L]$ achieves (t^L, t^S).*

4.2 Sleepy Communicating Clients (Fig. 1h)

Impossibility for Sleepy Communicating Clients

Theorem 8. *In a synchronous network with sleepy validators and sleepy communicating clients, no protocol can achieve (t^L, t^S) with $t^L + t^S \geq 1$ and $t^S \geq 1/2$.*

The proof is similar to Theorem 3. Suppose a protocol can achieve $t^L = 25\%, t^S = 75\%$. Let P and Q be two disjoint sets of $0.75n$ and $0.25n$ validators respectively, and k_1, k_2 be two clients awake since the start. Consider two worlds, 1 and 2, where the (P, k_1) and (Q, k_2) are adversary respectively. In both worlds, the adversary parties initially do not communicate with honest parties. Note that liveness must hold in world 2 because only 25% validators are adversary, and in world 1 because the 75% adversary validators appear indistinguishable from sleepy honest validators. Thus, in each world, client k_i outputs transaction tx_i in its log. In both worlds, a client k_3 awakes after round u and hears from *all parties* including the adversary ones. However, the two worlds are indistinguishable for k_3 because $P - Q$ and $k_1 - k_2$ exchange their roles, implying that its log must be the same in both worlds, and it contains tx_2 as world 2 has liveness, leading to a safety violation in at least one world. The full proof is in App. D.2.1.

Achievability for Sleepy Communicating Clients (Liveness-Favoring).
The protocol Π_{live}^* in Sect. 3.2 does not rely on the validators for its liveness, and its safety only requires safety and liveness of the internal protocol in a closed-box manner. Therefore, the same protocol, when instantiated with an internal protocol for sleepy validators (*e.g.*, Sleepy Consensus [49]), achieves the following.

Theorem 9. *In a synchronous network with sleepy validators and sleepy communicating clients, for all (t^L, t^S) with $t^L \leq 1, t^S < 1/2$, Π_{live}^* (Sect. 3.2) with the Sleepy Consensus protocol [49] as its internal protocol achieves (t^L, t^S).*

Proof. Follows from [49, Theorem 1] and Lems. 4 and 5. □

4.3 Always-on Communicating Clients (Fig. 1k)

Achievability for Always-on Communicating Clients. We show that the SMR protocol based on Dolev-Strong (Sect. 3.3, Alg. 5) achieves any $t^L < 1, t^S < 1$ even under sleepy validators. Under sleepy validators with always-on communicating clients, when a majority of the awake validators are adversary, the clients must output safe and live logs even though the validators themselves may not agree on a log (since validators are sleepy and communicating, the impossibility in Fig. 1h applies to them). Thus, the challenge is to design the validator's code to behave correctly even without knowing what happened while it was sleeping.

This challenge resolves itself due to the following observations. First, while the SMR protocol (Alg. 5) runs instances of Dolev-Strong one after the other, each instance does not depend on the previous instances. Second, within an instance, since the Dolev-Strong protocol (Alg. 4) guarantees agreement and validity when all but one validator are adversary under always-on validators (Lem. 6), it does so even when only one validator is honest and awake throughout the instance (all honest validators who sleep could be considered adversary). Moreover, we don't even require the same honest validator to be awake throughout the instance but only require that for each round during the instance, *some* honest validator is awake. Finally, since each validator (including the leader) signs only one message per instance, it may sleep after it does so without affecting the protocol's remaining execution. Thus, sleepy validators can faithfully run Alg. 4. We explain these surprising observations and prove security in App. D.3.1.

Theorem 10. *In a synchronous network with sleepy validators and always-on communicating clients, for all (t^L, t^S) such that $t^L, t^S < 1$, Alg. 5 achieves (t^L, t^S).*

5 Related Work

No Clients. Much of the classic SMR literature [6,7,14,16,19,22,27,34,49] did not explicitly consider clients. Let's call this the 'no clients' model. In this model, validators (a.k.a. 'replicas' or 'nodes') output logs, and in any protocol with resilience $t^L + t^S < 1$, sleepy silent clients may learn the log by querying a quorum of $t^S n + 1$ validators [6,7,34] (see Fig. 1a). However, always-on and/or communicating clients may use other means to learn the log. For example, always-on communicating clients can run the same 'confirmation logic' that validators use. This makes the 'no clients' model equivalent to always-on communicating clients (Fig. 1j). However, under sleepy validators, the 'no clients' model is equivalent to sleepy communicating clients (Fig. 1h), possibly weaker than always-on communicating clients. Reliable broadcast and Byzantine agreement, typically defined without clients, can also apply to different client types (*e.g.*, Def. 10).

Sleepy Silent Clients. Sleepy clients have been called sleepy [49], late-spawning [16,48,55], and lazy [30]. It has been proven that no protocol with sleepy silent clients can achieve both $t^L \geq \frac{1}{2}$ and $t^S \geq \frac{1}{2}$ [48,49,51]. When safety and liveness are decoupled, [41,45] prove $t^L + t^S \geq 1$ is impossible. But their proofs require a stronger notion of security, *certifiability*, *i.e.*, the protocol produces *non-interactively* verifiable certificates (cf. Definition 4, [31]). Certifiable protocols are also secure for sleepy silent clients, but the converse is not true (*e.g.*, longest-chain consensus [16,19,43,49] supports sleepy silent clients, but lack certificates since clients must check for longer chains). Thus, the impossibility results of [41,45] apply to certifiable protocols, but not necessarily to sleepy silent clients. We prove (in Theorem 1) that $t^L + t^S \geq 1$ is impossible for both sleepy silent and always-on silent clients.

Sleepy Communicating Clients. The idea of sleepy clients gossiping out-of-band to detect liveness or safety violations isn't new [40], although we are the first to formalize the sleepy communicating client model and apply it to SMR. Validators in some protocols [7,14] with $1/2$ resilience also wait Δ to detect conflicts, but achieving $t^S = 99\%$ requires communicating clients. Concurrent work [29] proposes a variant of Bitcoin [43] (which supports sleepy validators) that achieves resilience $t^L < 1/2, t^S = 1$ in the *always-on* clients model. However, their protocol doesn't achieve this resilience for *sleepy* clients who awaken after the adversary has corrupted a majority of validators. In App. F, we show a concrete attack and prove that no protocol can achieve these resiliences under sleepy validators with *sleepy* clients throughout the execution (see also Fig. 1h and Sect. 4.2).[9]

Sleepy validators. Protocols achieving $t^L < 1/2, t^S < 1/2$ for sleepy validators appear in [17, 24, 37, 38, 42, 49, 50]. With sleepy validators and 'no clients', [48, 49] prove that no protocol can simultaneously achieve $t^S \geq 1/2, t^L \geq 1/2$.

Appendices

Full version with appendices: https://eprint.iacr.org/2024/1799 [53].

References

1. 51% attacks. https://dci.mit.edu/51-attacks. Accessed 15 Jan 2025
2. Tendermint spec (2022). https://github.com/tendermint/tendermint/blob/main/spec/README.md#p2p-and-network-protocols. Accessed 14 Jan 2025
3. CometBFT (2023). https://github.com/cometbft/cometbft/blob/2cd0d1a33cdb6a2c76e6e162d892624492c26290/state/validation.go#L45-L51. Accessed 14 Jan 2025
4. CometBFT (2024). https://github.com/cometbft/cometbft/blob/2cd0d1a33cdb6a2c76e6e162d892624492c26290/consensus/state.go#L1711-L1714. Accessed 14 Jan 2025
5. Ethereum consensus specs: Phase 0 – networking (2024). https://github.com/ethereum/consensus-specs/blob/dev/specs/phase0/p2p-interface.md#global-topics. Accessed 15 Dec 2024
6. Abraham, I., Devadas, S., Nayak, K., Ren, L.: Brief announcement: practical synchronous byzantine consensus. In: DISC. LIPIcs, vol. 91, pp. 41:1–41:4. Schloss Dagstuhl - Leibniz-Zentrum für Informatik (2017)
7. Abraham, I., Malkhi, D., Nayak, K., Ren, L., Yin, M.: Sync HotStuff: simple and practical synchronous state machine replication. In: SP, pp. 106–118. IEEE (2020)

---

[9] The model we use assumes a known set of validators of which f are corrupted while the model in [29] instead uses proof-of-work and assumes limited adversary hashing power. Although these models are incomparable, our impossibility proof (Theorem 8) applies to that model as well (see detailed discussion in App. F).

8. Bitcoin Project: Bitcoin developer guide – P2P network – initial block download – headers-first (2020). https://web.archive.org/web/20230314181737/https://developer.bitcoin.org/devguide/p2p_network.html#headers-first
9. Buchman, E., Kwon, J., Milosevic, Z.: The latest gossip on BFT consensus. arXiv:1807.04938v3 [cs.DC] (2018)
10. Budish, E., Lewis-Pye, A., Roughgarden, T.: The economic limits of permissionless consensus. arXiv:2405.09173v2 [cs.DC] (2024)
11. Buterin, V.: A guide to 99% fault tolerant consensus (2018). https://vitalik.eth.limo/general/2018/08/07/99_fault_tolerant.html. Accessed 11 Oct 2024
12. Buterin, V., Griffith, V.: Casper the friendly finality gadget. arXiv:1710.09437v4 [cs.CR] (2017)
13. Castro, M., Liskov, B.: Practical byzantine fault tolerance and proactive recovery. ACM Trans. Comput. Syst. **20**(4), 398–461 (2002)
14. Chan, B.Y., Shi, E.: Streamlet: textbook streamlined blockchains. In: AFT, pp. 1–11. ACM (2020)
15. Coretti, S., Kiayias, A., Moore, C., Russell, A.: The generals' scuttlebutt: byzantine-resilient gossip protocols. In: CCS, pp. 595–608. ACM (2022)
16. Daian, P., Pass, R., Shi, E.: Snow White: robustly reconfigurable consensus and applications to provably secure proof of stake. In: Goldberg, I., Moore, T. (eds.) FC 2019. LNCS, vol. 11598, pp. 23–41. Springer, Cham (2019). https://doi.org/10.1007/978-3-030-32101-7_2
17. D'Amato, F., Neu, J., Tas, E.N., Tse, D.: Goldfish: No more attacks on ethereum?! In: FC (1). LNCS, vol. 14744, pp. 3–23. Springer, Cham (2024)
18. Danezis, G., Kokoris-Kogias, L., Sonnino, A., Spiegelman, A.: Narwhal and tusk: a DAG-based mempool and efficient BFT consensus. In: EuroSys, pp. 34–50. ACM (2022)
19. David, B., Gaži, P., Kiayias, A., Russell, A.: Ouroboros praos: an adaptively-secure, semi-synchronous proof-of-stake blockchain. In: Nielsen, J.B., Rijmen, V. (eds.) EUROCRYPT 2018. LNCS, vol. 10821, pp. 66–98. Springer, Cham (2018). https://doi.org/10.1007/978-3-319-78375-8_3
20. Dolev, D., Strong, H.R.: Authenticated algorithms for byzantine agreement. SIAM J. Comput. **12**(4), 656–666 (1983)
21. Dwork, C., Lynch, N.A., Stockmeyer, L.J.: Consensus in the presence of partial synchrony. J. ACM **35**(2), 288–323 (1988)
22. Garay, J.A., Kiayias, A., Leonardos, N.: The Bitcoin backbone protocol: analysis and applications. J. ACM **71**(4), 25:1–25:49 (2024)
23. Gilbert, S., Lynch, N.A.: Brewer's conjecture and the feasibility of consistent, available, partition-tolerant web services. SIGACT News **33**(2), 51–59 (2002)
24. Goyal, V., Li, H., Raizes, J.: Instant block confirmation in the sleepy model. In: Borisov, N., Diaz, C. (eds.) FC 2021. LNCS, vol. 12675, pp. 65–83. Springer, Heidelberg (2021). https://doi.org/10.1007/978-3-662-64331-0_4
25. Hou, R., Yu, H.: Optimistic fast confirmation while tolerating malicious majority in blockchains. In: SP, pp. 2481–2498. IEEE (2023)
26. Hou, R., Yu, H., Saxena, P.: Using throughput-centric byzantine broadcast to tolerate malicious majority in blockchains. In: SP, pp. 1263–1280. IEEE (2022)
27. Kiayias, A., Russell, A., David, B., Oliynykov, R.: Ouroboros: a provably secure proof-of-stake blockchain protocol. In: Katz, J., Shacham, H. (eds.) CRYPTO 2017. LNCS, vol. 10401, pp. 357–388. Springer, Cham (2017). https://doi.org/10.1007/978-3-319-63688-7_12
28. Lamport, L., Shostak, R.E., Pease, M.C.: The byzantine generals problem. ACM Trans. Program. Lang. Syst. **4**(3), 382–401 (1982)

29. Leshno, J.D., Shi, E., Pass, R.: On the viability of open-source financial rails: economic security of permissionless consensus. arXiv:2409.08951v1 [cs.GT] (2024)
30. Lewis-Pye, A.: Consensus in 50 pages (rough draft) (2022). https://lewis-pye.com/wp-content/uploads/2023/01/consensus-in-50-pages7-1.pdf. Accessed 11 Oct 2024
31. Lewis-Pye, A., Roughgarden, T.: How does blockchain security dictate blockchain implementation? In: CCS, pp. 1006–1019. ACM (2021)
32. Lewis-Pye, A., Roughgarden, T.: Byzantine generals in the permissionless setting. In: FC (1). LNCS, vol. 13950, pp. 21–37. Springer, Cham (2023)
33. Lewis-Pye, A., Roughgarden, T.: Permissionless consensus. arXiv:2304.14701v5 [cs.DC] (2023)
34. Liu, S., Viotti, P., Cachin, C., Quéma, V., Vukolic, M.: XFT: practical fault tolerance beyond crashes. In: OSDI, pp. 485–500. USENIX Association (2016)
35. Liu-Zhang, C., Matt, C., Maurer, U., Rito, G., Thomsen, S.E.: Practical provably secure flooding for blockchains. In: ASIACRYPT (1). LNCS, vol. 13791, pp. 774–805. Springer, Cham (2022)
36. Liu-Zhang, C., Matt, C., Thomsen, S.E.: Asymptotically optimal message dissemination with applications to blockchains. In: EUROCRYPT (3). LNCS, vol. 14653, pp. 64–95. Springer, Cham (2024)
37. Losa, G., Gafni, E.: Consensus in the unknown-participation message-adversary model. arXiv:2301.04817v2 [cs.DC] (2023)
38. Malkhi, D., Momose, A., Ren, L.: Towards practical sleepy BFT. In: CCS, pp. 490–503. ACM (2023)
39. Malkhi, D., Nayak, K.: Extended abstract: HotStuff-2: optimal two-phase responsive BFT. Cryptology ePrint Archive, Paper 2023/397 (2023)
40. Mazières, D., Shasha, D.E.: Building secure file systems out of byzantine storage. In: PODC, pp. 108–117. ACM (2002)
41. Momose, A., Ren, L.: Multi-threshold byzantine fault tolerance. In: CCS, pp. 1686–1699. ACM (2021)
42. Momose, A., Ren, L.: Constant latency in sleepy consensus. In: CCS, pp. 2295–2308. ACM (2022)
43. Nakamoto, S.: Bitcoin: a peer-to-peer electronic cash system (2008). https://bitcoin.org/bitcoin.pdf. Accessed 11 Oct 2024
44. Neu, J., Sridhar, S., Yang, L., Tse, D.: Optimal flexible consensus and its application to Ethereum. In: SP, pp. 3885–3903. IEEE (2024)
45. Neu, J., Tas, E.N., Tse, D.: The availability-accountability dilemma and its resolution via accountability gadgets. arXiv:2105.06075v1 [cs.CR] (2021)
46. Neu, J., Tas, E.N., Tse, D.: Ebb-and-flow protocols: a resolution of the availability-finality dilemma. In: SP, pp. 446–465. IEEE (2021)
47. Neu, J., Tas, E.N., Tse, D.: The availability-accountability dilemma and its resolution via accountability gadgets. In: Financial Cryptography. LNCS, vol. 13411, pp. 541–559. Springer, Cham (2022)
48. Pass, R., Shi, E.: Rethinking large-scale consensus. In: CSF, pp. 115–129. IEEE Computer Society (2017)
49. Pass, R., Shi, E.: The sleepy model of consensus. In: Takagi, T., Peyrin, T. (eds.) ASIACRYPT 2017. LNCS, vol. 10625, pp. 380–409. Springer, Cham (2017). https://doi.org/10.1007/978-3-319-70697-9_14
50. Pass, R., Shi, E.: **Thunderella**: blockchains with optimistic instant confirmation. In: Nielsen, J.B., Rijmen, V. (eds.) EUROCRYPT 2018. LNCS, vol. 10821, pp. 3–33. Springer, Cham (2018). https://doi.org/10.1007/978-3-319-78375-8_1
51. Schneider, F.B.: Implementing fault-tolerant services using the state machine approach: a tutorial. ACM Comput. Surv. **22**(4), 299–319 (1990)

52. Spiegelman, A., Giridharan, N., Sonnino, A., Kokoris-Kogias, L.: Bullshark: DAG BFT protocols made practical. In: CCS, pp. 2705–2718. ACM (2022)
53. Sridhar, S., Tas, E.N., Neu, J., Zindros, D., Tse, D.: Consensus under adversary majority done right. Cryptology ePrint Archive, Paper 2024/1799 (2024)
54. Sridhar, S., Zindros, D., Tse, D.: Better safe than sorry: recovering after adversarial majority. Cryptology ePrint Archive, Paper 2023/1556 (2023)
55. Tas, E.N., Tse, D., Gai, F., Kannan, S., Maddah-Ali, M.A., Yu, F.: Bitcoin-enhanced proof-of-stake security: possibilities and impossibilities. In: SP, pp. 126–145. IEEE (2023)
56. Yin, M., Malkhi, D., Reiter, M.K., Golan-Gueta, G., Abraham, I.: HotStuff: BFT consensus with linearity and responsiveness. In: PODC, pp. 347–356. ACM (2019)

On the (in)security of Proofs-of-Space Based Longest-Chain Blockchains

Mirza Ahad Baig$^{(\boxtimes)}$ and Krzysztof Pietrzak

ISTA, Klosterneuburg, Austria
{mbaig,pietrzak}@ist.ac.at

Abstract. The Nakamoto consensus protocol underlying the Bitcoin blockchain uses proof of work as a voting mechanism. Honest miners who contribute hashing power towards securing the chain try to extend the longest chain they are aware of. Despite its simplicity, Nakamoto consensus achieves meaningful security guarantees assuming that at any point in time, a majority of the hashing power is controlled by honest parties. This also holds under "resource variability", i.e., if the total hashing power varies greatly over time.

Proofs of space (PoSpace) have been suggested as a more sustainable replacement for proofs of work. Unfortunately, no construction of a "longest-chain" blockchain based on PoSpace, that is secure under dynamic availability, is known. In this work, we prove that without additional assumptions no such protocol exists. We exactly quantify this impossibility result by proving a bound on the length of the fork required for double spending as a function of the adversarial capabilities. This bound holds for any chain selection rule, and we also show a chain selection rule (albeit a very strange one) that almost matches this bound.

Concretely, we consider a security game in which the honest parties at any point control $\phi > 1$ times more space than the adversary. The adversary can change the honest space by a factor $1 \pm \varepsilon$ with every block (dynamic availability), and "replotting" the space (which allows answering two challenges using the same space) takes as much time as ρ blocks.

We prove that no matter what chain selection rule is used, in this game the adversary can create a fork of length $\phi^2 \cdot \rho/\varepsilon$ that will be picked as the winner by the chain selection rule.

We also provide an upper bound that matches the lower bound up to a factor ϕ. There exists a chain selection rule (albeit a very strange one) which in the above game requires forks of length at least $\phi \cdot \rho/\varepsilon$.

Our results show the necessity of additional assumptions to create a secure PoSpace based longest-chain blockchain. The Chia network in addition to PoSpace uses a verifiable delay function. Our bounds show that an additional primitive like that is necessary.

This research was funded in whole or in part by the Austrian Science Fund (FWF) 10.55776/F85.

Supplementary Information The online version contains supplementary material available at https://doi.org/10.1007/978-3-032-07035-7_8.

© International Financial Cryptography Association 2026
C. Garman and P. Moreno-Sanchez (Eds.): FC 2025, LNCS 15752, pp. 127–142, 2026.
https://doi.org/10.1007/978-3-032-07035-7_8

1 Introduction

Bitcoin was the first successful digital currency. What set it apart from previous attempts like Digicash [7] was the fact that it is permissionless. This means it is decentralized – so no single entity can shut it down or censor transactions – and moreover, everyone can participate in maintaining and securing the currency.

The key innovation in Bitcoin is the blockchain which realizes a "decentralized ledger". In the case of a digital currency, this ledger simply records all the transactions, but it can also hold richer data like smart contracts [13]. A blockchain is a hash-chain $b_0 \hookleftarrow b_1 \hookleftarrow b_2 \ldots \hookleftarrow b_j$ where each b_i is a data block that contains a "payload" (transactions, a time stamp, etc.), a hash $h_i = H(b_{i-1})$ of the previous block, and a "proof of work" (PoW) π_i.

The collision-resistance of the hash function H ensures that a block b_i commits all the previous blocks. The main novelty is the way proofs of work are used to make it computationally costly to add a block: To create a valid block b_i one must find a value π_i such that the hash of the previous block and π_i is below some threshold

$$0.H(b_{i-1}, \pi_i) < 1/D$$

here we think of the hash as a binary string: if the difficulty D is 2^k, then the hash $H(b_{i-1}, \pi_i)$ must start with at least k 0's. Parties called miners compete to find PoWs to extend the latest block. They are incentivized by rewards (block rewards and transaction fees) to contribute computing power towards this task. Bitcoin is permissionless in the sense that everyone can be a miner and the protocol does not need to know who currently participates [11]. Bitcoin can be shown to be secure (in particular, it does not allow for double spending), assuming that a majority of the hashing power is controlled by honest parties who follow the protocol rules. The most important rule just states that a miner should always work towards extending the heaviest valid chain (typically, the heaviest chain is also the longest one, hence the name "longest chain") they are aware of. Blockchains following this general rule are called "longest-chain blockchains", the protocol itself is referred to as "Nakamoto consensus".

Alternative Proof Systems. Nakamoto consensus uses computation as a resource so that a miner who holds an α fraction of the total resource will contribute an α fraction of all blocks in expectation, and thus get roughly an α fraction of the rewards.

Using computation as a resource has several negative implications. The main one is the ecological impact: currently Bitcoin mining is burning roughly as much energy as the Netherlands. It is thus natural to look for a more "sustainable" resource that could replace hashing power in a longest-chain blockchain.

The most investigated alternative are *proofs of stake* (PoStake), where the coins as recorded on the blockchain serve as a resource. More precisely, miners can stake their coins, which takes them temporarily out of circulation. They can then participate in the mining process, getting a fraction of the rewards which is proportional to the fraction of their stakes coins.

PoStake is extremely appealing as it is basically wasteless as it is not a "physical" resource, but it raises many technical questions and conceptual issues. One argument that is often raised is that PoStake is not really permissionless as the only way to participate in mining lies in acquiring coins from a limited supply in the first place.

In [9] *proofs of space* (PoSpace) were introduced. A PoSpace is a proof system where a prover convinces a verifier that it "wastes" disk space. The motivation for this notion was a replacement for proofs of work which is still a "physical resource", and thus does not share many of the shortcomings of PoStake, but is also much more sustainable than proofs of work.

Proofs of Space. A proof of space [9] is an interactive protocol between a prover P and a verifier V. The main protocol parameter is a value N determining the disk space of an (honest) prover (a typical value would be $N = 2^{43}$ bits, which corresponds to one TB). In an initialization phase, which is executed once, the honest prover initializes his disk space of size N with a file S, called a "plot". This phase should be very efficient for the verifier (or not involve the verifier at all [2]), while the prover should run in time $\tilde{O}(N)$. This is basically optimal as they must run in time N to just "touch" the entire disk space.

After the initialization phase, the prover can create valid proofs for random challenges very efficiently, in particular, only accessing a tiny portion of its local file S. The security property of a PoSpace states that any prover who instead of S stores some data S' of some size that is "sufficiently" smaller than S, will fail to "efficiently" create a proof for a random challenge with "significant" probability.

We will not discuss what exactly "sufficiently" and "significant" means here. Let us mention that for the application to longest-chain blockchains it is sufficient that for any $0 < \alpha < 1$, a prover storing $\alpha \cdot N$ bits will fail on a $1 - \alpha$ fraction of the challenges.

Concerning the "efficiently" in the statement above, note that a malicious prover can always create a valid proof even when storing almost nothing by simply running the initialization procedure after getting the challenge to create the plot S, and then computing the proof using the honest algorithm. Thus the best we can hope for is that a malicious prover needs $\Omega(\tilde{N})$ computational work (i.e., the cost of computing the plot) when only storing a sufficiently compressed plot S'.

The observation above also implies that a prover with N space can "pretend" to have $k \cdot N$ space by creating k different plots sequentially using $k \cdot \tilde{O}(N)$ work. Note that when attacking a blockchain, one would need to do the replotting afresh for every block, as the challenge for a block is only known once the previous block is computed. Thus, creating a proof using such a *replotting attack* is extremely expensive compared to creating proofs honestly, and this attack is presumably not an issue when blocks arrive sufficiently frequently. *The results of this paper show that this intuition is wrong.*

Longest-Chain Blockchains from Proofs of Space. To construct a longest-chain blockchain from PoSpace we can use Nakamoto consensus, but replace the PoW with PoSpace. There are various challenges one must address which we outline below.

Interactive Resource Initialization: In Bitcoin, a miner with some mining hardware can start participating in mining at any time. For PoSpace this is in general not the case as there's an initialization phase. The earliest PoSpace longest-chain proposal (which remained purely academic) is Spacemint [12], which uses the pebbling-based PoSpace from [9]. This PoSpace has an interactive initialization phase after which the verifier holds a type of commitment to the plot created by the prover. In Spacemint the chain plays the role of the verifier, and the commitment must be uploaded by a miner to the chain as a special transaction before they can start mining. The function-inversion-based PoSpace from [2] has a non-interactive initialization, i.e., the verifier is not involved at all, and thus it can be used like a PoW in Bitcoin. This PoSpace is used in the Chia network [8] blockchain.

Bock-Arrival Times: In Bitcoin, the arrival time of blocks can be controlled by setting the difficulty. Unlike PoW, PoSpace (also PoStake) are efficient proof systems, where once the resource (a plot or staked coins) is available, creating a proof is cheap and fast, so we need another mechanism. The easiest approach is to simply assume all parties have clocks and specify that blocks are supposed to arrive in specific time intervals, say once every minute. This is the approach taken by Spacemint [12] or Ouroboros [10], while in the Chia network [8] verifiable-delay functions (VDFs) are used to enforce some clock-time between the creation of blocks.

Costless Simulation/Grinding: The key difference between PoW and "efficient" proof systems like PoSpace or PoStake is the fact that producing proofs for $k > 1$ different challenges require k times as much of the resource in PoW, but it makes hardly a difference for PoSpace or Postake, as producing a proof is extremely cheap compared to acquiring the resource in the first place. This "costless simulation" property creates various issues in the blockchain setting. One such issue is grinding attacks. Consider a setting where an adversary can influence the challenge, a typical example is a blockchain like Bitcoin where the challenge for the next block depends on the current block, and the miner that creates the current block can e.g. choose which transactions to add. Such an attacker can "grind" through many different blocks until they find one that gives a challenge they like (say because with this challenge they can also win the next block).

A canonical countermeasure against grinding first proposed in Spacemint [12] is to "split" the chain in two. One chain only holds canonical values like proofs and is used for creating challenges, while another chain holds all the "grindable" values (transactions, time-stamps, etc.).

Costless Simulation/Double-Dipping: Even once grinding is no longer an issue, with costless simulation an adversary can still cheaply try to extend many of the past blocks, this way growing a tree rather than a chain. This strategy has been proven to virtually increase the adversarial resource by a factor of $e = 2.72$ [8]. An elegant countermeasure against this attack was proposed in [4], the basic idea is to only use the kth block for computing challenges, this "correlated randomness" technique decreases the advantage as k increases.

Costless Simulation/Bootstrapping: An adversary having some resource (space or stake) N can immediately create a long chain. Typically one would make up the time-stamps for this chain so it looks like a legit chain that has been created over a long period. In context of PoStake this is a well-known problem, while Spacemint [12] was the first instance this appeared in literature for PoSpace.

Replotting: In PoSpace a prover who has space of size N and gets a challenge c can pretend to have much more space by re-initializing the same space k times with different identifiers, this way creating k proofs pretending to have $k \cdot N$ bits of space. As replotting is fairly expensive, in a context like Blockchains, where challenges arrive frequently, it seems impossible (or at least not rational) to continuously replot. In this paper we show that this intuition is flawed; replotting attacks, in combination with bootstrapping, are used in our lower bound showing no PoSpace longest-chain blockchain is secure under resource variability. This was identified as a problem in [12].

1.1 Resource Variability

In this work, we prove that no PoSpace based longest-chain blockchain can be secure. Resource variability means that the amount of the resource dedicated to mining changes over time.

Bitcoin can be shown to be secure under resource variability as long as the honest parties hold more hashing power than a potential adversary at any point in time.

With PoStake the situation is more interesting. A PoStake based longest-chain protocol using the Bitcoin chain-selection rule where one picks the "heaviest" chain is not secure due to bootstrapping attacks.[1] On the positive side, the paper on Ouroboros Genesis [3] shows that a completely different chain selection rule does imply security even for PoStake based chains (with some additional assumptions, like assuming honest parties delete old keys). Their chain selection rule basically says that given two chains A and B one only looks at the weight of a short subchain starting at the point where A and B fork, and picks the chain whose subchain is heavier.

---

[1] More precisely, assume there's a point in time where a very high amount of coins is staked, say at the ith block the honest parties staked c_i^h coins, while the adversary $\mathcal{A}$ controls a $1/\phi < 1$ fraction of that, i.e., $c_i^a = c_i^h/\phi$. At this point, $\mathcal{A}$ bootstraps a private fork $b_i \hookleftarrow b_{i+1} \ldots \hookleftarrow b_{i+T}$ of some length T, each block having weight c_i^a. If for the next T blocks the amount staked by the honest parties is (on average) sufficiently smaller than c_i^a, the chain created by the honest parties will look lighter than the private fork of $\mathcal{A}$ at block $i + T$, and at this point $\mathcal{A}$ can release his private fork which will be adapted by all honest parties.

For PoSpace based chains the genesis chain selection rule is *not* secure, in fact, unlike the heaviest chain rule, the genesis rule is insecure even without resource variability (i.e. when we assume the space of the honest and adversarial parties is static). There is a simple attack exploiting bootstrapping and *replotting*, which we'll sketch below. Informally, the reason this attack does not apply in the PoStake or PoW settings is that there's no analog of replotting in PoStake, while in the PoW setting, we do not have bootstrapping.

1.2 Modelling a Longest-Chain PoSpace Blockchain

To model a PoSpace based longest-chain blockchain we will make a few idealizing assumptions. As our main result is a lower bound, this only makes our result stronger, concretely

Resource: We assume the chain grows by exactly one fresh block per time unit, and each block exactly reflects the amount of space that was used. In reality, a blockchain like Chia or Bitcoin (in the PoW setting) only approximately reflects this amount. One can get a very good approximation of the space used by looking at a sufficiently long subsequence (this idea is used when recalibrating the difficulty). Alternatively one could consider a blockchain design where each block contains the best k proofs for some $k > 1$. The larger k, the lower the variance and thus the better the approximation. With "block" we do not necessarily model a single block, but rather the appearance of a fresh challenge, and this challenge can be used for multiple blocks (e.g. in Chia we have a fresh challenge every 10 min, but as Chia uses the correlated randomness technique to prevent double dipping, this challenge is used for up to 64 actual blocks).

Attacks: While we model bootstrapping and replotting, we assume there is no grinding or double dipping. This is justified as we have techniques to mostly prevent griding and double dipping, while there's no simple way to prevent replotting, and to prevent bootstrapping we need additional primitives like VDFs.

Resource Variability: The adversary can control the change in resource, but is restricted to change it only within some $1+\varepsilon$ factor with each block, where $\varepsilon > 0$. The quantitative lower bound and the matching upper bound depend crucially on this parameter.

1.3 Approach for Lower Bound

To prove our lower bound we let an adversary specify two possible forks, A and B of a chain by specifying how the space of the honest parties changes over time in both cases. Now assume we show that (for given ranges of parameters) by exploiting bootstrapping and replotting it is possible to create such forks where B can be "faked" using a fraction (say half) of the space the honest parties had in A, and vice versa, i.e., A can be faked using half the space of B.

This means that an adversary in a hypothetical world where A is the honest chain could fake chain B and vice versa, thus, no matter which chain selection rule is used, in one of the two worlds the adversary's fork will succeed (say the chain rule prefers A over B, then in a "world" where B is the correct profile, the adversary can create a fork A which will win over B).

For our upper bound, we show that a particular chain selection rule is secure almost up to the parameters for which our lower bound applies.

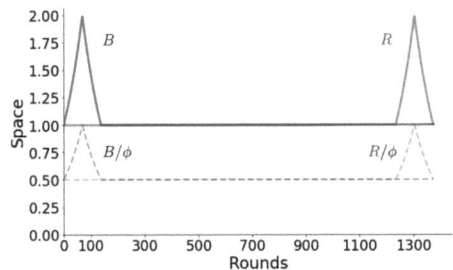

Fig. 1. Two profiles as used in our lower bound for $\varepsilon = 0.01, \phi = 2$ and $\rho = 4$.

1.4 Proof Sketch for Lower Bound

To prove our lower bound, we specify two profiles R and B reflecting the space honest users have, and then outline a strategy for how (by using bootstrapping and replotting) one can create profile R using a profile B/ϕ, where only a $1/\phi$ fraction of the space in B is available (i.e., the space the adversary has in world A) and vice versa. Moreover, in the profiles B and R the space is only allowed to change by a $1+\varepsilon$ per block. We will sketch the main idea using the profiles in Fig. 1. The profile R is plotted by the light red solid line and profile B is plotted by the light blue solid line. The solid lines show how much space honest parties control and the dashed lines of the respective colors show how much adversary controls for the respective solid space profile. The honest parties start at space 1, then we let the profile B increase to ϕ as fast as allowed (i.e., by a factor $1+\varepsilon$ per step), then we go back to 1 as fast as possible, and then there is a long flat part (the length will depend on our parameters). Profile R is the mirrored version of B.

Let us now sketch how the R (shown by light red solid line in Fig. 1) profile can be faked using a $1/\phi$ fraction of B (shown by solid light blue in Fig. 1). This is illustrated in the figures in Fig. 2(a) and 2(b). The adversary does nothing until block 70 when its space B/ϕ reaches its maximum.

At this point $B/\phi \geq 1$ and the adversary can bootstrap the flat part of R for 1233 steps as shown in the top left graph of Fig. 2. At this point, the adversary only needs to fake the "tent" in the last 140 steps of the R profile. For this, it uses replotting.

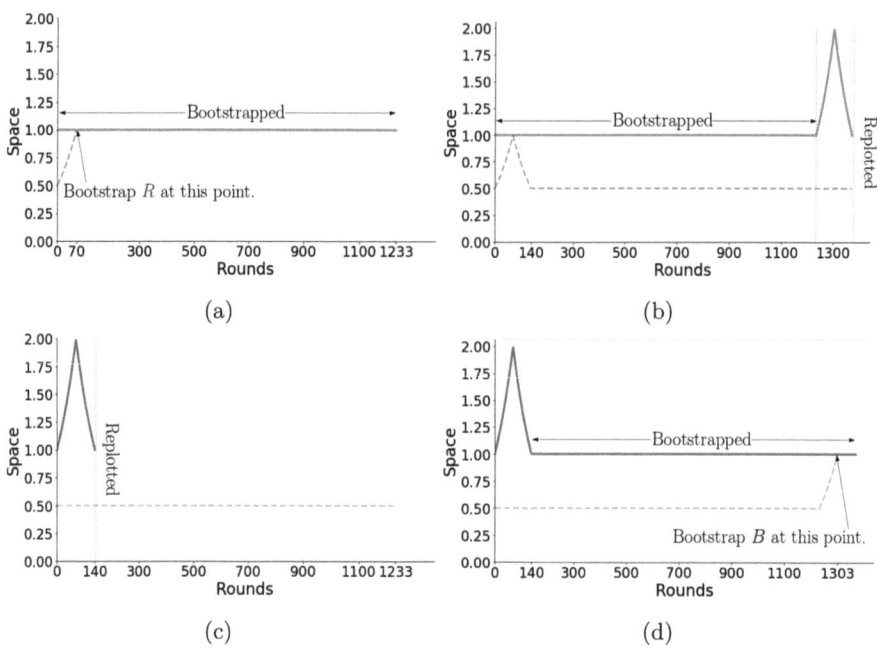

Fig. 2. The figs (a), (b) outline how the red profile from Fig. 1 is faked using the blue profile for parameters $\varepsilon = 0.01, \phi = 2$ and $\rho = 4$. In the first step, we use bootstrapping to create the flat part of the solid red profile (once the solid blue profile reaches the "peak", a $1/\phi$ fraction of the solid blue profile is as high as the flat part of the solid red profile, and thus it can be bootstrapped). Then we use replotting to create the "tent" of the solid red profile (as $\rho = 4$, i.e., replotting takes four steps, it is sufficient that the remaining area below the blue profile is as large as the area under the red "tent". The two figures (b), and (c) illustrate how the blue profile is faked using the red one. (Color figure online)

2 Model

2.1 Basic Notation for Chains

In the abstract model of the chain, we assume that time progresses in discrete steps $t_0, t_1, t_2, \ldots$. During the ith step $(t_{i-1}, t_i]$ the honest parties add a (super)block b_i. We'll always indicate the position of a block in the chain with a subscript like here.

The space available to the honest parties and the adversary at time i is denoted with $s_i^{\mathcal{H}}$ and $s_i^{\mathcal{A}}$, respectively. We assume that each block b_i perfectly reflects the amount of space that was used to create it, which is denoted by $s(b_i)$ (for the genesis block b_0 we set $s(b_0) = 1$).

We denote with $b_i \hookleftarrow b_{i+1}$ that b_{i+1} is extending (i.e., contains a hash of) block b_i. For a chain
$$\mathcal{C}_0^\ell = b_0 \hookleftarrow \ldots \hookleftarrow b_\ell,$$

we denote with $\mathcal{S}(\mathcal{C}_0^\ell)$ the *space-profile* of chain $\mathcal{C}_0^\ell$ which is defined as $(s(b_i))_{i=0}^\ell$, the sequence of space used to create each block b_i. We'll often use the notation $\mathcal{C}_i^j = b_i \hookleftarrow \ldots \hookleftarrow b_j$ to denote subchains.

> **Glossary:**
> $s_i^\mathcal{H} \in \mathbb{R}_{>0}$: The space available to the honest parties at step i.
> $s_i^\mathcal{A} \in \mathbb{R}_{>0}$: The space available to the adversary $\mathcal{A}$ at step i.
> $\phi > 1$: The honest/adversarial space ratio $\forall i : s_i^\mathcal{H}/s_i^\mathcal{A} = \phi$
> $\varepsilon > 0$: The rate of change of the space $\forall i : s_i^\mathcal{H} \cdot \frac{1}{1+\varepsilon} \leq s_{i+1}^\mathcal{H} \leq s_i^\mathcal{H} \cdot (1+\varepsilon)$
> $\rho \in \mathbb{N}_{\geq 2}^+$: Number of steps required for replotting

2.2 Chain Selection Rules

A chain selection rule takes as input two chains of the same length and outputs bit indicating the "winner"

$$\Lambda \colon \mathcal{C} \times \mathcal{C} \to \{0, 1\}$$

Consider two chains $\mathcal{C}_0^\ell, \tilde{\mathcal{C}}_0^\ell$

$$\mathcal{C}_0^\ell = b_0 \hookleftarrow \ldots \hookleftarrow b_\ell \qquad \tilde{\mathcal{C}}_0^\ell = \tilde{b}_0 \hookleftarrow \ldots \hookleftarrow \tilde{b}_\ell$$

The Bitcoin chain selection rule simply picks the chain of higher weight, adapted to our space setting this "highest weight rule" Λ_w is

$$\Lambda_w(\mathcal{C}_0^\ell, \tilde{\mathcal{C}}_0^{\ell'}) = 0 \iff \sum_{i=0}^\ell s(b_i) > \sum_{i=0}^{\ell'} s(\tilde{b}_i)$$

Note that the two chains may not always be of the same length but for our lower bound result we can assume without loss of generality that they are equal.

Most proposed and deployed longest-chain blockchains use a highest weight rule like this, in some cases augmented with checkpointing or finality gadgets that prevent miners from replacing their current chain with another chain that forks too far in the past even if it has a higher weight. An interesting exception is the rule suggested in Ouroboros Genesis [3] which, for some parameter $k \in \mathbb{N}$, chooses the winning chain based only on the weight of the k blocks following the forking point of the two chains. We'll denote the forking point (i.e., the index of the first blocks that differs) by λ as it looks like a forking chain, let

$$\lambda \stackrel{\text{def}}{=} \min\{i \; : \; b_i \neq \tilde{b}_i\}$$

The genesis chain selection rule, adapted to our setting, can now be defined as

$$\Lambda_{\text{genesis}}^k(\mathcal{C}_0^j, \tilde{\mathcal{C}}_0^j) = 0 \iff \sum_{i=\lambda+1}^{\min(j,\lambda+k)} s(b_i) > \sum_{i=\lambda+1}^{\min(j,\lambda+k)} s(\tilde{b}_i)$$

The Ouroboros genesis rule was introduced as a proof-of-stake based longest-chain blockchain that is secure under resource variability. In Lemma 2 we observe that for a proof-of-space based chain, this rule is not secure, and our impossibility result from Theorem 1 shows that in fact, no secure rule exists.

2.3 Adversarial Options

We consider an experiment where honest farmers create a chain (the "honest chain") following the rules, while an adversary tries to create a private fork that can at some point be released and will be chosen as the winner over the honest chain by the chain selection rule.

Before specifying the game let us describe the option the adversary has in this game. Concerning the honest chain, if the adversary doesn't contribute at all, the honest parties at the end of the jth step (i.e., time t_j) will have created and agreed on a chain

$$b_0 \hookleftarrow b_1 \hookleftarrow \ldots b_j \text{ where } \forall i \in [j] \ : \ s(b_i) = s_i^{\mathcal{H}}$$

The adversary could contribute to the honest chain, which would create a chain where

$$b_0 \hookleftarrow b_1 \hookleftarrow \ldots b_j \text{ where } \forall i \in [j] \ : \ s_i^{\mathcal{H}} \leq s(b_i) \leq s_i^{\mathcal{H}} + s_i^{\mathcal{A}}$$

Intuitively, for the chain selection rule, there shouldn't be any advantage for an adversary to contribute to the honest mining as it should only make the honest chain better, and this will be the case in our attack proving the lower bound.

While the honest parties will always create the ith block in the chain at time i, the adversary $\mathcal{A}$ who creates his private fork must not adhere to this, his only constraint is that his fork must have the same length as the honest chain when it is released.

In a PoSpace based chain, there are two ways in which $\mathcal{A}$ can exploit this, bootstrapping and replotting, outlined below.

Bootstrapping. If at time i $\mathcal{A}$ knows of a (prefix of a) chain $\mathcal{C}_0^j = b_0 \hookleftarrow \ldots \hookleftarrow b_j$, they can extend it immediately to a longer chain. The only constraint is that the space profile of the new blocks is at most the space available to $\mathcal{A}$, i.e., the new chain satisfies

$$\mathcal{C}_0^j \hookleftarrow b_{j+1} \hookleftarrow \ldots \hookleftarrow b_k \text{ where } \forall i > j \ : \ s(b_i) \leq s_i^{\mathcal{A}}$$

Replotting. The replotting parameter $\rho \in \mathbb{N}^+$ specifies how many time steps it takes $\mathcal{A}$ to replot its space. By replotting the space k times – which requires $k \cdot \rho$ steps – they can create a superblock that looks as if they had $k+1$ times the space they actually hold. Formally, using replotting, at time i, they can start extending a chain $\mathcal{C}_0^j$ with an extra block $\mathcal{C}_0^j \hookleftarrow b_{j+1}$ where $s(b_{j+1}) \le k \cdot s_i^{\mathcal{A}}$, and this will be done by time $i + k \cdot \rho$.[2]

2.4 The Forking Game

We now define the game in which an adversary $\mathcal{A}$ forks the honest chain with the goal of fooling the chain selection rule Λ to accept their fork as the winner.

Remark 1 (Probabilitsic vs. Deterministic). When analyzing actual blockchains there's always some probabilistic argument, e.g., in Bitcoin the probability that an adversary controlling $X\%$ (for $X < 50$) of the hashing power can double spend decreases exponentially with the confirmation time, but it is technically never 0. Our "game" on the other hand is completely deterministic (for given parameters and fork length $\mathcal{A}$ can win with probability 0 or 1) because we assume that each block perfectly reflects the amount of the resource (i.e., space) that was available to create it. While our analysis can be adapted to a probabilistic setting, we don't do so as it does not lead to any more interesting insight.

The game is parameterized by $\varepsilon > 1$, controlling how fast the amount of honest space changes; the changes are controlled by the adversary but allowed to change only by a factor $(1 + \varepsilon)$ per step.[3] The parameter $\phi > 1$ controls the amount of honest vs. adversarial space while $\rho \in \mathbb{N}^+$ is the number of steps required for replotting.

The $(\phi, \varepsilon, \rho, \Lambda)$-game is defined as follows:

1. – The round counter is set to $i := 0$ and the "replotting lock" $lock := 0$.
   – The honest and adversarial chains are initialized with the genesis block $\mathcal{C}_0^0 = \tilde{\mathcal{C}}_0^0 = b_0$ (where w.l.o.g. $s(b_0) = 1$).

---

[2] In an actual chain, the parameter $\rho = T_{replot}/T_{block}$ is defined by T_{replot}, the clock time required to replot, divided by T_{block}, the clock time in-between challenges (which is simply the block arrival time if the challenge for a block depends on the previous block like in Bitcoin). In practice, T_{block} should be large enough for a message to spread across the network, which is a few seconds. How large T_{replot} is, depends on many things, most importantly, on the type of PoSpace used. In the PoSpace based on function inversion [2] initialization is parallelizable, and thus T_{replot} can be in the order of seconds if the attacker has enough compute power (in particular, GPUs). As a consequence, ρ can only be assumed to be a small constant. In pebbling-based PoSpace [9], initialization is inherently sequential, and T_{replot} (and thus ρ) is much larger.

[3] Assuming that an adversary can precisely control the change of honest space is a strong assumption. But for our lower bound (i.e., an attack for any chain selection rule), arguably natural space profiles suffice. In particular, our attack works for any profile where the honest space stays below some bound s for a longer period of time, with the exception of a "peak" of height $\phi \cdot s$ in the middle (the more "narrow" this peak is, the shorter the overall period where the profile is below s can be). To break particular chain selection rules, even less demanding profiles are enough, e.g. for the rule used in Spacemint, it's sufficient that the profile at some point in time starts to decrease sufficiently much.

- $\mathcal{A}$ chooses its initial space $s_0^{\mathcal{A}}$ and we set the honest space to $s_0^{\mathcal{H}} := s_0^{\mathcal{A}} \cdot \phi$.
2. In each round
    - Increase the round counter $i := i+1$.
    - $\mathcal{A}$ chooses the space adjustment γ_i in the range $\frac{1}{(1+\varepsilon)} \leq \gamma_i \leq (1+\varepsilon)$ and the space is set to

    $$s_i^{\mathcal{A}} := s_{i-1}^{\mathcal{A}} \cdot \gamma_i \quad , \quad s_i^{\mathcal{H}} := s_i^{\mathcal{A}} \cdot \phi$$

    - The honest chain is extended

    $$\mathcal{C}_0^i := \mathcal{C}_0^{i-1} \hookleftarrow b_i$$

    with a block with space profile $s(b_i) = s_i^{\mathcal{H}}$
    - If $lock > 0$ (i.e., replotting is going on) set $lock := lock - 1$, otherwise $\mathcal{A}$ can extend its current chain $\tilde{\mathcal{C}}_0^j$ in two ways

    bootstrap: Extend $\tilde{\mathcal{C}}_0^j$ to

    $$\tilde{\mathcal{C}}_0^{j'} = \mathcal{C}_0^j \hookleftarrow \tilde{b}_{j+1} \hookleftarrow \ldots \hookleftarrow \tilde{b}_{j'}$$

    where $\forall t, j+1 \leq t \leq j' : s(\tilde{b}_t) \leq s_i^{\mathcal{A}}$.

    replot: $\mathcal{A}$ can call a replot request by which the last block $\tilde{b}_j$ is replaced with a block $\tilde{b}'_j$ with space profile

    $$s(\tilde{b}'_j) \leq s(\tilde{b}_j) + s_i^{\mathcal{A}}$$

    Set the replotting lock to $lock := \rho - 1$.
    - if $lock = 0$ (i.e., no replotting going on) and the length j of the adversarial chain $\tilde{\mathcal{B}}_0^j$ is at least $j \geq i$, then $\mathcal{A}$ can stop the game.

If the chain selection rule prefers the current (i block prefix of the) adversarial chain to the honest one, i.e.,

$$\Lambda(\mathcal{C}_0^i, \tilde{\mathcal{C}}_0^i) = 1$$

then we say the game is ℓ-winning for the $\mathcal{A}$, where ℓ denotes the length of the fork (i.e., length of chain minus the length of the common prefix)

$$\ell = i - \max\{k : b_k = \tilde{b}_k\}.$$

2.5 Forking Existing Rules

In this section, we'll observe that the forking game can be won against the highest weight Λ_w and the genesis $\Lambda_{\text{genesis}}^k$ chain selection rules that we discussed in Sect. 2.2. To break Λ_w one only requires bootstrapping (but no replotting) and resource variability, i.e. a $\varepsilon > 0$. For $\Lambda_{\text{genesis}}^k$ the ϕ can be 1.

Lemma 1. *The $(\phi, \varepsilon, \rho, \Lambda_w)$-game can be ℓ-won for $\ell = \left\lceil \frac{\phi}{\varepsilon} \right\rceil$*

Proof. To win $(\phi, \varepsilon, \rho, \Lambda_w)$-game, $\mathcal{A}$ simply bootstraps a long chain and then reduces the amount of space dynamically in order to make the honest chain have weight less than the adversarial chain. $\mathcal{A}$ never contributes to the honest chain.

Concretely, in each step $i > 0$ the adversary decreases the space by the maximum allowed amount $s_{i+1}^{\mathcal{H}} = \frac{1}{(1+\varepsilon)} \cdot s_i^{\mathcal{H}}$. At $i = 1$ $\mathcal{A}$ bootstraps

$$\tilde{\mathcal{C}}_0^j = \mathcal{C}_0^0 \hookleftarrow \tilde{b}_1 \hookleftarrow \tilde{b}_2 \hookleftarrow \cdots \hookleftarrow \tilde{b}_j$$

where $s(\tilde{b}_t) = s_0^{\mathcal{H}}/\phi = 1/\phi$ for all $t \in [1, j]$. After this adversary simply lets $\mathcal{C}_0$ catch up. The game ends on round j. This gives,

$$\text{Weight of } \mathcal{C}_0^j = \sum_{t=0}^{j} \left(\frac{1}{(1+\varepsilon)} \right)^t = \frac{1 - \frac{1}{(1+\varepsilon)^{j+1}}}{1 - \frac{1}{(1+\varepsilon)}} < \frac{1}{1 - \frac{1}{(1+\varepsilon)}}$$

while

$$\text{Weight of } \tilde{\mathcal{C}}_0^j = 1 + \frac{j}{\phi}$$

Thus when $j \geq \left\lceil \frac{1}{(1+\varepsilon)-1} \cdot \phi \right\rceil$ the weight of the adversarial chain is higher than the weight of the honest chain. Hence $\Lambda_w(\mathcal{C}_0^j, \tilde{\mathcal{C}}_0^j) = 1$. □

Lemma 2. *The $(\phi, \varepsilon, \rho, \Lambda_{\text{genesis}}^k)$-game can be ℓ-won for $\ell = \lceil \phi \rceil \cdot k \cdot \rho$*

Proof. To win $(\phi, \varepsilon, \rho, \Lambda_{\text{genesis}}^k)$-game, $\mathcal{A}$ simply replots many times to get an adversarial chain which in its k blocks after the fork has enough weight to be larger than the weight of the honest chain in the corresponding k blocks.

Concretely, the game runs till $l = \lceil \phi \rceil \cdot k \cdot \rho$. Throughout the game, $\mathcal{A}$ does not use the resource variability; $s_i^{\mathcal{H}}, s_i^{\mathcal{A}}$ remain constant at $1, \frac{1}{\phi}$ respectively. Further, $\mathcal{A}$ doesn't contribute to the honest chain. This produces

$$\mathcal{C}_0^j = b_0 \hookleftarrow b_1 \hookleftarrow \cdots \hookleftarrow b_l$$

such that $s(b_i) = 1 \forall i \in [0, l]$.
$\mathcal{A}$ does the following:

1. On round $i = 1$, it forks the chain to create

$$\tilde{\mathcal{C}}_0^1 = b_0 \hookleftarrow \tilde{b}_1$$

where $s(\tilde{b}_1) = \frac{1}{(1+\varepsilon)}$. Set $j := 1$
2. Starting with round $i = 1$ and ending on round l, it does the following steps:
   (a) If $(i-1) \mod \lceil \phi \rceil \cdot \rho = 0$ and $i > 1$, put $j := j + 1$ and add a new block $\tilde{b}_j$, with $s(\tilde{b}_j) = \frac{1}{\phi}$ to the adversarial chain

$$\tilde{\mathcal{C}}_0^j := b_0 \hookleftarrow \tilde{b}_1 \hookleftarrow \cdots \hookleftarrow \tilde{b}_{j-1} \hookleftarrow \tilde{b}_j.$$

Then $\mathcal{A}$ puts $lock := \rho - 1$ and starts replotting on $\tilde{b}_j$.

(b) For next $\lceil \phi \rceil \cdot \rho - 1$ rounds $\mathcal{A}$ repeats replotting on $\widetilde{b}_j$ to increase its space to $\lceil \phi \rceil / \phi \geq 1$. Go back to step (a).
3. In the last round $\mathcal{A}$ bootstraps the chain to create additional $l - k$ blocks to get a chain of length $l + 1$.

The adversarial chain now is

$$\widetilde{\mathcal{C}}_0^l = b_0 \hookleftarrow \widetilde{b}_1 \hookleftarrow \cdots \hookleftarrow \widetilde{b}_{l-1} \hookleftarrow \widetilde{b}_l.$$

Here $\lambda = 0$ as the chains $\mathcal{C}_0^l, \widetilde{\mathcal{C}}_0^l$ forked at the first block. Thus we get $\sum_{i=1}^{\min(l,k)} s(b_i) = k$ while $\sum_{i=1}^{\min(l,k)} s(\widetilde{b}_i) \geq k$. Hence $\Lambda_{\text{genesis}}^k(\mathcal{C}_0^j, \widetilde{\mathcal{C}}_0^j) = 1$ and $\mathcal{A}$ wins. □

2.6 Our Contribution

Having introduced the forking game, we can now state our main result that under resource variability, no PoSpace longest-chain blockchain is secure.

Theorem 1 (Impossibility Result). *For every chain selection rule Λ, there exists an adversary $\mathcal{A}$ that wins the $(\phi, \varepsilon, \rho, \Lambda)$-forking game in*

$$\ell = \left\lceil \rho \cdot \phi^2 \cdot (1 + \varepsilon) \cdot \left(\frac{(1+\varepsilon) - \frac{1}{\phi}}{\varepsilon} \right) \right\rceil$$

$$+ \left\lceil \rho \cdot \phi^2 \cdot \left(\frac{(1+\varepsilon) - \frac{1}{\phi}}{\varepsilon} \right) \right\rceil + 2 \cdot \left\lceil \frac{\log \phi}{\log(1+\varepsilon)} \right\rceil \text{ steps.}$$

We sketched the general proof idea in Sect. 1.4. The full proof can be found in Appendix A.2 of the full version of our paper [5]. While the expression in the theorem is somewhat complicated, typically we'd assume that ε is small, say < 0.1, while ϕ is bounded away from 1, say $\phi \geq 1.1$. In this case the bound becomes

$$\ell \leq O(\rho \cdot \phi^2 / \varepsilon).$$

Next, we prove that the fork length in the attack from Theorem 1 is an optimal attack up to a factor ϕ. We show this by providing a simple chain selection rule Λ_{tent} such that $\mathcal{A}$ can not win a $(\phi, 1 + \varepsilon, \rho, \Lambda_{\text{tent}})$ if the fork length is less than $\rho \left(\phi \cdot (1+\varepsilon) \cdot \frac{1 - \frac{1}{\phi}}{\varepsilon} - \left\lceil \frac{\log \phi}{\log(1+\varepsilon)} \right\rceil \right)$.

Before we give proof, we'll make a definition that will be useful. A $\Gamma = (\phi, x, y)$-tent, with $x \in \mathbb{N}$, $y \in \mathbb{R}_{>0}$, is the infinite sequence

$$\ldots, y_{x-1}, y_x, y_{x+1}, \ldots$$

where for $i > x$, $y_i = y_{i-1}/\phi$ and for $i < x$, $y_{2x-i} = y_{2x-i+1}/\phi$ (for an illustration see Fig. 1, where the first 36 steps of the dark blue curve are part of a $(\phi = 1.02, x = 18, y = 2)$ tent. We say y is the size of the tent $\Gamma = (\phi, x, y)$ and that tent $\Gamma = (\phi, x, y)$ is larger than tent $\Gamma' = (\phi, x', y')$ if $y > y'$.

Theorem 2 (The attack from Theorem 1 is tight up to ϕ). *For any $(\phi, 1 + \varepsilon, \rho)$ there's a chain selection rule Λ_{tent} for which no adversary can win the $(\phi, 1 + \varepsilon, \rho, \Lambda_{\text{tent}})$ forking game in less than*

$$\rho \left(\phi \cdot (1 + \varepsilon) \cdot \frac{1 - \frac{1}{\phi}}{\varepsilon} - \left\lceil \frac{\log \phi}{\log(1 + \varepsilon)} \right\rceil \right) \text{ steps}$$

The full proof can be found in Appendix A.2 of the full version of our paper [5].

3 Discussion and Open Problem

In this paper, we showed that there's no chain selection rule that guarantees security (against double spending) for a permissionless longest-chain blockchain based on proofs of space assuming honest parties always hold more space than an adversary.

Overcoming Our No-Go Result. Recall that our attacker can replot space and bootstrap the chain. Two existing PoSpace based chains, Chia and Filecoin, avoid our impossibility in different ways. Chia prevents bootstrapping by additionally using proofs of time, while Filecoin avoids replotting by using a BFT (rather than longest-chain) type protocol as we'll elaborate below.

Chia [8] combines proofs of space with "proofs of time", where the latter are instantiated with verifiable delay functions [6]. One can think of (a simplified version of) Chia as simply alternating PoSpace with VDFs, where the challenge for the next VDF (PoSpace) is computed from the previous PoSpace (VDF output). Bootstrapping such a chain is not possible as the main security property of a VDF requires that computing its output requires time.

In Filecoin parties must register their space before it can be used for mining. Moreover, parties must constantly compute and publish proofs for their registered space. Blocks are then created by the parties who registered space in a BFT-type protocol. Informally, this prevents replotting as only registered space can be used, and registering more space than one actually controls is not possible as one must constantly prove that space is available. Using the classification from [11], one can see our results as being in the fully permissionless setting (where the protocol has no knowledge about current participation), while Filecoin works in a quasi-permissionless setting (where parties must be known to the protocol and be always available).

A question one can ask is whether simply committing to space without periodic checks would overcome our impossibility result. This would correspond to *dynamic availability* setting in [11]. The answer is no: an adversary can simply plot and commit to many different proofs of space in the honest chain and then later replot them when launching an attack. Thus our result precludes PoSpace based Nakamoto like longest chain blockchain in both fully permissionless and dynamic availability setting.

Open Problems. Our upper and lower bounds are separated by a gap ϕ, we believe this gap can be closed by coming up with a more sophisticated chain selection rule for Theorem 2.

References

1. The chia network blockchain (2019). https://docs.chia.net/green-paper-abstract/
2. Abusalah, H., Alwen, J., Cohen, B., Khilko, D., Pietrzak, K., Reyzin, L.: Beyond Hellman's time-memory trade-offs with applications to proofs of space. In: Takagi, T., Peyrin, T. (eds.) ASIACRYPT 2017. LNCS, vol. 10625, pp. 357–379. Springer, Cham (2017). https://doi.org/10.1007/978-3-319-70697-9_13
3. Badertscher, C., Gazi, P., Kiayias, A., Russell, A., Zikas, V.: Ouroboros genesis: composable proof-of-stake blockchains with dynamic availability. In: Lie, D., Mannan, M., Backes, M., Wang, X. (eds.) Proceedings of the 2018 ACM SIGSAC Conference on Computer and Communications Security, CCS 2018, Toronto, ON, Canada, 15–19 October 2018, pp. 913–930. ACM (2018). https://doi.org/10.1145/3243734.3243848
4. Bagaria, V.K., et al.: Proof-of-stake longest chain protocols: security vs predictability. In: Soares, J.M., Song, D., Vukolic, M. (eds.) Proceedings of the 2022 ACM Workshop on Developments in Consensus, ConsensusDay 2022, Los Angeles, CA, USA, 7 November 2022, pp. 29–42. ACM (2022). https://doi.org/10.1145/3560829.3563559
5. Baig, M.A., Pietrzak, K.: On the (in)security of proofs-of-space based longest-chain blockchains (2025). https://arxiv.org/abs/2505.14891
6. Boneh, D., Bonneau, J., Bünz, B., Fisch, B.: Verifiable delay functions. In: Shacham, H., Boldyreva, A. (eds.) CRYPTO 2018. LNCS, vol. 10991, pp. 757–788. Springer, Cham (2018). https://doi.org/10.1007/978-3-319-96884-1_25
7. Chaum, D.: Blind signatures for untraceable payments. In: Chaum, D., Rivest, R.L., Sherman, A.T. (eds.) Advances in Cryptology, pp. 199–203. Springer, Boston, MA (1983). https://doi.org/10.1007/978-1-4757-0602-4_18
8. Cohen, B., Pietrzak, K.: The chia network blockchain (2019). https://docs.chia.net/files/Precursor-ChiaGreenPaper.pdf, this is an early proposal and differs significantly from the implemented version [1]
9. Dziembowski, S., Faust, S., Kolmogorov, V., Pietrzak, K.: Proofs of space. In: Gennaro, R., Robshaw, M. (eds.) CRYPTO 2015. LNCS, vol. 9216, pp. 585–605. Springer, Heidelberg (2015). https://doi.org/10.1007/978-3-662-48000-7_29
10. Kiayias, A., Russell, A., David, B., Oliynykov, R.: Ouroboros: a provably secure proof-of-stake blockchain protocol. In: Katz, J., Shacham, H. (eds.) CRYPTO 2017. LNCS, vol. 10401, pp. 357–388. Springer, Cham (2017). https://doi.org/10.1007/978-3-319-63688-7_12
11. Lewis-Pye, A., Roughgarden, T.: Permissionless consensus (2024). https://arxiv.org/abs/2304.14701
12. Park, S., Kwon, A., Fuchsbauer, G., Gaži, P., Alwen, J., Pietrzak, K.: SpaceMint: a cryptocurrency based on proofs of space. In: Meiklejohn, S., Sako, K. (eds.) FC 2018. LNCS, vol. 10957, pp. 480–499. Springer, Heidelberg (2018). https://doi.org/10.1007/978-3-662-58387-6_26
13. Wood, G.: Ethereum: a secure decentralised generalised transaction ledger

Constellation: Peer-to-Peer Overlays for Federated Byzantine Agreement Systems

Giuliano Losa[1], Yifan Mao[2], Shaileshh Bojja Venkatakrishnan[2], and Yunqi Zhang[2]

[1] Stellar Development Foundation, San Francisco, USA
giuliano@stellar.org
[2] The Ohio State University, Columbus, USA
{mao.360,bojjavenkatakrishnan.2,zhang.8678}@osu.edu

Abstract. A federated Byzantine agreement (FBA) system is a permissionless system in which each participant declares unilateral agreement requirements that collectively determine a set of quorums. The resulting quorums can be used in a consensus algorithm (such as the Stellar Consensus Protocol) to build a permissionless blockchain system without resorting to proof-of-work or proof-of-stake. Like most permissionless systems, FBA systems must rely on a secure peer-to-peer overlay network for communication between network nodes, yet this topic has received little attention in the FBA setting.

In this paper, we address the problem of connecting the nodes in an FBA system to each other in order to construct an overlay topology that securely and efficiently supports gossip protocols, a popular class of protocols for disseminating data across blockchain overlays. We present Constellation, an algorithm that computes an overlay topology whose fault tolerance matches that of the FBA quorum system. Constellation minimizes node degree, which reduces redundant traffic in gossip protocols, and it ensures a maximum diameter of 2, which is crucial for achieving low-latency consensus.

Keywords: Overlay Network · Federated Byzantine Agreement · Blockchain

1 Introduction

A federated Byzantine agreement system (FBA system, or FBAS) [25,30] is an open, permissionless distributed system in which nodes intend to reach agreement—e.g., on the next block of a blockchain—subject to *agreement requirements* that each node is free to choose for itself. Roughly speaking, each node declares its agreement requirements in the form of a set of so-called *quorum slices*, each of which is a set of other nodes, with the intent to never agree to anything unless at least one of its quorum slices unanimously agrees to it. For a set of nodes to make progress on its own, it must therefore contain at least one slice of each of its members. Such sets are called *quorums*. Thus, an FBAS gives rise to a set of quorums, which can be used in a voting-based Byzantine Fault-Tolerant (BFT) consensus algorithm such as the Stellar Consensus Protocol [30].

A fundamental challenge in an FBA system, and most blockchain systems, is the design of an efficient and fault-tolerant peer-to-peer (p2p) overlay network. In a p2p overlay, nodes establish connections with each other through the Internet, and those connections are then used by a protocol—often a gossip protocol [13, 20]—to disseminate information throughout the system. The characteristics of the p2p overlay, e.g., its diameter and degree distribution, heavily impact overall system performance; moreover, failure to keep the overlay connected may lead to a loss of liveness for parts of or for the entire system. While several works study consensus or reliable broadcast protocols for FBA systems [7,15,16,25,26,30] or related models [7,10,21], the problem of building an efficient p2p overlay for the FBA model has received little attention.

In practice, a popular approach to constructing p2p overlays is for each node to connect to a random sample of the peers it knows about. The Stellar network [3]—currently the largest deployed FBA system—uses such a random approach. While this is simple to implement and robust in benign scenarios, it is hard to give any guarantees when under Byzantine or Sybil attacks.

In an FBA system, we would like the overlay to remain functional despite failures as long as the failures are not severe enough to preclude meeting the agreement requirements of the nodes that remain well-behaved. Otherwise, the p2p overlay would cripple the liveness guarantees of the BFT consensus algorithm running on top. A random overlay cannot guarantee this property unless nodes connect to an excessive number of peers, which could severely impact system performance. For example, as of January 3rd, 2025, the subgraph formed by the top-tier nodes[1] of the Stellar network has an average degree of 4.3; unfortunately, this allows failure scenarios in which the well-behaved nodes form a quorum, and thus they should be able to make progress, but progress is impossible because the overlay becomes disconnected.

In this work, we investigate how to build efficient p2p overlay networks for FBA systems. We refer to the structure of a p2p overlay, seen as a graph, as its topology. We consider two key requirements.

First, we require the set of all well-behaved nodes to remain connected to each other as long as they form a quorum. In this case, we say that the overlay is *FBA-resilient*. A naïve approach is for a node to try to connect with all the nodes appearing in its quorum slices, but this creates too many connections. A better approach might be for a node to choose neighbors such that there is a connection to at least one node from each of its quorum slices; under the assumption that the node belongs to at least one fully well-behaved quorum—which we can make, as the node would otherwise not be able to reach agreement anyway—this ensures at least one available, well-behaved neighbor. However,

---
[1] See Sect. 2.2 for a discussion of top-tier nodes.

we aim for the stronger requirement of having a path (of well-behaved nodes) between any two well-behaved nodes.

Second, we require the overlay to have as low a diameter and node degrees as possible. A low diameter ensures messages published in the network are received by the nodes quickly, which is crucial for latency-sensitive messages like votes in a consensus algorithm. Similarly, a low node degree reduces bandwidth utilization, which in turn minimizes congestion and its associated delays. While the choice of gossip protocols (e.g., pull-based or eager push) used for message dissemination does impact efficiency, the p2p topology is a more fundamental parameter on which gossip protocol performance depends. In this work, we consider only the problem of topology optimization and not gossip-protocol design.

To build overlays satisfying the two requirements above, we present Constellation, a decentralized blockchain-assisted topology-construction algorithm for computing an overlay with a low diameter and low average node degree. Importantly, Constellation exploits the agreement requirements of nodes for neighbor selection, resulting in an overlay that is resilient to failures and malicious attacks. In symmetric cases, we show that the overlay remains connected provided well-behaved nodes form a quorum; in non-symmetric cases, simulation shows that this is likely to hold too.

Similarly to how proof-of-stake systems track stakers and their stake on chain, Constellation tracks nodes and their agreement requirements on chain. Given global agreement on the nodes' agreement requirements, as provided by the blockchain, each node locally applies the Constellation overlay-building algorithm, which is deterministic, and obtains a graph that determines which nodes it should connect to or accept connections from. However, even with global knowledge of the agreement requirements of each node, finding an optimal overlay topology that satisfies our requirements is a hard combinatorial problem.

To tractably compute an overlay, Constellation first conservatively approximates each node's quorum slices using a family of sets that can be described succinctly using simple thresholds (in practice, we expect quorum slices to be specified in this form already, as is the case in the Stellar network). Then, to avoid combinatorial explosion, Constellation searches for an optimal overlay that follows a predefined template. The template assigns nodes to clusters whose membership depends on the threshold parameters of their members; moreover, it creates inter-node edges that result in high interconnection within clusters and more sparse connections across clusters. If all nodes have the same threshold, the connectivity between any two clusters forms a bipartite matching, with each cluster being a partite.

The graphs obtained by Constellation bear resemblance to the Cartesian product of complete graphs, whose strong connectivity properties have been extensively studied in the literature [18,22,27,31,37]. In fact, in the main technical result of the paper, we leverage these existing results on the connectivity of Cartesian products of graphs to prove that, when all nodes have the same threshold, Constellation produces an FBA-resilient overlay. Moreover, the diameter of a Constellation overlay is 2 by construction, and we show that it remains below 3 even under a significant fraction of failures. Finally, we also show that the average node degree in Constellation is close to optimal.

We have evaluated Constellation using simulations and on a real-world testbed running stellar-core [2], a production implementation of a blockchain over an FBA system. Our results show that overlays generated by Constellation achieve higher transaction throughput compared to random overlays while also guaranteeing connectivity as long as the FBA agreement requirements can be met.

Our work is the first to propose a structured p2p overlay for blockchains that is secure under the same failure assumptions as the blockchain's consensus protocol. In a proof-of-stake setting, Coretti et al. [12] as well as Liu-Zhang et al. [23,24] propose to construct random graph overlays in which each node's degree is proportional to the amount of stake it has. It is unclear how such a construction can be adapted to an FBA system with subjective agreement requirements. Overlays using a distributed hash table (DHT; e.g., KadCast [35], which uses the Kademlia DHT [29]) are common, but they ignore the trust preferences of nodes.

Software and instructions to reproduce our evaluation results (both simulations and testbed experiments) are available online [4].

2 Background: Federated Byzantine Agreement Systems

In this paper we are interested in overlays for federated Byzantine agreement systems (FBAS) [25,30], as most prominently used in the Stellar network [3]. In this section, we briefly cover both theoretical and practical aspects of FBA systems that are necessary to understand the rest of the paper.

2.1 Federated Byzantine Agreement in Theory

An FBA system consists of a set of nodes that attempt to reach agreement on some value (typically, the next block in a blockchain). Nodes communicate using an underlying network such as the Internet. Each node is either well-behaved or Byzantine. Well-behaved nodes follow their assigned algorithm and remain available (i.e., responsive); Byzantine nodes may behave arbitrarily, modeling nodes controlled by an attacker.

Each node declares agreement requirements by specifying a collection of sets of nodes called *quorum slices*, with the intent not to agree to anything unless at least one of its quorum slices unanimously agrees to it. Thus, for a set of nodes Q to reach agreement even when the rest of the system is unavailable, Q must satisfy the following property: for every node n in Q, n must have a quorum slice that is a subset of Q. In other words, Q must satisfy the agreement requirements of all its members. We call such sets quorums:

Definition 1 (Quorum). *A set Q is a quorum when every node in Q has a quorum slice that is a subset of Q.*

Under the assumption that all quorums suitably intersect (see [25,26,30] for precise definitions) and that the set of well-behaved nodes forms a quorum, consensus algorithms like the Stellar Consensus Protocol (SCP) [25,30] or the algorithm of [26] solve consensus under eventual synchrony[2].

In this work, given an FBA system, our goal is to create an overlay that guarantees connectivity and diameter 2 in all situations where a consensus algorithm can be expected to make progress, i.e., under the assumption that the set of well-behaved nodes forms a quorum.

2.2 Federated Byzantine Agreement in Practice

We expect nodes in a real FBAS to belong to known, real-world organizations that run them, with a single operator per organization, and for most node operators to configure their node's quorum slices using a simple threshold of organizations. We formalize this assumption in Definition 2 with the notion of a regular FBAS, which we illustrate in Example 1.

Definition 2 (Regular FBAS). *A regular FBAS consists of a set of organizations $\mathcal{O}$, each running disjoint sets of nodes. For each organization $O \in \mathcal{O}$, let $n(O)$ be the set of nodes run by organization O, and let $N = \cup_{O \in \mathcal{O}} n(O)$ be the set of all nodes. We assume that the operator of the nodes belonging to an organization O chooses a set of organizations $\mathcal{T}_O \subseteq \mathcal{O}$ to trust, called O's universe, and an integer threshold $0 < t_O \leq |\mathcal{T}_O|$. This determines the quorum slices of every node $n \in n(O)$ as follows: n's quorum slices are the sets obtained by (a) picking t_O organizations among $\mathcal{T}_O$ and (b) for each picked organization O', picking a strict majority of O''s nodes.*

Example 1. Suppose that there are 4 organizations O_i, for i from 1 to 4, each running 3 nodes $n(O_i) = \{n_i^a, n_i^b, n_i^c\}$, and suppose that for all i, $\mathcal{T}_{O_i} = \{O_1, O_2, O_3, O_4\}$ and $t_{O_i} = 3$. Then each node has a set of quorum slices obtained by picking 3 organizations out of the four and then picking 2 nodes out of 3 (i.e., a strict majority) from each picked organization. For instance, $\{n_1^a, n_1^b, n_2^b, n_2^c, n_4^a, n_4^c\}$ is a quorum slice, but $\{n_1^a, n_2^b, n_2^c, n_3^a, n_3^b, n_3^c\}$ is not. Note that in this example, quorum slices and minimal quorums coincide, but this is not always the case.

In practice, we observe that most nodes in the Stellar network follow the structure above. The universe $\mathcal{T}_O$ and threshold t_O associated with an organization O correspond to what is called a *quorum set*[3] in Stellar's terminology[4].

Finally, when all organizations in a regular FBAS have the same universe, we say that the FBAS is a *single-universe* regular FBAS, and if, additionally, all organizations have the same threshold, we say that the FBAS is *symmetric*.

---
[2] Technically, to ensure termination, SCP additionally assumes that Byzantine nodes eventually stop interfering.
[3] Technically, Stellar's quorum sets can have a more refined structure, but it is rarely used in practice.
[4] The name "quorum set" used by Stellar is unfortunate, as a "quorum set" is not a set of quorums but instead encodes a set of quorum slices.

Top-Tier and Second-Tier Nodes. In practice in the Stellar network, we observe that a small subset of the nodes can be classified as top-tier nodes, while we call other nodes second-tier nodes. Top-tier nodes only require agreement from other top-tier nodes, while second-tier nodes require agreement from the top-tier nodes and sometimes other second-tier nodes.

The top-tier nodes in the Stellar network are nodes run by organizations such as the Stellar Development Foundation, the infrastructure provider Blockdaemon, or the investment firm Franklin Templeton, which are well-known in the Stellar community. As of January 3rd, 2025, there were 23 top-tier nodes belonging to 7 organizations and 458 second-tier nodes[5]. Due to how communities in the real world often coalesce around a few key players, we expect that most FBA systems in practice will have a similar structure.

The fact that the large number of second-tier nodes require agreement from the top-tier nodes but not vice versa poses a problem from the point of view of building an overlay that guarantees nodes can communicate with those they require agreement from. This is because the small top tier would need to be densely connected to the much larger rest of the network, meaning that top-tier nodes would have a very large degree. Unfortunately, this is intrinsic to our requirements, and there is no way around this problem. Worse, in an open system like the Stellar network, nothing can prevent a Sybil adversary from creating arbitrarily many second-tier nodes to further overload the top-tier nodes.

Faced with this conundrum, we suggest using a best-effort random-overlay approach to connect second-tier nodes to each other and to top-tier nodes, and to give resilience guarantees only to top-tier nodes. In the rest of the paper, we follow this approach, and the novel aspects of our work concern building overlays connecting the top-tier nodes together. We note that Liu-Zhang et al. face a similar issue in the context of proof-of-stake [23, Section 5]. They observe that nodes may exist in the system that have no stake (in some sense, those cannot be trusted because they have nothing at stake) but that nevertheless need to be connected to the overlay because legitimate users depend on them. They conclude that no guarantees can be given to those nodes without additional assumptions limiting Sybil attacks.

3 Model and Problem Formulation

We consider a regular FBAS $\mathcal{F}$ (Definition 2) consisting of a set of nodes N, also called validators, and we define the set of top-tier nodes TT as the union of all minimal quorums of the FBAS. The set of top-tier nodes also determines the set of top-tier organizations TO, where an organization is top tier when all its nodes are top-tier nodes. When an organization or node is not top tier, we

---

[5] This data was obtained using surveying functionality built into stellar-core [2] (Stellar's blockchain implementation), and communicated to the authors privately by the Stellar Development Foundation. Note that https://stellarbeat.io reports fewer than 200 nodes as of January 2025, and this is because many nodes do not accept inbound overlay connections from its crawler.

say it is second tier (moreover, note that in a regular FBAS, either all nodes of an organization are top tier or none are). We further assume that no second-tier organization appears in the universe of any top-tier organization. This means that the top tier TT forms a regular FBAS on its own.

We say that the top tier TT tolerates the failure of a set of nodes B when $TT \setminus B$ is a quorum (equivalently, every top-tier node not in B has a quorum slice disjoint from B). We are concerned with computing an *FBA-resilient overlay* over TT, which is a graph whose nodes are the members of TT and that satisfies the following definition.

Definition 3 (FBA-Resilient Overlay). *We say that an overlay over a set of nodes is* FBA-resilient *when, if we remove from the graph a set of nodes B such that the FBAS tolerates the failure of B, the graph remains connected.*

In other words, if Q is a quorum, then removing every edge with an endpoint not in Q should not disconnect the overlay graph.

The problem that we address with Constellation is to connect the top-tier nodes to form an overlay that (a) is FBA-resilient, (b) minimizes the average and maximum degree of the nodes, and (c) has a diameter of at most 2. Moreover, when taking the union with a random overlay connecting the second-tier nodes (e.g., an Erdős–Rényi graph spanning all the nodes), the combined overlay must allow a consensus algorithm to achieve high performance in practice.

In the next section, we present the Constellation algorithm, which, given a regular FBAS, computes an efficient and FBA-resilient overlay. Then, in Sect. 5, we discuss how to deploy this algorithm to obtain a practical solution to create and maintain an overlay connecting the nodes of a FBA system implementing a blockchain, like the Stellar network.

4 The Constellation Algorithm

The Constellation algorithm takes a regular FBAS (Definition 2) as input and computes an overlay graph over the FBAS nodes. The first step in the Constellation algorithm is to conservatively simplify the FBAS by setting $T_O = \mathcal{O}$ for each organization O, without modifying t_O, thereby obtaining a single-universe, regular FBAS. Note that this transformation ensures that if the well-behaved nodes form a quorum in the original FBAS $\mathcal{F}_1$, they also form a quorum in the new FBAS $\mathcal{F}_2$. Consequently, if an overlay is FBA-resilient in $\mathcal{F}_2$, then it is also FBA-resilient in $\mathcal{F}_1$.

Next, the Constellation algorithm determines a graph over the nodes of the (now single-universe) FBAS by instantiating the *Constellation Topology Template*. To instantiate the template, the Constellation algorithm performs a brute-force search over the template parameters to find an instantiation that minimizes the average degree of the resulting overlay.

In the rest of this section, we present the Constellation Topology Template, discuss how to instantiate it for a given FBAS, and present key properties that hold for a symmetric FBAS. Proofs are available in the full version of the paper.

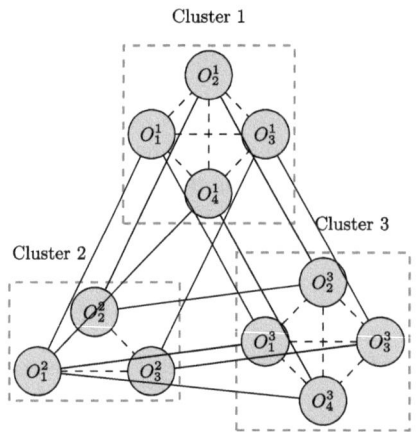
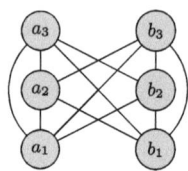

(b) Node-level intra-cluster connections (dotted edges) between two organizations A and B with three nodes each (a_1, a_2, and a_3 and b_1, b_2, and b_3, respectively).

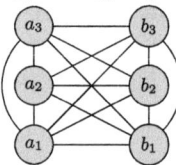

(a) Overlay construction for a symmetric system of 11 organizations with a threshold of $\lceil 2 \cdot 11/3 \rceil = 8$. Dotted and solid edges correspond to the two inter-organization connection patterns depicted in Figures 1b and 1c, respectively.

(c) Node-level inter-cluster connections (solid edges) between two organizations A and B with three nodes each (a_1, a_2, and a_3 and b_1, b_2, and b_3, respectively)

Fig. 1. Example of the cluster-based network structure produced by Constellation. The two types of intra-organization edges (dotted and solid) appearing on Fig. 1a are realized at the node level as shown on Figs. 1b and 1c.

4.1 The Constellation Topology Template

Creating Hyperedges. Let $G(N, E)$ denote the undirected graph of the overlay topology generated by Constellation. The high-level structure of G can be understood as a hypergraph[6] H defined on the set of organizations $\mathcal{O}$. For every two organizations O_1, O_2, we say there is a hyperedge (O_1, O_2) between O_1 and O_2 if there are edges between nodes in O_1 and O_2 in G. Conversely, there is no hyperedge between O_1 and O_2 if none of the nodes in O_1 are connected to any nodes in O_2 in G.

Constellation partitions the set of organizations $\mathcal{O}$ into a set of clusters $\mathcal{C}_1, \ldots, \mathcal{C}_k$ where $k > 0$ is a parameter. Within each cluster $\mathcal{C}_i$, the organizations form a complete hypergraph, i.e., $(O_1, O_2) \in H$ for all $O_1, O_2 \in \mathcal{C}_i$. Additionally, each organization $O \in \mathcal{C}_i$ has a hyperedge to at least one organization in each of the other clusters $\mathcal{C}_j, j \neq i, j \in \{1, \ldots, k\}$. This last requirement can be satisfied in many ways. However, to avoid excessive hyperedges on a single organization, hyperedges between two clusters $\mathcal{C}_i, \mathcal{C}_j$ are distributed evenly (as much as possible) among the constituent organizations: If $\{O_1, \ldots, O_{|\mathcal{C}_i|}\}$ and $\{O'_1, \ldots, O'_{|\mathcal{C}_j|}\}$

---

[6] By hypergraph we simply mean a graph whose vertices are organizations and not nodes.

are the organizations in $\mathcal{C}_i$ and $\mathcal{C}_j$ respectively, we have $(O_l, O'_{l \bmod |\mathcal{C}_j|}) \in H$ for all $l \in \{1, \ldots, |\mathcal{C}_i|\}$ and $(O_{l \bmod |\mathcal{C}_i|}, O'_l) \in H$ for all $l \in \{1, \ldots, |\mathcal{C}_j|\}$.

Note that the hypergraph is parameterized by the number of clusters k and the assignment of organizations to clusters. These are the parameters we will later optimize. Figure 1a shows an example of a Constellation hypergraph when there are 11 organizations and 3 clusters.

From Hyperedges to Node-Level Edges. Consider any two organizations O_1 and O_2 that belong to the same cluster. To realize the hyperedge connecting them, we construct a bipartite graph between O_1 and O_2 such that (1) each validator $v \in O_i$ is connected to at least half of the validators in $O_j, j \neq i, j \in \{1, 2\}$, and (2) the degrees of the nodes in each partite are evenly distributed (as much as possible). Letting $\{v_1, \ldots, v_{|O_1|}\}$ and $\{v'_1, \ldots, v'_{|O_2|}\}$ be the validators in O_1 and O_2, respectively, we include edges $(v_i, v'_{i \bmod |O_2|}), (v_i, v'_{i+1 \bmod |O_2|}), \ldots, (v_i, v'_{i+\lfloor |O_2|/2 \rfloor \bmod |O_2|})$ in the bipartite graph for all $i \in \{1, \ldots, |O_1|\}$. Similarly, we include edges $(v_{i \bmod |O_1|}, v'_i), (v_{i-1 \bmod |O_1|}, v'_i), \ldots, (v_{i-\lfloor |O_1|/2 \rfloor \bmod |O_1|}, v'_i)$ in the bipartite graph. For organizations O_1, O_2 that belong to different clusters but have a hyperedge between them, we let each validator $v \in O_i$ have an edge to all the validators in $O_j, j \neq i, j \in \{1, 2\}$. Each validator in an organization has an edge to all other validators in the organization. Figures 1b and 1c illustrate the connections between two organizations when they belong to the same cluster and different clusters, respectively.

Our first result is that, regardless of how the topology parameters are selected, the graph we obtain has a diameter of 2:

Proposition 1. *Regardless of how organizations are partitioned into clusters, the graph $G(N, E)$ constructed by Constellation has a diameter of 2.*

4.2 Ensuring Connectivity and Low Diameter Under Failures

Having defined the Constellation Topology Template in the previous section, we now show how to instantiate it for a given FBAS. Our goal is to find a number of clusters k and an assignment of organizations to clusters (i.e., a partition of the organizations) such that the resulting overlay topology minimizes the number of edges, is FBA-resilient (Definition 3), and has a low diameter even under failures.

We propose partitioning the organizations to ensure that, in the resulting overlay, each node has at least one connection to each of its quorum slices. Despite this seemingly weak (local) requirement, we show in the rest of this section that, for a symmetric FBAS (i.e., when all organizations have the same universe and threshold), the obtained overlay is FBA-resilient (i.e., it guarantees global connectivity under maximal failures tolerated by the FBAS). Moreover, we show that (again, for a symmetric FBAS) the resulting overlay has near-optimal average degree and maintains a diameter of 3 even under many failures.

Recall that Constellation first conservatively approximates the regular FBAS formed by the top-tier nodes to a single-universe, regular FBAS, where each validator $v \in N$ has the universe $\mathcal{T}_v = \mathcal{O}$ (the set of all top-tier organizations) and a threshold $t_v = t_O$, where O is v's organization, with $0 < t_O \leq |\mathcal{O}|$.

For an organization $O \in \mathcal{O}$ with a threshold of t_O, we require O to be part of at least $|\mathcal{O}| - t_O + 1$ hyperedges. This ensures O has a hyperedge to at least one available organization, even when $|\mathcal{O}| - t_O$ organizations are unavailable. Similarly, whenever $(O, O') \in H$ for any organization $O' \in \mathcal{O}$, we require validators $v \in O$ to form edges with at least half of the validators in O'. This ensures v has an edge to at least one available validator within each available organization.

A key challenge is computing the total number of clusters and assignments of organizations to those clusters such that the hypergraph degree requirements described above are satisfied without excessively increasing the degree. For a symmetric FBAS, we can derive an analytic formula for the optimal number of clusters k by solving for the optimal k satisfying $k + \frac{|\mathcal{O}|}{k} - 1 \geq |\mathcal{O}| - t + 1$ (where $\mathcal{O}$ is the universe of the symmetric FBAS and t the threshold). The left-hand side of inequality above counts the number of hyperedges an organization has outside its cluster $(k-1)$ and within its cluster $(|\mathcal{O}|/k - 1)$, plus one implicit self hyperedge, while the right-hand side is the desired degree requirement.

The full version of this paper presents a number of results about this constructions. First, the resulting topology remains connected under the maximal failures of $|\mathcal{O}| - t$ organizations allowed by the FBA model[7]:

Theorem 1. *For symmetric thresholds $t_v = t$, $\mathcal{T}_v = \mathcal{O}$ for all $v \in N$, $t \geq 2|\mathcal{O}|/3$, each cluster having the same number of organizations, and each organization having the same number of validators, the number of organizations that must be removed to disconnect the Constellation network is at least $|\mathcal{O}| - t + 1$.*

Second, we provide bounds on how far the resulting degree is from optimal. In simulations, for thresholds close to $2|O|/3$, the degree of the Constellation overlay converges below 3 times the optimal as $|O|$ increases.

Finally, we show that the diameter is at most 3 even under a significant number of failures:

Proposition 2. *For k clusters, with each cluster having the same number of organizations, the diameter of the Constellation network is at most 3 even under failure of $|\mathcal{O}|/k + k - 2$ organizations.*

Combined with the result of Theorem 1, Proposition 2 shows that the diameter of Constellation is near-optimal even when the number of failed nodes approaches that needed to disconnect the network.

When the FBAS is not symmetric, computing the cluster assignments that minimize degree is not straightforward. We propose a brute-force search approach to find good solutions. We discuss this approach in the full version of the paper and evaluate degree, diameter, and failure resilience using simulations.

---

[7] This results relies on Liouville's formula [18,22], which gives the mininum number of vertices that must be removed to disconnect cartesian-product graphs.

5 Deployment of Constellation in an FBA Blockchain

As we have seen, the Constellation algorithm takes as input a regular FBAS forming the top-tier (i.e., the union of all minimal quorums) of an FBA system, and then computes an overlay connecting the top-tier nodes.

To deploy Constellation in an FBA blockchain network, we use the blockchain to store each node's configuration (in practice, nodes submit special configuration-registration transactions to the blockchain which, when executed, update a shared data structure indicating each registered node's configuration). As long as a superset of the top-tier registers their configurations, this ensures that all nodes can compute the top-tier (Constellation includes an implementation using a SAT solver). Moreover, since the Constellation algorithm is deterministic, every node can compute the Constellation overlay locally and arrive at the same result. Finally, nodes establish and accept connections according to the Constellation algorithm's output. If a node receives an unexpected connection request not prescribed by the Constellation algorithm, it can simply reject it.

In the Stellar network, nodes typically execute a new transaction set (i.e., a block) every 5 s, while changes to top-tier node configurations are comparatively infrequent (having changed only a handful of times in the last 3 years). To balance adaptivity and network load, we propose recomputing the overlay topology daily. Thanks to Constellation's resilience guarantees, the system will remain operational as long as the set of nodes that fail or leave within a day is a set that the FBAS tolerates, according to their configuration at the beginning of the day. Note that this is similar to how proof-of-stake blockchains manage the list of stakers and their stake on chain. Moreover, recent work on overlay networks for proof-of-stake systems [12,23,24] also relies on the list of stakers and their stake, maintained on the blockchain, to derive overlay connections.

Since this scheme relies on the blockchain to set up the overlay, and the blockchain relies on the overlay to run, we need to bootstrap the system in some way. Moreover, we need to connect second-tier nodes, which the Constellation algorithm does not handle. An easy solution is to bootstrap the system with the same random-connections scheme currently used in the Stellar network. Specifically, we can instruct nodes to accept a fixed maximum number of connection requests beyond those prescribed by Constellation, and we can require newly joining nodes to establish a fixed number of random connections to bootstrap their inclusion in the overlay (after obtaining a list of nodes by contacting at least one existing node provided by their operator). Besides enabling system bootstrap, this approach also allows nodes to join during the daily reconfiguration period. However, this random scheme is best-effort and provides no guarantees.

6 Evaluation

In this section we evaluate Constellation empirically against random and greedy overlay-building strategies using simulations. The full version of the paper also evaluates Constellation on a real-world testbed on Amazon EC2.

To evaluate the degree of Constellation overlays, we consider a number of organizations ranging from 7 to 100, each consisting of 3 nodes and forming a single-universe, regular FBAS. For each number of organizations, we conduct experiments where we assign organizations random FBA thresholds between $|O|/2$ and $5|O|/6$, and we compare the maximum and average degree achieved with 3 different algorithms: a random algorithm, a greedy algorithm, and Constellation. We use random and greedy overlay-building strategies as our baselines because existing blockchain p2p overlay configurations (e.g., in Ethereum [5] or Bitcoin [19]) do not attempt to match the fault-tolerance of the consensus protocol running on top and are therefore not directly comparable to our approach.

In the random algorithm, each node picks k neighbors uniformly at random, and we repeat the experiment, incrementing k each time, until we obtain an overlay with diameter 2 that is FBA-resilient. In the greedy algorithm, we first build a graph over organizations, starting with an empty graph. We repeatedly sort the organizations in a list $O_1, O_2, ..., O_{|\mathcal{O}|}$ in descending order by the number of connections to other organizations still needed (recall that the minimum number of connections required for a threshold t_O is $c_O = |\mathcal{O}| - t_O + 1$). Then, letting c_1 be the number of additional connections needed by O_1, we connect O_1 to the first c_1 organizations in the list that O_1 is not yet connected to. This concludes one iteration of the loop. We exit the loop when all organizations have at least their required number of connections. Next, we make node-to-node connections: for each edge (O_1, O_2) in the hypergraph, we use the pattern of Fig. 1c, and we connect the 3 nodes of each organization using 2 edges. Finally, we repeatedly connect the most distant pairs of nodes until the diameter is at most 2.

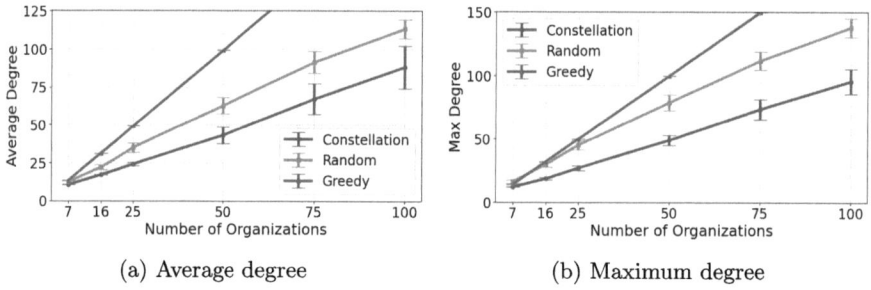

(a) Average degree   (b) Maximum degree

Fig. 2. Overlay degrees achieved with the Constellation algorithm, the greedy algorithm, and the random algorithm. Errors bars show standard deviation.

The results appear in Fig. 2. Constellation consistently achieves better average and maximum degrees than the random and greedy strategies, and the gap increases as the number of organizations increases. The greedy strategy is not competitive and, at 100 organizations, Constellation achieves an average degree roughly 22% lower than the random algorithm and a maximum degree roughly 30% better.

The full version of this paper presents additional simulations demonstrating Constellation's robustness under Byzantine failures.

7 Related Work

Classic structured p2p overlays such as Chord, CAN, Tapestry, Kademlia, and Pastry have been fundamental in shaping the landscape of distributed systems [29,34,36,38,45]. In particular, Kademlia [29] has been widely adopted by the blockchain community. For example, Ethereum uses Kademlia for address discovery [1], while the Interplanetary File System (IPFS) uses it for data discovery and routing [39]. KadCast proposes a Kademlia-based p2p overlay for faster message dissemination in blockchains [35]. Kadabra [43] builds upon Kademlia and allows nodes to improve their peer configurations by learning from and adapting to their environment.

While Ethereum uses Kademlia for peer discovery, consensus nodes disseminate data using gossipsub, which uses a random mesh [5,6]. Bitcoin also uses a random overlay [19]. Recent works have proposed new unstructured p2p overlay designs for blockchains, particularly to account for node heterogeneity. Perigee [28] proposes an adaptive topology-updating algorithm that uses an exploration-exploitation framework to discover efficient topologies. Zarin et al. [42] propose an overlay design in which nodes are segmented into distinct domains based on their type and resource availability, while using Kademlia for node discovery. All of these works ignore inherent consensus-level relationships, such as FBA's agreement requirements, that may exist between nodes.

Few works build Byzantine-resilient overlays that are secure under the same assumptions used by the consensus protocol. Notable exceptions include recent works by Coretti et al. [12] and Liu-Zhang et al. [23], which propose random graph overlays where each node's degree is proportional to its stake. Cohen et al. [11] and Tsimos et al. [40] propose efficient Byzantine-resilient gossip protocols for PKI settings.

Networking in FBA systems has received limited attention. Vytautas Tumas et al. [41] investigate network-level attacks in the XRP Ledger, which uses a model different from FBA but where nodes can also make subjective trust assumptions. The study introduces a novel robustness metric to assess resilience to node failures, revealing vulnerabilities in the XRP Ledger Consensus Protocol and proposing mitigation strategies to enhance robustness. André Gaul et al. [17] focus on assessing the level of decentralization in FBA networks using centrality measures. They explore three approaches for obtaining centrality measures for FBAS nodes, including adaptations of established graph and hypergraph-based measures, along with a newly developed measure based on node intactness—a crucial aspect of the FBAS model. Florian et al. [14] study the dynamics of reconfiguration in FBA systems.

Sophisticated view-maintenance and view-sampling algorithms [8,9,32,33,44] can provide resilience against Byzantine network-level attacks such as eclipse attacks [19] under Sybil-resilience assumptions (e.g., limited adversarial resources like IP addresses or proof-of-work). It would be interesting to consider adapting these algorithms to connect second-tier nodes in FBA systems.

8 Conclusion

We have presented and evaluated Constellation, an algorithm to construct overlays for Federated Byzantine Agreement (FBA) systems that are both performant in the normal case and resilient to failures, along with a practical scheme to deploy the Constellation algorithm in FBA systems such as the Stellar network.

For symmetric FBA systems, we have shown that Constellation guarantees connectivity of the overlay under all failures that must be tolerated according to the FBA model, and that it achieves an average degree close to optimal. In the general case, we have shown that Constellation overlays maintain a diameter of 3 under a large fraction of failures. Finally, performance metrics collected both in simulation and on a live testbed show that Constellation achieves better node degree and higher measured transaction throughput under realistic latencies than random overlays.

In future work, it would be interesting to investigate probabilistic solutions that guarantee resilience only probabilistically but achieve much lower degree (perhaps with higher diameter), and to investigate more decentralized solutions that do not rely on using the blockchain to agree on the FBA configuration.

Acknowledgments. We thanks Marta Lokhava and Brett Boston for numerous discussions that helped improve this work.

References

1. Ethereum Peer Discovery Protocol (2024). https://github.com/ethereum/devp2p/blob/master/discv5/discv5.md
2. The stellar-core github repository (2024). https://github.com/stellar/stellar-core/
3. Website of the Stellar Development Foundation (2024). https://stellar.org/
4. Artifacts for the paper "Constellation: Peer-to-Peer Overlays for Federated Byzantine Agreement Systems" (2025). https://doi.org/10.5281/zenodo.14873486
5. Ethereum Consensus Specs (2025). https://ethereum.github.io/consensus-specs/
6. Gossipsub (2025). https://github.com/libp2p/specs/tree/master/pubsub/gossipsub
7. Alpos, O., Cachin, C., Tackmann, B., Zanolini, L.: Asymmetric distributed trust. Distrib. Comput. **37**(3), 247–277 (2024). https://doi.org/10.1007/s00446-024-00469-1
8. Auvolat, A., Bromberg, Y.D., Frey, D., Mvondo, D., Taïani, F.: Basalt: a rock-solid byzantine-tolerant peer sampling for very large decentralized networks. In: Proceedings of the 24th International Middleware Conference, Middleware 2023, pp. 111–123. Association for Computing Machinery, New York (2023). https://doi.org/10.1145/3590140.3629109

9. Bortnikov, E., Gurevich, M., Keidar, I., Kliot, G., Shraer, A.: Brahms: byzantine resilient random membership sampling. Comput. Netw. **53**(13), 2340–2359 (2009). https://doi.org/10.1016/j.comnet.2009.03.008
10. Cachin, C., Losa, G., Zanolini, L.: Quorum systems in permissionless networks. In: Hillel, E., Palmieri, R., Rivière, E. (eds.) 26th International Conference on Principles of Distributed Systems (OPODIS 2022). Leibniz International Proceedings in Informatics (LIPIcs), vol. 253, pp. 17:1–17:22. Schloss Dagstuhl – Leibniz-Zentrum für Informatik, Dagstuhl, Germany (2023). https://doi.org/10.4230/LIPIcs.OPODIS.2022.17
11. Cohen, R., Loss, J., Moran, T.: Efficient agreement over byzantine gossip. In: Clark, J., Shi, E. (eds.) Financial Cryptography and Data Security, pp. 74–91. Springer, Cham (2025). https://doi.org/10.1007/978-3-031-78676-1_5
12. Coretti, S., Kiayias, A., Moore, C., Russell, A.: The generals' scuttlebutt: byzantine-resilient gossip protocols. In: Proceedings of the 2022 ACM SIGSAC Conference on Computer and Communications Security, CCS 2022, pp. 595–608. Association for Computing Machinery, New York (2022). https://doi.org/10.1145/3548606.3560638
13. Demers, A., Greene, D., Hauser, C., Irish, W., Larson, J.: Epidemic algorithms for replicated database maintenance. In: Proceedings of the Sixth Annual ACM Symposium on Principles of Distributed Computing, PODC 1987, pp. 1–12. ACM Press, Vancouver, British Columbia, Canada (1987). https://doi.org/10.1145/41840.41841
14. Florian, M., Henningsen, S., Ndolo, C., Scheuermann, B.: The sum of its parts: analysis of federated byzantine agreement systems. Distrib. Comput. **35**(5), 399–417 (2022). https://doi.org/10.1007/s00446-022-00430-0
15. García-Pérez, Á., Gotsman, A.: Federated byzantine quorum systems. In: Cao, J., Ellen, F., Rodrigues, L., Ferreira, B. (eds.) 22nd International Conference on Principles of Distributed Systems (OPODIS 2018). Leibniz International Proceedings in Informatics (LIPIcs), vol. 125, pp. 17:1–17:16. Schloss Dagstuhl – Leibniz-Zentrum für Informatik, Dagstuhl, Germany (2019). https://doi.org/10.4230/LIPIcs.OPODIS.2018.17
16. García-Pérez, Á., Schett, M.A.: Deconstructing stellar consensus. In: Felber, P., Friedman, R., Gilbert, S., Miller, A. (eds.) 23rd International Conference on Principles of Distributed Systems (OPODIS 2019). Leibniz International Proceedings in Informatics (LIPIcs), vol. 153, pp. 5:1–5:16. Schloss Dagstuhl – Leibniz-Zentrum für Informatik, Dagstuhl, Germany (2020). https://doi.org/10.4230/LIPIcs.OPODIS.2019.5
17. Gaul, A., Liesen, J.: Centrality of nodes in Federated Byzantine Agreement Systems (2020). https://doi.org/10.48550/arXiv.2012.03913
18. Govorčin, J., Škrekovski, R.: On the connectivity of Cartesian product of graphs. ARS Mathematica Contemporanea **7**(2), 293–297 (2014). https://doi.org/10.26493/1855-3974.313.e10
19. Heilman, E., Kendler, A., Zohar, A., Goldberg, S.: Eclipse attacks on Bitcoin's peer-to-peer network. In: Proceedings of the 24th USENIX Conference on Security Symposium, SEC 2015, pp. 129–144. USENIX Association, USA (2015)
20. Karp, R., Schindelhauer, C., Shenker, S., Vocking, B.: Randomized rumor spreading. In: Proceedings 41st Annual Symposium on Foundations of Computer Science, pp. 565–574 (2000). https://doi.org/10.1109/SFCS.2000.892324
21. Li, X., Chan, E., Lesani, M.: Quorum subsumption for heterogeneous quorum systems. In: Oshman, R. (ed.) 37th International Symposium on Distributed Computing (DISC 2023). Leibniz International Proceedings in Informatics (LIPIcs),

vol. 281, pp. 28:1–28:19. Schloss Dagstuhl – Leibniz-Zentrum für Informatik, Dagstuhl, Germany (2023). https://doi.org/10.4230/LIPIcs.DISC.2023.28
22. Liouville, B.: Sur la connectivité des produits de graphes (1978)
23. Liu-Zhang, C.D., Matt, C., Maurer, U., Rito, G., Thomsen, S.E.: Practical provably secure flooding for blockchains. In: Agrawal, S., Lin, D. (eds.) Advances in Cryptology – ASIACRYPT 2022, pp. 774–805. Springer, Cham (2022). https://doi.org/10.1007/978-3-031-22963-3_26
24. Liu-Zhang, C.D., Matt, C., Thomsen, S.E.: Asymptotically optimal message dissemination with applications to blockchains. In: Joye, M., Leander, G. (eds.) Advances in Cryptology – EUROCRYPT 2024, pp. 64–95. Springer, Cham (2024). https://doi.org/10.1007/978-3-031-58734-4_3
25. Lokhava, M., et al.: Fast and secure global payments with stellar. In: Proceedings of the 27th ACM Symposium on Operating Systems Principles, SOSP 2019, pp. 80–96. Association for Computing Machinery, Huntsville, Ontario, Canada (2019). https://doi.org/10.1145/3341301.3359636
26. Losa, G., Gafni, E., Mazières, D.: Stellar consensus by instantiation. In: Suomela, J. (ed.) 33rd International Symposium on Distributed Computing (DISC 2019). Leibniz International Proceedings in Informatics (LIPIcs), vol. 146, pp. 27:1–27:15. Schloss Dagstuhl–Leibniz-Zentrum fuer Informatik, Dagstuhl, Germany (2019). https://doi.org/10.4230/LIPIcs.DISC.2019.27
27. Lü, M., Wu, C., Chen, G.L., Lv, C.: On super connectivity of Cartesian product graphs. Networks **52**(2), 78–87 (2008). https://doi.org/10.1002/net.20224
28. Mao, Y., Deb, S., Venkatakrishnan, S.B., Kannan, S., Srinivasan, K.: Perigee: efficient peer-to-peer network design for blockchains. In: Proceedings of the 39th Symposium on Principles of Distributed Computing, PODC 2020, pp. 428–437. Association for Computing Machinery, New York (2020). https://doi.org/10.1145/3382734.3405704
29. Maymounkov, P., Mazières, D.: Kademlia: a peer-to-peer information system based on the XOR metric. In: Druschel, P., Kaashoek, F., Rowstron, A. (eds.) IPTPS 2002. LNCS, vol. 2429, pp. 53–65. Springer, Heidelberg (2002). https://doi.org/10.1007/3-540-45748-8_5
30. Mazieres, D.: The Stellar Consensus Protocol: A Federated Model for Internet-Level Consensus. Stellar Development Foundation (2015)
31. Parsonage, E., Nguyen, H.X., Bowden, R., Knight, S., Falkner, N., Roughan, M.: Generalized graph products for network design and analysis. In: 2011 19th IEEE International Conference on Network Protocols, pp. 79–88 (2011). https://doi.org/10.1109/ICNP.2011.6089084
32. Pigaglio, M., Bruneau-Queyreix, J., Bromberg, Y.D., Frey, D., Rivière, E., Réveillère, L.: RAPTEE: leveraging trusted execution environments for Byzantine-tolerant peer sampling services. In: 2022 IEEE 42nd International Conference on Distributed Computing Systems (ICDCS), pp. 603–613 (2022). https://doi.org/10.1109/ICDCS54860.2022.00064
33. Pilet, A.B., Frey, D., Taïani, F.: Foiling sybils with HAPS in permissionless systems: an address-based peer sampling service. In: 2020 IEEE Symposium on Computers and Communications (ISCC), pp. 1–6 (2020). https://doi.org/10.1109/ISCC50000.2020.9219606
34. Ratnasamy, S., Francis, P., Handley, M., Karp, R., Shenker, S.: A scalable content-addressable network. In: Proceedings of the 2001 Conference on Applications, Technologies, Architectures, and Protocols for Computer Communications, SIGCOMM 2001, pp. 161–172. Association for Computing Machinery, New York (2001). https://doi.org/10.1145/383059.383072

35. Rohrer, E., Tschorsch, F.: Kadcast: a structured approach to broadcast in blockchain networks. In: Proceedings of the 1st ACM Conference on Advances in Financial Technologies, AFT 2019, pp. 199–213. Association for Computing Machinery, New York (2019). https://doi.org/10.1145/3318041.3355469
36. Rowstron, A., Druschel, P.: Pastry: scalable, decentralized object location, and routing for large-scale peer-to-peer systems. In: Guerraoui, R. (ed.) Middleware 2001. LNCS, vol. 2218, pp. 329–350. Springer, Heidelberg (2001). https://doi.org/10.1007/3-540-45518-3_18
37. Špacapan, S.: Connectivity of Cartesian products of graphs. Appl. Math. Lett. **21**(7), 682–685 (2008). https://doi.org/10.1016/j.aml.2007.06.010
38. Stoica, I., Morris, R., Karger, D., Kaashoek, M.F., Balakrishnan, H.: Chord: a scalable peer-to-peer lookup service for internet applications. SIGCOMM Comput. Commun. Rev. **31**(4), 149–160 (2001). https://doi.org/10.1145/964723.383071
39. Trautwein, D., et al.: Design and evaluation of IPFS: a storage layer for the decentralized web. In: Proceedings of the ACM SIGCOMM 2022 Conference, pp. 739–752 (2022)
40. Tsimos, G., Loss, J., Papamanthou, C.: Gossiping for communication-efficient broadcast. In: Dodis, Y., Shrimpton, T. (eds.) Advances in Cryptology – CRYPTO 2022, pp. 439–469. Springer, Cham (2022). https://doi.org/10.1007/978-3-031-15982-4_15
41. Tumas, V., Rivera, S., Magoni, D., State, R.: Federated byzantine agreement protocol robustness to targeted network attacks. In: 2023 IEEE Symposium on Computers and Communications (ISCC), pp. 443–449. IEEE Computer Society, Los Alamitos, CA, USA (2023). https://doi.org/10.1109/ISCC58397.2023.10217935. https://doi.ieeecomputersociety.org/10.1109/ISCC58397.2023.10217935
42. Zarin, N., Sheff, I., Roos, S.: Blockchain Nodes are Heterogeneous and Your P2P Overlay Should be Too: PODS (2023). https://doi.org/10.48550/arXiv.2306.16153
43. Zhang, Y., Bojja Venkatakrishnan, S.: Kadabra: adapting kademlia for the decentralized web. In: Baldimtsi, F., Cachin, C. (eds.) Financial Cryptography and Data Security, pp. 327–345. Springer, Cham (2024). https://doi.org/10.1007/978-3-031-47751-5_19
44. Zhang, Y., Venkatakrishnan, S.B.: Honeybee: Byzantine Tolerant Decentralized Peer Sampling with Verifiable Random Walks (2025). https://doi.org/10.48550/arXiv.2402.16201
45. Zhao, B., Huang, L., Stribling, J., Rhea, S., Joseph, A., Kubiatowicz, J.: Tapestry: a resilient global-scale overlay for service deployment. IEEE J. Sel. Areas Commun. **22**(1), 41–53 (2004). https://doi.org/10.1109/JSAC.2003.818784

Short Paper: A New Way to Achieve Round-Efficient Asynchronous Byzantine Agreement

Simon Holmgaard Kamp(✉)

CISPA Helmholtz Center for Information Security, Saarbrücken, Germany
simonhkamp@gmail.com

Abstract. We translate the *expand-and-extract* framework by Fitzi, Liu-Zhang, and Loss (PODC 21) to the asynchronous setting. While they use it to obtain a synchronous BA with $2^{-\lambda}$ error probability in $\lambda + 1$ rounds, we achieve asynchronous BA in $\lambda + 3$ rounds. At the heart of their solution is a *proxcensus* primitive, which is used to reach graded agreement with $2^r + 1$ grades in r rounds by reducing proxcensus with $2s - 1$ grades to proxcensus with s grades in one round. The *expand-and-extract* paradigm relies on proxcensus to *expand* binary inputs to $2^\lambda + 1$ grades in λ rounds before *extracting* a binary output by partitioning the grades using a λ bit common coin. However, this proxcensus protocol does not translate to the asynchronous setting without lowering the corruption threshold or using more rounds in each recursive step.

Instead, we define validated proxcensus and show that it can be instantiated in asynchrony with the same recursive structure and round complexity as synchronous proxcensus. The main technique is to attach *justifiers* to all messages which forces the adversary to choose between only sending useful messages or being ignored.

1 Introduction

Following the *expand-and-extract* paradigm by Fitzi, Liu-Zhang, and Loss [9] we present a concretely round efficient asynchronous Monte Carlo style BA which runs for a fixed number of rounds, $\lambda + 3$, before reaching agreement on a binary decision with probability at least $1 - 2^\lambda$ using signatures and a common coin.

The expand-and-extract paradigm generalizes Feldman and Micali [8] (FM) in which the parties iteratively run *crusader agreement* to obtain either the input of an honest party or an inconclusive value "?", with the guarantee that no two honest parties get different bits. They then flip a coin and parties that had output "?" use the coin as input to the next FM iteration. With probability $> 1/2$ this makes the system enter a *univalent* configuration, in which honest parties input the same bit to all future iterations. While it is possible to detect this univalent

---

This work was done while the author was at Aarhus University and is partially funded by the Concordium Foundation.

state and terminate in an expected constant number of rounds: in order to enter this state and reach agreement with probability $1 - 2^{-\lambda}$, the protocol must run λ FM iterations which corresponds to 2λ rounds of communication.

Fitzi et al. cut this worst case round complexity almost in half to $\lambda + 1$ by introducing proxcensus which generalizes crusader agreement and graded agreement to any number of grades, while still guaranteeing that all honest outputs are distributed between two adjacent grades. They observe that you can remove all but one of the coin flip rounds by first using proxcensus to *expand* to $2^\lambda + 1$ grades in λ rounds and then flip a single λ-bit coin to *extract* a bit decision based on the value of the coin and each party's grade in a manner that is consistent with probability $1 - 2^{-\lambda}$. Their expansion technique is inherently synchronous, but we adapt it to tolerate asynchrony, while retaining the asymptotic communication complexity and the concrete round complexity up to needing one extra round to implement validated BA (VBA) as defined in [4] or two extra rounds to implement a full-fledged BA.

To compare with the FM approach in the asynchronous setting: observe that crusader agreement followed by a coin flip does not on its own solve BA in asynchrony. This is because the adversary is assumed to learn the output of the coin as soon as some honest party wishes to flip the coin. From a *bivalent* configuration (where at least two honest parties have different inputs) the adversary can make an honest party output "?" in order to learn the coin c and then let other honest parties receive output $1 - c$ to indefinitely maintain the bivalent configuration. This can be solved by using graded agreement with at least 4 grades, which requires an extra round of communication before flipping the coin. The resulting FM iterations use 3 rounds each and give a worst case round complexity of 3λ. The expand and extract technique improves on the worst case round complexity of this asynchronous BA by almost a factor 3 to $\lambda + 3$.

In the synchronous BA by Fitzi et al., the λ rounds spent on flipping a 1-bit coin in each FM iteration are removed and then replaced with a single round used to flip a λ-bit coin after expanding. The resulting round complexity is $\lambda + 1$ instead of 2λ. In the same vein we can view our VBA protocol as removing both the round spent on coin flipping and the round spent on upgrading crusader agreement to graded consensus with more grades from each of the λ FM iterations. In the end a (worst case) total of 2λ rounds are replaced by just two rounds after the expansion phase, that each functionally stand in for λ rounds and in combination result in a round complexity of $\lambda + 2$ rather than 3λ.

Techniques. The expand-and-extract approach first *expands* to $2^\lambda + 1$ grades and then uses a λ-bit coin to *extract* a decision. In the expansion step the parties input their bit to a *proxcensus* protocol which outputs a bit and a grade that serves as an indicator of confidence in the bit. Crusader agreement and graded agreement are well-known special cases of proxcensus with 3 and 5 grades respectively. If all honest parties input the same bit 0 (or 1), their output must be the minimal (or maximal) grade. All honest parties are guaranteed to have graded agreement in the sense that they have adjacent integer outputs. After expanding to a large space of $2^\lambda + 1$ grades, the output bit is *extracted* by splitting the space in two using a random coin. If the obtained grade is strictly greater than the coin, the output is 1, otherwise it is 0. This means that if a party has the minimal (or maximal) grade, then they output 0 (or 1) regardless of the coin. Hence, the validity of BA reduces to the validity of proxcensus.

When we enter the extraction phase, a more general version of the attack on the FM approach in asynchrony described above also applies to asynchronous expand-and-extract. As we cannot wait to flip the coin until all honest parties are done expanding: each party must initiate the coin flip when they are done expanding and this leaks the value of the common coin to adversary. The output grades of proxcensus are guaranteed to be adjacent, but when the first honest party gives output, there are still potentially two candidates for the adjacent grade. This gives the adversary two shots at guessing the random coin instead of one, doubling the error probability. However, adding an extra round to expand to twice as many grades recovers this lost bit of security. Finally, an additional round is used to reduce BA to VBA by establishing a threshold signature on the input bit as suggested in [4].

Related Work. Expand-and-extract along with the notion of proxcensus were introduced in [9]. Proxcensus is in turn an adaption of the proxcast definition used in [6]. The logic used to get validated proxcensus draws on the partially synchronous BA in [12], although the network model and definitions of justifiers are quite different. The result of [9] has later been improved by Ghinea et al. [10], but Attiya and Censor-Hillel [1] show that the asymptotic improvement cannot carry over to asynchrony. There has not been much recent progress on the concrete round efficiency of Monte Carlo style BA in the asynchronous setting. However, the recent work of Erbes and Wattenhofer [7] provides a 2^λ graded consensus protocol with $6(\lambda+1)$ rounds and suggests that [2] and [3] can be combined into a 2^λ graded consensus using $3(\lambda+1)$ rounds. We improve on this by a factor of 3 (see Corollary 1).

1.1 Preliminaries

We describe protocols for n parties $\mathsf{P}_1, \ldots, \mathsf{P}_n$ where $t < n/3$ can be adaptively Byzantine corrupted. We assume an asynchronous network where message delivery is handled by the adversary with no upper bound on the delay. Liveness properties hold under eventual delivery of the messages.

Threshold Signatures and Common Coin. These primitives are standard and we only give brief informal descriptions. For simplicity we treat them as unconditionally secure. We assume key shares of a threshold signature scheme for multiple different thresholds have been setup between the parties. We will be using thresholds $n-t$ and $t+1$ and assume that (partial) signatures have a size of λ bits. We also assume the parties can run a common coin primitive Π_{CC} that allow the parties to flip a λ bit coin which is unpredictable to the adversary until the first honest party initiates the protocol. This can be instantiated from threshold signatures following [5].

Justifiers. We use justifiers as defined in [11]. These are ways to demonstrate some notion of validity of a protocol message by providing relevant context. A simple example is justifying the input bit to VBA protocol using threshold signatures as suggested in [4].

Definition 1 (Justifier[11]). *For a message identifier* mid *we say that* J^{mid} *is a justifier if the following properties hold.* J^{mid} *is a predicate depending on the message m and the local state of a party. When we write pseudo-code then we write* $J^{\mathsf{mid}}(m)$ *to denote that the party* P *executing the code computes* J^{mid} *on m using its current state. In definitions and proofs we write* $J^{\mathsf{mid}}(m, \mathsf{P}, \tau)$ *to denote that we apply* J^{mid} *to m and the local state of* P *at time* τ.

Monotone: *If for an honest* P *and some time* τ *it holds that* $J^{\mathsf{mid}}(m, \mathsf{P}, \tau) = \top$ *then at all* $\tau' \geq \tau$ *it holds that* $J^{\mathsf{mid}}(m, \mathsf{P}, \tau') = \top$.
Propagating: *If for honest* P *and some point in time* τ *it holds that* $J^{\mathsf{mid}}(m, \mathsf{P}, \tau) = \top$, *then eventually the execution will reach a time* τ' *such that* $J^{\mathsf{mid}}(m, \mathsf{P}', \tau') = \top$ *for all honest parties* P'.

In our protocols all justifiers are explicit certificates based on threshold signatures and some auxiliary information sent along with the message. We therefore omit the party and time from the justifiers. The following two definitions provide a framework to reason about properties of justified messages.

Definition 2 (Possible Justified Messages [11]). *Let* Π *be a protocol. When we say that an* ℓ*-ary predicate P holds for all possible justified messages we mean: Run the protocol* Π *under attack by the adversary. At some point the adversary may output a sequence of triples* $(\mathsf{P}^1, \mathsf{mid}^1, m^1), \ldots, (\mathsf{P}^\ell, \mathsf{mid}^\ell, m^\ell)$. *We say that the adversary wins if the message identifiers* $\mathsf{mid}^1, \ldots, \mathsf{mid}^\ell$ *identify messages of* Π, $\mathsf{P}^1, \ldots, \mathsf{P}^\ell$ *are honest (but not necessarily distinct) parties, for* $j = 1, \ldots, \ell$ *it holds that* $J^{\mathsf{mid}_j}(m^j) = \top$ *at* P^j, *and* $P(m^1, \ldots, m^\ell) = \bot$. *Otherwise the adversary looses the game. Any PPT adversary should win with negligible probability.*

Definition 3 (Possible Justified Outputs [11]). *Let* Π *be a protocol with output justifier J. When we say that an* ℓ*-ary predicate P holds for all possible justified outputs we mean: Let* Π' *be the protocol* Π *with only change being that each party on getting output, sends their output to all parties if this was not already done. Run the protocol* Π' *under attack by the adversary. At some point the adversary may output a sequence of triples* $(\mathsf{P}^1, |^1, m^1), \ldots, (\mathsf{P}^\ell, |^\ell, m^\ell)$. *We say that the adversary wins if the* $|^1, \ldots, |^\ell$ *are identified with outputs of* Π, $\mathsf{P}^1, \ldots, \mathsf{P}^\ell$ *are honest (but not necessarily distinct) parties, for* $j = 1, \ldots, \ell$ *it holds that* $J^{|_j}(m^j) = \top$ *at* P^j, *and* $P(m^1, \ldots, m^\ell) = \bot$. *Otherwise the adversary looses the game. Any PPT adversary should win with negligible probability.*

The protocol in Fig. 1 corresponds to the procedure for justifying inputs in [4]. The parties multicast their input bits and initially try to collect signature shares on some input bit from $t+1$ parties, implying that it is the input of an honest party. At the same time (assuming $n > 3t$) it is guaranteed that parties eventually receive $t+1$ shares for one of the two inputs, since the bit input by the majority of the honest parties will account for at least $t+1$ shares. Using the definition of justifiers from [11] we can say that the Π_{IVG} in Fig. 1 has the liveness property that if all honest parties start running the protocol, then eventually they receive a justified bit as output. It also has the safety property that any *possible justified output* satisfying $\Pi_{\text{IVG}}.J_{\text{OUT}}$ was the input of an honest party.

Input validation gadget Π_{IVG}.

- On input b_i, P_i multicasts b_i with a signature and a partial signature with threshold $t+1$.
- On receiving b for some bit b from $t+1$ distinct parties: P_i combines the shares of the $t+1$ threshold signature scheme and outputs b justified by the threshold signature.

Fig. 1. An input validation gadget reducing BA to VBA.

2 Validated Proxcensus

In this section we define validated proxcensus, which is to the definition of proxcensus in [9] what VBA [4] is to BA. To ease the notation in the protocol and proofs we define the output over the integers, such that $VProx-(G)$ has outputs in $\{0, \ldots, G-1\}$ rather than a bit (or '?') with a grade up to $\lfloor G/2 \rfloor$.

We will follow the approach of reducing the problem of $VProx - (2s-1)$ to $VProx - (s)$ using one round of communication.

Definition 4 (Validated Proxcensus). *Let $\Pi_{\text{VPROX}-(G)}(J_{\text{IN}})$ be a protocol for n parties, parameterized by an input justifier J_{IN}, and outputting $y \in \{0, \ldots, G-1\}$ satisfying an output justifier J_{OUT}. We say that $\Pi_{\text{VPROX}-(G)}(J_{\text{IN}})$ solves VProx-(G) if the following holds:*

Liveness. *If every honest party P_i have justified input $x \in \{0,1\}$ where $J_{\text{IN}}(x) = \top$, then eventually every honest party P_j will have justified output $y \in \{0, \ldots, G-1\}$ where $J_{\text{OUT}}(y) = \top$.*
Justified Graded Agreement. *For all possible justified outputs y and y': $|y - y'| \leq 1$.*
Justified Validity. *If b is the only possible J_{IN} justified bit, then $y = b \cdot (G-1)$ for all possible justified outputs y.*

Remark 1. It is easy to map from an output $y \in [G]$ to the (b,g) representation used in [9]. In our case G is always odd, so we can define a middle grade $G' = \lfloor G/2 \rfloor$ and map y to (b,g) where $g = |G' - y|$ and $b = \begin{cases} ? & \text{if } y = G' \\ 0 & \text{if } y < G' \\ 1 & \text{if } y > G' \end{cases}$.

To motivate the definition and the use of justifiers, let us first consider the simplest (non-trivial) version of proxcensus: Crusader Agreement. Parties have input in $\{0,1\}$ and outputs in $\{0,1,2\}$. If we use the logic from Fitzi et al. in the asynchronous setting we run into problems with validity, liveness or agreement (unless we assume fewer corruptions or use more than one round).

First, a party should not output $2b$ unless it has seen $n-t$ votes for b. Otherwise graded agreement is easily broken. The validity property says that if all honest parties have input b, then the only valid output is $2b$. In order to make sure that you pick a valid output you can only "trust" your own input, or alternatively the other input if it is seen from at least $t+1$ parties. But what do you do if you had input b, only see $n-t$ votes, and the majority but not all of these votes are on b? You do not have enough information to know that $1-b$ is an honest input and thus that 1 is a valid output, but neither do you have the $n-t$ votes for b that would allow outputting $2b$. As the protocol is asynchronous, there is no way to wait for more than $n-t$ votes. While it could be solved by assuming $n > 4t$, or by using two rounds in each step of the recursion[1] it would be preferable to maintain the round complexity and resilience.

For this purpose, consider a *validated* flavour of Crusader Agreement which is to Crusader Agreement what VBA is to BA. Namely, where inputs satisfy a predicate and Justified Validity says that if only input b is justifiable, then $2b$ should be the only justifiable output bit. With this definition: if you see a justifier for both possible input bits, you can output bottom without violating Justified Validity. You can additionally justify it by forwarding the 2 justifiers. To ensure agreement: simply require seeing $n-t$ votes for the same bit b in order to output $2b$. Finally, for Liveness observe that you will eventually see $n-t$ votes from honest parties. Either these $n-t$ votes are on the same bit, or you saw two votes for different bits. In either case you obtain a valid output.

Let us generalize this idea to solve validated proxcensus. We now reinterpret the consensus rules as doubling an input that is seen n-t times, or taking the double of the average of two different inputs. Note that after giving output: since all justified outputs are on at most two different adjacent integers, we are essentially in the same situation as when we started with 0 and 1 being those two integers. If we apply this new interpretation of the consensus rules to those integers and use the invariant that all justifiable outputs of an iteration are adjacent integers, we can keep threading the justified outputs of each instance of validated crusader agreement into the next one. The maximum grade now doubles every round. To see why justified validity is maintained: there is only something to show if the only justified input is b. And in that case each round doubles the unique justified input and the only justified output after r rounds will be $2^r \cdot b$.

We describe the general protocol in detail in Fig. 2 as reducing VProx-$(2s-1)$ to VProx-(s). As the base case for the recursion, define $\Pi_{\text{VPROX}-(2)}(J_{\text{IN}})$ to output its input with $J_{\text{OUT}} = J_{\text{IN}}$. Rephrasing the above: the main insight is that *all*

---

[1] The validated proxcensus protocol in Fig. 2 if combined with the protocol in Fig. 1 would be such a recursive solution with two rounds in each step.

possible justified outputs of VProx-(s) are on at most 2 adjacent grades, so we can double the grade if we only receive the same grade from $n - t$ parties, or double the average of 2 justified grades.

Reduction from $\Pi_{\text{VProx}-(2s-1)}$ to $\Pi_{\text{VProx}-(s)}$ for $s \geq 2$.

- On input x_i where $J_{\text{IN}}(x_i) = \top$, P_i runs $\Pi_{\text{VPROX}-(s)}(J_{\text{IN}})$ with input x_i.
- On output z_i from $\Pi_{\text{VPROX}-(s)}(J_{\text{IN}})$, P_i multicasts (PROPOSAL, z_i) with a signature and a partial signature with threshold $n - t$.
- On receiving justified (PROPOSAL, z) and (PROPOSAL, $z + 1$) P_i lets $y_i = 2z + 1$ and terminates with output y_i justified by the justifiers for z and $z + 1$.
- On receiving justified (PROPOSAL, z) from $n-t$ distinct parties, P_i lets $y_i = 2z$ and terminates with output y_i justified by a $n - t$ threshold signature on z.

Fig. 2. A recursive description of the validated proxcensus protocol.

The protocol in Fig. 2 satisfies VProx-($2^i + 1$) as defined in Definition 4 for any nonnegative integer i, using i rounds of communication. For the base case $i = 0$ define $\Pi_{\text{VPROX}-(2)}(J_{\text{IN}})$ to be the zero round protocol that just returns the input with output justifier $J_{\text{OUT}} = J_{\text{IN}}$ trivially satisfying Definition 4. We first show the induction step.

Lemma 1. *If $\Pi_{\text{VPROX}-(s)}(J_{\text{IN}})$ satisfies Definition 4, then $\Pi_{\text{VPROX}-(2s-1)}(J_{\text{IN}})$ satisfies Definition 4*

Proof. For liveness we observe that $n - t$ honest parties $\Pi_{\text{VPROX}-(s)}(J_{\text{IN}}).J_{\text{OUT}}$ justified values z_i which by Justified Graded Agreement are either all identical or split between two adjacent integers, so when these are propagated every party has a set of $n - t$ values that allow defining y_i through one of the two cases. Justified Validity follows from Justified Validity of $\Pi_{\text{VPROX}-(s)}(J_{\text{IN}})$, as the input justifier is shared. So since all justified z are identical, every party gets the same y. In particular, if the only justified input to the inner protocol is b then the only $\Pi_{\text{VPROX}-(s)}(J_{\text{IN}}).J_{\text{OUT}}$-justified output is $z = b \cdot (s - 1)$, thus the only $\Pi_{\text{VPROX}-(2s-1)}(J_{\text{IN}}).J_{\text{OUT}}$-justified output is $2b \cdot (s - 1) = b \cdot (2s - 2)$. For Justified Graded Agreement we again rely on Justified Graded Agreement of the $\Pi_{\text{VPROX}-(s)}(J_{\text{IN}})J_{\text{OUT}}$-justified z values to say that and for any justified z_i and z_j we have $|z_i - z_j| \leq 1$. We only need to argue that there cannot be $n - t$ parties who send some z_i and $n-t$ parties who sent $z_j = z_i - 1$. But such two sets would overlap on at least one honest party as $n > 3t$. Thus, by definition of step 3 all justified outputs y_i and y_j satisfy $|z_i - z_j| \leq 1$. □

In the full version we show that the justifiers remain constant size which allows the asynchronous validated proxcensus to match the complexity of the synchronous proxcensus for $n > 3t$ parties presented in [9].

Corollary 1. *For any $r \geq 0$, $\Pi_{\text{VPROX}-(2^r+1)}(J_{\text{IN}})$ solves VProx-(2^r+1) with r rounds of communication and $O(rn^2(\lambda + |J_{\text{IN}}|))$ bits of communication, where $|J_{\text{IN}}|$ is the size of the input justifier. When using Π_{IVG} to establish J_{IN}, it solves Prox-(2^r+1) as defined in [9] in $r+1$ rounds with $O(rn^2\lambda)$ bits of communication.*

3 Validated BA

We give a brief description of the extraction phase, which follows [9] but requires an extra round of communication to expand to $2^{\lambda+1}+1$ grades in order to make up for the error probability being doubled in asynchrony. (In contrast to the $2^\lambda + 1$ that suffice in the synchronous case.) As the proxcensus is validated, the combined expand-and-extract procedure only yields a validated BA protocol. A full BA protocol is given in Sect. 4. We first define validated BA.

Definition 5 (Validated BA). *Let $\Pi_{\text{VBA}}(J_{\text{IN}})$ be a protocol for n parties parameterized by an input justifier J_{IN} outputting $y \in \{0,1\}$ satisfying an output justifier J_{OUT}. We say that $\Pi_{\text{VBA}}(J_{\text{IN}})$ is a secure VBA protocol if the following properties hold:*

Liveness. *If every honest party P_i has justified input $x_i \in \{0,1\}$ where $J_{\text{IN}}(x_i) = \top$, then eventually every honest party P_j will have justified output $y \in \{0,1\}$ where $J_{\text{OUT}}(y) = \top$.*
Justified Agreement. *For all possible justified outputs y and y': $y = y'$.*
Justified Validity. *If $J_{\text{OUT}}(y) = \top$, then $J_{\text{IN}}(y) = \top$.*

The protocol Π_{VBA} in Fig. 3 satisfies Definition 5 except with probability $2^{-\lambda}$. As mentioned the parties first expand to $2^{\lambda+1} + 1$ grades. Then Π_{CC} is run to obtain output c and the grades are compared with $2c$. This mitigates the security loss caused by the adversary being free to choose between more than two grades at the time the coin is flipped. The adversary can still learn c when the first honest party P_i gets their grade g_i and then decide to give some P_j grade $g_j \in \{g_i - 1, g_i, g_i + 1\}$ based on the value of c. But note that since $2c$ is even, agreement can only be broken if there are justified grades g and $g' = g+1$ where g is even. So even if the adversary has the ability to to choose between $g_i - 1$ and $g_i + 1$ becoming justified grades after learning the value of c. At most one of the two grades can result in conflicting bit decisions, so the adversary has no chance of breaking agreement beyond guessing the exact value of c before any honest party initiates Π_{CC}.

Theorem 1. *Π_{VBA} (Fig. 3) is a secure VBA as defined in Definition 5 except with probability $2^{-\lambda}$. It uses $\lambda+2$ rounds of communication and $O(\lambda n^2(\lambda+|J_{\text{IN}}|))$ bits of communication, where $|J_{\text{IN}}|$ is the size of the input justifier.*

Proof. Since we expand to $2^{\lambda+1} + 1$ grades and double the value of the coin: even if the adversary can choose between 3 different grades when the coin is leaked, the adversary needs to guess the value of the coin to split agreement. Justified validity reduces to justified validity of validated proxcensus: If b is the only justified input, then the only justified possible justified grade is $b \cdot (G-1)$ and the only possible justified output is b.

Validated BA protocol Π_{VBA}

- On input b_i, P_i initiates $\Pi_{\text{VPROX}-(2^{\lambda+1}+1)}$ with input b_i.
- On output g_i from $\Pi_{\text{VPROX}-(2^{\lambda+1}+1)}$, P_i initiates Π_{CC}.
- On output c_i from Π_{CC}, P_i lets $d_i = 1$ if $g_i > 2c_i$.

Fig. 3. A validated BA using expand-and-extract.

4 Binary Agreement

We finally solve BA using the recipe from [4] where a justifier is formed using a threshold signature before running VBA. This resulting BA has a slightly stronger security definition than standard BA: the output comes with a justifier and only one output can be justified.

Binary Agreement protocol Π_{BA}.

- On input b_i, P_i initiates Π_{IVG} with input b_i.
- On output x_i from Π_{IVG}, P_i initiates $\Pi_{\text{VBA}}(\Pi_{\text{IVG}}.J_{\text{OUT}})$ with input x_i.
- On output y_i from d_i $\Pi_{\text{VBA}}(\Pi_{\text{IVG}}.J_{\text{OUT}})$, P_i outputs d_i.

Fig. 4. A Binary Agreement protocol.

Definition 6 (BA). *Let Π_{BA} be a protocol for n parties outputting $y \in \{0,1\}$ satisfying an output justifier J_{OUT}. We say that Π_{BA} is a secure BA protocol if the following properties hold:*

Liveness. *If every honest party P_i has input $x_i \in \{0,1\}$, then eventually every honest party P_j will have justified output $y_i \in \{0,1\}$ where $J_{\text{OUT}}(y_i) = \top$.*
Justified Agreement. *For all possible justified outputs y and y': $y = y'$.*
Validity. *If $J_{\text{OUT}}(y) = \top$, then some honest party gave input y.*

We give a protocol Π_{BA} in Fig. 4 which implements BA except with probability $2^{-\lambda}$. The security follows as a corollary from Theorem 1.

Corollary 2. *Π_{BA} given in Fig. 4 implements a secure BA as defined in Definition 6 except with probability $2^{-\lambda}$. It uses $\lambda + 3$ rounds of communication and $O((n\lambda)^2)$ bits of communication.*

Acknowledgements. I would like to thank Jesper Buus Nielsen for many helpful discussions.

References

1. Attiya, H., Censor-Hillel, K.: Lower bounds for randomized consensus under a weak adversary. SIAM J. Comput. **39**(8), 3885–3904 (2010)
2. Attiya, H., Welch, J.L.: Multi-valued connected consensus: a new perspective on crusader agreement and adopt-commit. In: OPODIS. LIPIcs, vol. 286, pp. 6:1–6:23. Schloss Dagstuhl - Leibniz-Zentrum für Informatik (2023)
3. Bandarupalli, A., Bhat, A., Bagchi, S., Kate, A., Liu-Zhang, C., Reiter, M.K.: Delphi: efficient asynchronous approximate agreement for distributed oracles. In: DSN, pp. 456–469. IEEE (2024)
4. Cachin, C., Kursawe, K., Petzold, F., Shoup, V.: Secure and efficient asynchronous broadcast protocols. In: Kilian, J. (ed.) CRYPTO 2001. LNCS, vol. 2139, pp. 524–541. Springer, Heidelberg (2001). https://doi.org/10.1007/3-540-44647-8_31
5. Cachin, C., Kursawe, K., Shoup, V.: Random oracles in constantinople: practical asynchronous byzantine agreement using cryptography. J. Cryptol. **18**(3), 219–246 (2005). https://doi.org/10.1007/s00145-005-0318-0
6. Considine, J., Fitzi, M., Franklin, M.K., Levin, L.A., Maurer, U.M., Metcalf, D.: Byzantine agreement given partial broadcast. J. Cryptol. **18**(3), 191–217 (2005). https://doi.org/10.1007/S00145-005-0308-X
7. Erbes, M.M., Wattenhofer, R.: Asynchronous approximate agreement with quadratic communication (2024)
8. Feldman, P., Micali, S.: An optimal probabilistic protocol for synchronous byzantine agreement. SIAM J. Comput. **26**(4), 873–933 (1997)
9. Fitzi, M., Liu-Zhang, C.D., Loss, J.: A new way to achieve round-efficient byzantine agreement. In: Miller, A., Censor-Hillel, K., Korhonen, J.H. (eds.) 40th ACM PODC, pp. 355–362. ACM (2021). https://doi.org/10.1145/3465084.3467907
10. Ghinea, D., Goyal, V., Liu-Zhang, C.D.: Round-optimal byzantine agreement. In: Dunkelman, O., Dziembowski, S. (eds.) EUROCRYPT 2022, Part I. LNCS, vol. 13275, pp. 96–119. Springer, Cham (2022). https://doi.org/10.1007/978-3-031-06944-4_4
11. Kamp, S.H., Nielsen, J.B.: Byzantine agreement decomposed: Honest majority asynchronous total-order broadcast from reliable broadcast. IACR Cryptol. ePrint Arch. 1738 (2023)
12. Kamp, S.H., Nielsen, J.B., Thomsen, S.E., Tschudi, D.: Enig: player replaceable finality layers with optimal validity. Cryptology ePrint Archive, Report 2022/201 (2022). https://eprint.iacr.org/2022/201

Proof-of-X and Rewards

Blink: An Optimal Proof of Proof-of-Work

Lukas Aumayr[1,4], Zeta Avarikioti[2,4], Matteo Maffei[2,5], Giulia Scaffino[2,4,5](✉), and Dionysis Zindros[3,4]

[1] University of Edinburgh, Edinburgh, UK
[2] TU Wien, Vienna, Austria
giulia.scaffino@gmail.com
[3] Stanford University, Stanford, USA
[4] Common Prefix, Vienna, Austria
[5] CDL-BOT, Hamburg, Germany

Abstract. Designing light clients to securely and efficiently read Proof-of-Work blockchains has been a foundational problem since the inception of blockchains. Nakamoto themselves, in the original Bitcoin paper, presented the first client protocol, i.e., the Simplified Payment Verification, which consumes an amount of bandwidth, computational, and storage resources that grows linearly in the system's lifetime $\mathcal{C}$.

Today, the blockchain ecosystem is more mature and presents a variety of applications and protocols deployed on-chain and, often, cross-chain. In this landscape, light clients have become the cornerstone of decentralized bridges, playing a pivotal role in the security and efficiency of cross-chain operations. These new use cases, combined with the growth of blockchains over time, raise the need for more minimalist clients, which further reduce the resource requirements and, when applicable, on-chain costs. Over the years, the light client resource consumption has been reduced from $\mathcal{O}(\mathcal{C})$ to $\mathcal{O}(\text{polylog}(\mathcal{C}))$, and then down to $\mathcal{O}(1)$ with zero-knowledge techniques at the cost of often assuming a trusted setup.

In this paper, we present Blink, the first *interactive provably secure $\mathcal{O}(1)$ PoW light client without trusted setup*. Blink can be used for a variety of applications ranging from payment verification and bootstrapping, to bridges. We prove Blink secure in the Bitcoin Backbone model, and we evaluate its proof size demonstrating that, at the moment of writing, Blink obtains a commitment to the current state of Bitcoin by downloading only 1.6KB, instead of 67.3 MB and 197 KB for SPV and zk-based clients, respectively.

1 Introduction

Blockchain systems run consensus protocols among a large and varying set of mutually distrusting participants, favoring decentralized trust over efficiency. To engage with blockchains, users need to read the latest state of the chain to find out, e.g., how many coins they own, if they got paid by another user, or, in more modern chains, which is the current state of a contract. To do so, they can use different techniques with different trade-offs. One approach is to run a full node, which downloads, re-executes, and stores the entire history of the ledger. This is the most secure way but, obviously, also the most inefficient. It is like reading a whole long book from the beginning just to know if the protagonist defeats the villain at the end. An alternative way for a user to read the blockchain is to run a light node, which only downloads and validates block headers, trading off some security to gain efficiency. In our analogy, it is like skimming through the book, finding the page of interest, and only reading the sentence "Voldemort was dead, killed by his own rebounding curse" [1]. In the real world, users often have few resources and cannot read an entire (however good) book when checking a payment or trading assets. Users cannot be asked to run full nodes on their resource-constrained phones to use their wallet.

In the seminal Bitcoin white paper [2], Satoshi Nakamoto already predicted the need for efficiency and designed a *light client* called the Simplified Payment Verification (SPV) protocol, which decouples the download of the execution layer data (transactions) from the consensus layer data (block headers). An SPV client retrieves all block headers and verifies them according to the longest chain consensus rule, consuming an amount of resources that grows linearly with the system's lifetime. Several subsequent works optimized this concept, introducing *superlight clients* whose resource requirements are only polylogarithmic in the lifetime of the system [3–6]. Nevertheless, these protocols are not out-of-the-box compatible with Bitcoin and require a consensus fork. The increased performances of zero-knowledge techniques have also lead to *ultralight clients* [7–9] which, however, often rely on a trusted setup, trading off trust to gain efficiency.

As blockchains grow, and with them also the number of on-chain and cross-chain applications, the need for more efficient clients has become more pressing. Indeed, in today's more mature ecosystem, light clients are not only used by wallets, but they have become a pivotal component of many bridge protocols, whose operating costs are often dominated by the (inefficient) reads and verifications of blockchain data. Designing a client that only requires constant communication, computation, and storage resources has unfortunately remained an elusive goal over the past dozen years. This paper fills this gap, enabling critical resource optimizations for blockchain clients as well as reduced on-chain costs for cross-chain applications.

Contributions. In this work, we present Blink, a novel *interactive PoW light client with constant communication, computational, and storage complexity*. In a nutshell, the Blink client connects to multiple full nodes, so that at least one of them can be assumed honest. The client locally samples a random value η, includes it in a transaction Tx_η, and sends it to the full nodes. For instance, η could be a new, fresh address sampled with high entropy and Tx_η can be a payment to the vendor that owns this fresh address. Then, Blink waits for Tx_η to be included on-chain in a block and confirmed. The full nodes respond to the client with a proof π consisting of only $2k+1$ consecutive block headers, with the header of the block including Tx_η sitting in the middle (see Fig. 1); k is the *common prefix* security parameter [10], e.g., the conventional 6 confirmation blocks in Bitcoin. The constant-sized proof π ensures that *the first block in the proof is stable* and, therefore, it can be considered as a checkpoint or as a new genesis. Contrary to the $\mathcal{O}(1)$ zero-knowledge based clients, *Blink does not require any trusted setup*.

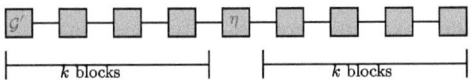

Fig. 1. Structure of the Blink's proof π. The proof π consists of $2k + 1$ consecutive block headers, with the one of the block including the entropy η in the middle, and k block headers before and after it. The block $\mathcal{G}'$ identified by the first header of the proof is stable in the chain and can act as a new genesis block.

Blink is proven secure in the *static population*, i.e., static difficulty, Bitcoin Backbone model [10] against an *adaptive minority adversary*. In this paper, we refine the problem of Proofs of Proofs-of-Work [3], i.e., techniques often used by light clients to prove on-chain inclusion by succinctly verifying the amount of Proof-of-Work done. We prove that Blink has a constant-sized proof verifiable in constant time, and constitutes therefore the first provably secure *Optimal Proof of Proof-of-Work (OPoPoW) without trusted setup*.

Furthermore, we showcase how Blink can be leveraged to develop a plethora of applications with enhanced efficiency compared to state-of-the-art protocols. For instance, it allows, for the first time, to securely and efficiently bootstrap light miners and full nodes, by providing a commitment to the state of the ledger with a short, constant-sized proof, bringing down the synchronization time from several days to a few hours. Furthermore, with Blink users can trustlessly verify their payments in a resource-constrained environment such as their phone with only a $\mathcal{O}(1)$ overhead, instead of $\mathcal{O}(\mathcal{C})$. Finally, Blink can replace SPV clients as a key component for bridges, further reducing the verification and storage costs incurred by contracts, while retaining the same security.

We provide a Proof-of-Concept *implementation* of Blink for Bitcoin, and evaluate its communication cost for the conventional $k = 6$ blocks. We underscore that Blink improves on all previous light client solutions in terms of proof size (and computational resources to verify it); at the time of writing, an SPV client has a proof size of 67MB, superlight clients [3,6] of 5-10KB, zk clients [9] of 197KB, and Blink of only 1.6KB.

In Sect. 7, we discuss practicality, limitations, and extensions of Blink to the variable difficulty setting.

Related Work. The description of Nakamoto's SPV client appears already in the Bitcoin whitepaper [2]. A series of optimizations followed. The first succinct construction was the interactive *Proofs of Proof-of-Work protocol* [5] with polylogarithmic costs. Later work removed this interactivity and achieved security against 1/2 adversaries but succinctness only in the optimistic setting (against no adversaries) [3]. This construction was subsequently optimized [4], made practical [11], and redesigned with backwards compatibility in mind [12]. The optimistic setting limitation was alleviated in a follow-up work, achieving succinctness against all adversaries up to a 1/3 threshold [13]. An alternative construction was also proposed, enabling security and succinctness against a 1/2 adversary, and adding support for variable difficulty [6]. All these solutions require polylogarithmic costs, whereas Blink requires only constant.

Recently, generic (recursive) zero-knowledge (ZK) techniques were utilized to build $\mathcal{O}(1)$ light clients [7,8,14]. However, these approaches incur prohibitively high computational costs (or necessitate specialized blockchain deployments [7,8] utilizing ZK-friendly cryptographic primitives [15]) and additionally require a trusted setup to generate and prove verification keys (which can only be removed if polylogarithmic communication is acceptable). Blink removes the trusted setup assumption.

Towards a $\mathcal{O}(1)$ light client without a trusted setup, the idea of using only a small segment of the chain near the tip was proposed [16]. However, the proposed construction was shown to be susceptible to pre-mining attacks and thus insecure [17]. Recently, Glimpse [17] has combined the idea of [16] with the injection of a *high-entropy* transaction Tx_η to prove the provided segment of the chain is "fresh" and not pre-mined. Nevertheless, we show that Glimpse suffers from safety and liveness attacks. In Blink we leverage and extend these ideas, proposing the first provably secure light client that consumes only a constant amount of resources and that does not require a trusted setup.

Finally, a similar quest for proof of stake light clients has achieved polylogarithmic complexity in an interactive setting [18]. For a review of the longstanding light client problem, see [19]. Light clients are also a cornerstone for building trustless bridges between chains, a question that has been explored in a multitude of works [20–23]. In this work, we demonstrate how Blink can serve as a building block for efficient optimistic bridges.

Comparison. In Table 1, we compare Blink with existing light client protocols. We denote by $\mathcal{C}$ the lifetime of the system (informally, the length of the blockchain) and by k the security parameter. According to the Bitcoin Backbone model, k is *constant* in the lifetime of the system, albeit with the trade-off of logarithmically increasing the probability of failure.

We first observe that Glimpse [17] consumes $\mathcal{O}(k)$ resources, but it is not secure (see Sect. 3); its exact resilience, if any, remains unknown. ZK clients, unlike Blink, rely on the trusted setup assumption. Blink consumes $\mathcal{O}(k)$ resources, it is finally provable secure, but requires one round of interaction.

Finally, contrary to other clients, Blink requires to publish on-chain the transaction Tx_η and wait for it to be k confirmed; despite this, in most real-world applications, all clients have the same latency as any payment or cross-chain request is considered final only after having k confirmation blocks. In Sect. 7, we propose practical solutions to reduce the costs of publishing Tx_η.

Table 1. Comparison of light client solutions.

	SPV [2]	KLS [5], NIPoPoW [3,13] FlyClient [6]	Plumo [7], Mina [8], Coda [14]	ZeroSync [9]	Glimpse [17]	Blink
Resources	$\mathcal{O}(\mathcal{C})$	$\mathcal{O}(k\,\text{polylog}(\mathcal{C}))$	$\mathcal{O}(1)$	$\mathcal{O}(1)$	$\mathcal{O}(k)$	$\mathcal{O}(k)$
No Trusted Setup	✓	✓	✗	✓	✓	✓
Adv. Resilience	1/2	1/2	1/2	1/2	✗(?)	1/2
Rounds of Interactivity	0	0	0	0	1	1
On-Chain Transactions	None	None	None	None	1	1
Proof size	67 MB	5–10 MB	22 KB	197 KB	1.2 KB	1.6KB

2 Preliminaries and Model

Notation. The bracket notation $[n]$ refers to the set $\{1, \ldots, n\}$ for a natural number n. $A[i]$ denotes the i-th element (starting from 0) of a sequence A, while negative indices like $A[-i]$ refer to the i-th element from the end. $A[i:j]$ represents the subsequence of A from index i (inclusive) to j (exclusive), while $A[i:]$ and $A[:j]$ represent the subsequences from i onwards and up to j, respectively. The notation $|A|$ denotes the size of the sequence A. The symbols $A \preceq B$ and $A \prec Y$ indicate that A is a prefix or a strict prefix of B or Y, respectively. We denote with $\mathcal{C}_r^\cap[:-k]$ the intersection of the view of the blockchain of all honest parties at round r, pruned of the last k blocks; likewise, $\mathcal{C}_r^\cup[:-k]$ is the union of the view of the blockchain of all honest parties at r, pruned of the last k blocks.

Ledger Model. We assume a synchronous network, i.e., all honest parties are guaranteed to receive messages sent by honest parties within a known delay. We consider the protocol execution to proceed in discrete rounds.

Definition 1 (Ledger). *A* ledger *is a sequence of transactions.*

Definition 2 (Distributed Ledger Protocol). *A distributed ledger protocol is an Interactive Turing Machine exposing to all parties the following methods:*

- execute: *Executes 1 round of the protocol, during which the machine can communicate with other parties.*
- write(Tx): *Takes transaction* Tx *as input.*
- read(): *Outputs a ledger.*

For all correct nodes, a distributed ledger protocol that returns a total order of the transactions on input satisfies two security properties: safety and liveness. The notation $\mathcal{L}_r^P$ denotes the output of the read() method invoked on party P at the end of round r.

Definition 3 (Safety). *A distributed ledger protocol is* safe *if it fulfills the following properties:*

Self-consistency *For any correct party P and any rounds $r_1 \leq r_2$, it holds that $\mathcal{L}_{r_1}^P \preceq \mathcal{L}_{r_2}^P$.*

View-consistency *For any correct parties P_1, P_2 and any round r, it holds that either $\mathcal{L}_r^{P_1} \preceq \mathcal{L}_r^{P_2}$ or $\mathcal{L}_r^{P_2} \preceq \mathcal{L}_r^{P_1}$.*

Definition 4 (Liveness). *A distributed ledger protocol is live with liveness parameter u if all transactions written by any correct party at round r, appear in the ledgers of all correct parties by round $r + u$.*

The ledger uniquely defines the current state of the system. Consider an empty ledger $\mathcal{L}_0$ with genesis state S_0. To ascertain the i-th state S_i of a ledger $\mathcal{L}_i$, with $i > 0$, transactions $[\mathsf{Tx}_1, \ldots, \mathsf{Tx}_i]$ are applied as follows:

$$S_i := \delta(\ldots \delta(\delta(S_0, \mathsf{Tx}_1), \mathsf{Tx}_2) \ldots, \mathsf{Tx}_i).$$

As shorthand notation, we use $S_i := \delta^*(S_0, \mathcal{L}_i)$ to denote successive application of all transactions $\mathsf{Tx} \in \mathcal{L}_i$ to S_0. We consider PoW ledgers whose block headers include state commitment, i.e., a succinct, constant size representation of the state of the ledger. We stress that state commitments are necessary for Blink only to extract the ledger's state and not to create a secure proof.

Prover-Verifier Model. A client protocol is an interactive protocol between the client, acting as verifier V, and a set $\mathcal{P}$ of full nodes, acting as provers. We focus on a client V that, when it bootstraps on the network for the first time, it is only aware of the genesis state. We assume that the client is honest, and in the set $\mathcal{P}$ there is at least one honest prover (existential honesty assumption). The client does not know which prover is honest. While honest parties adhere to the correct protocol execution, the adversary can execute any probabilistic polynomial-time algorithm.

Ledger Client Security. We now define what it means for a client of a ledger $\mathcal{L}$ to be *secure*. Among all the honest parties' ledgers, let $\mathcal{L}_r^{\cup}$ be the longest and $\mathcal{L}_r^{\cap}$ be the shortest at the end of round r.

Definition 5 (Ledger Client Security) [24]. *An interactive Prover-Verifier protocol $\Pi(\mathcal{P}, V)$ is secure with safety parameter v if, when the protocol terminates ar r, V outputs a commitment to a state of the ledger $\mathcal{L}$ that, $\forall r' \geq r + v$, satisfies the following properties:*

Safety: *$\mathcal{L}$ is a prefix of $\mathcal{L}_{r'}^{\cup}$.*
Liveness: *$\mathcal{L}_r^{\cap}$ is a prefix of $\mathcal{L}$.*

When a protocol $\Pi(\mathcal{P}, V)$ correctly executes by downloading and verifying asymptotically less data in $\mathcal{L}$, it is a *light client* protocol. We measure the performance of a client protocol by defining the *communication cost* for the verifier; the computational and storage costs of a client are linear in the amount of data downloaded during the protocol.[1]

---

[1] For full nodes, assume transaction execution has a constant upper bound on the computation.

Definition 6 (Client Communication Cost). *We define* $\mathsf{cost}(\mathcal{E}, V)$ *to be the communication cost in bits of an execution* $\mathcal{E}$ *of a protocol* $\Pi(\mathcal{P}, V)$ *for* V.

A client protocol has *optimal communication cost* if $\mathsf{cost}(\mathcal{E}, V) = \mathcal{O}(1)$, i.e., if V only receives a constant amount of data per protocol execution.

Definition 7 (Optimal Proof of Proof-of-Work (OPoPoW)). *A light client protocol is an* Optimal Proof of Proof-of-Work *when it is secure (Definition 5) and has optimal communication cost (Definition 6).*

Chain Client Security. To model the Proof-of-Work setting we closely follow [10]. Importantly, we operate in the static model, where the number of consensus nodes remains fixed throughout the protocol execution. Furthermore, each of them is assumed to have an equal computational power (flat model). The static model implies *static difficulty*. For a thorough description of the PoW blockchain model, see Appendix B.1 in the full version of this paper [25]. Throughout this work, we will use the term block to mean a block header. Towards defining the security of a client for blockchain protocols, we first define the notion of *admissible block*.

Definition 8 ((u, k)-Admissible Block at r). *Consider* $u, k \in \mathbb{N}$. *Any block* B *that, at round* r, *fulfils the following properties is an* admissible block at r:

Safety : $\mathsf{B} \in \mathcal{C}_{r+u}^{\cup}[: -k]$
Liveness : $\mathsf{B} \notin \mathcal{C}_r^{\cap}[: -k]$

In other words, for $r \leq r^*$, a block B is admissible at round r^* if B is seen as stable by at least one honest party at round $r + u$ (safety), and B is not yet seen by all parties at round r (liveness). In the above definition, u and k are free parameters. From the proofs in Appendix D in the full version of this work [25], it turns out that admissibility holds with u being the "wait time" parameter of liveness, and k the "depth" parameter of safety [10].

Definition 9 (Chain Client Security). *An interactive Prover-Verifier protocol* $\Pi(\mathcal{P}, V)$ *is* secure *if, when the protocol terminates at* r^*, V *outputs a block* B *that is* admissible *at* $r \leq r^*$.

We consider PoW blockchains whose blocks include state commitments. State commitments are a succinct representation of the state of the ledger, and they are assumed to be of constant size. In the account model of, e.g., Ethereum, an example of state commitment is the Merkle root of account balances; in the UTXO model of, e.g., Bitcoin, an example is the Merkle root of the UTXO Tree [2,24]. Equipped with state commitments, client protocols satisfying Definition 9 also satisfy Definition 5. We stress, however, that state commitments are necessary in Blink only for efficiently reading elements of the ledger's state, and not for creating a secure proof.

3 Blink

The ultimate goal of an OPoPoW client is to identify a recent, correct block of the ledger, by only receiving a constant-sized proof. We recall that in PoW blockchains, blocks are considered final if they have at least k confirmations, where k is the security parameter - in Bitcoin folklore $k = 6$.

A Naive Construction. We start considering a simple, naive construction. The provers give to the client the last $k+1$ consecutive blocks in their longest chain. The client verifies the validity of these sequences of blocks and, among the valid ones, takes the sequence whose blocks have the greatest height, and considers safe and live the first block in the sequence. This construction trivially breaks safety: an adversarial prover may have pre-mined $k+1$ fake blocks and can therefore trick the client into accepting a block that is not part of the chain.

Preventing Safety Attacks. To prevent this pre-mining attack, the client V needs to randomize the tip of the chain and to only accept blocks in the randomized suffix. In this way, the adversary is not able to predict the random value and therefore it is required to produce fresh blocks. Therefore, V locally samples a random string $\eta \xleftarrow{\$} \{0,1\}^\lambda$, defines a timeout T after which it stops accepting incoming proofs, and sends (η, T) to the provers [17]. The provers embed η into an *entropy transaction* Tx_η, broadcast Tx_η to the blockchain network, and wait for Tx_η to be included in a block B_η and confirmed. As soon as a prover P sees B_η with k confirmation blocks, if T has not expired, it sends to V a proof π consisting of B_η with its k confirmation blocks. Finally, V considers B_η safe and live, and it extracts from it the commitment to the state of the ledger.

Randomizing the proof rules out pre-mining attacks but, unfortunately, it does not result in a secure client protocol. Consider an adversary that controls $t < n/2$ of the n total participants in the PoW game. The adversary has a probability $t/n < 1/2$ of being elected as block proposer, which results in a non-negligible probability of censoring Tx_η in the next $k-1$ blocks. If by T the chain is extended by fewer than $2k$ consecutive blocks, the adversary can violate the liveness of the client protocol with probability t/n, as honest parties do not have time to produce $k+1$ blocks by T. Figure 2 shows this attack.

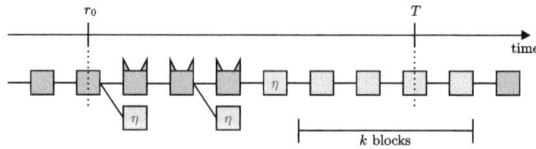

Fig. 2. Consider $k = 4$. The light client broadcasts η at round r_0. With non-negligible probability, a minority adversary can censor Tx_η in the next $k-1$ blocks. Honest parties do not have time to generate a proof of $k+1$ blocks before T expires.

Preventing Liveness Attacks. To protect the client from liveness attacks, one could remove the timeout T and ask V to accept the first incoming proof that consists of B_η and at least k confirmation blocks. Alternatively, one could ask V to accept the proof that, by T, has the most confirmation blocks on top of B_η. While both these attempts safeguard the liveness of the client, the client's safety is now broken again, as V might accept a block that is not part of any honest party's chain. We describe the safety attack for the case where T is removed, but a similar logic applies to the other case as well.

After Tx_η is broadcast, honest parties include it in the next block they create. The adversary, instead, extends the chain with blocks that censors Tx_η and it keeps these blocks private. Being k the security parameter, with non-negligible probability the adversary can privately mine $k - l$ blocks, with $0 < l < k - 1$. Meanwhile, honest parties can mine B_η with at most $k - l - 2$ confirmations. Then, the adversary broadcasts the private chain, causing all honest parties to switch to the adversarial chain, as per the longest chain rule. Honest parties include Tx_η in the new longest chain and keep mining on top of it. At the same time, the adversary starts privately mining on top of the chain abandoned by the honest parties, i.e., the one that included Tx_η early on. Now, to create a valid proof, the adversary only needs to mine $l + 2 < k + 1$ blocks, whereas honest parties need to mine $k+1$ blocks. As a result, with non-negligible probability the adversary can find the first k confirmation blocks on top of (an abandoned) B_η, and trick the client into considering safe and live a block that will never be part of the longest chain, thereby breaking security. Figure 3 illustrates this attack. This attack breaks the security of Glimpse [17].

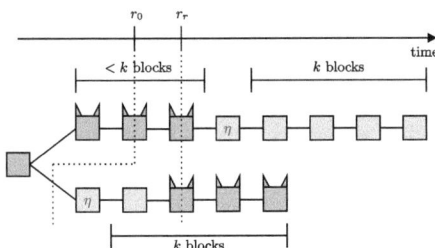

Fig. 3. Consider $k = 4$ and $l = 1$. The client broadcasts η at r_0. The adversary privately mines 3 blocks censoring Tx_η, while honest parties mine 2 blocks, the first of which includes Tx_η. The adversary releases the private chain at r_r and honest parties switch to it. Honest parties need to mine 5 blocks to find a valid proof, while the adversary only needs to mine 3 blocks. The adversary finds the proof first.

Blink. We recall that our goal is to let the client securely identify a block that is *safe*, i.e., already k deep in at least one honest party's chain [10], and *live*, i.e., sufficiently close to the tip of the chain. In the safety attack we just described, the adversary delays the inclusion of Tx_η in the main chain, but this censorship only succeeds for a limited time, specifically for less than k consecutive blocks:

a private chain longer than k and longer than the honest parties' chain would break safety of the ledger [10]. This means that any honest majority will create k blocks faster than any minority adversary.

Knowing that Tx_η can only be censored for $k-1$ blocks and that it takes k additional blocks for it to become safe (Fig. 3), in our final construction we modify the proof such that it consists of $2k+1$ blocks, with B_η in the middle, as depicted in Fig. 1. To avoid the safety attack, the client now considers safe and live the first block of the first valid proof it receives, and not B_η as before; this is because a proof of $2k+1$ blocks must necessarily contain a safe block, i.e., a block that is at least k deep in the chain of all honest parties. To be precise, the first proof that the client gets contains at least one block that was safe even before Tx_η was broadcast: the honest abandoned subchain has length at most $k-2$ and at least 1, therefore the first block in the proof was already part of the honest parties' stable chain (Fig. 4). Importantly, this is true even if the proof comes from the adversary. For any proof coming from an honest party, any block before B_η is already safe. We also note that the first block in the proof is live, as the block with η comes shortly after, and attached to genesis, otherwise honest parties would not have extended it.

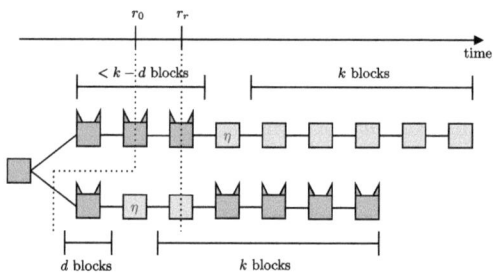

Fig. 4. Consider $k=5$. The adversary censors Tx_η by $k-d$ blocks on the top branch and by d blocks on the lower branch, with the overall number of adversarial blocks before Tx_η being smaller than k ($d \leq k-1$). This shows why taking fewer than k blocks before Tx_η is not sufficient.

To conclude, the first block of the first valid proof seen by the client is always safe, i.e., it has at least k confirmations in the view of an honest party, and live, i.e., it is at most k blocks far back from B_η.

We observe that the client receives a proof that consists of $2k+1$ blocks, with the number of blocks remaining constant in the system's lifetime (*optimal proof size*). After broadcasting η, the clients needs to wait for k blocks to be mined, but this waiting time is standard to all clients that want to have finality guarantees for a transaction. Finally, Blink can extract the state commitment from the first block of the proof. In Fig. 5 we present the pseudocode of the Blink protocol. In Appendix A of this paper's full version [25] we show the algorithms run by the client and provers of Blink.

Proof Construction
1. V samples $\eta \xleftarrow{\$} \{0,1\}^\lambda$.
2. V broadcasts η to $\mathcal{P}$.
3. $\mathcal{P}$ creates a transaction Tx_η that includes η and broadcast it to the network.
4. When a party $P \in \mathcal{P}$ sees a block B_η including Tx_η and having k confirmations, P sends to V a proof consisting of B_η and the k blocks before and after it.

State Commitment Extraction
5. V accepts the first incoming proof π that consists of $2k+1$ consecutive well-formed blocks, with the block in the middle containing η, i.e., $\pi[k] = \mathsf{B}_\eta$.
6. V extracts the state commitment from $\mathsf{B} := \pi[0]$ and terminates.

Fig. 5. The Blink protocol.

4 Applications

Payment Verification. Consider a vendor that wants to check if its customer (the buyer) has paid for the purchase of a good, and that will ship the good only after the client's payment has been verified and finalized. The vendor gives the buyer a new, fresh address η sampled with high entropy, and uses Blink to efficiently read the chain and verify the payment. Blink only guarantees safety for the first block of the first proof it receives, and not for the block including Tx_η. Fortunately, the safety guarantees of Blink are strong and they help our vendor nonetheless: the first block in the Blink proof behaves as a secure checkpoint or as a new genesis: this means that it will never be reverted and the consensus rules applied to genesis are consistent with the consensus rules applied to the new genesis (we prove this in Appendix D.1 of [25]). Therefore, upon accepting a proof and identifying the new genesis $\mathcal{G}'$, the Blink client can broadcast $\mathcal{G}'$ to the provers, and provers start sending to the client the blocks descending from $\mathcal{G}'$. The client now maintains the longest chain descending from $\mathcal{G}'$, temporarily running an SPV client on top of $\mathcal{G}'$, bootstrapped in $\mathcal{O}(1)$. When Tx_η is in a block k-deep in the longest chain, the client considers the payment final and terminates. This protocol retains the proof optimality of Blink (Tx_η is final at most $3k$ consecutive blocks after $\mathcal{G}'$), albeit with one more round of communication. Blink has the same latency of an SPV: k blocks during normal operation, and $2k$ in case of adversarial attack. This construction can be used out-of-the-box in the Bitcoin Backbone protocol in the static difficulty setting, without assuming block headers include a commitment to the state of the ledger. We refer to Sect. 7 for the variable difficulty setting and practical deployments.

Bootstrapping via Blink. In blockchains, there is interplay between different types of parties: consensus nodes (or miners) run the ledger protocol, full nodes verify the ledger by re-executing transactions, and light nodes query full nodes to verify transaction inclusion or account balances. Bootstrapping consensus and full nodes is resource-intensive, requiring a lot of bandwidth, compute, and disk space. Blink can be used for efficient bootstrapping of nodes: by identifying a recent block that behaves as a new genesis, SPV nodes can pinpoint the tip of the chain in $\mathcal{O}(1)$ and then run their protocol on top of it. Consensus nodes and full nodes, on the other hand, can use Blink to identify the new genesis and from it extract the commitment to the whole state of the ledger. Then, upon receiving from other nodes the state of the ledger, e.g., the set of UTXOs, they can verify its validity, without downloading and re-executing the entire history of transaction.

State Verification. As noted in Sect. 2, Blink assumed state commitments are embedded in each block to extract the global ledger state. Commitments come in different flavors (Merkle trees, accumulators, vector commitments), and they are used to efficiently download and validate the state of the ledger without having to receive and re-execute a complete copy of the ledger. In a chain with state commitments, *Blink verifies account balances and read the current state of on-chain contracts in $\mathcal{O}(1)$*. For a discussion on chains that have state commitments and how to introduce them to systems like Bitcoin, see Sect. 7.

Historical Transaction Verification. Though rare, some applications may need to verify transactions from, say, a day ago. With Blink, this involves locating the new genesis and traversing blocks backward until the target transaction is found—an approach with linear overhead in the transaction's age. More efficient are *proofs of ancestry*, which embed commitments (e.g., Merkle Mountain Ranges or vector commitments) in block headers, enabling backward navigation with logarithmic or constant overhead. Integrating such proofs with Blink improves historical transaction verification.

Bridging with Blink. Light clients have become key to bridge protocols, enabling efficient blockchain reads in a resource-constrained setting—the chain itself. High-volume bridges aim to relay one transaction per block, using SPV-like proofs. To reduce on-chain costs, optimistic bridges skip default block verification, checking blocks only when disputed. We now show how Blink enables succinct fraud proofs for optimistic bridges. Consider a PoW source blockchain $\mathcal{C}_S$ equipped with ancestry proofs and a destination chain $\mathcal{C}_D$. *Relayers* of the bridge optimistically relay a block B from $\mathcal{C}_S$ to the bridge contract in $\mathcal{C}_D$, along with a random string η_R freshly sampled for the block. Should a *challenger* notice that relayers submitted an invalid block, they have a time window to trigger a challenge, pinpointing the contested block B, and revealing a newly sampled random string η_C. The challenger also publishes a transaction Tx_η on $\mathcal{C}_S$, which includes $\eta := \eta_R \oplus \eta_C$ ($\oplus$ is bit-wise xor). The bridge contract will accept the first valid Blink proof received and, via ancestry proof, verify whether the contested block B is an ancestor of the first block in π. If this is not the case, B is removed from the bridge contract. We note that both parties need to contribute with a random string to prevent each of them from cheating, i.e., pre-mining a fake proof. Honest behavior can be incentivized through collateral that is slashed or redistributed in case of misbehavior.

5 Analysis

We now present the main theorems and an overview on the proof strategy. For model and definitions from the Bitcoin Backbone, for the general results, and the complete analysis of Blink security, see Appendix B, Appendix C, and Appendix D in the full version of this paper [25], respectively. In this work, we prove the following main theorem:

Theorem 1 (Ledger Client Security for Blink). *Blink is* ledger client secure *as per Definition 5, with the safety parameter v being the wait time parameter u of liveness.*

We start by identifying a special type of block: a *convergence event at round r*. A convergence event is an honestly produced block that, by r, has no acceptable parallel block; a block is *acceptable* if it is valid and there is at least one honest party who may extend it. Convergence events have interesting properties: (i) acceptable blocks at r descend from all convergence events at r; (ii) let $\tilde{\mathsf{B}}$ be a convergence event at r_c, and $\hat{\mathsf{B}}$ be an existing valid block whose height is larger than the one of $\tilde{\mathsf{B}}$ by at least k. Then, $\tilde{\mathsf{B}}$ is destined to become stable for all honest parties, even if $\hat{\mathsf{B}}$ is only known to the adversary; (iii) for any block, the prior convergence event is always less than k blocks back. These properties they are general and not specific to our construction, therefore they might be of independent interest. We prove the admissibility of $\pi[0]$, arguing about its liveness and safety. Towards proving safety of $\pi[0]$, we show that $\pi[k:]$ always extends $\tilde{\mathsf{B}}$ which, at the time that π is found, is the convergence event closest to $\pi[k:]$. Since $\pi[k]$ is fewer than k blocks in the future from its closest convergence event, $\tilde{\mathsf{B}} \in \pi$. Also, $\tilde{\mathsf{B}}$ will become stable, and thus $\pi[0]$ is safe. Towards proving liveness for $\pi[0]$, we know that $\pi[k]$ is fresh because it contains the newly sampled η; $\pi[0]$ is k blocks distant, and thus fresh. As a result of honest majority, a proof extending $\tilde{\mathsf{B}}$ is found first. To conclude, assuming that block include state commitments, we prove by reduction that any client construction that fulfills the chain client security definition, also fulfills the ledger client security definition.

Theorem 2. *Blink has optimal* communication cost, *i.e., $\mathcal{O}(k)$.*

The *communication cost* (Definition 6) measures the bits sent/received by V during an execution $\mathcal{E}$ of a protocol $\Pi(\mathcal{P}, V)$. V sends η whose size is $\mathcal{O}_\lambda(1)$ to all provers, and it receives (at most) one proof consisting of $2k+1$ block headers for each $P \in \mathcal{P}$, plus an inclusion proof for Tx_η which is of size $\log N$, with N being the average number of transactions in a block; $\log N$ can be considered a constant. This makes for a total size of $\mathcal{O}(k)$. Note that in any light client, the communication cost increases linearly in the number of provers. Nevertheless, the *communication cost* of Blink remains constant in the system's lifetime. From Theorems 1 and 2, Blink is an Optimal Proof of Proof-of-Work (Definition 7).

6 Evaluation

We evaluate Blink by measuring its proof size and waiting time for Bitcoin. A Proof-of-Concept implementation of Blink is available at [26], and entropy transactions broadcast during the evaluation can be inspected here [27]. The client uses the python-bitcoin-utils library [28] to create entropy transactions and communicates via RPC APIs using the python request HTTP library [29].

Experimental Setup. We deployed two mainnet Bitcoin full nodes running Bitcoin Core 25.0 and acting as untrusted provers: one was operated in-house on our own hardware (Central Europe) and the other one on a Vultr virtual machine (UK). We use two different deployments to emulate more realistic network conditions. The nodes maintain a complete copy of the ledger and they allow us to broadcast transactions to the Bitcoin network as well as retrieve blocks, transactions, and inclusion proofs. We ran our custom implementation client on commodity hardware. The client begins by sampling uniformly at random a 160-bit string η and creating Tx_η by placing η in an OP_RETURN output. The size of Tx_η is 222 bytes. Then, the client connects to the two Bitcoin full nodes, broadcasts Tx_η, and waits for it to be k-confirmed. We set $k=6$ according to Bitcoin folklore. When one of the two full nodes reports Tx_η k-deep, the client downloads and verifies the Blink proof ($2k+1$ block headers) by checking their parent-child relation and the PoW inequality. The client additionally downloads and verifies the inclusion proof of Tx_η in the middle block.

Proof Size. We measure all the data received by the client from the full node that first reports Tx_η with k confirmations. This data amounts to 7728 bytes (7360 for the Blink proof, 368 for verifying transaction inclusion).

The 7728 bytes are due to full nodes using the inefficient JSON format and to the available standard RPC endpoints of the bitcoin daemon full node. Using an optimized data transmission that avoids superfluous data, the total amount of data transmitted over the network can be brought down to 1646 bytes per prover (1040 bytes for the 13 headers of 80 bytes each, 384 bytes for the Merkle inclusion proof consisting of 12 sibling SHA256 hashes of 256 bits each, and 222 bytes for the transaction Tx_η). In Table 2, for height 841368, we compare the amount of data downloaded by Blink (1.6 KB) to the one of a full node (684 GB), to an SPV client (67.3 MB), to NIPoPoW and FlyClient clients (10.0 KB and ~5 KB, respectively), and, finally, to a PoW ZK-STARK client (ZeroSync [9], 197KB). Importantly, *the differences between these clients increase as the blockchain grows*.

Table 2. Amount of data light clients download for Bitcoin at height 841368, $k=6$.

Full node	SPV [2]	KLS [5], NIPoPoW [3], Mining LogSpace [13]	FlyClient [6]	ZK ZeroSync Client [9]	Blink
684 GB	67.3 MB	10 KB	~5 KB	197 KB	1.6 KB

Waiting Time. We measure the time it takes the client algorithm to run, averaging it over 10 runs. We broadcast the entropy transaction with a high-priority fee, which allows Tx_η to be included in the next 1 or 2 blocks. The average waiting time for the client to accept a proof is 59 min, with a standard deviation of 17 min, in accordance with the Bitcoin folklore of 6 blocks per hour. Any node that waits for 6 confirmations to report transactions final incurs the same waiting time.

7 Practicality, Limitations, and Extensions of Blink

State Commitments. Some applications in Sect. 4 assume that each block contains a state commitment. While chains like ZCash, Nimiq, and Ethereum PoW do, Bitcoin—the largest PoW chain—does not. NIPoPoWs [3,6] could be added via a velvet fork [12,30], and similarly, introducing state commitments for Blink this way is promising, though its practical deployment remains uncertain.

Entropy Transaction. We observe that to make light clients more efficient, the computational and storage complexity is often shifted from the light client to the full nodes or to the consensus nodes: for instance, NIPoPoW clients require consensus nodes to augment the chain with an interliking structure, FlyClient requires full nodes to store and update an MMR where each leaf is a block of the chain (plus additional metadata), and zk clients require full nodes to compute heavy proofs. In this respect, Blink has *optimal resource consumption for all the parties involved*: the light client, the full nodes, and the consensus nodes. Blink only requires to post on-chain a transaction with high entropy.

The Blink's entropy transaction does not need to have a Blink-specific format, but it can be, for instance, a transaction that sends money to a fresh address sampled with high entropy. In this case, the fee required to publish the entropy transaction is absorbed by the fee of performing a payment. If the entropy transaction is posted with the sole purpose of injecting entropy on-chain (e.g., by using the `OP_RETURN` opcode), fees can be paid in the form, for instance, of an anyone-can-spend output. Furthermore, dedicated contracts or untrusted services can mitigate the clients' costs by batching different requests and compressing multiple entropy values into a single transaction: Multiple random strings can be ordered in a Merkle tree, and only the root be published on-chain in an entropy transaction. For this to be safe, each client needs a proof of inclusion of its randomness in the tree.

Interactivity. Blink demands one round of interactivity between the client and the full nodes, unlike its predecessors that operate non-interactively [3,5,6]. This is the trade-off we incur for achieving a constant-sized proof. We could remove the interactivity by introducing additional assumptions, e.g.: (i) a trusted committee service operates the client, similarly to what Chainlink provides for oracles, (ii) a random beacon acts as global entropy source and serves Blink clients. However, both solutions come with drawbacks, i.e., centralization or a strong non-practical cryptographic primitive, respectively. It remains an open question whether designing a $\mathcal{O}(1)$ non-interactive client is possible without extra assumptions.

Variable Difficulty. Blink is analyzed in the static setting [10], i.e., the PoW difficulty remains the same throughout the protocol execution. In practice, Bitcoin uses a variable difficulty recalculation. Blink can still be used safely if we assume that parties agree on the difficulty beforehand by looking it up on a trusted service, or making assumptions on the computational power of the adversary. Ideally, designing a secure client in the variable difficulty setting [31] should be possible by using *difficulty balloons* to succinctly measure the current difficulty [32]. This approach utilizes entropy proofs to estimate (within some error) the current PoW difficulty of the network, by which point Blink can be applied as is. However, we anticipate that such an approach would only be secure under a weaker adversary, i.e., one that controls up to $1/3$ of the computational power of the system. To provide an intuition behind this threshold, consider an adversary $t < 1/2$ that abstains from mining while the clients measures the difficulty, thus creating a false sense of the total computational power and of the number of blocks they can create in a set of rounds. Then, the adversary takes advantage of this false estimation to mine privately the required proof, violating the safety of Blink. We estimate that this adversarial advantage may be mitigated if honest nodes can produce double as many blocks as the adversary.

Alternatively, one could change the selection rule for the proof: the client can choose the proof with the most work after taking the intersection of all proofs within a timeout. We conjecture such an approach may alleviate the possible attack vectors of a minority adversary, and we plan to explore it in future work.

Acknowledgments. We thank Joachim Neu and Kostis Karantias for discussions in the early phase of the work. The work was supported by CoBloX Labs, by the European Research Council (ERC) under the European Union's Horizon 2020 research (agreement 771527-BROWSEC), by the Austrian Science Fund (FWF) through the SFB SpyCode project F8510-N and F8512-N and the project CoRaF (agreement ESP 68-N), by the Austrian Federal Ministry for Digital and Economic Affairs, the National Foundation for Research, Technology and Development and the Christian Doppler Research Association through the Christian Doppler Laboratory Blockchain Technologies for the Internet of Things (CDL-BOT), by the WWTF through the project 10.47379/ICT22045, and by Input Output (http://iohk.io) through their funding of the Edinburgh Blockchain Technology Lab.

References

1. Rowling, J.K.: Harry Potter and the Deathly Hallows, Chapter 36 (2009)
2. Nakamoto, S.: Bitcoin: a peer-to-peer electronic cash system (2009). http://bitcoin.org/bitcoin.pdf
3. Kiayias, A., Miller, A., Zindros, D.: Non-interactive proofs of proof-of-work. In: Bonneau, J., Heninger, N. (eds.) FC 2020. LNCS, vol. 12059, pp. 505–522. Springer, Cham (2020). https://doi.org/10.1007/978-3-030-51280-4_27
4. Karantias, K., Kiayias, A., Zindros, D.: Compact storage of superblocks for NIPoPoW applications. In: Pardalos, P., Kotsireas, I., Guo, Y., Knottenbelt, W. (eds.) Mathematical Research for Blockchain Economy. SPBE, pp. 77–91. Springer, Cham (2020). https://doi.org/10.1007/978-3-030-37110-4_6

5. Kiayias, A., Lamprou, N., Stouka, A.-P.: Proofs of proofs of work with sublinear complexity. In: Clark, J., Meiklejohn, S., Ryan, P.Y.A., Wallach, D., Brenner, M., Rohloff, K. (eds.) FC 2016. LNCS, vol. 9604, pp. 61–78. Springer, Heidelberg (2016). https://doi.org/10.1007/978-3-662-53357-4_5
6. Bünz, B., Kiffer, L., Luu, L., Zamani, M.: FlyClient: super-light clients for cryptocurrencies. In: IEEE Symposium on Security and Privacy (2020)
7. Vesely, P., et al.: Plumo: an ultralight blockchain client. In: Eyal, I., Garay, J. (eds.) FC 2022. LNCS, vol. 13411, pp. 597–614. Springer, Cham (2022). https://doi.org/10.1007/978-3-031-18283-9_30
8. Mina docs (2023). https://docs.minaprotocol.com/about-mina
9. Robin, L., Lukas, G., Andrew, M., Tino, S.: ZeroSync - STARK proofs for Bitcoin (2024). https://github.com/ZeroSync/header_chain
10. Garay, J., Kiayias, A., Leonardos, N.: The bitcoin backbone protocol: analysis and applications. Association for Computing Machinery (2024)
11. Daveas, S., Karantias, K., Kiayias, A., Zindros, D.: A gas-efficient superlight bitcoin client in solidity. In: Proceedings of the 2nd ACM Conference on Advances in Financial Technologies (2020)
12. Kiayias, A., Polydouri, A., Zindros, D.: The velvet path to superlight blockchain clients. In: Proceedings of the 3rd ACM Conference on Advances in Financial Technologies. Association for Computing Machinery (2021)
13. Kiayias, A., Leonardos, N., Zindros, D.: Mining in logarithmic space. In: Proceedings of the 2021 ACM SIGSAC Conference on Computer and Communications Security. Association for Computing Machinery (2021)
14. Bonneau, J., Meckler, I., Rao, V., Shapiro, E.: Coda: decentralized cryptocurrency at scale. IACR Cryptol. ePrint Arch. (2020)
15. Grassi, L., Khovratovich, D., Rechberger, C., Roy, A., Schofnegger, M.: Poseidon: a new hash function for zero-knowledge proof systems. In: 30th USENIX Security Symposium 2021. USENIX Association (2021)
16. How to validate Bitcoin payments in Ethereum (for only 700k gas!) (2018). https://shorturl.at/6a00G
17. Scaffino, G., Aumayr, L., Avarikioti, Z., Maffei, M.: Glimpse: on-demand PoW light client with constant-size storage for DeFi. In: 32nd USENIX Security Symposium 2023. USENIX Association (2023)
18. Agrawal, S., Neu, J., Tas, E.N., Zindros, D.: Proofs of proof-of-stake with sublinear complexity. In: 5th Conference on Advances in Financial Technologies. Schloss Dagstuhl – Leibniz-Zentrum für Informatik (2023)
19. Panagiotis Chatzigiannis, P., Baldimtsi, F., Chalkias, K.: SoK: blockchain light clients. In: Eyal, I., Garay, J. (eds.) FC 2022. LNCS, vol. 13411, pp. 615–641. Springer, Cham (2022). https://doi.org/10.1007/978-3-031-18283-9_31
20. Xie, T., et al.: zkBridge: trustless cross-chain bridges made practical. In: ACM SIGSAC Conference on Computer and Communications Security, CCS (2022)
21. Zamyatin, A., Harz, D., Lind, J., Panayiotou, P., Gervais, A., Knottenbelt, W.: XCLAIM: trustless, interoperable, cryptocurrency-backed assets. In: 2019 IEEE Symposium on Security and Privacy (SP) (2019)
22. Kiayias, A., Zindros, D.: Proof-of-work sidechains. In: IACR Cryptology ePrint Archive (2019)
23. Gaži, P., Kiayias, A., Zindros, D.: Proof-of-stake sidechains. In: 2019 IEEE Symposium on Security and Privacy (SP) (2019)
24. Tas, E.N., Tse, D., Yang, L., Zindros, D.: Light clients for lazy blockchains. In: Clark, J., Shi, E. (eds.) FC 2024. LNCS, vol. 14745, pp. 3–21. Springer, Cham (2025). https://doi.org/10.1007/978-3-031-78679-2_1

25. Aumayr, L., Avarikioti, Z., Maffei, M., Scaffino, G., Zindros, D.: BLINK: an optimal proof of proof-of-work. Cryptology ePrint Archive, Paper 2024/692 (2024)
26. Blink Implementation (2024). https://github.com/scaffino/Blink
27. Bitcoin Address. https://shorturl.at/9gQP2
28. Bitcoin Utils (2024). https://pypi.org/project/bitcoin-utils/
29. Python Request Library (2024). https://pypi.org/project/requests/
30. Zamyatin, A., Stifter, N., Judmayer, A., Schindler, P., Weippl, E., Knottenbelt, W.J.: A wild velvet fork appears! Inclusive blockchain protocol changes in practice. In: Zohar, A., et al. (eds.) FC 2018. LNCS, vol. 10958, pp. 31–42. Springer, Heidelberg (2019). https://doi.org/10.1007/978-3-662-58820-8_3
31. Garay, J., Kiayias, A., Leonardos, N.: The bitcoin backbone protocol with chains of variable difficulty. In: Katz, J., Shacham, H. (eds.) CRYPTO 2017. LNCS, vol. 10401, pp. 291–323. Springer, Cham (2017). https://doi.org/10.1007/978-3-319-63688-7_10
32. Zindros, D.: Decentralized Blockchain Interoperability. Ph.D. thesis, University of Athens (2020)

Reward Schemes and Committee Sizes in Proof of Stake Governance

Georgios Birmpas[1], Philip Lazos[2], Evangelos Markakis[2,3], and Paolo Penna[3(✉)]

[1] University of Liverpool, Liverpool, UK
[2] London, UK
[3] Input Output Global (IOG), Zurich, Switzerland
paolo.penna@iohk.io

Abstract. We investigate the impact of reward schemes and committee sizes on governance systems over blockchain communities. We introduce a model of elections with a binary outcome space, where there is a ground truth (i.e., a "correct" outcome), and where stakeholders can only choose to delegate their voting power to a set of delegation representatives (DReps). Moreover, the effort (cost) invested by each DRep positively influences both (i) her ability to vote correctly and (ii) the total delegation that she attracts, thereby increasing her voting power. This model constitutes a natural counterpart of delegated proof-of-stake (PoS) protocols, where delegated stakes are used to elect the block builders.

As a way to motivate the representatives to exert effort, a reward scheme can be used based on the delegation attracted by each DRep. We analyze both the game-theoretic aspects and the optimization version of this model. Our primary focus is on selecting a committee that maximizes the probability of reaching the correct outcome, given a fixed monetary budget allocated for rewarding the delegates. Our findings provide insights into the design of effective reward mechanisms and optimal committee structures (i.e., how many DReps are enough) in these PoS-like governance systems.

Keywords: Nash equilibria · reward schemes · effort games

1 Introduction

Our work falls under the broader topic of selecting an appropriate set of representatives out of a voting population. This has been a prominent research agenda in social choice theory over the years and has been already investigated from various angles. As indicative directions, the performance of randomly selected committees has been extensively studied and there also exist various formulations of finding the optimal number of representatives either as an optimization problem or via game-theoretic models (described in our related work section).

P. Lazos—Work done while at IOG.

At the same time this is also complemented by empirical research and the study of real world practices, spanning a horizon of several decades, see e.g. [24].

We focus on addressing such questions for governance systems in Proof-of-Stake (PoS) blockchain protocols (see e.g. [15]). Several blockchain communities have already implemented or are currently designing governance policies, where stakeholders can propose a referendum on any relevant issue, which can then lead to an election. We believe there are some important aspects that can jointly differentiate such elections from other more traditional settings. First, in blockchain communities, voting among stakeholders is usually a weighted voting process, with the voting power corresponding to the stake owned by each user. This moves away from the classic "one person-one vote" paradigm, which cannot be enforced due to the anonymity of users (someone could vote with several identities by splitting her stake). Secondly, in some blockchains, elections are implemented only by delegating voting power to representatives (known a priori) who will then vote with a weight equal to their total delegation they collected. This is done both in order to avoid having a huge number of transactions in the long run (a delegation can remain valid for future elections too, for as long as the user wants) but also to give the option to users who are not well-informed on an election topic to transfer their rights to someone that they trust their opinion. Third, it has been acknowledged that the users who act as representatives should be given some monetary compensation. The reason for this is two-fold. Representatives need to exert an effort to advertize their opinion and attract voters. But more importantly, the elections under consideration may often concern a technical topic (like protocol parameter changes), where the representatives may need to spend time so as to become more informed and shape an opinion.

The features highlighted in the previous discussion, motivate various interesting questions for the design of appropriate policies. In particular, an important question that arises is how to design a reward scheme for the representatives, given an available budget. What are the relevant parameters that the reward should depend on? Ideally, we would like a reward scheme to induce good quality Nash equilibria, meaning that the representatives are incentivized to exert a sufficient amount of effort so that their vote contributes to making a good decision for the blockchain protocol. Therefore the rewards need to account for the fact that effort can be costly. At the same time, another relevant question is to understand how many representatives can be enough under such a scenario. Qualitatively, what we are interested in is whether a relatively small set of representatives can be sufficient or whether a large number of them is necessary to ensure a good election outcome, i.e., to ensure that the weighted majority of the representatives vote for the ground truth.

1.1 Contribution

Our work is motivated by the ongoing design of the governance system in an actual blockchain community, namely of the Cardano cryptocurrency [1]. In Sect. 2 we introduce a game-theoretic model for capturing the main aspects of the elections under consideration. We focus on the scenario where the outcome space is binary and there is a *ground truth*, i.e., there is a correct outcome (say for the long-term evolution of the protocol), not a priori known to the representatives. The representatives can exert effort in order to find out the correct outcome which however comes at a cost (for information acquisition). At the same time, the exerted effort leads to a higher level of attracted delegations and in turn to (potentially) higher rewards, as we focus on reward schemes that depend on the volume of delegations (similarly to delegated PoS protocols).

In Sects. 3 and 4, we analyze natural reward schemes under this setting regarding their equilibria. In Sect. 3, we demonstrate, to our surprise, that perhaps the most natural rule where the representatives split the total budget in a proportional manner to their attracted delegations, is not so appropriate. The reason is that it induces low quality equilibria where not enough effort is made. In Sect. 4, we advocate the use of a better mechanism where rewards are given only to voters who reach a desired threshold of delegations (and thus up to k of them, for some parameter k). We characterize the set of pure equilibria, and show that under any equilibrium, the representatives exert a significant effort, and hence contribute towards electing the correct outcome. We also comment on relevant variants of this mechanism.

As the scheme of Sect. 4 imposes an upper bound on the representatives who will make an effort at equilibrium, this motivates the algorithmic question of how to select the number of representatives. We investigate this in Sect. 5, as a budget constrained problem. We study various classes of cost functions for the exerted effort, including concave, convex and concave-convex costs and highlight the different behavior of the optimal solution under these classes. One of our main conclusions is that in many cases, a small number of representatives suffices for achieving a good quality outcome, e.g., this holds for concave costs and also for concave-convex functions. Another interesting finding is that in the convex domain the answer is heavily dependent on the available budget. Finally, we also demonstrate our findings in Sect. 6 for a particular class of concave-convex cost functions that is motivated by works on experimental psychology.

1.2 Related Work

The topic of incentivizing committee members or delegates in elections to exert more effort has recently attracted attention partly due to applications over blockchain protocols and partly due to the overall rise of proxy voting and liquid democracy. The works most related to ours along these lines are [8,11] and [12]. In [11], a similar cost model to ours is used for acquiring information over an election topic. There are however substantial differences in most other modeling aspects. In their work, a committee is chosen randomly among a given population, and with the same voting power per member, whereas in our case the voting power depends on the effort exerted. Secondly, they consider a different game in which the rewards are dependent on the tally difference between the two alternatives, which is quite different from our model, where the reward depends on the attracted delegation. Furthermore, the payments are transfers from the remaining population and not by some external source. In a recent follow up work [12], a similar model to [11] is studied, but where the monetary transfers depend on observed information acquisition costs. In both of these works, the particular structure of the underlying equilibria is studied and despite the differences with our setting, the conclusions made on the appropriate committee size are qualitatively of a similar flavor. Finally, in the work of [8], a different model is considered where the voters are categorized into well-informed and mis-informed agents, with different cost functions each. The reward scheme considered there is also different, with no delegation involved, and where the payments are dependent on the fraction of other voters who voted the same alternative.

A different approach is taken in [3] for determining a reward scheme and a committee size. Namely, a mechanism design model is presented where a committee is picked at random from the population, and where the rewards are obtained as the outcome of a truthful mechanism. For the question of finding the optimal number of representatives, there have also been other attempts that are not based on rewarding the voters. A game-theoretic model along this direction is presented in [17]. In [22], a different model is studied where the optimal committee set is derived as the one maximizing the probability of voting for the correct outcome, given competence levels from some distribution. A similar idea is also used in [16] under constraints on the feasible sets of delegates. Yet another approach is explored in [26] by adding the dimension of a social network for defining an optimal set of representatives in elections.

When there is no a priori ground truth, alternative methodologies within proxy voting have also been considered for selecting a committee size. These approaches are based on optimizing the total welfare of the electorate. As an example, the performance of the *Sortition* method (randomly pick a subset of the voters of a given size) is studied in [18]. The work [20] considers the performance of proxy voting, focusing on understanding when the proxy-elected outcome coincides with the outcome of direct voting. Finally, in [2] welfare guarantees are provided for a small number of representatives under incomplete preferences.

The topic of incentivizing effort has been extensively studied in economics within the field of contract theory [23]. The models there typically involve a principal who can offer a contract to an agent for performing some task. Recently there has been a renewed interest in such problems from an algorithmic viewpoint, and we refer to [9] for an upcoming survey. These models however are only distantly related to our work, as the effort there is not tied to attracting delegations or voting power. In our model, rewards cannot depend on the "correct answer/success" as the latter cannot be verified. This contrasts with prior contract theory (principal-agent) models, where reward schemes are tied to the success of the project.

Finally another relevant stream of literature is in the field of prediction markets. These are markets where people can bet on contracts that pay based on the outcomes of unknown future events. The common element with our work is that prediction markets can be seen as a tool for discovering a future outcome (in our case, we want to steer the agents to discover the correct outcome in an election). Besides this somewhat common goal however, the overall approaches in the relevant studies are quite different. For an overview of the literature, we refer to the book by [25] and the survey by [13].

2 Our Delegation Model

We are considering a voting scenario with a binary choice, consisting of a 'good' and a 'bad' outcome. This is initially unknown to laypeople voters, but delegates are ready to step up, using their expertise and effort to steer the community towards the right choice.

Suppose that we have n delegation representatives (DReps) competing for votes. Each delegate can choose to exert some effort x_i, which leads to two positive effects: an increased chance of voting for the right outcome and an increased number of voters delegating to i. In particular, an effort $x_i \in [0, 1/2]$ leads to a probability of $p_i = 1/2 + x_i$ for i to vote for the right outcome. At the same time, the DRep manages to accumulate delegation (and subsequently voting power) equal to

$$w_i = \frac{x_i}{\sum_j x_j}, \tag{1}$$

with $\mathbf{w} = (w_1, \ldots, w_n)$. If none of the representatives exert any positive effort, then we assume $w_i = 0$ for all i. The underlying assumption here is that a more informed and knowledgeable DRep is more likely to attract voters as well (a different interpretation is that voters follow DReps based on their long term performance on voting for the 'supposedly good' outcome). We assume that, even after the vote, the system has no way to detect if the answer is correct (thus rewards cannot directly depend on this information).

The effort x_i also comes with a cost, described by a cost function[1] $c(x_i)$, for which we assume that it is strictly increasing, continuous and differentiable. We will consider various cases for the cost function in the sequel, such as linear, convex, concave, and concave-convex types observed in experimental psychology.

Remark 1. A more accurate model would be to consider two types of effort, the effort for information acquisition and the effort to attract delegates. This in turn would lead to having two different cost functions. We find it instructive in this first step of studying these problems to focus on a unifying model regarding the effort and the cost.

We focus on reward mechanisms that provide a monetary payment to each DRep based on the delegation vector $\mathbf{w}$. Such mechanisms are easy to implement as the total attracted delegation for each DRep can be measured (the effort x_i cannot). If f_i is the reward function for the payment to DRep i, her final utility is

$$u_i = f_i(\mathbf{w}) - c(x_i) \tag{2}$$

---

[1] Following the relevant literature [11,12], we also consider a common cost function for all voters.

A pure Nash equilibrium for a particular combination of reward functions f_i, and cost function c is defined as an effort vector $\mathbf{x} \in [0, 1/2]^n$ such that for any player i and $x'_i \neq x_i$ we have that: $u_i(\mathbf{x}) \geq u_i(x'_i, \mathbf{x_{-i}})$.

Budget Constraint. The total rewards given should be limited, such that given an available budget B:

$$\sum_{i=1}^{n} f_i(\mathbf{w}) \leq B. \tag{3}$$

Objective. Our social objective is to maximize the probability that the 'good' outcome is selected by the election. Since each DRep i has a voting power equal to w_i, the right outcome is selected only when the total weight of the DReps voting correctly is at least $1/2$. For the case where it is exactly $1/2$, we assume a random tie-breaking, so that the correct outcome is selected with probability $1/2$. Therefore, given a profile $\mathbf{x} = (x_1, x_2, \ldots, x_n)$, the probability of success is the following quantity:

$$P_{succ}(\mathbf{x}) := \Pr\left[\sum_{i=1}^{n} w_i \cdot X_i > \frac{1}{2}\right] + \frac{1}{2} \Pr\left[\sum_{i=1}^{n} w_i \cdot X_i = \frac{1}{2}\right], \tag{4}$$

where X_i is a Bernoulli random variable with $\Pr[X_i = 1] = 1/2 + x_i$. To give an idea of how the success probability looks like as a function of $\mathbf{x}$, the first term in the right hand side of (4) equals

$$\Pr\left[\sum_{i=1}^{n} w_i \cdot X_i > \frac{1}{2}\right] = \sum_{S: \sum_j w_j > 1/2} \left(\prod_{i \in S: x_i > 0} (1/2 + x_i) \cdot \prod_{i \notin S: x_i > 0} (1/2 - x_i) \right).$$

An equivalent formulation of $P_{succ}(\mathbf{x})$, that will be convenient in some sections is

$$P_{succ}(\mathbf{x}) = \Pr\left[\sum_{i=1}^{n} Z_i > 0\right] + \frac{1}{2} \Pr\left[\sum_{i=1}^{n} Z_i = 0\right], \tag{5}$$

where each Z_i is a random variable with $\Pr[Z_i = x_i] = p_{x_i} := 1/2 + x_i$ and $\Pr[Z_i = -x_i] = p_{-x_i} = 1/2 - x_i = 1 - p_{x_i}$. The interpretation when using the Z_i variables, is that a voter i contributes a weight of x_i when voting for the correct outcome, and a weight of $-x_i$ otherwise.

Optimization Benchmark. Given a cost function $c(\cdot)$ and budget B, the optimization benchmark is defined by maximizing the probability $P_{succ}(x)$, subject to the following *benchmark budget constraint*:

$$\sum_i c(x_i) \leq B . \tag{6}$$

We denote the corresponding optimum as $OPT(c, B) := P_{succ}(\mathbf{x}^*)$, where $\mathbf{x}^*$ is an optimal solution to this problem.

Remark 2. Any reward sharing scheme that guarantees nonnegative utilities for the DReps and the budget constraint (3) must satisfy the benchmark budget constraint (6).

We will also consider variants with (*i*) *symmetric* efforts and (*ii*) a *maximum number k of DReps*,

$$x_i \in \{x, 0\} \quad \text{for all } i \text{ and for some } x \text{ (symmetry)} ; \quad (7)$$
$$|i : x_i > 0| \leq k \quad \text{(maximum number of DReps)} . \quad (8)$$

We denote by $OPT^\star(c, B)$ the optimum for the symmetric version (7), by $OPT_k(c, B)$ the optimum for the one with at most k DReps (8), and by $OPT_k^\star(c, B)$ the one in which we have both. By definition, the following relations hold: $OPT(c, B) \geq OPT^\star(c, B) \geq OPT_k^\star(c, B)$ and $OPT(c, B) \geq OPT_k(c, B) \geq OPT_k^\star(c, B)$, which correspond to the optimality of symmetric solutions, and to the optimality of a fixed number of DReps, and combinations thereof.

Finally observe that $x_i \leq x_{\max}(c, B)$ where $x_{\max}(c, B)$ is the largest $x \leq 1/2$ such that $c(x) \leq B$.

3 Warmup: Equilibrium Analysis of Proportional Sharing

We first analyze a very simple and natural reward mechanism where each representative obtains a reward equal to the percentage of the overall delegation that she accumulated, i.e., $f_i(\mathbf{w}) = w_i \cdot B$. Such approaches have been considered in many problems in the context of profit sharing games [4], project games [5], contests [6], etc., due to their simplicity, and usually they also provide good guarantees in terms of performance.

The purpose of this section is to exhibit that this reward rule is not an appropriate incentive scheme if we are interested in maximizing the probability of the correct outcome, in the sense that it can induce low quality equilibria.

For smooth reward functions f_i and cost function c, we can derive the first order conditions that should hold at an equilibrium. If c' is the derivative of c, these are

$$\frac{\partial f_i(\mathbf{x})}{\partial x_i} = c'(x_i),$$

To illustrate our negative result, let us assume that the cost function is linear, $c_i(x_i) = ax_i$. We focus below on the symmetric Nash equilibria that may arise, i.e., profiles where all players exert the same effort.

Theorem 1. *The only symmetric Nash equilibrium under the proportional reward sharing rule, with a linear cost function, is the strategy profile with $x_i = x = \frac{B(n-1)}{an^2}$ for every i, as long as $x \in [0, 1/2]$.*

When the parameters B and a are constants independent of n, the next theorem shows that for a large enough population of voters, the proportional sharing rule can induce bad equilibria. The reason is that the effort of each DRep is $O(1/n)$ as identified in Theorem 1, and hence the probability of each DRep voting correctly is only $1/2+O(1/n)$. As a result, the probability of having the correct outcome elected goes to $1/2$ as n becomes large, as established below.

Theorem 2. *Under the symmetric equilibrium profile of the proportional sharing rule, the probability of selecting the right outcome, as $n \to \infty$, tends to $1/2$.*

Remark 3. An analogous conclusion also holds for concave functions of the form $c(x) = x^b$, with $b < 1$. There the effort per player at a symmetric equilibrium can be even worse, and bounded by $O((1/n)^{1/b})$, using the same proof as in Theorem 2.

4 Equilibrium Analysis of Threshold Mechanisms

Given the previous conclusions, we suggest that in order to incentivize the delegates to elect the correct outcome, we need a payment rule that induces more competition among them, so that they need to make an effort to attract delegations.

4.1 Equilibria Under the Threshold(k) Mechanism

Consider the mechanism where a delegate receives a reward only if she managed to get at least a $1/k$-fraction of the total delegation. The reward received by a voter i is:

$$f_i(w_i) = \begin{cases} B/k & \text{if } w_i \geq 1/k \\ 0 & \text{otherwise} \end{cases}.$$

What kind of equilibria do we expect to have under this mechanism? Naturally, we cannot have equilibria with more than k delegates exerting positive efforts, since only up to k delegates can be paid, and the remaining would not have any incentive to make any effort. Instead, we will see that we can have equilibria with exactly k delegates making an effort that are also symmetric as in (7).

The following theorem characterizes the set of pure Nash equilibria of the Threshold(k) mechanism. In particular, it demonstrates that in every equilibrium the set of players that exerts positive effort is of specific size, while it also provides specific conditions which the efforts of the players must obey.

Theorem 3. *For the Threshold(k) reward rule, every pure Nash equilibrium must be a symmetric Nash equilibrium in which exactly k voters exert positive effort. Moreover, for any $x \in (0, 1/2]$ there exists an equilibrium where k voters make effort equal to x if and only if one of the following conditions hold:*

- *either $c(\frac{k}{k-1}x) \geq B/k \geq c(x)$ and $\frac{k}{k-1}x \in (0, 1/2]$,*
- *or $B/k \geq c(x)$ and $\frac{k}{k-1}x > 1/2$,*

Proof (Sketch). The proof is given in the full version of this work [7]. Here we just describe the main intuition and ideas. First, no equilibrium can have more than k players exerting positive effort (since only the k with the highest effort get rewarded). Also, no equilibrium can have strictly less than k players exerting positive effort (otherwise the player with highest effort can improve her utility by reducing slightly her effort). Hence, any equilibrium must have exactly k players that exert positive effort. Imposing that deviating to zero effort is not profitable, together with $\sum_i w_i = 1$, we get that all equilibria are of the form $(x, \ldots, x, 0, \ldots, 0)$, up to a renaming of the players. The bounds on $c(x)$ are then obtained by considering deviations restricted to equlibria of this form (and that $w_i \geq 1/k$ is necessary to get the reward B/k). □

There are some positive things that we can claim for this mechanism, showing that there are some advantages against the proportional scheme. The first one is that in all its equilibria, the DReps who decide to exert a positive effort are making a much higher effort than in the symmetric equilibrium of the proportional scheme identified in Theorem 1. As an example, when k is much smaller than n, and under a linear cost function, the effort in Threshold(k) can be seen to be $\Omega(1/k)$, which is significantly higher than $O(1/n)$ under the proportional scheme, from Theorem 1. Hence we expect to have a higher probability of selecting the correct outcome.

Secondly, the next corollary shows that equilibria always exist and in fact all of them are close to the optimal effort under the constraint of using exactly k DReps. This motivates further the question of identifying the optimal k for maximizing the success probability for electing the correct outcome, which is the focus of Sect. 5.

Corollary 1. *Let $x^*(k)$ be the optimal effort for the optimization benchmark in which we impose a committee of size exactly equal to k.*

- *The profile where k people exert effort equal to $x = x^*(k)$ is an equilibrium.*
- *For any equilibrium profile with effort x, such that $\frac{k}{k-1}x \leq 1/2$, it holds that $x \geq (1 - \frac{1}{k})x^*(k)$.*

4.2 Variants of Threshold(k)

There are two variations of Threshold(k) that are also of interest. We still feel however that Threshold(k) has a higher appeal, as we demonstrate below. Both variations require that we spend all the budget in contrast to Threshold(k), where we may end up spending less. In the first variant below, the budget is split up to exhaustion, among the DReps who collected delegations that are at least a fraction of $1/k$:

$$f_i(w_i) = \begin{cases} \frac{B}{|j : w_j \geq 1/k|}, & \text{if } w_i \geq 1/k \\ 0, & \text{otherwise} \end{cases} \quad \text{(Variant 1)}$$

This variant turns out to have the following negative aspects.

Theorem 4. *For any continuous and strictly increasing cost function c, the mechanism of Variant 1 does not possess pure Nash equilibria.*

Consider now a different variation, where again up to k DReps may receive a reward but the budget is then split proportionately among them:

$$f_i(w_i) = \begin{cases} B \cdot \dfrac{w_i}{\sum_{j:w_j \geq 1/k} w_j}, & \text{if } w_i \geq 1/k \\ 0, & \text{otherwise} \end{cases} \quad \text{(Variant 2)}$$

Using similar arguments as in Theorem 4, we can have again a negative result, albeit a bit weaker.

Theorem 5. *For any continuous and strictly increasing cost function c, the mechanism of Variant 2 does not always possess pure Nash equilibria that are symmetric for the voters who exert positive effort.*

Remark 4. In contrast to Variant 1, there might exist non-symmetric equilibria. The difference with Variant 1 is that the reward of a player i when $w_i \geq 1/k$, is now affected by the effort that she exerts. The equilibrium conditions for the existence or not of such equilibria then highly depend on the cost function $c(\cdot)$, something that (along with their more complex nature) makes this variant less appealing than Threshold(k).

5 Optimizing the Number of DReps

Motivated by the previous results on the Threshold(k) mechanism and Corollary 1, we investigate now the problem from an optimization perspective. Hence, we focus on determining the optimal number k of DReps for a given budget. That is, the problem of maximizing the probability of success in the symmetric case, where the effort exerted is the same for all the DReps who do so as described by (7) (which in some cases turns out to be the optimal even under the more general solution space where the voters could exert different efforts).

5.1 General Bounds

We start with proving a general upper bound on the probability of success which applies to any number of DReps and to the *non-symmetric* case (Theorem 6). This result plays a key role for the analysis of concave costs (Sect. 5.2) as well as for the more general concave-convex ones (Sect. 5.3). By a slight abuse of notation, in the sequel, for effort vectors of the form $\mathbf{x} = (x_1, 0, \ldots, 0)$, we will use $P_{succ}(x_1)$ instead of $P_{succ}(\mathbf{x})$, and similarly for $P_{succ}(x_1, x_2, \ldots, x_n)$.

Theorem 6. *For any number of DReps with (possibly non-symmetric) efforts $\mathbf{x} = (x_1, x_2, \ldots, x_n)$, it holds that*

$$P_{succ}(\mathbf{x}) \leq P_{succ}(y) = 1/2 + y, \qquad y = x_1 + x_2 + \cdots + x_n. \quad (9)$$

Note that the above result implies that a single DRep is optimal whenever effort y does not violate the budget constraint, i.e., if $c(y) \leq B$. The dependency on the budget B is somewhat unavoidable, even for the case of convex costs (Sect. 5.4).

5.2 Concave (and Linear) Case: One DRep is Optimal

An immediate consequence of Theorem 6 is that for concave (and thus also for linear) cost functions, the optimal solution consists of a single DRep. Indeed, for any concave cost function $c(\cdot)$, and any effort vector $(x_1,\ldots,x_n)$, the solution which utilizes a single DRep with effort $y = x_1 + \cdots + x_n$ still satisfies the budget constraint (6), thus implying the following.

Corollary 2. *For any concave cost function, there is always an optimal solution consisting of a single DRep with effort x_1 such that $c(x_1) = B$, where B is the budget. Hence, using asymmetric efforts does not help in this case. Moreover, for the strictly concave case, one DRep is strictly better than several DReps.*

Corollary 2 reveals an extreme scenario, where if one cares for the absolute maximum for the probability of electing the correct outcome, just one delegate suffices. Clearly, practical considerations would enforce larger committees, but the main intuition behind the corollary is that a small committee size suffices to have a good quality outcome under concave costs.

5.3 Concave-Convex Case: Too Many DReps are Not Optimal

In this section, we consider the more general class of cost functions, namely, concave-convex ones, which arise in many real world settings as a means to capture more accurately the cost of information acquisition (in Sect. 6 we elaborate on this). An example showing the shape of concave-convex functions can be seen in Fig. 1. We shall prove below general bounds on the maximum number of DReps that produce optimal solutions, and the corresponding efforts. The main message of this section is that the optimal number of DReps cannot be too high, and can be upper bounded by appropriate parameters with a geometric interpretation that we define below (and hence also establishing lower bounds on the minimal effort at an optimal solution).

For $x > 0$, the maximum number of DReps with equal effort x that we can use, given a cost function $c(\cdot)$ and budget B, is equal to $k_{\max}(x, c) := \left\lfloor \frac{B}{c(x)} \right\rfloor$.

The following lemma states some natural properties of the success probability.

Lemma 1. *The success probability $P_{succ}(x, k)$ is monotone increasing in both the effort x and in the number of DReps k. That is, $P_{succ}(x, k) \leq P_{succ}(x, k+1)$ and $P_{succ}(x, k) < P_{succ}(x', k)$ for all $x' > x$.*

Our first result (Theorem 7 below) is based on a geometric argument shown in Fig. 1, and formally captured by this definition.

Definition 1. *For any concave-convex cost function $c(\cdot)$ and for any budget B, we let $c_{lin}(x) = \alpha_{c,B} \cdot x$ be the linear cost function such that $c(\cdot)$ and $c_{lin}(\cdot)$ take the same value B at some common point $x_1 > 0$, i.e., $c(x_1) = B = c_{lin}(x_1)$. Then, we denote by $x_{int} = x_{int}(c, B)$ the largest value x such that $c_{lin}(x) \leq c(x)$ for all $x \in [0, x_{int}(c, B)]$ such that $c(x) \leq B$.*

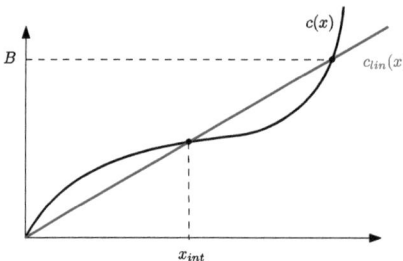
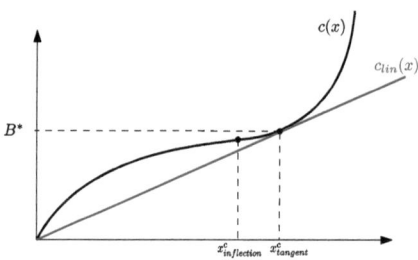

Fig. 1. The idea of Theorem 7.

Fig. 2. The idea of Theorem 8 with the inflection point $x^c_{inflection}$ and point $x^c_{tangent}$.

We first provide a general lower bound on the minimum effort for the optimal symmetric solutions, thus implying that the number of DReps cannot be too large.

Theorem 7. *For any concave-convex cost function $c(\cdot)$ and any budget B, the optimal symmetric solution with identical efforts must use at least an effort level of x_{int}, and thus at most $k_{\max}(x_{int}, c)$ DReps, where $x_{int} = x_{int}(c, B) > 0$ is given in Definition 1.*

Remark 5. Note that for smaller values of B, the bounds provided by the previous theorem get better, as the critical value $x_{int} = x_{int}(c, B)$ increases (see Fig. 1), which rules out more values from the optimum. Conversely, for increasing values of the budget B, the bounds of the previous theorem become weaker, as the opposite happens.

Moving on, the influence of the budget B suggested by the previous remark is the main focus of the remaining of this (and the next) section. We first note that Theorem 7 implies a *stronger* version of the result for concave costs. The idea is shown in Fig. 1, and formalized by the next definition.

Definition 2. *For any concave-convex cost function $c(\cdot)$, let $x^c_{inflection}$ denote its inflection point (where the switch from concave to convex occurs). Moreover, let $x^c_{tangent}$ be the largest point such that the line from the origin passing through $x^c_{tangent}$ is entirely below the cost function, and the two curves intersect at $x^c_{tangent}$. That is, the linear cost $c_{lin}(\cdot)$ such that $c_{lin}(x^c_{tangent}) = c(x^c_{tangent})$ satisfies $c_{lin}(x) \leq c(x)$ for all x such that $c(x) \leq B$.*

Observe that for $B = B^* := c(x^c_{tangent})$, the point $x_{int}(c, B)$ in Theorem 7 coincides with $x^c_{tangent}$, and $k_{\max}(x_{int}, c) = 1$; the same is true for $B < B^*$ as we consider the cost function restricted to a smaller interval – condition $c(x) \leq B$ in Definitions 1 and 2.

Corollary 3. *For any concave-convex cost function $c(\cdot)$, and for any budget $B \leq B^*$, there is always an optimal solution consisting of a single DRep with effort x_1 such that $c(x_1) = B$, where $B^* = c(x_{tangent}^c)$.*

We note that for concave functions, the condition on the budget required by the previous corollary is always satisfied, and therefore Corollary 3 generalizes Corollary 2.

We conclude this section by considering an arbitrarily large budget B and an improved version of the result in Theorem 7, if the following condition holds.

Assumption 1 (monotonicity). *For any linear cost function $c_{lin}(x) = a \cdot x$ with $a > 0$, the success probability is monotone decreasing with the number of DReps (while using the same corresponding maximum effort per DRep). That is, for any $x \leq x'$, $P_{succ}(x, k) \leq P_{succ}(x', k')$, where $k = k_{\max}(x, c_{lin})$ and $k' = k_{\max}(x', c_{lin})$.*

The next theorem provides better bounds for large B, showing that the optimal solution with equal efforts is situated in the region where $x_{tangent}^c > x_{int}(c, B)$. This result is conditioned on the above assumption, which we verified experimentally for several values of a and k, although we have not been able to formally prove it. The full version of this work provides further evidence for this assumption by proving a slightly weaker version of it (see [7]). The idea of the proof of the next theorem is shown in Fig. 2,

Theorem 8. *Suppose Assumption 1 holds. Then, for any concave-convex cost function $c(\cdot)$, and any budget B, the optimal solution with identical efforts must use at least $x_{tangent}^c$ effort level and thus at most $k_{\max}(x_{tangent}^c, c)$ DReps.*

5.4 Convex Case: The Budget Matters for the Optimal Number of DReps

One might conjecture that the convex case behaves inversely to the concave case, implying that many DReps are superior to fewer. However, we demonstrate that this presumption does not hold true, revealing a more intricate scenario (shown in Theorem 9 below). In particular, it holds that:

1. For certain convex costs, the superiority of three DReps over one hinges on the budget B.
2. The resolution of the former inquiry is contingent upon the specific convex function, even within costs of the form $c(x) = x^\beta$, parameterized in $\beta > 1$.

This indicates that a straightforward "monotonicity" argument asserting the supremacy of larger committees does not universally apply in the convex case.

The next lemma allows us to compare $k = 3$ with $k = 1$ on general cost functions, and it will also be used in Sect. 6 for a specific class of concave-convex cost functions.

Lemma 2. *Given any cost function $c(x)$ and any budget B, three DReps are better than one DRep (w.r.t. the success probability) if and only if the corresponding optimal efforts, $x^*(1)$ and $x^*(3)$, satisfy*

$$x^*(1) < \frac{3x^*(3) - 4x^*(3)^3}{2}. \tag{10}$$

The above lemma yields the following result for convex costs. We note that the result is analogous to the one obtained in [12], which also considers convex costs though in a slightly different setting.

Theorem 9. *For the family of convex cost functions $c(x) = x^\beta$, with $\beta > 1$, and for $\beta^\star := \frac{\ln(3)}{\ln(3)-\ln(2)} \approx 2.7095$, the following holds:*

1. *For $\beta < \beta^\star$, one DRep is always better than three DReps, regardless of B.*
2. *For $\beta > \beta^\star$, three DReps with equal effort are better than a single DRep if and only if the budget B is at most $B^\star = 3^{3/2} \cdot \left(\frac{3^{1-1/\beta}-2}{4}\right)^{\beta/2}$.*

We provide a numerical example for a simple (low degree) convex cost function.

Example 1 (budget-dependence for convex functions). Consider the convex cost function $c(x) = x^4$. By applying Theorem 9, we have that three DReps with equal effort are better than a single DRep if and only if the budget B is at most $B^\star = \left(\frac{3^{\frac{3}{2}} - 2 \cdot 3^{\frac{3}{4}}}{4}\right)^2 \approx 0.0254$. Moreover, the largest benefit for three DReps against a single DRep is for a budget equal to $B^{\star\star} = \left(\frac{4\sqrt[4]{3}x^2 - 3^{\frac{3}{4}}+2}{2}\right)^4$. □

Overall, the question of determining the optimal committee size with convex functions seems quite challenging. Even generalizing Theorem 9, to understand e.g. if k'' DReps are better than k' DReps for $k'' > k' > 3$, leads to a more complex analysis, since one needs to account for all the different probability events that can lead to the correct outcome. We leave this as an interesting open problem for future work.

6 Application to S-Shaped Learning Curves

In this section, we focus on certain classes of concave-convex costs which are derived by some *S-shaped learning curves* considered in the literature of experimental psychology [19]. Specifically, [19] proposes the following family of exponential learning curves, for learning over time a new task (in our case, learning the correct outcome),

$$p_\xi(t) = [1 - \exp(-\mu t)]^\xi \tag{11}$$

where the above success probability depends on the following parameters:

1. t is the time spent on learning (cost);
2. μ is the learning rate (potentially different for each individual);
3. ξ is a complexity parameter (equal for all individuals).

The complexity parameter $\xi > 1$ is crucial in order to obtain S-shaped learning curves, which have been often observed in practice. As pointed out by [19], several prior theoretical models [10,14,21] assume a "vanilla" exponential function with $\xi = 1$, i.e., $p(t) = 1 - \exp(-\mu t)$. The major shortcoming of these theoretical models is the mismatch with the S-shape observed by experimentalists. Intuitively speaking, the refined model in [19] assumes that $\xi = 1$ corresponds to acquiring some "elementary skills", while the actual tasks to be solved require some complex *combination* of these skills. The latter is captured by a parameter $\xi > 1$.

Remark 6 (homogeneous μ). Though the above model starts with the assumption of a different learning rate per individual, the actual experiments in [19] are conducted by isolating groups of people with *similar learning rate* and then fit the data of the group in order to estimate the complexity parameter ξ (the same ξ is used across all groups). In the following, we shall consider μ as homogeneous across all individuals, which is in line with the methodology in [19].

We next derive a concave-convex cost function $c(x)$ which corresponds to the above family of functions in (11). In our notation, $t = c(x)$. Moreover, we consider $x = p_\xi(t)/2$ so that the success probability for our two-outcomes setting, $1/2 + x = 1/2 + p_\xi(t)/2$, attains its minimum of $1/2$ when the cost for the corresponding player is zero. We thus have this relation: $2x = p_\xi(t) = [1-\exp(-\mu c(x))]^\xi$, which is equivalent to $\exp(-\mu c(x)) = 1 - (2x)^{1/\xi}$. The latter identity leads to the next definition for $c(x)$.

Definition 3. *The cost function associated to the exponential-learning curve (11) with complexity ξ and learning rate μ is defined as*

$$c_\xi(x) := -\frac{1}{\mu}\ln\left(1 - (2x)^{1/\xi}\right) . \qquad (12)$$

The next lemma provides useful features of these cost functions.

Lemma 3. *For every complexity parameter $\xi > 1$, the cost function c_ξ in (12) is a concave-convex function whose inflection point does not depend on the (individual) learning parameter μ but only on ξ. In particular, the inflection point is $\tilde{x} = \frac{1}{2}(1 - 1/\xi)^\xi$ and the corresponding cost is $c_\xi(\tilde{x}) = \ln(\xi)/\mu$.*

We next quantify the optimal symmetric efforts for this family of functions.

Lemma 4. *For the cost function c_ξ in (12) the optimal symmetric effort $x^*(k)$, given a budget B, is equal to $x^*(k) = \frac{p_\xi(B/k)}{2} = \frac{[1-\exp(-B\mu/k)]^\xi}{2}$.*

The next result concerns the optimality of one DRep when the budget is "not too high". Note that the result applies to a range of values for the budget, for which the largest feasible effort can be bigger than the inflection point, and thus we are still effectively considering a concave-convex cost function.

Corollary 4. *For the cost function c_ξ in (12) one DRep is optimal for any budget $B \leq B^*$, where B^* is defined as in Corollary 3 and it satisfies $B^* > \ln(\xi)/\mu$. In this case, the optimal probability of success is equal to $1/2 + p_\xi(B)/2 = 1/2 + \frac{[1-\exp(-B\mu)]^\xi}{2}$.*

Similarly to the convex case in Sect. 5.4, one DRep *is not* always optimal, and this depends on the budget B. In particular, Lemma 2 leads to the following:

Observation 1. *There exists a value B_{three} such that, for any budget $B \geq B_{three}$ three DReps are better than one DRep. This is because, for sufficiently large B, we are in the region where the curve gets sufficiently steep, and condition (10) of Lemma 2 is satisfied for the values given by Lemma 4. For example, this happens at $B_{three} \approx 4.35$ for parameters $\mu = 1$ and $\xi = 2$.*

Finally, we can also use Theorem 3 to obtain a characterization of the equilibria of the Threshold(k) mechanism. This can be found in the Appendix.

7 Conclusions

We have explored the questions of designing reward schemes and determining an appropriate number of representatives both from a game-theoretic and an optimization viewpoint. For proposing reward schemes, our results reveal that threshold-like mechanisms are more preferred as they seem to incentivize better the DReps on exerting more effort. Regarding the question of determining optimal committee sizes, our findings differ based on the type of cost function and on the available budget. In many cases however, as revealed in Sect. 5, a small number of representatives suffices for increasing the chances to select the correct outcome in the underlying election.

References

1. A first step towards on-chain decentralized governance (2024). https://cips.cardano.org/cip/CIP-1694
2. Amanatidis, G., Filos-Ratsikas, A., Lazos, P., Markakis, E., Papasotiropoulos, G.: On the potential and limitations of proxy voting: delegation with incomplete votes. In: Proceedings of the 23rd International Conference on Autonomous Agents and Multiagent Systems, AAMAS 2024, pp. 49–57. ACM (2024)
3. Auriol, E., Gary-Bobo, R.: On the optimal number of representatives. Public Choice **153**(3), 419–445 (2012)
4. Bachrach, Y., Syrgkanis, V., Vojnović, M.: Incentives and efficiency in uncertain collaborative environments. In: Chen, Y., Immorlica, N. (eds.) WINE 2013. LNCS, vol. 8289, pp. 26–39. Springer, Heidelberg (2013). https://doi.org/10.1007/978-3-642-45046-4_4
5. Bilò, V., Gourvès, L., Monnot, J.: Project games. In: Heggernes, P. (ed.) CIAC 2019. LNCS, vol. 11485, pp. 75–86. Springer, Cham (2019). https://doi.org/10.1007/978-3-030-17402-6_7

6. Birmpas, G., Kovalchuk, L., Lazos, P., Oliynykov, R.: Parallel contests for crowdsourcing reviews: existence and quality of equilibria. In: Proceedings of the 4th ACM Conference on Advances in Financial Technologies, AFT 2022, Cambridge, MA, USA, 19–21 September 2022, pp. 268–280. ACM (2022)
7. Birmpas, G., Lazos, P., Markakis, E., Penna, P.: Reward schemes and committee sizes in proof of stake governance (2024). https://arxiv.org/abs/2406.10525
8. Caragiannis, I., Schwartzbach, N.I.: Outsourcing adjudication to strategic jurors. In: Proceedings of the Thirty-Second International Joint Conference on Artificial Intelligence, IJCAI 2023, 19th–25th August 2023, Macao, SAR, China, pp. 2546–2553. ijcai.org (2023)
9. Dutting, P., Feldman, M., Cohen, I.: Algorithmic contract theory: a survey. In: Foundations and Trends in Theoretical Computer Science (FnTTCS) (forthcoming)
10. Estes, W.K.: Toward a statistical theory of learning. Psychol. Rev. **57**(2), 94–107 (1950). https://doi.org/10.1037/h0058559
11. Gersbach, H., Mamageishvili, A., Tejada, O.: Appointed learning for the common good: optimal committee size and monetary transfers. Games Econ. Behav. **136**, 153–176 (2022)
12. Gersbach, H., Mamageishvili, A., Tejada, O.: Do we need a committee? Available at SSRN 4699709 (2024)
13. Horn, C.F., Ivens, B.S., Ohneberg, M., Brem, A.: Prediction markets: a literature review. J. Predict. Mark. **8**(2), 89–126 (2014)
14. Hull, C.L.: Principles of behavior: an introduction to behavior theory (1943)
15. Larangeira, M., Karakostas, D.: The security of delegated proof-of-stake wallet and stake pools. In: Ruj, S., Kanhere, S.S., Conti, M. (eds.) Blockchains. Advances in Information Security, vol. 105, pp. 225–260. Springer, Cham (2023). https://doi.org/10.1007/978-3-031-32146-7_8
16. Magdon-Ismail, M., Xia, L.: A mathematical model for optimal decisions in A representative democracy. In: Annual Conference on Neural Information Processing Systems, NeurIPS 2018, pp. 4707–4716 (2018)
17. Martinelli, C.: Would rational voters acquire costly information? J. Econ. Theory **129**(1), 225–251 (2006)
18. Meir, R., Sandomirskiy, F., Tennenholtz, M.: Representative committees of peers. J. Artif. Intell. Res. **71**, 401–429 (2021)
19. Murre, J.M.: S-shaped learning curves. Psychonom. Bull. Rev. **21**, 344–356 (2014). https://doi.org/10.3758/s13423-013-0522-0
20. Pivato, M., Soh, A.: Weighted representative democracy. J. Math. Econ. **88**, 52–63 (2020)
21. Rescorla, R.A.: A theory of pavlovian conditioning: variations in the effectiveness of reinforcement and non-reinforcement. Classical Condition. Curr. Res. Theory **2**, 64–69 (1972)
22. Revel, M., Lin, T., Halpern, D.: How many representatives do we need? The optimal size of a congress voting on binary issues. In: Thirty-Sixth AAAI Conference on Artificial Intelligence, AAAI 2022, pp. 9431–9438. AAAI Press (2022)
23. Ross, S.A.: The economic theory of agency: the principal's problem. Am. Econ. Rev. **63**, 134–139 (1973)
24. Taagepera, R.: The size of national assemblies. Soc. Sci. Res. **1**(4), 385–401 (1972)
25. Williams, L.V. (ed.): Prediction Markets: Theory and Applications. Routledge International Studies in Money and Banking (2011)
26. Zhao, L., Peng, T.: An allometric scaling for the number of representative nodes in social networks. In: Proceedings of the 6th International Winter School and Conference on Network Science, NetSci-X, pp. 49–59 (2020)

Mining Power Destruction Attacks in the Presence of Petty-Compliant Mining Pools

Roozbeh Sarenche[✉], Svetla Nikova, and Bart Preneel

COSIC, KU Leuven, Leuven, Belgium
{roozbeh.sarenche,svetla.nikova,bart.preneel}@esat.kuleuven.be

Abstract. Bitcoin's security relies on its Proof-of-Work consensus, where miners solve puzzles to propose blocks. The puzzle's difficulty is set by the difficulty adjustment mechanism (DAM), based on the network's available mining power. Attacks that destroy some portion of mining power can exploit the DAM to lower difficulty, making such attacks profitable. In this paper, we analyze three types of mining power destruction attacks in the presence of petty-compliant mining pools: selfish mining, bribery, and mining power distraction attacks. We analyze selfish mining while accounting for the distribution of mining power among pools, a factor often overlooked in the literature. Our findings indicate that selfish mining can be more destructive when the non-adversarial mining share is well distributed among pools. We also introduce a novel bribery attack, where the adversarial pool bribes petty-compliant pools to orphan others' blocks. For small pools, we demonstrate that the bribery attack can dominate strategies such as selfish mining or undercutting. Lastly, we present the mining distraction attack, where the adversarial pool incentivizes petty-compliant pools to abandon Bitcoin's puzzle and mine for a simpler puzzle, thus wasting some part of their mining power. Similar to the previous attacks, this attack can lower the mining difficulty, but with the difference that it does not generate any evidence of mining power destruction, such as orphan blocks.

Keywords: Selfish mining · Bribery · Distraction attack

1 Introduction

Bitcoin [27] was the starting point of the exciting journey into the blockchain and cryptocurrency era. Despite the introduction of many new cryptocurrencies, Bitcoin has maintained the highest market capitalization [1] and remains the most famous cryptocurrency. Any serious attack that threatens Bitcoin's progress not only harms Bitcoin users but also impacts users of other cryptocurrencies and blockchain platforms. Although Bitcoin has operated smoothly since its emergence, the absence of a serious attack thus far does not guarantee that

---

The full version of this paper is available at [32].

its security will not be compromised in the future. Since the introduction of Bitcoin, numerous research papers [4, 13, 14] have analyzed its security and explored potential attacks [5, 11, 23, 30] that could target it. Identifying potential flaws in Bitcoin's underlying mechanism and studying possible solutions benefit Bitcoin's progress while serving as inspiration for new cryptocurrencies.

Several attacks have been introduced in the literature aimed at destroying the efforts of other miners in producing valid blocks, which we refer to as *mining power destruction attacks*. Examples include selfish mining [11, 30], block withholding [10, 29], power adjusting withholding and bribery selfish mining [12], block denial of service (BDoS) [25], undercutting [9], eclipse attack [28], Pitchforks [19], and script puzzle distraction attack [34]. While these attacks differ in their specific methods, they all share the common goal of destroying the mining power of other miners. The intuition behind the profitability of these attacks is the principle that mining rewards are distributed among the participating mining powers in proportion to their contributions to the chain extension. By destroying another miner's share, the adversary increases its own relative contributions, which consequently boosts its revenue. No mining power destruction attacks can be more profitable than following the honest strategy during the initial difficulty epoch [16, 33]. The adversary must wait for the subsequent difficulty adjustment mechanism to observe the impact of these attacks on its revenue. In contrast to attacks such as double spending, where the adversary receives revenue immediately upon a successful attack, mining power destruction attacks must be continued for at least two weeks (the length of one epoch) to become profitable.

In this paper, we analyze mining power destruction attacks in Bitcoin within the context of *petty-compliant mining pools*, referred to as a semi-rational setting. The analysis of these attacks in a semi-rational setting differs in two important ways from their analysis in the presence of altruistic mining pools. First, in semi-rational settings, we cannot naively assume that mining pools will always follow honest behavior, especially when they are the victims of an attack. As petty-compliant pools, they may choose to deviate from the honest strategy to defend against mining power destruction attacks and protect their mining efforts. Second, an adversarial mining pool in such settings may carry out incentive manipulation attacks [21], such as bribery, to convince non-victim petty-compliant mining pools to adopt its desired strategy, thereby increasing the success likelihood for its mining power destruction attacks. This potential for incentive manipulation allows adversarial mining pools even with a limited share of mining power to effectively attack the network. In this paper, we present a selfish mining analysis from a new perspective and introduce two novel mining power destruction attacks: bribery and mining power distraction attacks.

Selfish Mining Attack (Sect. 3): Selfish mining, introduced by Eyal et al. [11], is a well-studied attack in the context of Bitcoin. Numerous papers [6, 11, 16, 30, 31, 37] have analyzed the impact of selfish mining on the adversarial block ratio and profitability. However, most of these studies assume that, apart from the adversarial mining nodes, all the remaining mining nodes in the network follow the honest fork choice rule, meaning they always mine on the longest chain or the earliest of the longest forks. Carlsten et al. [9] introduced the concept of petty-compliant mining nodes, highlighting that, in a fork race, these mining nodes choose the fork that offers the highest return.[1] To the best of our knowledge, the first analysis of selfish mining in the presence of petty-compliant mining nodes was conducted by Bar-Zur et al. [7]. They showed that in a semi-rational setting, the mining share threshold for a profitable deviation from the honest strategy is reduced.

Despite considering petty-compliant mining nodes, the analysis in [7] is based on the implicit assumption that each mining node controls only an infinitesimal share of the total mining power, thereby overlooking the presence of any petty-compliant *mining pools*. A mining pool can be viewed as a group of infinitesimal mining nodes working together. Assuming no petty-compliant mining pools exist, the analysis can simply presume that, during a fork race, if the adversary places a bribe on top of the adversarial fork, almost all the network's mining power will mine on top of the adversarial fork. This is because the mining nodes that do not adopt the adversarial fork are only those that own a block in the non-adversarial fork, with a total mining share that is infinitesimal. However, when considering the existence of mining pools, the presence of a bribe offered by the adversary does not guarantee that all the network's mining power will mine on top of the adversarial fork. If a mining pool has already mined a block in the non-adversarial fork, it will continue to mine on top of that fork with its entire mining power, which can no longer be assumed to be infinitesimal. Figure 1 intuitively illustrates the mining share distributions between forks in a fork race, in the altruistic setting, in the presence of infinitesimally small petty-compliant mining nodes, and in the presence of petty-compliant mining pools.

In this paper, we analyze selfish mining in the presence of petty-compliant mining pools and examine the effect of mining power decentralization on selfish mining profitability. Our theoretical and Markov Decision Process (MDP)-based analysis shows that selfish mining is more destructive in settings where the non-adversarial mining pools are more decentralized. This suggests that the greater the gap in mining power share between the adversarial mining pool and the other pools, the more profitable selfish mining becomes.

Bribery Attack (Sect. 4): In the blockchain literature, various bribery attacks have been introduced for different purposes. These attacks can range from attempts to censor a single transaction, as seen in [26,35], to efforts aimed at rewriting the history of blockchain blocks to facilitate a successful double-spending attack [8,20,23,24]. The former requires a relatively small bribe to incentivize miners not to include a specific transaction, while the latter necessitates a substantial budget to persuade miners to abandon the longest chain and mine on top of a block that is deep within the chain. In this paper, we introduce a novel bribery attack aimed at destroying mining hash power. In our attack, the adversarial mining pool bribes petty-compliant mining pools to orphan the blocks of other mining pools, with the sole intention of wasting a portion of their

---

[1] [9] uses the concept of petty-compliant nodes in the undercutting attack analysis, overlooking them in the selfish mining analysis.

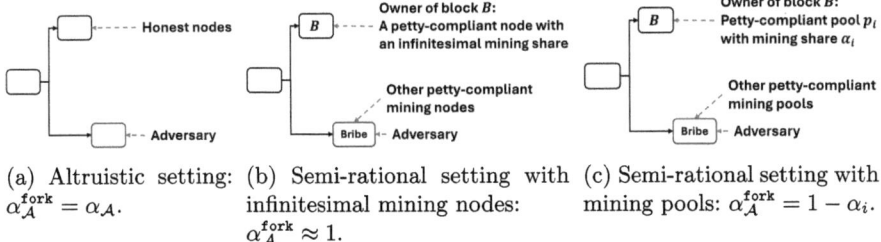

Fig. 1. Mining share distribution between forks in a block race. The adversarial block, denoted in red, is published later than the rival block in the block race. We denote by $\alpha_\mathcal{A}$, α_i, and $\alpha_\mathcal{A}^{fork}$ the mining shares of the adversarial mining pool, mining pool p_i, and all mining nodes extending the adversarial fork, respectively. (Color figure online)

mining power. Orphaning these blocks can reduce mining difficulty, resulting in revenue that compensates for the bribe paid. Our bribery attack is similar to selfish mining, except that instead of gambling on its own block to orphan another, the adversary pays a bribe less than the block reward to orphan a block. The advantage of the bribery attack over attacks such as selfish mining and feather forking is that it is risk-free for the adversarial pool, meaning the attacker does not risk losing its block or bribing budget. Additionally, a mining pool with any arbitrary share can always exploit other pools with a lesser share, making the attack profitable even for small mining pools.

Distraction Attack (App. F of [32]): As discussed in the literature [16,33], modifying the Bitcoin Difficulty Adjustment Mechanism (DAM) to adjust the difficulty based on the total active mining power—both wasted and effective—can mitigate mining power destruction attacks that generate valid proof of mining power destruction. For instance, selfish mining and the introduced bribery attack become unprofitable under such a modified DAM, as the orphan blocks generated during these attacks serve as evidence of mining power destruction. However, there are other types of mining strategies and attacks discussed in the literature, such as smart mining [15], coin hopping [17,18,22], and distraction attacks [34], which can destroy mining power without leaving evidence of destruction. In smart mining, a miner alternates between being idle and mining honestly, while in coin hopping, the miner switches between mining on different networks. Both strategies aim to manipulate and reduce the mining difficulty level. In distraction attacks, the adversary incentivizes miners to stop mining the Bitcoin puzzle and instead mine an alternative one. An example of a distraction attack is the script puzzle [34], where the adversary bribes miners through a smart contract-based puzzle to divert them from the Bitcoin chain. The goal of the script puzzle attack is to facilitate a double-spending attack or gain majority control of the network, which requires both a significant share of mining power and a substantial bribe (equivalent to six Bitcoin block rewards) for successful execution. These strategies and attacks can target Bitcoin without leaving any evidence, making them difficult to mitigate without relying on external trusted platforms.

In this paper, we introduce a novel distraction attack that aims to destroy a portion of mining power without leaving any evidence of power destruction. In our attack, the adversarial mining pool publishes a Proof-of-Work (PoW) puzzle with lower difficulty on another platform and incentivizes petty-compliant mining pools to mine the lower-difficulty puzzle. This attack can be carried out with minimal bribes, less than the value of a block reward.

2 Preliminaries and System Model

In our system model, time is divided into smaller units referred to as rounds. We use λ to denote the block mining rate of the network, representing the number of blocks mined per unit of time. We denote by $\text{REV}_i(t; \pi)$ and $\text{COST}_i(t; \pi)$ the revenue and the cost of mining pool p_i in round t under strategy π, respectively. If all the mining pools follow the honest strategy, the average per-round revenue of the mining pool p_i with mining share α_i is equal to $\alpha_i \cdot \lambda R$, where R denotes the block reward. If mining pool p_i mines with its whole mining power, its average mining cost per round is equal to $\alpha_i \cdot c_i$, where c_i denotes the average normalized mining cost of pool p_i per round.

Definition 1 (Time-averaged profit). *The time-averaged profit (per-round profit) of pool p_i following strategy π is defined as follows:*

$$\text{PROFIT}_i^t(\pi) = \frac{\sum_{t'=0}^{t-1} \left(\text{REV}_i(t'; \pi) - \text{COST}_i(t'; \pi) \right)}{t}, \quad (1)$$

$$\text{PROFIT}_i(\pi) = \lim_{t \to \infty} \text{PROFIT}_i^t(\pi) \ .$$

We define honest, petty-compliant, and adversarial mining pools as follows.

Definition 2 (Honest mining pool). *An honest mining pool is defined as a mining pool that i) always chooses the longest chain available in its view (in case of a tie, it chooses the block that was seen first) as its canonical chain to mine on top of, and ii) once it mines a new block, it immediately publishes the block to all other mining pools.*

Definition 3 (Chain expected return). *Let π_C and r_C denote the strategy of mining on top of a given chain C, and its expected return, respectively. The expected return r_C is defined as follows:*

$$r_C = \sum_{t=0}^{\infty} \gamma^t \text{REV}_i(t; \pi_C) \ , \quad (2)$$

where γ is a decaying factor set by each mining pool.[2]

---

[2] The presence of γ in the expected return definition makes it subjective to each mining pool's view of profitability. This reflects reality, as some pools prefer immediate rewards (low γ), while others prioritize long-term profit (with γ close to 1). In our paper analysis, we assume γ is close to 1 and that petty-compliant pools do not account for the impact of difficulty adjustment on the chain expected return.

For a given chain C, we denote by $|C|$ the length of the chain.

Definition 4 (Semi-rational fork choice rule). *Let C^{long} denote the longest chain available in the view of petty-compliant mining pool p_i (if there are multiple chains of equal length, consider the one that was seen first by the mining pool). Also, let CH^D denote the set of all the chains C in the view of petty-compliant mining pool p_i that satisfy $|C^{long}| - |C| \leq D$. According to the (ϵ, D)-semi-rational fork choice rule, if there is a chain $C^* \in CH^D$ that satisfies the following conditions:*

1. $r_{C^*} \geq r_C$ for all $C \in CH^D$, and
2. $r_{C^*} - r_{C^{long}} > \epsilon \alpha_i R$,

then C^* is the canonical chain. Otherwise, C^{long} is the canonical chain.

We refer to ϵ as the incentivizing factor, representing the threshold of normalized loss a mining pool tolerates before deviating from the honest strategy. A discussion of the parameters ϵ and D, as well as their role in the semi-rational fork choice definition is provided in App. A of [32].

Definition 5 (Petty-compliant mining pool). *An (ϵ, D)-petty-compliant mining pool is defined as a mining pool that i) follows the (ϵ, D)-semi-rational fork choice rule to select the canonical chain to mine on top of, and ii) once it mines a new block, it immediately publishes the block to all other mining pools unless it is incentivized not to do so.*

In this paper, petty-compliant pools are restricted to specific strategies defined for each attack and cannot act arbitrarily.

Definition 6 (Adversarial mining pool). *The adversarial mining pool may arbitrarily deviate from the honest strategy (for example, by delaying the publication of its blocks) or execute an incentive manipulation attack to induce petty-compliant mining pools to deviate from the honest strategy.*

Definition 7 (Semi-rational environment). *An (ϵ, D)-semi-rational environment is an environment in which any non-adversarial mining pool is an (ϵ', D)-petty-compliant mining pool, where $\epsilon' \leq \epsilon$. If $D = \infty$, we simply denote the environment as the ϵ-semi-rational environment.*

System Model. We assume our model operates within an (ϵ, D)-semi-rational environment. The system comprises a set of petty-compliant mining pools, denoted by p_i for i in $1, 2, \cdots, N$, alongside an adversarial mining pool denoted by $p_\mathcal{A}$. We denote by α_i and $\alpha_\mathcal{A}$ the mining power share of the ith petty-compliant mining pool and the adversarial mining pool, respectively, where $\alpha_\mathcal{A} + \sum_{i=1}^{N} \alpha_i = 1$. Our model assumes a fixed block reward of R; however, the adversarial mining pool may also place a bribe on top of any block. A discussion of the limitations of our system model is provided in App. B of [32].

Definition 8 (Normalized bribe). *The normalized bribe* $\mathtt{br}$ *is defined as the amount of bribe divided by the block reward* R.

According to Definition 8, a normalized bribe of $\mathtt{br}$ implies that the total amount of the bribe is equal to $\mathtt{br}R$.

3 Selfish Mining Attack

In this section, we analyze selfish mining in the presence of petty-compliant mining pools. Selfish mining results in a fork race between the adversarial and non-adversarial forks, with only one eventually being included in the canonical chain. The presence of petty-compliant mining pools offers some benefits to an adversarial pool. During a fork race, the adversary can bribe these pools to mine on the adversarial fork, boosting its chances of winning. The adversary can use in-band methods such as whale transactions [23] (discussed in App. C.1 of [32]) or out-of-band methods such as smart contracts [24,36] to bribe miners. It may also leave transaction fees in mempool as bribes for others [7,9].

Analyzing selfish mining in the presence of petty-compliant mining pools requires revisiting the selfish mining analysis typically applied to altruistic settings or semi-rational settings with infinitely many infinitesimal mining nodes. Under the altruistic assumption, the adversarial mining pool is guaranteed to win the fork race if its fork is longer than the competing fork. Additionally, if the adversarial pool propagates its fork faster, it increases its chances of winning a same-height fork race. In semi-rational settings with infinitely many infinitesimal mining nodes, the analysis may assume that the adversary can incentivize **all** petty-compliant nodes to abandon the non-adversarial fork with a bribe, as the mining share of infinitesimal miners in the non-adversarial fork is negligible.

However, the scenarios that can actually occur when selfish mining takes place in practice, particularly in the presence of petty-compliant mining pools, may differ significantly from the analyses conducted under the simplified assumptions of altruistic and infinitesimal miners. In the presence of petty-compliant mining pools, the adversary is not necessarily guaranteed to win the fork race solely based on the length of its fork, the speed at which it propagates its fork, or even the minimal bribe placed on its fork. Petty-compliant mining pools select the fork to mine based on its expected return, where the longest, fastest-propagated, or bribed chain may not always offer the highest expected return. For instance, consider a fork race between the non-adversarial fork with length $l_{\overline{A}}$ and the adversarial fork with length $l_A > l_{\overline{A}}$. If the petty-compliant mining pool p_i has $n > 0$ blocks in the non-adversarial fork, although the non-adversarial fork is shorter than the adversarial fork, p_i may still be incentivized to continue mining on top of the non-adversarial fork to revive its n blocks included in it. This example suggests that in the presence of petty-compliant mining pools, the strategy employed by the selfish pool and its profitability differ from those in altruistic settings or in environments with infinitely many infinitesimal nodes.

3.1 Theoretical Analysis

To analyze the selfish mining attack in the presence of petty-compliant mining pools, we first introduce metrics to assess the distribution of mining power among these pools.

Definition 9 (Centralization factor). *Let $\mathcal{P} = \{p_1, p_2, \cdots, p_N\}$ denote the set of all mining pools available in the environment. Also, let α_{p_i} denote the corresponding mining power share of mining pool $p_i \in \mathcal{P}$. The centralization factor, which is denoted by β, is defined as follows:*

$$\beta = \sum_{p_i \in \mathcal{P}} \alpha_{p_i}^2 . \tag{3}$$

The centralization factor β can take on values in the range of $(0, 1)$, with higher β values indicating a more centralized network. In a fully decentralized network, β approaches 0. Within a network where the maximum mining share of its mining pools is denoted by α, the centralization factor β is less than or equal to α, with the upper bound case of $\beta = \alpha$ occurring when all mining pools possess a mining share exactly equal to α.

Definition 10 (Residual centralization factor, Pool advantage). *Let $\mathcal{P}_{\bar{i}} = \{p_1, p_2, \cdots, p_N\} \setminus \{p_i\}$ denote the set of all mining pools excluding mining pool p_i whose mining power share is denoted by α_{p_i}. Also, let α_{p_j} denote the corresponding mining power share of mining pool $p_j \in \mathcal{P}_{\bar{i}}$. The residual centralization factor w.r.t. mining pool p_i, which is denoted by β_i, is defined as follows:*

$$\beta_i = \frac{\sum_{p_j \in \mathcal{P}_{\bar{i}}} \alpha_{p_j}^2}{1 - \alpha_{p_i}} . \tag{4}$$

The mining advantage of pool p_i is defined to be $1 - \beta_i$.

In the following, we demonstrate that a mining pool with a lower residual centralization factor (i.e., higher mining advantage) has a higher chance of conducting a successful selfish mining attack. To get the intuition of why pool advantage is defined as above, we first review the following lemma.

Lemma 1. *Consider a fork race within an ϵ-semi-rational environment, where the length of both semi-rational and adversarial forks is equal to 1, and a normalized bribe (see Definition 8) of $\bm{br} = \epsilon$ is available on top of the adversarial fork. The probability of the event that the next block is mined on top of the adversarial fork is equal to the mining advantage of the adversarial mining pool.*

The proof of Lemma 1 is presented in App. C.2 of [32]. In Def. 12 presented in App. C.3 of [32], we introduce a simple selfish mining strategy π^{selfish} suitable for an $(\epsilon, D = 1)$-semi-rational environment. As already discussed, strategies designed for an altruistic environment cannot be easily applied in a semi-rational setting. The outcome of each action that the adversarial mining pool takes in the semi-rational environment must be evaluated from the perspective of all petty-compliant mining pools. The following theorem examines the effect of the adversarial centralization factor on the profitability of strategy π^{selfish}.

Theorem 1. *Assume an $(\epsilon, D = 1)$-semi-rational environment[3] in which the mining share of each pool, excluding the adversarial pool, is less than 0.4302. In this environment, the selfish mining strategy π^{selfish} for an adversarial mining pool with mining share α_A and residual centralization factor β_A can dominate the honest mining if the following inequality holds:*

$$\beta_A < \frac{\alpha_A - \epsilon(1-\alpha_A)^2}{(1-\alpha_A)(1-\epsilon)} . \tag{5}$$

The proof of Theorem 1 is presented in App. C.5 of [32]. The assumption that the mining share of each non-adversarial mining pool is less than 0.4302 ensures that if an $(\epsilon, D = 1)$-petty-compliant mining pool has a single block in a fork that lags behind the longest fork by one block, it is incentivized to abandon its fork and adopt the longest fork (Lemma 2 of [32]).

Note that strategy π^{selfish} is not the optimal selfish mining strategy that an adversarial mining pool can follow in an $(\epsilon, D = 1)$-semi-rational environment. The main goal of Theorem 1 is to show that a mining pool with a lower residual centralization factor has a higher chance of successfully executing a selfish mining attack. This implies that the profitability of selfish mining in a semi-rational environment depends not only on the mining share of the adversarial pool but also on the distribution of mining power among the remaining mining pools.

Corollary 1. *Let P_1 and P_2 denote the first and second mining pools with the highest mining share in the network, whose corresponding mining shares are denoted by α_1 and α_2, respectively. Then, we can obtain the following statements for an ϵ-semi-rational environment:*

- *For $\epsilon > 0$, selfish mining dominate honest mining for mining pool P_1 if $\frac{\alpha_1}{1-\alpha_1} > \alpha_2 + \epsilon(1-\alpha_1-\alpha_2)$.*
- *For $\epsilon = 0$, selfish mining always dominate honest mining for mining pool P_1.*

The proof of Corollary 1 is presented in App. C.6 of [32]. According to Corollary 1, selfish mining is the dominant strategy for the largest mining pool if the network incentivizing threshold ϵ is less than the difference between the mining shares of the largest and the second largest mining pools. An important consideration in the literature on selfish mining is the minimum threshold of mining power required for a profitable attack. Perhaps the most well-known example is that, in an altruistic setting, a miner with a normal communication capability needs at least 25% of the network's mining power to successfully execute selfish mining [11]. These thresholds might suggest that if no mining pool holds a share above the threshold, selfish mining cannot threaten the network. However, Theorem 1 and Corollary 1 show that in practice, where multiple mining pools aim to maximize their payoffs, mining share alone is not the only factor determining

---

[3] $D = 1$ implies that the best chain in a mining pool view is a chain that is at most one block shorter than the longest chain.

the threat of selfish mining. The distribution of mining power among pools and the gap between their shares also play a critical role. Even if all mining pools hold less mining power than these well-known thresholds, a pool with a sufficiently large gap between its share and that of others can still find selfish mining profitable.

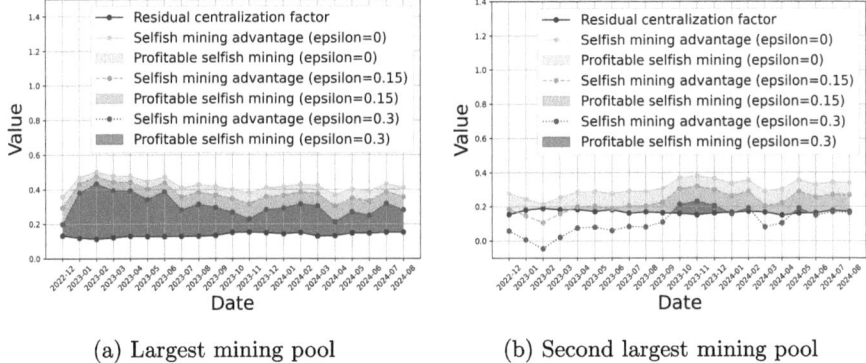

(a) Largest mining pool   (b) Second largest mining pool

Fig. 2. Periods of profitable selfish mining. According to Theorem 1, selfish mining becomes more profitable than honest mining when the selfish mining advantage of a mining pool (defined as the right-hand side of inequality (5)) surpasses its residual centralization factor (defined in Definition 10).

We define the ϵ-selfish mining advantage of the adversary as the right-hand side of inequality (5). According to Theorem 1, selfish mining dominates honest mining if the adversary's ϵ-selfish mining advantage exceeds its residual centralization factor. The mining power distribution for the first 8 months of 2024, obtained from [2], is presented in Table 1 in App. C.7 of [32]. Figure 2 depicts both the centralization factor and the ϵ-selfish mining advantage for the largest and second-largest mining pools over the months from December 2022 to August 2024. To generate Fig. 2, we used data on the number of blocks mined by the respective pools during these months to calculate their corresponding mining shares for each month. This figure illustrates in which months selfish mining could be considered profitable based on different values of the network incentivizing factor. As shown in Fig. 2a, selfish mining is always the dominant strategy for the largest pool, even with a high incentivizing factor of $\epsilon = 0.3$. If we assume $\epsilon = 0$, as can be seen in Fig. 2b, selfish mining is also the dominant strategy for the second-largest pool. However, as the incentivizing factor increases, some months are excluded from the profitable selfish mining period.

In App. C.8 of [32], we present our MDP-based implementation, available at [3], to derive the optimal selfish mining strategy in the semi-rational setting. In App. C.10 of [32], we discuss the duration of the initial financial loss associated with selfish mining and the cost incurred by the adversarial mining pool during this period.

4 Bribery Attack

Based on the selfish mining results from our MDP implementation presented in Table 4 of [32], the profitability of selfish mining drastically decreases as a pool's mining share decreases. The main reason for the marginal profitability of selfish mining for smaller pools is that, in selfish mining, an adversary is gambling on its own blocks, with no guarantee of winning the fork race. In other words, when an adversary withholds a block to initiate a fork race, it either collects the block reward R or loses it entirely. For larger mining pools, the probability of winning the fork race is high, making selfish mining profitable. However, smaller pools face a significantly higher risk of losing the block reward in the fork race. As a result, small mining pools prefer not to initiate a fork race unless they know the competing mining pool in the fork race is also small.

Knowing that selfish mining is a marginally-profitable mining power destruction attack for smaller pools, this section introduces a novel bribery attack that (similar to selfish mining) aims to waste a portion of the network's hash power. However, unlike selfish mining, this bribery attack is risk-free for the adversary and is not limited to times when the adversary has mined a block, thereby allowing the adversary to increase its profitability. In this attack, an adversarial mining pool pays a bribe to any other mining pool that can orphan a specific block targeted by the adversarial pool. In other words, the adversarial pool incentivizes petty-compliant mining pools to orphan a block mined by another mining pool. The profitability of the bribery attack is based on the same principle as selfish mining. In both of these attacks, the adversary aims to waste part of the network's hash power to exploit the difficulty adjustment mechanism, thereby reducing mining difficulty. The key difference is that in selfish mining, the adversarial pool uses its own blocks to carry out the attack, whereas in the bribery attack, it uses its budget to incentivize other mining pools to conduct the attack. The bribery attack offers two key advantages over selfish mining. First, it is risk-free for the adversary, as the bribe is only paid to collaborating pools upon successfully orphaning a block. Second, it can be executed by pools with small mining shares, enabling them to exploit weaker pools.

Definition 11 (Target and rival blocks). *Let B_1 represent the head of the canonical chain that is mined on top of block B_0. Additionally, suppose an adversarial mining pool offers a bribe for publishing a block B_1' on top of B_0, where B_1' differs from B_1. In this case, B_1 and B_1' are referred to as the target block and the rival block of a bribery attack, respectively.*

When an adversarial mining pool targets a block B_1 for a bribery attack, it is not guaranteed that a rival block will always be mined for the target block B_1. If no rival block is mined, the attack fails. However, if a rival block B_1' is mined for the target block B_1, the attack succeeds. In a successful bribery attack, both the target and rival blocks undergo a fork race. Note that the success of this bribery attack is independent of the outcome of the fork race, as neither of the blocks involved in the fork race is adversarial. Since only one block between the target and rival blocks can be included in the canonical chain, the orphaning of one block is definite, implying that the occurrence of the fork race is enough to consider the attack successful. The following theorem determines the maximum bribe the adversary can spend on the bribery attack while keeping it profitable.

Theorem 2. *Consider an adversarial mining pool with a mining share α_A that allocates a normalized bribe br for each target block B, which is payable only upon the successful mining of a rival block for block B. Assume k is the average number of target blocks per epoch for which a rival block is mined under the bribery attack. The time-averaged profit of the adversarial pool under the bribery attack exceeds the honest mining profit as long as $br < \alpha_A$, for any value of k.*

The proof of Theorem 2 is presented in App. D.1 of [32]. The idea behind the proof of Theorem 2 is to demonstrate that for each non-adversarial block that gets orphaned, the adversarial mining pool receives an additional revenue of $\alpha_A R$ on average. Therefore, if the bribe spent on orphaning each non-adversarial block is less than $\alpha_A R$, the adversarial mining pool can still earn a profit.

The question that arises is how the adversary can effectively use this bribe budget to incentivize other petty-compliant pools to mine a rival block for a target block. In the following section, we introduce a bribery attack and analyze it in the setting where all mining pools are aware of which pool has mined the target block B. Once a mining pool mines a block, it can reveal its identity in the coinbase transaction. According to the statistical information presented in [2], the ratio of unknown blocks in the first 8 months of 2024 is less than 8%, indicating that the majority of mining pools reveal their identity in their blocks. In App. D.2 of [32], we analyze the bribery attack in the setting where the miner of the target block is unknown.

4.1 Bribery Attack Under the Assumption of Known Miners

In this section, we present a smart-contract-based bribery attack under the assumption that the miners of target blocks are known. Appendix D.3 of [32] discusses a bribery attack using whale transactions.

Description of Bribery Attack Using Smart Contracts. Let α_A represent the mining share of the adversarial mining pool p_A. Assume block B_1 denotes the head of the canonical chain and is mined by mining pool p_i with mining share α_i. From the perspective of the adversarial mining pool, block B_1 can be considered a valid target block for the smart contract-based bribery attack if the following conditions hold: 1) B_1 is a non-adversarial block, and 2) $\alpha_A > \alpha_i + 2\epsilon$. If these conditions are not satisfied, the attack is not applicable, and the adversarial mining pool waits for the next block. If block B_1 is a valid target block, the adversarial mining pool proceeds with the bribery attack. Let B_0 denote the parent of the target block B_1. The adversarial mining pool deploys a smart contract and publishes it for all the mining pools. The smart contract stores three parameters: the hash of block B_0 denoted by $\text{Hash}(B_0)$, the hash of block

B_1 denoted by $\text{Hash}(B_1)$, and a difficulty target denoted by Target that is equal to the difficulty target of the epoch to which block B_1 belongs. The adversary deposits 2 normalized bribes $\text{br}_1 = \alpha_i + \epsilon$ and $\text{br}_2 = \epsilon$ in the smart contract. Anyone who submits a witness that proves the mining of a rival block B_{rival} for block B_1 can withdraw br_1. A valid witness includes a Bitcoin nonce, a Merkle root MR, a Bitcoin coinbase transaction tx, a Merkle inclusion proof, and a payout address add in the host blockchain, and satisfies the conditions:

1. Demonstrates valid evidence of power destruction[4]:
   - A valid rival block is mined on top of block B_0:
     $\text{Hash}(B_{\text{rival}}) = \text{Hash}\big(\text{Hash}(B_0), \text{MR}, \text{nonce}\big) \leq \text{Target}$.
   - The rival block differs from the target block: $\text{Hash}(B_{\text{rival}}) \neq \text{Hash}(B_1)$.
2. Includes a payout address that belongs to the compliant miner:
   - The coinbase transaction is included in the list of block transactions, i.e., a valid Merkle inclusion proof is available that proves coinbase transaction tx is a leaf of a Merkle tree with Merkle root MR.
   - The payout address add is included in the coinbase transaction.

If the witness transaction satisfies the conditions above, bribe br_1 will be transferred from the smart contract deposit to the payout address add, and the rival block hash $\text{Hash}(B_{\text{rival}})$ gets stored in the contract as the hash of the rival block. Anyone who submits a witness that proves the mining of a valid supporting block on top of the rival block B_{rival} can withdraw br_2. The witness verification is similar to the previous case with the difference that the hash of the parent block should be equal to $\text{Hash}(B_{\text{rival}})$. Note that this smart contract should have a time lock, after the expiration of which the adversarial mining pool is able to withdraw the deposits. This is to prevent any loss if the attack fails. During this attack, the adversarial mining pool follows the following strategy: if no rival block is published, it mines on top of the target block. Once a rival block is published, it switches to mining on top of the rival block.

Theorem 3. *In an ϵ-semi-rational environment, an adversarial mining pool with mining share α_A is incentivized to conduct a smart contract-based bribery attack on any target block B if block B is mined by a mining pool with mining share α_i, where $\alpha_A > \alpha_i + 2\epsilon$.*

The proof of Theorem 3 is presented in App. D.4 of [32]. The proof demonstrates that the adversarial mining pool must pay a normalized bribe of $\alpha_i + 2\epsilon$ to incentivize petty-compliant pools to mine a rival block for a target block mined by a pool with share α_i. Each bribery attack orphans one non-adversarial block, granting the adversary additional normalized revenue of α_A. Thus, if this additional revenue α_A exceeds the bribe $\alpha_i + 2\epsilon$, the attack becomes profitable.

According to Theorem 3, assuming $\epsilon = 0$, an adversarial mining pool can perform a bribery attack on blocks mined by any mining pool whose mining

---
[4] Verifying the transactions in the rival block is unnecessary. Any user who solves a new PoW puzzle (not necessarily a valid Bitcoin block) deserves the bribe.

power is less than the adversarial pool's mining share. The bribery attack is similar to the undercutting attack introduced in [9]. The key difference is that in undercutting, the adversarial mining pool uses its own block to undercut a target block. However, in the bribery attack, the adversarial mining pool incentivizes other mining pools to undercut a target block. Note that the undercutting attack is a subset of the possible actions considered in our selfish mining MDP analyzer introduced in App. C.8 of [32]. The Markov chain analysis of both the introduced bribery attack and the undercutting attack in the presence of petty-compliant pools is presented in App. D.5 and App. D.6 of [32], respectively.

Figure 3a, illustrates the percentage increase in reward share for the smart contract-based bribery attack, the selfish mining attack, and the undercutting attack, calculated for the 8 largest mining pools, based on the mining distribution in Table 1 of [32] and incentivizing factor $\epsilon = 0$. Figure 3b depicts the reward share that an adversarial mining pool can achieve in the presence of infinitesimal petty-compliant mining nodes. As can be seen in both Figs. 3a and 3b, the bribery attack can dominate both selfish mining and undercutting in an ϵ-semi-rational environment when the adversarial mining pool's share is small. The higher profitability of the bribery attack can be attributed to two main factors. First, in the bribery attack, the adversarial mining pool does not risk losing its blocks. Second, the bribery attack is not limited to the times when the adversarial mining pool has mined a block. In the undercutting attack, once the tip of the blockchain is a valid target block, the adversarial pool must mine the next block to successfully undercut the target block. This probability is relatively low, especially if the adversarial mining pool is small. In contrast, in the bribery attack, the adversarial mining pool can incentivize all mining pools, except the target block miner, to undercut the target block. Compared to other bribery attacks in the literature [8,20,23,24], where double-spent transactions compensate the adversary, in the introduced bribery attack, the protocol itself compensates the adversary, eliminating the need for performing deep block reorganizations. Addi-

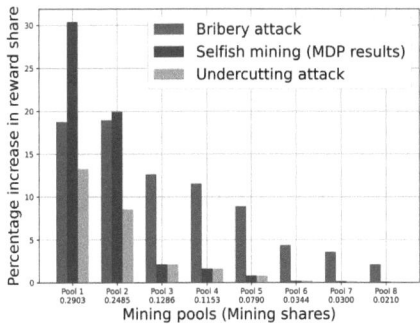
(a) Petty-compliant mining pools (real-world mining power distribution).

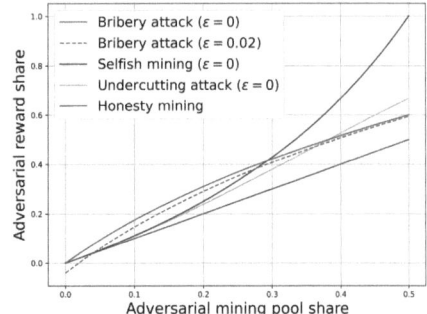
(b) A single adversarial pool and infinitesimal petty-compliant nodes.

Fig. 3. The adversarial reward share obtained from different attacks.

tionally, the budget for each instance of the introduced bribery attack is only a fraction of a block reward, significantly less than the double-spending bribes, which require several block rewards. In App. D.9 of [32], we discuss the duration of the initial financial loss associated with the bribery attack and the cost incurred by the adversarial mining pool during this period.

A discussion on the absence of major mining power destruction attacks on Bitcoin to date, potential solutions to mitigate such attacks, and the impact of DAM on the profitability of selfish mining and bribery attacks is presented in App. E and App. E.1 of [32]. We also introduce a novel distraction attack in App. F of [32], which destroys mining power without generating any evidence of destruction.

5 Conclusion

This paper discussed how an adversarial mining pool can use various methods to destroy a portion of the network's mining power. To execute a mining power destruction attack, the adversarial mining pool must invest some resources, which can be viewed as an initial cost. These resources may include withholding a block in selfish mining or offering a bribe in a bribery attack. However, this initial cost can be compensated, as the destruction attack lowers mining difficulty, resulting in an increased block production rate for the adversarial mining pool. Victims of destruction attacks can take countermeasures to mitigate them. For example, hiding their identity as block miners is a simple yet effective strategy. Additionally, mining pools can collaborate on mutual agreements, such as dividing larger pools into smaller ones or adopting a more secure difficulty adjustment mechanism. However, for every wise solution, there may be an equally clever counterattack.

References

1. Bitcoin market cap (2024). https://www.binance.com/en/price/bitcoin
2. Pools' mining share (2024). https://www.blockchain.com/explorer/charts/pools
3. Our selfish mining MDP implementation (2025). https://github.com/RoozbehSrnch/Selfish-Mining-Petty-Compliant-Pools
4. Badertscher, C., Garay, J., Maurer, U., Tschudi, D., Zikas, V.: But why does it work? A rational protocol design treatment of bitcoin. In: Nielsen, J.B., Rijmen, V. (eds.) EUROCRYPT 2018. LNCS, vol. 10821, pp. 34–65. Springer, Cham (2018). https://doi.org/10.1007/978-3-319-78375-8_2
5. Bag, S., Ruj, S., Sakurai, K.: Bitcoin block withholding attack: analysis and mitigation. IEEE Trans. Inf. Forensics Secur. **12**(8), 1967–1978 (2016)
6. Bar-Zur, R., Abu-Hanna, A., Eyal, I., Tamar, A.: WeRLman: to tackle whale (transactions), go deep (RL). In: Proceedings of the 15th ACM International Conference on Systems and Storage, pp. 148–148 (2022)
7. Bar-Zur, R., Dori, D., Vardi, S., Eyal, I., Tamar, A.: Deep bribe: predicting the rise of bribery in blockchain mining with deep rl. In: 2023 IEEE Security and Privacy Workshops (SPW), pp. 29–37. IEEE (2023)

8. Bonneau, J.: Why buy when you can rent? Bribery attacks on Bitcoin-style consensus. In: Clark, J., Meiklejohn, S., Ryan, P.Y.A., Wallach, D., Brenner, M., Rohloff, K. (eds.) FC 2016. LNCS, vol. 9604, pp. 19–26. Springer, Heidelberg (2016). https://doi.org/10.1007/978-3-662-53357-4_2
9. Carlsten, M., Kalodner, H., Weinberg, S.M., Narayanan, A.: On the instability of Bitcoin without the block reward. In: Proceedings of the 2016 ACM SIGSAC Conference on Computer and Communications Security, pp. 154–167 (2016)
10. Eyal, I.: The miner's dilemma. In: 2015 IEEE Symposium on Security and Privacy, pp. 89–103. IEEE (2015)
11. Eyal, I., Sirer, E.G.: Majority is not enough: bitcoin mining is vulnerable. Commun. ACM **61**(7), 95–102 (2018)
12. Gao, S., Li, Z., Peng, Z., Xiao, B.: Power adjusting and bribery racing: novel mining attacks in the Bitcoin system. In: Proceedings of the 2019 ACM SIGSAC Conference on Computer and Communications Security, pp. 833–850 (2019)
13. Garay, J., Kiayias, A., Leonardos, N.: The bitcoin backbone protocol with chains of variable difficulty. In: Katz, J., Shacham, H. (eds.) CRYPTO 2017. LNCS, vol. 10401, pp. 291–323. Springer, Cham (2017). https://doi.org/10.1007/978-3-319-63688-7_10
14. Garay, J.A., Kiayias, A., Leonardos, N.: The Bitcoin backbone protocol: analysis and applications. J. ACM (2015)
15. Goren, G., Spiegelman, A.: Mind the mining. In: Proceedings of the 2019 ACM Conference on Economics and Computation, pp. 475–487 (2019)
16. Grunspan, C., Pérez-Marco, R.: On profitability of selfish mining. arXiv preprint arXiv:1805.08281 (2018)
17. Grunspan, C., Pérez-Marco, R.: Profit lag and alternate network mining. In: The International Conference on Mathematical Research for Blockchain Economy, pp. 115–132. Springer, Heidelberg(2023). https://doi.org/10.1007/978-3-031-48731-6_7
18. Ilie, D.I., Werner, S.M., Stewart, I.D., Knottenbelt, W.J.: Unstable throughput: when the difficulty algorithm breaks. In: 2021 IEEE International Conference on Blockchain and Cryptocurrency (ICBC), pp. 1–5. IEEE (2021)
19. Judmayer, A., Stifter, N., Schindler, P., Weippl, E.: Pitchforks in cryptocurrencies: enforcing rule changes through offensive forking-and consensus techniques (short paper). In: Garcia-Alfaro, J., Herrera-Joancomartí, J., Livraga, G., Rios, R. (eds.) DPM/CBT -2018. LNCS, vol. 11025, pp. 197–206. Springer, Cham (2018). https://doi.org/10.1007/978-3-030-00305-0_15
20. Judmayer, A., et al.: Pay to win: cheap, crowdfundable, cross-chain algorithmic incentive manipulation attacks on PoW cryptocurrencies. Cryptology ePrint Archive (2019)
21. Judmayer, A., et al.: SoK: algorithmic incentive manipulation attacks on permissionless PoW cryptocurrencies. In: Bernhard, M., et al. (eds.) FC 2021. LNCS, vol. 12676, pp. 507–532. Springer, Heidelberg (2021). https://doi.org/10.1007/978-3-662-63958-0_38
22. Kwon, Y., Kim, H., Shin, J., Kim, Y.: Bitcoin vs. bitcoin cash: coexistence or downfall of bitcoin cash? In: 2019 IEEE Symposium on Security and Privacy (SP), pp. 935–951. IEEE (2019)
23. Liao, K., Katz, J.: Incentivizing blockchain forks via whale transactions. In: Brenner, M., et al. (eds.) FC 2017. LNCS, vol. 10323, pp. 264–279. Springer, Cham (2017). https://doi.org/10.1007/978-3-319-70278-0_17

24. McCorry, P., Hicks, A., Meiklejohn, S.: Smart contracts for bribing miners. In: Zohar, A., et al. (eds.) FC 2018. LNCS, vol. 10958, pp. 3–18. Springer, Heidelberg (2019). https://doi.org/10.1007/978-3-662-58820-8_1
25. Mirkin, M., Ji, Y., Pang, J., Klages-Mundt, A., Eyal, I., Juels, A.: BDoS: blockchain denial-of-service. In: Proceedings of the 2020 ACM SIGSAC conference on Computer and Communications Security, pp. 601–619 (2020)
26. Nadahalli, T., Khabbazian, M., Wattenhofer, R.: Timelocked bribing. In: Borisov, N., Diaz, C. (eds.) FC 2021. LNCS, vol. 12674, pp. 53–72. Springer, Heidelberg (2021). https://doi.org/10.1007/978-3-662-64322-8_3
27. Nakamoto, S.: Bitcoin: a peer-to-peer electronic cash system (2008). https://bitcoin.org/bitcoin.pdf
28. Nayak, K., Kumar, S., Miller, A., Shi, E.: Stubborn mining: generalizing selfish mining and combining with an eclipse attack. In: 2016 IEEE European Symposium on Security and Privacy (EuroS&P), pp. 305–320. IEEE (2016)
29. Rosenfeld, M.: Analysis of Bitcoin pooled mining reward systems. arXiv preprint arXiv:1112.4980 (2011)
30. Sapirshtein, A., Sompolinsky, Y., Zohar, A.: Optimal selfish mining strategies in bitcoin. In: Grossklags, J., Preneel, B. (eds.) FC 2016. LNCS, vol. 9603, pp. 515–532. Springer, Heidelberg (2017). https://doi.org/10.1007/978-3-662-54970-4_30
31. Sarenche, R., Nikova, S., Preneel, B.: Deep selfish proposing in longest-chain proof-of-stake protocols. Accepted at Financial Cryptography and Data Security 2024 (2024). https://eprint.iacr.org/2024/622
32. Sarenche, R., Nikova, S., Preneel, B.: Mining power destruction attacks in the presence of petty-compliant mining pools. arXiv preprint arXiv:2502.07410 (2025)
33. Sarenche, R., Zhang, R., Nikova, S., Preneel, B.: Selfish mining time-averaged analysis in bitcoin: is orphan reporting an effective countermeasure? IEEE Trans. Inf. Forensics Secur. **20**, 449–464 (2025). https://doi.org/10.1109/TIFS.2024.3518090
34. Teutsch, J., Jain, S., Saxena, P.: When cryptocurrencies mine their own business. In: Grossklags, J., Preneel, B. (eds.) FC 2016. LNCS, vol. 9603, pp. 499–514. Springer, Heidelberg (2017). https://doi.org/10.1007/978-3-662-54970-4_29
35. Tsabary, I., Yechieli, M., Manuskin, A., Eyal, I.: MAD-HTLC: because HTLC is crazy-cheap to attack. In: 2021 IEEE Symposium on Security and Privacy (SP), pp. 1230–1248. IEEE (2021)
36. Velner, Y., Teutsch, J., Luu, L.: Smart contracts make bitcoin mining pools vulnerable. In: Brenner, M., et al. (eds.) FC 2017. LNCS, vol. 10323, pp. 298–316. Springer, Cham (2017). https://doi.org/10.1007/978-3-319-70278-0_19
37. Zur, R.B., Eyal, I., Tamar, A.: Efficient MDP analysis for selfish-mining in blockchains. In: Proceedings of the 2nd ACM Conference on Advances in Financial Technologies, pp. 113–131 (2020)

A Theoretical Basis for MEV

Massimo Bartoletti[1(✉)] and Roberto Zunino[2]

[1] Università degli Studi di Cagliari, Cagliari, Italy
bart@unica.it
[2] Università di Trento, Trento, Italy

Abstract. Maximal Extractable Value (MEV) refers to a wide class of economic attacks to public blockchains, where adversaries with the power to reorder, drop or insert transactions in a block can "extract" value from smart contracts. Empirical research has shown that mainstream DeFi protocols are massively targeted by these attacks, with detrimental effects on their users and on the blockchain network. Despite the increasing real-world impact of these attacks, their theoretical foundations remain insufficiently established. We propose a formal theory of MEV, based on a general, abstract model of blockchains and smart contracts. Our theory is the basis for proofs of security against MEV attacks.

1 Introduction

Most blockchain protocols delegate the construction of blocks to consensus nodes that can freely pick users' transactions from the *mempool*, possibly add their own, and propose blocks containing these transactions in a chosen order. This arbitrariness in block construction can turn consensus nodes into adversaries, which exploit their transaction-ordering powers to maximize their gain at the expense of users. In the crypto jargon these attacks are referred to as "extracting" value, and the adversaries' gain is called *Maximal Extractable Value*, or MEV.

This issue is not purely theoretical: indeed, mainstream DeFi protocols like Automated Market Makers and Lending Pools are common targets of MEV attacks, which overall have led to attacks worth more than 1.2 billion dollars so far [1]. Notably, the profits derived from MEV attacks largely exceed those given by block rewards and transaction fees [16].

MEV attacks are so profitable that currently most Ethereum blocks proposals are due to centralized private relay networks that outsource the identification of MEV opportunities to anyone, and use their large networks of validators to include the MEV-extracting transactions in blocks [27,34]. While this systematic MEV extraction has some benefits (e.g., it has decreased transaction fees for users at the expense of MEV seekers [35]), it is detrimental to blockchain decentralization, transparency, and network congestion [28].

Given the practical relevance of MEV, various research efforts have focused on improving its understanding. Most approaches are preeminently empirical, and focus on heuristics to extract value from certain types of contracts [4,7,17,23,38], on the quantification of their impact in the wild [29,32,33,36,37], or on techniques to mitigate MEV attacks [5,10–13,15,20]. All these works, however, do not answer one fundamental question: *what is MEV, exactly?* This contrasts with fundamental principles of modern cryptography, where formal definitions of security properties and of adversaries' powers are essential to the study of cryptographic schemes. In the absence of a rigorous definition, it is impossible to prove that a contract is *MEV-free*, i.e., secure w.r.t. MEV attacks. Formalizing MEV is challenging, as it requires a complex characterization of the adversary: (i) as an entity who can control the construction of blocks, where they can craft and insert their own transactions; (ii) whose actual identity and current wealth are immaterial w.r.t. MEV extraction. This complexity requires a comprehensive formalization of the adversary powers, knowledge, and their MEV attacks. Existing MEV definitions [3,25,31] are partial (e.g., they do not formalize adversarial knowledge), and they wrongly classify some types of contracts (see Sect. 4).

Contributions. We summarise our contributions as follows:

- An abstract model of contracts, equipped with key economic notions like wealth and gain. We keep our model general in order to make it applicable to different blockchains and contract languages.
- An adversary model that includes a formalization of the adversaries' knowledge, i.e., the transactions that they can deduce by combining their private knowledge with that of the mempool. This improves over [3,25,31], where adversaries can craft blocks either by using their own knowledge or playing verbatim the transactions in the mempool, but cannot combine these two sources of information, so losing some potential attacks.
- A formal definition of the MEV extractable by a *given* set of users. We give this definition in two variants, depending on whether extracting MEV requires or not to exploit transactions in the mempool. This allows us to distinguish between the "legit" MEV that is intended in normal contract interactions, and the "bad" MEV that is not. To the best of our knowledge, this is the first work that attempts to separate "legit" MEV from "bad" MEV. We show that our definitions capture new attacks, not covered by [3,25,31].
- A formal definition of *universal* MEV, i.e., the maximal gain that can be achieved by *any* adversary, regardless of their actual identity and current wealth. Our MEV definition has a game-theoretic flavour: honest players try to minimize the damage, while adversaries try to maximize their gain. We support our notion through a theoretical study of its main properties, like monotonicity and finiteness;
- Proofs for MEV-freedom: we assess our MEV theory on real-world contracts such as crowdfunding, bounties, AMMs, and Lending Pools.

Overall, our formalization is a necessary first step towards the construction of analysis tools for the MEV-freedom of contracts. Because of space constraints, we provide our benchmark of use cases, additional results and the proofs of all our statements in a separated technical report [9].

2 Blockchain Model

We introduce below a formal model for reasoning about MEV. Aiming at generality and agnosticism of actual blockchains, rather than providing a concrete contract language we abstractly model contracts as state transition systems.

We assume a countably infinite set $\mathbb{A}$ of *actors* ($\mathsf{A}, \mathsf{B}, \ldots$), a set $\mathbb{X}$ of *transactions* ($\mathsf{X}, \mathsf{X}', \ldots$), and a set $\mathbb{T}$ of *token types* ($\mathsf{T}, \mathsf{T}', \ldots$). Actors are active entities, such as honest contract users or adversaries trying to extract MEV. We assume that tokens are *fungible*, i.e. units of the same type are interchangeable; NFTs are a special case of fungible tokens that are minted in a single indivisible unit.

We use calligraphic uppercase letters for sets (e.g., a set of actors $\mathcal{A}$, a set of transactions $\mathcal{X}$), and bold calligraphic uppercase for finite sequences (e.g., a sequence of transactions $\boldsymbol{\mathcal{X}}$). Pointwise sum of functions is denoted by $+$ and $\sum$.

We model the token holdings of a set of actors as a *wallet* $w : \mathbb{T} \to \mathbb{N}$, i.e., a map from token types to non-negative integers. A *wallet state* $W : \mathbb{A} \to (\mathbb{T} \to \mathbb{N})$ maps each actor to a wallet. We write $W(\mathcal{A})$ for $\sum_{\mathsf{A} \in \mathcal{A}} W(\mathsf{A})$, i.e., the pointwise addition of the wallets of the actors in $\mathcal{A}$. A *blockchain state* consists of a wallet state and a contract state. For the general results in this paper, the actual structure of contract states is immaterial, and therefore we do not specify it in Definition 1. When reasoning about specific contracts, we will make this structure explicit, including data and tokens. We model contracts as transition systems between blockchain states, with transitions triggered by transactions.

Definition 1 (Contract). *A contract is a triple made of:*

- $\mathbb{S} = \mathbb{C} \times \mathbb{W}$, *a set of* blockchain states, *where $\mathbb{C}$ is a set of* contract states, *and $\mathbb{W}$ is a set of wallet states;*
- $\mapsto : (\mathbb{S} \times \mathbb{X}) \to \mathbb{S}$, *a partial transition function that, given a blockchain state and a transaction, gives the next blockchain state;*
- $\mathbb{S}_0 \subseteq \mathbb{S}$, *a set of initial blockchain states.*

We denote by $\omega(S)$ the wallet state of a blockchain state S, and with $\omega_\mathsf{A}(S)$ the wallet of an actor A in S, i.e., $\omega_\mathsf{A}(S) = \omega(S)(\mathsf{A})$.

A transaction X is *valid* in a state S if S has an outgoing transition $\mapsto$ labelled X. In real-world contract platforms like Ethereum, invalid transactions can be included in blocks, but have no effect on the state of the contract. To model this behaviour, we transform $\mapsto$ into a (deterministic and) total relation $\to : (\mathbb{S} \times \mathbb{X}^*) \to \mathbb{S}$ between blockchain states; $\to$ is labelled with *sequences* of transactions. For an empty sequence ε, we let $S \xrightarrow{\varepsilon} S$, i.e., doing nothing has no effect. For a non-empty sequence $\boldsymbol{\mathcal{Y}}\mathsf{X}$, we let $S \xrightarrow{\boldsymbol{\mathcal{Y}}\mathsf{X}} S'$ when either:

$S \xrightarrow{\boldsymbol{\mathcal{Y}}} S''$ for some S'', and $S'' \xmapsto{\mathsf{X}} S'$ or $S \xrightarrow{\boldsymbol{\mathcal{Y}}} S'$ and X is not valid in S'

A state S is *reachable* if $S_0 \xrightarrow{\mathcal{X}} S$ for some initial state S_0 and sequence $\mathcal{X}$. We implicitly assume that all the states mentioned in our results are reachable.

Our model does not allow actors to freely exchange tokens, but this is not a limitation: if desired, this can be encoded in the contract transition function. This is coherent with how Ethereum handles e.g., ERC20 tokens, whose transfer capabilities are programmed in the contract.

Our model is quite general, and also includes some behaviors that are not meaningful in practice: e.g., there may be states where the total amount of tokens in actors' wallets is *infinite*. To rule out these cases, we require the following *finite tokens axiom*, ensuring that the overall amount of tokens in wallets is finite:[1]

$$\sum_{\mathrm{T}} W(\mathbb{A})(\mathrm{T}) \in \mathbb{N} \qquad (1)$$

As a consequence of the axiom, $\omega_\mathcal{A}(S)$ has finite support for all $\mathcal{A}$ and S. Hereafter, we denote by $\mathbb{N}^{(\mathbb{T})}$ the set of finite-support functions from $\mathbb{T}$ to $\mathbb{N}$.

Measuring the effect of an attack to a contract requires to estimate the *wealth* of the adversary before and after the attack. To account for the fact that different token types can have different prices, we assume an additive function $\$$ that, given a wallet w, determines its *wealth* $\$w$.[2]

Definition 2 (Wealth). *We say that* $\$: \mathbb{N}^{(\mathbb{T})} \to \mathbb{N}$ *is a wealth function if* $\$(w_0 + w_1) = \$w_0 + \$w_1$ *holds for all* $w_0, w_1 \in \mathbb{N}^{(\mathbb{T})}$.

Let $\mathbf{1}_\mathrm{T}$ be the wallet that contains exactly one token of type T. Then, we can write any wallet w as the (potentially infinite) sum:

$$w = \sum_{\mathrm{T}} w(\mathrm{T}) \cdot \mathbf{1}_\mathrm{T} \qquad (2)$$

If w has finite support, then the sum in (2) has only a finite number of non-zero terms. From additivity of $\$$, it follows that the wealth of a (finite-support) w is the sum of the amount of each token T in w, times the *price* of T, i.e., $\$\mathbf{1}_\mathrm{T}$:

$$\$w = \sum_{\mathrm{T}} \$(w(\mathrm{T}) \cdot \mathbf{1}_\mathrm{T}) = \sum_{\mathrm{T}} w(\mathrm{T}) \cdot \$\mathbf{1}_\mathrm{T} \qquad (3)$$

We measure the success of a MEV attack in terms of *gain*, i.e., the difference of the attackers' wealth before and after the attack.

---

[1] The finite tokens axiom applies only to the wallet state, while the tokens stored within the contract are unconstrained. Our theory works fine under this milder hypothesis, since to reason about MEV we do not need to count the tokens within the contract, but only the gain of actors.

[2] Note that $\mathbb{A}$'s wealth only depends on $\mathbb{A}$'s wallet, neglecting other parts of the state. As a result, actors with the same tokens have the same wealth, and wealth is insensitive to price fluctuations. This is because our notion of MEV is designed to capture attacks occurring in a *single* block. We discuss long-range attacks in Sect. 5.

Definition 3 (Gain). *We define the gain of $\mathcal{A}$ upon performing a sequence $\mathcal{X}$ of transactions from state S as $\gamma_{\mathcal{A}}(S, \mathcal{X}) = \$\omega_{\mathcal{A}}(S') - \$\omega_{\mathcal{A}}(S)$ if $S \xrightarrow{\mathcal{X}} S'$.*

The following proposition establishes some basic properties of gain. In particular, the maximal gain can always be extracted by a *finite* set of actors.

Proposition 1. *$\gamma_{\mathcal{A}}(S, \mathcal{X})$ is always defined and has a finite integer value, given by $\gamma_{\mathcal{A}}(S, \mathcal{X}) = \sum_{A \in \mathcal{A}} \gamma_A(S, \mathcal{X})$. Furthermore, there exists $\mathcal{A}_0 \subseteq_{fin} \mathcal{A}$ (finite subset of $\mathcal{A}$) such that, for all $\mathcal{B}$, if $\mathcal{A}_0 \subseteq \mathcal{B} \subseteq \mathcal{A}$ then $\gamma_{\mathcal{A}_0}(S, \mathcal{X}) = \gamma_{\mathcal{B}}(S, \mathcal{X})$.*

3 Maximal Extractable Value

Formalizing MEV is challenging, because it requires a twofold characterization of the adversary as a set of actors with the ability to reorder, drop and insert transactions, and whose actual identity and wealth are immaterial to MEV extraction. We then find it convenient to divide our formalization into three steps:

1. We define the set of transactions $\kappa_{\mathcal{A}}(\mathcal{X})$ that actors $\mathcal{A}$ can *deduce* by combining their private knowledge with that of the mempool $\mathcal{X}$ (Definition 4).
2. We define the MEV of a *given* set of actors $\mathcal{A}$ in a state S and mempool $\mathcal{X}$ as the *maximal gain* that $\mathcal{A}$ can achieve from S by firing a sequence of transactions in their deducible knowledge $\kappa_{\mathcal{A}}(\mathcal{X})$ (Definition 5). We also provide a variant, dubbed "bad" MEV, which models the case where the attack is only possible by exploiting transactions in the mempool.
3. We define the *universal* MEV in a state S and mempool $\mathcal{X}$ as the MEV that an *arbitrary* set of actors can achieve regardless of identity, only assuming they have (or can buy) the tokens needed to carry out the attack (Definition 9).

3.1 Adversary Model

Given a mempool $\mathcal{X}$, adversaries $\mathcal{A}$ can craft new transactions by mauling the transactions data in $\mathcal{X}$ (e.g., method arguments in Ethereum transactions). To this goal, $\mathcal{A}$ can reuse any piece of data in $\mathcal{X}$, with the constraints that they cannot forge signatures, and cannot deduce any value that is not efficiently computable from the previous ones (e.g., inverting a hash).

In our abstract model, we generalize this inference with an axiomatization of the set $\kappa_{\mathcal{A}}(\mathcal{X})$ of transactions deducible by the adversary $\mathcal{A}$ from a given mempool $\mathcal{X}$. We start by requiring **extensivity**, **idempotence** and **monotonicity** on $\mathcal{X}$, so making $\kappa_{\mathcal{A}}(\cdot)$ an upper closure operator for any $\mathcal{A}$. In particular, these axiom imply that $\kappa_{\mathcal{A}}(\mathcal{X})$ include all the transactions in the mempool $\mathcal{X}$, and that larger mempools lead to larger adversarial inferences. The **continuity** axiom is a standard structural requirement: in our theory, it is pivotal to prove that MEV can always be extracted from a finite mempool. The **finite causes** axiom ensures that any *finite* set of transactions can be deduced by a *finite* set of actors that only use their private knowledge. Abstractly, the private knowledge is the set of transactions deducible from an empty mempool $\mathcal{X}$ (in practice, this corresponds to the set of transactions that $\mathcal{A}$ can craft by using their private keys). The **private knowledge** axiom states that a larger private knowledge requires a larger set of actors: hence, if two sets of actors can deduce exactly the same transactions, then they must be equal. Finally, the **no shared secrets** axiom formalises a separation between the private knowledge of different actors: namely, it implies that if a transaction can be deduced by two disjoint sets of actors, then it can be deduced by anyone.

Definition 4 (Transaction deducibility). *We say that* $\kappa : 2^{\mathbb{A}} \times 2^{\mathbb{X}} \to 2^{\mathbb{X}}$ *is a transaction deducibility function if it satisfies the following axioms:*

```
contract BadHTLC {
  commit(a pays 1:T,b,c) { // a must send 1:T to the contract
    require balance(T)==1; commitment=c; // prevents multiple commits
  }
  reveal(a sig,y) { // a must sign the transaction and reveal the secret y
    require balance(T)>0 && H(y)==commitment; // y must be a preimage
    transfer(a,balance(T):T); // send all T balance to a
  }
  timeout(a sig,Oracle sig) { // a and Oracle must sign the transaction
    require balance(T)>0; // the contract must have some tokens T
    transfer(a,balance(T):T); // send all T balance to a
  }
}
```

Fig. 1. A Hash Time Locked Contract.

Extensivity $\mathcal{X} \subseteq \kappa_\mathcal{A}(\mathcal{X})$
Idempotence $\kappa_\mathcal{A}(\kappa_\mathcal{A}(\mathcal{X})) = \kappa_\mathcal{A}(\mathcal{X})$
Monotonicity *if* $\mathcal{A} \subseteq \mathcal{A}'$, $\mathcal{X} \subseteq \mathcal{X}'$, *then* $\kappa_\mathcal{A}(\mathcal{X}) \subseteq \kappa_{\mathcal{A}'}(\mathcal{X}')$
Continuity *for all chains* $\mathcal{X}_0 \subseteq \mathcal{X}_1 \subseteq \mathcal{X}_2 \subseteq \cdots$, $\kappa_\mathcal{A}(\bigcup_{i \in \mathbb{N}} \mathcal{X}_i) = \bigcup_{i \in \mathbb{N}} \kappa_\mathcal{A}(\mathcal{X}_i)$
Finite causes $\forall \mathcal{X}_0 \subseteq_{fin} \mathbb{X}. \ \exists \mathcal{A}_0 \subseteq_{fin} \mathbb{A}. \ \mathcal{X}_0 \subseteq \kappa_{\mathcal{A}_0}(\emptyset)$
Private knowledge *if* $\kappa_\mathcal{A}(\emptyset) \subseteq \kappa_{\mathcal{A}'}(\emptyset)$, *then* $\mathcal{A} \subseteq \mathcal{A}'$
No shared secrets $\kappa_\mathcal{A}(\mathcal{X}) \cap \kappa_\mathcal{B}(\mathcal{X}) \subseteq \kappa_{\mathcal{A} \cap \mathcal{B}}(\mathcal{X})$

We illustrate $\kappa_\mathcal{A}(\mathcal{X})$ through an example. For simplicity, in the contract language used in our examples we drop all the features of Solidity that are inessential to the understanding of MEV; still, the language is expressive enough to express real-world use cases like those found in DeFi see [9]. Our contract language has a formal semantics. While this semantics is crucial to prove the presence or absence of MEV in our benchmark of use cases, for now it will be sufficient to rely on its intuitive understanding.

Example 1. The BadHTLC contract in Fig. 1 implements a Hash-Time Locked Contract, where a committer promises that she will either reveal a secret within a certain deadline, or pay a penalty of 1:T to anyone after the deadline. Let S be a state where the secret has been committed to $H(s)$ but not revealed yet, and assume the mempool $\mathcal{X}$ contains a transaction $\mathsf{X_A} = \mathtt{reveal}(\mathtt{A\ sig}, s)$ sent by A to redeem the deposit. Since the secret s is public in the mempool, any adversary M can craft a transaction $\mathsf{X_M} = \mathtt{reveal}(\mathtt{M\ sig}, s)$ by combining their own knowledge (to provide M's signature) with that of $\mathcal{X}$ (to provide s). Hence, $\mathsf{X_M} \in \kappa_{\{\mathsf{M}\}}(\mathcal{X})$, and so M can extract MEV by front-running $\mathsf{X_A}$ with $\mathsf{X_M}$. Note instead that M *alone* cannot deduce the transaction that would allow her to trigger the timeout (see [9] for details). We remark that this attack requires the adversary to combine private and mempool knowledge, which does not seem to be properly accounted for in current MEV formalizations [3,25,31]. ◇

Proposition 2 establishes some key properties of κ, which will be instrumental to prove more complex properties about MEV. Item (1) states that different sets of actors have a different private knowledge. Item (2) implies that transactions that can be deduced by disjoint sets of actors can be deduced by anyone. Item (3) states that two groups of actors joining forces could infer more transactions than they could independently infer. Item (4) states that a group $\mathcal{B}$ that can exploit both a mempool $\mathcal{X}$ and the inference of a larger group $\mathcal{A}$ on a smaller mempool $\mathcal{Y}$ cannot infer more transactions than $\mathcal{A}$ infer from $\mathcal{X}$. Remarkably, Item (5) rules out the case where, to deduce a transaction X, a set of actors needs to combine knowledge from an *infinite* mempool $\mathcal{X}$ (the proof exploits the continuity of κ).

Proposition 2. *For all $\mathcal{A}$, $\mathcal{B}$, $\mathcal{X}$ and $\mathcal{Y}$, we have that:*

(1) *if $\mathcal{A} \neq \mathcal{B}$, then $\kappa_\mathcal{A}(\emptyset) \neq \kappa_\mathcal{B}(\emptyset)$*
(2) $\kappa_\mathcal{A}(\mathcal{X}) \cap \kappa_\mathcal{B}(\mathcal{X}) = \kappa_{\mathcal{A} \cap \mathcal{B}}(\mathcal{X})$
(3) $\kappa_\mathcal{A}(\mathcal{X}) \cup \kappa_\mathcal{B}(\mathcal{X}) \subseteq \kappa_\mathcal{A}(\kappa_\mathcal{B}(\mathcal{X})) \subseteq \kappa_{\mathcal{A} \cup \mathcal{B}}(\mathcal{X})$
(4) *if $\mathcal{B} \subseteq \mathcal{A}$ and $\mathcal{Y} \subseteq \mathcal{X}$, then $\kappa_\mathcal{B}(\kappa_\mathcal{A}(\mathcal{Y}) \cup \mathcal{X}) \subseteq \kappa_\mathcal{A}(\mathcal{X})$*
(5) $\forall \mathsf{X} \in \kappa_\mathcal{A}(\mathcal{X}).\ \exists \mathcal{X}_0 \subseteq_{\mathit{fin}} \mathcal{X}.\ \mathsf{X} \in \kappa_\mathcal{A}(\mathcal{X}_0)$

3.2 MEV Extractable by a Given Set of Actors

The axiomatization of adversarial knowledge is the core of our MEV definition. Namely, the MEV of a *given* set of actors $\mathcal{A}$ is the maximal gain that $\mathcal{A}$ can achieve by firing a sequence of transactions *deducible* by $\mathcal{A}$ using their private knowledge and that of the mempool.

Definition 5 (MEV). *The MEV extractable by a set of actors $\mathcal{A}$ from a mempool $\mathcal{X}$ in a state S is given by:*

$$\mathrm{MEV}_\mathcal{A}(S, \mathcal{X}) = \max\left\{\gamma_\mathcal{A}(S, \mathcal{Y}) \mid \mathcal{Y} \in \kappa_\mathcal{A}(\mathcal{X})^*\right\} \qquad (4)$$

By allowing $\mathcal{A}$ to fire arbitrary bundles in $\kappa_\mathcal{A}(\mathcal{X})^*$ (the set of finite sequences of transactions in $\kappa_\mathcal{A}(\mathcal{X})$), we are actually empowering $\mathcal{A}$ with the ability to reorder, drop and insert transactions. This is coherent with the practice, where miners/validators are commonly in charge for assembling blocks.[3]

Note that the max in (4) may not exist: for instance, consider a contract where each transaction (fireable by anyone) increases by 1 : T the tokens in A's wallet. The wallet states reachable in this contract satisfy the finite tokens axiom (1), but the MEV of A is unbounded, because for each fixed n, there exists a reachable state where A's gain is greater than n. A sufficient condition for the existence of the max in (4) is that, in any reachable state, the wealth of all actors is bounded by a constant:

$$\forall S_0 \in \mathbb{S}_0.\ \exists n.\ \forall S.\ S_0 \to \cdots \to S \implies \$\omega_\mathbb{A}(S) < n \qquad (5)$$

Hereafter, we assume that contracts satisfy (5), namely they are $-bounded. We now establish some key properties of MEV. First, MEV is always defined for $-bounded contracts.

Proposition 3. $\mathrm{MEV}_\mathcal{A}(S,\mathcal{X})$ *is defined and has a non-negative value.*

The MEV is preserved by removing from $\mathcal{X}$ all the transactions that the actors $\mathcal{A}$ can generate by themselves:

Proposition 4. $\mathrm{MEV}_\mathcal{A}(S,\mathcal{X}) = \mathrm{MEV}_\mathcal{A}(S, \mathcal{X} \setminus \kappa_\mathcal{A}(\emptyset))$

MEV is monotonic w.r.t. the mempool $\mathcal{X}$. This follows from the monotonicity of transactions deducibility κ, since a wider knowledge gives more opportunities to increase one's gain.

Proposition 5. *If* $\mathcal{X} \subseteq \mathcal{X}'$, *then* $\mathrm{MEV}_\mathcal{A}(S,\mathcal{X}) \le \mathrm{MEV}_\mathcal{A}(S,\mathcal{X}')$.

Perhaps surprisingly, MEV is *not* monotonic w.r.t. the set $\mathcal{A}$ of actors who are extracting it. For instance, if A has a positive gain by firing a transaction that yields a negative opposite gain for B (and B has no other ways to have a positive gain), then the MEV of {A} is positive, while that of {A, B} is zero.

In general, MEV is *not* even monotonic w.r.t. the amount of tokens in wallets, i.e., being richer does not always increase one's ability of extracting MEV. In particular, A might be able to extract MEV in a state $A[w] \mid S$, but not in a state $A[w + w_\Delta] \mid S$. For instance, this may happen when the contract enables the MEV-extracting transaction only in states containing an exact number of tokens in users' wallets. In fact, in most real-world contracts the effect of transactions never depends on tokens which are not controlled by the contract. We formalise this property of contracts by requiring that each transaction enabled in a certain wallet state W produces the same effect in a "richer" wallet state $W + W_\Delta$.

---

[3] Some blockchain networks instead do not allow the current leader node to propose a block, but use special protocols that ensure a fair ordering of transactions [22,24,30].

Definition 6 (Wallet-monotonic contract). *A contract is* wallet-monotonic *if for all W, W', W_Δ, C, C' and $\mathcal{X}$:*

$$(W, \texttt{C}) \stackrel{\mathcal{X}}{\mapsto} (W', \texttt{C}') \implies (W + W_\Delta, \texttt{C}) \stackrel{\mathcal{X}}{\mapsto} (W' + W_\Delta, \texttt{C}')$$

This naturally extends to sequences of valid transactions. For this class of contracts, MEV is monotonic w.r.t. wallets.

Proposition 6. *Let $S = (W, \texttt{C})$ and let $S_\Delta = (W + W_\Delta, \texttt{C})$. If the contract is wallet-monotonic, then* $\text{MEV}_\mathcal{A}(S, \mathcal{X}) \leq \text{MEV}_\mathcal{A}(S_\Delta, \mathcal{X})$.

In general, a single actor could not be able to extract MEV, since the contract could require the interaction between multiple actors in order to trigger a payment. Proposition 7 shows that the (maximal!) MEV can always be obtained by a *finite* set of actors.

Proposition 7. *For all $\mathcal{A}$, $\mathcal{X}$ and S, there exists $\mathcal{A}_0 \subseteq_{fin} \mathcal{A}$ such that, for all $\mathcal{B}$, if $\mathcal{A}_0 \subseteq \mathcal{B} \subseteq \mathcal{A}$ then:* $\text{MEV}_{\mathcal{A}_0}(S, \mathcal{X}) = \text{MEV}_\mathcal{B}(S, \mathcal{X})$.

We also show that MEV can always be extracted from a *finite* mempool. This follows from the continuity of κ, and in particular from its consequence Proposition 2(5), which ensures that each transaction in the sequence used to obtain the max gain can be deduced from a finite subset of the mempool.

Proposition 8 (Mempool finiteness). *For all $\mathcal{A}$, $\mathcal{X}$ and S, there exists some $\mathcal{X}_0 \subseteq_{fin} \mathcal{X}$ such that* $\text{MEV}_\mathcal{A}(S, \mathcal{X}_0) = \text{MEV}_\mathcal{A}(S, \mathcal{X})$.

Not all MEV is always considered an attack: e.g., the MEV that derives from arbitrage on AMMs and liquidations on Lending Pools is rather considered an incentive for users to keep the contract aligned with its ideal functionality. In these cases, the MEV is extracted without using the mempool. To isolate the part of MEV that is agreeably considered an attack, we remove from the overall $\text{MEV}_\mathcal{A}(S, \mathcal{X})$ the part that can be extracted without knowledge of the mempool, i.e., $\text{MEV}_\mathcal{A}(S, \emptyset)$. We dub this new notion as "bad MEV".

Definition 7 (Bad MEV). *The "bad MEV" extractable by a set of actors $\mathcal{A}$ from a mempool $\mathcal{X}$ in a state S is given by:*

$$\text{MEV}^{\text{bad}}_\mathcal{A}(S, \mathcal{X}) = \text{MEV}_\mathcal{A}(S, \mathcal{X}) - \text{MEV}_\mathcal{A}(S, \emptyset) \tag{6}$$

Proposition 9. *All the previous results about MEV, except Proposition 6, also hold for* MEV^{bad}. *Furthermore,* $\text{MEV}^{\text{bad}}_\mathcal{A}(S, \mathcal{X}) \leq \text{MEV}_\mathcal{A}(S, \mathcal{X})$.

3.3 Universal MEV

Definition 5 parameterises MEV over a set of actors $\mathcal{A}$. In this way, the same state $(S, \mathcal{X})$ could admit different MEVs for different sets of actors. This dependency on the set of actors contrasts with the practice, where the actual identity of miners or validators is unrelated to their ability to extract MEV.

For instance, consider the Whitelist contract in Fig. 2. In any state S where M has at least $1:\mathrm{T}$ and the contract has $n:\mathrm{T}$ with $n > 0$, any set of actors $\mathcal{B}$ including A has MEV. More precisely, $\mathrm{MEV}_{\mathcal{B}}(S, \mathcal{X}) = n \cdot \$1_\mathrm{T}$. However, this way of extracting MEV is *not* considered an attack in practice, since the recipient of the tokens is not arbitrary, but an actor (A) who is *hard-coded* in the contract. By contrast, the contract Blacklist is attackable, provided that the adversary $\mathcal{B}$ includes some $\mathtt{M} \neq \mathtt{A}$ who has at least $1:\mathrm{T}$. The fact that the hard-coded actor A cannot extract MEV is irrelevant, since the adversary can easily create a pseudonym which is different from the blacklisted ones.

As another example of a non-attack, consider the Bank contract in Fig. 2, which allows users to deposit and withdraw tokens, and to transfer them to others. Let S be a state where A has deposited $n:\mathrm{T}$ in the contract, while the balances of the other users are zero. We have that $\mathrm{MEV}_{\{\mathtt{A}\}}(S, \emptyset) = n \cdot \$1_\mathrm{T}$ and in general any set of actors including A can extract MEV. However, even this way of extracting MEV is *not* considered an attack, since any adversary $\mathcal{B}$ not including A has $\mathrm{MEV}_\mathcal{B}(S, \mathcal{X}) = 0$, for every mempool $\mathcal{X}$ (unless $\mathcal{X}$ includes an explicit xfer from A to $\mathcal{B}$). Unlike in the Blacklist example, the Bank has no hard-coded names, but some names become bound in the contract states upon transactions. For instance, after A has deposited $n:\mathrm{T}$, we have $\mathtt{Bank}[n:\mathrm{T}, \mathtt{acct} = \{\mathtt{A} \mapsto n\}]$.

In general, if the ability to extract MEV is subject to the existence of specific actors in the set $\mathcal{A}$, this is *not* considered an attack. Even when the identity of actors is immaterial, the amount of tokens in their wallets is not: e.g., actors may lose the capability of extracting MEV when spoiled from their tokens. Therefore,

```
contract Whitelist {
  pay(a pays 1:T) { require a==A; transfer(a,balance(T):T); }
}
contract Blacklist {
  pay(a pays 1:T) { require a!=A; transfer(a,balance(T):T); }
}
contract Bank {
  deposit(a pays amt:T) { // a sends amt:T to the contract
    if acct[a]==null then acct[a]=amt else acct[a]=acct[a]+amt
  }
  xfer(a sig,amt,b) { // a transfers amt:T to b
    require acct[a]>=amt && acct[b]!=null && amt>0;
    acct[a]=acct[a]-amt; acct[b]=acct[b]+amt
  }
  wdraw(a sig,amt) { // a withdraws amt:T
    require acct[a]>=amt && amt>0;
    acct[a]=acct[a]-amt; transfer(a,amt:T);
  }
}
```

Fig. 2. Whitelist, Blacklist and Bank contracts.

we consider as universal MEV the max gain that can be extracted by the adversary after a suitable *redistribution* of tokens in wallets. To stay on the safe side, we always consider the optimal token redistribution for the adversary. In this way, we never consider a state S as MEV-free just because the adversary has not enough tokens in S to carry the attack: this would be unsafe, since the attack could have been possible in a state S' where the adversary has redistributed the tokens in their wallets. Formally, a *token redistribution* is a relation $S \approx_\$ S'$ which holds when all the tokens in the wallets in S are reassigned in S'.

Definition 8 (Token redistribution). *Let $S = (W, \mathtt{C})$, $S' = (W', \mathtt{C}')$. We write $S \approx_\$ S'$ when $W(\mathbb{A}) = W'(\mathbb{A})$ and $\mathtt{C} = \mathtt{C}'$.*

We now formalise the key notion of *universal MEV*. States with no universal MEV are called *MEV-free*.

Definition 9 (Universal MEV). *The universal MEV extractable from a mempool $\mathcal{X}$ in a state S is given by:*

$$\mathrm{MEV}(S, \mathcal{X}) = \min_{\substack{\mathcal{B} \text{ cofinite}}} \max_{\substack{\mathcal{A} \subseteq \mathcal{B} \\ S \approx_\$ S'}} \mathrm{MEV}_\mathcal{A}(S', \mathcal{X}) \qquad (7)$$

We say that $(S, \mathcal{X})$ is MEV-free when $\mathrm{MEV}(S, \mathcal{X}) = 0$. We define $\mathrm{MEV}^{\mathrm{bad}}(S, \mathcal{X})$ and $\mathrm{MEV}^{\mathrm{bad}}$-free similarly.

To ensure that the identities of actors extracting MEV are immaterial, in (7) we take the *minimum* w.r.t. all sets $\mathcal{B}$ of actors. We restrict to *infinite* sets $\mathcal{B}$ to grant the attacker an unbounded amount of fresh identities, which can be used to avoid the ones handled in a special way by the contract. More specifically, since real-world contracts treat, in each state, only a finite number of actors as special, we let $\mathcal{B}$ range over *cofinite* sets. Once the set $\mathcal{B}$ of adversaries is fixed, we take the *maximum* MEV of $\mathcal{A} \subseteq \mathcal{B}$ w.r.t. all the possible token redistributions. In this way, we ensure that the adversary has enough tokens to carry the attack, if any. Note that (7) follows the *minimax* principle of game theoretic definitions. Intuitively, the honest players choose $\mathcal{B}$ in the min so to prevent the adversary from using privileged identities. Then, the adversary chooses, in the max, the identities $\mathcal{A}$ from $\mathcal{B}$ which are actually used for the attack: this allows the adversary to remove the actors with negative gain.

The universal MEV is always defined under a strengthened $-boundedness assumption which considers token redistributions:

$$\forall S_0 \in \mathbb{S}_0.\ \exists n.\ \forall S.\ S_0 \to_{\approx_\$} \cdots \to_{\approx_\$} S \implies \$w_\mathbb{A}(S) < n \qquad (8)$$

where the relation $\to_{\approx_\$}$ allows to redistribute tokens at each step.

Additionally, universal MEV is monotonic with respect to mempools and wallets.

Proposition 10. *For all $\mathcal{X}$ and S satisfying (8), $\mathrm{MEV}(S, \mathcal{X})$ and $\mathrm{MEV}^{\mathrm{bad}}(S, \mathcal{X})$ are defined and have a non-negative value.*

Table 1. MEV analysis of our benchmark of contracts.

Contract	MEV-free?	MEV^{bad}-free?	Contract	MEV-free?	MEV^{bad}-free?
Bad HTLC	✗	✗	Crowdfund	✓	✓
HTLC	✓	✓	AMM	✗	✗
Whitelist	✓	✓	Price Bet [3,8]	✗	✓
Blacklist	✗	✓	Naïve bounty	✗	✗
Bank	✓	✓	Bounty	✓	✓
Coin Pusher	✗	✗	Lending Pool	✗	✓

Theorem 1. *If* $\mathcal{X} \subseteq \mathcal{X}'$ *then* $\text{MEV}(S, \mathcal{X}) \leq \text{MEV}(S, \mathcal{X}')$ *(similarly for* MEV^{bad}*).*

Theorem 2. *Let* $S = (W, \mathtt{C})$ *and let* $S + W_\Delta$ *be* $(W + W_\Delta, \mathtt{C})$. *If the contract is wallet-monotonic, then:* $\text{MEV}(S, \mathcal{X}) \leq \text{MEV}(S + W_\Delta, \mathcal{X})$.

3.4 Proving MEV-Freedom

We now apply our MEV theory. Because of space constraints, here we just summarize the results of our analysis in Table 1 and refer to [9] for the technical details. In the column "MEV-free?", we mark with a ✗ those cases where a (universal) MEV attack exists with respect to some state and mempool, and with ✓ when no such attack exist. The column "MEV^{bad}-free?" uses a similar notation.

The ✗ in the AMM is witnessed by a sandwich attack in a state where the AMM is in balanced state (i.e., the internal exchange rate equals to that of an external page oracle). This is a case of "bad" MEV, since the attack exploits the mempool. When the AMM is unbalanced, there is a case of "legit" MEV, i.e., anyone can perform arbitrage and have a positive MEV with an empty mempool. The ✗ in the Lending Pool is witnessed by liquidations of under-collateralized borrowers. The Price Bet contract in [3,8] shows an interesting case where (universal) MEV is extractable without exploiting the mempool. In this contract, a player bets on the future exchange rate between two tokens, determined through an AMM acting as a price oracle. The attacker bets on a given price, then unbalances the AMM to obtain the desired exchange rate, and finally re-balances the AMM. In this way, the attacker can win the bet, extracting MEV. Note that this attack is possible whenever in the state there are enough tokens to unbalance the AMM as required. The Bounty contract, which rewards the first user who submits the solution to a puzzle, is a paradigmatic case where a naïve implementation leads to "bad" MEV attacks that makes the adversary able to steal a submitted solution. Fixing the contract requires to devise a non-trivial commit-reveal protocol, through which we eventually achieve MEV-freedom.

4 Related Work

The first (partial) formal definition of MEV was given by Babel, Daian, Kelkar and Juels [3]. Transliterated into our notation, it is:

$$\mathrm{MEV}_{\mathtt{A}}^{\mathrm{BDKJ}}(S) = \max\{\gamma_{\mathtt{A}}(S, \mathcal{Y}) \mid \mathcal{Y} \in \mathrm{Blocks}(\mathtt{A}, S)\} \tag{9}$$

where Blocks($\mathtt{A}, S$) represents the set of all valid blocks that $\mathtt{A}$ can construct in S, and $\mathtt{A}$ is allowed to own multiple wallets. A first key difference w.r.t. our work is that, while Blocks($\mathtt{A}, S$) is not specified in [3], we provide an axiomatization of this set in Definition 4. Notably, our axiomatization allows us to prove key properties of MEV, as monotonicity (w.r.t. mempools and wallets) and actors/mempool finiteness. The dependence of Blocks($\mathtt{A}, S$) on the mempool is left implicit in [3], while we make the mempool a parameter of MEV. This allows our attackers to craft transactions by combining their private knowledge with that of the mempool, as in the attack to the `BadHTLC`in [9]. Instead, in [3] the transactions in Blocks($\mathtt{A}, S$) are either generated by $\mathtt{A}$ using only her private knowledge, or taken from the (implicit) mempool.

Another key difference is that [3] does not provide a notion of *universal* MEV, i.e., the MEV that can be extracted by anyone, regardless of their identity and current token balance. Indeed, this is the kind of MEV which is most relevant in practice. The intuition of [3] is to compute $\mathrm{MEV}_{\mathtt{A}}^{\mathrm{BDKJ}}(S)$ w.r.t. an actor $\mathtt{A}$ who is "external" to the contract. However, the intuition is not supported by a formalization, which is not straightforward to achieve in general. Instead, our Definition 9 exactly characterises this universal MEV, making it identity-agnostic and token-agnostic.

Before ours, a version of universal MEV was proposed by Salles [31], and it has the following form:

$$\mathrm{MEV}^{\mathrm{Salles}}(S) = \min_{\mathtt{A} \in \mathbb{A}} \mathrm{MEV}_{\mathtt{A}}^{\mathrm{BDKJ}}(S) \tag{10}$$

By taking the minimum over all actors, (10) no longer depends on the identity of the attacker. As noted in [31], a drawback is that such definition classifies as MEV-free contracts that intuitively are not: e.g., the `Blacklist` contract would be considered MEV-free, since performing the attack requires upfront costs, that not all actors can afford. Note instead that we correctly classify `Blacklist` as *not* MEV-free. A fix proposed in [25,31] is to parameterise MEV by a constant n, which restricts the set of attackers to those who own at least n tokens:

$$\mathrm{MEV}^{\mathrm{Salles}}(S, n) = \min\{\mathrm{MEV}_{\mathtt{A}}^{\mathrm{BDKJ}}(S) \mid \mathtt{A} \in \mathbb{A}, W(\mathtt{A}) \geq n\} \tag{11}$$

where $W(\mathtt{A})$ is the number of tokens in $\mathtt{A}$'s wallet. We note that also this fix has drawbacks. A first issue is that the set of actors who own at least n tokens in a state S is always *finite*. Hence, a contract that blacklists all these actors preventing them to withdraw tokens would be MEV-free according to $\mathrm{MEV}^{\mathrm{Salles}}(S,n)$. Instead, Definition 9 correctly classifies it as *not* MEV-free, since for all cofinite $\mathcal{B}$, the tokens can be *redistributed* to some $\mathcal{A} \subseteq \mathcal{B}$ who are not blacklisted, and can then extract MEV. Another issue of making the min in (11) range over all actors is the following. Consider a variant of Blacklist where calling pay requires zero tokens. Since the min in (11) must take also the hard-coded A into account, and A's MEV is zero (since she is blacklisted) then the min would be 0, and so (11) would incorrectly classify the contract as MEV-free. Instead, our redistribution game allows us to rule out such A.

The notion of MEV in [8] is based on ours, but it uses an alternative approach to make MEV independent from the wealth of adversaries: rather than using a token redistribution, it takes the maximum MEV over all possible user wallets. Unlike ours, [8] does not provide a model of the adversarial knowledge.

Using redistributions like ours is also helpful to solve another issue of [31]: namely, blacklisting could also be based on the number of tokens held in wallets, e.g., preventing actors with more than 100 tokens from extracting MEV. In this case, $\mathrm{MEV}^{\mathrm{Salles}}(S,n)$ would be zero for all n, since the minimum would also take into account the blacklisted actors with zero MEV, while our notion correctly classifies the contract as *not* MEV-free.

As discussed in Sect. 3.3, our notion of universal MEV is game-theoretic. Another approach based on game theory—but with substantially different goals—is followed in [25]. This work models the priority gas auction arising from MEV extraction as a game, and studies the Nash equilibria ensuring that adversaries have the same MEV opportunities. Our goal instead is to formalize MEV so to analyse contracts w.r.t. MEV attacks.

5 Limitations and Conclusions

While designing our MEV model, we strove to capture the most important aspects of MEV in common smart contracts. However, our model still has some limitations, which we discuss below.

Long-Range Attacks. Our notion of MEV models the value extractable by adversaries in a single block: indeed, in Definition 5 we allow the adversary to perform a sequence $\mathcal{Y}$ of transactions (which models the block), but we neglect additional transactions happening after $\mathcal{Y}$. This does not consider long-range attacks spanning across multiple blocks. E.g., the adversary could perform some actions in one block that do not extract any MEV immediately, but affect the state of a time-based contract that will eventually give MEV. Precisely addressing long-range attacks would require some extensions to our theory. First, the notion of wealth should take into account token price fluctuations, which are irrelevant within a single block. Second, the knowledge κ should also depend on the blockchain state, e.g., to take revealed secrets into account. Third, MEV should depend on the strategies of the honest actors, i.e., on the transactions that they would send to the mempool in a given state. Actually, not considering these strategies, and just assuming that any actor is always willing to perform any contract action, would result in a gross over-approximation of MEV. An additional complication is that in certain contracts, like e.g., in gambling games, such strategies could be probabilistic. There, defining MEV in terms of the best possible future state for the adversary would again provide an over-approximation of MEV, since it would assume an unrealistically lucky adversary. E.g., consider a guessing game where an actor commits to a secret number, and then the adversary must guess its parity to win. Taking the *maximal* gain over all possible futures effectively provides the adversary with the knowledge of the secret.

Computational Adversaries. Our notion of adversarial knowledge in Definition 4 is *sharp*: any piece of data is either known to the adversary or completely inaccessible to them. This assumption is common in symbolic models of cryptographic protocols, but it does not always perfectly model the real-world adversaries. Indeed, an adversary could be able to obtain some data but only at the cost of a long computation. For instance, a contract could require the adversary to solve a moderately hard cryptographic puzzle to extract MEV. Modeling this kind of computational adversaries would require to refine the notions of adversarial knowledge and MEV to take costs into account.

Cost of MEV. Our notion of universal MEV evaluates the MEV that can be extracted by an arbitrarily wealthy adversary. To this purpose, Definition 9 uses token redistributions, which allow the adversary to use *all* tokens in the state, even those belonging to honest actors. In this way, we are effectively assuming that the adversary always has, either in their wallet or by buying them from honest actors, all the tokens needed to carry the attack. An alternative definition, which does not require to grab the tokens of honest actors, would be to allow the adversary to mint the tokens needed in the attack, similarly to the definition of MEV^∞ in [8]. In scenarios where tokens are used as credentials to perform given actions, we could restrict token redistribution to avoid giving such special tokens to the adversary. We also remark that transaction fees do not contribute to MEV, similarly to [3,31]. Encompassing fees would allow to declassify as MEV attacks those where the fees needed to carry the attack exceed the adversarial gain. In practice, fees may be quite costly in private mempools like Flashbots [35]. Adversaries can extract MEV also by front-running a transaction in the mempool so to increase the amount of gas needed to validate it.

Good *vs.* Bad MEV. There is an open debate about what exactly constitutes MEV, and how to separate "good MEV" from "bad MEV" [6,14,18,21,26,33]. In the absence of an agreement about these notions, our definition of "bad MEV" in Definition 7 formally captures some of the arguments used in this debate. In particular, we classify as "good" the MEV obtained through arbitrage in AMMs, since it does not exploit the mempool. Furthermore, we classify the liquidations on Lending Pools obtained without exploiting the mempool as "good" MEV. These classifications seem coherent with discussions in the community: MEV is good when it is an incentive for *any* user to perform actions (e.g., arbitrage, liquidations) that serve to the purpose of the protocol (e.g., aligning prices for AMMs, repaying loans for Lending Pools). Instead, we classify as "bad" the MEV resulting from sandwich attacks to AMMs [38] and from liquidations that back-run interest-accruing transactions in Lending Pools: this is correct in our view, because these attacks require the privileges of block proposers (by contrast, plain arbitrages and liquidations can be performed by any user with sufficient tokens). We stress that not all the intuitively bad MEVs are classified as such by our Definition 7: this is the case, e.g., of the DAO attack [2], where MEV results from a bug in the contract implementation. On the other side, we are not aware of any real-world contracts that have "bad MEV" (according to our definition), but where the MEV is considered beneficial to the contract functionality.

Private Order Flows. The "no shared secret" axiom in Definition 4 forbids actors to share private information (e.g., keys). It also rules out *private order flows* [19]: if the same order flow is sent to A and B, they might infer some common transactions that are not public knowledge. This simplifying assumption can be relaxed by making variables A represent secrets rather than actors, and modelling actors as the set of secrets $\mathcal{A}$ that they know.

Acknowledgments. Work partially supported by the MUR National Recovery and Resilience Plan funded by the European Union – NextGenerationEU, projects SERICS (PE00000014) and PRIN 2022 DeLiCE (F53D23009130001).

References

1. MEV-explore: Flashbots transparency dashboard. https://explore.flashbots.net/. Accessed 11 Oct 2024
2. Understanding the DAO attack (2016). http://www.coindesk.com/understanding-dao-hack-journalists/
3. Babel, K., Daian, P., Kelkar, M., Juels, A.: Clockwork finance: automated analysis of economic security in smart contracts. In: IEEE Symposium on Security and Privacy, pp. 622–639. IEEE Computer Society (2023). https://doi.org/10.1109/SP46215.2023.00036
4. Babel, K., Javaheripi, M., Ji, Y., Kelkar, M., Koushanfar, F., Juels, A.: Lanturn: measuring economic security of smart contracts through adaptive learning. In: ACM SIGSAC Conference on Computer and Communications Security (CCS), pp. 1212–1226. ACM (2023). https://doi.org/10.1145/3576915.3623204
5. Babel, K., et al.: PROF: protected order flow in a profit-seeking world. CoRR arxiv:2408.02303 (2024). https://doi.org/10.48550/ARXIV.2408.02303
6. Barczentewicz, M.: MEV on ethereum: a policy analysis (2023). https://doi.org/10.2139/ssrn.4332703

7. Bartoletti, M., Chiang, J.H., Lluch-Lafuente, A.: Maximizing extractable value from automated market makers. In: Financial Cryptography. LNCS, vol. 13411, pp. 3–19. Springer, Heidelberg (2022). https://doi.org/10.1007/978-3-031-18283-9_1
8. Bartoletti, M., Marchesin, R., Zunino, R.: DeFi composability as MEV non-interference. In: Financial Cryptography. LNCS, vol. 14744. Springer, Heidelberg (2024). https://doi.org/10.1007/978-3-031-78679-2_20
9. Bartoletti, M., Zunino, R.: A theoretical basis for MEV. CoRR arxiv:2302.02154 (2023). https://doi.org/10.48550/ARXIV.2302.02154
10. Baum, C., yu Chiang, J.H., David, B., Frederiksen, T.K., Gentile, L.: SoK: mitigation of front-running in decentralized finance. Cryptology ePrint Archive, Report 2021/1628 (2021). https://ia.cr/2021/1628
11. Baum, C., David, B., Frederiksen, T.K.: P2DEX: privacy-preserving decentralized cryptocurrency exchange. In: Sako, K., Tippenhauer, N.O. (eds.) ACNS 2021. LNCS, vol. 12726, pp. 163–194. Springer, Cham (2021). https://doi.org/10.1007/978-3-030-78372-3_7
12. Breidenbach, L., Daian, P., Tramèr, F., Juels, A.: Enter the hydra: towards principled bug bounties and exploit-resistant smart contracts. In: USENIX Security Symposium, pp. 1335–1352. USENIX Association (2019)
13. Canidio, A., Danos, V.: Commitment against front-running attacks. Manag. Sci. **70**(7), 4429–4440 (2024). https://doi.org/10.1287/MNSC.2023.01239
14. Chiplunkar, A., Gosselin, S.: A new game in town (2023). https://frontier.tech/a-new-game-in-town
15. Ciampi, M., Ishaq, M., Magdon-Ismail, M., Ostrovsky, R., Zikas, V.: Fairmm: a fast and frontrunning-resistant crypto market-maker. In: Cyber Security, Cryptology, and Machine Learning (CSCML). LNCS, vol. 13301, pp. 428–446. Springer, Heidelberg (2022). https://doi.org/10.1007/978-3-031-07689-3_31
16. Daian, P., et al.: Flash boys 2.0: frontrunning in decentralized exchanges, miner extractable value, and consensus instability. In: IEEE Symposium on Security and Privacy, pp. 910–927. IEEE (2020).https://doi.org/10.1109/SP40000.2020.00040
17. Eskandari, S., Moosavi, S., Clark, J.: SoK: transparent dishonesty: front-running attacks on blockchain. In: Bracciali, A., Clark, J., Pintore, F., Rønne, P.B., Sala, M. (eds.) FC 2019. LNCS, vol. 11599, pp. 170–189. Springer, Cham (2020). https://doi.org/10.1007/978-3-030-43725-1_13
18. Flashbots: Develop an MEV taxonomy (2021). https://github.com/flashbots/mev-research/issues/24
19. Gupta, T., Pai, M.M., Resnick, M.: The centralizing effects of private order flow on proposer-builder separation. In: Advances in Financial Technologies (AFT). LIPIcs, vol. 282, pp. 20:1–20:15. Schloss Dagstuhl - Leibniz-Zentrum für Informatik (2023). https://doi.org/10.4230/LIPICS.AFT.2023.20
20. Heimbach, L., Wattenhofer, R.: Sok: preventing transaction reordering manipulations in decentralized finance. In: Advances in Financial Technologies (2022)
21. Ji, Y., Grimmelmann, J.: Regulatory implications of MEV mitigations. In: Financial Cryptography Workshops. LNCS, vol. 14746, pp. 335–363. Springer, Heidelberg (2024). https://doi.org/10.1007/978-3-031-69231-4_21
22. Kelkar, M., Zhang, F., Goldfeder, S., Juels, A.: Order-fairness for byzantine consensus. In: Micciancio, D., Ristenpart, T. (eds.) CRYPTO 2020. LNCS, vol. 12172, pp. 451–480. Springer, Cham (2020). https://doi.org/10.1007/978-3-030-56877-1_16
23. Kulkarni, K., Diamandis, T., Chitra, T.: Towards a theory of Maximal Extractable Value I: constant function market makers. CoRR arxiv:2207.11835 (2022). https://doi.org/10.48550/arXiv.2207.11835

24. Li, Z., Pournaras, E.: Sok: Consensus for fair message ordering. CoRR arxiv:2411.09981 (2024). https://doi.org/10.48550/ARXIV.2411.09981
25. Mazorra, B., Reynolds, M., Daza, V.: Price of MEV: towards a game theoretical approach to MEV. In: ACM CCS Workshop on Decentralized Finance and Security, pp. 15–22. ACM (2022). https://doi.org/10.1145/3560832.3563433
26. Monoceros Venture: The MEV book: a comprehensive guide to Maximal Extractable Value (2024). https://www.monoceros.com/insights/maximal-extractable-value-book
27. Öz, B., Sui, D., Thiery, T., Matthes, F.: Who wins Ethereum block building auctions and why? In: Advances in Financial Technologies (AFT). LIPIcs, vol. 316, pp. 22:1–22:25. Schloss Dagstuhl - Leibniz-Zentrum für Informatik (2024). https://doi.org/10.4230/LIPICS.AFT.2024.22
28. Qin, K., Zhou, L., Gervais, A.: Quantifying blockchain extractable value: how dark is the forest? In: IEEE Symposium on Security and Privacy, pp. 198–214. IEEE (2022). https://doi.org/10.1109/SP46214.2022.9833734
29. Qin, K., Zhou, L., Livshits, B., Gervais, A.: Attacking the DeFi ecosystem with flash loans for fun and profit. In: Borisov, N., Diaz, C. (eds.) FC 2021. LNCS, vol. 12674, pp. 3–32. Springer, Heidelberg (2021). https://doi.org/10.1007/978-3-662-64322-8_1
30. Raikwar, M., Polyanskii, N., Müller, S.: Fairness notions in DAG-based DLTs, pp. 1–8. IEEE (2023). https://doi.org/10.1109/BRAINS59668.2023.10316937
31. Salles, A.: On the formalization of MEV (2021). https://writings.flashbots.net/research/formalization-mev
32. Torres, C.F., Camino, R., State, R.: Frontrunner jones and the raiders of the dark forest: an empirical study of frontrunning on the ethereum blockchain. In: USENIX Security Symposium, pp. 1343–1359 (2021)
33. Torres, C.F., Mamuti, A., Weintraub, B., Nita-Rotaru, C., Shinde, S.: Rolling in the shadows: analyzing the extraction of MEV across layer-2 rollups. In: ACM SIGSAC Conference on Computer and Communications Security (CCS), pp. 2591–2605. ACM (2024). https://doi.org/10.1145/3658644.3690259
34. Wahrstätter, A., Zhou, L., Qin, K., Svetinovic, D., Gervais, A.: Time to bribe: measuring block construction market. CoRR arxiv:2305.16468 (2023). https://doi.org/10.48550/ARXIV.2305.16468
35. Weintraub, B., Torres, C.F., Nita-Rotaru, C., State, R.: A Flash(Bot) in the pan: measuring maximal extractable value in private pools. In: ACM Internet Measurement Conference, pp. 458–471. ACM (2022). https://doi.org/10.1145/3517745.3561448
36. Werner, S., Perez, D., Gudgeon, L., Klages-Mundt, A., Harz, D., Knottenbelt, W.J.: SoK: decentralized finance (DeFi). In: ACM Conference on Advances in Financial Technologies, (AFT), pp. 30–46. ACM (2022). https://doi.org/10.1145/3558535.3559780
37. Zhou, L., Qin, K., Cully, A., Livshits, B., Gervais, A.: On the just-in-time discovery of profit-generating transactions in DeFi protocols. In: IEEE Symposium on Security and Privacy, pp. 919–936. IEEE (2021). https://doi.org/10.1109/SP40001.2021.00113
38. Zhou, L., Qin, K., Torres, C.F., Le, D.V., Gervais, A.: High-frequency trading on decentralized on-chain exchanges. In: IEEE Symposium on Security and Privacy, pp. 428–445. IEEE (2021). https://doi.org/10.1109/SP40001.2021.00027

Short Paper: Rewardable Naysayer Proofs

Gennaro Avitabile[1](✉), Luisa Siniscalchi[2], and Ivan Visconti[3]

[1] IMDEA Software Institute, Madrid, Spain
gennaro.avitabile@imdea.org
[2] Technical University of Denmark (DTU), Copenhagen, Denmark
luisi@dtu.dk
[3] Sapienza University of Rome, Rome, Italy
ivan.visconti@uniroma1.it

Abstract. Combining verifiable computation with optimistic approaches is a promising direction to scale blockchain applications. The basic idea consists of saving computations by avoiding the verification of proofs unless there are complaints.

A key tool to design systems in the above direction has been recently proposed by Seres, Glaeser and Bonneau [FC'24] who formalized the concept of a Naysayer proof: an efficient to verify proof disproving a more demanding to verify original proof.

In this work, we discuss the need of rewarding naysayer provers, the risks deriving from front-running attacks, and the failures of generic approaches trying to defeat them. Next, we introduce the concept of verifiable delayed naysayer proofs and show a construction leveraging proofs of sequential work, without relying on any additional infrastructure.

1 Introduction

In most blockchains the cost of a transaction for the end user depends on the amount of storage and computations of the invoked on-chain programs. To make an on-chain application successful and scalable, developers are therefore highly incentivized to minimize such costs for the end users. To this end, verifiable computation [19] has become a very popular tool. Verifiable computation outsources an expensive computation to an untrusted party which provides the result together with a *succinct* non-interactive proof (SNARK) that the result is correct. In the blockchain setting, this leads to a system where smart contracts verify proofs, which is much more efficient than executing the computations themselves.

An important application of this paradigm is zk-rollups (e.g., [21,28]). A zk-rollup is a scaling solution that involves batching several transactions into a *single* one that updates the state of the blockchain to the one resulting from the execution of all the transactions. To guarantee that the state is not compromised, a succinct proof that the new state is correct is also provided by a rollup coordinator. However, verifying such proofs is often wasteful, as in blockchain applications an incentive mechanism can always be put in place to punish whoever publishes incorrect proofs. Therefore, optimistic paradigms [5,24,27] assuming that coordinators are unlikely to publish incorrect information on-chain seem a promising avenue to reduce costs.

Seres et al. [27] recently proposed a new paradigm called *naysayer proofs*. In naysayer proofs, the verifier (i.e., the smart contract) optimistically accepts a proof without verifying it, opening a dispute period in which the proof can be rejected and the state reverted. Instead, off-chain validators will verify the proof and, if it is incorrect, they will submit a *naysayer proof* certifying its *incorrectness*. The naysayer verifier checks the naysayer proof and, if it is correct, rejects the original proof. We call these off-chain validators naysayer provers. The advantage of naysayer proofs is two-fold: first, in most cases, the naysayer proof will not be generated at all since the sole fact that they can be generated disincentivizes attempts of generating incorrect proofs; second, should the proof be challenged, naysayer proofs are more efficient to verify than the original proofs.

Naysayer Proofs vs Fraud Proofs. A concept related to naysayer proofs is the one of *fraud proofs* that is used in the context of *optimistic rollups* [5,24]. Fraud proofs operate under the optimistic assumption that a computation is correct unless someone challenges it. In case of a challenge, (some of) the steps of the computation are re-executed to resolve the dispute. Although naysayer proofs and fraud proofs are conceptually similar, there are some differences coming from the fact that what is disputed is a proof about a computation rather than the computation itself. In naysayer proofs, unlike fraud proofs, dispute resolution is *witness independent* [27]. Indeed, for fraud proofs, the entire input of the computation (i.e., the witness) must be made available at least to the challenger. On the other end, to verify a naysayer proof only the original statement and proof are required, which are usually much shorter than the witness.

Naysayer Proofs and Front-Running Attacks. To work in a permissionless setting, the naysayer paradigm requires an incentive mechanism ensuring that participation is profitable for the naysayer provers. The naysayer provers who post correct naysayer proofs should be rewarded and should be penalized in case they transmit incorrect proofs. Additionally, whoever posts a proof which is later proved incorrect by a naysayer prover must also be penalized[1].

Generally, all applications in which any user can obtain a reward by submitting a transaction before other participants are targets of *front-running* attacks [16,18]. Here the front-runner uses knowledge of unprocessed transactions to get her transactions executed ahead of the unprocessed ones. Therefore, when considering systems rewarding naysayer provers, the attacker could steal the naysayer proof from the transactions pool and rush the publication of her naysayer proof to cash the reward, without doing the hard work of a naysayer prover (i.e., without validating huge amounts of original proofs).

---

[1] The reward for posting correct naysayer proofs must be lower than the penalty given to users who post incorrect proofs. Otherwise, one could profit by posting an incorrect proof and shortly after a corresponding naysayer proof.

Solutions to Front-Running. Several techniques with various trade-offs have been proposed to mitigate generic and specific front-running attacks [6]. A common approach consists of batching blinded transactions, so that all transactions submitted within a confirmation period are independent from each other, preventing any adversarial ordering of the transactions. For instance, *commit and reveal* approaches [1,4,7,14] involve a first round where all inputs are committed and a second round where such commitments are opened so that rewards can be paid accordingly. When implemented with standard commitments, this technique requires multiple rounds of interaction between users and the blockchain. Additionally, this approach requires one to enforce the concept of *epoch*. That is, there must be a fixed time interval during which users are allowed to submit committed inputs. After this epoch has expired, no new committed inputs are allowed, and users can only submit openings for previously registered commitments. Some scenarios (e.g., auctions) have clearly defined epochs, while for some others it might not be immediately clear how to define an epoch[2]. Finally, while preventing front-running attacks, the commit-and-reveal approach introduces selective opening attacks that can be mitigated through additional complexity such as the use of timed-release cryptography (e.g., timed commitments [9] or delay encryption [10]), ensuring that the inputs can always be recovered after a certain time, or by relying on threshold encryption [11] and a committee where the majority of the members is assumed to be honest, or by a multi-party computation of an anonymous committed broadcast functionality [22].

Ensuring Delay to Prevent Front-Running. Another method to prevent front-running does not blind the transactions' inputs, but it instead focuses on making the creation of a valid transaction slow [12,26]. The central tool in this approach are verifiable delay functions (VDFs) [8]. A VDF takes a prescribed amount of time t (even in the presence of massive parallelism) to compute and can be verified in time much less than t. The overall idea is to tie the input of the VDF to the transaction as well as some user's identifying information. A transaction is then considered valid only if it comes with a proof of the VDF. Therefore, every time attackers want to front-run a transaction, they have to start a long-running computation. The time parameter t is set so that by the time the attacker finalizes her transaction, the transaction of the honest user will already be confirmed in the blockchain. The advantage of this approach is that it does not require a user to submit a second transaction. Unfortunately, the above generic use of a VDF to defeat front-running attacks suffers from the following technical caveat: the sequentiality of a VDF is only guaranteed when it is evaluated on a random input. This generally requires an external trusted infrastructure providing a publicly verifiable randomness beacon [13]. It is therefore interesting to study scenarios where no trusted external infrastructure (i.e., no additional points of failure) is available and still front-running scenarios can be defeated via delays.

---

[2] In the context of naysayer proofs, an intuitive way to define an epoch is to set it identically to the dispute period. However, this restriction will delay the punishment of the misbehaving original prover for an unnecessary amount of time.

1.1 Our Contribution

In this paper, we study the problem of front-running attacks against rewarding mechanisms associated to naysayer proofs. We make the following contributions:

- *Front-running resistant naysayer proofs:* we define the notion of verifiable delayed naysayer proofs (VDNs). VDNs are naysayer proofs that when plugged in a natural reward-based system are resilient to front-running attacks. We design a compiler which, starting from proofs of sequential works (PoSWs) [23] and a naysayer proof with minimal additional requirements, gives a VDN. Our solution does not add any setup assumption and, being tied to the setting of naysayer proofs, it does not require randomness beacons (or any other type of external infrastructure).
- *Generic front-running protection approaches can be harmful:* We show that applying a generic front-running protection technique can hurt the requirements of the underlying reward-based system. In particular, we observe that naysayer proofs have a crucial efficiency requirement (i.e., they should be faster to verify than the original proofs) that is not necessarily preserved when a front-running protection approach is applied on top of them.

Verifiable Delayed Naysayer Proofs. In VDNs, the naysayer prover takes as input an additional time parameter t and a prover-chosen watermark μ. The naysayer verifier also takes such additional values as input. Apart from completeness and soundness, we require the VDN to be sequential. By sequential we mean that given a sufficiently unpredictable statement/proof pair (stm, π) that can be naysayed, it is unfeasible to compute an accepting naysayer proof for (stm, π), with a watermark μ, in less than time t. This holds even when the adversary is provided with oracle access to fast generation of VDN proofs, except of course on (stm, π, μ)[3]. When using the VDN in a reward-based setting, it suffices to additionally verify that the prover-chosen watermark matches with the public key which submits the transaction. Indeed, sequentiality guarantees that even if the front-runner $\mathcal{F}$ sees a VDN proof of an honest user $\mathcal{H}$ (w.r.t. her public key $\mathsf{pk}_\mathcal{H}$), $\mathcal{F}$ will not be able to produce a valid proof (w.r.t. her public key $\mathsf{pk}_\mathcal{F}$) before the transaction submitted by $\mathcal{H}$ is finalized in the blockchain.

Our VDN. We combine naysayer proofs with PoSWs to construct a VDN. PoSWs are publicly verifiable proofs attesting that a certain amount of sequential work was performed starting from a specific challenge. VDFs can be seen as a special case of PoSWs offering the additional guarantee of a unique output. We observe that PoSWs suffice for front-running prevention. Indeed, we do not need a unique output since such output is merely verified to ensure that a long sequential computation was carried out, but the result of the computation is not used elsewhere. Unlike VDFs, we know PoSWs that are unconditionally secure in the random oracle model and do not require any setup [2,3,15,17,23].

---

[3] This requirement is similar to the one of watermarkable VDFs [20,30], with the difference that the output is not unique.

Our construction is very simple: the prover of the VDN runs the underlying naysayer prover over (stm, π) and gets a naysayer proof π_{nay}. Then, it calls a random oracle (RO) over $(\pi_{\mathsf{nay}}||\mathsf{stm}||\pi||\mu)$ to get the challenge χ for the PoSW. The PoSW π_{PoSW} is then computed w.r.t. χ and time parameter t. The VDN proof simply consists of both π_{nay} and π_{PoSW}, which are then individually verified by the verifier of the VDN. The caveat of this solution is that the security of PoSWs is formulated for uniformly random χ. Even if χ is derived from a RO, χ is a random string only if $(\pi_{\mathsf{nay}}, \mathsf{stm}, \pi, \mu)$ has high min-entropy. Generally, it is unclear how to find a high min-entropy source for all the users of a system.

Whenever a reward is connected to the punishment of another party, as in the naysayer setting, it is actually possible to find a source of high min-entropy. For example, in the rollup application discussed above, stm is a succinct representation (e.g., a cryptographic hash) of several transactions, which likely contain cryptographic material with high min-entropy such as digital signatures. Furthermore, there are generally many valid proofs π for the same stm. The malicious rollup coordinator is incentivized to use good entropy to create (stm, π), so that this pair is distributed similarly to honest proofs, and thus less likely to be verified by a naysayer prover. Moreover, we can include in π the digital signature used to authorize the rollup transaction. On an intuitive level, such a signature must be unpredictable; otherwise it would not be unforgeable and an attacker could damage the coordinators posting wrong proofs on their behalf.

Front-Running and Efficiency in Naysayer Proofs. The verification algorithm of our VDN is slower than the one of the underlying naysayer proof system since it additionally verifies a PoSW. Therefore, to prove that our VDN is a naysayer proof system we have to assume that the verification algorithm of the PoSW is asymptotically faster than the verification algorithm of the original proof[4].

This is not a problematic assumption, since the verification time of state-of-the-art PoSWs [3,15,17] scales logarithmically in t and as a small polynomial in the security parameter. However, this highlights that not all front-running compilers are necessarily compatible with every reward-based system. For example, one could artificially create a PoSW whose verification time depends on a high-degree polynomial in the security parameter while still being logarithmic in t, making it asymptotically slower than the verification of the original proof. The resulting construction would still prevent front-running attacks but it would also make the naysayer reward-based system useless since verifying regular proofs would be less expensive than verifying naysayer proofs.

Practical Considerations. Both VDFs and PoSWs are good candidates to enforce delays in our VDN. One can pick between the two depending on several tradeoffs. VDFs usually require setups and number-theoretic assumptions [25,30], but have more compact proofs [30]. PoSWs do not require setups and are based on symmetric primitives, but have larger proofs [2,3,15,17]. Another measure to

---

[4] Recall that the verification of a naysayer proof must be faster than the verification of the original proof.

consider is the gap between the actual work done by the honest prover and the level of sequential security that the primitive gives. In VDFs, the honest prover has to do more work than t *sequential* computations, while in PoSWs this gap can be reduced to 0 [2,17]. Obviously, as in all applications of timed primitives, estimating the right value of t is very challenging. However, we feel that this issue will naturally be better understood as these primitives get used in practice.

Future Work. While we focused on defining and constructing a VDN, we think it is important to investigate the practicality of our solutions. We leave to future work a performance evaluation study on how verification gas costs would increase when implementing our construction with state-of-the-art PoSWs, as well as a study to quantify the concrete parameters of the timed primitives.

2 Definitions and Tools

We start with the definition of non-interactive proof, then we report the definition of naysayer proof of [27] and then we define PoSWs similarly to [17].

Definition 1. *A non-interactive proof system Π for some NP relation $\mathcal{R}$ consists of the following PPT algorithms:*

$\mathsf{crs} \leftarrow \mathsf{Setup}(1^\lambda)$: *on input a security parameter λ, output crs.*
$\pi \leftarrow \mathsf{Prove}(\mathsf{crs}, \mathsf{stm}, w)$: *on input crs, stm, and w, output π.*
$0/1 \leftarrow \mathsf{Verify}(\mathsf{crs}, \mathsf{stm}, \pi)$: *on input crs, stm, and π output $1/0$ to accept/reject.*
We require Π to be correct and sound, we defer to [29] for formal definitions.

Definition 2. *Given a non-interactive proof system $\Pi = (\mathsf{Setup}, \mathsf{Prove}, \mathsf{Verify})$ for some NP relation $\mathcal{R}$, the corresponding naysayer proof system Π_{nay} consists of the PPT algorithms defined as follows. We define τ to be a tuple $(\mathsf{crs}, \mathsf{stm}, \pi)$, where $\mathsf{crs}, \mathsf{stm}, \pi$ are a common reference string, a statement, and a proof of the proof system Π. We call τ a naysayer tuple.*

- $\mathsf{crs}_{\mathsf{nay}} \leftarrow \mathsf{NSetup}(1^\lambda)$: *on input security parameter 1^λ, output $\mathsf{crs}_{\mathsf{nay}}$.*
- $\pi_{\mathsf{nay}} \leftarrow \mathsf{Naysay}(\mathsf{crs}_{\mathsf{nay}}, \tau)$: *on input $\mathsf{crs}_{\mathsf{nay}}$, and a naysayer tuple τ, output π_{nay}.*
- $0/1 \leftarrow \mathsf{NVerify}(\mathsf{crs}_{\mathsf{nay}}, \tau, \pi_{\mathsf{nay}})$: *on input $\mathsf{crs}_{\mathsf{nay}}$, a naysayer tuple τ, and π_{nay}, outputs 1 to accept and 0 to reject.*

We define the polynomial-time language $\mathcal{L}_{\mathsf{nay}}^{\Pi} := \{\tau = (\mathsf{crs}, \mathsf{stm}, \pi) : \Pi.\mathsf{Verify}(\mathsf{crs}, \mathsf{stm}, \pi) = 0\}$ and require the following properties to hold:

- *Naysayer Completeness: a naysayer proof system Π_{nay} w.r.t a non-interactive proof system Π is complete if for all $\tau \in \mathcal{L}_{\mathsf{nay}}^{\Pi}$ it holds that:*

$$\Pr\left[\mathsf{NVerify}(\mathsf{crs}_{\mathsf{nay}}, \tau, \pi_{\mathsf{nay}}) = 1 \; \middle| \; \begin{array}{l} \mathsf{crs}_{\mathsf{nay}} \leftarrow \mathsf{NSetup}(1^\lambda); \\ \pi_{\mathsf{nay}} \leftarrow \mathsf{Naysay}(\mathsf{crs}_{\mathsf{nay}}, \tau) \end{array}\right] = 1.$$

- *Naysayer Soundness:* a naysayer proof system Π_{nay} w.r.t a non-interactive proof system Π is sound if for all PPT adversaries $\mathcal{A}$ it holds that:

$$\Pr\left[\begin{array}{l}\mathsf{NVerify}(\mathsf{crs}_{\mathsf{nay}},\mathsf{crs},\tau)=1 \wedge \\ \tau \notin \mathcal{L}_{\mathsf{nay}}^{\Pi}\end{array} \middle| \begin{array}{l}\mathsf{crs}_{\mathsf{nay}} \leftarrow \mathsf{NSetup}(1^\lambda); \\ (\pi_{\mathsf{nay}},\tau) \leftarrow \mathcal{A}(\mathsf{crs}_{\mathsf{nay}})\end{array}\right] \leq \mathsf{negl}(\lambda).$$

- *Efficiency:* $\mathsf{NVerify}$ must be asymptotically faster than Verify.

Definition 3. *A proof of sequential work (PoSW) is a pair of PPT oracle-aided algorithms* $\mathsf{Prove}, \mathsf{Verify}$, *executed by a prover* P *and a verifier* V *as follows:*

Common Input: P and V get as common input $\lambda, t \in \mathbb{N}$. All parties have access to a random oracle $\mathsf{H}: \{0,1\}^* \to \{0,1\}^\lambda$.
Statement: V samples a random statement $\chi \leftarrow \{0,1\}^\lambda$ and sends it to P.
Prove: P computes $\pi \leftarrow \mathsf{Prove}^{\mathsf{H}}(\chi, t)$ and sends π to V.
Verify: V computes and outputs $\mathsf{Verify}^{\mathsf{H}}(\chi, t, \pi)$.

We require the PoSW to be complete, sound, and succinct as follows:

- *Completeness:* for all $\lambda, t \in \mathbb{N}$, and all $\chi \in \{0,1\}^\lambda$ it holds that
  $\Pr\left[\mathsf{Verify}^{\mathsf{H}}(\chi, t, \pi) = 1 \mid \pi \leftarrow \mathsf{Prove}^{\mathsf{H}}(\chi, t)\right] = 1.$
- *Soundness:* a PoSW is sound if for all $\lambda, t \in \mathbb{N}$ and $\alpha > 0$, for all $\mathcal{A}$ that make $(1-\alpha)t$ sequential[5] queries to H, it holds that
  $\Pr\left[\mathsf{Verify}^{\mathsf{H}}(\chi, t, \pi) = 1 \mid \chi \leftarrow \{0,1\}^\lambda, \pi \leftarrow \mathcal{A}^{\mathsf{H}}(\chi)\right] \leq \mathsf{negl}(\lambda).$
- *Succinctness:* for all $\lambda, t \in \mathbb{N}$ and every honestly generated proof π for parameter t, we have $|\pi| \leq \mathsf{poly}(\lambda, \log t)$, $\mathsf{Prove}^{\mathsf{H}}$ runs in time[6] $\mathsf{poly}(\lambda, t)$, and $\mathsf{Verify}^{\mathsf{H}}$ runs in time $\mathsf{poly}(\lambda, \log t)$.

3 Verifiable Delayed Naysayer Proofs

Definition 4. *Given a non-interactive proof system* $\Pi = (\mathsf{Setup}, \mathsf{Prove}, \mathsf{Verify})$ *for some NP relation* $\mathcal{R}$, *the corresponding verifiable delayed naysayer proof system* Π_{VDN} *consists of the oracle-aided PPT algorithms defined as follows:*

- $\mathsf{crs}_{\mathsf{VDN}} \leftarrow \mathsf{VDNSetup}(1^\lambda)$: *on input security parameter* 1^λ, *output a common reference string* $\mathsf{crs}_{\mathsf{VDN}}$.
- $\pi_{\mathsf{VDN}} \leftarrow \mathsf{VDNaysay}^{\mathsf{H}}(\mathsf{crs}_{\mathsf{VDN}}, t, \tau, \mu)$: *on input common reference string* $\mathsf{crs}_{\mathsf{VDN}}$, *time parameter* t, *naysayer tuple* τ, *and watermark* μ, *output a proof* π_{VDN}.

---

[5] Notice that no restriction is posed on the number of *parallel* queries $\mathcal{A}$ can make. In a nutshell, the budget of sequential queries gets reduced whenever a new query includes the output of a previously asked RO query as a sub-string.
[6] To simplify the notation, in accordance to [17], we give t as input to all the algorithms. However, we implicitly mean that, whenever required to comply with the efficiency requirements, the time parameter t is passed in unary.

- $0/1 \leftarrow \mathsf{VDNVerify}^{\mathsf{H}}(\mathsf{crs}_{\mathsf{VDN}}, t, \tau, \mu, \pi_{\mathsf{VDN}})$: on input common reference string $\mathsf{crs}_{\mathsf{VDN}}$, time parameter t, naysayer tuple τ, watermark μ, and a proof π_{VDN}, output 1 to accept or 0 to reject.

Completeness, soundness, and efficiency are analogous to the ones of Definition 2. While $\mathcal{Z}$-Watermarked Sequentiality is defined as follow: For all $\lambda, t \in \mathbb{N}$ and $\alpha > 0$, and for an auxiliary input distribution $\mathcal{Z}$, we define the following game applied to an adversary $\mathcal{A} := (\mathcal{A}_0, \mathcal{A}_1)$:

$$\mathsf{crs}_{\mathsf{VDN}} \leftarrow \mathsf{VDNSetup}(1^\lambda), st \leftarrow \mathcal{A}_0^{\mathsf{H}}(\mathsf{crs}_{\mathsf{VDN}}, t), \tau \leftarrow \mathcal{Z}(\mathsf{crs}_{\mathsf{VDN}}, t)$$

$$(\pi_{\mathsf{VDN}}^*, \mu^*) \leftarrow \mathcal{A}_1^{\mathsf{H}(\cdot), \mathsf{VDNaysay}^{\mathsf{H}}(\mathsf{crs}_{\mathsf{VDN}}, t, \cdot, \cdot)}(st, \tau)$$

We say that $\mathcal{A}$ wins the game if $\mathsf{VDNVerify}^{\mathsf{H}}(\mathsf{crs}_{\mathsf{VDN}}, t, \tau, \mu^*, \pi_{\mathsf{VDN}}^*) = 1$ and $\mathcal{A}$ did not query the oracle over (τ, μ^*). Π_{VDN} satisfies $\mathcal{Z}$-watermarked sequentiality if no pair of randomized algorithm $\mathcal{A}_0$ which runs in total time $\mathsf{poly}(t, \lambda)$, and $\mathcal{A}_1$ that makes at most $(1-\alpha)t$ sequential queries to H, can win the above game with probability greater than $\mathsf{negl}(\lambda)$.

Our PoSW-based construction. Our construction works as follows:

- $\mathsf{crs}_{\mathsf{VDN}} \leftarrow \mathsf{VDNSetup}(1^\lambda)$: $\mathsf{crs}_{\mathsf{nay}} \leftarrow \Pi_{\mathsf{nay}}.\mathsf{Setup}(1^\lambda), \mathsf{crs}_{\mathsf{VDN}} := \mathsf{crs}_{\mathsf{nay}}$.
- $\pi_{\mathsf{VDN}} \leftarrow \mathsf{VDNaysay}^{\mathsf{H}}(\mathsf{crs}_{\mathsf{VDN}}, t, \tau, \mu)$: parse $\mathsf{crs}_{\mathsf{VDN}} := \mathsf{crs}_{\mathsf{nay}}$, $\pi_{\mathsf{nay}} \leftarrow \Pi_{\mathsf{nay}}.\mathsf{Naysay}(\mathsf{crs}_{\mathsf{nay}}, \tau)$, $\chi = \mathsf{H}(\pi_{\mathsf{nay}} || \tau || \mu)$, $\pi_{\mathsf{PoSW}} \leftarrow \mathsf{PoSW}.\mathsf{Prove}^{\mathsf{H}}(\chi, t)$, $\pi_{\mathsf{VDN}} := (\pi_{\mathsf{nay}}, \pi_{\mathsf{PoSW}})$.
- $0/1 \leftarrow \mathsf{VDNVerify}^{\mathsf{H}}(\mathsf{crs}_{\mathsf{VDN}}, t, \tau, \mu, \pi_{\mathsf{VDN}})$: parse $\mathsf{crs}_{\mathsf{VDN}} := \mathsf{crs}_{\mathsf{nay}}$ and $\pi_{\mathsf{VDN}} := (\pi_{\mathsf{nay}}, y, \pi_{\mathsf{PoSW}})$, $\chi = \mathsf{H}(\pi_{\mathsf{nay}} || \tau || \mu)$, output $\mathsf{PoSW}.\mathsf{Verify}^{\mathsf{H}}(\chi, t, \pi_{\mathsf{PoSW}}) \wedge \Pi_{\mathsf{nay}}.\mathsf{NVerify}(\mathsf{crs}_{\mathsf{nay}}, \tau, \pi_{\mathsf{nay}})$.

Theorem 1. *If Π_{nay} is a naysayer proof system w.r.t. Π, if PoSW is a proof of sequential work, if $\mathcal{Z}$ is the distribution of naysayable proofs generated with high min-entropy, and if $\mathsf{PoSW}.\mathsf{Verify}^{\mathsf{H}}$ is asymptotically faster than $\Pi.\mathsf{Verify}$, then the above construction is a VDN.*

Proof Sketch. **Completeness:** it follows by inspection.
Soundness: it follows from the soundness of Π_{nay}.
$\mathcal{Z}$-Watermarked Sequentiality: it follows from the fact that a $\pi_{\mathsf{nay}} || \tau || \mu$ with high min-entropy gives a uniformly distributed χ when hashed down with a random oracle, and from the soundness of the PoSW. Intuitively, all the polynomially many queries of $\mathcal{A}_0$ do not give it any insight on χ, as well as the polynomially many queries done by $\mathcal{A}_1$ to $\mathsf{VDNaysay}^{\mathsf{H}}(\mathsf{crs}_{\mathsf{VDN}}, \mathsf{crs}, t, \cdot, \cdot)$ over $(\tau', \mu') \neq (\tau, \mu^*)$. Therefore, one can simply reduce watermarked sequentiality to the soundness of PoSW.
Efficiency: the running time of $\mathsf{VDNVerify}^{\mathsf{H}}$ is the sum of the running times of the verification algorithms of Π_{nay} and PoSW, which are both asymptotically faster than $\Pi.\mathsf{Verify}$, the same holds for $\mathsf{VDNVerify}^{\mathsf{H}}$.

Acknowledgments. We thank Hamza Abusalah for insightful discussions and the anonymous reviewers of FC 2025 for their feedback. This work has been supported by the grants PID2022-142290OB-I00 (ESPADA project co-funded by FEDER, EU), JDC2023-050791-I (co-funded by the ESF+), and TED2021-132464B-I00 (PRODIGY project, co-funded by the European Union NextGenerationEU/PRTR), all funded by MCIN/AEI/10.13039/501100011033. It has also received funding from the European Research Council (ERC) under the European Union's Horizon 2020 research and innovation programme (PICOCRYPT project, Grant No. 101001283). Ivan Visconti is member of the Gruppo Nazionale Calcolo Scientifico-Istituto Nazionale di Alta Matematica and his contribution on this work was in part supported under the National Recovery and Resilience Plan (NRRP), Mission 4, Component 2, Investment 1.1, Call for tender No. 104 published on 2.2.2022 by the Italian Ministry of University and Research (MUR), funded by the European Union -NextGenerationEU - Project Title "PARTHENON" - CUP D53D23008610006 - Grant Assignment Decree No. 959.

References

1. Abraham, I., Pinkas, B., Yanai, A.: Blinder - scalable, robust anonymous committed broadcast. In: Ligatti, J., Ou, X., Katz, J., Vigna, G. (eds.) ACM CCS 2020, pp. 1233–1252. ACM Press (2020)
2. Abusalah, H., Cini, V.: An incremental PoSW for general weight distributions. In: Hazay, C., Stam, M. (eds.) EUROCRYPT 2023. Part II, volume 14005 of LNCS, pp. 282–311. Springer, Cham (2023)
3. Abusalah, H., Kamath, C., Klein, K., Pietrzak, K., Walter, M.: Reversible proofs of sequential work. In: Ishai, Y., Rijmen, V. (eds.) EUROCRYPT 2019. Part II, volume 11477 of LNCS, pp. 277–291. Springer, Cham (2019)
4. Ambrona, M., Beunardeau, M., Toledo, R.R.: Timed commitments revisited. Cryptology ePrint Archive, Report 2023/977 (2023)
5. Arbitrum. Docs. https://docs.arbitrum.io
6. Baum, C., Chiang, J.H., David, B., Frederiksen, T.K., Gentile, L.: Sok: mitigation of front-running in decentralized finance. In: Matsuo, S., et al. (eds.) FC 2022 International Workshops, LNCS. vol. 13412, pp. 250–271. Springer, Heidelberg (2022). https://doi.org/10.1007/978-3-031-32415-4_17
7. Bebel, J., Ojha, D.: Ferveo: threshold decryption for mempool privacy in BFT networks. Cryptology ePrint Archive, Report 2022/898 (2022)
8. Boneh, D., Bonneau, J., Bünz, B., Fisch, B.: Verifiable delay functions. In: Shacham, H., Boldyreva, A. (eds.) CRYPTO 2018. LNCS, vol. 10991, pp. 757–788. Springer, Cham (2018). https://doi.org/10.1007/978-3-319-96884-1_25
9. Boneh, D., Naor, M.: Timed commitments. In: Bellare, M. (ed.) CRYPTO 2000. LNCS, vol. 1880, pp. 236–254. Springer, Heidelberg (2000). https://doi.org/10.1007/3-540-44598-6_15
10. Burdges, J., De Feo, L.: Delay encryption. In: Canteaut, A., Standaert, F.-X. (eds.) EUROCRYPT 2021. LNCS, vol. 12696, pp. 302–326. Springer, Cham (2021). https://doi.org/10.1007/978-3-030-77870-5_11
11. Canetti, R., Goldwasser, S.: An efficient *threshold* public key cryptosystem secure against adaptive chosen ciphertext attack (extended abstract). In: Stern, J. (ed.) EUROCRYPT 1999. LNCS, vol. 1592, pp. 90–106. Springer, Heidelberg (1999). https://doi.org/10.1007/3-540-48910-X_7

12. Chen, E., Chon, A.: Injective protocol: a collision resistant decentralized exchange protocol (2018)
13. Choi, K., Manoj, A., Bonneau, J.: SoK: distributed randomness beacons. In: 2023 IEEE Symposium on Security and Privacy, pp. 75–92. IEEE Computer Society Press (2023)
14. Choudhuri, A.R., Garg, S., Piet, J., Policharla, G.V.: Mempool privacy via batched threshold encryption: attacks and defenses. In: Balzarotti, D., Xu, W. (eds.) USENIX Security 2024. USENIX Association (2024)
15. Cohen, B., Pietrzak, K.: Simple proofs of sequential work. In: Nielsen, J.B., Rijmen, V. (eds.) EUROCRYPT 2018. LNCS, vol. 10821, pp. 451–467. Springer, Cham (2018). https://doi.org/10.1007/978-3-319-78375-8_15
16. Daian, P., et al.: Flash boys 2.0: frontrunning in decentralized exchanges, miner extractable value, and consensus instability. In: 2020 IEEE Symposium on Security and Privacy, pp. 910–927. IEEE Computer Society Press (2020)
17. Döttling, N., Lai, R.W.F., Malavolta, G.: Incremental proofs of sequential work. In: Ishai, Y., Rijmen, V. (eds.) EUROCRYPT 2019. LNCS, vol. 11477, pp. 292–323. Springer, Cham (2019). https://doi.org/10.1007/978-3-030-17656-3_11
18. Eskandari, S., Moosavi, S., Clark, J.: SoK: transparent dishonesty: front-running attacks on blockchain. In: Bracciali, A., Clark, J., Pintore, F., Rønne, P.B., Sala, M. (eds.) FC 2019. LNCS, vol. 11599, pp. 170–189. Springer, Cham (2020). https://doi.org/10.1007/978-3-030-43725-1_13
19. Gennaro, R., Gentry, C., Parno, B.: Non-interactive verifiable computing: outsourcing computation to untrusted workers. In: Rabin, T. (ed.) CRYPTO 2010. LNCS, vol. 6223, pp. 465–482. Springer, Heidelberg (2010). https://doi.org/10.1007/978-3-642-14623-7_25
20. Hoffmann, C., Pietrzak, K.: Watermarkable and zero-knowledge verifiable delay functions from any proof of exponentiation. Cryptology ePrint Archive, Paper 2024/481 (2024)
21. Linea. Documentation. https://docs.linea.build/
22. Lu, D., Yurek, T., Kulshreshtha, S., Govind, R., Kate, A., Miller, A.: Honeybadgermpc and asynchromix: practical asynchronous mpc and its application to anonymous communication. In: Proceedings of the 2019 ACM SIGSAC Conference on Computer and Communications Security, CCS '19, pp. 887–903. Association for Computing Machinery, New York (2019)
23. Mahmoody, M., Moran, T., Vadhan, S.P.: Publicly verifiable proofs of sequential work. In: Kleinberg, R.D. (ed.) ITCS 2013, pp. 373–388. ACM (2013)
24. Optimism. Docs. https://docs.optimism.io/
25. Pietrzak, K.: Simple verifiable delay functions. In: Blum, A. (ed.) ITCS 2019, vol. 124, pp. 60:1–60:15. LIPIcs (2019)
26. Sariboz, E., Panwar, G., Vishwanathan, R., Misra, S.: FIRST: frontrunning resilient smart contracts. CoRR arxiv:2204.00955 (2022)
27. Seres, I.A., Glaeser, N., Bonneau, J.: Short paper: Naysayer proofs. In: Clark, J., Shi, E. (eds.) FC 2024, March 2024, Revised Selected Papers, Part II. LNCS, vol. 14745, pp. 22–32. Springer, Heidelberg (2024). https://doi.org/10.1007/978-3-031-78679-2_2
28. StarkEx. Documentation. https://docs.starkware.co/starkex/overview.html
29. Thaler, J.: Proofs, Arguments, and Zero-Knowledge (2023)
30. Wesolowski, B.: Efficient verifiable delay functions. In: Ishai, Y., Rijmen, V. (eds.) EUROCRYPT 2019. Part III. LNCS, vol. 11478, pp. 379–407. Springer, Cham (2019)

Signatures and Threshold Cryptography

Verification-Efficient Homomorphic Signatures for Verifiable Computation over Data Streams

Gaspard Anthoine[1,2], Daniele Cozzo[1(✉)], and Dario Fiore[1]

[1] IMDEA Software Institute, Madrid, Spain
{gaspard.anthoine,daniele.cozzo,dario.fiore}@imdea.org
[2] Universidad Politécnica de Madrid, Madrid, Spain

Abstract. Homomorphic signatures for NP (HSNP) allow proving that a signed value is the result of a non-deterministic computation on signed inputs. At CCS'22, Fiore and Tucker introduced HSNP, showed how to use them for verifying arbitrary computations on data streams, and proposed a generic HSNP construction obtained by efficiently combining zkSNARKs with linearly homomorphic signatures (LHS), namely those supporting linear functions. Their proposed LHS however suffered from an high verification cost.

In this work we propose an efficient LHS that significantly improves on previous work in terms of verification time. Using the modular approach of Fiore and Tucker, this yields a verifier-efficient HSNP. We show that the HSNP instantiated with our LHS is particularly suited to the case when the data is taken from consecutive samples, which captures important use cases including sliding window statistics such as variances, histograms and stock market predictions.

1 Introduction

We consider the problem of verifiable computation on data streams (VCS) in which a data provider $\mathcal{D}$ streams a large amount of data to a server $\mathcal{S}$, which later computes on portions of this stream in order to reply to the queries of a client $\mathcal{C}$. This problem emerges in a variety of applications that require the continuous monitoring and analysis of vast, dynamically generated, data. Notable examples include financial data (e.g., stock-market, blockchains transactions), health or environmental sensors, network traffic, and smart metering – all fields that demand efficient and reliable solutions.

More in detail, cryptographic solutions for VCS aim to achieve five main properties: (1) Workflow: the communication from $\mathcal{D}$ to $\mathcal{S}$ is unidirectional and the stream is ordered, and $\mathcal{C}$ can verify the queries without having to follow the stream (i.e., it does not need to stay online). (2) Security: the client accepts the correct result while trusting the data provider but not trusting the server. (3) Efficiency: the communication from $\mathcal{S}$ to $\mathcal{C}$ is at most logarithmic in the size of the stream, and $\mathcal{C}$'s cost to verify the queries is smaller than the cost of running the computation. (4) <u>Privacy-preserving</u>: the verifier does not learn any information about the input stream beyond the received output. (5) <u>Non-deterministic</u>: the server can execute and prove non-deterministic computations of the form $\exists w : y = f(x, w)$.

In a recent work [5], Fiore and Tucker proposed a solution to VCS through a new primitive that they called *homomorphic signatures for NP* (HSNP). HSNP essentially generalize classical homomorphic signatures [1,7], mainly to support non-deterministic computation (i.e., statements in NP as opposed to P) and efficient verification. The application of HSNP to VCS is natural and proceeds as follows. The data provider $\mathcal{D}$ uses a secret key to sign each element x_i of the stream and gives (x_i, σ_i) to the server. Upon a client's request of computing a function f on a portion Q of the stream, the HSNP scheme enables the server to derive a short signature σ_y that vouches for the correctness of statements of the form $\exists w$ such that $y = f(\{x_j\}_{j \in Q}, w)$ and for the fact that each input $\{x_j\}_{j \in Q}$ is legitimately signed by $\mathcal{D}$. Then any client can publicly check the correctness of y by using (f, Q, y, σ_y) and $\mathcal{D}$'s public key. Notably, this configuration satisfies the workflow property of VCS. Also, HSNP signatures are guaranteed to be short and can be efficiently verified without knowledge of the inputs, which satisfies the efficiency requirement of VCS.

Fiore and Tucker [5] proposed a generic HSNP construction based on a combination of commit-and-prove (CaP) SNARKs and linearly-homomorphic signatures for committed outputs (ComLHS)[1], and then proposed and implemented an efficient pairing-based instantiation, dubbed SPHinx. In their experiments, they confirm that SPHinx features a proof generation that, depending on the application, is between 15× and 1 300× faster than a straw-man approach in which one uses a general-purpose SNARK to prove the correctness of the computation and the validity of the signatures. However, the fast prover of SPHinx comes at the price of high verifier's costs. For a computation on a stream's portion of t values, verification is largely dominated by a multi-exponentiation of length t. Concretely, for $t \approx 1{,}000{,}000$ verification approaches 20 s whereas the SNARK solution enjoys a cheap verification of 11 ms.

1.1 Our Results

In this work we continue this line of research on efficient HSNP for verifiable computation on data streams. Our main result is the construction of two new HSNP solutions that achieve fast proof generation without the need of sacrificing the verification. Our new schemes feature a verification time that is up to 88× faster than SPHinx. Therefore our HSNP solutions improve over the SNARK-based one on all fronts, without any tradeoff.

More in detail, our contributions are the following. Our first (and main technical contribution) is a new ComLHS scheme that can be replaced in the SPHinx

---

[1] ComLHS are LHS for the non-deterministic computation that checks that a commitment opens to the result of a linear function s on signed messages x, i.e., $\exists r : c = \mathsf{Commit}(\langle x, s \rangle; r)$.

construction. Indeed, it turns out that the slow verification process of SPHinx is entirely due to slow verification in their ComLHS scheme which requires the verifier to perform a multi-exponentiation of length t. We solve this issue by proposing the first pairing-based (Com)LHS in which the verifier needs to perform only $O(t)$ *field operations*, which are way faster than exponentiations. More precisely, our scheme supports two verification profiles: (A) when verifying the output of an arbitrary linear function verification costs $O(t)$ field operations and constant group operations and pairings; (B) for structured linear functions described by a vector of powers $(1, s, s^2, \ldots, s^{t-1})$ verification costs $O(\log t)$. Our technique to enable verification based on field operations requires the prover to hold an auxiliary information with which it can help the verifier. Interestingly, this condition comes for free in the streaming setting where the signer streams signed elements in order to the prover. We formally call this model *streaming-friendly correctness*. We refer to Sect. 3 for more details.

An immediate application of our ComLHS (with (A)-type verification) is to replace the ComLHS in SPHinx. We dub the resulting scheme SPHinx$^+$ and show that it has 2 to 88 times faster verification than SPHinx, at the small price of 7% more expensive prover.

Next, we revisit the generic HSNP construction of [5] in order to be instantiated with our new ComLHS with (B)-type verification and thus to achieve even an asymptotic exponential speedup in verification, from $O(t)$ to $O(\log t)$. Their generic HSNP requires a CaP SNARK in which committed vectors are encoded with polynomials based on (univariate or multivariate) interpolation techniques. In Sect. 4 we generalize this construction to work with any vector encoding. This generalization allows us to capture the case where the vectors is encoded in the coefficients of a polynomial (so-called monomial-base encoding). Thanks to this change we can instantiate the HSNP generic construction with (monomial-base) (CaP) SNARKs and our new LHS with (B)-type verification. We dub this scheme SPHinx^{++}. On the other hand, for the techniques underlying both verification (A) and (B) to work, we need to assume that the portion of inputs $\{x_i\}_{i \in Q}$ to compute over is consecutive, i.e. $Q = \{\delta + 1, \ldots, \delta + t\}$ for a fixed δ. Even though this seems a restriction at the application level, it captures important use cases like sliding window statistics over data streams (histograms, variance, stock prices predictions), where one is interested in analyzing the "window" of the last t items of the stream. Importantly, these use cases with consecutive labels arise in several application scenarios where a faster verification can be of crucial importance, e.g., whenever signatures must be verified in real time. Concretely, consider for example a scenario where a medical device receives statistics computed from values streamed by health sensors which can be labeled using consecutive time instants, hence consecutive labels. In such cases, verifying the authenticity of the data and computation results is essential for security, while fast and efficient verification ensures that critical decisions can be made on-the-fly.

Finally, as the last contribution, we implement our schemes and evaluate them experimentally on the set of applications of HSNP for sliding window statistics.

2 Preliminaries

2.1 Notation

For a $n \in \mathbb{N}$, $[n]$ denotes the set $\{1, \ldots, n\}$. Vectors are in bold. We denote by v_i the i-th coefficient of the vector $\mathbf{v}$. The inner product between two vectors $\mathbf{x}$ and $\mathbf{y}$ is denoted by $\langle \mathbf{x}, \mathbf{y} \rangle$. Let D be a distribution over a set X. For a $x \in X$, we say $x \leftarrow D$ to say that the element x is sampled from X according to D. All algorithms are assumed to be PPT machines.

A universal relation $\mathcal{R}$ is a set of triples (R, y, w) where R is a relation over $\mathcal{Y} \times \mathcal{W}$, y is called the instance and w the witness. We write $(y, w) \in \mathsf{R}$ to denote that R holds on the pairs (y, w), otherwise $(y, w) \notin \mathsf{R}$. When discussing schemes that prove statements on committed values, the witness can be a pair $(x, w) \in \mathcal{X} \times \mathcal{W}$, with x being the value committed into y. We sometimes use a finer grained specification of $\mathcal{X}$, assuming it splits over ℓ domains $\mathcal{X}_1 \times \cdots \times \mathcal{X}_\ell$ for some arity ℓ.

2.2 Bilinear Groups

We denote by $\mathbb{G}_1, \mathbb{G}_2, \mathbb{G}_T$ cyclic groups of prime order and $e : \mathbb{G}_1 \times \mathbb{G}_2 \to \mathbb{G}_T$ is a bilinear map that is non-degenerate and efficiently computable. For the formal definition and the d-Power-DLog assumption we refer the reader to the full version.

Assumption 2.1. *Given a group generator $\mathcal{G}$, any polynomial p, and any PTT adversary $\mathcal{A}$ making $t = p(\lambda)$ queries, and for large enough λ:*

$$\Pr\left[g_1^a \leftarrow \mathcal{A}\left(\begin{array}{c} \mathsf{pp}_\mathcal{G}, \boldsymbol{\omega}, g_1, \{g_1^{c^i}\}_{i \in [t]}, \{g_1^{a(c^i + \omega_i)}\}_{i \in [t]}, \\ h, h^a, g_2, \{g_2^{c^i}\}_{i \in [t]}, g_2^{1/a} \end{array}\right)\right] = \mathsf{negl}(\lambda).$$

for the random choice of $\mathsf{pp}_\mathcal{G} = (\mathbb{G}_1, \mathbb{G}_2, \mathbb{G}_T, e, p) \leftarrow \mathcal{G}(1^\lambda)$, $g_1 \leftarrow \mathbb{G}_1$, $h \leftarrow \mathbb{G}_1$, $g_2 \leftarrow \mathbb{G}_2$, $\boldsymbol{\omega} \leftarrow \mathbb{Z}_p^t$, $c \leftarrow \mathbb{Z}_p$, $a \leftarrow \mathbb{Z}_p$.

In the full version we prove that Assumption 2.1 holds in the Algebraic group model (AGM) [6].

2.3 Commitment Schemes

A commitment scheme Com is a tuple (Setup, Commit, VerCom) where $\mathsf{ck} \leftarrow \mathsf{Setup}(1^\lambda)$ generates a commitment key; $(\mathsf{cm}, \mathsf{o}) \leftarrow \mathsf{Commit}(\mathsf{ck}, x)$ generates a commitment cm and an opening o, given a input message x; $b \leftarrow \mathsf{VerCom}(\mathsf{ck}, \mathsf{cm}, x, \mathsf{o})$ checks if o is a valid opening for cm to x. In this work, unless otherwise specified, we use commitments that are computationally binding - it is hard to open the same cm to two distinct messages - and statistically hiding - cm leaks no information about the message x.

A succinct argument of knowledge (SNARK) with specializable universal SRS for a universal relation $\mathcal{R}$ is a tuple of algorithms Π = (Setup, Derive, Prove, Verify), where srs ← Setup($1^\lambda, \mathcal{R}$) outputs a universal structured reference string srs; (ek$_R$, vk$_R$) ← Derive(srs, R) takes a universal srs and a relation R ∈ $\mathcal{R}$, and outputs a specialized SRS consisting of an evaluation key and a verification key; π ← Prove(ek$_R$, R, y, w) takes an evaluation key for a relation R, a relation R, an instance y, and a witness w such that (y, w) ∈ R, and returns a proof π; b ← VerProof(vk$_R$, y, π) takes a specialized verification key, an instance y, and a proof π, and accepts ($b = 1$) or rejects ($b = 0$). A SNARK satisfies the properties of completeness, succinctness, knowledge soundness and composable zero-knowledge. In the full version we recall these standard definitions.

2.4 Homomorphic Signature for NP Relations

HSNP extend classical homomorphic signatures (HS) to support the evaluation of non-deterministic computations on signed data. Informally, this means that anyone who knows inputs $x_1, \ldots, x_n$ and signatures $\sigma_1, \ldots, \sigma_n$ on them, can compute $y = f(x_1, \ldots, x_n, w)$ where w is a non-deterministic input, and then derive a signature $\hat{\sigma}$ on y which guarantees that there exists a w and validly authenticated $x_1, \ldots, x_n$ such that $y = f(x_1, \ldots, x_n)$. For an HSNP we consider a privacy notion which guarantees that (σ, y) leaks no information about $(x_1, \ldots, x_n)$ beyond what can be inferred from the result of the computation y.

An interesting feature of HSNP is that they can prove statements about signed inputs that are committed to. For example, one can authenticate commitments to outputs of functions on signed data, i.e., authenticate cm$_y$ which commits to $y = f(x, w)$. This property plays an important role for composing building blocks in large protocols, see for example Sect. 2.4 and Sect. 3.

An important class of HSNP are those for linear relations, namely when the function f is a linear function of the inputs **x**. To emphasize the commit-and-proof feature, we will refer to these as ComLHS.

Labelled Relations . In the context of homomorphic signatures it is important that inputs are labelled. Such a technicality was introduced in [3] for the sake of verifying computations on datasets. Concretely, any data element x_i is signed with respect to the position τ_i it occupies within the stream or dataset. The verifier knows the labels $(\tau_1, \ldots, \tau_n)$ (e.g. the locations of the data in the stream or database) corresponding to the actual data $(x_1, \ldots, x_n)$ which are unknown to it, yet it wants to be assured that a computation $y = f(x_1, \ldots, x_n, w)$ was done on the inputs associated with the labels $(\tau_1, \ldots, \tau_n)$. To give an intuition on why when computing on authenticated data just signing inputs is not enough, suppose that one needs to compute a linear function **a** = $(a_1, \ldots, a_n)$ on signed inputs $x_1, \ldots, x_n$ as $\sum_{i=1}^{n} a_i x_i$. If it happens that $x_i = x_j$ for some $i \neq j$ then this might lead to ambiguity.

Let $\mathcal{R} = \{R : R \subset \mathcal{Y} \times \mathcal{M}^t \times \mathcal{W}\}$ be a universal relation, for some $t \in \mathbb{N}$. A *labelled relation* is a tuple $(R, (\tau_1, \ldots, \tau_t))$, where $R \in \mathcal{R}$ and τ_i is a label for the i-th slot of $\mathcal{M}^t$. We will denote by $R_{id} := (x, x, \emptyset)$ the identity relation on $\mathcal{Y} \times \mathcal{M}^t \times \mathcal{W}$.

Definition 2.1 (HSNP). *A homomorphic signature scheme for NP consists of the following PPT algorithms:*

- $(\mathsf{sk}, \mathsf{vk}) \leftarrow \mathsf{KeyGen}(1^\lambda, \mathcal{L}, \mathcal{R})$: *on input $\lambda \in \mathbb{N}$, a set of labels[2] $\mathcal{L}$, and a universal relation $\mathcal{R}$, outputs a secret signing key sk, and a public key vk.*
- $\sigma \leftarrow \mathsf{Sign}(\mathsf{sk}, \tau, m)$: *on input the signing key sk, a label τ, and a message m, outputs a signature σ.*
- $\sigma \leftarrow \mathsf{Eval}(\mathsf{vk}, R, y, \sigma_1, \ldots, \sigma_t, w)$: *on input the verification key vk, a relation $R \in \mathcal{R}$ over $\mathcal{Y} \times \mathcal{M}^t \times \mathcal{W}$ for some $t \leq |\mathcal{L}|$, a statement $y \in \mathcal{Y}$, signatures $\{\sigma_1, \ldots, \sigma_t\}$, and a witness $w \in \mathcal{W}$, outputs a new signature σ.*
- $b \leftarrow \mathsf{Verify}(\mathsf{vk}, (R, \tau_1, \ldots, \tau_t), y, \sigma)$: *on input a verification key vk, a labelled relation $(R, \tau_1, \ldots \tau_t)$ where $R \in \mathcal{R}$ is over $\mathcal{Y} \times \mathcal{M}^t \times \mathcal{W}$, a statement $y \in \mathcal{Y}$, and a signature σ, outputs 0 (reject) or 1 (accept).*

These algorithms must satisfy the following properties:

Definition 2.2 (Authentication correctness). *For any $(\mathsf{vk}, \mathsf{sk}) \leftarrow \mathsf{KeyGen}(1^\lambda, \mathcal{L}, \mathcal{R})$, $\tau \in \mathcal{L}, x \in \mathcal{M}$, if $\sigma_\tau \leftarrow \mathsf{Sign}(\mathsf{sk}, \tau, x)$ then $\mathsf{Verify}(\mathsf{vk}, (R_{id}, \tau), x, \sigma_\tau) = 1$.*

Definition 2.3 (Evaluation correctness). *Consider any $(\mathsf{vk}, \mathsf{sk}) \leftarrow \mathsf{KeyGen}(1^\lambda, \mathcal{L}, \mathcal{R})$, any $R \in \mathcal{R}$, and any set of label/message/signature triples $\{\tau_i, x_i, \sigma_{\tau_i}\}_{i=1}^t$ satisfying $\mathsf{Verify}(\mathsf{vk}, (R_{id}, \tau_i), x_i, \sigma_{\tau_i}) = 1$. If $(y, (x_{\tau_i}, \ldots, x_{\tau_t}), w) \in R$, and $\sigma = \mathsf{Eval}(\mathsf{vk}, R, y, \sigma_{\tau_1}, \ldots, \sigma_{\tau_t}, w)$ then $\mathsf{Verify}(\mathsf{vk}, (R, \tau_1, \ldots, \tau_t), y, \sigma) = 1$.*

Definition 2.4 (Succinctness). *The size of the evaluated signatures depends at most logarithmically on the size of the signed and non-deterministic inputs.*

Definition 2.5 (Efficient verification). *After a preprocessing step that depends on the size of the relation being proved, the verification algorithm can be efficiently run independently on the input size.*

Definition 2.6 (Adaptive security). *This definition can be seen as an adaptation of the standard notion of unforgeability for HSNP. Intuitively, the evaluator should only be able to compute valid signatures for statements y for which it received signatures for data items $x_1, \ldots, x_t$ and knows a witness w satisfying $(y, (x_1, \ldots, x_t), w) \in R$. The idea is to have an adversary $\mathcal{A}$ which can adaptively query signatures for labelled messages of its choice. Now assume that $\mathcal{A}$ outputs a valid signature σ for a statement y as output of some labelled relation $(R, \tau_1, \ldots, \tau_t)$ for some $t \geq 1$. Then with overwhelming probability (i) $\mathcal{A}$ must have queried signatures for each label τ_i; and, denoting these queries $\{\tau_i, x_i\}_{i \in [t]}$ (ii) the adversary $\mathcal{A}$ must know a witness w such that $(y, (x_1, \ldots, x_t), w) \in R$.*

---

[2] In our construction in Sect. 3, we do not need to specify in advance the labels.

Definition 2.7 (Zero-knowledge). *The zero-knowledge property guarantees that evaluated signatures do not reveal anything about the signed inputs and the non-deterministic input beyond the fact that the signed statement satisfies the relation. The intuition is the following. The adversary queries the* Sign *algorithm on labelled messages on its choice. Then it chooses a statement y, a labelled relation $(\mathsf{R}, \tau_1, \ldots, \tau_t)$ (where each τ_i must have been queried along with an input x_i resulting in the signature σ_{τ_i}) and a witness w satisfying $(y, (x_1, \ldots, x_t), w) \in \mathsf{R}$. Then $\mathcal{A}$ is given a signature σ for the statement y, which is either the result of the computation of the relation R on the signatures $\sigma_{\tau_1}, \ldots, \sigma_{\tau_t}$ or the output of the simulator that receives the secret key* sk *and $y, (\mathsf{R}, \tau)$ but does not have access to the signed inputs. The scheme is zero-knowledge if it is hard for $\mathcal{A}$ to tell which is the case.*

A Generic HSNP from ComLHS. In [5] Fiore and Tucker construct a generic HSNP using a commit-and-prove zkSNARK, a polynomial commitment and a ComLHS as building blocks. Here we sketch the idea behind their construction (with a simple generalization of it that enables more instantiations). For a complete description, we refer the reader to the full version.

Let $\mathbb{T} = \{\tau_1, \ldots, \tau_t\}$ be a set of labels. Let $\mathsf{Dec} : \mathbb{F}[X_1, \ldots, X_n] \to \mathbb{F}^t$ be a decoding function and $\chi(X_1, \ldots, X_n)$ be a list of t n-variate polynomials satisfying the following properties:

- Dec is $\mathbb{F}$-linear and $\mathsf{Dec}(\chi_i) = \mathbf{e}_i$, where $\mathbf{e}_i$ is the ith vector of the canonical basis of $\mathbb{F}^t$;
- $\deg(\chi_i(X_1, \ldots, X_n))/|\mathbb{F}|$ is negligible for all $i = 1, \ldots, t$;
- $\forall \mathbf{r} \in \mathbb{F}^n$ then $\chi_i(\mathbf{r})$ is computable in $O(t)$ $\mathbb{F}$-operations.

We define $\tilde{x}(X_1, \ldots, X_t) = \langle \mathbf{x}, \chi(X_1, \ldots, X_n) \rangle$ as the polynomial encoding of a vector $\mathbf{x}$.

The first condition, the existence of a decoding function Dec, is our generalization. In SPHinx, it is instead assumed the existence of a public set $\mathbb{H} = \{h_1, \ldots, h_t\}$ such that $\chi_i(h_j) = 1$ if $i = j$ and 0 otherwise. Namely, the polynomials χ_i are the Lagrange polynomials corresponding to the set $\mathbb{H}$. For instance, in the univariate case $\chi_i(X) = \frac{h_i(X^{|\mathbb{H}|}-1)}{|\mathbb{H}|(X-h_i)}$, and thus $\mathbf{x} = \mathsf{Dec}(\tilde{x}(X))$.

The building blocks for their generic HSNP are:

1. A commitment scheme $\mathsf{Com} = (\mathsf{KeyGen}, \mathsf{Commit}, \mathsf{Open}, \mathsf{VerCom})$ for committing to n-variate polynomials with coefficients in $\mathbb{F}$.
2. A universal commit-and-prove (CaP) zkSNARK $\mathsf{CP}_\mathcal{R}$ for Com and relation $\mathcal{R}$. Specifically, given a statement y and a commitment $\mathsf{cm}_{\tilde{x}}$, $\mathsf{CP}_\mathcal{R}$ proves the existence of witnesses $\tilde{x}(X_1, \ldots, X_n) \in \mathbb{F}[X_1, \ldots, X_n]$, $\mathsf{o}_{\tilde{x}}$ and w such that

$$(y, \mathsf{Dec}(\tilde{x}), w) \in \mathsf{R} \wedge \mathsf{VerCom}(\mathsf{ck}, \mathsf{cm}_{\tilde{x}}, \tilde{x}, \mathsf{o}_{\tilde{x}}) = 1.$$

3. A universal CP zkSNARK $\mathsf{CP}_{\mathsf{ev}}$ for committed polynomial evaluations. Specifically, given a statement $\mathbf{r} \in \mathbb{F}^n$ and commitments $\mathsf{cm}_{\tilde{x}}, \mathsf{cm}_z$ to $\tilde{x} \in \mathbb{F}[X_1, \ldots, X_n]$ and $z \in \mathbb{F}$, it proves that

$$z = \tilde{x}(\mathbf{r}) \wedge \mathsf{VerCom}(\mathsf{ck}, \mathsf{cm}_{\tilde{x}}, \tilde{x}, \mathsf{o}_{\tilde{x}}) = 1 \wedge \mathsf{VerCom}(\mathsf{ck}, \mathsf{cm}_z, z, \mathsf{o}_z) = 1$$

4. A ComLHS scheme ComLHS = (KeyGen, Sign, Eval, Verify) for the relation

$$\mathcal{R}_{\text{com-ip}} = \{\mathsf{R}^{t,\mathbf{s}}_{\text{com-ip}} := \{(\mathsf{cm}, \mathbf{x}, \mathsf{o}) \; : \; \mathsf{VerCom}(\mathsf{ck}, \mathsf{cm}, \langle \mathbf{x}, \mathbf{s} \rangle, \mathsf{o}) = 1\} \; : \; t \leqslant N, \mathbf{s} \in \mathbb{F}^t\}$$

For a relation R that can be encoded as a circuit $F : \mathbb{F}^{t+|w|} \to \mathbb{F}$, given t signed inputs $x_1, \ldots, x_t$ with labels $\tau_1, \ldots, \tau_t$, to compute a signature on the output $y = F(x_1, \ldots, x_t, w)$, where w is a witness, the evaluator proceeds as follows. It commits to the polynomial $\tilde{x}$, say $\mathsf{cm}_{\tilde{x}}$. It then computes a proof π using $\mathsf{CP}_\mathcal{R}$ for the relation $\mathcal{R}$ to prove that the computation was performed correctly on the inputs $\mathbf{x} = \mathsf{Dec}(\tilde{x}(X))$ with witness w. Then it proves that these inputs are signed. For this, it gets a random challenge $\mathbf{r}$, computes $z = \tilde{x}(\mathbf{r}) = \langle \mathbf{x}, \chi(\mathbf{r}) \rangle$, commits to z in, say, cm_z, and uses $\mathsf{CP}_{\mathsf{ev}}$ to prove this committed evaluation. Finally, the ComLHS is used to prove that cm_z opens to the signed result of the linear function $\langle \mathbf{x}, \chi(\mathbf{r}) \rangle$ of the signed inputs $\mathbf{x}$.

3 Linearly Homomorphic Signature

We present our construction of a linearly-homomorphic signature for committed outputs (ComLHS), which is an HSNP for the family of relations

$$\mathcal{R}_{\text{com-ip}} := \{\mathsf{R}^{(t,\mathbf{s})}_{\text{com-ip}} := (c, \mathbf{x}, \mathsf{o}) \; : \; \mathsf{VerCom}(\mathsf{ck}, c, \langle \mathbf{x}, \mathbf{s} \rangle, \mathsf{o}) = 1, t \leqslant N, \mathbf{s} \in \mathbb{F}^t\}$$

where Com = (Setup, Commit, Open, VerCom) is a commitment scheme.

Our scheme supports labels that are integers, without an a-priori fixed upper bound, and has streaming-friendly correctness. Namely, when evaluating on a set of labels $\mathbb{T} = \{\tau_1, \ldots, \tau_t\} \in \mathbb{N}^t$, it achieves correctness if the evaluator has received (a stream of) signatures with labels $1, 2, \ldots, \tau_t$.

We construct our scheme in bilinear groups, and we additionally make use of a secure (EUF-CMA) signature $\Sigma = (\Sigma.\mathsf{KG}, \Sigma.\mathsf{Sign}, \Sigma.\mathsf{Verify})$, and a proof system NIZK = (K, P, V) for the relation $\mathsf{R}_c = \{(y,(z,w)) \; : \; y = g_1^z h^w\}$. Concretely, we will instantiate Σ with Schnorr's signature and NIZK with Okamoto's sigma protocol [8].

We describe our ComLHS in Fig. 1. Below we provide an intuition of the construction, comparing it to the scheme proposed in [5].

Previous LHS. First, we will sketch the LHS proposed in [5]. We will only include the parts that are important to understand our improvement. A key generation phase produces secret keys a, b along with a public key consisting among other things of $\Gamma_1 = h_1^a, \Gamma_2 = g_2^{1/a}, B = g_1^b$. To sign an input x with label τ, the signer first hashes the label τ to obtain $C_\tau \leftarrow H(\tau)$. It computes $\Lambda_\tau = (C_\tau g_1^{br_\tau + x})^a$, where r_τ is obtained from applying a PRF to τ. The signature on x, τ is then (Λ_τ, r_τ). To compute a linear function with public coefficients $\mathbf{s} \in \mathbb{Z}_p^t$ on signed inputs $(x_1, \ldots, x_t)$ with labels $\tau_1, \ldots, \tau_t$, given a commitment $y = g_1^{\langle \mathbf{x}, \mathbf{s} \rangle} h^w$, the evaluator first applies the linear function to the pseudo-randomness $(r_{\tau_1}, \ldots, r_{\tau_t})$ resulting in $r = \langle \mathbf{r}, \mathbf{s} \rangle$. It then computes the product $\Lambda \leftarrow \Gamma_1^w \prod_{i=1}^{t} (\Lambda_i)^{s_i}$. The evaluated signature then includes (y, Λ, r). To verify the above signature with the public key, the verifier computes $C \leftarrow \prod_{i=1}^{t} (H(\tau_i))^{s_i}$ and then checks that $e(yB^rC, g_2) = e(\Lambda, \Gamma_2)$.

From the above description, it appears that the cost for both evaluating and verifying an evaluated signature is dominated by the computation of $C = \prod_{i=1}^{t} H(\tau_i)^{s_i}$ which is a multi-exponentiation of t factors, namely t $\mathbb{G}_1$-operations. This is the main bottleneck for SPHinx, making its verification orders of magnitude slower than that from a solution using general purpose SNARKs due to both hashing into the group t times and then computing the multi-exponentiation.

Our Algebraic LHS. Our idea to speed up verification is to delegate the computation of the term C to the prover and let it provide a proof of correct computation which is fast to verify. Notably, the challenge of achieving this is that we simultaneously want to keep the prover's cost in the same order of magnitude, that is we cannot use a general purpose delegation scheme which would likely need to encode the multi-exponentiation in a circuit, with prohibitive overhead.

Therefore, to achieve our goal we change the ComLHS scheme in such a way that the terms C_τ have a convenient algebraic form which leads more naturally to an efficient and succinct proof of correct computation. Our starting point is to replace the random oracle in the terms C_τ with $g_1^{c^\tau}$ for a secret c that is part of the secret key. This way, the term $C = \prod_{i=1}^{t}(g_1^{c^{\tau_i}})^{s_i}$ can be interpreted as a commitment to the polynomial $\sum_{i=1}^{t} s_i X^{\tau_i}$, for which the prover can provide a succinct proof using a KZG-style proof. The issue is that the terms C_{τ_i} in the product C depend on the size of the whole stream, while we want the computation as well as the verification to depend only on the size of the sample $\mathbb{T}$. To avoid this we need to make some restriction on the sample set $\mathbb{T}$. For simplicity, we focus on the case when the label set $\mathbb{T} = \{\tau_1, \ldots, \tau_t\}$ can be represented as consecutive labels[3], namely $\{\delta+1, \ldots, \delta+t\}$ for a $\delta \in \mathbb{N}$ which is possibly $O(N)$, where N is the size of the whole stream.

The key generation produces secret keys a, b, c along with a public key consisting among other things of $\Gamma_1 = h^a, \Gamma_2 = g_2^{1/a}, B = g_1^b$, with $\mathbb{G}_1 = (g_1), \mathbb{G}_2 = (g_2)$ and h being a random element from $\mathbb{G}_1$, and a PRF key κ.

To sign a data element x with label τ, the signer now computes $C_\tau^{(1)} := g_1^{c^\tau}$. It then computes r_τ from a PRF F_κ applied to τ and then computes the element $\Lambda_\tau = (C_\tau^{(1)} g_1^{br_\tau + x})^a$ as before. Note that this uniquely binds the Λ_τ to the label τ as long as c is secret. The signature σ_τ then includes $C_\tau^{(1)}, C_\tau^{(2)} := g_2^{c^\tau}, r_\tau, \Lambda_\tau$.

To compute a linear function with public coefficients $\mathbf{s} \in \mathbb{Z}_p^t$ on signed inputs $(x_{\delta+1}, \ldots, x_{\delta+t})$ with labels $\delta+1, \ldots, \delta+t$, given a commitment $y = g_1^{\langle \mathbf{x}, \mathbf{s} \rangle} h^w$, the

---

[3] In fact, in order to make the prover depend only on the size of $\mathbb{T}$ one can even allow gaps between labels provided they are of constant size. We will argue that both cases are enough to capture realistic use cases, for example the important case of sliding-window statistics.

evaluator proceeds as follows. As before, the evaluator applies the linear function on the pseudo-randomness $\mathbf{r}$, resulting in $r = \langle \mathbf{r}, \mathbf{s} \rangle$. The goal is to compute $g_1^{\bar{S}(c)}$ where $\bar{S}(X) = \sum_{i=1}^t s_i X^{\delta+i}$ and provide a succinct proof of this. Define the polynomial $S(X) := \sum_{i=1}^t s_i X^{i-1}$. Note that $\bar{S}(X) = X^{\delta+1} S(X)$ and that $S(X)$ does not depend on δ. The evaluator first computes $C_S := \prod_{i=0}^{t-1} (C_i^{(1)})^{s_{i+1}}$ and $C_{\bar{S}} := \prod_{i=1}^t (C_{\delta+i}^{(1)})^{s_i}$. It then computes a KZG-like proof $\pi_S := g_1^{q(u)}$ where $q(X)$ is the polynomial defined by $q(X) = \frac{S(X)-S(u)}{X-u}$ for a random point u, derived e.g. from a random oracle. Then it computes the product $\Lambda \leftarrow \Gamma_1^w \prod_{i=1}^t (\Lambda_i)^{s_i}$. The outputed evaluated signature then includes $C_S, C_{\bar{S}}, \pi_S, r, \Lambda$.

To verify the above signature, the verifier first derives the random point u from the RO. It then computes $S(u) = \sum_{i=1}^t s_i u^{i-1}$ and checks that $e(yB^r C_{\bar{S}}, g_2) = e(\Lambda, \Gamma_2)$ and that $e(\pi_S, g_2) = e(C_S g_1^{-S(u)}, g_2^{c-u})$ and $e(C_{\bar{S}}, g_2) = e(C_S, C_{\delta+1}^{(2)})$, the latter check testing that $\bar{S}(X) = X^{\delta+1} S(X)$. Note that the verifier cannot, in principle, check that the term $C_{\delta+1}^{(2)}$ is indeed $g_2^{c^{\delta+1}}$. To ensure this, we let the signer include as part of the output a signature, e.g. Schnorr's, that the value $C_\tau^{(2)}$ correspond to the label τ. The signature corresponding to the label $\delta + 1$ is then appended to the evaluated signature from the evaluator so the verifier just needs to check the validity of the signature on the element $C_{\delta+1}^{(2)}$ under the signer's public key, which it trusts.

It is clear that in our LHS now the verification only involves $O(t)$ field operations. We will later introduce further optimizations that allow reducing the verification cost to $O(\log t)$ field operations.

Further Comments. Here we explain some technical details in our LHS that we omitted in the above intuitive description.

In both [5] and our ComLHS, the evaluator uses a succinct NIZK for proving that $y = g_1^z h^w$, where $z = \langle \mathbf{x}, \mathbf{s} \rangle$. This is needed in the proof of adaptive security to extract the witness w.

In our ComLHS, the evaluator needs to compute the element $C'_{\bar{S}} = g_1^{\alpha \bar{S}(c)}$ so as to allow the extraction of the polynomial $\bar{S}(X)$ in the security proof. To do this, we include the elements g_1^α, g_2^α in the verification key, and let the signer produce and send the element $g_1^{\alpha c^\tau}$ for each label τ. A final pairing is needed to check that $C'_{\bar{S}} = C_{\bar{S}}^\alpha$.

To sign labelled inputs, we make use of a PRF $F_\kappa : \mathbb{N} \to \mathbb{Z}_p$ to generate the randomness r_τ. This is needed for proving the zero-knowledge property of the ComLHS. This makes the value $r = \langle \mathbf{r}, \mathbf{s} \rangle$ a deterministic function of the labels, the relation $\mathsf{R}_{\text{com-ip}}^{t,\mathbf{s}}$ and the secret key. All this information being known to the simulator, it can simulate r.

Theorem 3.1. *If NIZK is a proof of knowledge for R_c, Σ is a EUF-CMA signature, RO is modelled as a random oracle and F is a secure PRF, then the ComLHS scheme in Fig. 1 satisfies authentication correctness, evaluation correctness and adaptive security under Assumption 2.1. Furthermore, if NIZK is zero-knowledge, then the LHS is zero-knowledge.*

The proof of Theorem 3.1 is provided in the full version.

3.1 Cost of Our ComLHS

Here we give the costs for our ComLHS in Fig. 1 and compare it with the one in Table 1 of Fiore and Tucker [5].

Table 1. Comparison of our LHS with the one in [5]. Our construction improves on the verification cost by removing the expensive group operations that were the main bottleneck of previous work. At the cost of adding a constant overhead in the proving time and signature size. The values of the last column refer to our instantiation with the BLS12-381 curve. For evaluation and verification we do not include the costs that do not depend on t. Verification requires performing a constant number of pairings. These do not affect the efficiency of the scheme, as shown our experiments, see Sect. 5.

Scheme	Evaluation	Verifier	Evaluated sig. size	Evaluated sig. size (in Bytes)
[5]	$t\ \mathbb{G}_1$-operations	$t\ \mathbb{G}_1$-operations	$2\mathbb{G}_1$	255
	$2t\ \mathbb{F}$-operations		$4\mathbb{F}$	
This work arbitrary linear functions	$5t\ \mathbb{G}_1$-operations	$t\ \mathbb{F}$-operations	$8\mathbb{G}_1, 1\mathbb{G}_2$	478
	$3t\ \mathbb{F}$-operations		$4\mathbb{F}$	
This work structured linear functions	$4t\ \mathbb{G}_1$-operations	$\log t\ \mathbb{F}$-operations	$8\mathbb{G}_1, 2\mathbb{G}_2$	557
	$2t\ \mathbb{F}$-operations		$5\mathbb{F}$	

(A)-type Verification: Arbitrary Linear Functions. This is the case where the vector **s** is arbitrary. The cost for the evaluator is dominated by the computation of the elements $\Lambda, C_S, C_{\bar{S}}, C'_{\bar{S}}, \pi_S$, each one being a multi-exponentiation of size t. Using Pippenger's algorithm this takes around $t \log(q)/\log(t \log(q))$ group operations.

The cost for the verifier is dominated by the computation of the term ρ, which is an inner product of two vectors of size t. This requires $O(t)$ field operations.

An evaluated signature consists of the proof π_{NIZK} which counts for one group element and two field elements, the field elements r, and the group elements $y, \Lambda, C_S, C_{\bar{S}}, C'_{\bar{S}}, C^{(2)}_{\delta+1}, \pi_S$ and the signature $sig_{\delta+1}$.

Faster Prover. It is possible to verify π_S without the need of communicating C_S. Notice that line 2.4 of Verify checking that $q(X) = \frac{S(X)-S(u)}{X-u}$ and $\bar{S}(X) = X^{\delta+1}S(X)$ can be replaced by checking that $\bar{S}(X) - S(u)X^{\delta+1} = q(X)(X-u)X^{\delta+1} = \frac{S(X)-S(u)}{X-u}(X-u)X^{\delta+1}$. This can be checked by replacing line 2.4 with the check $e(C_{\bar{S}}, g_2)e(g_1^{-S(u)}, C^{(2)}_{\delta+1}) = e(\pi_S, C^{(2)}_{\delta+2}(C^{(2)}_{\delta+1})^{-u})$. For this, the

KeyGen($1^\lambda, \mathcal{R}_{\text{com-ip}}$):
1. $\text{pp}_{\mathcal{G}} := (\mathbb{G}_1 = \langle g_1 \rangle, \mathbb{G}_2 = \langle g_2 \rangle, \mathbb{G}_T, e, p) \leftarrow \mathcal{G}(1^\lambda), h \leftarrow \mathbb{G}_1$;
2. $\text{ck} := (\text{pp}_{\mathcal{G}}, h)$;
3. $\text{sk}_\Sigma, \text{pk}_\Sigma \leftarrow \Sigma.\text{KeyGen}(1^\lambda)$;
4. $\text{crs} \leftarrow \text{NIZK.K}(1^\lambda, \text{ck})$;
5. $\kappa \leftarrow \mathcal{K}$;
6. $a, b, c \leftarrow \mathbb{Z}_p, \alpha \leftarrow \mathbb{Z}_p$;
7. $\Gamma_1 \leftarrow h^a, \Gamma_2 \leftarrow g_2^{1/a}, B \leftarrow g_1^b$;
8. Return $\text{sk} := ((a, b, c), \alpha, \kappa, \text{sk}_\Sigma), \text{vk} := (\text{ck}, \text{crs}, \Gamma_1, \Gamma_2, B, g_1^c, g_2^c, g_1^\alpha, g_2^\alpha, \text{pk}_\Sigma)$;

Sign(sk, τ, x):
1. $C_\tau^{(1)} \leftarrow g_1^{c^\tau}, C_\tau' \leftarrow g_1^{\alpha c^\tau}, C_\tau^{(2)} \leftarrow g_2^{c^\tau}$;
2. $r_\tau \leftarrow F_\kappa(\tau)$;
3. $\Lambda_\tau \leftarrow \left(C_\tau^{(1)} g_1^{x+br_\tau}\right)^a$;
4. $sig_\tau \leftarrow \Sigma.\text{Sign}(\text{sk}_\Sigma, C_\tau^{(2)} \| \tau)$;
5. Return $\sigma_\tau = (x_\tau, \Lambda_\tau, r_\tau, C_\tau^{(1)}, C_\tau', C_\tau^{(2)}, sig_\tau, \emptyset)$;

Eval($\text{vk}, \mathcal{R}_{\text{com-ip}}^{t,\mathbf{s}}, \delta, y, \{\sigma_\tau\}_{\tau \in [N]}, w$):
1. Parse $\mathbf{s} \in \mathbb{Z}_p^t$ from $\mathcal{R}_{\text{com-ip}}^{(t,\mathbf{s})}$;
2. For $i \in [t]$ do:
   2.1 Parse $(x_{\delta+i}, \Lambda_{\delta+i}, r_{\delta+i}, C_{\delta+i}^{(1)}, C_{\delta+i}', C_{\delta+i}^{(2)}, sig_{\delta+i}, \emptyset) = \sigma_{\delta+i}$;
   2.2 Parse $(x_i, \Lambda_i, r_i, C_i^{(1)}, C_i', C_i^{(2)}, sig_i, \emptyset) = \sigma_i$;
3. Set $\mathbf{x} = (x_{\delta+1}, \ldots, x_{\delta+t}), \mathbf{r} = (r_{\delta+1}, \ldots, r_{\delta+t})$;
4. $z \leftarrow \langle \mathbf{x}, \mathbf{s} \rangle, r \leftarrow \langle \mathbf{r}, \mathbf{s} \rangle$;
5. $\pi_{\text{NIZK}} \leftarrow \text{NIZK}.P(\mathcal{R}_c, \text{crs}, y, (z, w))$;
6. $\Lambda \leftarrow \Gamma_1^w \cdot \prod_{i \in [t]} (\Lambda_{\delta+i})^{s_i}$;
7. Set $S(X) := \sum_{i=0}^{t-1} s_{i+1} X^i, \bar{S}(X) := \sum_{i=1}^{t} s_i X^{\delta+i}$;
8. $C_S \leftarrow g_1^{s_1} \cdot \prod_{i \in [t]} (C_{i-1}^{(1)})^{s_{i+1}}, C_{\bar{S}} \leftarrow \prod_{i \in [t]} (C_{\delta+i}^{(1)})^{s_i}, C_{\bar{S}}' \leftarrow \prod_{i \in [t]} (C_{\delta+i}')^{s_i}$;
9. $u \leftarrow RO(\text{vk}, \mathcal{R}_{\text{com-ip}}^{(t,\mathbf{s})}, \delta, sig_{\delta+1}, y, \Lambda, r, C_S, C_{\bar{S}}, C_{\bar{S}}', C_{\delta+1}^{(2)}, \pi_{\text{NIZK}})$;
10. Compute $q(X) = \sum_{i=0}^{t-2} q_i X^i := \frac{S(X) - S(u)}{X - u}$;
11. $\pi_S \leftarrow \prod_{i=0}^{t-2} \left(C_i^{(1)}\right)^{q_i}$;
12. Return $\sigma := (y, \Lambda, r, C_S, C_{\bar{S}}, C_{\bar{S}}', C_{\delta+1}^{(2)}, sig_{\delta+1}, \pi_{\text{NIZK}}, \pi_S)$;

Verify($\text{vk}, \mathcal{R}_{\text{com-ip}}^{(t,\mathbf{s})}, \delta, \sigma$):
1. If $\sigma = \sigma_\tau = (x, \Lambda_\tau, r_\tau, C_\tau^{(1)}, C_\tau', C_\tau^{(2)}, sig_\tau, \emptyset)$:
   1.1 If $\Sigma.\text{Verify}(\text{pk}_\Sigma, sig_\tau, C_\tau^{(2)} \| \tau) = 1 \wedge (e(g_1^x B^{r_\tau}, g_2) = e(\Lambda_\tau, \Gamma_2))$: return 1;
   1.2 Else: return 0;
2. Else if $\sigma = (y, \Lambda, r, C_S, C_{\bar{S}}, C_{\bar{S}}', C_{\delta+1}^{(2)}, sig_{\delta+1}, \pi_{\text{NIZK}}, \pi_S)$:
   2.1 $u \leftarrow RO(\text{vk}, \mathcal{R}_{\text{com-ip}}^{(t,\mathbf{s})}, \delta, y, \Lambda, r, C_S, C_{\bar{S}}, C_{\bar{S}}', C_{\delta+1}^{(2)}, \pi_{\text{NIZK}}, \pi_S)$;
   2.2 $\rho \leftarrow \sum_{i=0}^{t-1} s_{i+1} u^i$;
   2.3 If $\Sigma.\text{Verify}(\text{pk}_\Sigma, sig_{\delta+1}, C_{\delta+1}^{(2)} \| \delta + 1) \neq 1$: return 0;
   2.4 If $e(\pi_S, g_2^c g_2^{-u}) \neq e(C_S g_1^{-\rho}, g_2) \vee e(C_S, C_{\delta+1}^{(2)}) \neq e(C_{\bar{S}}, g_2)$: return 0;
   2.5 If $e(C_{\bar{S}}', g_2) \neq e(C_{\bar{S}}, g_2^\alpha)$: return 0;
   2.6 If $(\text{NIZK}.V(\mathcal{R}_c, \text{crs}, y, \pi_{\text{NIZK}}) = 1) \wedge e(y B^r C_{\bar{S}}, g_2) = e(\Lambda, \Gamma_2)$: return 1;
   2.7 Else: Return 0;

Fig. 1. Our new ComLHS

Eval algorithm should also send the element $C_{\delta+2}^{(2)}$ along with a signature. This saves one multi-exponentiation for the prover (since C_S is not needed) and one pairing for the verifier.

(B)-type Verification: Structured Linear Functions. If we assume now that the vector **s** has additional structure, for example $\mathbf{s} = (1, s, s^2, \ldots, s^{t-1})$, then we can further reduce the cost for both the prover and the verifier.

By exploiting the structure of **s**, the evaluator does not have to produce the proof π_S. The only two modifications in Fig. 1 are the following. In Eval the evaluator sends $(g_2^{c^t}, sig_t)$. In Verify the verifier needs to additionally check the signature sig_t and that $e(C_S, g_2(g_2^c)^{-s}) = e(g_1, g_2(g_2^{c^t})^{-s^t})$ which tests $S(c) = \frac{1-(sc)^t}{1-sc}$. This saves the computation of $u, q(X), \pi_S$ in Eval (lines 9, 10, 11) and of u, ρ and the check $e(\pi_S, g_2^c g_2^{-u}) \neq e(C_S g_1^{-\rho}, g_2)$ (lines 2.1, 2.2 and first part of line 2.4) in Verify.

In particular, the cost for the verifier is then dominated by computing the exponent s^t, which can be done in $O(\log t)$ field operations. Therefore, in this special case the verifier is succinct in the size of the sample set $\mathbb{T}$.

4 Application to Efficient HSNP

Here we use our ComLHS to obtain efficient HSNP schemes.

4.1 Our SPHinx$^+$ Instantiation with Our ComLHS and Marlin

Fiore and Tucker [5] give an efficient instantiation of their generic HSNP (see also Sect. 2.4, called SPHinx, obtained by instantiating the building blocks as follows: $\chi_i(X)$ are univariate Lagrange polynomials; Com is KZG; $\mathsf{CP}_\mathcal{R}$ is a commit-and-prove variant of Marlin that they propose; $\mathsf{CP}_{\mathsf{ev}}$ is a version of KZG with committed outputs, optmized from [4]; ComLHS is instantiated with their own scheme.

In our paper we exploit the modularity of the SPHinx scheme, by taking the same instantiation as above except that we replace their ComLHS with our new, verifier-efficient ComLHS scheme in Fig. 1. The rest of the building blocks remains the same. We dub this instantiation SPHinx$^+$. As we confirm in Sect. 5, the faster verification algorithm of our ComLHS based on field operations makes the SPHinx$^+$ HSNP very efficient for the verifier, removing the drawback of SPHinx.

4.2 Our SPHinx^{++} Instantiation with Our ComLHS and VOMarlin

We show a second HSNP instantiation, dubbed SPHinx^{++}, obtained using our ComLHS with the (B)-type verification. However, this requires the public linear function to be structured. To this end, to build SPHinx^{++} we set $\chi(X_1,\ldots,X_n) = \chi(X)$ univariate with $\chi_i(X) = X^{i-1}$. The polynomial $\tilde{x}(X)$ encoding the inputs $\mathbf{x}$ is then just the polynomial having $\mathbf{x}$ as coefficients, namely $\tilde{x}(X) = f_\mathbf{x}(X) := \sum_{i=1}^{t} x_i X^{i-1}$.

To support this choice, though, we should replace CP.Marlin with a zkSNARK that is commit-and-prove w.r.t. a polynomial commitment with such monomial-basis encoding of vectors. Recently, several PIOPs have been proposed that can be compiled with polynomial commitments in the monomial basis, for example Claymore [9] and the ones from vector oracles [10]. We focus on the latter, specifically those for R1CS relations (see the full version), that we name VOMarlin for the sake of clarity. To use this scheme in the HSNP construction, we make it commit-and-prove, following an approach similar to the one used in [5] for Marlin. We give the construction in the full version.

5 Applications and Experiments

HSNPs yield a natural application to verifiable computation on data streams. In this domain, most concrete use cases fall into so called sliding-window statistics, a method for continuously updating statistical measures over a subset of data, focusing on the t most recent items. They are essential for real-time data analysis across various applications as they provide dynamic and efficient insights into evolving data streams with limited computational resources. They are particularly valuable for continuous monitoring in fields such as finance, network security, and sensor data management.

Sliding-window statistics fit the requirements of our HSNP realizations in which the data owner can stream values with consecutive labels, and computation occurs on a portion of consecutive data. In this section, we evaluate the performance of our HSNP realizations using three benchmarks, that are the following three sliding-window statistics considered in [5]:

Variance: Measures the spread of a set of points from their average value within a given window. For example, this is useful in financial data analysis or sensor data monitoring, where sudden changes in variance could indicate important shifts or anomalies. Variance can be expressed by an R1CS circuit of $t + 2$ variables and $2t + 2$ constraints.

Histogram: Is useful for visualizing and understanding the distribution of data within each window. For example by plotting the frequency of data points in predefined intervals, histograms can reveal patterns or trends that evolve over time in the data stream. Denoting by k the number of intervals, histograms can be expressed by an R1CS circuit with $36tk$ constraints and $96tk$ variables.

Multi-linear Regression: Is a generalisation of linear regression that allows to take into account multiple factors before outputting a prediction. This is particularly relevant in scenarios where relationships between variables need to be analyzed dynamically as new data arrives. Previous work [5] showed that for n days, computing both k additional features and the prediction of the model can be represented by an $R1CS$ with $n(2k^2 + 8k + 4) + k^3 + 5k^2 + 9k + 6$ constraints, and $n\left(\frac{3}{2}k^2 + \frac{15}{2}k + 4\right) + k^3 + 4k^2 + 7k + 4$ variables.

5.1 Implementation and Experimental Setup

The implementation of our scheme extends the previous SPHinx library. It is done in Rust and based on the arkworks[4] libraries. Pairing-friendly curves are instantiated with BLS12-381 [2]. The experiments were run on a Debian GNU/Linux virtual machine running with 8 cores Xeon-Gold-6154 clocked at 3GHz and with 128 GB of RAM. All the reported timings correspond to the median of measurements over 10 executions.

We evaluate the performance of our implementation of SPHinx$^+$ on the three benchmarks above, comparing it with SPHinx and SigMarlin. The latter is a generic HSNP that uses Marlin to prove both the computation and that the corresponding inputs were signed. We simulate SigMarlin by running Marlin on R1CS with an additional 5,000 constraints per signed input to include the cost of verifying signatures. As explained in [5] it is important to note that the addition of 5,000 constraints per signed input is a lowered estimation, with state-of-the-art suggesting that the actual costs could be double this amount.

To benchmarks SPHinx and SPHinx$^+$ we executed all components of our HSNP protocol on the specified R1CS instance and include the associated costs.

5.2 Evaluation

Signing. For SPHinx$^+$ signing takes 1.7 ms which is around 3 times slower than SPHinx signing time as a result of few more group operations. However we argue that this trade off is worth in order to improve the verification time and unnoticeable in practice. The signature still remains of constant size.

---
[4] https://github.com/arkworks-rs

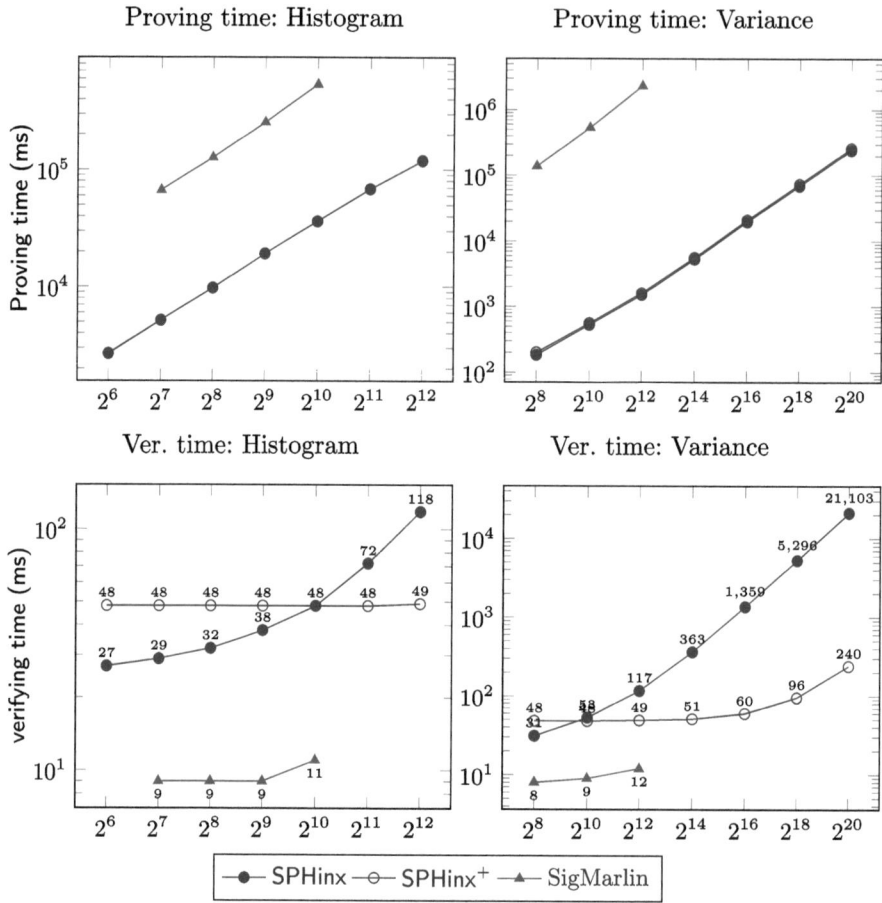

Fig. 2. Comparison of SPHinx, SPHinx⁺ and SigMarlin on: Histogram with 4 buckets and varying input (left), and variance (right). The x-axis displays the number of signed inputs. Plots in log-scale.

Proving and Verification Time. Figure 2 shows the verification time for histograms with 4 buckets and variance computation over varying input sizes. Verification time for MLR with 30 additional features is similar to the one of histograms and for lack of space is not included as a plot.

Our experiments show that SPHinx⁺ improves significantly on SPHinx performances from 2 times for histograms and MLR with $k = 4$ and $t = 2^{12}$ to 88 times faster for the biggest instance we tested (variance with $t = 2^{20}$), staying under a quarter of a second. The additional proving cost stays constant through any input size and is of around 7%, which is negligible compared to the cost of running Marlin. It is worth mentioning that the implementation does not currently use any batching or preprocessing of the pairings. We argue that this would further reduce the verification time bringing it closer to SigMarlin without inheriting its limitations on proving time and RAM usage. Compared to SPHinx$^+$, the advantage of SPHinx^{++} in terms of verification time is in the order of milliseconds, and t had to be increased significantly to see a noticeable difference. For this reason and for lack of space, we do not include it here.

Acknowledgments. We would like to thank Yuncong Zhang for clarifying some points in the VOProof paper and the anonymous reviewers for their comments. This work is supported by the PICOCRYPT project that has received funding from the European Re- search Council (ERC) under the European Unions Horizon 2020 research and innovation programme (Grant agreement No. 101001283), partially supported by projects PRODIGY (TED2021-132464B- I00) and ESPADA (PID2022-142290OB-I00) funded by MCIN/AEI/10.13039/501100011033/. This work is part of the grant JDC2023-050791-I, funded by MCIN/AEI/10.13039/501100011033 and the ESF+.

References

1. Boneh, D., Freeman, D.M.: Homomorphic signatures for polynomial functions. In: Paterson, K.G. (eds.) Advances in Cryptology – EUROCRYPT 2011. EUROCRYPT 2011. LNCS, vol. 6632, pp. 149–168. Springer, Berlin, Heidelberg (2011). https://doi.org/10.1007/978-3-642-20465-4_10
2. Bowe, S., Gabizon, A., Miers, I.: Scalable multi-party computation for zk-SNARK parameters in the random beacon model. Cryptology ePrint Archive, Report 2017/1050, 2017. https://eprint.iacr.org/2017/1050
3. Catalano, D., Fiore, D.: Practical homomorphic MACs for arithmetic circuits. In: Johansson, T., Nguyen, P.Q. (eds.) Advances in Cryptology – EUROCRYPT 2013. EUROCRYPT 2013. LNCS, vol. 7881, pp. 336–352. Springer, Berlin, Heidelberg (2013). https://doi.org/10.1007/978-3-642-38348-9_21
4. Fiore, D., Nitulescu, A., Pointcheval, D.: Boosting verifiable computation on encrypted data. In: Kiayias, A., Kohlweiss, M., Wallden, P., Zikas, V. (eds.) PKC 2020. LNCS, vol. 12111, pp. 124–154. Springer, Cham (2020). https://doi.org/10.1007/978-3-030-45388-6_5
5. Fiore, D., Tucker, I.: Efficient zero-knowledge proofs on signed data with applications to verifiable computation on data streams. In: Yin, H., Stavrou, A., Cremers, C., Shi, E. (eds.), ACM CCS 2022, pp. 1067–1080. ACM Press, 2022
6. Fuchsbauer, G., Kiltz, E., Loss, J.: The algebraic group model and its applications. In: Shacham, H., Boldyreva, A. (eds.) CRYPTO 2018. LNCS, vol. 10992, pp. 33–62. Springer, Cham (2018). https://doi.org/10.1007/978-3-319-96881-0_2
7. Johnson, R., Molnar, D., Song, D., Wagner, D.: Homomorphic signature schemes. In: Preneel, B. (ed.) CT-RSA 2002. LNCS, vol. 2271, pp. 244–262. Springer, Heidelberg (2002). https://doi.org/10.1007/3-540-45760-7_17
8. Okamoto, T.: Provably secure and practical identification schemes and corresponding signature schemes. In: Brickell, E.F. (ed.) CRYPTO 1992. LNCS, vol. 740, pp. 31–53. Springer, Heidelberg (1993). https://doi.org/10.1007/3-540-48071-4_3

9. Szepieniec, A., Zhang, Y.: Polynomial IOPs for linear algebra relations. In: Hanaoka, G., Shikata, J., Watanabe, Y. (eds.) Public-Key Cryptography – PKC 2022. PKC 2022. LNCS, vol. 13177, pp. 523–552. Springer, Cham (2022). https://doi.org/10.1007/978-3-030-97121-2_19
10. Zhang, Y., Szepeniec, A., Zhang, R., Sun, S.F., Wang, G., Gu, D.: VOProof: efficient zkSNARKs from vector oracle compilers. In: Yin, H., Stavrou, A., Cremers, C., Shi, E. (eds.), ACM CCS 2022, pp. 3195–3208. ACM Press, 2022

Rational Secret Sharing with Competition

Tiantian Gong[✉][ID] and Zeyu Liu[ID]

Yale University, New Haven, USA
{tiantian.gong,zeyu.liu}@yale.edu

Abstract. The rational secret sharing problem (RSS) considers incentivizing rational parties to share their received information to reconstruct a correctly shared secret. Halpern and Teague (STOC'04) demonstrate that solving the RSS problem deterministically with explicitly bounded runtime is impossible, if parties prefer learning the secret than not learning, and they prefer fewer other parties to learn.

To overcome this impossibility result, we propose RSS with *competition*. We consider a slightly different yet sensible preference profile: Each party prefers to learn the secret *early* and prefers fewer parties learning *before* them. This preference profile changes the information-hiding dynamics among parties in prior works: First, those who have learned the secret are indifferent towards or even prefer informing others later; second, the competition to learn the secret earlier among different access groups in the access structure facilitates information sharing inside an access group. As a result, we are able to construct the *first* deterministic RSS algorithm that terminates in *at most* two rounds. Additionally, our construction does not employ any cryptographic machinery (being fully game-theoretic and using the underlying secret-sharing scheme as a black-box) nor requires the knowledge of the parties' exact utility function. Furthermore, we consider general access structures.

1 Introduction

Secret sharing is one of the fundamental building blocks of modern cryptography. An m-out-of-n secret sharing scheme shares one secret among n parties and then m people together can reconstruct this secret. In this access structure, any m parties form an *access group*. However, this threshold secret sharing notion naturally assumes at least m parties are honest (i.e., follow the protocol exactly) to ensure a successful reconstruction. Such an assumption can be strong in some applications. Therefore, Halpern and Teague [10] proposed the rational secret sharing (RSS) problem.

In particular, RSS only assumes that the participants are rational, and aims to achieve *fair reconstruction*. Informally, a fair reconstruction in an RSS protocol run by rational (and possibly also malicious parties) allows rational parties to all learn the secret. Here, a rational party follows some preference profile when

---

T. Gong—This work is mostly done while the author was a Ph.D. candidate at Purdue University.

taking an action. As an example, the preference profile in [10] is that rational parties prefer learning the secret over not learning and prefer that fewer others also learn the secret. Under this profile, it was shown in [10] that it is impossible to build a fair reconstruction that is *deterministic* and runs for a *known bounded number of rounds*. Intuitively, this is because in the last round, not sharing dominates sharing when $(m-1)$ other parties share. Then via backward induction, the Nash equilibrium that survives iterated deletion of dominated strategies from the last to the first round is each rational party sharing no information.

To circumvent such an impossibility result, past works have taken a few different routes: (1) adding randomness so that reconstruction terminates probabilistically, and parties can penalize those not sending shares in the previous round by aborting [1,10,14], (2) considering different preference profiles, e.g., only preferring learning [1], (3) considering infinite or unknown rounds of reconstruction, where backward induction no longer applies, and defecting can always be penalized, or (4) discussing repeated reconstructions for many secrets where parties can penalize cheating parties in later runs reconstructing a different secret [20]. Among these approaches, (1), (3), and (4) share the same intrinsic rationale: parties who do not honestly help reconstruction get penalized, which promotes cooperation. Following this idea, one may also consider RSS to be part of a larger protocol where penalties can be applied outside RSS executions. However, one issue with this method together with approaches (3) and (4) is that they are not as generic as (1) and (2). Thus, we avoid such non-generic settings.

For approach (1), previous works have explored randomized RSS protocols based on Shamir's secret sharing scheme [24]. The protocol typically proceeds in rounds. In each round, each party decides whether to send their correct share to others or not. Each round is an actual reconstruction round for the secret with some probability $\alpha \in (0,1)$: If a round is not an actual reconstruction round, the secret is not successfully reconstructed, and parties start a new round. Parties abort if others deviate from sharing in the previous round. Otherwise, the protocol terminates when it hits an actual reconstruction round. Here, α is parameterized with parties' utility functions in a way such that rational parties are incentivized to share.

To design such a randomized RSS algorithm, past works have used some heavy tools, including simultaneous broadcast (SBC) [3] (or time-delayed encryption (TDE) [17], homomorphic time-lock puzzles (HTLP) [19], verifiable random function (VRF) [21]), along with a trusted mediator or a secure multiparty computation (MPC) protocol [7], and digital signatures [1,2,5,9,10,14–17,22] [12,13]. With these primitives and given a proper α, sending shares to others is made the equilibrium strategy (in the respective equilibrium in each past work). We give a more detailed description of these RSS protocols in Sect. 2. However, there are several major issues with these solutions: (1) they use heavy machinery and thus lack practicality; (2) α may be small, meaning that the protocol can potentially last many rounds (e.g., hundreds with $\alpha < 0.01$); (3) α is set according to the utility function of each party and thus the function must be known explicitly. These issues are also detailed in Sect. 2.

An Alternative Preference Profile. To avoid the above drawbacks, we choose the route of devising a different yet still sensible preference profile. In practice, information can be *time-sensitive*: People may not only prefer learning the information but also prefer learning it earlier than others, since this may give them advantages. For example, in stock markets, people who learn information earlier can front-run others and make a profit. Moreover, for people who have already learned and capitalized on the secret, they may still prefer others learning it than not. For instance, others buying the same stock after oneself increases the bid prices. On the other hand, people who have not learned still prefer learning than not learning. In the same example, not learning incurs opportunity costs.

With this intuition in mind, we consider a preference profile accounting for *time and competition*: Rational parties prefer learning the secret in earlier rounds and prefer fewer parties learning the secret before themselves. However, they still prefer learning it than not.

This profile especially applies to RSS in the following applications. (1) It applies where the secrets generate time-sensitive returns and can be capitalized fast, e.g., the reconstructed secret indicates investment opportunities. In this case, learning the secret earlier yields higher profits and one is indifferent towards informing others after acting on the information. (2) It also applies where parties benefit from others taking a certain predictable action after learning the secret, e.g., buying the same stocks as oneself. In this case, one prefers informing others after learning. (3) It also applies to applications where accomplishing computation tasks faster facilitates progress, e.g., distributed computing protocols [6] where a supermajority of parties reconstructing a secret– such as the randomness– early can form a committee to make progress.

1.1 Contributions

New Preference Profile. We first formally define the new preference profile that provides a new direction to circumvent the impossibility. Intuitively, under the updated preference profile, rational parties are naturally encouraged to share information inside their access groups to learn the secret quickly and before other access groups.[1] Indeed, we show that sharing information in the first or second round is the subgame perfect equilibrium (in the scheme below), which is *stronger* than the Nash equilibrium (NE) used in prior works.

Deterministic RSS Construction. With this new preference profile, we provide a *deterministic RSS* scheme (with general access structure, see Sect. 3.2 for details) that terminates in two rounds without requiring simultaneous communication. In particular, it has the following advantages:

- No heavy cryptographic machinery: Major previous works [1,9,10,14,15,17] [2,5,12,13,16,22] focus on probabilistic termination of the protocol and avoid

---

[1] Except for the singleton access structure (i.e., all parties need to participate to recover the secret).

parties' gaining information advantages in the reconstruction game by either enforcing simultaneous movements with SBC or other heavy tools including timed primitives and VRF.

In contrast, we lift all these requirements: we do not even request broadcast channels and allow parties to move sequentially. [2] We also do not need a trusted mediator or MPC functioning as a mediator during reconstruction.

- Knowledge about the utility function is not required. The previous randomized protocols require the knowledge of participants' exact utility functions to parameterize α, the protocol termination parameter, properly. Such knowledge is *not* needed in deterministic reconstruction.
- Arbitrary side information does not affect the protocol. As pointed out by Asharov and Lindell [2], access to auxiliary information about the secret motivates deviation from the equilibrium of information sharing in randomized RSS protocols that do not rely on SBC. Intuitively, the informed party can potentially reconstruct and recognize the secret without sharing and entering the next round. Lysyanskaya and Segal [16] circumvent this by utilizing TDE to hide the reconstructed output for a sufficiently long time. Our updated preference profile allows RSS to accommodate side information because each round is needed for actual reconstruction (unlike prior works where each round is only for actual reconstruction with some probability), and auxiliary information does not give informed parties an advantage.
- Small complexity overhead. The reconstruction of our scheme terminates in constant rounds. It also has little communication and computation overhead, and the share size is *unchanged* from generic secret sharing schemes. Furthermore, when the randomness of the schemes relies on secret sharing schemes (e.g., distributed randomness beacons and asynchronous distributed key generation), randomized RSS faces circularity or expensive setups, while our deterministic RSS avoids them.

2 Prior Work on RSS

We summarize the prior works, elaborate on each of them and show how they compare to our solution below. We also summarize the discussion in Table 1 in the full version [8] and describe the solution concepts used in prior works there.

First generation RSS. Halpern and Teague [10] consider the following preference profile for parties: (U1) rational parties' utilities only depend on the outcome of the reconstruction; (U2) each rational party prefers learning the secret than not; (U3) when one learns the secret, it prefers fewer other parties who

---

[2] Sequential actions further allow the reconstruction to operate in *network asynchrony*. However, since our preference profile is more reasonable in network synchrony (to make "time-sensitiveness" relevant), we only discuss asynchrony setting briefly in the full version [8]. .

also learn the secret. The *solution concept* utilized for solving the reconstruction game is Nash equilibrium (NE) where no party can increase their utility by unilaterally deviating from the equilibrium. They first show that the NE for the reconstruction game in a single access group is *parties not sending their shares to others*. They demonstrate that it is impossible to have a deterministic RSS protocol with a known finite number of rounds under preferences (U1)-(U3). The authors then devise a randomized RSS protocol where each round is an actual reconstruction round with probability α, and parties run the protocol until accomplishing an actual reconstruction round or after detecting deviating behaviors of not sending shares. In this way, rational parties are incentivized to broadcast shares. The RSS protocol applies to $n \geq 3$ parties (due to how the protocol realizes the probabilistic termination). It utilizes an *online dealer* who continuously issue shares, a *trusted mediator* for coordinating reconstruction, and SBC for enforcing simultaneous moves of parties. This first proposal has the following limitations:

1. An online trusted dealer is needed.
2. The protocol does not handle 2-out-of-2 secret sharing and does not have coalition resistance.
3. The protocol does not tolerate malicious parties.
4. SBC is needed.
5. The RSS designer needs to know the parties' utility functions to decide α.
6. The round complexity is $O(\alpha^{-1})$.

Second Generation RSS. Gordon and Katz [9] propose a simpler RSS protocol for $n \geq 2$ parties: In each round, an honest dealer shares the actual secret which is in some field with probability α and otherwise, she shares a random element outside this field. Lysyanskaya and Triandopoulos [17] consider malicious parties and propose a scheme that tolerates ($\lceil n/2 \rceil - 1$) malicious parties with MPC and zero-knowledge proofs. Abraham et al. [1] introduce the (k,t)-robustness notion for equilibrium strategies where a set of $k \geq 1$ parties form a coalition in playing the reconstruction game, and another set of t parties behave arbitrarily. For a base m-out-of-n Shamir's secret sharing scheme ($n \geq 2$), they propose a (k,t)-robust RSS protocol terminates in expected two rounds for $k < m \leq n - k$ and $O(\alpha^{-1})$ rounds for $k < m \leq n$ provided that parties' utility functions satisfy some additional conditions. This generation of protocols resolve issues 1, 2, 3 and partly 6 above. However, issues 4 and 5 remain unsolved. Besides, SBC is still the main inefficiency source, on top of other newly introduced heavy tools.

Third Generation RSS. Kol and Naor [14,15] remove the dependence on SBC in previous RSS protocols and adopt a stronger solution concept, strict NE[3] when solving the reconstruction game. However, [14,15] introduce high round complexity. Fuchsbauer et al. [5] utilize VRF [21] to remove the reliance on SBC and preserve the round complexity $O(\alpha^{-1})$. Moreover, the protocol applies to *asynchronous network*. However, without SBC, randomized RSS inherently does

---

[3] In a strict NE, each party's equilibrium strategy generates strictly higher utility.

not allow for access to *side information* since an informed party can recognize a reconstruction round before sharing [2].

To accommodate side information, Lysyanskaya and Segal [16] assume computationally bounded parties and network synchrony, and utilize TDE to hide reconstruction results until the next round. Additionally, they assume parties prefer *misleading others to wrong outputs and not learning the secret* to *everyone learning the secret*. De and Pal [4] build on [16], and continue to adopt TDE for hiding shares. Side information is distributed by the dealer to help parties decide whether the reconstructed secret is correct. Knapp and Quaglia [13] build upon [4] and improve on computation overhead by employing HTLP instead of TDE. In [11], Kawachi et al. build verifiable RSS upon another RSS plus verifiable/authenticated SS (and they use [5] as the underlying RSS) – which means that they inherit all the assumptions from the underlying RSS – and achieve constant rounds in expectation. While these works relax the SBC requirement resolving issue 4, and [11] solves issue 6 (but cannot tolerate side information), the constructions are still randomized and rely on other heavy cryptographic tools or additional assumptions on rational parties' preferences.

3 Model and Definitions

3.1 System and Network

There are n parties functioning as share holders. They can have *side information* about the secret of interest. The parties are either **rational** and act in a utility-maximizing manner or **malicious** and behave arbitrarily. We start by assuming that the parties are rational and consider malicious parties in Sect. 6.

Parties are connected via authenticated point-to-point channels. Their messages are digitally signed. The network is **synchronous**, meaning that there is a known finite time bound Δ: For a message sent at some time t, it is delivered by time $t + \Delta$. We define one round to be Δ time. We assume a party learning a secret in a round x can capitalize on the information faster than a party learning it in a higher round $\geq x+1$.

3.2 Secret Sharing

This section recalls the definition of secret sharing. In this paper, we consider a more general secret sharing setting, allowing a general access structure, instead of only the threshold setting (i.e., m-out-of-n secret sharing). At a high level, it means that there exist multiple sets of participants, and each of these individual sets of participants can reconstruct the secret among themselves. All these sets together form an access structure $\mathcal{A}$. m-out-of-n is a special access structure, where each individual set is simply m out of these n participants. These are defined more formally below.

Access Structure. Consider a secret sharing scheme run by n parties, $[n] = \{1, \ldots, n\}$. A general access structure $\mathcal{A} \subseteq 2^{[n]}$ is a subset of the power set of the party set. We address each set in $\mathcal{A}$ as an **access group**. The m-out-of-n threshold secret sharing scheme has access structure $\mathcal{A}^{(m)} = \{S \subseteq [n] : |S| \geq m\}$. For clarity in analysis, we consider only the minimal access groups in $\mathcal{A}$ where each party in the set is needed for reconstruction and truncate their strict supersets, which we denote as $\mathcal{A}^\star$. For example, the minimal threshold access structure is $\mathcal{A}^{\star(m)} = \{S \subseteq [n] : |S| = m\}$.

The n parties can have asymmetric status in $\mathcal{A}$ in terms of the number of ways to reconstruct the secret. For instance, one party can be present in every access group and is needed by each group for secret reconstruction while this party only needs shares from any group. We capture this asymmetry by defining a new notion, *rank*, and let function $\gamma(\cdot)$ compute the rank of the input.

Definition 1 (Rank). *The initial rank of a party i in a minimal access structure $\mathcal{A}^\star$ is $\gamma(i) = |\{S \in \mathcal{A}^\star : i \in S\}|$.*

A party present in *every* access group has rank $|\mathcal{A}^\star|$, and we say that such a party is *universal* when $|\mathcal{A}^\star| > 1$. We let the lowest possible rank be 1 for non-triviality. Parties in m-out-of-n Shamir's scheme have symmetric status: They have the same rank $\binom{n-1}{m-1}$.

Next, we define a reconstruction freedom notion to measure how much a party depends on another party to reconstruct the secret.

Definition 2 (Reconstruction Freedom). *For $i, j \in [n]$, the reconstruction freedom of a party j from party i is $\mathsf{free}_j(i) = |\{S \in \mathcal{A}^\star : j \in S, i \notin S\}|$.*

Secret Sharing Scheme. A secret sharing scheme is a tuple of two algorithms $(\mathsf{Share}(\cdot), \mathsf{Rec}(\cdot))$:

- $[\mathsf{s}] := (\mathsf{s}_1, \ldots, \mathsf{s}_n) \leftarrow \mathsf{Share}(\mathsf{m})$: Given the secret m as input, output the shares for each party.
- $\mathsf{m}' \leftarrow \mathsf{Rec}([\mathsf{s}]_A)$ where $[\mathsf{s}]_A$ are the shares held by parties in a set A: Given a set of shares, deterministically reconstructs a secret.

The security of a secret sharing scheme requires *correctness* where any group of parties in the access structure can reconstruct the secret successfully, i.e., $\mathsf{m}' = \mathsf{m}$ if $A \in \mathcal{A}$, and *privacy* where any group of parties that does not appear in $\mathcal{A}$ do not learn anything about the secret from their received shares.

We will assume a secure secret sharing scheme defined for honest and malicious parties, and develop a RSS reconstruction algorithm that makes closed-box use of its reconstruction function $\mathsf{Rec}(\cdot)$.

3.3 Reconstruction Game Definitions

This section introduces concepts that are needed for our proof, arguing why our construction satisfies our requirement via game theoretic arguments.

Game Representation. In game theory, a normal-form game captures the outcomes of participants playing certain strategies at the same time and receiving respective utilities. It can be formalized with (1) *the set of parties*, (2) *the actions available to each party*, and (3) *the utility function of each party*, which maps an outcome to a real number.

Our solution does not rely on SBC and therefore, allows the parties to move sequentially. Note that in the reconstruction game, sequential move does *not* mean that each party has to wait for other parties to act before taking an action but that they act in each round and take others' prior actions into consideration. When the game involves sequential moves of parties, we need to additionally capture a few more concepts, including the actions available at each point of the game, parties' knowledge of others' past actions and their own past moves, and parties' beliefs about others' future actions. Such a game is addressed and expressed as an extensive form game: It can be formalized with the three components (1)-(3) as before together with (4) the party's *knowledge of the past*, and (5) the party's *beliefs of the future* when it is her turn to move.

Solution Concepts. A *strategy* is a probability distribution over all available actions, and a *strategy profile* records the strategies of all parties. Strategy profiles that have certain desired properties are called equilibrium strategies or *solution Concepts.*, e.g., the equilibrium where no party increases her utility by unilaterally deviating from a strategy profile is called the Nash equilibrium (NE).

Definition 3 (NE). *Let* $(\{A_i\}_{i \in [n]}, \{u_i\}_{i \in [n]})$ *denote a game where* A_i *is party i's action space and* u_i *is utility function of i. Let* σ_i *be a probability distribution on actions in* A_i. *A vector of distributions* $\sigma = (\sigma_1, \ldots, \sigma_n)$ *is the NE if*

$$\forall i \in [n], \forall \sigma'_i \neq \sigma_i, u_i(\sigma) \geq u_i(\sigma'_i, \sigma_{-i})$$

Since NE is susceptible to empty threats, we turn to its refinements to solve sequential games. Specifically, the solution concept that we adopt for solving the reconstruction game is subgame perfect equilibrium (SPE [23]), where the equilibrium strategy profile specifies the NE strategies for each rational party for *any* subgame.

Definition 4 (SPE). *A Nash equilibrium is said to be an SPE if and only if it is a NE in every subgame of the original game.*

Alternatively, one can consider *sequential equilirbium*: parties hold beliefs about others' past moves when selecting the utility-maximizing strategies at their turn to move, and their equilibrium strategy profile turns out to be consistent with each other's beliefs. We adopt SPE instead because parties can *observe* others' actions, e.g., sharing information or staying silent.

4 Preference Profiles

This section starts with the preference profiles introduced in prior works and what we modify to obtain a new preference profile that we work on.

Preference Profiles Assumed in Prior Works. Let $\text{out}_i(r)$ denote whether party i learns the secret in a complete run r of the reconstruction game, i.e., from the start of the reconstruction algorithm until reconstruction is no longer possible even if all remaining parties are honest. $\text{out}_i(r) = 1$ indicates that i learns the secret and 0 otherwise. We let $\text{out}(r)$ indicate the outcome for all parties in $[n]$. We denote the utility function of party i as $u_i(\cdot)$ and i's utility from obtaining the outcome of run r as $u_i(r)$. In prior works, the assumed preference profile for any rational party $i \in [n]$ is as follows:

- (U1) For any two runs r, r', if $\text{out}(r) = \text{out}(r')$, then $u_i(r) = u_i(r')$.
- (U2) For any two runs r, r', if $\text{out}_i(r) = 1$ and $\text{out}_i(r') = 0$, then $u_i(r) > u_i(r')$.
- (U3) For any two runs r, r', if $\text{out}_i(r) = \text{out}_i(r')$, $\forall j \neq i, \text{out}_j(r) \leq \text{out}_j(r')$ and $\exists j \neq i, \text{out}_j(r) < \text{out}_j(r')$, then $u_i(r) > u_i(r')$.

Here U1 means that each party's utility depends only on the overall outcome. U2 means that a party strictly prefers learning the secret. U3 means that parties *strictly* prefer fewer other parties who also learn the secret.

Our Preference Assumption. We update the preference profile U1 and U3 to take the *timing* of learning the secret into consideration: Parties prefer to learn the secret fast[4] and *strictly* prefer fewer parties who learn the secret before themselves. Note that a party still prefers learning the secret than not learning it, and thus U2 remains the same. Also note that we adopt a weaker assumption on the timing of learning: If parties *strictly* prefer learning the secret earlier, the analysis still applies.

Let $\text{it}_i(r)$ denote the earliest "round" where i learns the secret in a run r. Note that $\text{it}_i(r) = \infty$ if i does not learn the secret. The updated preference profile is as follows:

- (U1*) For any two runs r, r' where $\text{out}(r) = \text{out}(r')$, if $\text{it}_i(r) = \text{it}_i(r')$, then $u_i(r) = u_i(r')$, and if $\text{it}_i(r) < \text{it}_i(r')$, then $u_i(r) \geq u_i(r')$.
- (U3*) For any two runs r, r' where $\text{out}(r) = \text{out}(r')$, if $|\{j \in [n] \wedge j \neq i : \text{it}_j(r) < \text{it}_i(r)\}| < |\{j \in [n] \wedge j \neq i : \text{it}_j(r') < \text{it}_i(r')\}|$, then $u_i(r) > u_i(r')$.

Here we do not explicitly formalize a party's preference towards letting others learn after learning the secret. However, we have assumed that parties learning the secret earlier profit from it earlier (Sect. 3.1). Then naturally, a party is indifferent to informing others after acting on the knowledge of the secret. In certain applications, they may find it strictly preferable to share with others, such as in the example in Sect. 1.

5 Fair Reconstruction Under the New Preference Profile

5.1 Order of Events

To argue the security of our scheme, we need to first define a *secret reconstruction game* (see Sect. 3.3 for a game definition).

---
[4] This is because we assumed that parties learning the secret in earlier rounds can profit from it faster (Sect. 3.1).

In the reconstruction game, the action space for each party includes: (1) abort, (2) enter a new round, and (3) send one's share(s) to one or more parties.[5] During reconstruction, one can tell if a party has taken actions (1) and (2) due to network synchrony, and action (3) directly if they are one of the recipient(s). This allows us to adopt SPE as the solution concept since rational parties can observe others' prior actions.

Given network synchrony, we can describe the reconstruction game in *rounds*. Specifically, we consider running the reconstruction algorithm among the parties only for a finite known number of rounds, $T \geq 1$. Note that if we let T be infinite, parties sending their shares or fair reconstruction can be made the equilibrium [18] with punishment on deviators. We focus on a finite known T because it is harder to encourage cooperation in this setting, which is also indicated by the impossibility result [10].

Now, consider the following **secret reconstruction game** $\mathcal{G}$ (proceeding in rounds) given a pre-defined integer $T \geq 1$.

<u>In each round $i = 1, \ldots, T+1$</u>:

(1) If $i = T + 1$ or if each access group in $\mathcal{A}^*$ has at least one aborted party, the game terminates.
(2) The parties in each access group with no aborted members decide whether to take one of the three actions in time Δ (after which a round ends). After each party takes an action, enter the next round and go to step (1).

One might notice that in Step (1), checking if the game has terminated may induce a computation complexity that is exponential in the number of parties due to the size of the access structure. We note that this game is conceptual and only for reasoning about parties' actions. It does not indicate the computation complexity of our actual RSS protocol (to be presented in Fig. 1).

5.2 Game Analysis

Now, we discuss the intuition of why under the preference profile introduced in Sect. 4, rational parties intend to reconstruct the secret in $\mathcal{G}$. As in prior works, we aim for a fair reconstruction where all rational parties learn the secret.

Intuitions. We start with a simple case: consider an access structure with a *universal* party (who appears in every group, with rank $|\mathcal{A}^*| > 1$). Let $u \in [n]$ be one universal party. u can ensure that it becomes the first to learn the secret by committing to only sharing information after receiving all other shares from (at least) one access group. Note that this may not be credible. After recovering the secret, u can then send all shares from one access group to other non-universal parties so that they all learn the secret after u. Then non-universal parties are

---

[5] Note that here we do not consider sending a fake share, since if the underlying base secret-sharing scheme is not verifiable, the transformed RSS scheme is not verifiable. To obtain verifiable RSS, one can simply use a verifiable secret-sharing scheme and our transformation naturally extends to the verifiable setting.

better off sending their shares in the first round, since the universal party would send them the shares afterwards. We later show that this strategy profile is an SPE, and the reconstruction game terminates in two rounds without requiring SBC (case (b) in Theorem 1).

Next, consider a non-singleton access structure ($|\mathcal{A}^\star| > 1$) with only non-overlapping parties (i.e., every party has rank 1). In this case, parties are incentivized to share information in the first round. This is because (1) learning the secret faster generates higher returns, (2) deviating from sharing does not improve one's utility (since others would learn at most as fast as them but not sooner), and (3) deviating from the sharing strategy may even decrease one's utility if other access groups successfully reconstruct in the first round. The *competition* among access groups who do not need each other's shares promotes cooperation in secret reconstruction inside an access group. The strategy profile of sharing information in the first round is an SPE, and the reconstruction game terminates in one round without requiring SBC. This is formalized as case (a) in Theorem 1.

Finally, consider a non-singleton access structure with only non-universal parties who have ranks $\in [1, |\mathcal{A}^\star| - 1]$, and at least one party has rank > 1. Consider a party i with rank $x > 1$, i.e., $\mathsf{rank}(i) = x > 1$. Let $A_1, \ldots, A_x$ be the x access groups that i is in, and $A = \cup_{j=1}^{x} A_j$. If for any party $j \neq i$ in set A, $\mathsf{free}_j(i) = 0$. Then i is a locally universal party for parties in set A. The reasoning in the first case described in the beginning applies: i sends everyone else shares after receiving all the other shares from at least one group. If there exists a party j such that $\mathsf{free}_j(i) > 0$, i now has incentives to share in the first round because otherwise, other access groups may reconstruct before it. This is formalized as case (c) in Theorem 1. Note that this includes m-out-of-n threshold secret sharing for all $m < n$.

Solve for SPE. We now formally state and prove the main results for RSS under preference profile U1*, U2, and U3*.

Theorem 1. *Consider a secret sharing scheme with minimal access structure $\mathcal{A}^\star$ on party set $[n]$ where $|\mathcal{A}^\star| > 1$. Suppose rational parties have preference profiles U1*, U2, and U3*, and the reconstruction algorithm is run for at most a finite T rounds for some finite integer $T > 1$.*

(a) *If $\forall i \in [n], \gamma(i) = 1$, there exists a deterministic RSS scheme that terminates in 1 round.*
(b) *If $\exists i \in [n]$ such that $\gamma(i) = |\mathcal{A}^\star|$, there exists a deterministic RSS scheme that terminates in at most 2 rounds.*
(c) *In other cases, there exists a deterministic RSS scheme that terminates in at most 2 rounds.*

Proof. We use backward induction to solve for the SPE. For clarity, let party i receive utility ω^i from learning the secret in the first round, lose ϵ_k^i when k parties learn the secret before themselves ($0 \leq k \leq n-1$), lose τ_j^i if one learns the secret in the j-th round ($1 \leq j \leq T$), and lose τ_{T+1}^i if i does not learn the secret. We have $0 = \tau_1^i \leq \tau_2^i \leq \ldots \leq \tau_T^i < \tau_{T+1}^i$ to reflect party i's desire to learn the secret sooner, and $0 = \epsilon_0^i < \epsilon_1^i < \ldots < \epsilon_{n-1}^i$ to express its preference of not learning after others. For example, if party i learns the secret after $(n-2)$ other parties in the second round, its utility equals $(\omega^i - \epsilon_{n-2}^i - \tau_2^i)$.

Setting (a): We first show that in setting (a), the SPE in the reconstruction game is that parties sen their shares to each other in the first round. The equilibrium strategy of sharing information in the first round gives each party utility ω. Without loss of generality (abbreviated as WLOG hereon), consider an access group A with m parties $\{1, \ldots, m\}$. Consider any party $i \in A$.

- In round T, all parties in A sharing gives each party $i \in A$ utility $(\omega^i - \epsilon_{n-m}^i - \tau_T^i)$ in the worst case where other access groups have already learned the secret (i.e., all the other $m - n$ parties have learned) and $(\omega^i - \tau_T^i)$ in the best case where no other access groups have successfully reconstructed. More generally, suppose x parties have already learned the secret in prior rounds, this quantity is $(\omega^i - \epsilon_x^i - \tau_T^i)$. All parties sharing in round T is a NE of the remaining game since no party can increase their utility by deviating towards the action of entering the next round without sharing. Each party not sharing or any $\leq (m-2)$ parties sharing are also NEs since no party can increase their utility unilaterally, which is at most $-\tau_{T+1}^i$. However, the latter NEs will be eliminated when we reason backwards.
- In round $(T-1)$, all parties in A sharing gives each party i utility $(\omega^i - \epsilon_x^i - \tau_{T-1}^i)$ when x parties from other groups have already learned. All parties in A sharing is an NE of the remaining game given any $x \in [0, n-m]$, because $(\omega^i - \epsilon_x^i - \tau_{T-1}^i) \geq (\omega^i - \epsilon_x^i - \tau_T^i) > (\epsilon_0^i - \tau_{T+1}^i)$.

Intuitively, if all parties are going to share in the last round or $\leq m-2$ parties share, then sharing in the second to last round provides higher utility. We apply this reasoning until round 1. Sharing in round 1 is a NE of the remaining subgame since $\omega^i \geq \omega^i - \epsilon_x^i - \tau_2^i$ for each party $i \in A$ where x is the number of parties that have learned the secret in round 1. We can apply this reasoning in each non-overlapping access group. This then concludes the SPE for setting (a). We give the RSS protocol for setting (a) in Fig. 1.

Setting (b): We next show that in the setting described in (b), the SPE is as follows: In the first round, non-universal parties send their shares to universal parties, and universal parties send shares among each other; in the second round, universal parties send collected shares to non-universal parties that have sent them shares in round one. First, consider the case where there is exactly one universal party. WLOG, let this party be party 1. Consider any access group A with m parties $\{1, \ldots, m\}$.

We have established that after learning the secret, sharing is at least a weakly dominant strategy for the universal party since we assume parties learning the secret earlier can capitalize on it earlier (discussed by the end of Sect. 4). Next, the universal party 1 can adopt the following strategy: only after learning the secret, share the collected shares with parties who have sent shares to it in the next round (if not already). This is *credible* until the round $1 < R \leq T$ where $\tau_R^1 > \tau_1^1$ and $\tau_{R-1}^1 = \tau_1^1$ with $R > 2$, and for any other party i, $\tau_{R-1}^i - \tau_1^i > \epsilon_1^i$. This means that the universal party does not mind delaying learning the secret to a round $R - 1$ as long as it can learn first, while others prefer learning the secret earlier even if they have to let one party learn before them.

We first consider the non-credible case. Since the threat is completely non-credible, we treat the universal party as normal parties. Similar to setting (a), in round T, all parties in A sharing or any $\leq m - 2$ parties sharing are the NEs. In round $T - 1$ to round 1, all parties in A sharing is the NE.

We next reason about the case with a credible universal party.

- In round T, all parties in A (including party 1) sharing is an NE for the subgame if party 1 has not yet learned the secret, where each non-universal party i earns utility $(\omega^i - \epsilon_x^i - \tau_T^i)$ when $0 \leq x \leq n - m$ parties in $B = [n] \backslash A$ have learned the secret. Any $\leq m - 3$ parties sharing (regardless of whether party 1 has learned the secret or not) are also NEs for the remainder of the reconstruction game, where each non-universal party in A earns $(-\epsilon_x^i - \tau_{T+1}^i)$.
- In round $(T - 1)$ until round $(R - 1)$, we have the same NEs as round T.
- In round $(R - 2)$, the universal party 1 plays the strategy in the threat. If 1 has learned the secret, non-universal parties in A sending shares to the universal party is the NE as sharing produces higher utility in some scenarios, e.g., when some other parties who have not yet learned the secret send shares to 1 in round $(R - 2)$, and at least the same utility as not sharing in other scenarios. If 1 has not yet learned the secret, all parties in A sharing is an NE if $(\tau_{R-1}^i - \tau_{R-2}^i) > \epsilon_1^i$ for all non-universal party $i \in A$. Any $\leq m - 3$ parties sharing are also NEs for the remainder of the game regardless of the relationship between $(\tau_{R-1}^i - \tau_{R-2}^i)$ and ϵ_1^i
- In round 1, no party has learned the secret yet, and party 1 plays the strategy in the threat. If non-universal parties in A send shares to 1, they learn the secret in round 2. If all others learn the secret in a round ≤ 2, sharing produces strictly higher utility as learning in later rounds 3, 4 and so on. If there exists some other party who learns in a higher round, then sharing produces at least the same utilities.

Next, we consider the scenario where there are multiple universal parties. WLOG, we let there be $k_u > 1$ universal parties and denote them as $1, \ldots, k_u$. Consider any access group A with m parties $\{1, \ldots, k_u, \ldots, m\}$, and we can apply the above reasoning in the same way. Note that same as before, we only consider universal parties who can issue credible threats, i.e., $\tau_{R_u}^u < \tau_1^u$ and $\tau_{R_u-1}^u = \tau_1^u$ for each universal party u with $R_u > 2$ as well as $\tau_{R-1}^i - \tau_1^i > \epsilon_{k_u}^i$ where $R = \min\{R_1, \ldots, R_{k_u}\}$ for any other party $i \in A$.

- In round T, if universal parties have not learned the secret, all parties in A sharing is an NE for the subgame. Any $\leq m - k_u - 2$ parties (excluding the universal parties) sharing are also NEs.
- In round $(T - 1)$ until round $(R - 1)$, we have the same NEs as round T.

- In round $(R-2)$, the universal parties play the strategy in the threat. If universal parties have learned the secret, the non-universal parties in A sending shares to the universal parties is the NE as sharing produces higher utility in some scenarios, e.g., when some other parties who have not yet learned the secret send shares to universal parties in round $(R-2)$, and at least the same utility as not sharing in other scenarios. If universal parties have not learned the secret, all parties in A sharing is an NE if $(\tau_{R-1}^i - \tau_{R-2}^i) > \epsilon_{k_u}^i$ for all non-universal party $i \in A$. Any $\leq m-3$ parties sharing are also NEs for the remainder of the game regardless of the relationship between $(\tau_{R-1}^i - \tau_{R-2}^i)$ and $\epsilon_{k_u}^i$.
- In round 1, no party has learned the secret yet, and universal parties play the strategy in the threat. Same as the previous case of a single universal party, sharing and learning the secret in round 2 produces at least the same utility as not sharing and learning in later rounds. Similar to case (a), the universal parties share with each other in round 1. Briefly, sharing among universal parties in the last round is an NE, and sharing earlier produces at least the same utility as sharing in the last round T.

Then the equilibrium strategy profiles take at most two rounds. This concludes the SPE for setting (b). We give the RSS protocol for setting (b) in Fig. 1.

Setting (c): We finally analyze setting (c). We say a subset of k_u parties in a group A, denoted as $A_u \subset A$, is *locally universal* if the following holds: (1) any party $u \in A_u$ has rank > 1, and for each party u, there exists a round $R_u > 2$ such that $\tau_{R_u-1}^u = \tau_1^u$ and $\tau_{R_u}^u > \tau_1^u$; (2) for any other party $i \in A \setminus A_u$, $\text{free}_j(u) = 0 \forall u \in A_u$, i.e., other parties have to rely on this group's shares in reconstruction, and $(\tau_{R-1}^j - \tau_1^j) > \epsilon_{k_u}^i$ where $R = \min\{R_1, \ldots, R_{k_u}\}$. Combining the analysis for settings (a) and (b), the SPE in scenario (c) is as follows: For access groups with locally universal parties, in the first round, parties that are not locally universal send their shares to the locally universal parties, who send shares among themselves in the first round and send their shares to the non-locally universal parties in the second round; For access groups without universal parties, parties send their shares to their group members in the first round.

5.3 RSS Protocols

Let the secret message m of length ℓ be in space $\{0,1\}^\ell$. Consider any base secret sharing scheme $(\mathsf{Share}(\cdot), \mathsf{Rec}(\cdot))$ with respect to minimal access structure $\mathcal{A}^\star$. In the sharing phase, the dealer generates shares $[\mathbf{s}] \leftarrow \mathsf{Share}(\mathsf{m})$ and distributes shares $\mathbf{s}_i$ to each party $i \in [n]$. We give the simple reconstruction routines under settings (a)-(c) in Fig. 1.

Communication and Computation Complexity. In all three settings, the protocol terminates in at most two rounds. In the worst case, each party needs to send its share to all other parties, resulting in quadratic communication complexity. The computation complexity is bounded by the reconstruction algorithm $\mathsf{Rec}(\cdot)$ of the underlying secret sharing algorithm.

Reconstruction routine 1

▷ Applicable to setting (a), setting (b) and (c) where universal parties are not credible and setting (c) where an access group has no locally universal parties.

1. Each party i multicasts (i.e., sends a message to one or more parties) s_i to all parties in their access groups. Wait for Δ time (i.e., one round):
   - If i collects all the shares s_A for its access group, denoted as $A \in \mathcal{A}^\star$, i reconstructs to obtain $\mathsf{m} \leftarrow \mathsf{Rec}(s_A)$ and terminates.
   - Otherwise, i aborts.

Reconstruction routine 2

▷ Applicable to setting (b) with credible universal parties. Note that non-credible universal parties are treated as normal parties.

1. Each non-universal party i multicasts s_i to to all parties in their access groups. Each universal party u with multicast s_u to all the other universal parties. Wait for Δ time (i.e., one round):
   - If a universal party u collects all the shares in any of its access group, denoted as $A \in \mathcal{A}^\star$, u reconstructs to obtain $\mathsf{m} \leftarrow \mathsf{Rec}(s_A)$ and enters into round 2. Otherwise, u aborts.
   - Non-universal parties enter into round 2.
2. u multicasts s_A to parties who have sent u shares in round 1 and terminates. Non-universal parties reconstruct $\mathsf{m} \leftarrow \mathsf{Rec}(s_A)$ and terminates.

Reconstruction routine 3

▷ Applicable to setting (c) with credible locally universal parties. Note that non-credible universal parties are treated as normal parties.

1. Each party i who is not locally universal multicasts s_i to all parties in their acccess groups. Each locally universal party u sends s_u to other locally universal parties present in the same access groups. Wait for Δ time (i.e., one round).
   - If a locally universal party u collects all the shares in any of the access group $A \in \mathcal{A}^\star$, u reconstructs to obtain $\mathsf{m} \leftarrow \mathsf{Rec}(s_A)$, and enters into round 2. Otherwise, u aborts.
   - Non-locally-universal parties enter into round 2.
2. u multicasts s_A to parties who have sent u shares. Non-locally-universal parties reconstruct $\mathsf{m} \leftarrow \mathsf{Rec}(s_A)$ and terminates.

Fig. 1. RSS reconstruction algorithms.

6 Extension

Coalitions. Due to the preference profile, the analysis applies to any coalition size. We only need to treat the coalition as a single party in analysis, including determining its rank and steps to take in reconstruction.

Malicious Parties. A malicious party can act arbitrarily, including *rushing* (as we do not require SBC or timed primitives) and never sending their shares.

For malicious parties, consider the hypergraph constructed from $\mathcal{A}$: each party is a vertex; each access group is a hyperedge. The minimum cover $t^\star$ of this graph gives the maximum number of tolerable malicious parties $t^\star - 1$. This means that when there exist universal parties in $\mathcal{A}$, we cannot tolerate even one malicious corruption. Note that commonly used access structures such as the threshold structure do not have a universal party intrinsically because of the need for robustness. Thus, to tolerate malicious parties, we first require that all the malicious parties together do not cover all access groups. Then, we slightly modify the current reconstruction algorithm: Instead of letting parties abort after learning the secrets, we let each party eventually multi-cast the secret in round T. This then makes sure at least one rational group recovers the secret, and other rational parties also learn the secret. Hence, the analysis of the rational parties remain unchanged.

MPC. Halpern and Teague [10] and Abraham et al. [1] note that the results for secret sharing apply to secure multi-party computation assuming a trusted third party and correct inputs from rational parties. The trusted mediator can perform the computation and secret-share the result among participants.

Consider the Sharing Phase. We follow prior RSS protocols and focus on designing a (fair) reconstruction algorithm, as it involves multiple interacting parties. Moreover, in our deterministic protocol, we do not require the dealer to re-issue actual or fake secrets as in prior works with randomized protocols. The dealer only sends shares to parties once and no more interaction is needed afterward. However, as an interesting future direction, one can examine the sharing phase of RSS as a part of a larger protocol such as MPC where the dealer can also be a share holder.

Verifiable Secret Sharing (VSS). Replacing the underlying secret sharing scheme in our construction with VSS *does not* change our analysis or scheme. In the analysis, first, the action of "sending a wrong share" is equivalent to "entering the next round" without sharing due to share verifiability. Second, our scheme does not employ any cryptographic tools (unlike prior works), and our solution concept does not depend on computational assumptions on parties (i.e., our SPE holds for computationally bounded parties as well). In the protocol, our construction uses the underlying secret sharing scheme as a closed-box: what happens inside is orthogonal to our analysis.

When $|\mathcal{A}| = 1$. One condition not discussed in Theorem 1 is when there is only one access group (e.g., n-out-of-n secret sharing). In this case, no competition exists. Therefore, the proof in Sect. 5.2 does not intuitively work. To make our construction work, we simply modify our preference profile for the parties to *strictly* prefer learning the secrets sooner than later. In other words, changing U1* to the following (difference marked in blue): (U1**) For any two runs r, r' where $\mathsf{out}(r) = \mathsf{out}(r')$, if $\mathsf{it}_i(r) = \mathsf{it}_i(r')$, then $u_i(r) = u_i(r')$, and if $\mathsf{it}_i(r) < \mathsf{it}_i(r')$, then $u_i(r) > u_i(r')$.

References

1. Abraham, I., Dolev, D., Gonen, R., Halpern, J.: Distributed computing meets game theory: robust mechanisms for rational secret sharing and multiparty computation. In: Proceedings of the Twenty-fifth Annual ACM Symposium on Principles of Distributed Computing (2006)
2. Asharov, G., Lindell, Y.: Utility dependence in correct and fair rational secret sharing. J. Cryptol. (2011)
3. Chor, B., Goldwasser, S., Micali, S., Awerbuch, B.: Verifiable secret sharing and achieving simultaneity in the presence of faults. In: 26th Annual Symposium on Foundations of Computer Science (sfcs 1985) (1985)
4. De, S.J., Pal, A.K.: Achieving correctness in fair rational secret sharing. In: International Conference on Cryptology and Network Security (2013)
5. Micciancio, D.: TCC 2010. LNCS, vol. 5978. Springer, Heidelberg (2010). https://doi.org/10.1007/978-3-642-11799-2
6. Gagol, A., Leśniak, D., Straszak, D., Świetek, M.: Aleph: efficient atomic broadcast in asynchronous networks with byzantine nodes. In: Proceedings of the 1st ACM Conference on Advances in Financial Technologies (2019)
7. Goldreich, O., Micali, S., Wigderson, A.: How to play any mental game, or a completeness theorem for protocols with honest majority. In: Providing Sound Foundations for Cryptography: on the Work of Shafi Goldwasser and Silvio Micali (2019)
8. Gong, T., Liu, Z.: Rational secret sharing with competition. Cryptology ePrint Archive, Paper 2025/242 (2025). https://eprint.iacr.org/2025/242, full version of this paper that appeared at FC'25
9. Gordon, S.D., Katz, J.: Rational secret sharing, revisited. In: De Prisco, R., Yung, M. (eds.) SCN 2006. LNCS, vol. 4116, pp. 229–241. Springer, Heidelberg (2006). https://doi.org/10.1007/11832072_16
10. Halpern, J., Teague, V.: Rational secret sharing and multiparty computation. In: Proceedings of the thirty-sixth annual ACM STOC (2004)
11. Kawachi, A., Okamoto, Y., Tanaka, K., Yasunaga, K.: General constructions of rational secret sharing with expected constant-round reconstruction. Comput. J. **60**(5), 711–728 (12 2016)
12. Kawachi, A., Okamoto, Y., Tanaka, K., Yasunaga, K.: General constructions of rational secret sharing with expected constant-round reconstruction. Comput. J. (5) (2017)
13. Nguyen, K., Wu, W., Lam, K.Y., Wang, H.: ProvSec 2020. LNCS, vol. 12505. Springer, Cham (2020). https://doi.org/10.1007/978-3-030-62576-4
14. Kol, G., Naor, M.: Cryptography and game theory: designing protocols for exchanging information. In: Canetti, R. (ed.) TCC 2008. LNCS, vol. 4948, pp. 320–339. Springer, Heidelberg (2008). https://doi.org/10.1007/978-3-540-78524-8_18
15. Kol, G., Naor, M.: Games for exchanging information. In: Proceedings of the fortieth annual ACM STOC (2008)
16. Lysyanskaya, A., Segal, A.: Rational secret sharing with side information in point-to-point networks via time-delayed encryption. Cryptol. ePrint Archive (2010)
17. Lysyanskaya, A., Triandopoulos, N.: Rationality and adversarial behavior in multi-party computation. In: Dwork, C. (ed.) CRYPTO 2006. LNCS, vol. 4117, pp. 180–197. Springer, Heidelberg (2006). https://doi.org/10.1007/11818175_11
18. Mailath, G.J., Samuelson, L.: Repeated games and reputations: long-run relationships. Oxford university press (2006)

19. Malavolta, G., Thyagarajan, S.A.K.: Homomorphic time-lock puzzles and applications. In: Boldyreva, A., Micciancio, D. (eds.) CRYPTO 2019. LNCS, vol. 11692, pp. 620–649. Springer, Cham (2019). https://doi.org/10.1007/978-3-030-26948-7_22
20. Maleka, S., Shareef, A., Rangan, C.P.: Rational secret sharing with repeated games. Lecture Notes Comput. Sci. (2008)
21. Micali, S., Rabin, M., Vadhan, S.: Verifiable random functions. In: 40th Annual Symposium on Foundations of Computer Science (cat. No. 99CB37039) (1999)
22. Ong, S.J., Parkes, D.C., Rosen, A., Vadhan, S.: Fairness with an honest minority and a rational majority. In: Reingold, O. (ed.) TCC 2009. LNCS, vol. 5444, pp. 36–53. Springer, Heidelberg (2009). https://doi.org/10.1007/978-3-642-00457-5_3
23. Selten, R.: Spieltheoretische behandlung eines oligopolmodells mit nachfrageträgheit: Teil i: Bestimmung des dynamischen preisgleichgewichts. Zeitschrift für die gesamte Staatswissenschaft/Journal of Institutional and Theoretical Economics (H. 2) (1965)
24. Shamir, A.: How to share a secret. Commun. ACM (11) (1979)

The Latency Price of Threshold Cryptosystem in Blockchains

Zhuolun Xiang[1]([✉]), Sourav Das[2], Zekun Li[1], Zhoujun Ma[1], and Alexander Spiegelman[1]

[1] Aptos Labs, Palo Alto, USA
xiangzhuolun@gmail.com
[2] University of Illinois Urbana-Champaign, Urbana-Champaign, IL, USA

Abstract. Threshold cryptography is essential for many blockchain protocols. For example, many protocols rely on threshold common coin to implement asynchronous consensus, leader elections, and randomized applications. Similarly, threshold decryption and threshold time-lock puzzles are often necessary for privacy.

In this paper, we study the interplay between threshold cryptography and a class of blockchains that use Byzantine-fault tolerant (BFT) consensus protocols with a focus on latency. More specifically, we focus on *blockchain-native threshold cryptosystem*, where the blockchain validators seek to run a threshold cryptographic protocol once for every block with the block contents as an input to the threshold cryptographic protocol. All existing approaches for blockchain-native threshold cryptosystems introduce a latency overhead of at least one message delay for running the threshold cryptographic protocol. In this paper, we first propose a mechanism to eliminate this overhead for blockchain-native threshold cryptosystems with *tight* thresholds, i.e., in threshold cryptographic protocols where the secrecy and reconstruction thresholds are the same. However, real-world proof-of-stake-based blockchain-native threshold cryptosystems rely on ramp thresholds, where reconstruction thresholds are strictly greater than secrecy thresholds. For these blockchains, we demonstrate that the additional delay is unavoidable. We then introduce a mechanism to minimize this delay in the optimistic case. We implement our optimistic protocol for the proof-of-stake distributed randomness scheme on the Aptos blockchain. Our measurements from the Aptos mainnet show that the optimistic approach reduces latency overhead by 71%, from 85.5 ms to 24.7 ms, compared to the existing method.

1 Introduction

Threshold cryptography plays a vital role in modern blockchains, where various applications rely on primitives such as distributed randomness and threshold decryption. In threshold cryptography, a secret is shared among a set of parties using a threshold secret sharing [8,26], and parties seek to collaboratively evaluate a function of the shared secret and some public input without revealing the shared secret. For security, the function of the shared secret and the public information is revealed only if a threshold fraction of parties contribute to the function evaluation.

In this paper, we study the interplay between threshold cryptography and a class of blockchains that use Byzantine-fault tolerant (BFT) consensus protocols with a focus on latency. More specifically, we focus on *blockchain-native threshold cryptosystem*, where the blockchain validators seek to run a threshold cryptographic protocol TC once for every block with the block's content as an input to TC protocol. We focus on schemes where the secret is shared using the Shamir secret sharing scheme [26], and the threshold cryptographic protocol is non-interactive, i.e., parties send a single message during the threshold cryptography protocol.

One concrete example of a blockchain-native threshold cryptosystem is the recent distributed randomness protocol for proof-of-stake blockchains [13], that has been deployed in the Aptos blockchain [5]. In [13], parties collaboratively compute a threshold verifiable random function (VRF) to generate shared randomness for each block, using the cryptographic hash of the block as an input to the threshold VRF. Similarly, Kavousi et al. [22] propose to use threshold decryption to mitigate Maximal Extractable Value (MEV) attacks by the block proposers. Specifically, in [22] blockchain validators first order a set of encrypted transactions using a consensus protocol. Next, upon ordering, block validators run a threshold decryption protocol to decrypt the finalized transactions and execute them.

One limitation of existing blockchain-native threshold cryptosystem is that parties participate in the TC protocol only after the block is finalized. Hence, all existing protocol introduces at least one additional message delay before the output of the TC protocol is available, for the parties to exchange their TC shares. As a result, blockchains that seek to use the output of the TC protocol to execute the finalized transactions also incur this additional latency. For blockchains [3,11] with optimal consensus latency of three-message delay [2,24,25], the additional round of communication adds at least 33% latency overhead, which is significant.

This paper studies whether the additional delay is inherent to support threshold cryptography in BFT-based blockchains. More specifically, let TC be a threshold cryptography scheme. Then, the *secrecy threshold* of TC is the upper bound on the number of TC messages an adversary can learn without learning the output of the TC protocol. Alternatively, the *reconstruction threshold* is the number of TC messages an honest party requires to be able to compute the TC output. Committee-based blockchains where the parties have equal weights (stakes), such as Dfinity [20], can use blockchain-native threshold cryptosystem with the same secrecy threshold as the reconstruction threshold. For a wide variety of these blockchains, we present a protocol in which the parties can compute the TC output simultaneously with the block finalization time. More specifically, our protocol applies to all BFT consensus protocols in which a value is finalized if and only if a threshold number of parties *prefinalize* the value.

However, many proof-of-stake blockchains [5,16,28,31] where parties have unequal stakes, will rely on threshold cryptography with *ramp* thresholds [9], i.e., use threshold cryptographic protocols where the reconstruction threshold is strictly larger than the secrecy thresholds. The ramp nature of threshold cryptography in these protocols is because these protocols assign to each party an approximate number of shares proportional to their stake [32]. This approximate assignment of a number of shares to each party introduces a gap between the secrecy and reconstruction threshold, as the assignment process may allocate more shares to the corrupt parties and fewer shares to honest ones. Somewhat surprisingly, we prove a lower bound result illustrating that for blockchain-native threshold cryptosystem with ramp thresholds, the extra latency incurred by existing protocols is inherent for a wide family of consensus protocols.

To circumvent this impossibility result, we propose a mechanism to design blockchain-native threshold cryptosystem protocols with ramp thresholds that achieve small latency overhead under optimistic executions. To demonstrate the effectiveness, we implement our solution atop the distributed randomness protocol (based on threshold VRF) used in the Aptos blockchain and evaluate its performance with their prior protocol. Our evaluation with real-world deployment illustrates that our optimistic approach reduces latency overhead by 71%.

In summary, we make the following contributions:

- We propose a mechanism (Algorithm 2) to remove the latency overhead for blockchain-native threshold cryptosystem with *tight* secrecy and reconstruction thresholds. The result applies to committee-based blockchain systems where parties have *equal* weights.
- We prove an impossibility result (Theorem 1) indicating that the latency overhead is inherent for blockchain-native threshold cryptosystem with *ramp* thresholds, and present a solution (Algorithm 3) that can remove the latency overhead under optimistic scenarios. The results apply to proof-of-stake blockchain systems where parties have *unequal* weights.
- We implement our solution of ramp thresholds for distributed randomness and present evaluation numbers from the Aptos mainnet deployment. The evaluation demonstrates that the solution significantly improves the randomness generation latency overhead by 71%, from 85.5 to 24.7 ms.

2 Preliminaries

Notations. For any integer a, we use $[a]$ to denote the ordered set $\{1, 2, \ldots, a\}$. For any set S, we use $|S|$ to denote the size of set S. We use λ to denote the security parameter. A machine is probabilistic polynomial time (PPT) if it is a probabilistic algorithm that runs in time polynomial in λ. We use $\mathsf{negl}(\lambda)$ to denote functions that are negligible in λ. We summarize the notations in Table 1.

System Model. We consider a set of n parties labeled $1, 2, ..., n$, where each party executes as a state machine. For brevity, we present the results for parties with *equal* weights, which can be easily extended to the case with *unequal* weights.

Table 1. Table of Notations.

Symbol	Description
MBB	multi-shot Byzantine broadcast (Definition 1)
$\mathsf{MBB_{FT}}$	MBB with finalization threshold (Definition 4)
TC	threshold cryptosystem (Definition 5)
BTC	blockchain-native threshold cryptosystem (Definition 8)
$\mathsf{BTC_{FT}}$	BTC with finalization threshold (Definition 10)
t_{sec}	secrecy threshold in TC (Definition 5)
t_{rec}	reconstruction threshold in TC (Definition 5)
t_{fin}	finalization threshold in $\mathsf{MBB_{FT}}$ (Definition 4)
GFT_r	global finalization time of round r in MBB (Definition 3)
GRT	global reconstruction time in TC (Definition 7)
GRT_r	global reconstruction time of round r in BTC
L_r	latency of round r in BTC (Definition 9)

The parties communicate with each other by message passing, via pairwise connected communication channels that are authenticated and reliable. We consider a *static* adversary $\mathcal{A}$ that can corrupt up to t parties before the execution of the system. A corrupted party can behave arbitrarily, and a non-corrupted party behaves according to its state machine. We say that a non-corrupted party is *honest*. We use $\mathcal{C}$ to denote the set of corrupted parties, and $\mathcal{H}$ to denote the set of honest parties. The network is assumed to be *partially synchronous*, where there exists a known message delay upper bound Δ, and a global stabilization time (GST) after which all messages between honest parties are delivered within Δ [15]. The adversary can receive messages from any party instantaneously.

2.1 Blockchain Definitions

We define Multi-shot Byzantine Broadcast under partial synchrony as follows to capture the consensus layer of many real-world blockchains that assume a partial synchronous network. We will use Multi-shot Byzantine Broadcast and consensus interchangeably throughout the paper. Intuitively, Multi-shot Byzantine Broadcast consists of infinite instances of Byzantine Broadcast with rotating broadcasters and guarantees a total ordering among all instances. The primary reason for introducing a new definition, rather than relying on existing ones such as Byzantine Atomic Broadcast, is the necessity of incorporating *rounds* into the definition, as rounds will be referenced in later definitions (Definition 4, Definition 8). The definition of Multi-shot Byzantine Broadcast captures many existing partially synchronous leader-based BFT protocols, or with minor modifications[1], such as [10–12,14,18,19,21,34], as well as DAG-based BFT protocols, such as [6,7,23,29,30].

Definition 1 (Multi-shot Byzantine Broadcast). *Multi-shot Byzantine Broadcast is defined for a message space $\mathcal{M}$ where $\perp \notin \mathcal{M}$, and rounds $r = 0, 1, 2, \ldots$ where each round $r \in \mathbb{N}$ has one designated broadcaster B_r who can call* bcast(r, m) *to broadcast a message $m \in \mathcal{M}$. For any round $r \in \mathbb{N}$, each party can output* finalize(r, m) *once to finalize a message $m \in \mathcal{M} \cup \{\perp\}$. The Multi-shot Byzantine Broadcast problem satisfies the following properties.*

- *Agreement. For any round $r \in \mathbb{N}$, if an honest party i outputs* finalize(r, m) *and an honest party j outputs* finalize(r, m'), *then $m = m'$.*
- *Termination. After GST, for any round $r \in \mathbb{N}$ each honest party i eventually outputs* finalize(r, m_i) *where $m_i \in \mathcal{M} \cup \{\perp\}$.*
- *Validity. If the broadcaster B_r of round r is honest and calls* bcast(r, m) *for any $m \in \mathcal{M}$ after GST, then all honest parties eventually output* finalize(r, m).
- *Total Order. If an honest party outputs* finalize(r, m) *before* finalize(r', m'), *then $r < r'$.*

A Multi-shot Byzantine Broadcast protocol MBB defines the state machine for each party to solve Multi-shot Byzantine Broadcast. Now we define an *execution* of an MBB protocol, and the *globally finalization* of a message for a round.

Definition 2 (Execution, Multivalent and Univalent State). *A configuration of the system consists of the state of each party, together with all the messages in transit. Each execution of a Multi-shot Byzantine Broadcast protocol is uniquely identified by the sequence of configurations.*

During the execution of a Multi-shot Byzantine Broadcast protocol, the system is in a multivalent state for round r, if there exist two possible executions $\mathcal{E} \neq \mathcal{E}'$ both extending the current configuration, where some honest party output differently in $\mathcal{E}, \mathcal{E}'$; the system is in a univalent state of $m \in \mathcal{M} \cup \{\perp\}$ for round r, if for all executions extending the current configuration, all honest parties always outputs finalize(r, m).

Definition 3 (Global Finalization). *During the execution of a Multi-shot Byzantine Broadcast protocol, a message $m \in \mathcal{M} \cup \{\perp\}$ is globally finalized for round r, if and only if the system is in the univalent state of m for r. The global finalization time* GFT$_r$ *of round r is defined as the earliest physical time when a message is globally finalized for r.*

We say that a party locally finalizes m for round r when it outputs finalize(r, m).

---

[1] Many chained BFT protocols such as HotStuff [34] and Jolteon [18] achieve a weaker Validity property. In these protocols, the finalization of the message proposed by the broadcaster of round r requires multiple consecutive honest broadcasters starting from round r. This weaker Validity does not affect the results we present in this paper.

Intuitively, a message is globally finalized for a round r in Multi-shot Byzantine Broadcast when it is the only message that can be the output of r. Global finalization is a global event that may not be immediately known to any honest party, but must occur no later than the moment that any honest party outputs finalize$(r, \cdot)$. Compared to local finalization, which occurs when any honest party outputs finalize$(r, \cdot)$, global finalization is more fundamental.

Multi-shot Byzantine Broadcast with Finalization Threshold. The paper focuses on a family of MBB protocols that have a finalization threshold t_{fin} defined as follows, where t_{fin} is a parameter of the definition. We call such a protocol Multi-shot Byzantine Broadcast with finalization threshold, or MBB_{FT}.

Definition 4 (Finalization Threshold t_{fin}). *For any round $r \in \mathbb{N}$, the Multi-shot Byzantine Broadcast with finalization threshold, or MBB_{FT}, has a step where a party prefinalizes m for round r by sending $(\texttt{PREFIN}, r, m)$ to all parties, such that*

- *For any round r, there exists at most one $m \in \mathcal{M}$ such that any honest party may send $(\texttt{PREFIN}, r, m)$.*
- *For any round r, any honest party can send $(\texttt{PREFIN}, r, \bot)$ after sending $(\texttt{PREFIN}, r, m)$ for some $m \in \mathcal{M}$, but not the reverse.*
- *$m \in \mathcal{M} \cup \{\bot\}$ is globally finalized for r, if and only if there exist t_{fin} parties (or equivalently $t_{\text{fin}} - |\mathcal{C}|$ honest parties) that have sent $(\texttt{PREFIN}, r, m)$.*

Any honest party outputs finalize(r, m) to locally finalize a message $m \in \mathcal{M} \cup \{\bot\}$ for a round r when the party receives $(\texttt{PREFIN}, r, m)$ messages from t_{fin} parties, which implies that m is globally finalized for r.

We say t_{fin} is the finalization threshold of MBB_{FT}.

Intuitively, prefinalization is a local state of any party. When enough honest parties prefinalize a message, the message is globally finalized. A single party prefinalizing a message does not guarantee that the message will be finalized, and the party may finalize another message at the end. In many BFT protocols such as HotStuff [34] and Jolteon [18], prefinalization is also named *lock*. In PBFT [11], party prefinalizes a message when sending a *commit* for the message.

Examples of Multi-shot Byzantine Broadcast with finalization threshold. A larger number of MBB protocols used in partially synchronous blockchains fall into this family. As a concrete example, Jolteon [18] is a partially synchronous MBB_{FT} protocol deployed by blockchains such as Aptos [5] and Flow [17]. We explain in detail how Jolteon satisfies the definition of Multi-shot Byzantine Broadcast with finalization threshold with finalization threshold in the full version [33]. Other than Jolteon, numerous partially synchronous BFT protocols are also part of this family or can be easily adapted to fit into this family, such as PBFT [11], Tendermint [10], SBFT [19], HotStuff [34], Fast-Hotstuff [21], Moonshot [14] and many others. Additionally, another series of DAG-based consensus protocols also satisfy the definition of Multi-shot Byzantine Broadcast with finalization threshold with finalization threshold, such as Shoal++ [6], Sailfish [27], Cordial miners [23] and Mysticeti [7].

2.2 Cryptography Definitions

Next, we describe the syntax and security definitions for threshold cryptosystems. We focus on non-interactive threshold cryptographic protocols.

Definition 5 (Threshold Cryptosystem). *Let $t_{\text{sec}}, t_{\text{rec}}, n$ with $t_{\text{sec}} \leq t_{\text{rec}} \leq n$ be natural numbers. We refer to t_{sec} and t_{rec} as the secrecy and reconstruction threshold. Let $\mathcal{X}$ be a input space. Looking ahead, the input space $\mathcal{X}$ denotes the output space of the underlying Multi-shot Byzantine Broadcast protocol.*

A $(n, t_{\text{sec}}, t_{\text{rec}})$-threshold cryptosystem TC *is a tuple of PPT algorithms* TC = (Setup, ShareGen, Eval, PEval, PVer, Comb, Verify) *defined as follows:*

1. Setup(1^λ) $\to$ pp. *The setup algorithm takes as input a security parameter and outputs public parameters pp (which are given implicitly as input to all other algorithms).*
2. ShareGen(s) $\to \{\text{pk}, \text{pk}_i, [\![s]\!]_i\}_{i \in [n]}$. *The share generation algorithm takes as input a secret $s \in \mathcal{K}$ from a secret key space $\mathcal{K}$ and outputs a public key* pk, *a vector of threshold public keys* $\{\text{pk}_1, \ldots, \text{pk}_n\}$, *and a vector of secret shares* $([\![s]\!]_1, \ldots, [\![s]\!]_n)$. *The j-th party receives* $(\{\text{pk}_i\}_{i \in [n]}, [\![s]\!]_j)$.
3. Eval(s, val) $\to \sigma$. *The evaluation algorithm takes as input a secret share s, and a value* val $\in \mathcal{X}$. *It outputs a function output σ, which is called the* TC *output in the paper.*
4. PEval($[\![s]\!]_i$, val) $\to \sigma_i$. *The partial evaluation takes as input a secret share $[\![s]\!]_i$, and a value* val $\in \mathcal{X}$. *It outputs a function output share σ_i, which is called the* TC *output share in the paper.*
5. PVer(pk_i, val, σ_i) $\to 0/1$. *The partial verification algorithm takes as input a public key pk_i, a value* val, *and a* TC *output share σ_i. It outputs 1 (accept) or 0 (reject).*
6. Comb(S, val, $\{(\text{pk}_i, \sigma_i)\}_{i \in S}$) $\to \sigma/\bot$. *The combine algorithm takes as input a set $S \subseteq [n]$ with $|S| \geq t_{\text{rec}}$, a value* val, *and a set of tuples (pk_i, σ_i) of public keys and* TC *output shares of parties in S. It outputs a* TC *output σ or $\bot$.*
7. Verify(pk, val, σ) $\to 0/1$: *The verification algorithm takes as input a public key* pk, *input* val, *and evaluation output σ. It outputs 1 (accept) or 0 (reject).*

We require a threshold cryptosystem to satisfy the standard *Robustness* and *Secrecy* properties, as defined in the full version [33] due to space constraints.

Definition 6 (Ramp [9] and Tight Thresholds). *For any $(n, t_{\text{sec}}, t_{\text{rec}})$-threshold cryptosystem, we call it a* tight *threshold cryptosystem if $t_{\text{sec}} = t_{\text{rec}}$, and a* ramp *threshold cryptosystem if $t_{\text{sec}} < t_{\text{rec}}$.*

Definition 7 (Global Reconstruction). *For any $(n, t_{\text{sec}}, t_{\text{rec}})$-threshold cryptosystem with secret s and input* val, *we say* Eval(s, val) *is globally reconstructed if and only if the adversary learns* Eval(s, val) *(or equivalently $t_{\text{rec}} - |\mathcal{C}|$ honest parties reveal* TC *output shares to $\mathcal{A}$). The global reconstruction time* GRT *is defined to be the earliest physical time when* Eval(s, val) *is globally reconstructed (i.e., when $t_{\text{rec}} - |\mathcal{C}|$ honest parties reveal* TC *output shares to $\mathcal{A}$).*

We say that a party locally reconstructs Eval(s, val) *when it learns* Eval(s, val) *(or equivalently receiving t_{rec} valid shares).*

Double Sharing of the Secret. Looking ahead, we require our threshold cryptosystem to support double sharing of the same secret for two sets of thresholds $(t_\mathsf{sec}, t_\mathsf{rec})$ and $(t'_\mathsf{sec}, t'_\mathsf{rec})$ where $(t_\mathsf{sec}, t_\mathsf{rec}) \neq (t'_\mathsf{sec}, t'_\mathsf{rec})$. Threshold cryptosystems based on Shamir secret sharing [26] easily support double sharing.

3 Blockchain-Native Threshold Cryptosystem

We now formally define the problem of blockchain-native threshold cryptosystem. In such a system, a secret is shared among the participants in the blockchain protocol and these parties seek to collaboratively run a threshold cryptographic protocol, after every block, using the shared secret and the block as input.

Definition 8 (Blockchain-Native Threshold Cryptosystem). *Let* MBB *be a Multi-shot Byzantine Broadcast protocol as in Definition 1. Let* TC = (Setup, ShareGen, Eval, PEval, PVer, Comb, Verify) *be a* $(n, t_\mathsf{sec}, t_\mathsf{rec})$-*threshold cryptosystem as in Definition 5. A blockchain-native threshold cryptosystem protocol* BTC = (MBB, TC) *is defined as follows.*

1. *The parties start with a secret share of a secret key s as per* ShareGen(s).
2. *The parties run* MBB, *and may simultaneously execute the* TC *protocol.*
3. *Upon* MBB *outputs* finalize(r, m) *for any round $r \in \mathbb{N}$, after some possible delay, parties finish the* TC *protocol to compute* $\sigma = $ Eval$(s, (r, m))$ *and outputs* (r, m, σ).

We require BTC *to satisfy the following except for negligible probabilities.*

- **Agreement.** *For any round $r \in \mathbb{N}$, if an honest party outputs (r, m, σ) and another honest party outputs (r, m', σ'), then $m = m'$ and $\sigma = \sigma'$.*
- **Termination.** *After GST, for any round $r \in \mathbb{N}$ each honest party i eventually outputs (r, m_i, σ) where $m_i \in \mathcal{M} \cup \{\bot\}$.*
- **Validity.** *For any round $r \in \mathbb{N}$, if the designated broadcaster B_r is honest and calls* bcast(r, m) *for $m \in \mathcal{M}$ after GST, then all honest parties eventually output $(r, m, $Eval$(s, (r, m)))$.*
- **Total Order.** *If an honest party outputs (r, m, σ) before (r', m', σ'), then $r < r'$.*
- **Secrecy.** *If an honest party outputs (r, m, σ) where $m \in \mathcal{M} \cup \{\bot\}$, then $\sigma = $ Eval$(s, (r, m))$, and the adversary cannot compute* Eval$(s, (r, m'))$ *where $m \in \mathcal{M}$ and $m' \neq m$.*

For BTC = (MBB, TC), we use GRT$_r$ to denote the global reconstruction time of round r in TC, as defined in Definition 7.

Example of blockchain-native threshold cryptosystem. On-chain distributed randomness generates a shared randomness for every finalized block. TC for this application can be a threshold VRF scheme. Upon MBB (the blockchain consensus layer) outputs m (a block) for a round r, parties run the TC protocol to compute the shared randomness Eval$(s, (r, m))$.

Below we define the latency of a blockchain-native threshold cryptosystem to measure the introduced latency overhead. Intuitively, L_r is the maximum time difference, across all honest parties, between the time a honest party i finalizes in MBB and the time the same honest party i outputs. Since the transaction execution relies on the TC output of the threshold cryptosystem, by definition, a party may have to wait a period of L_r before executing the transactions finalized for round r, thus increasing the blockchain's transaction end-to-end latency.

Definition 9 (Latency of Blockchain-Native Threshold Cryptosystem). *During an execution of a blockchain-native threshold cryptosystem* BTC $=$ (MBB, TC), *for any round r and party i, let $T^F_{i,r}$ be the physical time when party i outputs* finalize(r, m) *for some m in* MBB, *and $T^O_{i,r}$ be the physical time when party i outputs (r, m, σ) for some m, σ in* BTC. *The latency for round r of the execution is defined to be* $L_r = \max_{i \in \mathcal{H}}(T^O_{i,r} - T^F_{i,r})$.

3.1 Blockchain-Native Threshold Cryptosystem with Finalization Threshold

This paper focuses on a family of blockchain-native threshold cryptosystem protocols defined as follows.

Definition 10 (Blockchain-Native Threshold Cryptosystem with Finalization Threshold). *A blockchain-native threshold cryptosystem with finalization threshold, or* BTC$_{FT}$ $=$ (MBB$_{FT}$, TC), *is a blockchain-native threshold cryptosystem (Definition 8) that uses an* MBB$_{FT}$ *protocol (Definition 4).*

We will henceforth shorten *blockchain-native threshold cryptosystem* as BTC, and *blockchain-native threshold cryptosystem with finalization threshold* as BTC$_{FT}$.

Some of the paper's results hold under optimistic conditions defined below.

Error-free. An execution of BTC is error-free if all parties are honest.

Synchronized Execution. An execution of BTC$_{FT}$ $=$ (MBB$_{FT}$, TC) is synchronized for a round r if all honest parties prefinalize the same message $m \in \mathcal{M}$ for r at the same physical time[2] in MBB$_{FT}$.

Optimistic. An execution of BTC$_{FT}$ is optimistic if the execution is error-free and synchronized for any round r, and all messages have the same delay.

3.2 A Strawman Protocol

As a warm-up, we first describe a strawman protocol for any blockchain-native threshold cryptosystem BTC $=$ (MBB, TC) (Definition 8) in Algorithm 1, which works for both tight and ramp thresholds. The protocol has a latency $L_r \geq \delta$

---

[2] This condition is defined solely for proving theoretical latency claims. In practice, different honest parties may prefinalize at different physical times, and the result of the paper still achieves latency improvements as in Sect. 6.1.

Algorithm 1. Slow Path for Blockchain-Native Threshold Cryptosystem

SETUP:
1: let $\bm{m} \leftarrow \{\}, \bm{\sigma} \leftarrow \{\}$ ▷ Maps that store outputs for rounds
2: let $queue \leftarrow \{\}$ ▷ A FIFO queue that stores the finalized rounds
3: let $(\{\mathsf{pk}_j\}_{j\in[n]}, [\![s]\!]_i) \leftarrow \mathsf{ShareGen}(s)$ for thresholds $t+1 \leq t_\mathsf{sec} \leq t_\mathsf{rec} \leq n - t$ ▷ s is unknown to any party

---

SLOW PATH:
1: **upon** $\mathsf{finalize}(r, m)$ **do**
2:     let $\bm{m}[r] \leftarrow m$ and $\sigma_i \leftarrow \mathsf{PEval}([\![s]\!]_i, (r, m))$
3:     $queue.push(r)$
4:     **send** $(\mathtt{SHARE}, r, m, \sigma_i)$ to all parties

---

RECONSTRUCTION:
1: **upon** receiving $(\mathtt{SHARE}, r, m, \sigma_j)$ from party j **do**
2:     **if** $\mathsf{PVer}(\mathsf{pk}_j, (r, m), \sigma_j) = 1$ **then**
3:         $S_{r,m} \leftarrow S_{r,m} \cup \{j\}$
4:         **if** $|S_{r,m}| \geq t_\mathsf{rec}$ and $\bm{\sigma}[r] = \{\}$ **then**
5:             let $\bm{\sigma}[r] \leftarrow \mathsf{Comb}(S_{r,m}, (r, m), \{(\mathsf{pk}_i, \sigma_i)\}_{i \in S_{r,m}})$
6:         **end if**
7:     **end if**

OUTPUT:
1: **upon** $\bm{\sigma}[queue.top()] \neq \{\}$ **do** ▷ Always running in the background
2:     let $r \leftarrow queue.pop()$
3:     **output** $(r, \bm{m}[r], \bm{\sigma}[r])$

---

for any round $r \in \mathbb{N}$ even in error-free executions with constant message delay δ between honest parties. To the best of our knowledge, all existing blockchain-native threshold cryptosystem follow this approach, such as the Dfinity [20] and Sui [31] blockchains for distributed randomness. For brevity, we refer to this protocol as the *slow path*.

As part of the setup phase, each party i receives $(\{\mathsf{pk}\}_{i\in[n]}, [\![s]\!]_i)$, where $[\![s]\!]_i$ is the secret share of party i and $\{\mathsf{pk}\}_{i\in[n]}$ is the vector of threshold public keys of all parties. Each party maintains a First-in-first-out (FIFO) $queue$ to record the finalized rounds awaiting the TC output. These rounds are pushed into the FIFO $queue$ in the order they are finalized, and only the head of the FIFO $queue$ will pop and be output. Looking ahead, this ensures Total Ordering, even when parties reconstruct TC outputs of different rounds in out of order. Each party additionally maintains two maps $\bm{m}$ and $\bm{\sigma}$ to store the finalized message and TC output shares of each parties of each round, respectively.

In the protocol, for any given round r, each party i waits until a message m is finalized by the MBB protocol in round r. Upon finalization, each party i computes its TC output share $\sigma_i \leftarrow \mathsf{PEval}([\![s]\!]_i, (r, m))$ and sends the SHARE message $(\mathtt{SHARE}, r, m, \sigma_i)$ to all parties. Party i also adds round r to $queue$ and updates $\bm{m}$ as $\bm{m}[r] \leftarrow m$. Next, upon receiving $(\mathtt{SHARE}, r, m, \sigma_j)$ from party

Algorithm 2. Tight Blockchain-Native Threshold Cryptosystem

SETUP is same as Algorithm 1 except that $t_\mathsf{sec} = t_\mathsf{rec} = t_\mathsf{fin}$.

PREFINALIZATION:
1: **upon** sending (PREFIN, r, m) to all parties **do**   ▷ Augment the consensus protocol
2:     let $\sigma_i \leftarrow \mathsf{PEval}(\llbracket s \rrbracket_i, (r, m))$
3:     send (SHARE, r, m, σ_i) to all parties
4: **upon** finalize(r, m) **do**
5:     let $\boldsymbol{m}[r] \leftarrow m$
6:     $queue.push(r)$
7:     **if** (SHARE, $r, *, *$) not sent **then**
8:         let $\sigma_i \leftarrow \mathsf{PEval}(\llbracket s \rrbracket_i, (r, m))$
9:         send (SHARE, r, m, σ_i) to each other party
10:    **end if**

RECONSTRUCTION and OUTPUT are same as Algorithm 1.

j, party i first validates σ_j using PVer algorithm and adds σ_j to the set $S_{r,m}$ upon successful validation. Finally, upon receiving t_rec valid SHARE messages for (m, r), party i computes the TC output σ using Comb algorithm and updates $\boldsymbol{\sigma}$ as $\boldsymbol{\sigma}[r] = \sigma$. Whenever party i has the TC output of round r that is the head of $queue$, party i pops the queue and outputs the result $(r, \boldsymbol{m}[r], \boldsymbol{\sigma}[r])$ for round r.

To ensure the Termination property, the reconstruction threshold must be no greater than $n - t$, i.e., $t_\mathsf{rec} \leq n - t$. Intuitively, this ensures that once the MBB outputs in a round, every honest party receives a sufficient number of TC output shares to reconstruct the TC output. Additionally, for Secrecy for the strawman protocol, the secrecy threshold must be greater than the number of TC shares controlled by the adversary, i.e., $t_\mathsf{sec} \geq t + 1$. Intuitively, this prevents the adversary from reconstructing the TC output on its own. The correctness of the protocol is straightforward and is omitted here for brevity.

We will now argue that the slow path has a latency overhead of at least δ even in error-free executions with constant message delay δ between honest parties. For any round r, any party needs to receive at least $t_\mathsf{rec} - |\mathcal{C}| \geq 1$ shares from the honest parties to compute σ. Consider the first honest party i that outputs finalize(r, m). In the strawman protocol, party i needs to wait for at least one message delay starting from finalization to receive the shares from the honest parties to compute σ, since other honest parties only send shares after finalization. Adding one additional message delay to the system represents a significant overhead as the MBB latency can be as short as three message delays

4 Tight Blockchain-Native Threshold Cryptosystem

In this section, we present a protocol for $\mathsf{BTC}_\mathsf{FT} = (\mathsf{MBB}_\mathsf{FT}, \mathsf{TC})$ (Definition 10) for tight thresholds that has low latency. In any round $r \in \mathbb{N}$ of any execution, the global finalization time of our protocol is same as the global reconstruction time, i.e., $\mathsf{GFT}_r = \mathsf{GRT}_r$. Moreover, in error-free executions[3], honest parties in our protocol learns the TC output simultaneously with the $\mathsf{MBB}_{\mathsf{FT}}$ output, i.e., $\mathsf{L}_r = 0$. We summarize our construction in Algorithm 2 and describe it next.

The setup phase is identical to that of Algorithm 1, except that the secrecy and reconstruction thresholds are set to be equal to the finalization threshold of $\mathsf{MBB}_{\mathsf{FT}}$. Note that, the Termination property of $\mathsf{MBB}_{\mathsf{FT}}$ requires $t_{\mathsf{fin}} \leq n - t$, as honest parties needs to finalize a message even when corrupted parties do not send any throughout the protocol. Next, unlike Algorithm 1, parties reveal their TC output shares when they prefinalize a message. More specifically, for every round r, each party i computes $\sigma_i \leftarrow \mathsf{PEval}(\llbracket s \rrbracket_i, (r, m))$ upon prefinalizing the value (r, m), and sends the SHARE message $(\mathsf{SHARE}, r, m, \sigma_i)$ to all parties in addition to sending the PREFIN message (PREFIN, r, m). When a party receives t_{fin} PREFIN messages (PREFIN, r, m), it finalizes the message m for round r, by adding round r to $queue$ and recording m in $\boldsymbol{m}[r]$. The party also computes and sends σ_i if it has not done so. The reconstruction and output phases are also identical to Algorithm 1, where parties collect and combine shares to generate TC output, and output the result round-by-round. We defer the protocol analysis to the full version [33] due to space constraints.

5 Ramp Blockchain-Native Threshold Cryptography

In this section, we present an impossibility result and a feasibility result for $\mathsf{BTC}_{\mathsf{FT}} = (\mathsf{MBB}_{\mathsf{FT}}, \mathsf{TC})$ (Definition 10) with ramp thresholds $t_{\mathsf{sec}} < t_{\mathsf{rec}}$.

5.1 Impossibility

First, we demonstrate the impossibility result, which says that no $\mathsf{BTC}_{\mathsf{FT}}$ protocol with ramp thresholds $t_{\mathsf{sec}} < t_{\mathsf{rec}}$ can always guarantee that global finalization and reconstruction occur simultaneously.

Theorem 1 *For any* $\mathsf{BTC}_{\mathsf{FT}} = (\mathsf{MBB}_{\mathsf{FT}}, \mathsf{TC})$ *with ramp thresholds, there always exists some execution where* $\mathsf{GRT}_r > \mathsf{GFT}_r$ *for each round* $r \in \mathbb{N}$.

Due to space constraints, the proof of Theorem 1 is deferred to the full version [33]. Theorem 1 states that for any blockchain-native threshold cryptosystem with finalization threshold and ramp thresholds, there always exists an execution where global reconstruction occurs after global finalization for each round. In fact, existing solutions for BTC with ramp thresholds all have a latency of at least one message delay, such as Das et al. [13].

5.2 Fast Path

Theorem 1 claims that no $\mathsf{BTC}_{\mathsf{FT}}$ protocol with ramp thresholds can *always* guarantee that the global finalization and reconstruction occur simultaneously, implying that the latency of $\mathsf{BTC}_{\mathsf{FT}}$ may be unavoidable. Fortunately, we can circumvent this impossibility result in optimistic executions. In this section, we describe

---
[3] We require error-free for the $\mathsf{L}_r = 0$ claim, otherwise malicious parties may cause honest parties to prefinalize at different times and lead to $\mathsf{L}_r > 0$.

Algorithm 3. Fast Path for Ramp Blockchain-Native Threshold Cryptosystem

SETUP:
1: let $\boldsymbol{m} \leftarrow \{\}, \boldsymbol{\sigma} \leftarrow \{\}, queue \leftarrow \{\}$
2: let $(\{\mathsf{pk}_j\}_{j \in [n]}, [\![s]\!]_i) \leftarrow \mathsf{ShareGen}(s)$ for $t+1 \leq t_{\mathsf{sec}} < t_{\mathsf{rec}} \leq n-t$ ▷ For slow path
3: let $(\{\mathsf{pk}'_j\}_{j \in [n]}, [\![s]\!]'_i) \leftarrow \mathsf{ShareGen}(s)$ for $t'_{\mathsf{sec}} = t_{\mathsf{fin}}, t'_{\mathsf{rec}} = \min(t'_{\mathsf{sec}} + (t_{\mathsf{rec}} - t_{\mathsf{sec}}), n)$ ▷ For fast path, s is unknown to any party

FAST PATH:
1: **upon** sending $(\mathtt{PREFIN}, r, m)$ to all parties **do** ▷ Augment the consensus protocol
2:    let $\sigma'_i \leftarrow \mathsf{PEval}([\![s]\!]'_i, (r, m))$
3:    **send** $(\mathtt{FAST\text{-}SHARE}, r, m, \sigma'_i)$ to each other party

SLOW PATH:
1: **upon** finalize(r, m) **do**
2:    let $\boldsymbol{m}[r] \leftarrow m$ and $\sigma_i \leftarrow \mathsf{PEval}([\![s]\!]_i, (r, m))$
3:    $queue.push(r)$
4:    **send** $(\mathtt{SLOW\text{-}SHARE}, r, m, \sigma_i)$ to each other party

RECONSTRUCTION:
1: **upon** receiving $(\mathtt{FAST\text{-}SHARE}, r, m, \sigma'_j)$ from party j **do** ▷ Fast path reconstruction
2:    **if** $\mathsf{PVer}(\mathsf{pk}'_j, (r, m), \sigma'_j) = 1$ **then**
3:        $S'_{r,m} \leftarrow S'_{r,m} \cup \{j\}$
4:        **if** $|S'_{r,m}| \geq t'_{\mathsf{rec}}$ and $\boldsymbol{\sigma}[r] = \{\}$ **then**
5:            let $\boldsymbol{\sigma}[r] \leftarrow \mathsf{Comb}(S'_{r,m}, (r, m), \{(\mathsf{pk}'_i, \sigma'_i)\}_{i \in S'_{r,m}})$
6:        **end if**
7:    **end if**
8: **upon** receiving $(\mathtt{SLOW\text{-}SHARE}, r, m, \sigma_j)$ from party j **do** ▷ Slow path reconstruction
9:    **if** $\mathsf{PVer}(\mathsf{pk}_j, (r, m), \sigma_j) = 1$ **then**
10:       $S_{r,m} \leftarrow S_{r,m} \cup \{j\}$
11:       **if** $|S_{r,m}| \geq t_{\mathsf{rec}}$ and $\boldsymbol{\sigma}[r] = \{\}$ **then**
12:           let $\boldsymbol{\sigma}[r] \leftarrow \mathsf{Comb}(S_{r,m}, (r, m), \{(\mathsf{pk}_i, \sigma_i)\}_{i \in S_{r,m}})$
13:       **end if**
14:   **end if**

OUTPUT is same as Algorithm 1

---

a simple protocol named *fast path* that, for any round r, achieves $\mathsf{GRT}_r = \mathsf{GFT}_r$ under synchronized executions, and $\mathsf{L}_r = 0$ under optimistic executions[4]. As we illustrate in Sect. 6.1, in practice, our new protocol achieves significantly lower latency compared to the strawman protocol.

The key observation from Theorem 1 is that, to ensure the same global finalization and reconstruction time, the secrecy threshold cannot be lower than the finalization threshold; otherwise, the TC output could be revealed before $\mathsf{MBB}_{\mathsf{FT}}$

---

[4] Similar to Sect. 4, we require error-free for the $\mathsf{L}_r = 0$ claim. However, the honest parties can reconstruct the TC output via fast path as long as $|\mathcal{H}| \geq t'_{\mathsf{rec}}$ (with $\mathsf{L}_r > 0$).

finalizes a message. A naive way to address this is to increase the secrecy threshold to match the finalization threshold, i.e., $t_{sec} = t_{fin}$. However, the issue is that, since the threshold is ramped, $t_{rec} > t_{sec} = t_{fin} = n - t$ (MBB$_{FT}$ protocols with optimal resilience typically have $t_{fin} = n - t$ to ensure quorum intersection for safety), there may not be enough honest shares for parties to reconstruct TC output upon finalizing the MBB$_{FT}$ output, violating the Termination property.

We address this issue as follows: First, we share the TC secret s among the parties twice, using independent randomness, with two different pairs of thresholds (t_{sec}, t_{rec}) and (t'_{rec}, t'_{sec}). The new thresholds are set to be $t'_{sec} = t_{fin}, t'_{rec} = \min(t'_{sec} + (t_{rec} - t_{sec}), n)$. Let $\{[\![s]\!]\}_{i \in [n]}$ and $\{[\![s]\!]'\}_{i \in [n]}$ be the secret shares of s with thresholds (t_{sec}, t_{rec}) and (t'_{sec}, t'_{rec}), respectively. Second, we add a *fast path*, where parties reveal their TC output shares they compute with $\{[\![s]\!]'\}_{i \in [n]}$ immediately upon prefinalizing a message.

Our final protocol is in Algorithm 3. The setup phase is similar to Algorithm 1, except the same secret s is shared twice, using independent randomness, for the slow path and fast path, respectively. Each party does the following:

- *Fast path:* When a party prefinalizes a message m for round r, it reveals its TC output share PEval($[\![s]\!]'_i, (r, m)$). Once a party receives t'_{rec} verified shares of the fast path, it reconstructs the TC output.
- *Slow path:* Upon MBB$_{FT}$ finalization for message m and round r, each party i reveals its TC output share PEval($[\![s]\!]_i, (r, m)$). Next, any party who has not received t'_{rec} verified TC output shares from the fast path waits to receive t_{rec} verified TC output shares from the slow path. Once the party receives t_{rec} verified shares of the slow path, it reconstructs the TC output.

Lastly, similarly to Algorithm 1, to guarantee Total Order, the parties push the finalized rounds into the FIFO *queue* and output the result round-by-round once either the fast path or slow path has reconstructed the TC output. So the latency of the protocol is the minimum latency of the two paths.

Note that, a party reveals its share of the slow path even if it has revealed its share of the fast path or reconstructed the TC output from the fast path. This is crucial for ensuring Termination, because with corrupted parties sending their TC output shares to only a subset $\mathcal{S}$ of honest parties, it is possible that only parties in $\mathcal{S}$ can reconstruct the TC output from the fast path. If honest parties in $\mathcal{S}$ do not reveal their shares of the slow path, the remaining honest parties cannot reconstruct the TC output, thereby losing the Termination guarantee. We defer the protocol analysis to the full version [33] due to space constraints.

6 Distributed Randomness: A Case Study

In this section, we implement and evaluate distributed randomness as a concrete example of blockchain-native threshold cryptosystem, to demonstrate the effectiveness of our solution in reducing the latency for real-world blockchains. We implement the fast path (Algorithm 3) for Das et al. [13], which is a distributed randomness scheme designed for proof-of-stake blockchains and is deployed in the Aptos blockchain [5] to enable smart contracts to use randomness [4]. We then compare our latency (using both micro-benchmarks and end-to-end evaluation) with the [13], that implements the strawman protocol (Algorithm 1).

In the rest of the section, we first provide a very brief overview of [13] and our implementation of fast-path protocol atop their scheme. Due to space constraints, more details are deferred to the full version [33].

Overview of Das et al. [13]. Das et al. [13] is a distributed randomness protocol for proof-of-stake blockchains where each party has a (possibly unequal) stake, and the blockchain is secure as long as the adversary corrupts parties with combined stake less than 1/3-th of the total stake. Since the total stake in practice can be very large, [13] first assigns approximate stakes of parties to a much smaller value called *weights*, and this process is called *rounding*. Parties in [13] then participate in a publicly verifiable secret sharing (PVSS) based distributed key generation (DKG) protocol to receive secret shares of a TC secret s. After DKG, Das et al. [13] implements the weighted extension of slow path (Algorithm 1) for blockchain-native threshold cryptosystem (Definition 10), where they use a distributed verifiable unpredictable function (VUF) as the TC protocol. More precisely, for each finalized block, each party computes and reveals its VUF shares. Next, once a party receives verified VUF shares from parties with combined weights greater than or equal to w, it reconstructs the VUF output.

Implementation of Fast Path (Algorithm 3). Recall that the fast path requires sharing the same secret with two sets of thresholds, i.e., $t_{\mathsf{sec}} < t_{\mathsf{rec}}$ for the slow path and $t'_{\mathsf{sec}} < t'_{\mathsf{rec}}$ for the fast path. Consequently, we augment the rounding algorithm of [13] to additionally take $(t'_{\mathsf{sec}}, t'_{\mathsf{rec}})$ as input, and output the weight threshold for the fast path. To setup the secret-shares of the TC secret, we use the DKG protocol of [13] with the following minor modifications. Each party starts by sharing the same secret independently using two weight thresholds w and w'. The rest of the DKG protocol is identical to [13], except parties agree on two different aggregated PVSS transcript instead of one. Note that, these doubles the computation and communication cost of DKG. As described in Algorithm 3, parties reveal their VUF shares (TC output shares) for the fast path upon prefinalizing a block, and for the slow path upon finalizing a block. For both paths, the parties collect the VUF shares and are ready to execute the block as soon as the randomness (TC output) is reconstructed from either path.

6.1 Evaluation Results

We implement our fast-path protocol (Algorithm 3) in Rust, atop the open-source Das et al. [13] implementation [5] on the Aptos blockchain. We worked with Aptos Labs to deploy and evaluate our protocol on the Aptos mainnet.

Setup and Metrics. As of July 2024, the Aptos blockchain is run by 140 validators, distributed 50 cities across 22 countries with the stake distributed described in [1]. The 50-th, 70-th and 90-th percentile (average) of round-trip latency between the blockchain validators is approximately 150ms, 230ms, and

Table 2. Latencies of Das et al. [13] and our fast-path on Aptos mainnet.

Scheme	Randomness Latency	Consensus Latency	Overhead on top of Consensus
Das et al. [13]	85.5 ms	362 ms	23.6%
our fast-path	24.7 ms	362 ms	6.8%

400ms, respectively. Due to space limitation, we defer other details of the evaluation setup to the full version [33]. We measure the *randomness latency* as the duration required to generate randomness for each block, as in Definition 9. It measures the duration from the moment the block is finalized by consensus to the when the randomness for that block becomes available. We report the average randomness latency (measured over a period of 12 h). We also measure and compare the setup overhead for Das et al. [13] and fast-path, using microbenchmarks on machines of the same hardware specs as the Aptos mainnet.

Randomness Latency. Table 2 summarizes the latency comparison of our fast-path and Das et al. [13]. As observed, fast-path significantly reduces the randomness latency of Das et al. by 71%, from 85.5 ms to 24.7 ms. As mentioned in Sect. 5.2, the small latency overhead of fast-path comes from the fact that honest parties may need to wait slightly longer after local finalization to receive additional shares from the fast path, since the reconstruction threshold of the fast path is higher than the finalization threshold. To show the significance of the latency improvement for consensus end-to-end latency, we also measure the consensus latency 362 ms as the duration of each block from proposed to finalized. As shown in the table, fast-path improves the latency overhead from 23.6% to 6.8% in terms of the consensus latency. The latency of the slow path in our fast-path protocol (Algorithm 3) is comparable to that of Das et al. [13] and is therefore omitted for brevity.

Acknowledgments. We would like to thank Alin Tomescu, Andrei Tonkikh, and Benny Pinkas for helpful discussions.

References

1. Aptos node distribution (2024). https://explorer.aptoslabs.com/validators?network=mainnet
2. Abraham, I., Nayak, K., Ren, L., Xiang, Z.: Good-case latency of Byzantine broadcast: A complete categorization. In: Proceedings of the 2021 ACM Symposium on Principles of Distributed Computing, pp. 331–341 (2021)
3. Androulaki, E., et al.: Hyperledger fabric: a distributed operating system for permissioned blockchains. In: Proceedings of the thirteenth EuroSys Conference, pp. 1–15 (2018)
4. Aptos: Aip-41 - move apis for public randomness generation (2023). https://github.com/aptos-foundation/AIPs/blob/main/aips/aip-41.md

5. Aptos: Official implementation in rust (2024). https://github.com/aptos-labs/aptos-core
6. Arun, B., Li, Z., Suri-Payer, F., Das, S., Spiegelman, A.: Shoal++: high throughput DAG BFT can be fast! arXiv preprint arXiv:2405.20488 (2024)
7. Babel, K., Chursin, A., Danezis, G., Kokoris-Kogias, L., Sonnino, A.: Mysticeti: low-latency DAG consensus with fast commit path. arXiv preprint arXiv:2310.14821 (2023)
8. Blakley, G.R.: Safeguarding cryptographic keys. In: 1979 International Workshop on Managing Requirements Knowledge (MARK), pp. 313–318. IEEE (1979)
9. Blakley, G., Meadows, C.: Security of ramp schemes. In: Proceedings of CRYPTO'84 on Advances in cryptology, pp. 242–268 (1985)
10. Buchman, E.: Tendermint: byzantine fault tolerance in the age of blockchains. Ph.D. thesis (2016)
11. Castro, M., Liskov, B.: Practical Byzantine fault tolerance. In: Proceedings of the third Symposium on Operating Systems Design and Implementation (OSDI), pp. 173–186. USENIX Association (1999)
12. Chan, B.Y., Shi, E.: Streamlet: textbook streamlined blockchains. In: Proceedings of the 1st ACM Conference on Advances in Financial Technologies (AFT) (2020)
13. Das, S., Pinkas, B., Tomescu, A., Xiang, Z.: Distributed randomness using weighted VRFs. Cryptology ePrint Archive (2024)
14. Doidge, I., Ramesh, R., Shrestha, N., Tobkin, J.: Moonshot: optimizing chain-based rotating leader BFT via optimistic proposals. arXiv preprint arXiv:2401.01791 (2024)
15. Dwork, C., Lynch, N., Stockmeyer, L.: Consensus in the presence of partial synchrony. J. ACM (JACM) **35**(2), 288–323 (1988)
16. Ethereum: Whitepaper (2024). https://ethereum.org/en/whitepaper/
17. Flow: Jolteon: advancing Flow's consensus algorithm (2023). https://flow.com/engineering-blogs/jolteon-advancing-flows-consensus-algorithm
18. Gelashvili, R., Kokoris-Kogias, L., Sonnino, A., Spiegelman, A., Xiang, Z.: Jolteon and ditto: network-adaptive efficient consensus with asynchronous fallback. In: International Conference on Financial Cryptography and Data Security, pp. 296–315. Springer (2022)
19. Gueta, G.G., et al.: SBFT: a scalable and decentralized trust infrastructure. In: 2019 49th Annual IEEE/IFIP International Conference on Dependable Systems and Networks (DSN), pp. 568–580. IEEE (2019)
20. Hanke, T., Movahedi, M., Williams, D.: Dfinity technology overview series, consensus system. arXiv preprint arXiv:1805.04548 (2018)
21. Jalalzai, M.M., Niu, J., Feng, C., Gai, F.: Fast-hotstuff: a fast and resilient Hotstuff protocol. arXiv preprint arXiv:2010.11454 (2020)
22. Kavousi, A., Le, D.V., Jovanovic, P., Danezis, G.: Blindperm: efficient MEV mitigation with an encrypted mempool and permutation. Cryptol. ePrint Archive (2023)
23. Keidar, I., Naor, O., Poupko, O., Shapiro, E.: Cordial miners: fast and efficient consensus for every eventuality. arXiv preprint arXiv:2205.09174 (2022)
24. Kuznetsov, P., Tonkikh, A., Zhang, Y.X.: Revisiting optimal resilience of fast Byzantine consensus. In: Proceedings of the 2021 ACM Symposium on Principles of Distributed Computing, pp. 343–353 (2021)
25. Martin, J.P., Alvisi, L.: Fast Byzantine consensus. IEEE Trans. Dependable Secure Comput. **3**(3), 202–215 (2006)
26. Shamir, A.: How to share a secret. Commun. ACM **22**(11), 612–613 (1979)

27. Shrestha, N., Shrothrium, R., Kate, A., Nayak, K.: Sailfish: towards improving the latency of DAG-based BFT. Cryptology ePrint Archive (2024)
28. Solana: Whitepaper (2024). https://solana.com/solana-whitepaper.pdf
29. Spiegelman, A., Aurn, B., Gelashvili, R., Li, Z.: Shoal: improving DAG-BFT latency and robustness. In: International Conference on Financial Cryptography and Data Security. Springer (2023)
30. Spiegelman, A., Giridharan, N., Sonnino, A., Kokoris-Kogias, L.: Bullshark: DAG-BFT protocols made practical. In: Proceedings of the 2022 ACM SIGSAC Conference on Computer and Communications Security, pp. 2705–2718 (2022)
31. Sui: official implementation in rust (2024). https://github.com/MystenLabs/sui
32. Tonkikh, A., Freitas, L.: Swiper: a new paradigm for efficient weighted distributed protocols. In: Proceedings of the 43rd ACM Symposium on Principles of Distributed Computing, pp. 283–294 (2024)
33. Xiang, Z., Das, S., Li, Z., Ma, Z., Spiegelman, A.: The latency price of threshold cryptosystem in blockchains. arXiv preprint arXiv:2407.12172 (2024)
34. Yin, M., Malkhi, D., Reiter, M.K., Gueta, G.G., Abraham, I.: Hotstuff: BFT consensus with linearity and responsiveness. In: Proceedings of the 2019 ACM Symposium on Principles of Distributed Computing, pp. 347–356. ACM (2019)

On Non-Interactive Blind Signatures in the Plain Model Using Complexity Leveraging

Kazuki Yamamura[1(✉)], Tetsuya Okuda[1], and Eiichiro Fujisaki[2]

[1] NTT Social Informatics Laboratories, Tokyo, Japan
`kazuki.yamamura@ntt.com`
[2] Japan Advanced Institute of Science and Technology, Ishikawa, Japan

Abstract. Blind signatures, introduced by Chaum (Crypto'82), are a fundamental cryptographic primitive with various applications such as e-voting, e-cash, anonymous credentials, and more. Although blind signatures inherently require interaction between both parties, Hanzlik (Eurocrypt'23) introduced the notion of non-interactive blind signatures (NIBS), which allow signatures on random messages to be issued blindly without interaction. While Hanzlik's NIBS constructions are provably secure in the random oracle model, instantiating a provably secure NIBS in the plain model remains an open problem.

In this paper, we introduce a non-interactive blind signature scheme in the plain model based on complexity leveraging. The key to our construction is the use of the non-uniform reductions employed by Garg et al. (Crypto'11), which enables us to instantiate a provably secure NIBS without relying on a trusted setup.

Furthermore, we investigate whether our construction can avoid the use of complexity leveraging by applying the idea proposed by Kalai and Khurana (Crypto'19), wherein complexity leveraging can be replaced with classical and quantum assumptions. We introduce a weaker blindness notion called non-adaptive blindness and show that this property allows our construction to avoid using complexity leveraging.

Of independent interest, we provide separation results demonstrating the existence of a NIBS construction that satisfies nonce blindness but not recipient blindness, and vice versa. This result implies that any NIBS construction should be proven to satisfy both nonce blindness and recipient blindness.

Keywords: Blind Signatures · Non-Interactive · Plain Model · Standard Model · Complexity Leveraging

1 Introduction

Blind signature schemes, introduced by Chaum [13], are a fundamental cryptographic primitive with several applications, such as e-voting [10], e-cash [12,13], and anonymous credentials [4]. Blind signature schemes can be viewed as an interactive protocol between a signer, holding a signing key, and a recipient, holding a message. Informally, the goal of blind signatures is for the user to obtain a signature from the signer without revealing the content of the message being signed. As such, blind signatures must satisfy two key security properties: Blindness, meaning the signer cannot learn the signed message, and Unforgeability, meaning the user can only obtain valid signatures through interaction with the signer.

As described, all existing blind signatures require interaction. However, Hanzlik introduced a groundbreaking cryptographic protocol called non-interactive blind signatures (NIBS) for random messages [27]. NIBS eliminates the need for online interactions. In the NIBS setting, both the signer and the recipient (i.e., the user) possess a pair of public and private keys. To create a valid message-signature pair, the signer creates a presignature on a nonce and the recipient's public key[1], and the recipient uses their secret key to derive a signature on a random message from the presignature.

NIBS has the potential to replace interactive blind signatures in applications where the choice of message is not critical. For instance, Privacy Pass [14,31] is a typical application of NIBS (for more details, see [27]). Other applications of NIBS include e-cash-like payment protocols [30]. Implementing NIBS allows for batch-issuing and offline issuance via hardware security modules (HSM) or cold wallets [27]. Given the security incidents at cryptocurrency exchanges, such as signing key leakage, utilizing NIBS can mitigate these risks through offline issuance in HSMs or cold wallets.

Hanzlik introduced two instantiations of NIBS schemes [27]: an efficient construction based on structure-preserving signatures of equivalence classes and a generic construction. Both are provably secure in the random oracle model. However, the question remains whether it is possible to design a NIBS scheme without relying on the random oracle model or the common reference string (CRS) model. Whether a cryptographic protocol requires a trusted setup assumption is a critical consideration since, in the trusted setup model, if an authority introduces a backdoor, security can no longer be guaranteed.

To explore NIBS schemes without any trusted setup, we first examine the existing round-optimal (interactive) blind signatures that do not require such setups. Fischlin and Schröder showed that under certain conditions, it is impossible to construct a three-move blind signature from falsifiable assumptions without any trusted setup [18]. However, Garg et al. demonstrated a round-optimal blind signature without any trusted setup by using complexity leveraging and non-uniform reductions [22][2]. Complexity leveraging refers to a type of reduction in which the reduction algorithm has more computational power than the adversary, and non-uniform reductions allow the algorithm to perform unbounded

---

[1] In the PKI model, the recipient never needs to send their public key, allowing them to create a valid message-signature pair without interaction.
[2] This does not contradict the impossibility result by Fischlin and Schröder [18], as it relies on complexity leveraging.

computation before it is given the problem instance (further details will be provided later).

In more recent work, Katsumata et al. demonstrated that it is possible to construct a round-optimal blind signature without relying on complexity leveraging, by employing both classical and quantum polynomial-time algorithms [33], building on the ideas of Kalai and Khurana [32]. Intuitively, their approach replaces super-polynomial security with quantum polynomial-time security, allowing the construction of round-optimal blind signatures in the plain model without using complexity leveraging.

Complexity Leveraging and Non-Uniform Reduction. Complexity leveraging exploits the gap between the computational power of an adversary and that of the reduction algorithm in security proofs. To create this gap, the building blocks must provide super-polynomial-time security. This allows the reduction algorithm—operating in super-polynomial time—to extract information from the adversary, who is constrained to polynomial time, thereby reducing the security proof to a cryptographic hard problem. Using this approach, Pass [35] introduced a two-move zero-knowledge argument system, which surpasses the barrier posed by the impossibility result by Goldreich and Oren [23]. Subsequently, several protocols have been instantiated using complexity leveraging [9,11,15,20–22,32,33].

Non-uniform reduction algorithms can be intuitively regarded as P/poly-machines. More specifically, in this setting, reduction algorithms are treated as two-stage processes: the pre-computation phase and the online phase. In the pre-computation phase, the reduction algorithm takes the security parameter as input and, using unbounded computational power, computes a polynomial-length advice string. In the online phase, the reduction algorithm takes the problem instance along with the advice string as input and attempts to solve the problem in polynomial time. Both Garg et al. [22] and Katsumata et al. [33] constructed round-optimal blind signatures in the plain model using this non-uniform reduction approach.

1.1 Our Result

In this paper, we present a non-interactive blind signature (NIBS) scheme in the plain model. Our construction relies on complexity leveraging. Unlike previous schemes [3,27], our construction does not require any setup assumptions, such as a common reference string or random oracle. Additionally, its security does not rely on interactive assumptions.

Furthermore, we explore whether our construction can avoid relying on complexity leveraging. Specifically, we investigate the possibility of constructing a NIBS scheme using a combination of classical and quantum hardness assumptions [32,33].While complexity leveraging necessitates a gap between the computational power of the adversary and the reduction algorithm in the security proof—requiring large parameters for the underlying building blocks—using both classical and quantum hardness assumptions can improve the overall efficiency of our construction. However, we observe that Hanzlik's blindness definition does not straightforwardly accommodate such techniques in our construction. On the other hand, a weaker notion of blindness, which we refer to as non-adaptive blindness, does allow these techniques to be applied. Further details are provided in Sect. 4.

Additionally, we analyze the distinction between two types of blindness definitions: recipient blindness and nonce blindness. A reader might wonder whether every scheme that satisfies recipient blindness also satisfies nonce blindness, or vice versa. To address this question, we present separation results demonstrating the existence of a NIBS scheme that satisfies nonce blindness but not recipient blindness, and vice versa. These findings suggest that any NIBS construction should be proven to satisfy both nonce blindness and recipient blindness. More details can be found in Sect. 2.1.

1.2 Technical Overview

Constructing NIBS in the Plain Model. We provide an overview of our construction. Our main contribution is the demonstration of the NIBS scheme in the plain model. Unlike Hanzlik's construction [27], our scheme does not rely on trusted setup assumptions, such as the random oracle model or the CRS model. To better understand our construction, we revisit the generic NIBS scheme proposed by Hanzlik [27]. In the key generation phase, the signer generates a standard signature key pair (spk, ssk) while the recipient generates a verifiable random function (VRF) key pair (vpk, vsk). During the issuance phase, the signer creates a digital signature psig on both a nonce nonce and the recipient's public key vpk, resulting in a presignature. In the obtaining phase, the recipient evaluates the VRF on the nonce nonce to obtain a message m, and then creates a dual-mode witness indistinguishable proof (DMWI) [26] π, using a common reference string $\mathsf{H}_{\mathsf{crs}}(0)$, where $\mathsf{H}_{\mathsf{crs}}$ is treated as a random oracle. The proof π demonstrates one of the following:

- the presignature psig is a standard digital signature on (nonce, vpk) and the message m is a result of the VRF evaluation,

or

- the random oracle value $\mathsf{H}_{\mathsf{crs}}(1)$ acts as a common reference string in binding mode.

An honest recipient proves the first case, while in a security reduction, the latter case is demonstrated by programming the random oracle $\mathsf{H}_{\mathsf{crs}}$. The recipient thus obtains the NIBS message-signature pair (m, π). In the verification phase, the verifier checks whether the proof π is valid.

Next, we review the security proof strategy for Hanzlik's generic construction. To prove the one-more unforgeability of the scheme, we need to construct a reduction that uses an adversary against one-more unforgeability to compute a forgery for the underlying standard signature scheme. This reduction requires programming the random oracle H_{crs} in such a way that it can extract the witness from the DMWI proofs computed by the adversary, which implies that the common reference string $H_{crs}(0)$ needs to be in binding mode. On the other hand, to prove the blindness of the scheme, we need to simulate DMWI proofs without a witness used by an honest prover (i.e., the latter case mentioned above). This requires programming the common reference string $H_{crs}(1)$ to be in binding mode.

Thus, Hanzlik's generic construction relies on a 'trapdoor' to simulate the DMWI proof within the security proof, necessitating a trusted setup, such as the common random string model or the random oracle model. However, to achieve a NIBS scheme in the plain model, we cannot rely on these trusted setups. This means that we can no longer extract the witness for the proof (in the one-more unforgeability proof) or simulate the proof (in the blindness proof).

To address this challenge, we employ complexity leveraging. Specifically, the signer and recipient exchange a 'trapdoor' with one another. Then, reductions running in super-polynomial time extract the trapdoor, enabling us to prove the security of the underlying schemes. In other words, these trapdoors allow the reduction in the one-more unforgeability proof to extract signatures from the underlying scheme, and the reduction in the blindness proof to simulate message-signature pairs for the adversary.

Let us introduce the idea of our construction based on the above strategy. In the key generation phase, a singer samples a random value $y \leftarrow \{0,1\}^\lambda$ as well as a standard signature key pair (spk, ssk), setting $((\mathsf{spk}, y), \mathsf{ssk})$ as a signer's key pair. (Why we require the signer's public key to include this random value y is described later.) Meanwhile, a recipient samples a secret key $R \leftarrow \{0,1\}^\lambda$ for a pseudorandom function F and computes a commitment to R^3; i.e., rpk ← Com($R; r_{\mathsf{rpk}}$) as a recipient's public key, where r_{rpk} is a randomness.

In the issue phase, the signer creates a standard digital signature psig on a nonce nonce and recipient's public key rpk to receive a presignature as in Hanzlik's construction. In the obtaining phase, the recipient evaluates the pseudorandom function F on input nonce to receive a message m. It also computes the following two commitments:

1. $\mathsf{com}^{(0)} \leftarrow \mathsf{Com}'((\mathsf{nonce}, \mathsf{rpk}, \mathsf{psig}); r^{(0)})$
2. $\mathsf{com}^{(1)} \leftarrow \mathsf{Com}'(0; r^{(1)})$,

where $r^{(0)}$ and $r^{(1)}$ are randomness for the commitments. Note that commitments Com and Com' are not identical, which reason we will describe later.

---

[3] Since VRF can be constructed in the plain model [24], even if we use a verifiable random function as a building block as in Hanzlik's construction then we can obtain NIBS in the plain model. However, we instead use a non-interactive commitment scheme and a pseudorandom function, which enables us to obtain a simpler and more general scheme.

Furthermore, it creates a non-interactive witness indistinguishable proof (NIWI)[4] π [6,16], which proves one of the following:

- The recipient's public key rpk is committed to the secret key R for the pseudorandom function F,
- The presignature psig is a standard digital signature on (nonce, rpk),
- The message m is the result of evaluating F_R on input nonce with R, and
- com$^{(0)}$ is committed to (nonce, rpk, psig),

or

- com$^{(1)}$ is committed to a preimage a such that $y = f(a)$ holds.

An honest recipient proves the former case, while the reduction in the security proof for blindness proves the latter case. Specifically, in the one-more unforgeability proof, the reduction, which aims to break the unforgeability of the underlying signature scheme, extracts a valid message-signature pair (nonce, rpk, psig) from the commitment com$^{(0)}$ as a forgery by running in super-polynomial time $T \cdot \text{poly}(\lambda)$. Here, note that the hardness of the one-way function f ensures that the adversary running inside the reduction cannot create a proof for the latter case. In the blindness proof, the reduction, running in super-polynomial time $T' \cdot \text{poly}(\lambda)$, extracts a value a from y such that $f(a) = y$, which allows us to create a NIWI proof proving the latter case.

However, this strategy presents a challenge. Suppose the one-way function f is super-polynomial-time $T \cdot \text{poly}(\lambda)$ secure, and the commitment scheme Com' is super-polynomial $T' \cdot \text{poly}(\lambda)$-time secure. We observe a contradiction: On one hand, T and T' must satisfy $T > T'$, as the one-more unforgeability proof requires the reduction to extract a preimage for f from the commitment com$^{(1)}$. On the other hand, T and T' must satisfy $T < T'$, as the blindness proof requires the reduction to invert $y = f(a)$ from the signer's public key to simulate a NIWI proof.

To address this conflicting requirement, we turn to the non-uniform setting, as observed by [21,22,33]. In the non-uniform setting, reduction algorithms are viewed as two-stage processes. In the pre-computation phase, the reduction algorithm takes the security parameter as input and, using unbounded computational power, generates an advice string of polynomial length. Then, in the online phase, the reduction algorithm uses this advice string, along with the problem instance, to solve the problem in polynomial time.

Revisiting the strategy under the assumption that $T < T'^5$, the one-more unforgeability holds since $T < T'$. Meanwhile, in the blindness game, the pre-computation phase of the non-uniform reduction algorithm inverts $y = f(a)$ and

---

[4] NIWI can be constructed from NIZK proofs and derandomization assumptions [6, 16], from bilinear pairings [25] and indistinguishablity obfuscation [8]. NIWI is a powerful tool for constructing several cryptographic protocols in the plain model (e.g., verifiable random functions [24] and ring signatures [2]) as NIWI does not require a trusted setup assumption.

[5] Indeed, the commitment scheme Com' only needs to be poly(λ)-secure.

outputs a as an advice string. In the online phase, given the problem instance and the advice string a, the algorithm can generate a NIWI proof demonstrating knowledge of the preimage a, meaning that the reduction can simulates the NIWI proof under the assumption that $T < T'$ (not $T > T'$).

Avoiding Complexity Leveraging. As discussed earlier, complexity leveraging exploits a gap between computational power of an adversary and that of the reduction. To create this gap, certain building blocks of the protocol must be secure against super-polynomial-time adversaries. This requirement necessitates large parameters, which negatively impact overall efficiency. To address this issue, Kalai and Khurana [32] replace complexity leveraging with classical and quantum assumptions. This approach eliminates the need for super-polynomial-time secure primitives, significantly improving efficiency. Indeed, Katsumata et al. [33] applies this idea to a round optimal blind signature in the plain model from standard (polynomial-time) assumptions.

Can we simply replace complexity leveraging with classical and quantum assumptions in the NIBS scheme discussed above? Unfortunately, this direct replacement does not work, as our protocol requires three security levels of underlying primitives (since $T < T'$) whereas Kalai and Khurana's approach [32] requires only two security levels to achieve the replacement. To overcome this obstacle, we introduce a weaker blindness notion that allows the NIBS scheme to incorporate Kalai and Khurana's idea [32]. Intuitively, this weaker definition forces adversaries to fix the signer's public key before receiving the recipient's public key. As a result, the scheme no longer requires $T < T'$, meaning that it suffices to set $T' = \mathsf{poly}(\lambda)$. This adjustment enables us to replace complexity leverainging with classical and quantum assumptions.

Separation Results ntuitively, recipient blindness ensures that a given message-signature pair cannot be linked to any particular recipient. Meanwhile, nonce blindness ensures that a message-signature pair cannot be linked to any presignatures issued to a particular recipient, allowing the signer to issue multiple presignatures per user.

It is evident that every NIBS scheme should satisfy Both blindness property. However, an important question arises: Does satisfying one blindness property necessarily imply satisfaction of the other? In other words, does a NIBS scheme with recipient blindness always satisfy nonce blindness, and vice versa? We answer this question by showing for each blindness property, there exists NIBS scheme which satisfies one but not the other (Theorem 1 and Theorem 2). Specifically, constructing a scheme with nonce blindness but not recipient blindness is straightforward—if a signature includes the recipient's public key, it can always be linked to the recipient, but this does not affect nonce blindness. However, constructing a scheme that satisfies recipient blindness but not nonce blindness requires more ingenuity. Our key idea is intuitively to incorporate a (one-time) ciphertext c that encrypts the nonce, defined as $c := \mathsf{rsk} + \mathsf{nonce}$, into the signature. This allows adversaries in the nonce blindness game to obtain two (one-time) ciphertexts, from which they can extract the nonce information.

Meanwhile, this adjustment does not compromise the recipient blindness of the scheme, since different recipients typically have distinct secret keys. As a result, the (one-time) ciphertexts perfectly conceal nonce information from adversaries in the recipient blindness game.

1.3 Related Work

Non-Interactive Blind Signatures. Hanzlik [27] introduced two NIBS schemes in the random oracle model: an efficient construction based on structure-preserving signatures on equivalence classes (SPS-EQ) [19], and a generic construction.

Hanzlik's efficient construction is pairing-based, and therefore does not provide post-quantum security. In contrast, Baldimtsi et al. proposed an efficient lattice-based construction [3]. Additionally, they revisited the definitional framework proposed by Hanzlik and introduced a stronger blindness definition for NIBS, which allows the adversary to issue Obtain queries—granting oracle access to the recipient's secret key. More recently, [29] introduced a NIBS scheme that supports RSA public keys as recipient public keys.

All of these schemes are provably secure in the random oracle model. As of now, no NIBS scheme exists in the plain model.

Round-Optimal Blind Signatures. A round-optimal blind signature is a two-move protocol in which the user and signer each send one message to the other. Although many round-optimal blind signatures have been proposed [1,7,13,17,21,28,33,34,37], all existing schemes rely on random oracles, setup assumptions, interactive assumptions, or complexity leveraging. Indeed, several impossibility results exist for constructing round-optimal blind signatures in the plain model [5,18,36]. In particular, Fischlin and Schröder discovered a surprising result: three-move schemes cannot be constructed from non-interactive assumptions under certain conditions [18].

Since NIBS can be regarded as a two-move protocol, one might expect these impossibility results to apply to NIBS as well. However, unlike standard blind signatures, in NIBS, the message depends on the nonce chosen by the signer and the recipient's secret key. Therefore, as discussed in [27], whether it is possible to construct NIBS in the plain model remains unclear and requires further investigation.

2 Preliminaries

The security parameter is $\lambda \in \mathbb{Z}$. All algorithms receive λ implicitly as input. We denote the first N natural numbers by $[N] := \{1, \cdots, N\}$. For a finite set S, we write $x \leftarrow S$ if x is sampled uniformly at random from S. For a probabilistic algorithm $\mathcal{A}$, we write $y \leftarrow \mathcal{A}(x)$ if y is output from $\mathcal{A}$ on input x with uniformly sampled initialized randomness. We write $y \leftarrow \mathcal{A}(x; \rho)$ to make the initialized randomness ρ explicit, and $y \in \mathcal{A}(x)$ means that y is a possible output of $\mathcal{A}(x)$. We also write $\mathcal{A}^{\mathcal{O}}(x)$ if $\mathcal{A}$ can access $\mathcal{O}$. We say that a function $f : \mathbb{N} \to \mathbb{R}_+$ is negligible in its input n, denoted by $f(n) = \mathsf{negl}(n)$, if $f \in n^{-\omega(1)}$. We use PPT and QPT to mean classical probabilistic polynomial time and quantum polynomial time.

In this section, we formally define non-interactive blind signatures (NIBS). Definitions of other cryptographic primitives can be found in the full version.

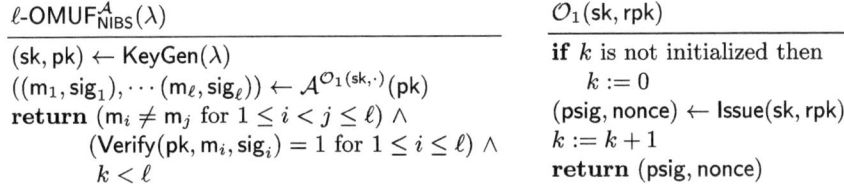

Fig. 1. ℓ-OMUF Games

2.1 Non-Interactive Blind Signature

We introduce NIBS schemes as proposed by Hanzlik [27].

Definition 1 (Non-Interactive Blind Signatures). *A non-interactive blind signature* NIBS = (KeyGen, RKeyGen, Issue, Obtain, Verify) *consists of the following PPT algorithms:*

KeyGen(λ) : *On input a security parameter λ, it outputs a signer's key pair* (pk, sk). *We assume that* pk *defines a nonce space* $\mathcal{N}_{\mathsf{pk}}$ *implicitly.*

RKeyGen(λ) : *On input a security parameter λ, it outputs a recipient's key pair* (rpk, rsk).

Issue(pk, sk, rpk, nonce) : *On input a signer's key pair* (pk, sk) *a recipient's public key* rpk, *and a nonce* nonce, *it outputs a presignature* psig.

Obtain(pk, rpk, rsk, nonce, psig) : *On input a signer's public key, a recipient's key pair* (rpk, rsk), *a nonce* nonce, *and a presignature* psig, *it outputs a valid message-signature pair* (m, sig) *or* $\bot$.

Verify(pk, m, sig) : *On input a signer's public key* pk *and a message-signature pair* (m, sig), *it outputs a bit b.*

We require that NIBS meets the following three properties: completeness, one-more unforgeability, and blindness:

Completeness. *We say that* NIBS *satisfies completeness if for all* (pk, sk) $\in$ KeyGen(λ), *all* (rpk, rsk) $\in$ RKeyGen(λ) *and all* nonce $\in \mathcal{N}_{\mathsf{pk}}$, *it holds that*

$$\Pr\left[\mathsf{Verify}(\mathsf{pk}, \mathsf{m}, \mathsf{sig}) = 1 \,\middle|\, \begin{array}{l} \mathsf{psig} \leftarrow \mathsf{Issue}(\mathsf{pk}, \mathsf{sk}, \mathsf{rpk}, \mathsf{nonce}); \\ (\mathsf{m}, \mathsf{sig}) \leftarrow \mathsf{Obtain}(\mathsf{pk}, \mathsf{rpk}, \mathsf{rsk}, \mathsf{nonce}, \mathsf{psig}) \end{array}\right] = 1$$

One-More Unforgeability. *A* NIBS *scheme is said to be ℓ-one-more unforgeable if, for every PPT adversary $\mathcal{A}$, the following advantage is negligible in λ:*

$$\mathbf{Adv}_{\mathsf{NIBS},\mathcal{A}}^{\ell\text{-OMUF}}(\lambda) := \Pr\left[\ell\text{-OMUF}_{\mathsf{NIBS}}^{\mathcal{A}}(\lambda) = 1\right],$$

where the game ℓ-OMUF is defined in Fig. 1. A scheme is one-more unforgeable if it satisfies ℓ-one-more unforgeability for all $\ell = \mathsf{poly}(\lambda)$.

Blindness. *We define two blindness properties: recipient blindness and nonce blindness.*

Recipient Blindness. *A* NIBS *scheme satisfies recipient blindness if, for all PPT adversaries $\mathcal{A}$, the following advantage is negligible in λ:*

$$\mathbf{Adv}_{\mathsf{NIBS},\mathcal{A}}^{\mathsf{rbnd}}(\lambda) := 2\Pr\left[\mathsf{RBND}_{\mathsf{NIBS}}^{\mathcal{A}}(\lambda) = 1\right] - 1,$$

where the game RBND *is defined in Fig. 2.*

Nonce Blindness. *A* NIBS *scheme satisfies nonce blindness if, for all PPT adversaries $\mathcal{A}$, the following advantage is negligible in λ:*

$$\mathbf{Adv}_{\mathsf{NIBS},\mathcal{A}}^{\mathsf{nbnd}}(\lambda) := 2\Pr\left[\mathsf{NBND}_{\mathsf{NIBS}}^{\mathcal{A}}(\lambda) = 1\right] - 1,$$

where the game NBND *is defined in Fig. 2.*

In this paper, we provide separation results between recipient blindness and nonce blindness. Specifically, Theorem 1 demonstrates the existence of a NIBS scheme that satisfies nonce blindness but not recipient blindness, while Theorem 2 shows the existence of a scheme that satisfies recipient blindness but not nonce blindness. The full proofs can be found in the full version.

Theorem 1. *If there exists a* NIBS *scheme which satisfies nonce blindness and one-more unforgeability, then there exists a scheme which satisfies these same properties but which does not satisfies recipient blindness.*

Theorem 2. *If there exists a* NIBS *scheme which satisfies recipient blindness and one-more unforgeability, then there exists a scheme which satisfies these same properties but which does not satisfies nonce blindness.*

3 Our Construction

In this section, we provide a NIBS scheme in the plain model from complexity leveraging. Fix two super-polynomial functions T_1 and T_2 such that $T_1 < T_2$. Our construction relies on the following building blocks:

- $f : \{0,1\}^\lambda \to \{0,1\}^\lambda$ is an one-way permutation with T_1-one-wayness and T_2-invertible

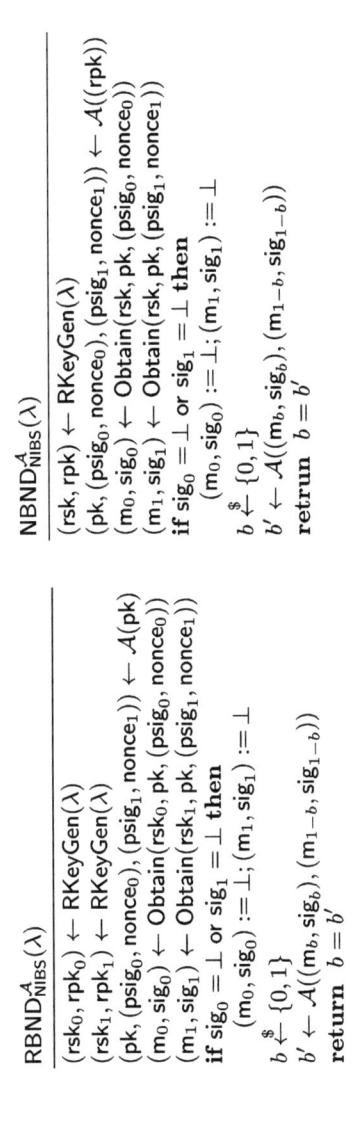

$\mathsf{RBND}_{\mathsf{NIBS}}^{\mathcal{A}}(\lambda)$

$(\mathsf{rsk}_0, \mathsf{rpk}_0) \leftarrow \mathsf{RKeyGen}(\lambda)$
$(\mathsf{rsk}_1, \mathsf{rpk}_1) \leftarrow \mathsf{RKeyGen}(\lambda)$
$(\mathsf{pk}, (\mathsf{psig}_0, \mathsf{nonce}_0), (\mathsf{psig}_1, \mathsf{nonce}_1)) \leftarrow \mathcal{A}(\mathsf{pk})$
$(m_0, \mathsf{sig}_0) \leftarrow \mathsf{Obtain}(\mathsf{rsk}_0, \mathsf{pk}, (\mathsf{psig}_0, \mathsf{nonce}_0))$
$(m_1, \mathsf{sig}_1) \leftarrow \mathsf{Obtain}(\mathsf{rsk}_1, \mathsf{pk}, (\mathsf{psig}_1, \mathsf{nonce}_1))$
if $\mathsf{sig}_0 = \bot$ **or** $\mathsf{sig}_1 = \bot$ **then**
$\quad (m_0, \mathsf{sig}_0) := \bot; (m_1, \mathsf{sig}_1) := \bot$
$b \xleftarrow{\$} \{0, 1\}$
$b' \leftarrow \mathcal{A}((m_b, \mathsf{sig}_b), (m_{1-b}, \mathsf{sig}_{1-b}))$
return $b = b'$

$\mathsf{NBND}_{\mathsf{NIBS}}^{\mathcal{A}}(\lambda)$

$(\mathsf{rsk}, \mathsf{rpk}) \leftarrow \mathsf{RKeyGen}(\lambda)$
$(\mathsf{pk}, (\mathsf{psig}_0, \mathsf{nonce}_0), (\mathsf{psig}_1, \mathsf{nonce}_1)) \leftarrow \mathcal{A}((\mathsf{rpk}))$
$(m_0, \mathsf{sig}_0) \leftarrow \mathsf{Obtain}(\mathsf{rsk}, \mathsf{pk}, (\mathsf{psig}_0, \mathsf{nonce}_0))$
$(m_1, \mathsf{sig}_1) \leftarrow \mathsf{Obtain}(\mathsf{rsk}, \mathsf{pk}, (\mathsf{psig}_1, \mathsf{nonce}_1))$
if $\mathsf{sig}_0 = \bot$ **or** $\mathsf{sig}_1 = \bot$ **then**
$\quad (m_0, \mathsf{sig}_0) := \bot; (m_1, \mathsf{sig}_1) := \bot$
$b \xleftarrow{\$} \{0, 1\}$
$b' \leftarrow \mathcal{A}((m_b, \mathsf{sig}_b), (m_{1-b}, \mathsf{sig}_{1-b}))$
retrun $b = b'$

Fig. 2. RBND and NBND Games

- SIG = (Gen, Sign, Verify) is a digital signature scheme with T_1-EUF-CMA security.
- Com is a non-interactive perfect binding commitment with T_2-hiding.
- Com' is a non-interactive perfect binding commitment with hiding against non-uniform PPT adversaries and T_1-extractability.
- $F_R : \{0,1\}^\lambda \to \{0,1\}^\lambda$ is a pseudorandom function with pseudorandomness against non-uniform PPT adversaries.
- NIWI = (Prove, Verify) is a non-interactive witness-indistinguishability proof system for the language $\mathcal{L}$ with witness-indistinguishability against non-uniform PPT adversaries.

Let us define the following NP language $\mathcal{L}$:

$$\mathcal{L} = \{(\mathsf{m}, \mathsf{pk} = (\mathsf{spk}, y), \mathsf{com}^{(0)}, \mathsf{com}^{(1)}) \mid (\mathsf{m}, \mathsf{spk}, \mathsf{com}^{(0)}) \in \mathcal{L}_0 \vee (y, \mathsf{com}^{(1)}) \in \mathcal{L}_1\},$$

where

$$\mathcal{L}_0 := \{(\mathsf{m}, \mathsf{spk}, \mathsf{com}^{(0)}) \mid \exists (\mathsf{nonce}, \mathsf{rpk}, \mathsf{psig}, R, r_{\mathsf{rpk}}, r^{(0)}), \; \mathsf{SIG.Verify}(\mathsf{spk}, (\mathsf{nonce}, \mathsf{rpk}), \mathsf{psig}) = 1$$
$$\wedge \mathsf{rpk} = \mathsf{Com}(R; r_{\mathsf{rpk}})$$
$$\wedge \mathsf{m} = F_R(\mathsf{nonce})$$
$$\wedge \mathsf{com}^{(0)} = \mathsf{Com}((\mathsf{nonce}, \mathsf{rpk}, \mathsf{psig}); r^{(0)})\}$$

and

$$\mathcal{L}_1 := \left\{(y, \mathsf{com}^{(1)}) \;\middle|\; \exists (a, r^{(1)}),\; y = f(a) \wedge \mathsf{com}^{(1)} = \mathsf{Com}(a; r^{(1)})\right\}.$$

Then our scheme NIBS = (KeyGen, RKeyGen, Issue, Obtain, Verify) is described as follows:

KeyGen(λ):
1. $(\mathsf{spk}, \mathsf{ssk}) \leftarrow \mathsf{SIG.Gen}(1^\lambda)$;
2. $y \leftarrow \{0,1\}^\lambda$;
3. $\mathsf{pk} := (\mathsf{spk}, y); \mathsf{sk} := (\mathsf{spk}, \mathsf{ssk})$;
4. Output $(\mathsf{pk}, \mathsf{sk})$.

RKeyGen(λ):
1. $R \leftarrow \{0,1\}^\lambda; r_{\mathsf{rpk}} \leftarrow \{0,1\}^\lambda$;
2. $\mathsf{rpk} \leftarrow \mathsf{Com}(R; r_{\mathsf{rpk}}); \mathsf{rsk} := (R, r_{\mathsf{rpk}})$;
3. Output $(\mathsf{rpk}, \mathsf{rsk})$.

Issue(sk, rpk, nonce):
1. $(\mathsf{spk}, \mathsf{ssk}) := \mathsf{sk}$;
2. $\mathsf{psig} \leftarrow \mathsf{SIG.Sign}(\mathsf{ssk}, (\mathsf{nonce}, \mathsf{rpk}))$;
3. Output psig;

Obtain(pk, rpk, rsk, nonce, psig):
1. $(R, r_{\mathsf{rpk}}) := \mathsf{rsk}$;
2. If $\mathsf{SIG.Verify}(\mathsf{spk}, (\mathsf{nonce}, \mathsf{rpk}), \mathsf{psig}) = 0$, then output $\bot$;
3. $\mathsf{m} \leftarrow F_R(\mathsf{nonce}); r^{(0)}, r^{(1)} \leftarrow \{0,1\}^\lambda$;
4. $\mathsf{com}^{(0)} \leftarrow \mathsf{Com}'((\mathsf{nonce}, \mathsf{rpk}, \mathsf{psig}); r^{(0)}); \mathsf{com}^{(1)} \leftarrow \mathsf{Com}'(0; r^{(1)})$;
5. $x := (\mathsf{m}, \mathsf{pk}, \mathsf{com}^{(0)}, \mathsf{com}^{(1)}); w := (\mathsf{nonce}, \mathsf{rpk}, \mathsf{psig}, R, r_{\mathsf{rpk}}, r^{(0)})$;

6. $\pi \leftarrow \mathsf{NIWI.Prove}(x, w)$;
7. $\mathsf{sig} \leftarrow (\mathsf{com}^{(0)}, \mathsf{com}^{(1)}, \pi)$;
8. Output message-signature pair $(\mathsf{m}, \mathsf{sig})$;

$\mathsf{Verify}(\mathsf{pk}, (\mathsf{m}, \mathsf{sig}))$:
1. $(\mathsf{com}^{(0)}, \mathsf{com}^{(1)}, \pi) := \mathsf{sig}$;
2. $x := (\mathsf{m}, \mathsf{pk}, \mathsf{com}^{(0)}, \mathsf{com}^{(1)})$;
3. Output $\mathsf{NIWI.Verify}(x, \pi)$.

3.1 Security

We show that our construction satisfies one-more unforgeability, recipient blindness, and nonce blindness. Within all proofs, we assume that $T_1 < T_2$. The full proof can be found in the full version.

Theorem 3. *Our scheme satisfies one-more-unforgeability assuming that the signature scheme* SIG *satisfies T_1-EUF-CMA security, one-way permutation f satisfies T_1-one-wayness, non-interactive witness indistinguishable proof system* NIWI *satisfies perfect soundness, and the perfect binding commitment scheme* Com' *is T_1-extractable.*

Theorem 4. *Our scheme satisfies recipient blindness assuming the commitment scheme* Com *satisfies T_2-hiding and the non-interactive indistinguishable proof system* NIWI *satisfies witness-indistinguishability against non-uniform PPT adversaries, the one-way permutation f satisfies T_2-invertible and F is pseudorandom against non-uniform PPT adversaries.*

Theorem 5. *Our scheme satisfies nonce blindness assuming the commitment scheme* Com *satisfies T_2-hiding and the non-interactive indistinguishable proof system* NIWI *satisfies witness-indistinguishability against non-uniform PPT adversaries, the one-way permutation f satisfies T_2-invertible and F is pseudorandom against non-uniform PPT adversaries.*

4 Observations

Constructing NIBS from Classical and Quantum Hardness Assumptions. Complexity leveraging requires a gap between the computational power of the adversary and the reduction algorithm in security proofs, necessitating large parameters for the building blocks. These large parameters reduce overall efficiency. To address this issue, Kalai and Khurana [32] suggest replacing complexity leveraging with quantum supremacy, converting super-polynomial hardness assumptions into quantum polynomial hardness. This approach allows the building blocks to avoid large parameters. Using this idea, Katsumata et al. [33] introduced a round-optimal blind signature in the plain model. This naturally raises the question:

Can the super-polynomial hardness assumptions in our construction be replaced with quantum polynomial hardness assumptions?

Unfortunately, this approach is not feasible in our case. Our security proof relies on complexity leveraging at two distinct points—T_1-hardness and T_2-hardness—requiring three levels of security for the underlying primitives. In contrast, combining classical and quantum polynomial hardness can provide only two security levels.

While prior work [33] encountered a similar obstacle, they skillfully avoided it using non-uniform reductions. Could this idea apply to our construction? Unfortunately, it does not. In the NIBS blindness game, adversaries receive the recipient's public key from the game before outputting any messages. This means that non-uniform reductions cannot extract meaningful information during the pre-computation phase, as the recipient's public key, a problem instance, is required in the pre-computation phase (refer to **Claim7** in the proof of Theorem 4). In contrast, in the blindness game for standard blind signatures, the adversary must first output the signer's public key before receiving any messages, allowing non-uniform reductions to extract useful information in the pre-computation phase without needing the problem instance. This distinction allows the construction in [33] to achieve security in the plain model.

We now consider how Hanzlik's blindness definition needs to be weakened to achieve security in the plain model from classical and quantum hardness assumptions. The main obstacle in the case of NIBS is that the adversary in the blindness game receives the recipient's public key before outputting the signer's public key. A natural solution is to modify the game such that the adversary must first output the signer's public key before receiving the recipient's public key. Based on this idea, we introduce a weaker blindness definition called non-adaptive blindness, with the formal definition provided in the full version. This non-adaptive blindness property allows us to extract useful information from the signer's public key during the pre-computation phase (as referenced in **Claim7** in the non-adaptive recipient blindness proof of Theorem 7), enabling us to overcome the challenge above.

4.1 Construction

We present a NIBS scheme with non-adaptive blindness from classical and quantum hardness assumptions. The construction remains the same as the one introduced in Sect. 3, except for the underlying primitive, which is defined as follows:

- $f : \{0,1\}^\lambda \to \{0,1\}^\lambda$ is an one-way permutation against QPT adversaries.
- SIG = (Gen, Sign, Verify) is a digital signature scheme with EUF-CMA security against QPT adversaries.
- Com is a non-interactive perfect binding commitment with computational hiding against non-uniform PPT adversaries.
- Com' is a non-interactive perfect binding commitment with computationally hiding against non-uniform PPT adversaries and QPT-extractability.

- $F_R : \{0,1\}^\lambda \to \{0,1\}^\lambda$ is a pseudorandom function with pseudorandomness against non-uniform PPT adversaries.
- NIWI = (Prove, Verify) is a non-interactive witness-indistinguishability proof system for the language $\mathcal{L}$ with witness-indistinguishability against non-uniform PPT adversaries.

Security. The full proof can be found in the full version.

Theorem 6. *Our scheme satisfies one-more-unforgeability assuming that the signature scheme* SIG *satisfies* EUF-CMA *against QPT adversaries, one-way permutation f satisfies one-wayness against QPT adversaries, non-interactive witness indistinguishable proof system* NIWI *satisfies perfect soundness, and the perfect binding commitment scheme* Com' *is* QPT-*extractable.*

Theorem 7. *Our scheme satisfies non-adaptive blindness assuming the commitment scheme* Com *satisfies computational hiding and the non-interactive indistinguishable proof system* NIWI *satisfies witness-indistinguishability against non-uniform PPT adversaries, the function f is a permutation and F is pseudorandom against non-uniform PPT adversaries.*

5 Open Problems

We leave open the question of whether it is possible to construct NIBS schemes with basic (not weaker) blindness, as introduced by Hanzlik [27], in the plain model using classical and quantum assumptions. Unlike standard blind signatures, the basic blindness of NIBS schemes requires adversaries to output their own signer's public key before receiving the recipient's public key, which prevents the approach used for constructing round-optimal blind signatures in the plain model [33] from being applied to NIBS. Overcoming this obstacle seems to be a significant challenge. We also leave as an open problem whether NIBS schemes with the stronger blindness introduced in [3] can be constructed in the plain model using complexity leveraging.

References

1. Agrawal, S., Kirshanova, E., Stehlé, D., Yadav, A.: Practical, round-optimal lattice-based blind signatures. In: Yin, H., Stavrou, A., Cremers, C., Shi, E. (eds.) Proceedings of the 2022 ACM SIGSAC Conference on Computer and Communications Security, CCS 2022, Los Angeles, CA, USA, November 7–11, 2022, pp. 39–53. ACM (2022)
2. Backes, M., Döttling, N., Hanzlik, L., Kluczniak, K., Schneider, J.: Ring signatures: logarithmic-size, no setup - from standard assumptions. In: Ishai, Y., Rijmen, V. (eds.) Advances in Cryptology - EUROCRYPT 2019 - 38th Annual International Conference on the Theory and Applications of Cryptographic Techniques, Darmstadt, Germany, May 19–23, 2019, Proceedings, Part III. Lecture Notes in Computer Science, vol. 11478, pp. 281–311. Springer (2019)

3. Baldimtsi, F., Cheng, J., Goyal, R., Yadav, A.: Non-interactive blind signatures: post-quantum and stronger security. In: Chung, K., Sasaki, Y. (eds.) Advances in Cryptology - ASIACRYPT 2024 - 30th International Conference on the Theory and Application of Cryptology and Information Security, Kolkata, India, December 9–13, 2024, Proceedings, Part II. Lecture Notes in Computer Science, vol. 15485, pp. 70–104. Springer (2024)
4. Baldimtsi, F., Lysyanskaya, A.: Anonymous credentials light. In: Proceedings of the 2013 ACM SIGSAC Conference on Computer & Communications Security, pp. 1087–1098 (2013)
5. Baldimtsi, F., Lysyanskaya, A.: On the security of one-witness blind signature schemes. In: Sako, K., Sarkar, P. (eds.) ASIACRYPT 2013. LNCS, vol. 8270, pp. 82–99. Springer, Heidelberg (2013). https://doi.org/10.1007/978-3-642-42045-0_5
6. Barak, B., Ong, S.J., Vadhan, S.: Derandomization in cryptography. In: Boneh, D. (ed.) CRYPTO 2003. LNCS, vol. 2729, pp. 299–315. Springer, Heidelberg (2003). https://doi.org/10.1007/978-3-540-45146-4_18
7. Beullens, W., Lyubashevsky, V., Nguyen, N.K., Seiler, G.: Lattice-based blind signatures: short, efficient, and round-optimal. In: Meng, W., Jensen, C.D., Cremers, C., Kirda, E. (eds.) Proceedings of the 2023 ACM SIGSAC Conference on Computer and Communications Security, CCS 2023, Copenhagen, Denmark, November 26–30, 2023, pp. 16–29. ACM (2023)
8. Bitansky, N., Paneth, O.: ZAPs and non-interactive witness indistinguishability from indistinguishability obfuscation. In: Dodis, Y., Nielsen, J.B. (eds.) TCC 2015. LNCS, vol. 9015, pp. 401–427. Springer, Heidelberg (2015). https://doi.org/10.1007/978-3-662-46497-7_16
9. Branco, P., Döttling, N., Wohnig, S.: Universal ring signatures in the standard model. IACR Cryptol. ePrint Arch. p. 1265 (2022)
10. Canard, S., Gaud, M., Traoré, J.: Defeating malicious servers in a blind signatures based voting system. In: International Conference on Financial Cryptography and Data Security, pp. 148–153. Springer (2006)
11. Chardouvelis, O., Malavolta, G.: The round complexity of quantum zero-knowledge. In: Nissim, K., Waters, B. (eds.) TCC 2021. LNCS, vol. 13042, pp. 121–148. Springer, Cham (2021). https://doi.org/10.1007/978-3-030-90459-3_5
12. Chaum, D.: Blind signatures for untraceable payments. In: CRYPTO, pp. 199–203 (1982)
13. Chaum, D.: Blind signature system. In: Advances in Cryptology: Proceedings of Crypto 83, pp. 153–153. Springer (1983)
14. Davidson, A., Goldberg, I., Sullivan, N., Tankersley, G., Valsorda, F.: Privacy pass: bypassing internet challenges anonymously. Proc. Priv. Enhancing Technol. (2018)
15. Dujmovic, J., Malavolta, G., Qi, W.: Registration-based encryption in the plain model. Cryptology ePrint Archive, Paper 2025/502 (2025)
16. Dwork, C., Naor, M.: Zaps and their applications. In: 41st Annual Symposium on Foundations of Computer Science, FOCS 2000, 12–14 November 2000, Redondo Beach, California, USA, pp. 283–293. IEEE Computer Society (2000)
17. Fischlin, M.: Round-optimal composable blind signatures in the common reference string model. In: Dwork, C. (ed.) CRYPTO 2006. LNCS, vol. 4117, pp. 60–77. Springer, Heidelberg (2006). https://doi.org/10.1007/11818175_4
18. Fischlin, M., Schröder, D.: On the impossibility of three-move blind signature schemes. In: Gilbert, H. (ed.) EUROCRYPT 2010. LNCS, vol. 6110, pp. 197–215. Springer, Heidelberg (2010). https://doi.org/10.1007/978-3-642-13190-5_10

19. Fuchsbauer, G., Hanser, C., Slamanig, D.: Structure-preserving signatures on equivalence classes and constant-size anonymous credentials. J. Cryptol. **32**(2), 498–546 (2019)
20. Fuchsbauer, G., Konstantinov, M., Pietrzak, K., Rao, V.: Adaptive security of constrained PRFs. In: Sarkar, P., Iwata, T. (eds.) ASIACRYPT 2014. LNCS, vol. 8874, pp. 82–101. Springer, Heidelberg (2014). https://doi.org/10.1007/978-3-662-45608-8_5
21. Garg, S., Gupta, D.: Efficient round optimal blind signatures. In: Nguyen, P.Q., Oswald, E. (eds.) EUROCRYPT 2014. LNCS, vol. 8441, pp. 477–495. Springer, Heidelberg (2014). https://doi.org/10.1007/978-3-642-55220-5_27
22. Garg, S., Rao, V., Sahai, A., Schröder, D., Unruh, D.: Round optimal blind signatures. In: Rogaway, P. (ed.) CRYPTO 2011. LNCS, vol. 6841, pp. 630–648. Springer, Heidelberg (2011). https://doi.org/10.1007/978-3-642-22792-9_36
23. Goldreich, O., Oren, Y.: Definitions and properties of zero-knowledge proof systems. J. Cryptol. **7**(1), 1–32 (1994). https://doi.org/10.1007/BF00195207
24. Goyal, R., Hohenberger, S., Koppula, V., Waters, B.: A generic approach to constructing and proving verifiable random functions. In: Kalai, Y., Reyzin, L. (eds.) TCC 2017. LNCS, vol. 10678, pp. 537–566. Springer, Cham (2017). https://doi.org/10.1007/978-3-319-70503-3_18
25. Groth, J., Ostrovsky, R., Sahai, A.: Non-interactive zaps and new techniques for NIZK. In: Dwork, C. (ed.) CRYPTO 2006. LNCS, vol. 4117, pp. 97–111. Springer, Heidelberg (2006). https://doi.org/10.1007/11818175_6
26. Groth, J., Sahai, A.: Efficient non-interactive proof systems for bilinear groups. In: Smart, N. (ed.) EUROCRYPT 2008. LNCS, vol. 4965, pp. 415–432. Springer, Heidelberg (2008). https://doi.org/10.1007/978-3-540-78967-3_24
27. Hanzlik, L.: Non-interactive blind signatures for random messages. In: Hazay, C., Stam, M. (eds.) Advances in Cryptology - EUROCRYPT 2023 - 42nd Annual International Conference on the Theory and Applications of Cryptographic Techniques, Lyon, France, April 23–27, 2023, Proceedings, Part V. Lecture Notes in Computer Science, vol. 14008, pp. 722–752. Springer (2023)
28. Hanzlik, L., Loss, J., Wagner, B.: Rai-choo! evolving blind signatures to the next level. In: Annual International Conference on the Theory and Applications of Cryptographic Techniques, pp. 753–783. Springer (2023)
29. Hanzlik, L., Paracucchi, E., Zanotto, R.: Non-interactive blind signatures from RSA assumption and more. In: Fehr, S., Fouque, P. (eds.) Advances in Cryptology - EUROCRYPT 2025 - 44th Annual International Conference on the Theory and Applications of Cryptographic Techniques, Madrid, Spain, May 4–8, 2025, Proceedings, Part II. Lecture Notes in Computer Science, vol. 15602, pp. 365–394. Springer (2025)
30. Heilman, E., Alshenibr, L., Baldimtsi, F., Scafuro, A., Goldberg, S.: Tumblebit: An untrusted bitcoin-compatible anonymous payment hub. In: Network and distributed system security symposium (2017)
31. IETF: Privacy Pass (privacypass). https://datatracker.ietf.org/wg/privacypass/documents/
32. Kalai, Y.T., Khurana, D.: Non-interactive non-malleability from quantum supremacy. In: Boldyreva, A., Micciancio, D. (eds.) CRYPTO 2019. LNCS, vol. 11694, pp. 552–582. Springer, Cham (2019). https://doi.org/10.1007/978-3-030-26954-8_18
33. Katsumata, S., Nishimaki, R., Yamada, S., Yamakawa, T.: Round-optimal blind signatures in the plain model from classical and quantum standard assumptions. In:

Canteaut, A., Standaert, F.-X. (eds.) EUROCRYPT 2021. LNCS, vol. 12696, pp. 404–434. Springer, Cham (2021). https://doi.org/10.1007/978-3-030-77870-5_15
34. Katsumata, S., Reichle, M., Sakai, Y.: Practical round-optimal blind signatures in the ROM from standard assumptions. In: Guo, J., Steinfeld, R. (eds.) Advances in Cryptology - ASIACRYPT 2023 - 29th International Conference on the Theory and Application of Cryptology and Information Security, Guangzhou, China, December 4–8, 2023, Proceedings, Part II. Lecture Notes in Computer Science, vol. 14439, pp. 383–417. Springer (2023)
35. Pass, R.: Simulation in quasi-polynomial time, and its application to protocol composition. In: Biham, E. (ed.) EUROCRYPT 2003. LNCS, vol. 2656, pp. 160–176. Springer, Heidelberg (2003). https://doi.org/10.1007/3-540-39200-9_10
36. Pass, R.: Limits of provable security from standard assumptions. In: Fortnow, L., Vadhan, S.P. (eds.) Proceedings of the 43rd ACM Symposium on Theory of Computing, STOC 2011, San Jose, CA, USA, 6–8 June 2011, pp. 109–118. ACM (2011)
37. del Pino, R., Katsumata, S.: A new framework for more efficient round-optimal lattice-based (partially) blind signature via trapdoor sampling. In: Dodis, Y., Shrimpton, T. (eds.) Advances in Cryptology - CRYPTO 2022 - 42nd Annual International Cryptology Conference, CRYPTO 2022, Santa Barbara, CA, USA, August 15–18, 2022, Proceedings, Part II. Lecture Notes in Computer Science, vol. 13508, pp. 306–336. Springer (2022)

Do Compilers Break Constant-Time Guarantees?

Lukas Gerlach[1(✉)], Robert Pietsch[2], and Michael Schwarz[1]

[1] CISPA Helmholtz Center for Information Security, Saarbrücken, Germany
{lukas.gerlach,michael.schwarz}@cispa.de
[2] Saarland University, Saarbrücken, Germany
robert.pietsch@uni-saarland.de

Abstract. Side-channel attacks are a significant concern for the implementation of cryptographic algorithms. Data-oblivious programming is a discipline that helps mitigate side-channel attacks by preventing data leakage over side channels. However, due to various optimizations in modern compilers, data-obliviousness cannot be guaranteed in high-level languages. This work investigates to which extent compiler optimizations violate data-obliviousness. To this end, we present <u>d</u>ata-<u>o</u>blivious <u>c</u>ompiler <u>c</u>hecker (DOCC), an automated binary testing pipeline for detecting data-obliviousness violations under different compiler configurations. We show that DOCC is applicable across 6 widely used compilers. Additionally, DOCC can retrofit existing analysis tools with advanced leakage models, such as data-dependent instruction execution times and data-obliviousness under speculation. We evaluate DOCC on 5 major cryptographic libraries and the recently proposed NIST lightweight cryptography primitives. We reveal data-obliviousness violations in 93 out of the 127 tested algorithms and 1845 out of the 12917 test cases across different cryptographic libraries, building blocks, and programming languages. We demonstrate that the choice of compiler and optimizations heavily influences the resulting binary's properties.

1 Introduction

Side-channel attacks threaten software security, compromising the confidentiality of functionally correct software systems. Examples of side-channels are the execution time of programs [12,34,60], the state of data in caches [47,67], and the processor's power consumption [35,42]. Attackers can observe side channels through software without physical access to the device. Side-channels often affect widely used libraries, such as OpenSSL [45], as evidenced by past CVEs such as CVE-2022-4304, CVE-2019-1547, and CVE-2018-5407. Side-channel leakage is typically discovered manually and addressed on a case-by-case basis. To prevent exploitation of such side channels, developers must write software in a side-channel-resilient manner. Constant-time or data-oblivious programming [28,51] prevents software side channels by making the execution time, code, and data access patterns of programs independent of secret values.

However, testing whether a program is data-oblivious is challenging for several reasons. While a variety of different checking tools provide non-formal [36, 53,61,63,64] as well as formal guarantees of data-obliviousness [14,16], these tools are not typically integrated into modern build systems and often have significant limitations both technically and from a usability perspective [24,29]. Moreover, many checking tools consider a limited execution model based solely on architectural observations and do not consider leakage in speculative execution [8]. Furthermore, current approaches rarely model variable execution time instructions, which can increase the attack surface [3]. Finally and most importantly, data-obliviousness can only be defined at the machine-code level, not for high-level C code [30]. This lack of a clear definition is due to the compiler's freedom to perform optimizations that do not alter observable behavior [19].

In this paper, we therefore ask the following question:

Do compilers influence data-obliviousness, and can we automatically detect violations by combining different detection techniques?

We present DOCC, a systematic approach assessing the data-obliviousness of compiled code under various compiler parameters. DOCC integrates different compilers and testing tools in a flexible and expandable framework. It includes binary-rewriting-based techniques that enhance existing and enable additional testing capabilities for data-obliviousness. As a result, our framework can check properties such as data-obliviousness in speculative execution or data-dependent instruction execution. DOCC is efficient because it implements testing in 3 stages. In the first stage, DOCC conducts computationally inexpensive heuristic tests to determine if the binary is data-oblivious. If the binary passes the heuristic tests, DOCC proceeds to the second stage, which involves dynamic execution. If the tests of the second stage are passed, the third stage employs symbolic execution to verify data-obliviousness formally. Ultimately, DOCC offers 2 outcomes: Failure at any stage indicates non-data-obliviousness, and successful verification at the third stage denotes data-obliviousness.

To evaluate DOCC, we analyze data-oblivious building blocks [5,66] and entire cryptographic algorithms from widely used libraries. We identify building blocks where seemingly data-oblivious code compiles to machine code violating data-obliviousness and also cases where code violating data-obliviousness compiles to data-oblivious executables. We evaluate the OpenSSL [45], BearSSL [49], mbedTLS [4], wolfSSL [65] and libsodium [38] cryptographic libraries. We analyze AES, Aria, ChaCha20, Camellia, and SHA implementations of OpenSSL, BearSSL, mbedTLS, wolfSSL, and libsodium using DOCC. We discover that OpenSSL's AES implementation exhibits key-dependent memory accesses when compiled using the `no-asm` flag. Similarly, AES, Aria, and Camellia commonly rely on non-data-oblivious lookup tables. In contrast, analyzing BearSSL and libsodium produces evidence supporting their data-obliviousness claims. Additionally, we analyze candidates of the NIST lightweight cryptography competition [43]. We discover that 9 out of the 10 reference implementations of the current NIST lightweight cryptographic competition are not data-oblivious.

Our evaluation shows that seemingly data-oblivious code only sometimes leads to data-oblivious binaries. We emphasize that employing DOCC enables automatic detection of issues, e.g., in a continuous-integration pipeline.

Contributions. The main contributions of this paper are:

1. We systematically evaluate how compilers influence data-obliviousness.
2. We introduce an extensible framework combining binary rewriting passes with data-obliviousness checkers in a 3-stage pipeline that outperforms single data-obliviousness checking tools.
3. We analyze the NIST lightweight cryptography finalists and 5 cryptographic libraries, revealing 1063 data-obliviousness violations in 53 of 76 algorithms.

We publish our DOCC framework as open source.[1]

Responsible Disclosure. We disclosed our findings to OpenSSL on August 30, 2023. Monero removed the OpenSSL `no-asm` flag from their codebase to guarantee a constant-time AES implementation.

2 Background

2.1 Software Side Channels

Software side-channel attacks leak meta-information during normal operation without physical access. Secret-dependent control and data flows are primary leakage sources [28]. *Timing attacks* exploit variations from secret-dependent branches or instruction latency (e.g., multiplication, division, shifting) [3,51]. *Cache attacks* infer secrets via timing differences between memory hits and misses (Flush+Reload [67], Prime+Probe [47]). *Branch-prediction attacks* mistrain predictors to reveal secret-dependent timing discrepancies [2].

2.2 Assisted Data-Oblivious Programming

To defend against side-channel attacks, *data-oblivious programming* [5,34,50,51] ensures that the sequence of memory accesses and control flow does not depend on secret data. In the past, programmers relied on manual auditing the compiler output for the absence of information leakage [29]. Nowadays, a wide variety of assistance methods to test for data-obliviousness has emerged [24].

Heuristic-Based Approach. DUDECT collects program execution times for different program arguments [53]. The resulting execution times are analyzed statistically for secret-dependent execution times. This approach is inherently limited to the path coverage generated by the respective program arguments.

Taint Tracking and Memory Tracing. Another approach is to trace memory and instruction access patterns during the program's execution. CTGRIND [36] performs *taint tracking* [17] to detect dependencies between memory accesses and

---
[1] https://github.com/cispa/constant-time-compilers.

program arguments. Taint tracking propagates additional information (taint) during program execution to determine whether program arguments labeled as secret end up in branches or memory accesses. Similarly, DATA [61] is built upon Intel's binary instrumentation framework PIN [27], which allows for *address-tracing*, capturing a trace of the instruction and memory accesses of a program. DATA performs statistic tests to determine if there is a difference between sets of traces collected on different secret program inputs. Both taint tracking and memory tracing are dynamic approaches that can only test the parts of a program covered by the inputs during testing.

Symbolic Execution. *Symbolic execution* [32] symbolizes the program state to derive logical constraints, which can be used with a logic solver to obtain guarantees for each possible program execution under test. Unlike dynamic testing, symbolic execution can derive strong guarantees that hold for the entire program under test. PITCHFORK [15] leverages symbolic execution to detect secret data flowing into address calculations or branch conditions.

2.3 Static Binary Rewriting

Binary rewriting is a technique that allows the modification of compiled binary code without recompilation [62]. The remainder of the paper builds upon e9patch [20] which uses trampolines patched into the code and, therefore, requires no changes to the control and data flow of the remaining unpatched code. Thus, the data-obliviousness properties of patched code remain unchanged.

3 Overview and Design of DOCC

We introduce DOCC, an automated approach testing data-obliviousness of machine code compiled with different compilers and compiler options under different testing strategies. We build a generic, extensible framework that performs compilation in different compiler configurations and tests the resulting binaries for data-obliviousness violations. In addition, DOCC supports binary rewriting passes to retrofit existing data-obliviousness analysis tools with new features, such as detecting violations under speculation or from instructions with non-constant runtimes. Moreover, our debranching technique can reduce the complexity of applications, improving testing performance.

At the core of our testing framework lies the code snippet under test. To determine how the snippet under test is compiled and run, we provide a checker- and compiler-agnostic testing specification. This specification must be provided once per snippet under test. Multiple compilers and architectures can be part of a generic pipeline layout. For the remainder of the paper, we focus on the x86 architecture due to the variety of available compilers.

We employ a 3-stage checking approach (with an additional optional binary rewriting pass), as shown in Fig. 1, to find violations reliably and quickly. Before testing, the binary can be rewritten to enable more efficient checking of

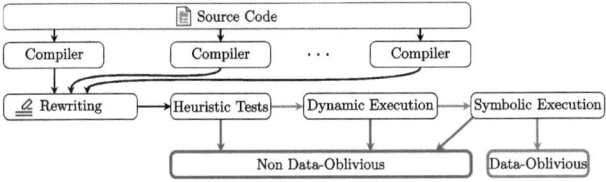

Fig. 1. Three-phase design of DOCC. The input code is compiled with different compilers, rewritten, and checked with increasingly powerful testing methods. Each code snippet is ultimately categorized as data-oblivious or not.

data-obliviousness violations or to test specific properties such as data operand-dependent instruction timing or data-obliviousness under speculative execution. The first 2 stages leverage heuristic tests and dynamic execution to find violations of data-obliviousness. The main intuition is that showing a violation of data-obliviousness requires only one such violating input (pair), while guaranteeing data-obliviousness requires showing that no such violating inputs exist. Hence, if DOCC cannot find inputs that violate data-obliviousness during a fixed test time or coverage, it resorts to the computationally more expensive verification of data-obliviousness in the third stage.

3.1 (Optional) Stage 0: Binary Rewriting

We introduce 4 novel rewriting approaches that broaden the applicability of already developed data-obliviousness analysis techniques. Instead of changing the checker, we change the binary under test such that the desired property can be evaluated using an off-the-shelf checker, while keeping its data-obliviousness properties. Our 4 rewriting strategies are:

- Rewriting non-constant-time instructions into data and control flow leakage.
- Debranching to reduce the false positive rate and increase the analysis speed of taint tracking and symbolic-execution-based checkers.
- Speculative execution emulation to evaluate the data-obliviousness properties of a binary under speculative execution.
- Coverage instrumentation to evaluate the completeness of the tests.

Non-Constant-Time Instruction Rewriting. Execution times for most instructions are typically independent of operand values, but there are exceptions, such as integer divisions and shift operations [1,51]. Such timing differences have been exploited in browser-based and cryptographic attacks [3]. However, such leakage is not detectable with off-the-shelf checkers. We present a two-stage approach to identify such non-constant-time instructions. First, we detect whether an instruction's execution time is influenced by its operands using statistical tests. Next, we make these instructions detectable via code rewriting.

Our testing method, inspired by test vector leakage assessment [55], involves evaluating instructions on two classes of inputs: one with fixed values and the other with randomly sampled values. Execution times are measured using randomly interleaved inputs from these two classes. A statistical test, specifically a Welsch t-test, is then applied to determine if there is a significant difference between the two sets of timing measurements. If the t-test reveals a significant difference (with a threshold of 4.5 [55]), the instruction's timing likely is operand dependent.

In the second step, we rewrite variable time instructions into data and control flow leakage. Each instruction is replaced with a snippet of code called a trampoline, which performs artificial data and control flow constructs. The trampoline is designed such that any bitwise change in the input arguments causes a change in data and control flow. After the trampoline, the patched instruction is executed normally. Therefore, the semantics of the binary under test do not change. In addition, the patching itself does not induce new secret-dependent control or data flow. Therefore, the data-obliviousness properties of the binary are only changed by the contents of the trampoline.

We tested our rewriting pass on the RC5 implementation [46] of OpenSSL, which contains secret-dependent shift instructions in both the E_RC5_32 and D_RC5_32 macro. We confirmed that the shift instruction has a different, operand-dependent runtime when executed on an Intel i9-12900K CPU. DOCC automatically rewrites the OpenSSL binary to detect the shift instruction in our patched version using DATA.

We additionally test our rewriting pass on the examples snippets tested in Sect. 5.1. These examples contain 296 shift instructions on average. However, using a combination of DATA and our rewriting pass, we verify that none of them are secret dependent. By manually verifing that no secret dependent shift instructions exist in the resulting binaries we find that our binary rewriting pass is effective for our examples.

Debranching. Both symbolic execution and taint tracking can produce false positives, such as in code like `if(never_taken & secret) func()`. Here, a secret value flows into a never-taken branch, leading to a false positive data-obliviousness violation. We implemented a binary rewriting strategy because addressing the issue at the source code level is tedious and ineffective; compiler optimizations can alter the binary's properties again.

Our approach benchmarks the program on random, well-formed inputs until sufficient coverage is achieved, using a custom Quiling-based tracer [23]. This tracer records all branches and whether they were taken, allowing us to identify branches that are always or never executed during regular operation. These static branches, often part of assertions, are then rewritten as unconditional branches. Since assertions are always true for valid input, they can safely be ignored in data-obliviousness tests.

We applied this technique to a base64 decoding routine in CTTK [50], where comparisons with whitespace—flagged as violations by both CTGRIND and PITCHFORK—were rewritten as unconditional branches, resolving the false positive. Similar issues were found and addressed in the mbedTLS base64 implementation and the hex decoding in libsodium. In all other tests debranching was not able to find and eliminates stale branches as they did not occur. In such cases, debranching does not reduce false positives as it simply has no effect.

Speculative Execution Emulation. Typically, data-obliviousness checks focus on architectural execution. However, speculative execution can expose additional attack surfaces [13,33]. An example of such a program contains a branch that is never architecturally taken, e.g.,an assertion statement. Under speculative execution, an attacker can trick the branch predictor into entering the branch. If the branch contains a non-data-oblivious statement leaking the secret variable, i.e.,a memory lookup, the attacker can leak the content of the variable [13,33].

Rather than integrating speculative execution checks into the tools used by DOCC, we use binary rewriting to emulate speculative execution in two steps. First, we execute the binary while recording all conditional branches and their coverage. Once sufficient coverage is achieved, we identify static branches that are candidates for speculative execution rewrites, particularly those never taken during normal execution but potentially vulnerable under speculation. We rewrite each static branch by inverting its condition, similar to the approach used in SpecFuzz [44], effectively emulating speculative execution. This process is repeated for all branches in the binary.

We evaluated the rewriting approach on the wolfSSL library, where the Poly1305 authenticated encryption showed additional leakage during speculation. However, this leakage induced by an error-checking branch without a speculative leakage gadget inside the branch is likely not exploitable.

Coverage Instrumentation. Dynamic testing methods only partially test a binary, resulting in data-obliviousness guarantees only for the covered code. We provide a coverage-instrumentation rewriting pass using bcov [10] to measure coverage. Rewriting the binary for coverage has the benefit that it is independent of the compiler. We tested our coverage of the mbedTLS [4] AES implementation and observed full test coverage on the encryption and decryption routines.

> **Takeaway** Binary rewriting of programs under test is a viable alternative to adding functionality to individual checkers.

3.2 Stage 1: Inexpensive Heuristic Checks

The first stage of our pipeline uses efficient heuristic checks to identify potential data-obliviousness violations quickly. We employ a customized version of DUDECT [53], which runs the code snippet while measuring execution time and tracking microarchitectural events through performance counters. Performance counters allow for tracking events that are hard to detect using timing only, such as cache misses. These events only produce timing differences on specifically crafted inputs, which are often not covered by DUDECT, as inputs for each execution are generated randomly for secret inputs and fixed for public inputs. If, during execution, the snippet induces statistically significant secret-dependent timing or counter differences, it is labeled as non-data-oblivious.

Despite its efficiency, this approach has limitations. False negatives may occur because simple heuristics might miss subtle violations, while false positives can arise due to measurement noise or runtime variance caused by external factors like interrupts. Stage 2 employs a more powerful dynamic test to verify negative results. In the case of false positives, the checks can be repeated or refined using more robust tests.

> **Takeaway** Heuristic checks can be extended using performance counters to detect more subtle data-obliviousness violations.

3.3 Stage 2: Moderately-Expensive Dynamic Execution

When heuristic tests fail to detect data-obliviousness violations, we move to more powerful dynamic execution methods. For instance, runtime-based heuristics are often insufficient for detecting secret-dependent memory accesses, as these do not always cause measurable timing differences—such as in small lookup tables where entries are mostly cached. Additionally, hardware optimizations like dynamic frequency scaling or prefetching can distort timing results, leading to inaccuracies.

We employ 2 different strategies of increasing computational power but also complexity, namely recording execution traces [61,63,64] and taint tracking [36]. Taint tracking can detect data-dependent edge cases that are unlikely to be found with trace recording as taint allows to track secret-dependent computations independent of concrete values.

While these techniques only cover executed code paths, this is not a significant problem, as cryptographic implementations contain few branches. Like previous work, generating random inputs is sufficient to achieve good coverage [53,61]. Our coverage instrumentation rewriting pass described in Sect. 3.1 can validate this. If dynamic execution finds no data-obliviousness violations, DOCC transitions to symbolic execution in Stage 3.

3.4 Stage 3: Expensive Symbolic Execution

If dynamic execution fails to detect data-obliviousness violations, we proceed to symbolic execution [7,32]. Symbolic execution explores all possible paths through a program, providing a complete analysis. The code is considered data-oblivious if no violations are found during this phase.

Symbolic execution for verifying data-obliviousness has been studied extensively in previous works [15,16]. Unlike taint tracking, which dynamically executes the program, symbolic execution solves constraints over inputs to determine whether a secret input can influence a branch or memory access. If it finds such a case, the program leaks sensitive information.

Symbolic execution is the only approach employed by DOCC to provide strong guarantees. However, to do so, the entire program must be explored, which is only feasible if the generated program contains a manageable number of branches. For more complex programs, symbolic execution suffers from the problem of path explosion [7]. It is, therefore, more helpful in finding data-obliviousness violations than in proving their absence.

3.5 Result Analysis and Option Triage

Our pipeline identifies the root cause of data-obliviousness violations at both the source-code and compiler-optimization levels. Source-level analysis uses existing checkers [36,61]. We automatically pinpoint the optimization flag that induces a violation by finding the threshold optimization level where data-obliviousness changes, then iteratively adding or removing flag subsets to isolate a minimal data-oblivious configuration. We evaluate on the examples from Sect. 5.1 using gcc. In every case, -fipa-pure-const converts code to constant time by eliminating constants. A similar procedure for clang found no single flag that toggles constant-time behavior; testing beyond three-flag combinations is infeasible due to pass ordering and interdependencies.

4 Implementation

In this section, we describe our proof-of-concept DOCC, used in Sects. 5.1 and 5.2. We support seven compilers—gcc, clang, icc, aocc, tcc, compcert, and zigcc—and four data-obliviousness checkers—DUDECT, DATA, CTGRIND, and PITCHFORK. Our compiler configurations include -O1, -O2, -O3, -Ofast, -Os, and CompCert's -Obranchless. The checkers cover heuristic testing, dynamic taint tracking, address tracing, and symbolic execution. All non-heuristic tests are parallelized up to available cores and memory; heuristic tests run serially to avoid precision loss under load.

5 Evaluation

In the following, we evalaute DOCC across a wide range of constant-time building blocks and cryptographic libraries. The normalized results of each tests are shown in Fig. 2, more detailed results are provided as part of our artifact.

5.1 Building-Block Analysis

In this section, we apply DOCC to 9 common building blocks for data-oblivious code and evaluate the non-constant-time instruction and debranching rewriting passes from Sect. 3.1. Our experiments identify 312 non-data-oblivious cases among 2525 tests across 14 of 24 code snippets. We assess building blocks from the literature [5,28,66] (see Appendix B) and the Constant Time Toolkit (CTTK) [50] in Appendix A. Our findings demonstrate that compiler optimizations can both break and restore data-obliviousness at the machine-code level.

> **Takeaway** Compiler options, e.g.,optimizations, influence the data-obliviousness properties of the resulting binaries in arbitrary ways.

33% of the samples produce a non-data-oblivious binary from ostensibly data-oblivious C code. In contrast, 56% of the samples that are not data-oblivious on the source level result in a data-oblivious binary. The CTTK library remained data-oblivious independent of compilation options, showing that it is possible to create robust and portable data-oblivious code.

Testing small snippets helps evaluate the effectiveness and precision of various data-obliviousness-checking methods. However, each method can yield false results for different reasons. Simple heuristics may produce false positives due to measurement noise, misinterpreting errors as secret-dependent differences.

More sophisticated methods, such as taint analysis and symbolic execution, may also be overly sensitive, misclassifying branches that are never taken—like assertions—as leakage. For instance, in testing the CTTK library, a branch that skips non-secret whitespace was incorrectly flagged as a violation. To address these issues, we propose binary rewriting, as discussed in Sect. 3.1.

> **Takeaway** Checkers disagree on data-obliviousness violations, but an ensemble of checkers can detect data-obliviousness violations reliably.

5.2 Cryptographic Library Analysis

This section analyzes cryptographic libraries as real-world case studies. We analyze implementations from the NIST lightweight cryptography competition,and 5 popular cryptographic libraries (OpenSSL, wolfSSL, Mbed TLS, BearSSL, and libsodium). Due to scalability issues these tests are all performed without the rewrtiting step.

NIST Lightweight Cryptography Finalists. We test all 10 NIST lightweight cryptography finalists implementing authenticated encryption with associated data (AEAD). These algorithms should work on devices with little computational power while still providing sufficient security properties. We test multiple implementations per candidate, leading to 28 tested code snippets. Only one finalist variant is free of data-obliviousness violations.

Test Setup. We test the 10 finalist submissions, including the optimized implementation, using all compilers and checkers described in Sect. 4. Each submission is tested for both encryption and decryption routines.

Results. In 11 of the 28 tested implementations, data-obliviousness depends on the compiler or compiler option. We find that 16 schemes are implemented in a non-data-oblivious way independent of the compiler. For example, the romolus and photon-beetle reference implementations use lookup tables, always resulting in non-data-oblivious binaries. Lastly, ascon is the only finalist that is data-oblivious across all compilers and compiler options (excluding a false positive with the `zig` compiler).

Common Cryptograpic Libraries. We evaluate DOCC on 5 commonly used cryptographic libraries: OpenSSL (3.1.1), wolfSSL (5.6.3-stable), Mbed TLS (v3.4.1), BearSSL (v0.6) and libsodium (1.0.19-stable). While previous work already focussed on manual and automatic testing of these libraries [53,61], we focus on the compilation process and options. As our results show, for OpenSSL, the presence of optimization may cause the resulting library to violate data-obliviousness after compilation.

Tested Functions. We evaluate the AES Aria, and Camellia block ciphers, the ChaCha20 stream cipher and its AEAD counterpart Poly1305. We also test utility functions like base64 encoding. These functions are valid attack targets for cache and timing attacks, making their data-oblivious implementation crucial [6, 69].

Results. Across all libraries, Aria and Camellia employ lookup tables, inherently violating data-obliviousness guarantees. Every library offers a data-oblivious AES implementation, but OpenSSL's `no-asm` flag breaks obliviousness (documented in version3.0.2). This flag is used by many projects (e.g., nginx, MoneroGUI) and OpenSSL defers responsibility to downstream users. ChaCha20 and Poly1305 remain data-oblivious in all tested libraries; DOCC verified both in 4 of 5 cases, with one timeout. SHA implementations are either data-oblivious or time out; manual inspection confirms obliviousness. Base64 encoding is data-oblivious across compilers, though CTGRIND and PITCHFORK report spurious branches (removable via binary debranching).

> **Takeaway** Not all cryptographic primitives, even in the most-common cryptographic libraries, are data-oblivious, and libraries may fall back to unsafe implementations silently.

6 Evaluation Outcome

In the following we evaluate the efficacy and performance of DOCC across all tests from Sect. 5.

Efficacy. We illustrate the efficacy of DOCC in Fig. 3a. Our pipeline can capture data-obliviousness violations in each stage, with the dynamic methods in Stage 2

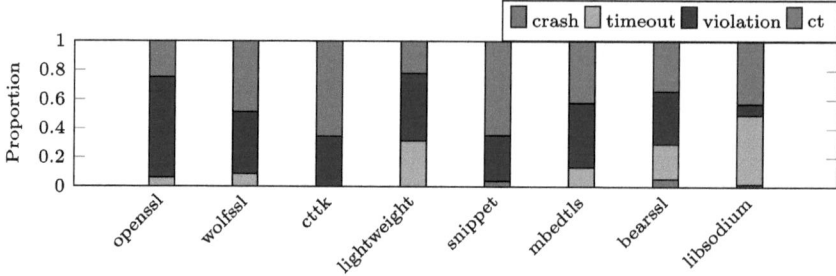

Fig. 2. Normalized data-obliviousness results for the accumulate function in all tested libraries. DOCC finds violations in all tested libraries.

being the most effective. Additionally, we observe that the third stage (symbolic execution) still discovers new data-obliviousness violations.

Figure 3b shows the number of violations observed for each compiler and optimization level. The significantly fewer violations in `compcert` and `zig` are due to the fewer code snippets they could compile. Overall, the relationship between optimization options and the number of violations varies by compiler. While `gcc` shows slightly more violations at lower optimization levels, LLVM-based compilers like `clang`, `icx`, and `aocc` exhibit slightly more violations at higher optimization levels.

> **Takeaway** Pipelined checks of increasing complexity efficiently and reliably dectect data-obliviousness violations.

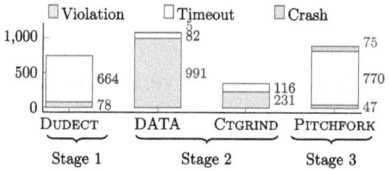

(a) Snippets grouped by result and pipeline stage. If a violation is detected, later pipeline stages are excluded.

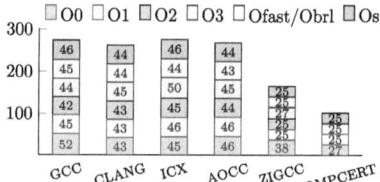

(b) Violations for each compiler and optimization level.

Fig. 3. Comparison of pipeline stages and compiler optimizations.

Performance. While high accuracy is desirable, it must be achievable within a practical timeframe for DOCC to be usable. We use an Intel Xeon Gold 6346 machine with 32 cores and 128 GB of memory running Ubuntu 22.04, with a test timeout of 2 min. In our tests, we find most violations within seconds, only requiring longer on branchy code or code that enters Stage 3. In addition, we parallelize testing, which scales with the number of cores on the test system. Running all tests in this paper takes around 100 h on our test system. With 12917 tests overall, this results in an average time of 27 s per test.

As shown in Fig. 3a, most timeouts occur in either Stage 1 (heuristic checks) or Stage 3 (symbolic execution). Still, Stage 1 is valuable to our pipeline, as it can capture secret-dependent instruction runtime differences.

7 Discussion

Potential Improvements. Input generation is the limiting factor for dynamic approaches. Fuzzing-based methods [25] with coverage-driven input generation could enhance coverage more quickly. Since DOCC manages input generation and provides coverage instrumentation, integrating this approach could improve efficiency without additional checker modifications.

Supporting more architectures in DOCC presents another avenue for future work. Different architectures come with unique instructions and optimizations, meaning C code that compiles to a data-oblivious binary on one architecture may not retain this property on another.

Related Work. Previous work manually analyzed the impact of compilation on data-obliviousness. Kaufmann [30] found that a seemingly data-oblivious implementation of curve25519 was vulnerable to a side-channel attack when compiled with the MSVC compiler. Additionally, Simon et al.[58] show that specific cryptographic code snippets are transformed to non data-oblivious ones by the compiler and devise ways to prevent this transformation. Concurrent work [54] analyzed the impact of compiler optimizations on data-obliviousness in cryptographic libraries. However, our focus lies more on the choice of testing tool and compiler, where they test more cryptographic libraries and architectures.

Jancar et al.[29] surveyed data-oblivious programming and automated testing frameworks to check for data-obliviousness. They find that most developers working on cryptographic implementations are unaware of such tools or do not use them. Similarly, Geimer et al.[24] show that using a single checking tool can lead to unreliable results. These results closely relate to our work, as we not only provide more thorough checking of binaries but also unify multiple checking frameworks such that a testing harness only has to be written once.

Much work has gone into automatically rewriting programs into their data-oblivious counterparts [21,22,26,31,39–41,52,59]. FaCT [14] is a programming language that guarantees that the resulting executable satisfies constant-time properties. Similarly, Barthe et al.[9] propose a framework to compile code to constant-time versions that are then proven correct using the Coq proof assistant. In addition, Wu et al.[66] rewrite a program's LLVM code to a data-oblivious version. Program synthesis based approaches have been used to synthesize a constant time instructions from a safe subset of instructions [18]. A similar approach is taken by Borrello et al.[11], where code is dynamically benchmarked to ensure more precise rewriting. Additionally approaches that require a special runtime to enable data-obliviousness have been proposed [37,56]. However, this approach trades provable data-obliviousness with performance and practicality. All compiler-based approaches require a modified compiler toolchain.

Work on extending the processor ISA [39,68] aims to fix the data-obliviousness problem on the ISA level.

8 Conclusion

In this work, we proposed DOCC, an automated pipeline for checking data-obliviousness under different compiler optimizations. DOCC efficiently detects violations of data-obliviousness while at the same time being able to give strong guarantees. In 3 case studies, we evaluated the capabilities of DOCC, revealing data-obliviousness violations in 93 of the 127 tested algorithms and 1845 of the 12917 test cases across cryptographic libraries and building blocks. We show that the choice of compiler and optimizations heavily influences the final binary's properties, making rigorous testing necessary to guarantee data-oblivious code.

Acknowledgment. We thank our reviewers and our shepherd for their valuable feedback. We thank Leon Trampert for fruitful discussions.

A Tested CTTK Library Functions

In this section, we discuss the tested CTTK primitives, including the testing results and challenges. CTTK is a small library that provides data-oblivious primitives for cryptographic applications.

De- and Encoding Functions. We test 2 standard functions to encode data, namely base64 and hex encoding.

Multiplication. Constant-time multiplication is necessary if the underlying processor does not provide a constant-time multiplication in its instruction set. Some hardware architectures [51] do not or only partially provide constant-time multiplications, so these operations must be emulated by software.

Oblivious RAM (ORAM). ORAM [48,57] provides a way to perform memory accesses in a data-oblivious way. The implementation provided by CTTK accesses each element in memory when performing a single memory access while arithmetically masking the result.

B Tested Building Blocks

We present building blocks designed to stress compiler optimizations and serve as ground truth for DOCC, each with data-oblivious and non-oblivious variants [66].

Array Lookup. Performs a secret-indexed lookup into a `uint32_t` array; the oblivious version accesses all elements and selects via arithmetic. Used in primitives like T-table AES.

String Comparison. Compares two-byte strings for equality; widely used and vulnerable to timing attacks [53].

Conditional Select. Selects one operand based on a condition; used to eliminate branches where `cmov` or inline assembly is unavailable.

Maximum of Integers. Computes the maximum of two numbers; commonly used in cryptographic code, such as BearSSL's `inner.h`.

References

1. Abel, A.: Automatic generation of models of microarchitectures (2020)
2. Acıiçmez, O., Seifert, J.P., Koç, C.K.: Predicting secret keys via branch prediction. In: CT-RSA (2007)
3. Andrysco, M., Kohlbrenner, D., Mowery, K., Jhala, R., Lerner, S., Shacham, H.: On subnormal floating point and abnormal timing. In: S&P (2015)
4. ARM.: mbed TLS (2020). https://tls.mbed.org
5. Aumasson, J.P.: Cryptocoding (2023). https://github.com/veorq/cryptocoding
6. Bae, D., Hwang, J., Ha, J.: Flush+ reload cache side-channel attack on block cipher aria. J. Korea Inst. Inf. Secur. Cryptology (2020)
7. Baldoni, R., Coppa, E., D'elia, D.C., Demetrescu, C., Finocchi, I.: A survey of symbolic execution techniques. CSUR (2018)
8. Barthe, G., et al.: High-assurance cryptography in the Spectre era. In: S&P (2021)
9. Barthe, G., Grégoire, B., Laporte, V.: Secure compilation of side-channel countermeasures: the case of cryptographic "constant-time". In: CSF (2018)
10. Ben Khadra, M.A., Stoffel, D., Kunz, W.: Efficient binary-level coverage analysis. In: FSE (2020)
11. Borrello, P., D'Elia, D.C., Querzoni, L., Giuffrida, C.: Constantine: automatic side-channel resistance using efficient control and data flow linearization. In: SIGSAC (2021)
12. Brumley, B.B., Tuveri, N.: Remote timing attacks are still practical. In: ESORICS (2011)
13. Canella, C., et al.: A systematic evaluation of transient execution attacks and defenses. In: USENIX Security (2019). extended classification tree and PoCs at https://transient.fail/
14. Cauligi, S., et al.: FaCT: a flexible, constant-time programming language. In: IEEE cybersecurity development (SecDev), pp. 69–76. IEEE (2017)
15. Cauligi, S., et al.: Constant-time foundations for the new spectre era. In: SIGPLAN (2020)
16. Daniel, L.A., Bardin, S., Rezk, T.: Binsec/rel: efficient relational symbolic execution for constant-time at binary-level. In: S&P (2020)
17. Denning, D.E.: A lattice model of secure information flow. ACM Commun. (1976)
18. Dinesh, S., Garrett-Grossman, G., Fletcher, C.W.: Synthct: towards portable constant-time code. In: NDSS (2022)
19. Dos Reis, G., Stroustrup, B., Merideth, A.: Axioms: semantics aspects of c++ concepts. ISO/IEC JTC1/WG21 doc (2009)

20. Duck, G.J., Gao, X., Roychoudhury, A.: Binary rewriting without control flow recovery. In: ACM SIGPLAN (2020)
21. Fletcher, C.W., Dijk, M.V., Devadas, S.: A secure processor architecture for encrypted computation on untrusted programs. In: STC (2012)
22. Fletchery, C.W., Ren, L., Yu, X., Van Dijk, M., Khan, O., Devadas, S.: Suppressing the oblivious ram timing channel while making information leakage and program efficiency trade-offs. In: HPCA (2014)
23. Framework, Q.: Quiling: a True Instrumentable Binary Emulation Framework (2024). https://github.com/qilingframework/qiling
24. Geimer, A., Vergnolle, M., Recoules, F., Daniel, L.A., Bardin, S., Maurice, C.: A systematic evaluation of automated tools for side-channel vulnerabilities detection in cryptographic libraries. In: SIGSAC (2023)
25. He, S., Emmi, M., Ciocarlie, G.: CT-FUZZ: fuzzing for timing leaks. In: ICST (2020)
26. Hunger, C., Kazdagli, M., Rawat, A., Dimakis, A., Vishwanath, S., Tiwari, M.: Understanding contention-based channels and using them for defense In: HPCA (2015)
27. Intel Corporation.: Pin - A Dynamic Binary Instrumentation Tool (2012). https://software.intel.com/en-us/articles/pin-a-dynamic-binary-instrumentation-tool
28. Intel Corporation.: Guidelines for Mitigating Timing Side Channels Against Cryptographic Implementations (2020). https://www.intel.com/content/www/us/en/developer/articles/technical/software-security-guidance/secure-coding/mitigate-timing-side-channel-crypto-implementation.html
29. Jancar, J., et al.: "they're not that hard to mitigate": What cryptographic library developers think about timing attacks. In: SP (2022)
30. Kaufmann, T., Pelletier, H., Vaudenay, S., Villegas, K.: When constant-time source yields variable-time binary: exploiting curve25519-donna built with MSVC. In: CANS (2016)
31. Kim, T., Peinado, M., Mainar-Ruiz, G.: "{STEALTHMEM}:{System-Level} protection against {Cache-Based} side channel attacks in the cloud. In: USENIX (2012)
32. King, J.C.: Symbolic execution and program testing. ACM Commun. (1976)
33. Kocher, P., et al.: Spectre attacks: exploiting speculative execution. In: S&P (2019)
34. Kocher, P.C.: Timing attacks on implementations of diffe-hellman, RSA, DSS, and other systems. In: CRYPTO (1996)
35. Kogler, A., et al.: Collide+power: leaking inaccessible data with software-based power side channels. In: USENIX Security (2023)
36. Langley, A.: Checking that functions are constant time with Valgrind (2023). https://github.com/agl/ctgrind
37. Lee, H.B., Jois, T.M., Fletcher, C.W., Gunter, C.A.: Dove: a data-oblivious virtual environment. arXiv preprint arXiv:2102.05195 (2021)
38. libsodium.: libsodium (2023). https://libsodium.org
39. Liu, C., Harris, A., Maas, M., Hicks, M., Tiwari, M., Shi, E.: Ghostrider: a hardware-software system for memory trace oblivious computation. SIGPLAN (2015)
40. Liu, C., Hicks, M., Shi, E.: Memory trace oblivious program execution. In: CSF (2013)
41. Maas, M., et al.: Phantom: practical oblivious computation in a secure processor. In: SIGSAC (2013)
42. Mangard, S., Oswald, E., Popp, T.: Power Analysis Attacks: Revealing the Secrets of Smart Cards. Springer Science & Business Media, Berlin and Heidelberg (2008)

43. N. I. of Standards and Technology. "Lightweight cryptography," (2023). https://csrc.nist.gov/projects/lightweight-cryptography
44. Oleksenko, O., Trach, B., Silberstein, M., Fetzer, C.: SpecFuzz: bringing spectre-type vulnerabilities to the surface. In: USENIX Security Symposium (2020)
45. OpenSSL.: OpenSSL: The Open Source toolkit for SSL/TLS (2019). http://www.openssl.org
46. OpenSSL.: OpenSSL RC5 implementation (2024). https://github.com/openssl/openssl/tree/master/crypto/rc5
47. Osvik, D.A., Shamir, A., Tromer, E.: Cache Attacks and Countermeasures: the Case of AES. In: CT-RSA (2006)
48. Pinkas, B., Reinman, T.: Oblivious ram revisited. In: CRYPTO (2010)
49. Pornin, T.: BearSSL: a smaller SSL/TLS library (2022). https://www.bearssl.org
50. Pornin, T.: Constant-time toolkit (2022). https://github.com/pornin/CTTK
51. Pornin, T.: Why Constant-Time Crypto? (2022). https://www.bearssl.org/constanttime.html
52. Rane, A., Lin, C., Tiwari, M.: Raccoon: closing digital {Side-Channels} through obfuscated execution. In: USENIX (2015)
53. Reparaz, O., Balasch, J., Verbauwhede, I.: Dude, is my code constant time?. In: DATE (2017)
54. Schneider, M., Lain, D., Puddu, I., Dutly, N., Capkun, S.: Breaking bad: how compilers break constant-time implementations. arXiv preprint arXiv:2410.13489 (2024)
55. Schneider, T., Moradi, A.: Leakage assessment methodology: a clear roadmap for side-channel evaluations. In: CHES (2015)
56. Shaon, F., Kantarcioglu, M., Lin, Z., Khan, L.: Sgx-bigmatrix: a practical encrypted data analytic framework with trusted processors. In: Proceedings of the 2017 ACM SIGSAC Conference on Computer and Communications Security (2017)
57. Shi, E., Chan, T.H.H., Stefanov, E., Li, M.: Oblivious ram with o ((log n) 3) worst-case cost. In: ASIACRYPT (2011)
58. Simon, L., Chisnall, D., Anderson, R.: What you get is what you c: controlling side effects in mainstream c compilers. In: EuroS&P (2018)
59. Soares, L., Pereira, F.M.Q.: Memory-safe elimination of side channels. In: CGO (2021)
60. Song, D.X., Wagner, D., Tian, X.: Timing analysis of keystrokes and timing attacks on SSH. In: USENIX Security Symposium (2001)
61. Weiser, S., Zankl, A., Spreitzer, R., Miller, K., Mangard, S., Sigl, G.: DATA - differential address trace analysis: finding address-based side-channels in binaries. In: USENIX Security Symposium (2018)
62. Wenzl, M., Merzdovnik, G., Ullrich, J., Weippl, E.: From hack to elaborate technique—a survey on binary rewriting. CSUR (2019)
63. Wichelmann, J., Moghimi, A., Eisenbarth, T., Sunar, B.: MicroWalk: a framework for finding side channels in binaries. In: ACSAC (2018)
64. Wichelmann, J., Sieck, F., Pätschke, A., Eisenbarth, T.: Microwalk-ci: practical side-channel analysis for javascript applications. In: SIGSAC (2022)
65. wolfSSL.: wolfSSL: Embedded TLS Library (2023). https://www.wolfssl.com/
66. Wu, M., Guo, S., Schaumont, P., Wang, C.: Eliminating timing side-channel leaks using program repair. In: ISSTA (2018)
67. Yarom, Y., Falkner, K.: Flush+Reload: a High Resolution, Low Noise, L3 Cache Side-Channel Attack. In: USENIX Security Symposium (2014)

68. Yu, J., Hsiung, L., El Hajj, M., Fletcher, C.W.: Data oblivious ISA extensions for side channel-resistant and high performance computing. Cryptology ePrint Archive (2018)
69. Zhao, X.J., Wang, T., Zheng, Y.: Cache Timing Attacks on Camellia Block Cipher (2009)

Machine Learning

PrivGNN: High-Performance Secure Inference for Cryptographic Graph Neural Networks

Fuyi Wang[1,2], Zekai Chen[3], Mingyuan Fan[4], Jianying Zhou[2], Lei Pan[1], and Leo Yu Zhang[5(✉)]

[1] Deakin University, Geelong, Australia
[2] Singapore University of Technology and Design, Singapore, Singapore
[3] Fuzhou University, Fuzhou, China
[4] East China Normal University, Shanghai, China
[5] Griffith University, Gold Coast, Australia
leo.zhang@griffith.edu.au

Abstract. Graph neural networks (GNNs) are powerful tools for analyzing and learning from graph-structured (GS) data, facilitating a wide range of services. Deploying such services in privacy-critical cloud environments necessitates the development of secure inference (SI) protocols that safeguard sensitive GS data. However, existing SI solutions largely focus on convolutional models for image and text data, leaving the challenge of securing GNNs and GS data relatively underexplored. In this work, we design, implement, and evaluate PrivGNN, a lightweight cryptographic scheme for graph-centric inference in the cloud. By hybridizing additive and function secret sharings within secure two-party computation (2PC), PrivGNN is carefully designed based on a series of novel 2PC interactive protocols that achieve $1.5\times \sim 1.7\times$ speedups for linear layers and $2\times \sim 15\times$ for non-linear layers over state-of-the-art (SotA) solutions. A thorough theoretical analysis is provided to prove PrivGNN's correctness, security, and lightweight nature. Extensive experiments across four datasets demonstrate PrivGNN's superior efficiency with $1.3\times \sim 4.7\times$ faster secure predictions while maintaining accuracy comparable to plaintext graph property inference.

Keywords: Function secret sharing · Additive secret sharing · Secure inference · Graph neural networks

1 Introduction

Recently, the rapid development of graph neural network (GNN) techniques has significantly impacted various domains such as drug discovery [18], social networks [33], and recommendation systems [17]. For example, pharmaceutical enterprises can train the specific GNNs [8] on known drug compounds to predict the binding potential of new molecules with target proteins, such as those related to cancer. These well-trained GNNs can then be offered as AI-driven services on a pay-as-you-go basis, allowing end-users to enhance drug discovery or analyze complex molecular data. However, graph-structured (GS) data often represents sensitive and proprietary information, making end-users hesitant to outsource it to service providers due to privacy concerns. Also, highly specialized GNNs for graph-centric services are considered valuable intellectual property and should be protected against leakage while circumventing reverse engineering risks [34].

In response to these concerns, privacy-preserving deep learning (PPDL) schemes have been developed to enable secure inference (SI) using cryptographic techniques such as homomorphic encryption (HE) [25] and/or multi-party computation (MPC) [9]. However, HE-based schemes often suffer from heavy computational and communication overhead due to inefficient exponentiation and ciphertext expansion. As a result, recent efforts focus on leveraging MPC [9] for SI with secret-shared neural networks (NNs) and inputs, offering a more efficient alternative [22]. Advanced SI solutions [13,30,36], have successfully secured convolutional neural networks (CNNs) for unstructured data (e.g., images and text). However, SI of GNNs in the cloud for complex GS data, while explored in some initial studies [26,28,33,35], remains relatively underdeveloped.

Related Works and Challenges. Existing cryptographic GNN approaches primarily introduce HE [26,28] and MPC [33] to secure node features in graph data. However, they do not fully protect the relational structure of graphs, such as the maximum node degree [33] and the range of node degrees [28] (**Challenge** ①). For instance, while SecGNN [33] optimizes node representation by reducing the adjacency matrix size from $\mathcal{O}(N^2)$ to $\mathcal{O}(N \cdot d_{max})$—resulting in over 90% reduction for real-world datasets—it leaks the maximum degree d_{max} in the graph. Moreover, these approaches [26,28,33] often rely on cryptographic primitives that are computationally and communication-intensive, particularly for non-linear operations (**Challenge** ②). Non-linear operations, such as ReLU, implemented with primitives like garbled circuits in MPC or HE, are several orders of magnitude more expensive than linear layers in computation and communication [37]. While some optimizations have been proposed for non-linear operations [13,30,37], these approaches often impose heavy online computational burdens or require multiple communication rounds. Such constraints pose challenges to scalability and efficiency for real-world graph data containing millions or even billions of nodes and edges. Lastly, recent efforts like SecMPNN [18] and OblivGNN [35] optimize non-linear operations via lightweight secret sharing primitives in a fully outsourced setting, where a group of cloud servers jointly perform SI over encrypted/shared GNNs and inputs. However, this setup raises concerns about cloud-server collusion, relying on a strong non-collusion assumption for security models (**Challenge** ③). SecMPNN [18] also requires continuous third-party assistance during online phases, adding additional complexity.

To tackle the above challenges, we design, implement, and evaluate PrivGNN, a high-performance cryptographic scheme for secure GNN inference with a client-server setup. In this secure two-party computation (2PC) setup, PrivGNN distributes the SI workload between the client and the service provider, mitigating cloud-collusion risks and enhancing security. To improve efficiency, PrivGNN employs lightweight additive secret sharing (AddSS) and function secret sharing (FuncSS) in an offline-online paradigm, significantly reducing the computational overhead during the online phase. By carefully designing the offline phase, the online phase is reduced to only one round of interaction with lightweight computation. Specifically, we develop and optimize a line of secure protocols for both linear and non-linear computations. These protocols integrate seamlessly into various layers across various graph-centric services, reducing the online SI latency. In summary, our contributions are threefold.

- We present PrivGNN, a fast SI scheme for graph-centric services via the delicate synergy of GNNs and cryptography. PrivGNN employs lightweight AddSS to securely protect the graph structure, node features, and well-trained GNNs, without relying on a strong non-collusion assumption in the 2PC setup.
- With AddSS and FuncSS, we propose a set of secure protocols for multiplication, comparison-based activations, and sigmoidal activation variants. Our designs shift the computational-intensive operations to the offline phase and streamline online communication with only one-round interaction.
- We formally prove the correctness, efficiency, and security of PrivGNN. We conduct extensive experiments showing that our protocols outperform SotA works. Results on various datasets highlight PrivGNN's efficiency and scalability in applications like image classification and molecular property recognition.

2 Preliminaries

Additive Secret Sharing (AddSS) [6] divides a secret message over the plaintext space into multiple shares, each of which is distributed to different parties. AddSS's key property is that the shares can be combined (added) together to reconstruct the original secret, while no individual shareholder possesses adequate information to determine the secret message independently. This paper adopts the 2-out-of-2 AddSS over the ring $\mathbb{Z}_{2^l}$ and the definition is given below.

Definition 1. *A 2-out-of-2 AddSS scheme over the ring $\mathbb{Z}_{2^l}$ is a pair of probabilistic polynomial-time (PPT) algorithms* {Share, Reconstruct} *where*

- Share: *On the secret message $x \in \mathbb{Z}_{2^l}$, Share outputs shares $\{\langle x \rangle_0, \langle x \rangle_1\} \in \mathbb{Z}_{2^l}$, s.j. $x = \langle x \rangle_0 + \langle x \rangle_1 \pmod{2^l}$.*
- Reconstruct: *With 2 shares $\{\langle x \rangle_0, \langle x \rangle_1\} \in \mathbb{Z}_{2^l}$, Reconstruct outputs x over the plaintext space $\mathbb{Z}$.*

In the case of $l > 1$ (e.g., $l = 32$) which supports arithmetic operations (e.g., addition and multiplication), the arithmetic share pair is denoted by $\langle \cdot \rangle_\gamma$ ($\gamma \in \{0,1\}$). In the case of $l = 1$ which supports Boolean operations XOR ($\oplus$), NOT ($\neg$) and AND ($\otimes$), the Boolean share pair is denoted by $[\cdot]_\gamma$. In the following, we assume all arithmetic operations to be performed in the ring $\mathbb{Z}_{2^l}$ (i.e., all arithmetic operations are mod 2^l).

Function Secret Sharing (FuncSS) [3,4] within the 2PC setup divides a function $f : \mathbb{G}_{in} \to \mathbb{G}_{out}$ into 2 shares $\{f_0, f_1\}$, where $\mathbb{G}_{in}$ and $\mathbb{G}_{out}$ are input and output groups. Each party receives one of the function shares, and for any input x, there exists $f_0(x) + f_1(x) = f(x)$. The definition of FuncSS is given below.

Definition 2. *A 2PC FuncSS scheme over the ring $\mathbb{Z}_{2^l}$ is a pair of algorithms $\{\texttt{Gen}, \texttt{Eval}\}$ where*

- Gen: *With the security parameter κ and a function f, the PPT key generation algorithm $\texttt{Gen}(1^\kappa, f)$ outputs a pair of keys $\{k_0, k_1\}$, where each key implicitly represents $f_\gamma : \mathbb{G}_{in} \to \mathbb{G}_{out}$.*
- Eval: *With the party identifier $\gamma \in \{0,1\}$, the key k_γ (key defining f_γ), and the public input $x \in \mathbb{Z}_{2^l}$, the PPT evaluation algorithm $\texttt{Eval}(\gamma, k_\gamma, x)$ outputs $y_\gamma \in \mathbb{Z}_{2^l}$, i.e., the value of $f_\gamma(x)$, where $f(x) = \sum_{\gamma=0}^{1} y_\gamma$.*

3 System Overview

System Model. We consider the SI scenario with a client-server setup, where the client $\mathcal{C}$ (e.g., a drug laboratory) holds private GS data D, and the server $\mathcal{S}$ possesses a well-trained GNN model $\mathcal{N}$ with private weights W, illustrated in Fig. 1. $\mathcal{C}$ intends to utilize the model $\mathcal{N}(W, \cdot)$ to facilitate accurate results on its data D (i.e., $\mathcal{N}(W, D)$), while ensuring that $\mathcal{C}$'s data remains confidential. We regard $\gamma \in \{0,1\}$ as the identifier of a party, $\gamma = 0$ represents $\mathcal{C}$ and $\mathcal{S}$ otherwise. Specifically, ① To ensure the privacy of raw graph D, $\mathcal{C}$ uses AddSS to split D into two shares (i.e., $D = \langle D \rangle_0 + \langle D \rangle_1$), then sends the share $\langle D \rangle_1$ to $\mathcal{S}$ to issue a SI query. ② $\mathcal{C}$ and $\mathcal{S}$ collaboratively take charge of SI tasks via utilizing a series of secure computation protocols in PrivGNN. ③ After execution of PrivGNN, $\mathcal{S}$ returns the shared inference result $\langle O \rangle_1$ to $\mathcal{C}$. ④ Upon receiving $\langle O \rangle_1$, the client $\mathcal{C}$ reconstructs to get the final plaintext result via $O = \langle O \rangle_0 + \langle O \rangle_1$ to complete the prediction and inference services.

Threat Model. We assume that $\mathcal{C}$ and $\mathcal{S}$ in PrivGNN are semi-honest, i.e., they honestly obey the specification of the protocols, yet attempt to learn auxiliary information from intermediate shares. Non-collusion is unnecessary to assume, as collusion would imply a willingness to disclose their private data. The service provider (i.e., $\mathcal{S}$), operated by reputable vendors like Google, is incentivized to follow the protocols, as poor performance or violations of privacy regulations

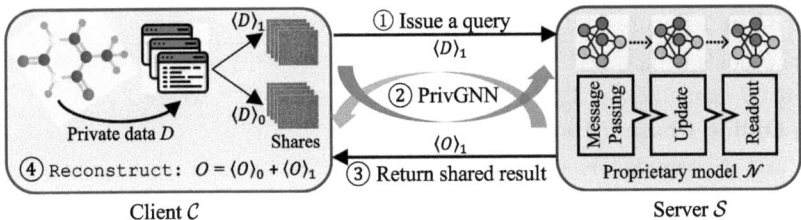

Fig. 1. A client-server secure inference scenario.

would have an irreversible negative impact on their credibility and profitability. Therefore, the semi-honest assumption is practical, as witnessed in existing secure outsourcing works [5,18,24,30,33]. We define security in the real/ideal world. In the real world, protocol $\prod$ is executed, yielding the output $\mathsf{Real}^{\prod}_{\mathcal{A}}(1^\kappa)$, while in the ideal world, the ideal functionality $\mathcal{F}$ is executed by a trusted third party, yielding the output $\mathsf{Ideal}^{\mathcal{F}}_{\mathsf{Sim}}(1^\kappa)$. Here, $\mathcal{A}$ is a stateful adversary, Sim is a stateful simulator, and $\kappa \in \mathbb{N}^+$ is the security parameter.

Definition 3. *Let $\mathcal{F} = \{\mathcal{F}_0, \mathcal{F}_1\}$ be a ideal-world function and $\prod$ be a real-world protocol computing $\mathcal{F}$. For any PPT adversary $\mathcal{A}$ in the real world, there exists a PPT simulator Sim in the ideal world, such that for corrupted party $\mathcal{P} \subset \{\mathcal{S}, \mathcal{C}\}$*

$$\mathsf{Ideal}^{\mathcal{F}}_{\mathsf{Sim}_\mathcal{P}}(1^\kappa, D, W) \equiv_c \mathsf{Real}^{\prod}_{\mathcal{A}_\mathcal{P}}(1^\kappa, D, W). \tag{1}$$

where $\equiv_c$ denotes computational indistinguishability against PPT adversaries except for a negligible advantage.

4 Our Approach

PrivGNN introduces the offline-online paradigm to minimize the online communication rounds and computational costs. This paradigm alleviates the computational burden on resource-constrained clients during the online phase, effectively enhancing the client experience. To achieve lightweight online performance, we use AddSS and FuncSS to design multiplication, quadratic polynomial, comparison protocols. In these protocols, the computational-intensive cryptographic operations, i.e., $\mathsf{Gen}^{\mathsf{BV}}$ for generating Beaver multiplication triples [2] and $\mathsf{Gen}^{\mathsf{key}}$ for generating FuncSS keys [4], are performed during the data-independent offline phase. These operations can be implemented using either a trusted third party [3,11,36] or specific 2PC protocols [5,23]. This paper opts for the former one. All these protocols integrate seamlessly into NN layers.

4.1 Secure Matrix Multiplication Protocol

Given the secret-shared $\langle X \rangle$ and the server's plaintext Y for secure matrix multiplication protocol SMatMul (i.e., $\langle Z \rangle = \langle X \times Y \rangle$), the key insight is that the

Algorithm 1 Secure Matrix Multiplication Protocol

Input: $\mathcal{C}$ holds $\langle X \rangle_0 \in \mathbb{Z}_{2^l}^{m_1 \times m_2}$. $\mathcal{S}$ holds $\langle X \rangle_1 \in \mathbb{Z}_{2^l}^{m_1 \times m_2}$, $Y \in \mathbb{Z}_{2^l}^{m_2 \times m_3}$.
Output: $\mathcal{C}$ learns $\langle Z \rangle_0 \in \mathbb{Z}_{2^l}^{m_1 \times m_3}$. $\mathcal{S}$ learns $\langle Z \rangle_1 \in \mathbb{Z}_{2^l}^{m_1 \times m_3}$, where $Z = X \times Y$.
 # Offline Phase: $\langle A \times Y \rangle$
1: $\mathcal{C}$ and $\mathcal{S}$ sample $A \xleftarrow{\$} \mathbb{Z}_{2^l}^{m_1 \times m_2}, B \xleftarrow{\$} \mathbb{Z}_{2^l}^{m_2 \times m_3}$, and then jointly invoke $\text{Gen}^{\text{BV}}(A, B) \to \{\langle C \rangle_0, \langle C \rangle_1\}$, where $C = A \times B$.
2: $\mathcal{S}$ computes $Y - B$ and sends its result to $\mathcal{C}$ and sets $\langle A \times Y \rangle_1 = \langle C \rangle_1$.
3: $\mathcal{C}$ computes $\langle A \times Y \rangle_0 = A \times (Y - B) + \langle C \rangle_0$.
 # Online Phase: $\langle X \times Y \rangle$
4: $\mathcal{C}$ computes $\langle X \rangle_0 - A$ and sends its result to $\mathcal{S}$. $\mathcal{C}$ sets $\langle Z \rangle_0 = \langle A \times Y \rangle_0$.
5: $\mathcal{S}$ computes $\langle Z \rangle_1 = (X - A) \times Y + \langle C \rangle_1 = (\langle X \rangle_0 + \langle X \rangle_1 - A) \times Y + \langle C \rangle_1$.

output $\langle Z \rangle$ and client's input $\langle X \rangle$ are secret-shared, while variable Y is the plaintext held by the server $\mathcal{S}$. We reformulate $X \times Y \to (X - A) \times Y + A \times Y$, where A is randomness held by the client $\mathcal{C}$. Thus, SMatMul's offline phase focuses on precomputing the shares of $A \times Y$, and then the online phase evaluates $(X - A) \times Y$ in plaintext by $\mathcal{S}$. Compared with [11,23], SMatMul reduces *one* unnecessary auxiliary randomness r, eliminating r-related offline computation and minimizing pseudorandom generator usage. Algorithm 1 presents the main steps and the details of SMatMul are described below.

- The offline phase aims to learn the shared $A \times Y$. Specifically, client and server sample A and B randomly, respectively, and then jointly invoke $\text{Gen}^{\text{BV}}(A, B)$ to generate matrix multiplication triples $\{A, \langle C \rangle_0\}$ for client and $\{B, \langle C \rangle_1\}$ for server, where $\langle C \rangle_0 + \langle C \rangle_1 = A \times B$. After that, the server sends $Y - B$ to the client. Next, the client locally compute $\langle A \times Y \rangle_0 = A \times (Y - B) + \langle C \rangle_0$ and the server sets $\langle A \times Y \rangle_1 = \langle C \rangle_1$.
- The online phase aims to learn the final shared $X \times Y$. The client computes $\langle X \rangle_0 - A$ and sends its result to the server. Finally, the client holds $\langle X \times Y \rangle_0 = \langle A \times Y \rangle_0$ directly and the server learns $\langle X \times Y \rangle_1 = (\langle X \rangle_0 + \langle X \rangle_1 - A) \times Y + \langle C \rangle_1$.

Secure Element-Wise Multiplication Protocol. Algorithm 1 is applicable for secure element-wise multiplication protocol SEleMul, with the modification of replacing matrix multiplication $\times$ with element-wise multiplication $\odot$, while ensuring that the sizes of X, Y, A, and B remain the same: $\langle Z \rangle = \text{SEleMul}(\langle X \rangle, Y)$, where $\langle z_{i,j} \rangle = \text{SMatMul}(\langle x_{i,j} \rangle, y_{i,j})$.

Secure Fully-Connected and Convolutional Layers. A fully-connected layer SecFC in NNs is essentially a matrix multiplication, thus SecFC is implemented directly using SMatMul: $\text{SecFC}(\langle D \rangle, W) = \text{SMatMul}(\langle D \rangle, W)$. A convolutional layer SecCONV can be expressed as a matrix multiplication with the help of reshape techniques [15]: $\text{SecCONV}(\langle D \rangle, W) = \text{ReshapeOutput}(\text{SMatMul}(\text{Reshape}(\text{Input}(\langle D \rangle), \text{ReshapeFilter}(W)))$.

4.2 Secure Quadratic Polynomial Protocol

We initially propose the secure quadratic polynomial protocol SQuaPol, which computes $z = p_2x^2 + p_1x + p_0$. In this protocol, both parties, $\mathcal{C}$ and $\mathcal{S}$, hold secret-shared inputs $\langle x \rangle$ and outputs $\langle z \rangle$, while $\mathcal{S}$ possesses the plaintext coefficients p_0, p_1, p_2. We then extend SQuaPol to support polynomials of arbitrary degrees. Inspired by the customized SMatMul in Sect. 4.1, we have the insight of the following reformulation:

$$\begin{aligned} z &= p_2x^2 + p_1x + p_0 = p_2(x-a+a)^2 + p_1(x-a+a) + p_0 \quad \triangleright f \leftarrow x-a \\ &= p_2(f+a)^2 + p_1(f+a) + p_0 = p_2 f^2 + \underline{p_2 a^2} + \underline{2p_2 a}f + p_1 f + \underline{p_1 a} + p_0, \end{aligned} \quad (2)$$

where a is the randomness held by the client $\mathcal{C}$ which is independent of the input x. Hence, SQuaPol can be efficiently divided into online and offline phases. The offline phase, which performs the computations labeled with underline in Eq. 2, is precomputed without knowing the input x, reducing the computational burden during the online phase. In the online phase, the client and server only need to compute the shared value f with minimal interaction, requiring just one round of communication and one message per party. This design significantly reduces both online communication overhead and latency, highlighting the efficiency and practicality of PrivGNN. Algorithm 2 presents the details of SQuaPol and the main steps are given below.

- The offline phase aims to learn the shared $\langle p_2 a^2 \rangle_\gamma$, $\langle 2p_2 a \rangle_\gamma$, $\langle p_1 a \rangle_\gamma$ ($\gamma \in \{0,1\}$) and precompute the parameter on the server side, which is used in the online phase of $\langle 2p_2 af \rangle$ in Eq. 2. Therefore, four sets of multiplication triples need to be generated by invoking Gen^{BV} four times.
- During the online phase, after one communication round, the client computes $\langle z \rangle_0 \leftarrow \langle p_2 a^2 \rangle_0 + 2(\underbrace{(a_4(e_4 + f_5) + \langle c_4 \rangle_0)}_{\langle p_2 af \rangle_0}) + \langle p_1 a \rangle_0$ and the server computes $\langle z \rangle_1 \leftarrow p_2(\underbrace{f_5 + \langle x \rangle_1}_{f})^2 + \langle p_2 a^2 \rangle_1 + 2(\underbrace{(f_5 + \langle x \rangle_1)(f_4 + \langle p_2 a \rangle_1) + \langle c_4 \rangle_1)}_{\langle p_2 af \rangle_1} + p_1(\underbrace{f_5 + \langle x \rangle_1}_{f}) + \langle p_1 a \rangle_1 + p_0$.

Extension to Higher-Degree Polynomials. Considering a d-degree polynomial $z = \sum_{i=0}^{d} p_i x^i \to \sum_{i=0}^{d} p_i (f+a)^i$, where $f = x - a$. We can use the binomial theorem [19] $((f+a)^i = \sum_{k=0}^{i} \binom{i}{k} a^k f^{i-k})$, then we obtain:

$$z = \sum_{i=0}^{d} p_i (f+a)^i = \sum_{i=0}^{d} \sum_{k=0}^{i} \binom{i}{k} p_i a^k f^{i-k}. \quad (3)$$

The secure computation rationale for Eq. 3 follows the same pattern as that of Eq. 2, with the protocol being divided into offline and online phases. Likewise, the underlined parts can be computed during the offline phase, where the

Algorithm 2 Secure Quadratic Polynomial Protocol

Input: $\mathcal{C}$ holds $\langle x \rangle_0 \in \mathbb{Z}_{2^l}$. $\mathcal{S}$ holds $\langle x \rangle_1 \in \mathbb{Z}_{2^l}$, $p_0, p_1, p_2 \in \mathbb{Z}_{2^l}$.
Output: $\mathcal{C}$ learns $\langle z \rangle_0$. $\mathcal{S}$ learns $\langle z \rangle_1$, where $z = p_2 x^2 + p_1 x + p_0$.

\# **Offline Phase:** $\langle p_2 a^2 \rangle$, $\langle p_2 a \rangle$, $\langle p_1 a \rangle$,

1: $\mathcal{C}$ and $\mathcal{S}$ sample $\{a, a_1, a_2, a_3, a_4\} \xleftarrow{\$} \mathbb{Z}_{2^l}^5$, $\{b_1, b_2, b_3, b_4\} \xleftarrow{\$} \mathbb{Z}_{2^l}^4$, and then jointly invoke $\text{Gen}^{\text{BV}}(a_i, b_i)$ ($\forall i \in \{1, 2, 3, 4\}$) to generate triples $\{a_i, \langle c_i \rangle_0\}$ for $\mathcal{C}$ and $\{b_i, \langle c_i \rangle_1\}$ for $\mathcal{S}$, where $c_i = a_i b_i$.
2: $\mathcal{S}$ computes $e_1 \leftarrow p_1 - b_1, e_2 \leftarrow p_2 - b_2, e_3 \leftarrow p_2 - b_3$, and sends $e = \{e_1, e_2, e_3\}$ to $\mathcal{C}$.
3: $\mathcal{C}$ computes $\langle p_1 a \rangle_0 \leftarrow a_1 e_1 + \langle c_1 \rangle_0, \langle p_2 a \rangle_0 \leftarrow a_2 e_2 + \langle c_2 \rangle_0, \langle p_2 a^2 \rangle_0 \leftarrow a_3 e_3 + \langle c_3 \rangle_0$, $f_1 \leftarrow a - a_1, f_2 \leftarrow a - a_2, f_3 \leftarrow a^2 - a_3, f_4 = \langle p_2 a \rangle_0 - a_4$, and sends $f = \{f_1, f_2, f_3, f_4\}$ to $\mathcal{S}$.
4: $\mathcal{S}$ computes $\langle p_1 a \rangle_1 \leftarrow p_1 f_1 + \langle c_1 \rangle_1, \langle p_2 a \rangle_1 \leftarrow p_2 f_2 + \langle c_2 \rangle_1, \langle p_2 a^2 \rangle_1 \leftarrow p_2 f_3 + \langle c_3 \rangle_1$.
\# **Online Phase:**
5: $\mathcal{S}$ computes $e_4 \leftarrow \langle x \rangle_1 - b_4$ and sends e_4 to $\mathcal{C}$.
  $\mathcal{C}$ computes $f_5 \leftarrow \langle x \rangle_0 - a$ and sends f_5 to $\mathcal{S}$.
6: $\mathcal{S}$ computes $\langle z \rangle_1 \leftarrow p_2 (f_5 + \langle x \rangle_1)^2 + \langle p_2 a^2 \rangle_1 + 2((f_5 + \langle x \rangle_1)(f_4 + \langle p_2 a \rangle_1) + \langle c_4 \rangle_1) + p_1 (f_5 + \langle x \rangle_1) + \langle p_1 a \rangle_1 + p_0$.
  $\mathcal{C}$ computes $\langle z \rangle_0 \leftarrow \langle p_2 a^2 \rangle_0 + 2(a_4 (e_4 + f_5) + \langle c_4 \rangle_0) + \langle p_1 a \rangle_0$.

---

client learns $\langle \binom{i}{k} p_i a^k \rangle_0$ and the server learns $\langle \binom{i}{k} p_i a^k \rangle_1$ ($\forall i \in \{1, 2, \cdots, d\}, k \in \{1, 2, \cdots, i\}$). In the online phase, the server reconstructs the plaintext f marked by a. At the end, only one-round online communication suffices to securely compute the arbitrary degree polynomial $\langle z \rangle = \sum_{i=0}^{d} \langle p_i x^i \rangle$.

4.3 Secure DReLU Protocol

Secure DReLU protocol SDReLU builds upon the FuncSS-based distributed comparison function $\mathcal{F}_{a,b}^{\text{cmp}}$ [3,14], that is, $\mathcal{F}_{a,b}^{\text{cmp}}(x) = b$ if $x < a$; otherwise, $\mathcal{F}_{a,b}^{\text{cmp}}(x) = 0$. Recall from Sect. 2, the two-party $\mathcal{F}_{a,b}^{\text{cmp}}$ involves a pair of algorithms: $\text{Gen}^<(a, b)$ and $\text{Eval}^<(\gamma, k_\gamma, x)$. $\text{Gen}^<(a, b)$ creates two keys k_0, k_1, then two parties learn the shared results $\mathcal{F}_\gamma^{\text{cmp}} \leftarrow \text{Eval}^<(\gamma, k_\gamma, x)$ of $\mathcal{F}_{a,b}^{\text{cmp}}(x)$. There are two challenges in employing $\mathcal{F}_{a,b}^{\text{cmp}}$ for SDReLU. *Challenge 1*: As x is in secret-shared form and needs to remain confidential, calling $\text{Eval}^>(\gamma, k_\gamma, x)$ by two parties poses a dilemma. *Challenge 2*: $\mathcal{F}_{a,b}^{\text{cmp}}$ is designed for less-than comparisons, whereas PrivGNN requires greater-than comparisons, as seen in layers like ReLU's comparison of x against 0 or maxpool's selection of the maximum value. Therefore, we made modifications to seamlessly integrate FuncSS-based $\mathcal{F}_{a,b}^{\text{cmp}}$ for efficient comparison of secret-shared data in PrivGNN. We present our approach below.

Addressing Challenge 1. For a signed l-bit $x \in \mathbb{Z}_{2^l}$, DReLU(x) is defined as:

$$\text{DReLU}(x) = 1\{x < 2^{l-1}\} = 1 \oplus \text{MSB}(x). \tag{4}$$

We first define an offset function $f^a(x) = f(x - a)$ and establish the FuncSS-centric scheme accordingly, where $a \xleftarrow{\$} \mathbb{Z}_{2^l}$ is randomly generated by $\mathcal{C}$ in $\mathbb{Z}_{2^l}$.

Specifically, $\mathcal{C}$ possesses the offset value of the input x and reveals the offset/masked input $x + a \to \hat{x}$. The FuncSS keys are subsequently computed for $f^a(x+a)$, which is essentially equivalent to evaluating $f(x)$ on x. Accordingly, the offset function of Eq. 4 can be formulated as:

$$\mathrm{DReLU}^{a,c}(\hat{x}) = \mathrm{DReLU}(\hat{x} - a \pmod{2^l}) = \mathrm{MSB}\left(\hat{x} - a \pmod{2^l}\right) \oplus 1 \oplus c.$$

where a and c are the input and output masks.

Addressing Challenge 2. Inspired by CrypTFlow2 [30], for shared $\langle x \rangle_0$ and $\langle x \rangle_1$ with $\langle y \rangle_0 = \langle x \rangle_0 \pmod{2^{l-1}}$ and $\langle y \rangle_1 = \langle x \rangle_1 \pmod{2^{l-1}}$, we reformulate $\mathrm{MSB}(x)$ as: $\mathrm{MSB}(x) = \mathrm{MSB}(\langle x \rangle_0) \oplus \mathrm{MSB}(\langle x \rangle_1) \oplus 1 \left\{ 2^{l-1} - \langle y \rangle_0 - 1 < \langle y \rangle_1 \right\}$. Then, we set $\langle x \rangle_0 = \hat{x} = x + a$ and $\langle x \rangle_1 = 2^l - a$, we learn:

$$\mathrm{DReLU}^{a,c}(\hat{x}) = \mathrm{MSB}(\hat{x}) \oplus 1 \left\{ 2^{l-1} - \langle y \rangle_0 - 1 < \langle y \rangle_1 \right\} \oplus \underline{\mathrm{MSB}\left(2^l - a\right) \oplus 1} \oplus c. \quad (5)$$

Hence, SDReLU is divided into online and offline phases, where the computations in the offline phase of Eq. 5 are labeled with underline as these are independent of the input x. Simultaneously, keys are prepared for online $\mathrm{Eval}^<$ (i.e., $\mathcal{F}^{\mathrm{cmp}}_{\langle y \rangle_1, 1}(2^{l-1} - \langle y \rangle_0 - 1)$) by invoking $\mathrm{Gen}^<$. In the online phase, through only one communication round, $\mathcal{C}$ and $\mathcal{S}$ jointly recover the plaintext $\hat{x}$ for $\mathcal{S}$ learning $\mathrm{MSB}(\hat{x})$. Meanwhile, with $\langle y \rangle_0 \leftarrow \hat{x} \pmod{2^{l-1}}$, $\mathcal{C}$ and $\mathcal{S}$ learn the Boolean-shared $1 \left\{ 2^{l-1} - \langle y \rangle_0 - 1 < \langle y \rangle_1 \right\}$ locally based on the respective key. Algorithm 3 presents the SDReLU protocol's main steps for executing $\mathrm{DReLU}^{a,c}(\hat{x})$.

Secure ReLU Layer. $\mathrm{ReLU}(x)$ can be expressed as $\mathrm{ReLU}(x) = x \cdot \mathrm{DReLU}(x)$. To learn the result of secure ReLU layer SecReLU over the secret-shared $\langle x \rangle$, $\mathcal{C}$ and $\mathcal{S}$ learn $[z] \leftarrow \mathrm{SDReLU}(\langle x \rangle)$ first and then multiply $[z]$ to $\langle x \rangle$: $\mathrm{SecReLU}(\langle x \rangle) \leftarrow [z] \cdot \langle x \rangle$. However, direct multiplication of arithmetic shares $\langle x \rangle$ and Boolean shares $[z]$ is not feasible due to their calculation with different moduli. Various approaches tackle this issue by converting Boolean to arithmetic shares, typically requiring two rounds of online communication (i.e., one for conversion and another for multiplication). Upon investigation, SBitXA protocol (Algorithm 1 in FssNN [36]) reduces this to one round, with only $n + 1$ bits of online communication per party. In this work, we leverage SBitXA as a black box to learn $\mathrm{SecReLU}(\langle x \rangle) \leftarrow \mathrm{SBitXA}(\langle x \rangle, [z])$.

Secure Max Pool Layer. The rationale of secure max pool layer SecMaxPool in NNs is to select the maximum value from n^2 shared elements with an $(n \times n)$-width pooling window. Given two elements $\langle x \rangle$ and $\langle y \rangle$, we reduce SecMaxPool to SecReLU according to below equation:

$$\begin{aligned}
\max(\langle x \rangle, \langle y \rangle) &= x \cdot 1\left\{\langle x \rangle > \langle y \rangle\right\} + y \cdot (1 - 1\left\{\langle x \rangle > \langle y \rangle\right\}) \\
&= (\langle x \rangle - \langle y \rangle) \cdot 1\left\{\langle x \rangle - \langle y \rangle > 0\right\} + \langle y \rangle.
\end{aligned} \quad (6)$$

Algorithm 3 Secure DReLU Protocol

Input: $\mathcal{C}$ holds $\langle x \rangle_0 \in \mathbb{Z}_{2^l}$. $\mathcal{S}$ holds $\langle x \rangle_1 \in \mathbb{Z}_{2^l}$.
Output: $\mathcal{C}$ learns $\langle z \rangle_0 \in \mathbb{Z}_2$. $\mathcal{S}$ learns $\langle z \rangle_1 \in \mathbb{Z}_2$, where $z = \text{DReLU}(x)$.

\# **Offline Phase:** $\text{Gen}^{\text{DReLU}}$
1: Sample $\langle a \rangle_0, \langle a \rangle_1 \xleftarrow{\$} \mathbb{Z}_{2^l}, b \leftarrow 1$, and $a = \langle a \rangle_0 + \langle a \rangle_1 \pmod{2}^l$
2: Let $\langle x \rangle_1 = 2^l - a \in \mathbb{Z}_{2^l}$, $\langle y \rangle_1 = 2^l - a \pmod{2^{l-1}} \in \mathbb{Z}_{2^{l-1}}$.
3: $\{\tilde{k}_0, \tilde{k}_1\} \leftarrow \text{Gen}^{<}(1^\kappa, \langle y \rangle_1, b)$.
4: Sample a Boolean randomness $c \xleftarrow{\$} \mathbb{Z}_2$.
5: Let $r = c \oplus \left\lfloor \frac{\langle x \rangle_1}{2^{l-1}} \right\rfloor \oplus 1$.
6: Sample $[r]_0, [r]_1 \leftarrow \mathbb{Z}_2$, s.t., $[r]_0 \oplus [r]_1 = r$.
7: $\forall \gamma \in \{0, 1\}, k_\gamma = \tilde{k}_\gamma \| [r]_\gamma$.
8: **Return** $\{\langle a \rangle_\gamma, k_\gamma\}$

\# **Online Phase:** $\text{Eval}^{\text{DReLU}}$
9: $\forall \gamma \in \{0, 1\}$, parse $k_\gamma = \tilde{k}_\gamma \| [r]_\gamma$.
10: $\mathcal{C}$ computes $\langle f \rangle_0 \leftarrow \langle x \rangle_0 + \langle a \rangle_0$ and sends $\langle f \rangle_0$ to $\mathcal{S}$.
11: $\mathcal{S}$ computes $\langle f \rangle_1 \leftarrow \langle x \rangle_1 + \langle a \rangle_1$ and sends $\langle f \rangle_1$ to $\mathcal{C}$.
12: $\mathcal{C}$ and $\mathcal{S}$ recover $f \leftarrow \langle f \rangle_0 + \langle f \rangle_1 \pmod{2^{l-1}}$.
13: $\forall \gamma \in \{0, 1\}, [\tilde{z}]_\gamma \leftarrow \text{Eval}^{<}(\gamma, \tilde{k}_\gamma, 2^{l-1} - f - 1)$.
14: $\forall \gamma \in \{0, 1\}, [z]_\gamma \leftarrow \gamma \left\lfloor \frac{x+a}{2^{l-1}} \right\rfloor \oplus [r]_\gamma \oplus [\tilde{z}]_\gamma$.

The underlined part in Eq. 6 can be learned by invoking SecReLU protocol. Hence, SecMaxPool can be achieved by invoking SecReLU $(n^2 - 1)$ times for each $(n \times n)$-width pooling window.

4.4 Secure Piecewise Polynomials Protocol

Sigmoidal activations in NNs pose challenges in 2PC due to the computational complexity of exponentiation and reciprocal, especially when working with blinded exponents. It is well-known that such activations can be approximated using piecewise continuous polynomials with negligible accuracy loss [20]. However, existing methods efficiently handle only low-degree polynomials, limiting approximation accuracy. To address this, we introduce a secure piecewise polynomial protocol SPiePol, that can be computed by our computational- and communication-saving designs. Given a piecewise polynomial function:

$$P(x) = P_1(x)\mathbf{1}_{x \in (-\infty, e_1)} + P_2(x)\mathbf{1}_{x \in [e_1, e_2)} + \cdots + P_k(x)\mathbf{1}_{x \in [e_{k-1}, \infty)}, \quad (7)$$

where $P_i(x) = p_{i0} + p_{i1}x + \ldots + p_{id}x^d$ ($\forall i \in \{1, \cdots, k\}$) is a d-degree polynomial applied to different intervals of x. The indicator function $\mathbf{1}_{x \in [e_{i-1}, e_i)}$ ensures that each polynomial $P_i(x)$ is active only within its designated interval $[e_{i-1}, e_i)$. The k piecewise polynomials in $P(x)$ are transformed into a construction by DReLU (Eq. 8), where each polynomial $P_i(x)$ is activated by an indicator s_i. For example, $P_2(x)$ in Eq. 7 is activated when $e_1 \leq x < e_2$, i.e., $s_2 = 1$ and all other indicators are "0". The indicator s_2 is derived from two DReLUs: $\neg c_1 \leftarrow \neg \text{DReLU}(e_1 - x) =$

Algorithm 4 Secure Piecewise Polynomials Protocol
Input: $\mathcal{C}$ holds $\langle x \rangle_0 \in \mathbb{Z}_{2^l}$. $\mathcal{S}$ holds $\langle x \rangle_1 \in \mathbb{Z}_{2^l}$.
Output: $\mathcal{C}$ learns $\langle z \rangle_0 \in \mathbb{Z}_2$. $\mathcal{S}$ learns $\langle z \rangle_1 \in \mathbb{Z}_2$, where $z = P(x)$.
1: $\mathcal{C}$ and $\mathcal{S}$ execute SDReLU $k-1$ times, resulting in $k-1$ shared comparison bits: $\forall i \in \{1, 2, \cdots, k-1\}, [c_i] \leftarrow \mathsf{SDReLU}(e_i - \langle x \rangle)$.
2: $\mathcal{C}$ and $\mathcal{S}$ execute SQuaPol k times, resulting in k shared polynomial results: $\forall i \in \{1, 2, \cdots, k\}, \langle f_i \rangle \leftarrow \mathsf{SQuaPol}(P_i(\langle x \rangle))$.
3: $\mathcal{C}$ and $\mathcal{S}$ compute the 1st-th polynomial via $\langle z_1 \rangle = \mathsf{SBitXA}([c_1], \langle f_1 \rangle)$.
4: **for** $1 < i < k$ **do**
5: $\quad$ $\mathcal{C}$ and $\mathcal{S}$ compute the i-th polynomial via $\langle z_i \rangle = \mathsf{SBitXA}([c_{i-1}] \oplus \gamma, \mathsf{SBitXA}([c_i], \langle f_i \rangle))$.
6: **end for**
7: $\mathcal{C}$ and $\mathcal{S}$ compute the k-th polynomial via $\langle z_k \rangle = \mathsf{SBitXA}([c_{k-1}] \oplus \gamma, \langle f_k \rangle)$.
8: $\mathcal{C}$ and $\mathcal{S}$ learn the AddSS-shared $P(\langle x \rangle)$: $\langle z \rangle \leftarrow \sum_{i=1}^{k} \langle z_i \rangle$.

1, indicating $e_1 \leq x$, and $c_2 \leftarrow \mathsf{DReLU}(e_2 - x) = 1$, indicating $x < e_2$, with $s_2 = \neg c_1 \otimes c_2$, where $\neg$ and $\otimes$ represent logical NOT and AND, respectively. Thus, $P(x)$'s expression is given by:

$$P(x) = \mathsf{DReLU}(e_1 - x) \cdot P_1(x) + \sum_{i=1}^{k-2} \neg \mathsf{DReLU}(e_i - x) \cdot \mathsf{DReLU}(e_{i+1} - x)$$
$$\cdot P_{i+1}(x) + \neg \mathsf{DReLU}(e_{k-1} - x) \cdot P_k(x). \tag{8}$$

To this end, we present the secure realization of SPiePol over the secret-sharing domain based on Eq. 8. Given the additive shares of each neuron output $\langle x \rangle$, and $p_{ij}(i \in [k], j \in [d])$ representing the plaintext weights held by the server $\mathcal{S}$, the client $\mathcal{C}$ and server $\mathcal{S}$ collaboratively compute $\langle z \rangle \leftarrow P(\langle x \rangle) = \mathsf{SPiePol}(\langle x \rangle)$. The main steps are outlined in ithm 4.

Secure Sigmoid and Tanh layers. The server offers an efficient alternative to the expensive exponentiation and reciprocal operations inherent in standard sigmoidal activations, i.e., Sigmoid and Tanh. By approximating these activations with piecewise continuous polynomials (e.g., splines [7]), the server learns the plaintext polynomial weights. As a result, secure Sigmoid and Tanh layers i.e., SecSig and SecTanh, can be implemented directly using SPiePol.

4.5 Putting Things Together

We are ready to integrate these blocks into the scheme PrivGNN. PrivGNN considers the most widely used GNN model for graph classification tasks, namely message passing neural networks (MPNNs). The client $\mathcal{C}$ first splits the graph-structured data $D = (G, E, H)$, where $G \in \mathbb{Z}_2^{n \times n}$ is the adjacency matrix, $E \in \mathbb{R}^{n \times n}$ represents the attributes of the edges, and $H \in \mathbb{R}^{n \times m}$ is the node feature matrix, with n as the number of nodes and m as the feature dimension. The data is split into random shared values $\langle D \rangle_0, \langle D \rangle_1$. At this point, the structure and data of the graph are fully protected. $\mathcal{C}$ then uploads $\langle D \rangle_1 = (\langle G \rangle_1, \langle E \rangle_1, \langle H \rangle_1)$ to the server to access PrivGNN services. Due to space limitations, we outline the secure inference (SI) process in MPNN-centric PrivGNN. The SI process involves three functions: secure message passing function (PRIVMF), secure update function (PRIVUF), and secure readout function (PRIVRF)—which are securely executed as detailed below.

- PRIVMF consists of two types of NN layers: SecFC and SecReLU for message passing. With GS data $\langle D \rangle$ and server-hold plaintext parameter W, PRIVMF's workflow is $(\langle D \rangle, W) \to [\text{SecFC} \to \text{SecReLU}] \times \iota \to \text{SecFC} \to \text{AGGREGATE}(\cdot) \to \langle M \rangle = \{\langle m_v \rangle | v \in V\} = \{\langle \sum_{u \in N(v)} m_{u \to v} \rangle | v \in V\}$, where ι denotes the number of repetitions, AGGREGATE represents the aggregation function, V is the set of nodes in graph, and $N(v)$ is the set of neighboring nodes of node v.
- PRIVUF sets up secure update gates and secure reset gates, using SecSig, SecTanh, and SEleMul to compute the update states of the two gates. For each node $v \in V$ (i.e., $m_v \in M$ and $h_v \in H$), PRIVUF's workflow is $(\langle m_v \rangle, \langle h_v \rangle, W^0) \to [\text{SecFC} \to \text{SecReLU}] + [\text{SecFC} \to \text{SecReLU}] \to \text{SecSig} \to \langle \varphi_v \rangle$, $(\langle m_v \rangle, \langle h_v \rangle, W^1) \to [\text{SecFC} \to \text{SecReLU}] + [\text{SecFC} \to \text{SecReLU}] \to \text{SecSig} \to \langle \eta_v \rangle$, $(\langle m_v \rangle, \langle h_v \rangle, W^2) \to [\text{SecFC} \to \text{SecReLU}] \odot \langle \eta_v \rangle + [\text{SecFC} \to \text{SecReLU}] \to \text{SecTanh} \to \langle \vartheta_v \rangle$, and $(\langle \varphi_v \rangle, \langle \vartheta_v \rangle, \langle h_v \rangle) \to (1 - \langle \varphi_v \rangle) \odot \vartheta_v + \langle \varphi_v \rangle \odot \langle h_v \rangle \to \langle \hat{h}_v \rangle$. The overall updated node feature matrix is $\langle \hat{H} \rangle = \{\langle \hat{h}_v \rangle | v \in V\}$.
- With updated $\hat{H}^{(1)}$ and $\hat{H}^{(T)}$, where $\hat{H}^{(t)}$ denotes the outputs of t executions of PRIVMF $\rightleftarrows$ PRIVUF, PRIVRF executes two paths: $(\langle \hat{H}^{(1)} \rangle | \langle \hat{H}^{(T)} \rangle, W_R) \to [\text{SecFC} \to \text{SecReLU}] \times \iota \to \text{SecFC} \to \langle \tilde{\mathcal{H}} \mathcal{H}^{\iota+1} \rangle$ and $(\langle \hat{H}^{(T)} \rangle, W_Z) \to [\text{SecFC} \to \text{SecReLU}] \times \iota \to \text{SecFC} \to \langle \tilde{\mathcal{H}}^{\iota+1} \rangle$, where ι denotes the number of repetitions and | denotes concatenation. PRIVRF then connect the results of the two paths: $\langle \mathcal{R} \rangle = \text{SMatMul}(\text{SEleMul}(\text{SecSig}(\langle \tilde{\mathcal{H}} \mathcal{H}^{\iota+1} \rangle), \langle \tilde{\mathcal{H}}^{\iota+1} \rangle), \text{SDReLU}(\langle \tilde{\mathcal{H}}^{\iota+1} \rangle))$.

5 Theoretical Analysis

Efficiency Analysis. We analyze the computational and communication complexity of key protocols (SMatMul, SQuaPol, SDReLU, and SPiePol) and compare them with SotA schemes. We define SMul and SFunC as AddSS-based multiplication and FuncSS-based comparison operations. HEnc, HDec, HAdd, and Hmul represent the operations for encryption, decryption, addition, and multiplication with homomorphic ciphertexts. There are five parameters involved in this analysis: (1) the bit length l of an AddSS share, (2) the bit l_h length of the homomorphic ciphertext, (3) the pieces k of piecewise polynomials, (4) the degree d of each piece, (5) the time complexity $\mathcal{T}$ of secure operations. Table 1 summarizes the analysis results. SQuaPol, SDReLU, and SPiePol show notable overall computational improvements, with most costs concentrated in the offline phase for generating cryptographic primitives like multiplication triples and keys. They also achieve lower overall communication costs compared to SotA.

Table 1. Computation and communication costs of supporting protocols in PrivGNN, PAPI [5], and FastSecNet [11].

Protocols	Benchmarks	Computation	Communication
SMatMul	PAPI	T_{SMul}	$2l$ (online: $2l$)
	PrivGNN	T_{SMul}	$2l$ (online: l)
SQuaPol	PAPI	$7T_{\text{HEnc}} + 3T_{\text{HDec}} + 7T_{\text{HAdd}} + 5T_{\text{HMul}} + T_{\text{SMul}}$	$5l_h + 2l$ (online: $2l$)
	PrivGNN	T_{SMul}	$9l$ (online: $2l$)
SDReLU	FastSecNet	$2T_{\text{SFunC}}$	$8(l+1)$ (online: $2l$)
	PrivGNN	$T_{\text{SFunC}} + T_{\text{SMul}}$	$2(2l+1)$ (online: $2l$)
SPiePol	FastSecNet	$2(k-1)T_{\text{SFunC}} + \frac{d(d+1)k}{2}T_{\text{SMul}}$	$8(k-1)(l+1) + d(d+1)kl$ (online: $2l(k-1) + \frac{d(d+1)kl}{2}$)
	PrivGNN	$(k-1)T_{\text{SFunC}} + (2k-1)T_{\text{SMul}}$	$6kl + 2k - 4l - 2$ (online: $4kl - 2l$)

Security Analysis. PrivGNN's pipeline integrates a variety of cryptographic protocols for different layers, with each layer's input and output in the additive secret-sharing domain. Using the sequential composition theorem [10], we deduce the overall security of PrivGNN's inference as stated in Theorem 1.

Theorem 1. *PrivGNN's secure inference scheme $\prod^{PrivGNN}$ securely realizes the ideal functionality $\mathcal{F}^{PrivGNN}$ in the presence of one semi-honest adversary $\mathcal{A}$ in the $(\prod_{SecCONV}, \prod_{SecReLU}, \prod_{SecMaxPool}, \prod_{SecSig}, \prod_{SecTanh}, \prod_{SecFC}, \prod_{SEleMul})$-hybrid model.*

We analyze the security of PrivGNN against two types of semi-honest adversaries, as described in Definition 1. Specifically, we consider the following two cases based on the potential adversary: (1) a corrupted client ($\mathcal{P} \leftarrow \mathcal{C}$) and (2) a corrupted server ($\mathcal{P} \leftarrow \mathcal{S}$). The security of PrivGNN under these two semi-honest adversaries is proven according to the cryptographic standard outlined in **Definition 1**.

6 Experimental Evaluation

Testbed. We implement a prototype of PrivGNN in Python 3.7 and PyTorch 1.9. Extensive experiments are conducted on two distinct servers with 64-core CPUs, 128GB RAM, and 2 NVIDIA GeForce RTX 2080Ti GPU. The environment simulates a local-area network with 1 Gbps bandwidth and 0.1 ms latency. Following prior work [11,21,31], we set the integer ring size of additive secret shares to $\mathbb{Z}_{2^{32}}$. Cleartext NN models are trained using PyTorch on an NVIDIA RTX 2080Ti GPU, using the standard SGD optimizer with a learning rate of 0.001, batch size of 128, momentum of 0.9, and weight decay of 1×10^{-6}.

Datasets and Models. We evaluate PrivGNN on MNIST, CIFAR-10, CIFAR-100, and QM9 [27] datasets. MNIST, CIFAR-10, and CIFAR-100, are utilized for image classification inference with CNNs. The QM9 dataset, comprising 134,000 stable organic molecules, is processed into molecular fingerprints using RDKit [1], and employed for molecular property inference with GNNs. The models include a 3-layer fully-connected network (FC-3) and a 4-layer CNN (CNN-4) [31] for MNIST, LeNet [16] and VGG-16 [32] for CIFAR10, ResNet-32 [12] and VGG-16 [32] for CIFAR-100, and the GNN in Sect. 4.5 for QM9.

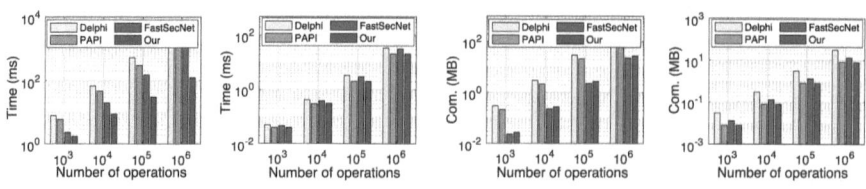

(a) Offline runtime (b) Online runtime (c) Offline com. cost (d) Online com. cost

Fig. 2. Performance comparison of SQuaPol protocol.

6.1 Microbenchmarks

Secure SQuaPol Protocol. Figure 2 compares the performance of SQuaPol with Delphi [23], PAPI [5], and FastSecNet [11] in terms of runtime and communication (com.) cost across operation scales from 10^3 to 10^6. SQuaPol outperforms in online computation, showing a ∼ 35% reduction in time compared to Delphi and FastSecNet, benefiting from a single-round interaction. Online com. of SQuaPol also excels, with costs 4× and 2× lower than Delphi and FastSecNet. For offline computation, SQuaPol achieves improvements by one order of magnitude over other schemes. While its offline com. cost is ∼ 20% higher than FastSecNet, SQuaPol prioritizes online efficiency, delivering strong overall performance.

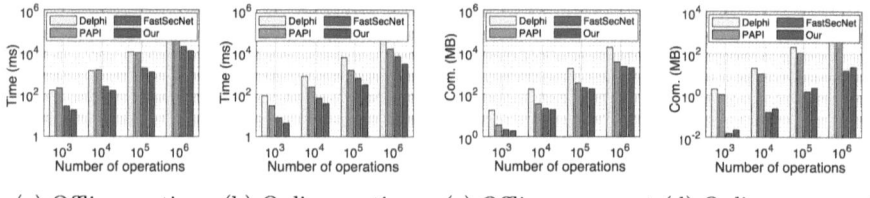

(a) Offline runtime (b) Online runtime (c) Offline com. cost (d) Online com. cost

Fig. 3. Performance comparison of SecReLU protocol.

Secure Comparison-Based Activations. Figure 3 reports the performance comparison of SecReLU. SecReLU achieves 2× ∼ 15× speedup in online runtime compared to Delphi, PAPI, and FastSecNet, with higher online com. costs than FastSecNet. Specifically, SecReLU requires one FuncSS-based comparison and one multiplication for $ReLU(x) = DReLU(x) \cdot x$, while FastSecNet uses two comparisons, trading online time for lower com. In contrast, Delphi and PAPI's use of garbled circuits and HE introduces higher overall costs. Further, SecReLU presents superior offline performance in both runtime and com. costs, stressing its overall efficiency.

Secure Sigmoidal Activations. Figure 4 reports the performance of SecSig (equivalent to SecTanh and SPiePol) compared to SiRNN [29] and MiniONN

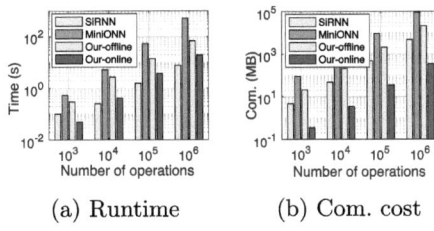

(a) Runtime (b) Com. cost

Fig. 4. Performance comparison of SecSig/SecTanh protocols: SiRNN uses a 3-piece polynomial, MiniONN a 12-piece linear approximation, while our protocol employs a 12-piece quadratic approximation, offering better accuracy due to the higher polynomial degree.

[20]. SecSig adopts a 12-piece spline, sufficient for maintaining cross-entropy loss [20]. We compare its online portion to the total costs of the fully online baselines. The online running time and com. cost of SecSig are both less than those of SiRNN and MiniONN for small scales. For 10^3 operations, the online running time of SecSig is 2× and 10.8× faster than SiRNN and MiniONN. The 3-piece spline of SiRNN shows sub-linear growth in latency but offers limited approximation accuracy. Regarding online com. cost, SecSig is 13.6× and 260× lower than SiRNN and MiniONN across all operation scales.

Table 2. Summary of inference accuracy (%)

	MNIST		CIFAR-10		CIFAR-100		QM9
	FC-3	CNN-4	LeNet-5	VGG-16	ResNet-32	VGG-16	GNN
Training Accuracy	96.96	99.16	96.81	88.03	74.90	72.22	98.17
Plain Inference	96.23	99.02	81.50	87.45	68.48	70.12	97.93
Secure Inference	96.12	99.00	80.57	87.40	68.16	70.12	96.42

6.2 Summary of Accuracy

Table 2 compares the inference accuracy of PrivGNN with plaintext inference across various datasets and models, delivering its robust SI capabilities. Specifically, for MNIST, PrivGNN achieves an inference accuracies of 96.12% and 99.00% for the FC-3 and CNN-4 models, respectively, only $\sim 0.1\%$ lower than their plaintext. On CIFAR-10, PrivGNN records accuracies of 80.57% for LeNet-5 and 87.40% for VGG-16, slightly below the plaintext accuracies of 81.50% and 87.45%, respectively, but still reasonable. For CIFAR-100, ResNet-32 achieves a SI accuracy of 68.16%, closely trailing the plaintext accuracy of 68.48%. VGG-16 matches the plaintext accuracy of 70.12%. On QM9 with the GNN model, PrivGNN reports an accuracy of 96.42%, slightly below the plaintext accuracy of 97.93%. The possible minor accuracy drop is from truncation errors caused by the fixed-point arithmetic and the reformulated activations used in PrivGNN.

6.3 Performance Comparison with SotA Schemes

Secure Convolutional Inference. We evaluate PrivGNN on CNN-4 (MNIST), VGG-16 (CIFAR-10), and ResNet-32 (CIFAR-100), and compare it with SotA works. The reported results of SotA are sourced directly from the respective papers. Table 3 shows that PrivGNN improves CNN-4's online runtime up to $1.2\times \sim 73.6\times$. For VGG-16, PrivGNN exhibits $2.6\times$ and $4.0 \times$ savings in online time when compared to the CrypTFlow2 [30] and Delphi [23], respectively. While PrivGNN's online runtime is 21.5% higher than PAPI [5] due to PAPI's optimization strategy of retaining a subset of ReLUs. For ResNet-32, PrivGNN outperforms prior works with online runtime reductions of $1.3\times \sim 4.7\times$, also enhancing online communication efficiency by $4.6\times \sim 23.9\times$.

Table 3. Performance comparison with SotA schemes (Scheme abbreviations: Medi = MediSC

	Model	MNIST (CNN-4)				CIFAR-10 (VGG-16)				CIFAR-100 (ResNet-32)				QM9 (MPNN)	
	Scheme	XONN	Medi	Fast	Ours	Cryp	Delp	PAPI	Ours	Cryp	Chet	PAPI	Ours	SecM	Ours
Time (s)	Offline	-	1.21	0.25	0.22	42.50	88.10	47.80	23.15	62.50	-	65.70	38.36	-	5.45
	Online	0.30	4.42	0.07	0.06	4.20	6.30	1.30	1.53	6.40	15.95	4.50	3.35	102.57	2.48
	Total	0.30	5.63	0.32	0.28	46.70	94.40	49.10	24.68	68.90	15.95	70.20	41.71	102.57	7.93
Com. (MB)	Offline	-	2.54	40.19	22.59	30.72	51.20	40.96	217.74	122.88	-	143.36	468.26	-	87.04
	Online	62.77	2.62	0.65	1.28	686.08	40.96	30.72	16.55	583.68	112.64	122.88	24.38	156.13	9.10
	Total	62.77	5.16	40.84	23.87	716.8	92.16	71.68	234.29	706.56	112.64	266.24	492.64	156.13	96.14

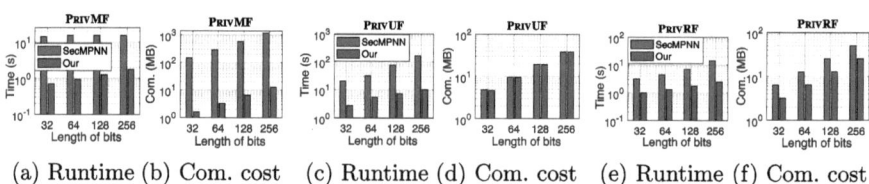

(a) Runtime (b) Com. cost (c) Runtime (d) Com. cost (e) Runtime (f) Com. cost

Fig. 5. Performance comparison of different functions in GNNs.

Secure Graph Inference. The overall performance is shown in the last column of Table 3. We evaluate three functions across four secret-sharing ring sizes ($l = 32, 64, 128, 256$ bits) to assess resource usage. Figure 5 shows that time and com. costs rise with larger secret-sharing ring sizes. As seen, the three functions PRIVMF, PRIVUF, and PRIVRF take 0.7, 2.7, and 1.0 seconds, respectively, to predict one molecule within the 32-bit ring. Overall, PrivGNN achieves an order of magnitude improvement over SecMPNN [18], attributed to the dual optimization of linear and non-linear layers. Notably, PRIVUF accounts for 50% ↑ of the overall SI runtime due to the costly piecewise approximations of sigmoidal activations like SecSig and SecTanh.

7 Conclusion

We introduced PrivGNN, a high-performance cryptographic inference framework designed for privacy-preserving GNNs in the semi-honest client-server setup. By carefully designing a line of secure offline-online protocols for both linear and non-linear layers with lightweight AddSS and FuncSS, PrivGNN performs fast and low-interactive inference during the online phase. Extensive experimental results on benchmark and real-world datasets shed light on the scalability and efficiency of PrivGNN, outperforming prior PPDL and secure GNN schemes. Our approach paves the way for secure, scalable AI-driven services in various domains, including drug discovery and beyond.

References

1. RDKit: Open-source cheminformatics. http://www.rdkit.org. Accessed 11 Apr 2024
2. Beaver, D.: Efficient multiparty protocols using circuit randomization. In: Advances in Cryptology—CRYPTO'91: Proceedings 11, pp. 420–432. Springer (1992)
3. Boyle, E., et al.: Function secret sharing for mixed-mode and fixed-point secure computation. In: Annual International Conference on the Theory and Applications of Cryptographic Techniques, pp. 871–900. Springer (2021)
4. Boyle, E., Gilboa, N., Ishai, Y.: Function secret sharing. In: Annual International Conference on the Theory and Applications of Cryptographic Techniques, pp. 337–367. Springer (2015)
5. Cheng, K., Xi, N., Liu, X., Zhu, X., Gao, H., et al.: Private inference for deep neural networks: a secure, adaptive, and efficient realization. IEEE Trans. Comput. (2023)
6. Demmler, D., Schneider, T., Zohner, M.: ABY-a framework for efficient mixed-protocol secure two-party computation. In: NDSS (2015)
7. Dierckx, P.: Curve and surface fitting with splines. Oxford University Press (1995)
8. Gilmer, J., Schoenholz, S.S., Riley, P.F., Vinyals, O., Dahl, G.E.: Neural message passing for quantum chemistry. In: International Conference on Machine Learning, pp. 1263–1272. PMLR (2017)
9. Goldreich, O.: Foundations of Cryptography, vol. 2. Cambridge University Press, Basic Applications (2009)
10. Goldreich, O., Micali, S., Wigderson, A.: How to play any mental game, or a completeness theorem for protocols with honest majority. In: Proceedings of the Nineteenth Annual ACM Symposium on Theory of Computing, pp. 218–229 (1987)
11. Hao, M., Li, H., Chen, H., Xing, P., Zhang, T.: FastSecNet: an efficient cryptographic framework for private neural network inference. IEEE TIFS **18**, 2569–2582 (2023)

12. He, K., Zhang, X., Ren, S., Sun, J.: Deep residual learning for image recognition. In: Proceedings of the IEEE Conference on Computer Vision and Pattern Recognition, pp. 770–778 (2016)
13. Huang, Z., Lu, W., Hong, C., Ding, J.: Cheetah: Lean and fast secure two-party deep neural network inference. In: USENIX Security, pp. 809–826 (2022)
14. Jawalkar, N., Gupta, K., Basu, A., Chandran, N., Gupta, D., Sharma, R.: Orca: Fss-based secure training and inference with GPUs. In: S&P, pp. 63–63. IEEE Comput. Soc. (2023)
15. Kumar, N., Rathee, M., Chandran, N., Gupta, D., Rastogi, A., Sharma, R.: Cryptflow: Secure tensorflow inference. In: S&P, pp. 336–353. IEEE (2020)
16. LeCun, Y., Bottou, L., Bengio, Y., Haffner, P.: Gradient-based learning applied to document recognition. Proc. IEEE **86**(11), 2278–2324 (1998)
17. Liao, X., Liu, W., Zheng, X., Yao, B., Chen, C.: PPGenCDR: A stable and robust framework for privacy-preserving cross-domain recommendation. In: Proceedings of the AAAI Conference on Artificial Intelligence. vol. 37, pp. 4453–4461 (2023)
18. Liao, X., Xue, J., Yu, S., Liu, X., Shu, J.: SecMPNN: 3-party privacy-preserving molecular structure properties inference. In: 2022 IEEE International Conference on Acoustics, Speech and Signal Processing, pp. 3004–3008. IEEE (2022)
19. Liu, C.s.: The essence of the generalized newton binomial theorem. Commun. Nonl. Sci. Numer. Simul. **15**(10), 2766–2768 (2010)
20. Liu, J., Juuti, M., Lu, Y., Asokan, N.: Oblivious neural network predictions via MiniONN transformations. In: CCS, pp. 619–631 (2017)
21. Liu, X., Zheng, Y., Yuan, X., Yi, X.: Towards secure and lightweight deep learning as a medical diagnostic service. In: 26th European Symposium on Research in Computer Security, pp. 519–541. Springer (2021)
22. Makri, E., Rotaru, D., Vercauteren, F., Wagh, S.: Rabbit: Efficient comparison for secure multi-party computation. In: International Conference on Financial Cryptography and Data Security, pp. 249–270. Springer (2021)
23. Mishra, P., Lehmkuhl, R., Srinivasan, A., Zheng, W., Popa, R.A.: **DELPHI**: a cryptographic inference service for neural networks. In: USENIX Security, pp. 2505–2522 (2020)
24. Ohata, S., Nuida, K.: Communication-efficient (client-aided) secure two-party protocols and its application. In: International Conference on Financial Cryptography and Data Security, pp. 369–385. Springer (2020)
25. Paillier, P.: Public-key cryptosystems based on composite degree residuosity classes. In: International Conference on the Theory and Applications of Cryptographic Techniques, pp. 223–238. Springer (1999)
26. Peng, H., Ran, R., Luo, Y., Zhao, J., Huang, S., et al.: LinGCN: Structural linearized graph convolutional network for homomorphically encrypted inference. Adv. Neural Inf. Process. Syst. **36** (2024)
27. Ramakrishnan, R., Dral, P.O., Rupp, M., Von Lilienfeld, O.A.: Quantum chemistry structures and properties of 134 kilo molecules. Sci. Data **1**(1), 1–7 (2014)
28. Ran, R., Wang, W., Gang, Q., Yin, J., Xu, N., Wen, W.: CryptoGCN: Fast and scalable homomorphically encrypted graph convolutional network inference. Adv. Neural. Inf. Process. Syst. **35**, 37676–37689 (2022)
29. Rathee, D., Rathee, M., Goli, R.K.K., Gupta, D., et al.: SiRnn: A math library for secure RNN inference. In: S&P, pp. 1003–1020. IEEE (2021)
30. Rathee, D., et al.: CrypTFlow2: Practical 2-party secure inference. In: CCS, pp. 325–342 (2020)
31. Riazi, M.S., Samragh, M., Chen, H., Laine, K., et al.: XONN:XNOR-based oblivious deep neural network inference. In: USENIX Security, pp. 1501–1518 (2019)

32. Simonyan, K., Zisserman, A.: Very deep convolutional networks for large-scale image recognition. arXiv preprint arXiv:1409.1556 (2014)
33. Wang, S., Zheng, Y., Jia, X.: Secgnn: Privacy-preserving graph neural network training and inference as a cloud service. IEEE Trans. Serv. Comput. **16**(4), 2923–2938 (2023)
34. Wu, F., Long, Y., Zhang, C., Li, B.: Linkteller: Recovering private edges from graph neural networks via influence analysis. In: S&P, pp. 2005–2024. IEEE (2022)
35. Xu, Z., Lai, S., Liu, X., Abuadbba, A., Yuan, X., Yi, X.: OblivGNN: Oblivious inference on transductive and inductive graph neural network. In: USENIX Security, pp. 2209–2226 (2024)
36. Yang, P., et al.: FssNN: communication-efficient secure neural network training via function secret sharing. Cryptology ePrint Archive (2023)
37. Zhou, L., Wang, Z., Cui, H., Song, Q., Yu, Y.: Bicoptor: Two-round secure three-party non-linear computation without preprocessing for privacy-preserving machine learning. In: S&P, pp. 534–551. IEEE (2023)

Linking Cryptoasset Attribution Tags to Knowledge Graph Entities: An LLM-Based Approach

Régnier Avice[1]((✉))[iD], Bernhard Haslhofer[2][iD], Zhidong Li[1][iD], and Jianlong Zhou[1][iD]

[1] University of Technology Sydney, Ultimo, Australia
`regnier.avice@student.uts.edu.au`, `{zhidong.li,jianlong.zhou}@uts.edu.au`
[2] Complexity Science Hub, Vienna, Austria
`haslhofer@csh.ac.at`

Abstract. Attribution tags form the foundation of modern cryptoasset forensics. However, inconsistent or incorrect tags can mislead investigations and even result in false accusations. To address this issue, we propose a novel computational method based on Large Language Models (LLMs) to link attribution tags with well-defined knowledge graph concepts. We implemented this method in an end-to-end pipeline and conducted experiments showing that our approach outperforms baseline methods by up to 37.4% in F1-score across three publicly available attribution tag datasets. By integrating concept filtering and blocking procedures, we generate candidate sets containing five knowledge graph entities, achieving a recall of 93% without the need for labeled data. Additionally, we demonstrate that local LLM models can achieve F1-scores of 90%, comparable to remote models which achieve 94%. We also analyze the cost-performance trade-offs of various LLMs and prompt templates, showing that selecting the most cost-effective configuration can reduce costs by 90%, with only a 1% decrease in performance. Our method not only enhances attribution tag quality but also serves as a blueprint for fostering more reliable forensic evidence.

Keywords: Forensics · LLM · Cryptoassets

1 Introduction

Attribution tags, which link pseudo-anonymous cryptoasset addresses to identifying information about real-world entities and services (e.g., cryptoasset exchanges), form the foundation of modern cryptoasset forensics [25]. Over the past decade, a multibillion-dollar industry has emerged, providing blockchain tracing tools for law enforcement investigations. These tools allow users to "follow the money", ultimately leading to the identification and potential conviction of perpetrators. As cryptoassets have gained increasing relevance across various crime sectors, these tools are now used in investigations related to ransomware [19,29], sextortion [30], and malware [13]. Attribution tags have also been employed to train machine learning models for automatically categorizing service providers, such as exchanges [13,15,24,43], miners [15,24,43], and ICO wallets [24,43]. Moreover, these models are used to classify addresses or transactions as illicit [2,5,18,22,24,41,43]. Consequently, the accuracy of attribution tags becomes a critical success factor in all these application domains.

Imprecise or incorrect tags can mislead investigations, result in inaccurate model predictions, or, in the worst case, lead to false accusations. As a result, the concept of *attribution tag quality* is gaining increased attention, especially as the scientific validity of crypto-tracing techniques is being more frequently questioned and scrutinized [4]. As with any digital forensic investigation that forms the basis for legal decisions, the collected evidence must be reliable [10], since poor data quality can lead to incorrect conclusions. Ensuring high data quality also guarantees that the methodologies used in digital forensics can be consistently tested and verified.

Since attribution tags originate from and are often shared among multiple stakeholders, data consistency becomes a critical aspect of data quality. A key challenge, for instance, is the inconsistent referencing of real-world entities across different parties [10,13]. For example, one party might refer to a specific exchange as *btc-e*, while another uses *btc-e.com*. While a human can easily recognize that both tags refer to the same entity, different tracing tools may interpret them as referring to two distinct entities. To harmonize their representation, reuse, and interpretation in forensic investigations or machine learning tasks, a suitable data format and a computational approach are needed to automatically eliminate potential data inconsistencies.

Given the semantic nature of this practical problem, knowledge graphs offer an effective solution. They represent entities as identifiable semantic concepts rather than plain strings and are widely used in search engines [14] and large knowledge bases [38]. The process of linking data to these well-defined entities is known as record linkage [9] or entity linking [35]. However, existing approaches often rely on heuristics or heavily labeled, domain-specific training datasets, which are not readily available in the context of cryptoasset attribution tags.

Therefore, in this paper, we present a novel computational approach based on Large Language Models (LLMs) that enables the linking of attribution tag datasets to well-defined knowledge graph concepts without requiring domain-specific fine-tuning. We implemented this approach by integrating several cutting-edge techniques—such as filtering, blocking, and LLMs—into an end-to-end pipeline. Our experiments, conducted on three datasets, demonstrate that:

1. Our end-to-end entity linking approach outperforms baseline methods across all three datasets, achieving up to a 37.4% improvement in F1-scores.
2. $BM25_3$ blocking and related-concept filtering reduce the number of candidates per tag to 5, with a recall of 93%, without requiring labeled data.
3. GPT-4o-based candidate selection achieves a 94% F1-score, while Mistral 7B-Instruct, which can run locally, achieves a 90% F1-score.

4. Using the most cost-effective prompt template reduces costs by 90%, with only a 1% drop in performance.

Our method not only enhances the quality of attribution tags but also seeks to inspire broader efforts toward improving data quality, ensuring accurate and reliable evidence in forensic investigations. To ensure reproducibility, we have made our code and datasets publicly available in the following GitHub repository: https://github.com/ravice234/cryptoasset-attribution-tag-linker.

2 Background

2.1 Attribution Tags

Attribution tags link pseudo-anonymous blockchain objects, such as addresses or transactions, to real-world actors or events. They provide additional context, such as the name of a service controlling an address (e.g., btc-e), some form of categorization (e.g., exchange), and any other information that might be useful in forensic investigations. Figure 1 illustrates an example in which two distinct attribution tags originating from different sources reference the same cryptoasset address 0x123 and describe the same real-world actor, a well-known cryptoasset exchange. One can observe that, despite describing the same entity, the attribution tag data records the name (btc-e vs. btc-e.com) and categorize the exchange differently (Exchange vs. Service).

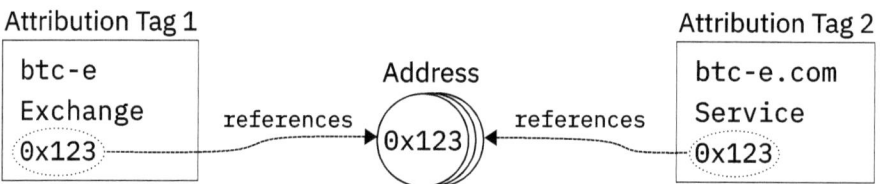

Fig. 1. Attribution Tag Example. Two attribution tags referencing the same cryptoasset address *0x123* owned by the real-world entity *BTC-e*.

Attribution tag data quality issues can occur at various levels [16]: technical heterogeneities, such as different data formats, can impede uniform processing; syntactic heterogeneities, like the use of different encoding schemes, can hinder uniform interpretation; and semantic heterogeneities, such as the use of different names to denote the same real-world concept (synonyms, homonyms, hypernyms, etc.), can lead to inconsistent interpretations. In this paper, we primarily focus on resolving semantic interoperability issues, assuming that technical and syntactic issues can be addressed using common data preprocessing procedures.

Introducing knowledge graphs to data management environments has become a common strategy to deal with semantic interoperability issues. A knowledge graph defines nodes representing real-world entities of interest and semantic relationships between these entities [17]. An example is eBay's product knowledge graph, which allows them to identify if two sellers sell the same products, or if the products are related otherwise (Fig. 2).

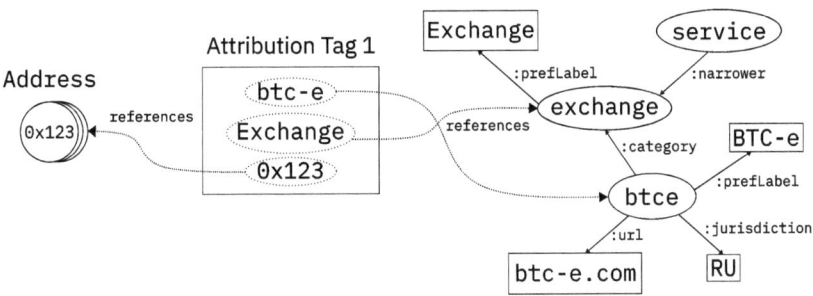

Fig. 2. Linking an Attribution Tag to the Knowledge Graph. Attribution tag instances are linked to concepts defined in the knowledge graph.

The process of linking text mentions to entities in a knowledge graph is called *entity linking* [35]. This process can be further broken down into: 1) generating a subset of entities (*candidates*) that are most likely to match, and 2) selecting which, if any, candidate matches to the text mention. Candidate set generation can be achieved by excluding implausible (*filtering*) and clustering similar (*blocking*) entities [28]. The selection of a matching candidate is typically performed using a decision function learned through machine learning. In this paper, the term *entity linking* is used to describe the process of linking tags to a knowledge graph; while our solution also encompasses techniques that stem from the closely related problem of linking database records (record linkage, entity matching), for the sake of simplicity, we will consistently refer to it as entity linking.

2.2 Related Work

Entity linking approaches where tuples are linked to knowledge base entities have utilized look-up methods [33], embedding comparisons [7], and hybrid approaches [8]. Record-based entity linking has seen advancements using classical machine learning [20], deep neural networks [26], and pre-trained language models [23]. In [37], a mixture-of-experts approach was proposed, utilizing the training results from various data integration matching tasks. For blocking, many state-of-the-art approaches use deep learning [3,23,36,39]. A simple tf-idf based blocker can achieve competitive results without training and labeled data as shown in [31].

More recently, researchers started to examine LLMs on data integration tasks. Studies have evaluated and proposed various models, including GPT-3 [27], Jellyfish variants [42], and others [32], on tasks such as entity linkage, data imputation, and error detection. Different matching strategies for LLMs in detail have also been explored in [32,40].

Within the specific domain of cryptoasset investigations, [13] described a method for resolving conflicting attribution tags. They use the edit distance to harmonize strings referring to the same entity. The application of LLMs in the context of cryptoassets and blockchains has been explored for multiple tasks, such as detecting anomalous Ethereum transactions [11], auditing smart contracts [6], and identifying discrepancies between smart contract bytecode and project documentation [12].

In this paper, we go beyond this approach, by linking attribution tag datasets to well-defined knowledge graph concepts using an LLM-based approach.

3 Data

In Table 1, we present a summary of the data we used to design and evaluate our approach. We utilized three datasets: the GraphSense TagPack, the WatchYourBack attribution tags, and the DeFi Rekt database. More details about the dataset can be found in the extended version of this paper [1].

Table 1. Overview of the three attribution tag datasets used in this study.

Dataset	Samples	Actor Links	Distinct Actors
GraphSense Tag Pack	2,570	2,570	484
Train	25	25	20
Validation	771	771	198
Test	1,774	1,774	361
WatchYourBack	126	67	58
Defi Rekt	100	32	32
Total	2,794	2,669	520

4 Approach

Our approach for linking attribution tags to knowledge graph concepts comprises two main components, as illustrated in Fig. 3: the *candidate set generator* and the *candidate selector* modules. The candidate set generator reduces the pool of potential actors in the knowledge graph that may correspond to an attribution tag by applying filtering and blocking techniques. Next, the candidate selector module determines which, if any, of the proposed entities match the attribution tag. The following sections offer a detailed explanation of each module.

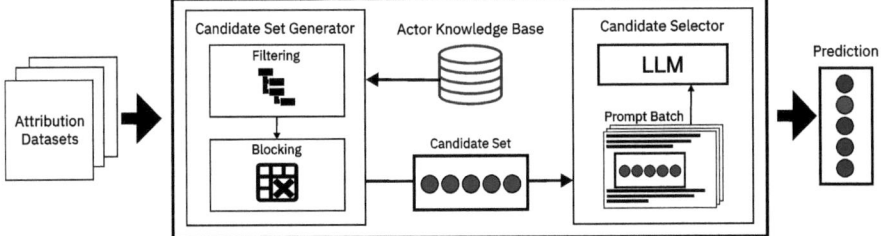

Fig. 3. Approach Overview. The *candidate set generator* filters potential entities and the *candidate selector module* identifies the matching entity.

4.1 Candidate Set Generator

The goal of the candidate set generator is to reduce the pool of candidates in the knowledge graph that potentially match a given attribution tag. Since LLM inference is expensive and pairwise comparison is of order $O(nm)$, where n is the number of records and m is the number of entities in the knowledge graph, an approach that minimizes the comparisons is required.

To reduce the overall cost, we limit the entities in each prompt to k candidates by applying *filtering* and *blocking* techniques, thereby reducing the problem complexity to $O(nk)$, where $k \ll m$. Filtering is the process of eliminating incorrect candidates, while blocking refers to similarity-based clustering that identifies likely and unlikely candidates [28].

Filtering. The candidate set can be narrowed down when both the attribution tag and the corresponding knowledge graph entity are associated with categorization information from the same controlled vocabulary. For example, an attribution tag might be categorized as "exchange" and a knowledge graph entity as "service", where the latter represents a semantically broader concept than the former. When such information is available, as in the GraphSense TagPack dataset, it can be leveraged for filtering. We define two possible filtering methods:

– *Same-Concept Filtering*: This method excludes actors that belong to a category different from the one specified in the attribution tag.
– *Related-Concept Filtering*: This approach is more flexible than same-concept filtering, as it leverages the taxonomy structure to exclude all actors associated with concepts unrelated to the attribution tag. Related concepts include both ancestors and descendants of the original concept, but exclude descendants of ancestor concepts that are not directly related.

Blocking. The basic idea behind blocking is to avoid comparing entities that are unlikely to match, significantly reducing the number of comparisons. This is done by partitioning the data into smaller subsets (*blocks*), where entities share some similarities or common attributes. Inspired by [31], who demonstrate that simple blocking methods—without requiring machine learning or pre-trained models—can achieve strong results, we apply two straightforward methods:

$BM25_3$. This method is based on the Okapi BM25 [34] that is part of the family of term frequency-inverse document frequency (tf-idf) scoring functions. We tokenize the document and query strings into trigrams as proposed in [3] to allow for approximate string matching. The overall score for a tokenized document D with respect to a tokenized query Q is given by:

$$\text{BM25}(D, Q) = \sum_{i=1}^{n} \text{idf}(q_i) \cdot \frac{f(q_i, D) \cdot (k_1 + 1)}{f(q_i, D) + k_1 \cdot (1 - b + b \cdot \frac{|D|}{\text{avgdl}})} \tag{1}$$

where $f(q_i, D)$ is the frequency of token q_i of query q in document D and avgdl is the average document length in the corpus. The inverse document frequency (IDF) is calculated as:

$$\text{idf}(q_i) = \log\left(\frac{N - n(q_i) + 0.5}{n(q_i) + 0.5} + 1\right) \tag{2}$$

We use the standard parameters $k_1 = 1.5$ and $b = 0.75$ defined in the implentation of the rank_bm25 library[1].

Overlap_3 This method measures the similarity between two strings based on the overlap $\frac{|A \cap B|}{\min(|A|, |B|)}$ of their trigram sets A and B.

4.2 Candidate Selector

The candidate selector module takes a set of candidates for each attribution tag and selects the best matching entity. Technically, this step is implemented using an LLM. In the first stage, the module constructs a batch of prompts, where each prompt corresponds to an attribution tag and includes all associated candidates. Optionally, the prompts can include examples (few-shot prompts) showcasing both matching and non-matching cases. This prompt batch is then fed to the LLM, which is tasked with either selecting the candidate that best matches the attribution tag or indicating that none of the candidates correspond to the tag.

Figure 4 shows the template used for this prompting task. It consists of an extended system message (SYS, SYS+), the few-shot examples (FEW-SHOT), a task description (TASK), a domain statement (DOMAIN), the input data (INPUT), the selection question (QUEST), and an extended output format reminder (OUT, OUT+).

---

[1] https://github.com/dorianbrown/rank_bm25.

SYS	You are an AI assistant that follows instruction extremely well.
SYS+	User will give you a question. Your task is to answer as faithfully as you can.
	Determine if the attribution tag label refers to any of the listed entities and, if so, to which one. The attribution tag describes an entity that is related to a blockchain address. Attribution Tag Label: compound_Pair_ETH_USDC
FEW-SHOT	[0] Compound [1] Morpho Aave/Compound [2] Tether (USDT) [3] BitLaunder.com [4] CryptoBounty.com [5] None of the entities above 0
DOMAIN	The attribution tag describes an entity that is related to a blockchain address.
TASK	Determine if the attribution tag label refers to any of the listed entities and, if so, to which one. Attribution Tag Label: curvefinance_UST-StableSwapUST
INPUT	[0] TrustSwap [1] Curve Finance [2] PancakeSwap (AMM, v2, Stableswap) [3] Zyberswap (AMM,Stableswap) [4] StableKoi [5] None of the entities above
QUEST	Choose your answer from: [0, 1, 2, 3, 4, 5].
OUT	Does the attribution tag refer to any of the listed entities and, if so, to which one?
OUT+	Before answering, make sure your answer only contains a number.

Fig. 4. Prompt template. The template used for prompting candidate selection. It consists of several parts (e.g., SYS, FEW-SHOT, INPUT, etc.) and defines the instructions provided to an LLM to guide its response or generated output.

5 Experiments

In this section, we present three experiments to evaluate the performance of our approach. Details to the experimental setup, including the models and prompt configurations can be found in the extended version of this paper [1].

5.1 Experiment 1: Candidate Set Generation

The goal of this experiment is to evaluate different filtering and blocking techniques (described in Sect. 4.1) and find an appropriate candidate set size. We run the experiment on the GraphSense Tag Pack validation dataset on candidate set sizes (k) of 1, 5, 10, and 25. The task is to predict the correct actor for each sample within the k candidates by comparing the tag label with the actor label, e.g., btc-e.com with BTC-e. To evaluate the performance of combined filtering and blocking techniques, we compute the ratio of attribution tags for which the correct actor link is included among the k candidates. This metric is often referred to as top-k accuracy. However, since each attribution tag has exactly one correct actor link, the proportion of correctly recovered actor links, *recall*, is equivalent in this context. Following prior works [28,31] on blocking methods, we refer to this metric as recall. Note that in this scenario, precision depends solely on k and recall, and thus does not provide additional information.

The results in Table 2 demonstrate that $BM25_3$ consistently outperforms $Overlap_3$ across all candidate set sizes k. Using the *same-concept* filter degrades performance, suggesting that it is overly restrictive. In contrast, the related-concept filter produces slightly better candidate sets than using no filtering. The

Table 2. Effectiveness of candidate set generation. Recall of candidate set generation for different candidate set sizes (k), blocking (BM25$_3$, Overlap$_3$), and filtering (*same-concept*, *related-concept*) techniques.

Filter	Blocker	Recall			
		$k=1$	$k=5$	$k=10$	$k=25$
No Filtering	Overlap$_3$	0.467	0.826	0.872	0.904
	BM25$_3$	0.765	0.899	0.916	**0.957**
same-concept	Overlap$_3$	0.553	0.739	0.763	0.774
	BM25$_3$	0.669	0.770	0.776	0.782
related-concept	Overlap$_3$	0.658	0.873	0.914	0.938
	BM25$_3$	**0.811**	**0.933**	**0.944**	0.955

candidate sets improve only marginally when their size exceeds 5. Therefore, we conclude that for our subsequent experiments, $k = 5$ is the optimal candidate set size and BM25$_3$ is the preferred blocking method. The related-concept filter will be applied where relevant. An illustration of the performance on the different candidate set sizes can be found in the appendix of the extended version [1].

This demonstrates that basic blocking techniques, such as the BM25$_3$ blocker, are effective in generating candidate sets with as little as 5 elements, achieving 90% recall, and that related-concept filtering can further improve recall to 93%.

5.2 Experiment 2: Candidate Selection

The goal of our second experiment is to assess the performance of different LLM-based candidate selectors using various prompt template configurations and few-shot examples. We run the experiment on the GraphSense TagPack validation set, using the candidate sets generated by the previous experiment. The model's task is to select the correct actor for each attribution tag from the candidate set if present, otherwise to predict that no candidate matches. The model selects a candidate by responding with the corresponding number, as illustrated in Fig. 4. Invalid responses are classified as no match, following the guidelines of [27,32]. We treat the task as a multiclass classification problem and evaluate the models using accuracy and macro-averages for recall, precision, and F1-score.

The results in Table 3 indicate that GPT-4o outperforms all other methods in both zero-shot and five-shot scenarios. Notably, while GPT-3.5 has the weakest performance with zero examples, it achieves the second-highest F1-score when five examples are included in the prompt. The Jellyfish 7B model ranks second in zero-shot F1-score, suggesting that its fine-tuning on diverse data preprocessing tasks positively impacts the entity selection task. In contrast, the Jellyfish 13B model underperforms compared to the other local models, despite having more parameters, confirming the findings of [42] that it performs worse on unseen tasks than its 7B counterpart. Among the local models, Mistral 7B-Instruct performs the best, achieving an F1 score of more than 90%.

Table 3. Candidate Selector results on the GraphSense TagPack validation set, showing recall (**R**), precision (**P**), F1-score (**F1**), and accuracy (**Acc.**) for each model's top-performing template (**T**). Best performance is in bold, second best is underlined.

Model	Zero-Shot					Five-Shot				
	T	R	P	F1	Acc.	T	R	P	F1	Acc.
GPT4o	1	**0.907**	**0.919**	**0.910**	**0.953**	7	**0.939**	**0.940**	**0.939**	**0.983**
GPT3.5	7	0.536	0.573	0.535	0.499	9	<u>0.929</u>	<u>0.928</u>	<u>0.927</u>	0.951
Jellyfish 7B	0	<u>0.804</u>	<u>0.802</u>	<u>0.797</u>	0.847	3	0.876	0.870	0.869	0.946
Jellyfish 13B	6	0.568	0.588	0.571	0.708	2	0.797	0.790	0.789	0.879
Llama 3 8B	0	0.744	0.743	0.738	0.827	0	0.868	0.859	0.861	0.947
Llama 3 8B-Inst	7	0.729	0.731	0.725	0.844	3	0.883	0.874	0.875	0.955
Mistral 7B	1	0.737	0.732	0.728	<u>0.850</u>	8	0.829	0.813	0.812	0.908
Mistral 7B-Inst	7	0.711	0.702	0.698	0.799	0	0.913	0.900	0.903	<u>0.958</u>

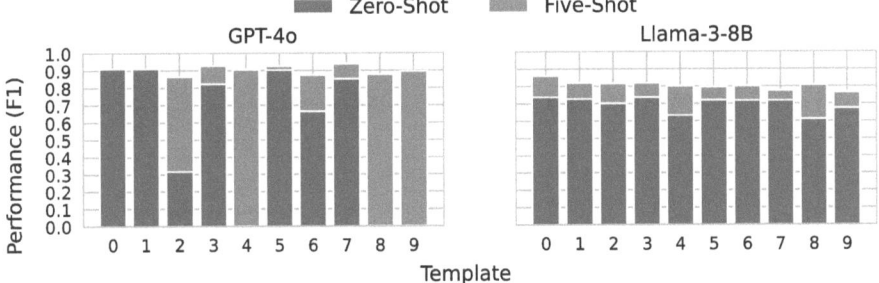

Fig. 5. Model Performance with different Templates. *GPT-4o's* zero-shot results vary significantly across different templates, while *Llama-3 8B* has a more stable performance.

In Fig. 5, we can see that the template choice can have a significant effect on some models. For example, GPT-4o zero-shot results are close to zero on some templates, while on others, they achieve F1-scores of over 90%. The Meta Llama 3 base model has the most stable performance and is the only model that achieves more than 60% F1-score on every template with zero examples. An overview of all models can be found in the appendix of the extended version [1].

Cost Analysis. Choosing more extensive template configurations and introducing few-shot examples increases the size of the prompts, and thus makes inference more expensive. For remote models, we define cost in $USD based on the OpenAI API usage policy[2] that charges based on the prompt size. The

---

[2] https://openai.com/api/pricing/.

current rates are (\$5,\$15) per 1 million input/output tokens for GPT-4o and (\$0.5,\$1.5) for GPT-3.5 Turbo.

For local LLMs, we use inference time as the cost metric. We define inference time as the time taken by the model to process all prompt batches and generate the responses, which includes tokenization but does not include the loading of the weights or any prompt pre/post-processing. We calculate the average run time of five runs for each template in both zero- and five-shot settings.

To determine which models and what configurations provide the best cost-performance value we first define value as:

$$V_{T/S} = F1_{T/S} * (1 - \tilde{C}_{T/S}) \qquad (3)$$

where T/S is the template/shot configuration and $\tilde{C} = \frac{C - \min(C)}{\max(C) - \min(C)}$ is the normalized cost. We normalize the cost for remote and local models separately.

Table 4. Template/Shots (**T/S**) configuration and cost and performance differences (Δ**C/F1**) between models with the highest F1-score and the one with the best cost-performance value (**V**). Local and remote models are compared separately

Model	T/S	F1	C	V	Δ(%)	
					C	F1
GPT-4o	7/5	0.939	\$3.359	0.116		
GPT-3.5	9/5	0.927	\$0.256	0.876	-92.380	-1.163
Mistral-7B-Inst	0/5	0.903	33.951 s	0.659		
Mistral-7B-Inst	9/5	0.899	22.777 s	0.797	-32.941	-0.390

In Table 4 we see that we can save over 90% on costs when using GPT-3.5 with template 9 while only losing 1% on the F1-score compared to the best GPT-4o configuration. The template configuration for local LLMs has less cost impact because we can reduce redundant computation to encode the large shared prefix of the prompts by using vLLM prefix caching [21]. However, using Mistral-7B-Inst with template 9 instead of template 0 still reduces inference time by more than 30%, with a performance decrease of less than 0.5%.

This experiment shows LLM-based entity linking is effective, with GPT-4o achieving a 94% F1-score. Aditionally, LLM's that can run locally in a consumer-grade GPU perform well, reaching 90% F1-score. Furthermore, we show that cost-performance analysis can yield a 90% cost reduction for only 1% of performance decrease.

5.3 Experiment 3: End to End Entity Linking

The goal of this experiment is to test our approach of linking attribution tags to a knowledge graph end-to-end and compare it to baseline solutions. We run the experiment on the GraphSense TagPack test set, WatchYourBack, and Defi Rekt datasets. All samples pass through the candidate generator, and the resulting batch of candidate sets are then fed to the candidate selector. For the candidate set generator, we employ the $BM25_3$ blocker. Additionally, we apply the *related-concept* filtering for the GraphSense dataset, while no filtering is used for the other datasets, because their categories are not linked to knowledge graph concepts. For the candidate selector, we use for each LLM the template that achieved the best performance in the previous experiment. We follow experiment 2's evaluation method, with the difference that a miss by the candidate set generator is counted as an error. We compare the LLMs with the following baseline methods:

$BM25_3$: We use the top ranking candidate of our $BM25_3$ blocker, and decide based on a threshold if it is a match or not. The threshold of *15.7238* was determined by evaluating the model's precision and recall on all top-candidate scores in the GraphSense TagPack validation set, and selecting the one that maximizes the F1-score.

UnicornPlus, UnicornPlusFT: UnicornPlus [37] is a DeBERTa-based mixture-of-expert model that is fine-tuned for data integration matching tasks. For a fair comparison, we apply the same candidate set generation process and perform pairwise matching between attribution tags and their candidates. In case multiple candidates match, we apply the softmax function on each prediction and choose the one with the highest probability. Furthermore, we create UnicornPlusFT, a fine-tuned version of the model. For this, we reshuffle our GraphSense train and validation sets with a 80/20 training/validation split and train the model for 10 epochs using the settings proposed in [37].

Table 5. Performance of various models on different datasets

Model	GraphSense		WatchYourBack		DeFi Rekt	
	F1	Acc.	F1	Acc.	F1	Acc.
$BM25_3$	0.718	0.789	0.495	0.516	0.393	0.510
UnicornPlus	0.667	0.445	0.558	0.651	0.352	0.670
UnicornPlusFT	0.783	0.873	0.542	0.603	0.419	0.610
GPT4o	**0.853**	**0.927**	**0.801**	**0.873**	**0.793**	**0.930**
GPT3.5	0.810	0.881	0.756	0.825	0.691	0.890
Llama 3 8B-Inst	0.814	0.921	0.625	0.746	0.516	0.710
Mistral 7B-Inst	0.821	0.918	0.692	0.786	0.547	0.770

Table 5 demonstrates that our end-to-end linking approach outperforms baseline methods across all datasets. Using $BM25_3$ blocking and GPT-4o as candidate selector, we achieve F1-scores of 79–85%. With Mistral 7B-Instruct, our best-performing local candidate selector, F1-scores range from 55–82%. Detailed results for all models and error type analysis are available in the appendix of the extended version [1].

This experiment shows that our approach outperforms baseline methods on all three datasets by up to 37.4% in F1-score. Furthermore, it demonstrates the generalization capabilities of our approach by achieving F1-scores of over 79% on all datasets.

6 Discussion and Conclusions

In this paper, we addressed the issue of *attribution tag quality*, with a particular focus on data inconsistencies that arise when attribution tags are shared among different parties. We argue that data quality issues can mislead forensic investigations and even result in false convictions if addresses are labeled incorrectly. To solve this, we proposed a novel computational approach based on Large Language Models (LLMs) that automatically links attribution tags to well-defined concepts in knowledge graphs, addressing the semantic nature of the problem. We implemented our approach in an end-to-end pipeline and demonstrated that, when combined with filtering and blocking techniques, it outperforms existing methods. Additionally, we showed that pre-trained LLMs running locally on consumer-grade hardware achieve performance comparable to remote models. Furthermore, we demonstrated that carefully designed prompts can significantly reduce costs with only a marginal decrease in performance. Overall, we believe our approach not only addresses the pressing issue of inconsistent attribution tags but also has the potential to inspire broader efforts to improve data quality in other forensic investigation tools and platforms.

One limitation of our approach is its binding to specific application domains; so far, we lack evidence that our method is generally applicable to all record linkage problems. However, we believe that a data- and measurement-driven approach would be valuable for assessing the broader suitability of this method. Another limitation is the assumption that different parties (e.g., exchanges, investigators) use the same knowledge graph when exchanging attribution tag records. If this is not the case, our approach does not harmonize the data but merely shifts the problem to a different abstraction level. However, significant efforts are being made to harmonize and adopt shared knowledge graphs within the field. For example, the Darkweb and Virtual Assets taxonomy developed by INTERPOL has been integrated into the Malware Information Sharing Platform (MISP) Galaxy[3]. This taxonomy helps categorize and enrich threat intelligence, with MISP Galaxies organizing related data clusters to describe higher-level concepts such as adversary groups, malware families, and vulnerabilities, simplifying complex data analysis for organizations.

Future work could include fine-tuning pre-trained LLMs to the cryptoasset domain, improving performance by recognizing semantically related terms that are syntactically different. Additionally, leveraging relationships like hypernyms

---

[3] https://misp-galaxy.org/interpol-dwva/.

and hyponyms in knowledge graphs could refine candidate matching. Extending the approach to automatically categorize cryptoasset addresses based on well-defined categories would also provide a more comprehensive solution.

Acknowledgments. Avice gratefully acknowledges funding from the Digital Finance CRC which is supported by the Cooperative Research Centres program, an Australian Government initiative. This research was partially funded by the Austrian security research program KIRAS of the Federal Ministry of Finance (BMF) under the project DeFiTrace (grant agreement number 905300) and the FFG BRIDGE project AMALFI (grant agreement number 898883).

Disclosure of Interests. The authors have no competing interests to declare that are relevant to the content of this article.

References

1. Avice, R., Haslhofer, B., Li, Z., Zhou, J.: Linking Cryptoasset attribution tags to knowledge graph entities: An LLM-based approach (2025). https://arxiv.org/abs/2502.10453
2. Bartoletti, M., Carta, S., Cimoli, T., Saia, R.: Dissecting Ponzi schemes on Ethereum: Identification, analysis, and impact. Futur. Gener. Comput. Syst. **102**, 259–277 (2020)
3. Brinkmann, A., Shraga, R., Bizer, C.: SC-Block: Supervised Contrastive Blocking Within Entity Resolution Pipelines, pp. 121–142. Springer Nature Switzerland (2024). https://doi.org/10.1007/978-3-031-60626-7_7
4. Tell congress: Stop the use of Chainalysis services. https://www.change.org/p/tell-congress-stop-the-use-of-chainalysis-services
5. Chen, W., Zheng, Z., Ngai, E.C.H., Zheng, P., Zhou, Y.: Exploiting blockchain data to detect smart ponzi schemes on Ethereum. IEEE Access **7**, 37575–37586 (2019). https://doi.org/10.1109/access.2019.2905769
6. David, I., Zhou, L., Qin, K., Song, D., Cavallaro, L., Gervais, A.: Do you still need a manual smart contract audit? (2023). https://doi.org/10.48550/arXiv.2306.12338
7. Deng, X., Sun, H., Lees, A., Wu, Y., Yu, C.: Turl: table understanding through representation learning. Proceedings of the VLDB Endowment **14**(3), 307–319 (2020). https://doi.org/10.14778/3430915.3430921
8. Efthymiou, V., Hassanzadeh, O., Rodriguez-Muro, M., Christophides, V.: Matching Web Tables with Knowledge Base Entities: From Entity Lookups to Entity Embeddings, pp. 260–277. Springer International Publishing (2017). https://doi.org/10.1007/978-3-319-68288-4_16
9. Elmagarmid, A.K., Ipeirotis, P.G., Verykios, V.S.: Duplicate record detection: a survey. IEEE Trans. Knowl. Data Eng. **19**(1), 1–16 (2007). https://doi.org/10.1109/tkde.2007.250581
10. Fröwis, M., Gottschalk, T., Haslhofer, B., Rückert, C., Pesch, P.: Safeguarding the evidential value of forensic cryptocurrency investigations. Forensic Science International: Digital Investigation **33**, 200902 (2020). https://doi.org/10.1016/j.fsidi.2019.200902
11. Gai, Y., Zhou, L., Qin, K., Song, D., Gervais, A.: Blockchain Large Language Models (2023). https://doi.org/10.48550/arXiv.2304.12749

12. Gan, R., Zhou, L., Wang, L., Qin, K., Lin, X.: DeFiAligner: Leveraging Symbolic Analysis and Large Language Models for Inconsistency Detection in Decentralized Finance. LIPIcs, Volume 316, AFT 2024 **316**, 7:1–7:24 (2024). https://doi.org/10.4230/LIPICS.AFT.2024.7
13. Gomez, G., Moreno-Sanchez, P., Caballero, J.: Watch your back: Identifying cybercrime financial relationships in bitcoin through back-and-forth exploration. In: Proceedings of the 2022 ACM SIGSAC Conference on Computer and Communications Security. pp. 1291–1305. CCS '22, ACM (2022). https://doi.org/10.1145/3548606.3560587
14. Google: Introducing the knowledge graph: Things, not strings (2012). https://blog.google/products/search/introducing-knowledge-graph-things-not/. Accessed: 2024-08-30
15. Harlev, M., Sun Yin, H., Langenheldt, K., Mukkamala, R., Vatrapu, R.: Breaking bad: De-anonymising entity types on the bitcoin blockchain using supervised machine learning. In: Proceedings of the 51st Hawaii International Conference on System Sciences 2018, pp. 3497–3506. In: Proceedings of the Annual Hawaii International Conference on System Sciences, Hawaii International Conference on System Sciences (HICSS), United States (2018). http://www.urbanccd.org/events/2018/1/3/hawaii-international-conference-on-system-sciences-hicss-51. The 51st Hawaii International Conference on System Sciences. HICSS 2018, HICSS2018 ; Conference date: 03-01-2018 Through 06-01-2018
16. Haslhofer, B., Klas, W.: A survey of techniques for achieving metadata interoperability. ACM Comput. Surv. **42**(2), 1–37 (2010)
17. Hogan, A., Blomqvist, E., Cochez, M., D'amato, C., Melo, G.D., Gutierrez, C., Kirrane, S., Gayo, J.E.L., Navigli, R., Neumaier, S., Ngomo, A.C.N., Polleres, A., Rashid, S.M., Rula, A., Schmelzeisen, L., Sequeda, J., Staab, S., Zimmermann, A.: Knowledge graphs. ACM Comput. Surv. **54**(4), 1–37 (2021)
18. Hu, S., Zhang, Z., Luo, B., Lu, S., He, B., Liu, L.: Bert4eth: A pre-trained transformer for ethereum fraud detection. In: Proceedings of the ACM Web Conference 2023. WWW '23, ACM (2023). https://doi.org/10.1145/3543507.3583345
19. Huang, D.Y., Aliapoulios, M.M., Li, V.G., Invernizzi, L., Bursztein, E., McRoberts, K., Levin, J., Levchenko, K., Snoeren, A.C., McCoy, D.: Tracking ransomware end-to-end. In: 2018 IEEE Symposium on Security and Privacy (SP). IEEE (2018). https://doi.org/10.1109/sp.2018.00047
20. Konda, P., et al.: Magellan: toward building entity matching management systems. Proc. VLDB Endowment **9**(12), 1197–1208 (2016). https://doi.org/10.14778/2994509.2994535
21. Kwon, W., Li, Z., Zhuang, S., Sheng, Y., Zheng, L., Yu, C.H., Gonzalez, J., Zhang, H., Stoica, I.: Efficient memory management for large language model serving with pagedattention. In: Proceedings of the 29th Symposium on Operating Systems Principles. SOSP '23, ACM (2023). https://doi.org/10.1145/3600006.3613165
22. Li, S., Gou, G., Liu, C., Hou, C., Li, Z., Xiong, G.: Ttagn: Temporal transaction aggregation graph network for ethereum phishing scams detection. In: Proceedings of the ACM Web Conference 2022. WWW '22, ACM (2022). https://doi.org/10.1145/3485447.3512226
23. Li, Y., Li, J., Suhara, Y., Doan, A., Tan, W.C.: Deep entity matching with pre-trained language models. Proc. VLDB Endow. **14**(1), 50–60 (2020). https://doi.org/10.14778/3421424.3421431
24. Liu, X., Tang, Z., Li, P., Guo, S., Fan, X., Zhang, J.: A graph learning based approach for identity inference in Dapp platform blockchain. IEEE Trans. Emerg. Top. Comput. **10**(1), 438–449 (2022)

25. Meiklejohn, S., et al.: A fistful of bitcoins: characterizing payments among men with no names. In: Proceedings of the 2013 conference on Internet measurement conference. IMC'13, ACM (2013). https://doi.org/10.1145/2504730.2504747
26. Mudgal, S., et al.: Deep learning for entity matching: A design space exploration. In: Proceedings of the 2018 International Conference on Management of Data. SIGMOD/PODS '18, ACM (2018). https://doi.org/10.1145/3183713.3196926
27. Narayan, A., Chami, I., Orr, L., Ré, C.: Can foundation models wrangle your data? Proc. VLDB Endowment **16**(4), 738–746 (2022). https://doi.org/10.14778/3574245.3574258
28. Papadakis, G., Skoutas, D., Thanos, E., Palpanas, T.: Blocking and filtering techniques for entity resolution: a survey. ACM Comput. Surv. **53**(2), 1–42 (2020)
29. Paquet-Clouston, M., Haslhofer, B., Dupont, B.: Ransomware payments in the bitcoin ecosystem. J. Cybersec. **5**(1) (2019). https://doi.org/10.1093/cybsec/tyz003
30. Paquet-Clouston, M., Romiti, M., Haslhofer, B., Charvat, T.: Spams meet cryptocurrencies: sextortion in the bitcoin ecosystem. In: Proceedings of the 1st ACM Conference on Advances in Financial Technologies. AFT '19, ACM (2019). https://doi.org/10.1145/3318041.3355466
31. Paulsen, D., Govind, Y., Doan, A.: Sparkly: A simple yet surprisingly strong tf/idf blocker for entity matching. Proc. VLDB Endowment **16**(6), 1507–1519 (2023). https://doi.org/10.14778/3583140.3583163
32. Peeters, R., Bizer, C.: Entity matching using large language models (2024). https://arxiv.org/abs/2310.11244v2
33. Ritze, D., Lehmberg, O., Bizer, C.: Matching html tables to Dbpedia. In: Proceedings of the 5th International Conference on Web Intelligence, Mining and Semantics. WIMS '15, ACM (2015). https://doi.org/10.1145/2797115.2797118
34. Robertson, S.E., Walker, S.: Some Simple Effective Approximations to the 2-Poisson Model for Probabilistic Weighted Retrieval, p. 232–241. Springer London (1994). https://doi.org/10.1007/978-1-4471-2099-5_24
35. Shen, W., Wang, J., Han, J.: Entity linking with a knowledge base: Issues, techniques, and solutions. IEEE Transactions on Knowledge and Data Engineering **27**(2), 443–460 (2015). https://doi.org/10.1109/tkde.2014.2327028
36. Thirumuruganathan, S., et al.: Deep learning for blocking in entity matching: a design space exploration. Proceedings of the VLDB Endowment **14**(11), 2459–2472 (2021). https://doi.org/10.14778/3476249.3476294
37. Tu, J., Fan, J., Tang, N., Wang, P., Li, G., Du, X., Jia, X., Gao, S.: Unicorn: A unified multi-tasking model for supporting matching tasks in data integration. Proc. ACM Manag. Data **1**(1), 1–26 (2023)
38. Vrandečić, D., Krötzsch, M.: Wikidata: a free collaborative knowledgebase. Commun. ACM **57**(10), 78–85 (2014)
39. Wang, R., Li, Y., Wang, J.: Sudowoodo: Contrastive self-supervised learning for multi-purpose data integration and preparation. In: 2023 IEEE 39th International Conference on Data Engineering (ICDE). vol. 14, p. 1502–1515. IEEE (2023). https://doi.org/10.1109/icde55515.2023.00391
40. Wang, T., et al.: Match, compare, or select? An investigation of large language models for entity matching (2024). https://arxiv.org/abs/2405.16884
41. Wu, J., Yuan, Q., Lin, D., You, W., Chen, W., Chen, C., Zheng, Z.: Who are the phishers? phishing scam detection on ethereum via network embedding. IEEE Trans. Syst. Man Cybern. Syst. **52**(2), 1156–1166 (2022)

42. Zhang, H., Dong, Y., Xiao, C., Oyamada, M.: Jellyfish: A large language model for data preprocessing (2024). https://arxiv.org/abs/2312.01678v4
43. Zhou, J., Hu, C., Chi, J., Wu, J., Shen, M., Xuan, Q.: Behavior-aware account deanonymization on ethereum interaction graph. IEEE Transactions on Information Forensics and Security **17**, 3433–3448 (2022). https://doi.org/10.1109/tifs.2022.3208471

CCBNet: Confidential Collaborative Bayesian Networks Inference

Abele Mălan[1(✉)], Thiago Guzella[2], Jérémie Decouchant[3], and Lydia Chen[1,3]

[1] University of Neuchâtel, Neuchâtel, Switzerland
{abele.malan,yiyu.chen}@unine.ch
[2] ASML, Eindhoven, Netherlands
thiago.guzella@asml.com
[3] Delft University of Technology, Delft, Netherlands
j.decouchant@tudelft.nl

Abstract. Effective large-scale process optimization in manufacturing industries requires close cooperation between different human expert parties who encode their knowledge of related domains as Bayesian network models. For instance, Bayesian networks for domains such as lithography equipment, processes, and auxiliary tools must be conjointly used to effectively identify process optimizations in the semiconductor industry. However, business confidentiality across domains hinders such collaboration, and encourages alternatives to centralized inference. We propose CCBNet, the first **C**onfidentiality-preserving **C**ollaborative **B**ayesian **Net**works inference framework. CCBNet leverages secret sharing to securely perform analysis on the combined knowledge of party models by joining two novel subprotocols: (i) CABN, which augments probability distributions for variables across parties by modeling them into secret shares of their normalized combination; and (ii) SAVE, which aggregates party inference result shares through distributed variable elimination. We extensively evaluate CCBNet via 9 public Bayesian networks. Our results show that CCBNet achieves predictive quality that is similar to the ones of centralized methods while preserving model confidentiality. We further demonstrate that CCBNet scales to challenging manufacturing use cases that involve 16–128 parties in large networks of 223–1003 variables, and decreases, on average, computational overhead by 23%, while communicating 71k values per request. Finally, we showcase possible attacks and mitigations for partially reconstructing party networks in the protocol.

1 Introduction

Improving productivity and quality standards in manufacturing demands effectively expressing complex interactions between domain items. Bayesian networks

---

Work partly done while graduating from TU Delft and interning at ASML.

(BNs) are commonly adopted to graphically model causality in manufacturing [20], with nodes representing variables and directed edges showing dependencies. An essential trait of these models is their ability to specify arbitrary input and output variables for each query instead of having them fixed.

In the semiconductor industry, the pursuit of smaller chips at a high yield [28] entails cooperation among specialized parties protecting their trade secrets. More specifically, fab operators encode their insight into settings dictating the production process in a BN. Similarly, vendors of equipment like scanners, construct BNs that describe the inner workings of their machines. Pooling together parties' knowledge allows to better optimize production environments, leading to new business opportunities. Simultaneously, the need to protect intellectual property expressed within party models calls for confidential collaboration.

Existing studies on collaborative inference for BNs **ignore model confidentiality** or limit the ability to merge party information. We consider confidentiality preserved if parties cannot infer from others the identity and structural connections of new variables, or parameters of other probability tables, even for variables they also define themselves. Most previous works detail a centralized combination of local BNs into a larger one [10,11] without protecting confidential knowledge within the input networks and global output. Models get stitched together based on common nodes, and remain in the final representation as largely unaltered submodels whose encoded knowledge is easily inspectable. Pavlin et al. [22] propose a distributed combination variant that partially preserves confidentiality by maintaining the locality of combined party models. However, it leaks information when combining them and does not allow merging inner graph nodes having both parents and children. Tedesco et al. [27] maintain the confidentiality of how nodes are linked within parties but only allow propagating information between them in a fixed sequential order. The approach of Kim and Ghahramani [17] has similar confidentiality properties but even greater compatibility restrictions by requiring models to have identical inputs and outputs.

In this paper, we propose CCBNet, the first confidential, collaborative BNs inference framework that combines knowledge of multiple parties involved in inference queries through a novel secret sharing scheme. CCBNet does not require a trusted third party, and protects confidentiality at both the levels of party models and data instances. The two key components of CCBNet are: (i) confidential sharing of aggregated variable probability distributions across all overlapping parties; and (ii) distributed inference based on variable elimination for aggregating party results. The novelty of the augmentation procedure lies in constructing discrete conditional probability distributions for all variables present in more than one party. These variables represent secret shares of a combined and normalized distribution from a centralized scenario without exposing any party's initial probability function. To evaluate CCBNet, we simulate knowledge compartmentalization over different public BNs. Moreover, we demonstrate possible attacks against the framework, their limitations, and possible mitigations.

In summary, we make the following contributions:

- We devise a confidential, collaborative framework for BNs, CCBNet, to satisfy the needs of industry use cases like process optimization in manufacturing.
- We design a novel secret sharing-based protocol, CABN, to confidentially augment the conditional probability function of overlapping variables in parties.
- We define SAVE, a method backed by variable elimination for performing distributed secret sharing inference on augmented party models.
- We evaluate CCBNet over various scenarios based on nine public BNs. Our results indicate that CCBNet's predictive accuracy is similar to those of non-confidential centralized alternatives and, for many collaborators in large networks, that CCBNet decreases the computational overhead by 23% on average when 71k values are communicated per request.
- We discuss possible attacks and mitigations on the two CCBNet subprotocols.

Our code is available at: https://github.com/AbeleMM/ccbnet

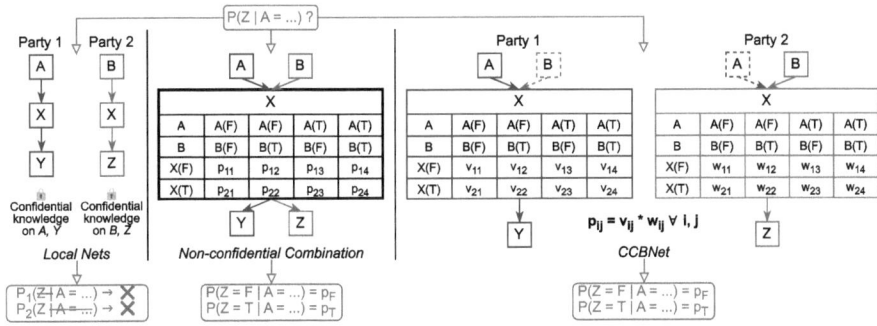

Fig. 1. Bayesian networks collaboration comparison: Variables are X (shared), A, B, Y, and Z. They all have two states, **F**alse and **T**rue. Entries p_{ij} are conditional probability values (e.g., $p_{11} = P(X = F \mid A = F, B = F)$). v_{ij} and w_{ij} are secret shares which multiplied reconstruct p_{ij}. After observing A, inferring Z's updated posterior $P(Z \mid A = ...)$ requires propagating information between A, B, and X, which is impossible by averaging model outputs. Meanwhile, the non-confidential approach reveals the combined graph and probability tables to parties. CCBNet exchanges minimal structural information among parties and runs distributed inference with secretly shared confidential values.

2 Background and Related Studies

2.1 Background

Bayesian Networks are probabilistic graphical models that maintain explicit conditional probability distributions (CPDs) for variables which form a directed acyclic graph [26]. Shown in Fig. 1, variables and the influences between them give the graph nodes and edges, respectively. Principally for performance and interpretability, variables in practical applications are generally discrete, with CPDs specifically embodying conditional probability tables. Learning may be driven by data, human experts, or both [8,18], as with other human-readable models like decision trees. Automated learning discovers the graph structure and then populates CPD parameters from training data. Manual learning is desirable when incorporating concepts with known governing rules that need no approximation from observations.

Computation in discrete BNs relies on a few base operations for propagating information: normalization, reduction, marginalization, and products [18]. We outline them with help from the non-confidential combination in Fig. 1. Normalizing a CPD divides its entries by their column sum. Thus column summations, like $p_{11} + p_{21}$, would become 1. Reduction and marginalization remove variables from a CPD by fixing their states or, respectively, summing them out. Reducing or marginalizing A from X leaves B as its sole parent. Previous operations apply to both representations. Products operate on CPDs of the same variable or factors and create a new CPD/factor over the input variables' union, where each entry is the multiplication of the corresponding ones in the original representations. The product of X and Z's factors, thus, also contains A and B.

In the considered discrete scenario, a CPD with target variable X, and parents $A, B, ...$ is denoted as an $(S_X \times S_A \times S_B \times ...)$ array, accompanied by a mapping between dimensions to variables and indices to states. S_V is the number of states for variable V. Each entry specifies a probability value for the state combination it represents. The corresponding factor is identical but does not distinguish between a target and parents. Any continuous variables would need to have a globally agreed-upon discretization applied to them before usage.

Inference in BNs finds updated posterior probabilities for the states of target variables, given the observed states of any evidence variables [23,24]. As general inference is NP-Hard, approximate algorithms help decrease computation costs compared to exact ones while sacrificing some precision in the result. The main exact inference techniques are variable elimination (VE) and junction tree belief propagation, which decomposes the network into a tree of variable clusters, runs VE within them and then disseminates updates between neighbors by message-passing [18]. In Fig. 1's query, Z is the target, given some observed state of A. The VE algorithm performs three main steps over the factors corresponding to the model's CPDs. It first reduces the evidence from input factors. Reduction merely discards entries in the factor where evidence variables have a different state than specified. Then, it iteratively performs products between factors and marginalizes them for each non-query variable. Lastly, it takes the product between the leftover factors to get the final result factor.

Markov random fields (MRFs) are a sibbling model of BNs, backed by undirected graphs, into which every BN is easily transformable via moralization [19,25]. Apart from lacking acyclicity constraints, MRFs directly define parameters as factors and can deal with scenarios where edge directionality is unspecified, but BNs are more compact and efficient for generative use. For inference, BN properties and algorithms remain applicable. Thus, when aciclicity constraints are unsatisfiable, MRFs can still perform inference like in BNs.

2.2 Prior Art

We identify two high-level categories of collaborative analysis for BNs: single- and multi-model. The first creates one global model, while the other keeps local models separate, merging their results.

Single-model approaches harness party data instances or models but neglect model confidentiality. Federated learning discovers models [1,7,12,15,21] from private party instances with a coordinator. Fully decentralized formulations also exist [4,13]. Direct network combination fuses structure [2,10] and parameters [11] from party models.

Multi-model methods have parties work together during inference to produce a complete analysis result. Tedesco et al. [27] chain model without exchanging their contents but only allows using them one at a time in a predetermined order. Less confidential but more flexible, the work of Pavlin et al. [22] fuses party networks based on common nodes but still requires them to be roots or leaves in the party's directed acyclic graph. Ypma et al. [29] patent a collaborative solution for industrial processes, but only mention data confidentiality preservation by anonymization. Kim and Ghahramani [17] run models autonomously and only average their final outputs, maintaining confidentiality but expecting models to share inputs and outputs.

Single-model solutions break confidentiality by centralizing knowledge. Multi-model ones trade modeling power for confidentiality. CCBNet addresses both.

3 CCBNet

We propose, CCBNet, a framework for secure distributed analysis over a related set of confidential and discrete BNs. CCBNet is composed of two key steps, (i) CABN augments the BNs of parties through overlapping variables, and (ii) SAVE performs joint inference on them.

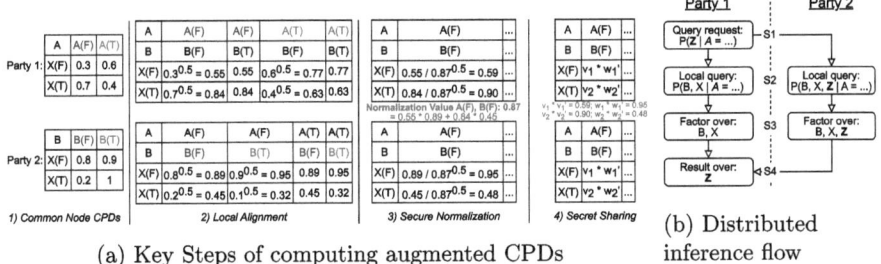

Fig. 2. CABN & SAVE steps for Fig. 1 scenario.

The assumptions we make are that variables from different parties have the same name only if they represent the same concept, and the independence, across parties, of distinct parents for the same node reasonably approximates the ground truth. These are shared by previous BN combination works. Thus, names identify the overlapping (common) nodes between models, giving the contact points for graph fusion. Since variables modeled by parties may be any subset of those from the full domain, modeling direct interactions between their non-overlapping variables requires great amounts of often unavailable information.

Our adversarial model includes semi-honest parties that follow the protocol while trying to abuse gained information [14] but do not collude. No trusted third party exists. The goal is to protect all network parameters and only disclose structure/state-name information among parties modeling the same variables.

Algorithm 1. CABN

Input: $P = \{p_1, p_2, \ldots, p_n\}$ – parties,
$CPD_p[T \mid A, B, \ldots]$ – CPD in party p for target var T with parent vars $\{A, B, \ldots\}$,
$weight_p$ – weight assigned by p to its BN (defaults to 1)
Output: updated $CPD_p[O \mid \ldots]$, $\forall$ overlap var O modeled by party p

1: **for each** var V of parties from P **do**
2:    $parties_V \leftarrow \emptyset$ {list of parties containing V}
3:    $states_V \leftarrow \emptyset$ {list of overlap states for V}
4: **for each** pair of parties (p, p') from P **do**
5:    **for each** var $O \in PSI$(vars of p, vars of p') **do**
6:      $parties_O \leftarrow parties_O \cup \{p, p'\}$
7: **for each** var O s.t. $parties_O \neq \emptyset$ **do**
8:    **for each** var set $\mathcal{V} = \{X, Y, \ldots\}$ s.t. $(p \in parties_O \land CPD_p[O \mid \mathcal{V}]$ exists) **do**
9:      $states_V \leftarrow states_V \cup \{v_0, v_1, \ldots\}$ {where v_i is a state of var V}
10:    $idCPD \leftarrow$ CPD for target var O and $states_V$ with all entries 1
11:    $wSum \leftarrow \sum_{p \in parties_O} weight_p$
12:    **for each** party $p \in parties_O$ **do**
13:      $CPD_p[O \mid \ldots] \leftarrow CPD_p[O \mid \ldots] \cdot idCPD$ {factor prod}
14:      $CPD_p[O \mid \ldots] \leftarrow CPD_p[O \mid \ldots]^{weight_p/wSum}$ {element-wise exp}
15:    **for each** parent config $\mathcal{S} = (X = x_i, Y = y_j, \ldots)$ s.t. $idCPD[O \mid \mathcal{S}]$ exists **do**
16:      $prodHE \leftarrow \odot_{p \in parties_O} HE_{enc}(CPD_p[O \mid \mathcal{S}])$ {enc element-wise prod}
17:      $norm \leftarrow HE_{dec}(\|prodHE\|_1)^{1/|parties_O|}$ {dec normalization scalar}
18:      **for each** party $p \in parties_O$ **do**
19:        $CPD_p[O \mid \ldots] \leftarrow CPD_p[O \mid \ldots] / norm$
20:    **for each** party $p \in parties_O$ **do**
21:      $CPD_p^0[O \mid \ldots], CPD_p^1[O \mid \ldots], \cdots \leftarrow$ secret share $CPD_p[O \mid \ldots]$
22:    **for each** party $p_i \in parties_O$ **do**
23:      $CPD_{p_i}[O \mid \ldots] \leftarrow \prod_{p \in parties_O} CPD_p^i[O \mid \ldots]$
24: **return** $CPD_p[O \mid \ldots]$, $\forall\, parties_O \neq \emptyset, p \in parties_O$

3.1 Confidentially Augmented Bayesian Networks

We now present the CABN[1] protocol, which updates local CPDs for overlap variables to hold secret shares of their combination, protecting the initial probabilities. Algorithm 1 details the four steps of the protocol, illustrated in Fig. 2 a: (i) private common node identification; (ii) local alignment; (iii) secure normalization; and (iv) secret sharing. The protocol updates parties when the number of changes in local networks passes a set threshold.

Overview. Structurally, CABN imitates a union of the involved networks of Del Sagrado and Moral [10]. Parameter-wise, it follows Feng et al. [11] but replaces the superposition operator with the geometric mean. We use the union instead of the more complex ruleset of Feng et al. to decide which overlapping node parents to retain. The more straightforward allows for combining more than two BNs at a time, lowering the number of communication rounds. It also reduces the attack surface area due to fewer checks on party data. For fusing probabilities, the geometric mean enables a multiplication-based secret sharing scheme in CABN. Reconstruction happens automatically during distributed inference when merging local results from parties. The mean also outperforms the superposition in our centralized tests.

Step 1: Private Common Node Identification. CABN starts with party pairs identifying their common nodes like in the central case, albeit privately. We use a private set intersection (PSI) protocol [9] to attain confidentiality (ll. 1-6). Only parties that have updates need to recalculate their intersection with the others. Outside the private intersection context, node and state names are communicated obfuscated to prevent information leakage about which parties model which nodes. Parties can choose any unique representation for non-overlapping nodes, but involved parties agree on an obfuscated representation for overlapping ones. Our implementation uses a commutative elliptic curve ElGamal cypher.

Step 2: Local Alignment. After parties know which local nodes overlap with which peers, they start solving overlaps by exchanging structure and weight information about their local CPDs and independently updating local representations accordingly (ll. 7-14). First, the obfuscated union of CPD nodes and states for overlapping CPDs is determined (ll. 8-9). From it, an identity CPD containing all the parents across parties gets created for the union (l. 10). An identity CPD (or factor) has all entries equal to 1, so its product with another replicates the later's columns over their joint state space. The initial CPD gets replaced by the product with the identity in each party, giving all overlap CPDs the same shape (l. 13), as seen in Fig. 2 a. Parties have a public weight representing confidence in their BN, which in the default unweighted case is 1. They compute the sum of their weights (l. 11) and individually raise the entries of their CPD to the ratio between their weight and the sum, computing the partial geometric mean (l. 14). By the exponent product rule $(XY)^k = X^k Y^k$, the CPDs' product already yields the unnormalized CPD of the central combination.

Model Weighting. As previously mentioned, CABN allows weighting CPDs through the geometric mean, unlike previous BN works that cover parameter

---
[1] **C**onfidentially **A**ugmented **B**ayesian **N**etworks.

fusion. A natural integration of unequal weighting of inputs is another advantage of using a geometric mean instead of Feng et al.'s superposition. We implement weights at the model level as 0–1 values, encoding the human expert's confidence in the network or data availability for algorithmic learning. Nevertheless, weighting can be applied at the CPD level.

Step 3: Secure Normalization. Homomorphic encryption (HE) [5] allows to privately compute column normalization values (ll. 15-19). One party is elected to generate the encryption key pair and another to perform the encrypted computation. All parties receive the public key and send their encrypted columns to the party that calculates normalization value ciphers (l. 16). The private key party decrypts the values and shares them with the rest (l. 17). A column normalization value is the sum of entries obtained by multiplying matching party columns element-wise. Letting P_{ij} denote party i CPD column j, we thus find $\|\odot_i P_{ij}\|_1$. Then, the K overlapping parties individually divide each column by the K-th root of the appropriate normalization value (l. 19), so their factor product is the normalized geometric mean. Figure 2 a shows an example. Our implementation relies on the CKKS [5] HE scheme for floating-point addition and multiplication.

Because local columns no longer sum to 1 after exponentiation, even in a two-party overlap where the variable has only two possible states, a party cannot reconstruct the other's entries by only knowing the normalization values and its own entries. Furthermore, vital for HE schemes in practice, we know that the number of consecutive multiplications needed for each column is equal to the party count, which allows configuring the scheme accordingly. Functional encryption, in which completing the desired computation also decrypts the output [3], can be a more viable choice, but existing implementations have overly stringent limits on the number of inputs and complexity of the applied functions. Using a secret sharing scheme (SSS) [6] instead of HE is also possible, but we favor decreasing the communication count over computing overhead for this step. An SSS has the advantage of requiring fewer computational resources and being more robust against collusion. However, it requires communication for each multiplication operation and, depending on the scheme, the presence of a third party. Despite the expectation that CABN needs to run more rarely than inference, we still favor optimizing for message count. High communication latency is likelier to be a bottleneck than processing for envisioned deployments.

The only extra role of the two elected parties, K and C, is to manage the private/public key pair and compute with the encrypted data, respectively. We elect both parties from those in the overlap, so their CPDs are also part of the calculation. They can be picked based on any criteria, like the order of joining the network. Party K forwards the public key to all others in the overlap, C excluded. Parties, K included, send their encrypted data to C, which calculates the normalization value. The result gets forwarded to K, which decrypts and shares it with all overlap parties. Apart from the normalization value, party K only ever has the chance to decrypt data it owns. The elected parties may also be outside the overlap as long as they are different entities.

Algorithm 2. SAVE

Input: $P = \{p_1, p_2, \ldots\}$ – parties,
$\mathcal{Q} = \{X, Y, \ldots\}$ – query vars, $\mathcal{E} = \{a_i, b_j, \ldots\}$ – evidence var states
Output: factor over $\mathcal{Q}$

1: **for each** party $p \in P$ **do**
2:     {receive $\mathcal{Q}$ & $\mathcal{E}$ from querying party}
3:     $inFacts_p \leftarrow$ set of CPDs in p as factors
4:     $\mathcal{Q}_p \leftarrow$ all overlap vars of p and their parents
5:     $outFact_p \leftarrow VE(\mathcal{Q} \cup \mathcal{Q}_p, \mathcal{E}, inFacts_p)$ {exec by p}
6:     {send $outFact_p$ to querying party}
7: **return** $VE(\mathcal{Q}, \{\}, \bigcup_{p \in P} outFact_p)$ {exec by querying party}

Step 4: Secret Sharing. Finally, to combat party parameter leaks at inference, we secret share [16] the CPD entries of parties in each overlap through a multiplication-based scheme (ll. 20-23). The scheme allows using the product operation needed for inference while exchanging a similar number of messages to HE and achieving much better computation scaling. The common shape of updated local CPDs facilitates the procedure. In the classic additive secret sharing scheme, a secret value is split into shares distributed among parties whose sum is the secret. It allows efficient and secure computation of expressions summing multiple secret values and applying other operations involving non-secret values. Parties perform the computation with their local share of each secret and all aggregate their results to reconstruct the answer. The utilized scheme functions similarly but uses multiplication as the base operation instead. Reconstruction happens implicitly during inference, with no extra overhead since other factors containing partial results from parties get incorporated into the final result via the same product operations. Figure 2 a exemplifies share splitting in CPDs.

Handling potential cycles. To avoid compatibility restrictions between combinable BNs, if solving overlaps creates a cycle, the distributed global network gets treated as an MRF, with no changes to the inference, which operates on factors regardless. Edges that form cycles in the BN are effectively incorporated into the moralized MRF and treated as undirected. Since the main target is to not share the complete combined network, the readability advantages of BNs are not a concern in the joint global model. Deciding which edge to remove from a cycle often requires unavailable information and threatens confidentiality. Alternatives like treating all nodes within a cycle as a single node [29] are coarse-grained and threaten confidentiality.

3.2 Share Aggregation Variable Elimination

SAVE[2] is the inference protocol wherein all parties run VE locally before aggregating their outputs into the final factor. Algorithm 2 describes its steps, and

---
[2] **S**hare **A**ggregation **V**ariable **E**limination.

Fig. 2 b visualizes an example query. Parties execute most of the process in parallel (algo. l. 1). They first receive the obfuscated target variables $\mathcal{Q}$ and evidence $\mathcal{E}$ from the querying party (algo. 1.2, S1 in fig.). Then, they prepare all their CPDs as factors (algo l. 3). They extend the queried variables set with local overlap variables and their parents (algo. l. 4). Extending the set avoids illegal marginalization operations within our SSS. Although the individual operations have no overhead via our scheme, the changed order of operations is less efficient, increasing the cost of VE. Parties each run VE over their factors and extended query set (algo. l. 5, S2 in fig.). To reduce overall communication strain, our implementation defaults to stopping VE early and returning a list of disjoint smaller factors instead of a single large one. Consequently, each party sends its result to the querying party (algo. l. 6, S3 in fig.). Finally, the querying party runs VE with the original set of query variables and received factors to get the query result factor (algo. l. 7, S4 in fig.).

Applying a *log* transform to values and using additive secret sharing instead of the multiplication-based variant would also work for products but cause even more marginalization issues. Allowing multiplications between shares and plaintext would require taking the *log* of all values, not just shares. Consequently, plaintext marginalization becomes impossible since addition has no correspondence under *log*. Fixed-point arithmetic keeps the scheme's theoretical guarantees by mapping fractional CPD values to integers. Within it, rounding avoids overflows from multiplication chains.

Queryable Nodes. To maintain confidentiality, parties can only specify modeled variables in inference by default, even if the result still reflects the effect of prior knowledge about others, so we propose mechanisms for expanding the set of possible queries. The first involves all parties that own a node agreeing to expose its unobfuscated name and states with select others to use as a target or evidence. Doing so only requires revealing a node's existence, not its place in the network(s). The other mechanism implicitly enhances evidence with the help of some key shared between parties (e.g., timestamp, product batch identifier). If a query request also includes a value for the shared key, parties incorporate any observations for the key's value as evidence during their local inference step. Parties do not have to disclose the value of the observed data, but the query output is the same as if it had been part of the initial evidence.

Communication Properties. The number of messages exchanged within an inference request is of magnitude $O(N)$ (where N is the number of parties), but the size of the messages varies. Regarding count, the requester sends out $N-1$ messages and receives the same amount of replies adding up to $2N-2$. The size of the messages, particularly replies, varies greatly depending on the number and complexity of the responder's overlaps and the query itself.

4 Performance Evaluation

Our main results show `CCBNet` achieving the predictive ability of centralized solutions in the confidential, collaborative setting and examine its ability to maintain reasonable computation and communication costs.

4.1 Setup

Table 1. Evaluation datasets with node/edge/parameter counts

Class	Name	#Nodes	#Edges	#Params
Small (< 20 Nodes)	ASIA	8	8	18
Medium (20–49 Nodes)	CHILD	20	25	230
	ALARM	37	46	509
	INSURANCE	27	52	1008
Large (50–99 Nodes)	WIN95PTS	76	112	574
Very Large (101–999 Nodes)	ANDES	223	338	1157
	PIGS	441	592	5618
	LINK	724	1125	14211
Massive (≥ 1000 Nodes)	MUNIN2	1003	1244	69431

Our experiments evaluate average predictive performance, computation overhead, and communication cost of inference in single-machine simulations. We measure prediction quality based on the Brier Score ($= \frac{1}{N}\sum_{t=1}^{N}\sum_{i=1}^{R}(f_{ti} - o_{ti})^2$, where N is the number of queries, R is the number of target variables state combinations, while f and o are predicted and reference probabilities). Note that, different from the original multi-category definition, we have probability values for all reference entries o instead of a binary value differentiating an observed (1) state from all others (0). We report the total processing time ratio between examined methods and the ground truth network for computation overhead. For communication we consider the count of factor values exchanged per query. We do not evaluate CABN time or communication as we expect it to be amortizable.

We test on public networks[3] (Table 1), and consider two variable splitting methods alongside multiple overlap variable ratios. **Related splits** assign to parties variables connected in the ground truth network. **Random splits** ensure parties have equal variable counts and share the same overlaps. Test sets contain 2000 queries, each with one random overlap variable as the target and 60% of the others fixed as evidence. Related splits attempt to simulate a realistic deployment in which the experts within clients have an incomplete but close-to-the-ground truth view of the interactions between their modeled variables (which also differ in number). Random splits aim for a worst-case scenario where the variables within clients (of roughly equal number) are not subgraphs of the complete network, generally giving more densely connected local networks and overlaps.

---
[3] https://www.bnlearn.com/bnrepository/.

4.2 Baselines

As the closest prior work is strictly centralized, our baselines are:

Centralized Combination (CC) iteratively combines parties by the method of [11] and treats the network as an MRF if cycles form.

Centralized Union (CU), the approach confidentially mimicked by CCBNet, is structurally based on the union of [10], combines parameters via geometric mean, and also applies the MRF principle.

Decentralized Output Mean (DOM) is a naïve approach that takes the geometric mean for each target variable's state probabilities over independently operating contained parties, trading long-range effect modeling for greater safety.

CCBNetJ is a degenerate CCBNet variant that stores fully combined central CPDs for overlaps in singular parties, trading some safety for faster inference.

4.3 CCBNet Performance Overview

In Fig. 3, we summarize Brier score, computation time, and communication cost results under two splitting methods, four parties, and a 30% overlap ratio.

Predictive Performance. Regardless of split type, CCBNet predictions often outperform or match the classic CC and always beat the naïve DOM. Figure 3 a gives results for related splits, CCBNet only scores worse than CC on the smallest network (0.015 versus 0.005) and gains a significant advantage over the larger ones (0.022 versus 0.009, 0.123 versus 0.114, and 0.006 versus 0.016). CCBNet has an advantage over DOM in all scenarios. Examining the random splits in Fig. 3 b, CCBNet still outscores CC in all but one of the smaller networks (0.031 vs 0.038) and maintains its lead over DOM in all but the smallest network, where the two tie. Since CCBNet yields the same predictive ability as its centralized counterpart CU, the differentiating points with CC are the structure combination policy and parameter combination operator. Over both splits, the pairing of the union selection and geometric mean aggregation in CCBNet fares better in most cases than the nondeterministic selection and superposition aggregation of CC, apart from some instances within small networks.

Computation Overhead. Regarding computation cost relative to centralized inference on the original network, average slowdowns are 1.63x for DOM, 1.15x for CCBNetJ, and 1.6x for CCBNet. Communication latency is unaccounted for as it can vary greatly based on the deployment. Still, we overestimate wall time by summing computation time across parties, as much processing would happen concurrently in reality. In the related splits from Fig. 3 c, across the board, CCBNetJ is the fastest, but others follow closely. CCBNet is the second best in all except the largest networks, where it fares worse than DOM (1.17x vs 1.3x slower). The networks also examined for random splits in Fig. 3 d show a similar trend, with somewhat higher general overhead, especially for CCBNet. Thus, as expected, CCBNetJ is faster than CCBNet, but both perform reasonably in most scenarios, even if the latter suffers more as overlaps increase in complexity. The DOM implementation does has a higher base overhead, but the gap to the other

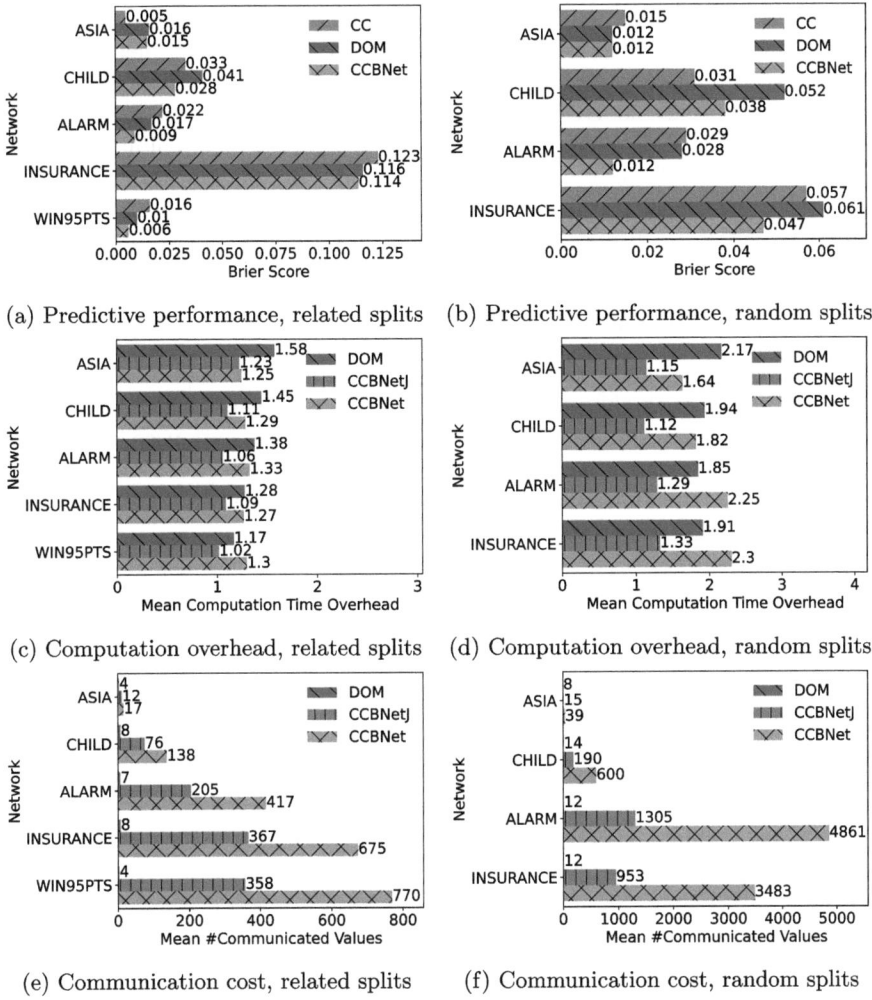

Fig. 3. Performance of decentralized methods relative to ground truth (lower is better); 4 parties, 30% of vars in > 1 party.

algorithms is often relatively contained. As for absolute total computation time, queries are slowest on the largest related splits dataset, as DOM averages 2.9 ms/query, CCBNetJ 2.5 ms, and CCBNet 3.2 ms.

Communication Cost. DOM averages merely 9 CPD values communicated per query, while CCBNetJ and CCBNet need orders of magnitude more at 387 and 1222, respectively. Since the number of communicated values depends on which party initiates a query, the reported figures include communication within the querying party to eliminate variability but overestimate reality. The number of messages to complete a query is the same for all methods. Furthermore, the raw data transmitted in bytes remain in the low megabyte range for hundreds of thousands of values before compression. Figure 3 e shows the mentioned discrepancy over related splits for all but the smallest network, in which the three methods are comparable. DOM merges complete party outputs and cannot propagate evidence between parties. Thus, it does not increase communication with the number of overlaps, and parties that do not contain any target variables send empty replies. The situation for random splits, illustrated in Fig. 3 f, is very similar, although the disadvantage of CCBNet over CCBNetJ widens considerably.

4.4 Party Weighting

Table 2 shows the weighted version of the proposed method having better predictive performance than the unweighted one in almost all scenarios with random splits. In weighting tests, we reduce the overall amount of data used for learning local BNs to ensure more variance and alternatingly assign parties a smaller or larger fraction of training data. Over the one scenario where the unweighted version performs better (0.079 versus 0.104), parties with lower data get overly punished for their perceived imprecision. Since each CPD has a single weight, all parents of a node within the party are still treated uniformly according to that value, even if there is a mismatch between the weight and the actual quality of the estimates. Similarly, if a party with lower overall confidence is the only one to model a highly influential parent, its importance is underrepresented in the final result. Nevertheless, despite these phenomena, which can adversely affect performance, weighting has a positive overall impact in tested scenarios.

Table 2. Unweighted (**UW**) & Weighted (**W**) Brier scores for CCBNet relative to original network – random splits, imbalanced learning data (lower is better)

#Parties	2				4			
Vars in >1 Party	10%		30%		10%		30%	
Method	UW	W	UW	W	UW	W	UW	W
Network ASIA	0.028	**0.018**	0.029	**0.009**	0.036	**0.020**	0.031	**0.011**
CHILD	**0.067**	**0.067**	0.088	**0.047**	0.084	**0.067**	0.097	**0.048**
ALARM	0.063	**0.058**	0.061	**0.050**	0.103	**0.092**	0.061	**0.057**
INSURANCE	**0.079**	0.104	**0.051**	**0.051**	0.112	**0.088**	0.135	**0.098**

4.5 Large Networks and Many Parties

Table 3. Metrics for large networks & many parties – related splits, 10% of vars in >1 party (lower is better)

Networks/Parties	Brier Score			Avg Comp Time Overhead			Avg #Comm Values		
	CC	DOM	CCBNet	DOM	CCBNetJ	CCBNet	DOM	CCBNetJ	CCBNet
ANDES/16	0.040	0.039	**0.035**	0.58	0.62	0.68	4	317	445
PIGS/32	0.103	0.092	**0.076**	0.39	0.51	1.34	7	4202	37838
LINK/64	0.144	**0.125**	0.126	0.25	0.35	0.39	6	2402	4549
MUNIN2/128	0.016	**0.015**	**0.015**	0.20	0.41	0.67	11	88581	242788

Lastly, in Table 3, our tests for challenging use cases with large networks (223–1003 variables), many parties (16–28), and related variable splits, but lower overlaps reconfirm prediction/communication trends, yet computation improves over original networks. In larger networks, CCBNet's predictions outperform CC, and communication size increases with parties and network size, averaging 71k values per request. Computation overhead is always <1, for a mean speedup of 21%. The hardness of inference makes approximating a big network by splitting it into chunks faster, even before considering parallel party solving.

5 Attacks on CCBNet

Carelessly combining related BNs into a single global model has a high risk of leaking confidential information to all parties that can access it. As illustrated in the middle of Fig. 1: (i) at a purely structural level the centralized combination can contain a large amount of the local party information; and (ii) at a parameter level, probability functions for any non-overlap nodes remain unmodified. Since BNs are human-readable, inspection can compromise sensitive information even before any inference. We review two attacks that respectively reconstruct CPDs during CABN and SAVE, along with their implications in CCBNet and CCBNetJ. The attacks do not bypass the obfuscation of unowned variable names and states but still expose potentially sensitive information via the recovered probability values. We execute these attacks as visualized in Fig. 4 on a corner case of **two-party ASIA and CHILD network instances**.

The CABN **attack** allows a party to reconstruct a peer's CPD for an overlap variable without inference, assuming no other parties are involved in the overlap, the attacker holds the combined CPD, and the protocol is CCBNetJ. The attacker first runs CABN to compute the combined CPD. Then, it removes its contribution from the geometric product that yielded the CPD, marginalizes any parents that should not be present in the victim's version, and normalizes to get the final result. With any secure computation scheme, if one input parties knows

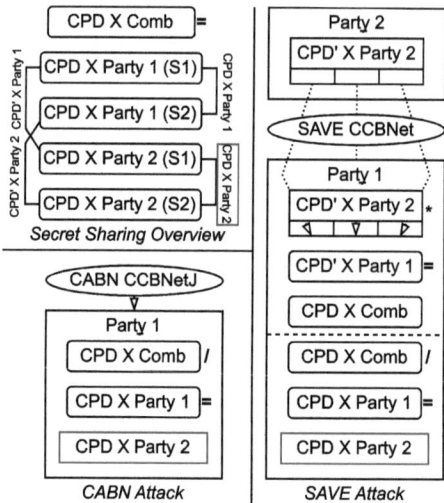

Fig. 4. CABN & SAVE attacks visualization.

the output and the applied operations are reversible, it can find the other input. With three or more parties, the attacker can only reconstruct an aggregation of the other involved CPDs. Even when the attack is possible, name obfuscation still hides the real-world meaning of the variables. Should any party outside the overlap exist, in the assumed no collusion setting, having it compute and store the combined CPD instead gives a minimum-change fix. CCBNet is not vulnerable, as it does not join shares before applying inference operations.

The **SAVE attack** reconstructs a peer's CPD for an overlap variable via inference assuming that the overlap contains no other parties but also applies to CCBNet. As one of the two parties in the overlap, the attacker begins by querying for the overlap variable as the only target, specifying a state for each of its parents in the evidence. With all parents fixed, no other variables in the victim's network can affect the transmitted result. Thus, the attacker receives one row from the victim's share of the combined target CPD. The attacker repeats the procedure for all other configurations of parent states, building up the victim's complete CPD share. It then obtains the full combined CPD as the product of its share and the one recovered from the other party. Finally, like in the previous attack, it removes the contribution of its whole local CPD from the combination, marginalizes any parents not in the victim, and normalizes to find the result. Also similar to the previous attack, obfuscation limits the damage that can be done, while with the involvement of more than two parties, the attacker is able to compromise their shares, but not the contribution of each, before sharing the secrets. Thus, secret sharing avoids the attack for overlaps with three or more parties. As the attack requires a series of specific queries, redundant in most real applications, a simple defense has parties limit the number of requests serviced that target some node and assign all parents in the evidence.

6 Conclusion

We propose CCBNet to address the issue of collaborative analysis for BNs in confidential (manufacturing) settings. The framework allows distributed analysis spanning multiple models without revealing their contents. It has no model compatibility restrictions and allows unequally weighting parties. Results show CCBNet outperforming/matching distributed/centralized baselines while maintaining reasonable computation time that decreases to 23% of centralized formulations in large networks with many parties but produces much larger messages the distributed baseline, averaging 71k communicated values per request. Altogether, CCBNet offers centralized-like predictive performance in a distributed setting and ensures a base for protecting parties' private information.

Acknowledgments. This research was partly funded by the NWO Perspectief project, DepMAT, and the SNSF project, Priv-GSyn 200021E_229204.

References

1. Abyaneh, A., Scherrer, N., Schwab, P., Bauer, S., Schölkopf, B., Mehrjou, A.: Fed-cd: federated causal discovery from interventional and observational data (2022)
2. Alrajeh, D., Chockler, H., Halpern, J.Y.: Combining experts' causal judgments. Artif. Intell. **288**, 103355 (2020)
3. Boneh, D., Sahai, A., Waters, B.: Functional encryption: definitions and challenges. In: Theory of Cryptography, pp. 253–273 (2011)
4. Campbell, T., How, J.P.: Approximate decentralized bayesian inference (2014)
5. Cheon, J.H., Kim, A., Kim, M., Song, Y.: Homomorphic encryption for arithmetic of approximate numbers. In: Takagi, T., Peyrin, T. (eds.) ASIACRYPT 2017. LNCS, vol. 10624, pp. 409–437. Springer, Cham (2017). https://doi.org/10.1007/978-3-319-70694-8_15
6. Cramer, R., Damgård, I.B., Nielsen, J.B.: Secure Multiparty Computation and Secret Sharing. Cambridge University Press (2015)
7. van Daalen, F., Ippel, L., Dekker, A., Bermejo, I.: Vertibayes: Learning bayesian network parameters from vertically partitioned data with missing values (2022)
8. Daly, R., Shen, Q., Aitken, S.: Learning bayesian networks: approaches and issues. Knowl. Eng. Rev. **26**(2), 99–157 (2011)
9. De Cristofaro, E., Tsudik, G.: Practical private set intersection protocols with linear complexity. In: Financial Cryptography and Data Security, pp. 143–159 (2010)
10. Del Sagrado, J., Moral, S.: Qualitative combination of bayesian networks. Int. J. Intell. Syst. **18**(2), 237–249 (2003)
11. Feng, G., Zhang, J.D., Shaoyi Liao, S.: A novel method for combining bayesian networks, theoretical analysis, and its applications. Pattern Recogn. **47**(5), 2057–2069 (2014)
12. Gao, E., Chen, J., Shen, L., Liu, T., Gong, M., Bondell, H.: Feddag: federated DAG structure learning (2021)
13. Gholami, B., Yoon, S., Pavlovic, V.: Decentralized approximate bayesian inference for distributed sensor network. In: Proceedings of the AAAI Conference on Artificial Intelligence, vol. 30, no. 1 (2016)

14. Goldreich, O.: Foundations of cryptography – a primer. Foundations and Trends in Theoretical Computer Science **1**(1), 1–116 (2005)
15. Huang, J., Yu, K., Guo, X., Cao, F., Liang, J.: Towards privacy-aware causal structure learning in federated setting (2022)
16. Kilbertus, N., Gascon, A., Kusner, M., Veale, M., Gummadi, K., Weller, A.: Blind justice: fairness with encrypted sensitive attributes. In: Proceedings of the 35th International Conference on Machine Learning. vol. 80, pp. 2630–2639 (2018)
17. Kim, H.C., Ghahramani, Z.: Bayesian classifier combination. In: Proceedings of the Fifteenth International Conference on Artificial Intelligence and Statistics. vol. 22, pp. 619–627 (2012)
18. Koller, D., Friedman, N.: Probabilistic graphical models: principles and techniques. MIT Press (2009)
19. Li, S.Z.: Markov random field modeling in image analysis. Springer Science & Business Media (2009)
20. Nannapaneni, S., Mahadevan, S., Rachuri, S.: Performance evaluation of a manufacturing process under uncertainty using bayesian networks. J. Clean. Prod. **113**, 947–959 (2016)
21. Ng, I., Zhang, K.: Towards federated bayesian network structure learning with continuous optimization (2021)
22. Pavlin, G., de Oude, P., Maris, M., Nunnink, J., Hood, T.: A multi-agent systems approach to distributed bayesian information fusion. Inform. Fusion **11**(3), 267–282 (2010)
23. Pearl, J.: Causality. Cambridge University Press, 2 edn. (2009)
24. Russell, S.J.: Artificial intelligence a modern approach. Pearson Education (2010)
25. Scutari, M., Denis, J.B.: Bayesian networks: with examples in R. CRC Press (2021)
26. Stephenson, T.A.: An introduction to bayesian network theory and usage. Tech. rep, Idiap (2000)
27. Tedesco, R., Dolog, P., Nejdl, W., Allert, H.: Distributed bayesian networks for user modeling. In: Proceedings of E-Learn: World Conference on E-Learning in Corporate, Government, Healthcare, and Higher Education 2006, pp. 292–299 (2006)
28. Yang, W.T.: An Integrated Physics-Informed Process Control Framework and Its Applications to Semiconductor Manufacturing. Université de Lyon, Theses (2020)
29. Ypma, A., Koopman, A.C.M., Middlebrooks, S.A.: Methods & apparatus for obtaining diagnostic information, methods & apparatus for controlling an industrial process (2018)

Author Index

A
Anthoine, Gaspard 264
Aumayr, Lukas 178
Avarikioti, Zeta 178
Avice, Régnier 380
Avitabile, Gennaro 252

B
Bachu, Brad 75
Baig, Mirza Ahad 132
Bartoletti, Massimo 233
Birmpas, Georgios 197
Buchwald, Aaron 94
Buttolph, Stephen 94

C
Chen, Lydia 398
Chen, Zekai 360
Cozzo, Daniele 264

D
Das, Sourav 302
Decouchant, Jérémie 398

F
Fan, Mingyuan 360
Feng, Yebo 2
Fiore, Dario 264
Fujisaki, Eiichiro 321

G
Garimidi, Pranav 20
Gerlach, Lukas 340
Gong, Tiantian 283
Guzella, Thiago 398

H
Haslhofer, Bernhard 380
Heimbach, Lioba 20, 55

K
Kamp, Simon Holmgaard 166
Kokoris-Kogias, Lefteris 37

L
Lazos, Philip 197
Lewis-Pye, Andrew 94
Li, Zekun 302
Li, Zhidong 380
Liu, Zeyu 283
Losa, Giuliano 148
Luo, Yichen 2

M
Ma, Zhoujun 302
Maffei, Matteo 178
Mălan, Abele 398
Mao, Yifan 148
Markakis, Evangelos 197
Milionis, Jason 55
Moallemi, Ciamac C. 75

N
Neu, Joachim 112
Nikova, Svetla 215

O
O'Grady, Patrick 94
Okuda, Tetsuya 321

P
Pan, Lei 360
Penna, Paolo 197

Pietrzak, Krzysztof 132
Pietsch, Robert 340
Preneel, Bart 215

R
Riva, Ben 37
Robinson, Dan 75
Roughgarden, Tim 20

S
Sarenche, Roozbeh 215
Scaffino, Giulia 178
Schwarz, Michael 340
Sekniqi, Kevin 94
Siniscalchi, Luisa 252
Sonnino, Alberto 37
Spiegelman, Alexander 302
Sridhar, Srivatsan 112

T
Tas, Ertem Nusret 112
Tasca, Paolo 2
Tse, David 112

V
Venkatakrishnan, Shaileshh Bojja 148
Visconti, Ivan 252

W
Wan, Xin 75
Wang, Fuyi 360

X
Xiang, Zhuolun 302
Xu, Jiahua 2

Y
Yamamura, Kazuki 321

Z
Zhang, Leo Yu 360
Zhang, Yunqi 148
Zhou, Jianlong 380
Zhou, Jianying 360
Zhu, Brian Z. 75
Zindros, Dionysis 112, 178
Zunino, Roberto 233

MIX
Papier aus verantwortungsvollen Quellen
Paper from responsible sources
FSC® C105338

If you have any concerns about our products,
you can contact us on
ProductSafety@springernature.com

In case Publisher is established outside the EU,
the EU authorized representative is:
**Springer Nature Customer Service Center GmbH
Europaplatz 3, 69115 Heidelberg, Germany**

Printed by Libri Plureos GmbH
in Hamburg, Germany